The Zohar

by
Rav Shimon bar Yochai
From The Book of Avraham

with
The Sulam Commentary

by
Rav Yehuda Ashlag

The First Ever Unabridged
English Translation with Commentary

Published by
The Kabbalah Centre International Inc.
Dean Rav S. P. Berg Shlita

Edited and Compiled by
Rabbi Michael Berg

Published by
The Kabbalah Centre International Inc.

155 E. 48th St., New York, NY 10017
1062 S. Robertson Blvd., Los Angeles, CA 90035

Director Rav Berg

First Printing 2001
Revised Edition 2008

Printed in USA

ISBN: 1-57189-159-5

With all our love for you

יעקב בן ליב יהודה הלוי

Johnny Newstead

May the light of the Zohar fill hearts with
happiness and joy, bringing peace to
all the world forever.

Your girls
Ingrid, Rachel, Hayley & Stephanie

APPLYING THE POWER OF THE ZOHAR

The Zohar is a book of great mystical power and wisdom. It is Universally recognized as the definitive work on the Kabbalah – and it is also so Much more.

The Zohar is a wellspring of spiritual energy, a fountainhead of metaphysical power that not only reveals and explains, but literally brings blessing, protection, and well-being into the lives of all those who read or peruse its sacred texts. All that is required is worthy desire, the certainty of a trusting heart, and an open and receptive mind. Unlike other books, including the great spiritual texts of other traditions, The Zohar is written in a kind of code, through which metaphors, parables, and cryptic language at first conceal but ultimately reveal the forces of creation.

As electrical current is concealed in wire and cable before disclosing itself as an illuminated light bulb, the spiritual Light of the Creator is wrapped in allegory and symbolism throughout the Aramaic text of the Zohar. And while many books contain information and knowledge, the Zohar both expresses and embodies spiritual Light. The very letters on its pages have the power to bring spiritual wisdom and positive energy into every area of our lives.

As we visually scan the Aramaic texts and study the accompanying insights that appear in English, spiritual power is summoned from above – and worlds tremble as Light is sent forth in response.

It's primary purpose is not only to help us acquire wisdom, but to draw Light from the Upper Worlds and to bring sanctification into our lives. Indeed, the book itself is the most powerful of all tools for cleansing the soul and connecting to the Light of the Creator. As you open these pages, therefore, do not make understanding in the conventional sense your primary goal.

Although you may not have a knowledge of Aramaic, look first at the Aramaic text before reading the English. Do not be discouraged by difficulties with comprehension. Instead, open your heart to the spiritual transformation the Zohar is offering you.

Ultimately, the Zohar is an instrument for refining the individual soul – for removing darkness from the earth – and for bringing well being and blessing to our fellow man.

Its purpose is not only to make us intellectually wise, but to make us spiritually pure.

Glossary of Hebrew words

Torah

Also known as the Five Books of Moses, the Torah is considered to be the physical body of learning, whereas the Zohar is the internal soul. The literal stories of the Torah conceal countless hidden secrets.` The Zohar is the Light that illuminates all of the Torah's sublime mysteries.

Beresheet	Genesis
Shemot	Exodus
Vayikra	Leviticus
Bemidbar	Numbers
Devarim	Deuteronomy

Prophets

Amos	Amos
Chagai	Haggai
Chavakuk	Habakkuk
Hoshea	Hosea
Malachi	Malachi
Melachim	Kings
Michah	Micah
Nachum	Nahum
Ovadyah	Obadiah
Shmuel	Samuel
Shoftim	Judges
Tzefanyah	Zephaniah
Yechezkel	Ezekiel
Yehoshua	Joshua
Yeshayah	Isaiah
Yirmeyah	Jeremiah
Yoel	Joel
Yonah	Jonah
Zecharyah	Zechariah

Writings

Daniel	Daniel
Divrei Hayamim	Chronicles
Eicha	Lamentations
Ester	Esther
Ezra	Ezra
Nechemiah	Nehemiah
Iyov	Job
Kohelet	Ecclesiastes
Mishlei	Proverbs
Rut	Ruth

Sir Hashirim	Songs of Songs
Tehilim	Psalms

The Ten Sfirot – Emanations

To conceal the blinding *Light* of the Upper World, and thus create a tiny point into which our universe would be born, ten *curtains* were fabricated. These ten *curtains* are called Ten Sfirot. Each successive Sfirah further reduces the emanation of *Light*, gradually dimming its brilliance to a level almost devoid of *Light* – our physical world known as *Malchut*. The only remnant of Light remaining in this darkened universe is a *pilot light* which sustains our existence. This Light is the life force of a human being and the force that gives birth to stars, sustains suns and sets everything from swirling galaxies to busy ant hills in motion. Moreover, the Ten Sfirot act like a prism, refracting the Light into many *colors* giving rise to the diversity of life and matter in our world.

The Ten Sfirot are as follows:

Keter	Crown
Chochmah	Wisdom
Binah	Understanding
Da'at	Knowledge
Zeir Anpin	Small Face,
	(includes the next six Sfirot):
Chesed	Mercy (Chassadim - plural)
Gvurah	Judgment (Gvurot - Plural)
Tiferet	Splendor
Netzach	Victory (Eternity)
Hod	Glory
Yesod	Foundation
Malchut	Kingdom

The Partzufim - Spiritual forms

One complete structure of the Ten Sfirot creates a *Partzuf* or Spiritual Form. Together, these forces are the building blocks of all reality. As water and sand combine to create cement, the Ten Sfirot combine to produce a Spiritual Form [*Partzuf*]. Each of the Spiritual Forms below are therefore composed of one set of Ten Sfirot.

These Spiritual Forms are called:

Atik	Ancient
Atik Yomin	Ancient of Days
Atika Kadisha	Holy Ancient
Atik of Atikin	Anceint of Ancients
Aba	Father
Arich Anpin	Long Face
Ima	Mother
Nukva	Female
Tevunah	Intelligence
Yisrael Saba	Israel Grandfather
Zachar	Male

These names are not meant to be understood literally. Each represents a unique spiritual force and building block, producing a substructure and foundation for all the worlds make up reality.

The Five Worlds

All of the above Spiritual Forms [*Partzufim*] create one spiritual world. There are Five Worlds in total that compose all reality, therefore, five sets of the above Spiritual Forms are required.

Our physical world corresponds to the world of: Asiyah – Action

Adam Kadmon	Primordial Man
Atzilut	Emanation
Briyah	Creation
Yetzirah	Formation
Asiyah	Action

The Five Levels of the soul

Nefesh	First, Lowest level of Soul
Ruach	Second level of Soul
Neshamah	Third level of Soul
Chayah	Fourth level of Soul
Yechidah	Highest, fifth level of Soul

Names of God

As a single ray of white sunlight contains the seven colors of the spectrum, the one Light of the Creator embodies many diverse spiritual forces. These different forces are called *Names of God*. Each Name denotes a specific attribute and spiritual power. The Hebrew letters that compose these Names are the interface by which these varied Forces act upon our physical world. The most common Name of God is the Tetragrammaton (the four letters, *Yud Hei Vav Hei* יהוה.) Because of the enormous power that the Tetragrammaton transmits, we do not utter it aloud. When speaking of the Tetragrammaton, we use the term *Hashem* which means, *The Name*.

Adonai, El, Elohim, Hashem, Shadai, Eheyeh, Tzevaot, Yud Hei Vav Hei

People

Er	The son of Noach
Rabbi Elazar	The son of Rabbi Shimon bar Yochai
Rabbi Shimon bar Yochai	Author of the Zohar
Shem, Cham, Yefet	Noach's children
Shet	Seth
Ya'akov	Jacob
Yishai	Jesse (King David's father)
Yitzchak	Isaac
Yosef	Joseph
Yitro	Jethro
Yehuda	Judah

Angels

Angels are distinct energy components, part of a vast communication network running through the upper worlds. Each unique Angel is responsible for transmitting various forces of influence into our physical universe.

Adriel, Ahinael, Dumah (name of Angel in charge of the dead), Gabriel, Kadshiel, Kedumiel, Metatron, Michael, Rachmiel,

Raphael, Tahariel, Uriel

Nations

Nations actually represent the inner attributes and character traits of our individual self. The nation of Amalek refers to the doubt and uncertainty that dwells within us when we face hardship and obstacles. Moab represents the dual nature of man. Nefilim refers to the sparks of Light that we have defiled through our impure actions, and to the negative forces that lurk within the human soul as a result of our own wrongful deeds.

Amalek, Moab, Nefilim

General

Aba	Father
	Refers to the male principle and positive force in our universe. Correlates to the proton in an atom.
Arvit	The Evening prayer
Chayot	Animals
Chupah	Canopy (wedding ceremony)
Et	The
Avadon	Hell
Gehenom	Hell
Sheol	Hell
	The place a soul goes for purification upon leaving this world.
Ima	Mother
	The female principle and minus force in our universe. Correlates to the electron in an atom.
Kiddush	Blessing over the wine
Klipah	Shell (negativity)
Klipot	Shells (Plural)
Kriat Sh'ma	The Reading of the Sh'ma
Mashiach	Messiah
Minchah	The Afternoon prayer
Mishnah	Study
Mochin	Brain, Spiritual levels of Light
Moed	A designated time or holiday
Negev	The south of Israel
Nukva	Female

Partzuf	Face
Shacharit	The Morning prayer
Shamayim	Heavens (sky)
Shechinah	The Divine presence, The female aspect of the Creator
Tefilin	Phylacteries
The Dinur river	The river of fire
Tzadik	Righteous person
Zion	Another name for Jerusalem
Yisrael	The land of Israel
	The nation of Israel or an individual Israelite
Zohar	Splendor

The Hebrew vowels

Chirik **א**, Cholam **וא א**, Kamatz **א**, Patach **א**, Segol **א**, Sh'va **א**, Shuruk **וא א**, Tzere **א**.

The Twelve Tribes

Asher, Dan, Ephraim, Gad, Issachar, Judah, Levi, Menasheh, Naphtali, Reuben, Shimon, Zebulun

Jewish Holidays

Rosh Hashanah	The Jewish New Year
Yom Kippur	Day of Atonement
Sukkot	Holiday of the Booths
Shmini Atzeret	The day of Convocation
Simchat Torah	Holiday on which we dance with the Torah
Pesach	Passover
Shavout	Holiday of the Weeks

כרך ז

פרשת ויחי

Vol. VII

Vayechi

A Prayer from The Ari

To be recited before the study of the Zohar

Ruler of the universe, and Master of all masters, The Father of mercy and forgiveness, we thank You, our God and the God of our fathers, by bowing down and kneeling, that You brought us closer to Your Torah and Your holy work, and You enable us to take part in the secrets of Your holy Torah. How worthy are we that You grant us with such big favor, that is the reason we plead before You, that You will forgive and acquit all our sins, and that they should not bring separation between You and us.

And may it be your will before You, our God and the God of our fathers, that You will awaken and prepare our hearts to love and revere You, and may You listen to our utterances, and open our closed heart to the hidden studies of Your Torah, and may our study be pleasant before Your Place of Honor, as the aroma of sweet incense, and may You emanate to us Light from the source of our soul to all of our being. And, may the sparks of your holy servants, through which you revealed Your wisdom to the world, shine.

May their merit and the merit of their fathers, and the merit of their Torah, and holiness, support us so we shall not stumble through our study. And by their merit enlighten our eyes in our learning as it stated by King David, The Sweet Singer of Israel: "Open my eyes, so that I will see wonders from Your Torah" (Tehilim 119:18). Because from His mouth God gives wisdom and understanding.

"May the utterances of my mouth and the thoughts of my heart find favor before You, God, my Strength and my Redeemer" (Tehilim 19:15).

XI

Vayechi

Names of the articles

1. "And Jacob lived"

A Synopsis
Rabbi Yosi opens a discussion on the meaning of the quotation, "And Jacob lived," which has high mysteries contained in it, because Jacob arrived at a hitherto unprecedented prophecy "and lived" in Egypt, among his exiled descendants. Rabbi Yosi next questions how this is possible when the name Jacob indicates smallness, while Yisrael indicates greatness. Rabbi Elazar responds by pointing out that scripture indicates Jacob purchased his birthright, which is tantamount to greatness. Rabbi Shimon further states that Jacob, not Yisrael, was chosen by God to be a sapphire in the Throne of Glory. Jacob's name was then changed to Yisrael, to reflect the Mercy of Judgment, since judgment is the cause of the revelation of mercy, and those banished to Egypt were judged and shown mercy by God. Rabbi Shimon concludes by saying that the whole of Jacob's life was 147 years, divided into three periods of exile, the first of which was seven years. The number seven is significant because it represents atonement by the holy children, exiled "seven times," according to the number of sins they perpetrated.

The Relevance of this Passage
The phrase "and he lived" is a code alluding to the fact that Jacob had attained a lofty level of spirituality and prophecy. This feat was achieved during his sojourn in Egypt, which itself is a code word representing negativity and the materialism of our physical existence. In most sections of Zohar, the names Jacob and Yisrael are two designations for the Patriarch, indicating two levels of his spirituality, Jacob being a lower level and Yisrael signifying a higher one. However, in this particular section of Zohar, the name Jacob is used to indicate an exalted spiritual level. The reason for this is to convey the different form of Light that is aroused when one ascends out of negativity and darkness. Hence, the underlying purpose of this passage is to imbue the reader with the spiritual fortitude necessary to elevate and climb out of any darkness or negativity currently in their life.

א. וַיְחִי יַעֲקֹב בְּאֶרֶץ מִצְרַיִם שְׁבַע עֶשְׂרֵה שָׁנָה וגו'. אָמַר רִבִּי יוֹסֵי, לְבָא חָמָא בִּנְבוּאָה, בְּמִצְרַיִם, דִּיהוֹן בְּנוֹהִי בְּכַמָּה גַּלְוָון, עַד הָכָא, וְעַד עִדָנָא דְּקֵץ מְשִׁיחָא.

1. "And Jacob lived in the land of Egypt seventeen years" (Beresheet 47:28). Rabbi Yosi said: Jacob's heart saw through prophecy in Egypt that

his descendants would suffer many exiles - NAMELY HE SAW ALL THE EXILES from then until now, until the End, and the time of the Coming of Messiah.

2. וְלָא מָטָא לִנְבוּאָה דְּוַיְחִי, אֶלָּא בְּמִצְרַיִם, וְהִיא נְבוּאָתָא מַעַלְיָיתָא, לָא אִתְנַבִּיאוּ דְּכַוָּותָה, וְלָא מָטָא לְהוּ שׁוּם אֵינִישׁ מִן בְּנֵי נְבִיאָה, אֶלָּא הוּא וּמֹשֶׁה, בְּמֹשֶׁה כְּתִיב, כִּי לֹא יִרְאַנִי הָאָדָם וָחָי. בְּיַעֲקֹב כְּתִיב, וַיְחִי יַעֲקֹב. וַיְחִי: נְבוּאָתָה דְּנַחֲתָא מֵאַסְפַּקְלַרְיָאה דְּנַהֲרָא.

2. Jacob arrived at the prophecy of "and...lived" only in Egypt. It was an excellent prophecy, the like of which was never prophesied before. None of the prophets was worthy of it except for him and Moses ALONE. It is written of Moses: "For no man shall see Me, and live" (Shemot 33:20). Of Jacob, it is written: "And Jacob lived" REFERRING TO the prophecy which descends from the shining mirror, TIFERET.

3. בָּעֵי לְמֵימַר נְבוּאָן דְּגָלוּתָא דְּעַרְעָן לִבְנוֹהִי בְּאַרְעָא דִּכְנָעַן, וּבְכָל אַרְעָא דְּאִתּוֹתַב בָּהּ, מֵאַרְעָא דְמִצְרַיִם הֲוָה תְּבִיר לִבֵּיה, דִּכְתִיב כִּי יֵשׁ שֶׁבֶר בְּמִצְרַיִם.

3. Jacob wanted to prophesy concerning the exiles of his children in the land of Canaan and in any land wherein they dwelt WHICH came from the land of Egypt; TO WIT, ALL EXILES ARE INCLUDED WITHIN EGYPT. His heart broke, as it is written: "Now Jacob saw that there was corn (also: 'breaking') in Egypt" (Beresheet 42:1).

4. וְע״ד מָטָא וַיְחִי יַעֲקֹב בְּמִצְרַיִם, וְלָא הֲוָה חָדֵי, כִּי בְּאַרְעָא הַהִיא סְפִיקָן דְּעַמְמִין, סַפִּירִין דְּכוּרְסֵי יְקָרָא, וְלָא מָטָא לְהוֹן שׁוּם אֵינִישׁ, לָא מִן עִלָּאָה, וְלָא מִן תַּתָּאָה, אֶלָּא מִן ח״י, וְרָזָא דָא, כִּי לֹא יִרְאַנִי הָאָדָם וָחָי.

4. Hence, when it came to pass that "Jacob lived in Egypt," he did not rejoice, because this land was the bond of the nations; TO WIT, ALL THE FILTH OF THE NATIONS LIES THERE. ALSO, the sapphires of the Throne of Glory, THE SECRET OF THE CAPTIVE SPARKS OF CHOCHMAH AMONGST

THEM, CALLED SAPPHIRES ACCORDING TO THE SECRET MEANING OF THE VERSE: "AND ABOVE THE FIRMAMENT THAT WAS OVER THEIR HEADS WAS THE LIKENESS OF A THRONE, IN APPEARANCE LIKE A SAPPHIRE STONE" (YECHEZKEL 1:26). Nobody came to SIFT them, neither from the upper nor from the lower, save the living. This is the secret of: "For no man shall see Me, and live."

5. כַּמָּה הוּא רָזָא עִלָּאָה בְּדָא קְרָא, וַאֲנַן חַבְרַיָּיא תְּמֵיהִין עֲלַיְיהוּ, עַל וַיְחִי דְּדָכוּר עֲמֵיה יַעֲקֹב, הֲוָה לֵיה לְמֵימַר קַמֵּי יִשְׂרָאֵל. יִשְׂרָאֵל מְנַיִן, דִּכְתִיב קֹדֶשׁ יִשְׂרָאֵל לַה' רֵאשִׁית וְגוֹ'. בְּנִי בְכוֹרִי יִשְׂרָאֵל. רִבִּי אֶלְעָזָר בְּרֵיה דְּרִבִּי שִׁמְעוֹן אֲמַר, וְכִי לָא אֲמַר קְרָא, וַיִּמְכֹּר אֶת בְּכֹרָתוֹ לְיַעֲקֹב.

5. There are high mysteries in this verse, and we friends wonder about them, for it says that Jacob lived instead of Yisrael, TO WIT 'AND ISRAEL LIVED.' FOR THE NAME JACOB INDICATES SMALLNESS, AND THE NAME ISRAEL INDICATES MOCHIN OF GREATNESS, WHILE "AND LIVED" ALLUDES TO THE LIGHT OF CHAYAH, WHICH IS THE MOCHIN OF GREATNESS. IT SHOULD HAVE SAID: 'AND ISRAEL LIVED.' How do we know that Yisrael INDICATES MOCHIN OF GREATNESS? From the verse: "Yisrael is holy to Hashem" (Yirmeyah 2:3), HOLY BEING AN ALLUSION TO GREATNESS. It also says, "Israel is My son, My firstborn" (Shemot 4:22), FIRSTBORN BEING AN ALLUSION TO GREATNESS. THUS, THE NAME ISRAEL IS MENTIONED WITH RELATION TO GREATNESS AND NOT JACOB, WHICH IS A NAME OF SMALLNESS, ACCORDING TO THE SECRET MEANING OF THE VERSE: "HOW SHALL JACOB STAND? FOR HE IS SMALL" (AMOS 7:2). Rabbi Elazar, the son of Rabbi Shimon, said: Yet scripture says, "and he sold his birthright to Jacob" (Beresheet 25:33), FOR WITH THE BIRTHRIGHT, WHICH IS GREATNESS, THE NAME JACOB IS MENTIONED. THUS IT IS NO QUESTION WHY IT SAYS "AND JACOB LIVED" INSTEAD OF 'AND ISRAEL LIVED.'

6. אֲמַר רִבִּי שִׁמְעוֹן אֲבוּהַ, בְּעִידְנָא דַּהֲווֹ יִשְׂרָאֵל קְשִׁיטִין וְזַכָּאִין וְעָבְדִין זְכוּ, וְלָא הֲווֹ רְתִיתִין יִשְׂרָאֵל, אֶלָּא יַעֲקֹב לְחוּדֵיה. בְּדִין טָבָאן דְּעָבְדִין, הֲוָה לְמֶעְבַּד לְהוּ טָבָאן סַגִּיאִין דָּא בְּדָא.

6. His father Rabbi Shimon said to him: When Yisrael were righteous men of truth and gave charity, they were not afraid, save Jacob alone, WHO, THE VERSE TELLS US, WAS AFRAID, SAYING: "FOR I FEAR HIM" (BERESHEET 32:12), WHILE YISRAEL IS A NAME OF GREATNESS, WITHOUT FEAR. IT IS due to the good deeds YISRAEL did, and the kindness amongst them THAT THEY HAD NO FEAR.

‫7. מִדְחָבוּ, וְאִתְגְּלִיאוּ עַל חוֹבֵיהוֹן, וְעַל עוֹבָדֵיהוֹן בִּישִׁין, לָא הֲווֹ סָבְלִין יָתֵיהּ, דְּלָא יֶהֱוַיִין לְעַלְמָא, בְּקוּשְׁטָא עַל חוֹבֵיהוֹן, וְעַל דָּא אָתֵי מְכִילְתָּא דְרַחֲמֵי וְדִינָא לְחוּד, יִשְׂרָאֵל, וְיָהֲבִית יַתְהוֹן בְּאַרְעָא גָּלוּתְהוֹן.‬

7. When they sinned and were exiled because of their transgressions and evil deeds, they could not bear THE FEAR that they would really stay forever IN EXILE for their sins. Thus came the aspect of Mercy and Judgment joined WHICH IS THE MEANING OF THE NAME Yisrael, and put them in exile.

‫8. יָאוֹת בָּעֵי בְּרִי, אֲבָל אִינִישׁ מִסְתַּכֵּל וְיִנְדַע יָתֵיהּ, יַעֲקֹב דְּמִתְלַף עִם וַיְחִי, קֹדֶשׁ. וְעַל דְּנָא רָזָא אָמְרִין, יַעֲקֹב בָּחַר יָתֵיהּ סַפִּירָא בְּכוּרְסֵי יְקָרָא.‬

8. Well asked, son, IN RELATION TO THE VERSE, "AND HE SOLD HIS BIRTHRIGHT TO JACOB." But whoever looks into it will know that Jacob attached to "and lived" represents holiness, LIKE THE NAME YISRAEL. In relation to this secret, it has been said that Jacob was chosen by the Holy One, blessed be He, to be a sapphire in the Throne of Glory, INSTEAD OF YISRAEL.

‫9. רִבִּי שִׁמְעוֹן פָּתַח וַאֲמַר, וְאֶת דַּכָּא וּשְׁפַל רוּחַ לְהַחֲיוֹת רוּחַ שְׁפָלִים וּלְהַחֲיוֹת לֵב נִדְכָּאִים. לֵב נִדְכָּאִים: דָּא יַעֲקֹב, כְּד"א, תְּחוֹת מִן דַּרְגָּא נְחִיתַת עֲלוֹהִי נְבִיאִין בִּרְכָאן בְּמִצְרַיִם.‬

9. Rabbi Shimon opened the discussion, saying: "Yet with him also that is of a contrite and humble spirit, to revive the spirit of the humble, and to revive the heart of the contrite ones" (Yeshayah 57:15). "The heart of the contrite ones" is Jacob, as it says "AND JACOB LIVED," FOR from beneath the grade prophecies and blessings descended upon him even in Egypt.

10. תָּנָא א״ר אַבָּא, לְבָּא חָמָא, דְּיַעֲקֹב דַּהֲוָה בְּמִצְרַיִם לֵית נְבוּאָתֵיה מַעַלְיוּתָא. אַרְעָא סַגִּיאָה.

10. We have learned that Rabbi Aba said: The heart sees that, while Jacob lived in Egypt, his prophecy was not sublime, for the land was detested.

11. תָּא חֲזֵי, לָא זָכֵי לְבָרֵךְ לְחַד מִבְּנוֹהִי, וְלָא הֲוָה בִּידֵיה רוּחָא לְבָרֵךְ, אֶלָּא בְּמִצְרַיִם, כַּד בָּרֵיךְ יַתְהוֹן כָּל חַד וְחַד בְּרָזָא. וְרָזָא וַיַּרְא יַעֲקֹב כִּי יֶשׁ שֶׁבֶר בְּמִצְרַיִם וַיֹּאמֶר יַעֲקֹב לְבָנָיו לָמָּה תִּתְרָאוּ. תָּא חֲזֵי, דְּלָא אִתְיְיהִיבַת נְבוּאָתָא, אֶלָּא לִתְבִירֵי לִבָּא, כְּד״א רְדוּ שָׁמָּה וְשִׁבְרוּ לָנוּ מִשָּׁם וְנִחְיֶה וְלֹא נָמוּת.

11. Come and behold: he did not deserve to bless any of his sons, and had no spirit with which to bless, except in Egypt. When he did, he blessed each of them according to a mystery, which is, "Now Jacob saw that there was corn (also: 'breaking') in Egypt. Jacob said to his sons, 'Why do you look at one another?'" Come and see, prophecy was given only to the broken - hearted, as it is written: "Go down there, and buy (also: 'break') us from there, that we may live, and not die" (Beresheet 42:2).

12. אָמַר רִבִּי יוֹסֵי, תְּחוֹת כָּרְסֵי יְקָרָא קַדִּישָׁא, יַעֲקֹב סַפִּיר, דְּאִיהִי מְכִילְתָּא דְּדִינָא לִסְטְרֵיה, אָתָא אָמַר לֹא יַעֲקֹב יֵאָמֵר עוֹד שִׁמְךָ כִּי אִם יִשְׂרָאֵל כִּי שָׂרִיתָ עִם אֱלֹקִים וְעִם אֲנָשִׁים וַתּוּכָל. אַתְּ מַשְׁכַּח, דְּיַעֲקֹב חָזָא לִסְטְרֵיה מְכִילְתָּא דְּדִינָא, וַיִּזְרַח לוֹ הַשֶּׁמֶשׁ כַּאֲשֶׁר עָבַר אֶת פְּנוּאֵל וְגוֹ', וְרָזָא דְּמִלָּה אוֹי לָנוּ כִּי פָנָה הַיּוֹם כִּי יִנָּטוּ צִלְלֵי עָרֶב.

12. Rabbi Yosi said: Under the Holy Throne of Glory is Jacob as a sapphire; THE SAPPHIRE pertains to his aspect of Judgment. Then scripture came and said: "And he said: 'Your name shall be called no more Jacob but Israel: for you have contended with Elohim and with men, and have prevailed'" (Beresheet 32:29). Now we find that Jacob found out there was Judgment within him, as it is written: "The sun rose upon him" (Ibid. 32). And the secret of the matter is: "Woe to us! For the day declines, for the shadows of the evening are lengthened" (Yirmeyah 6:4).

13. רִבִּי שִׁמְעוֹן אֲמַר, כַּד אִתְגְּלִיאוּ מִן יְרוּשְׁלֵם, וְאַעֲדִיאוּ תְּדִירָא, וְסָאֵיב מְסָנְאָה יַת הֵיכָלָא, בְּעִדָּנָא הַהִיא לָא סוֹבְלַת מַלְכוּתָא לְיִשְׂרָאֵל עַל חוֹבֵיהוֹן, אֶלָּא יִשְׂרָאֵל, בְּגִין דְּהִיא מִתְּרֵי גִיסָא: רַחֲמֵי וְדִינָא.

13. Rabbi Shimon said: When they were banished from Jerusalem, and the daily offering was no more, and the foe defiled the Temple, Malchut, THE NUKVA OF ZEIR ANPIN, could not then bear Yisrael and their sins. Only THE GRADE OF THE NAME, Yisrael COULD SUFFER THEM, because it is two - sided of Mercy and Judgment. SINCE THE JUDGMENT IS THE CAUSE OF THE REVELATION OF MERCY, THEREFORE THE JUDGMENT IS ALSO CONSIDERED AS MERCY.

14. וּמִלָּה דְּלָא יַעֲקֹב יֵאָמֵר עוֹד שִׁמְךָ כִּי אִם יִשְׂרָאֵל, כַּד אִתְפְּרִישׁ בְּסָבִירֵיהּ, יִשְׂרָאֵל יַעֲקֹב עִלָּאָה דָּא מִן דָּא, וּבְגִינֵיהוֹן הֲוָה חוּטְרָא דְּמֹשֶׁה גְּלִיפָא מִתְּרֵין סִטְרוֹי מִשְׁמֵיהּ קַדִּישָׁא, חַד רַחֲמֵי בְּדִינָא, וְחַד דִּינָא בְּדִינָא.

14. The words, "Your name shall be called no more Jacob but Israel," when clearly understood, mean that Israel is superior to Jacob, AND THEREFORE HE BLESSED HIM WITH THE NAME ISRAEL. And it is according to their meaning that the staff of Moses was engraved with the Holy Name on both sides, the one of Mercy of Judgment, THE GRADE OF ISRAEL, and the other Judgment of Judgment, THE GRADE OF JACOB.

15. וְרָזָא לֹא הִבִּיט אָוֶן בְּיַעֲקֹב וְלֹא רָאָה עָמָל בְּיִשְׂרָאֵל, מִדְּאַנַן בְּגָלוּתָא, דְּחִיקָן בֵּין שָׂנְאֵי, וְאִסְתַּלִּיקַת מַטְרוֹנִיתָא מִן מַלְכָּא, וְאִתְרְחִיקַת מִנֵּיהּ, הוּא יַשְׁרֵי שְׁכִינְתָּא בֵּינָנָא וִיפָרְקִינָנָא, וְרָזָא כֹּה אָמַר ה׳ מֶלֶךְ יִשְׂרָאֵל וְגוֹאֲלוֹ ה׳ צְבָאוֹת. וַיְחִי חַי, כֹּה אָמַר ה׳ הַשָּׁמַיִם כִּסְאִי וְהָאָרֶץ הֲדוֹם רַגְלָי.

15. This is the secret of: "He has not beheld iniquity in Jacob nor has He seen perverseness in Israel" (Bemidbar 23:21), WHICH MEANS HE DID NOT

BEHOLD INIQUITY IN JACOB, BUT DID SEE PERVERSENESS. YET IN ISRAEL, EVEN PERVERSENESS HE DID NOT BEHOLD, FOR IN IT JUDGMENT IS ALSO CONSIDERED MERCY. HE EXPLAINS, We are thrown into exile amidst enemies, and the Shechinah is gone from the King, ZEIR ANPIN, and separated from Him. EVENTUALLY He will cause the Shechinah to dwell among us and redeem us, FOR BANISHMENT BRINGS US TO REPENT, AND REPENTANCE BRINGS REDEMPTION. THEREFORE, JUDGMENT IN ISRAEL CHANGES INTO MERCY. THEREFORE SCRIPTURE SAYS, "NOR HAS HE SEEN PERVERSENESS IN ISRAEL," WHICH IS ALL MERCY. BUT THE GRADE OF JACOB IS NOT SO, FOR IT CONTAINS PERVERSENESS. HENCE THE ANGEL BLESSED HIM: "YOUR NAME SHALL BE CALLED NO MORE JACOB BUT ISRAEL," WHICH CONTAINS BOTH JUDGMENT AND MERCY, EXILE AND REDEMPTION, AND IS WHOLLY MERCIFUL. This is the secret of the verse, "Thus says Hashem, the King of Yisrael, and His redeemer, Hashem, Lord of Hoste Tzeva'ot" (Yeshayah 44:6): and lived, living. "Thus says Hashem, The heaven is My throne, and the earth is My footstool" (Yeshayah 66:1).

16. בִּנְיַן עִלָּאָה, שְׁתֵּ״י רַגְלֵי חַי, לִי׳ רַבָּתָא י׳ זְעֵירְתָּא, לְחֵ׳ תיו, ו״י לֵי׳, ו״ד לִי׳, הֲדָא הוּא דְּנָפֵיק מֵעֵלָּאָה.

16. Within the upper grade ISRAEL two legs, NETZACH AND HOD, live. NETZACH IS CALLED "AND LIVED (HEB. *VAYECHI, VAV YUD CHET YUD*)" AND HOD 'LIVING (HEB. *CHAI, CHET YUD*),' BOTH INCLUDED WITHIN THE WORD FOR "AND LIVED." HE EXPLAINS: Large *Yud* contains small *Yud*, large *Chet* contains *Tav*; there are *Vav* and *Yud* in *Vav*, and in *Yud* – *Vav* and *Dalet*. This comes from the upper one, ISRAEL.

17. תְּחוֹת כָּרְסֵיה יְקָרָא, מֵאֶבֶן טָבָא, בְּאֶרֶץ מִצְרַיִם, הַיְינוּ דִכְתִיב וְנָגַף ה׳ אֶת מִצְרַיִם וְגו׳, בּ׳ פְּרִישָׁא. כִּי טַל אוֹרֹת טַלֶּךָ א׳ פְּרִישָׁא.

17. THESE ARE THE TWO DIVISIONS INCLUDED within the precious stone SAPPHIRE underneath the Throne of Glory, which is in the land of Egypt. For it is written, "And Hashem shall smite Egypt" (Yeshayah 19:22), which is the second division, while the verse, "For your dew is as the dew on herbs" (Yeshayah 26:19) is the first division.

18. וּבְגִין דָּא מִתְלַף כַּחֲדָא, ב׳ פְּרִישָׁא גָלוּתָא, א׳ פְּרִישָׁא קַדְמַיְיתָא. תָּא חֲזֵי, מַאי דִכְתִיב בֵּית יַעֲקֹב לְכוּ וְנֵלְכָה בְּאוֹר ה׳, בְּגָלוּתָא, אַתְוָון דְּאִתְגְזַר עֲלֵיהוֹן, עַל חוֹבֵיהוֹן, בְּקוּשְׁטָא בְּדִינָא הֲוֹו, בְּאוֹרַיְיתָא תַּקַנְתָּא, וְתִפְקוּן מִן חַמְרָא טִינָא, דְּהִיא גָלוּתָא, וְתַהֲכוּ לְנַהֲרָא דַיי׳.

18. The second division, WHICH ALLUDES TO the exile, is therefore connected with the first division, WHICH ALLUDES TO REVIVAL AND REDEMPTION. Come and see the verse, "O house of Jacob, come, and let us walk in the light of Hashem" (Yeshayah 2:5), WHICH MEANS that the letters indicating the exile they were sentenced to for their sins, according to Truth and Justice, have a remedy within the Torah. And IF YOU KEEP IT, you shall come out of the filth and mud, which is exile; and walk by the light of Hashem, WHICH IS RESURRECTION AND REDEMPTION, SINCE THE EXILE CAUSED THE RETURN TO TORAH WHICH LEADS TO THE REDEMPTION, SO WE FIND BOTH DIVISIONS CONNECTED.

19. א׳ ר״ץ בָּאָרֶץ, אִתְצַפֵּי אָתָא בְּתִיגְנָא דְּסִיפְרָא דְאוֹרַיְיתָא. וְאִינוּן אִתְפַּלְגִין בָּאָרֶץ, לָא׳ ר״ץ. אַתְּ מַשְׁכַּח בְּתִיגְנָא דְסַפְרָא דְּאוֹרַיְיתָא, ר״ץ מִתְלַפִּין כַּחֲדָא גָלוּתָא. מַאי גָלוּתָא דְמִצְרָאֵי אַרְבַּע מְאָה שְׁנִין הֲוָה אֲמַר לְאַבְרָהָם, דְּיֵהֵא גָלוּתָא לִבְנוֹהִי בְּמִצְרָאֵי, וְכִי הֲוֵית מְנַיְתָא יַתְהוֹן מָאתָן וְתִשְׁעִין שְׁנִין הֲוֹו.

19. THE LETTERS Aleph and Resh - Tzakik of Eretz (lit. 'land') are the land which sadly goes INTO EXILE, by the decree of the book of the Torah; TO WIT, THE FOUR HUNDRED YEARS MENTIONED IN THE DECREE 'BETWEEN THE PIECES.' They are divided by land into Aleph and Resh - Tzakik. It may be found by the decree of the book of Torah that Resh - Tzakik come together in exile, MEANING THAT THEY WERE IN EXILE IN EGYPT RESH -TZAKIK (= 290) YEARS; WHICH, TOGETHER WITH ALEPH (OF ALEPH = 110), AMOUNTS TO FOUR HUNDRED YEARS. What is the Egyptian exile? Abraham was told his children would be in exile for four hundred years, yet if you count it, it amounts to only 290 years.

20. תָּא חֲזֵי וַיָּמָת יוֹסֵף בֶּן מֵאָה וָעֶשֶׂר שָׁנִים. ר״ש פָּתַח וְאָמַר, הִנֵּה הָעַלְמָה הָרָה וְיוֹלֶדֶת בֵּן וְקָרָאת שְׁמוֹ עִמָּנוּאֵל, עֲדוּי וְלֵידָה, דְּאִתְמְלֵי

לְגָלוּיָאן, וְעָקְתָן סַגִּיאִין, וְעֶדֶן בִּישִׁין, וְאע"ג דִּיהוּ בְּאִלֵּין מַטְרוּנִיתָא אִזְדַּעֲזְעַת וְאִתְרַחֲקַת מִן בַּעֲלָהּ, תְּהֵא עִמָּנָא בְּגָלוּתָא, בֶּן מֵאָה וְעֶשֶׂר הֲוָה גָּלוּפָא דְאִתּוֹסַף, יִתְרְעֵי לְמֵימַר וַהֲוָה עָבַר מִן גָּלוּתָא מֵאָה וְעֶשֶׂר שְׁנִין, וּמָאתָן וְתִשְׁעִין, הֲוֵי אַרְבַּע מְאָה שְׁנִין, וְלָא אִתְמְנֵי גָלוּתָא דְיַעֲקֹב, אֶלָּא מִדְּמִית יוֹסֵף, וְהַיְינוּ דָּא דָּא ע"ג דָּא דַּאֲמַר וּמֵעֵת הוּסַר הַתָּמִיד וְלָתֵת שִׁקּוּץ שׁוֹמֵם וְגו'.

20. "And Joseph died, being a hundred and ten years old" (Beresheet 50:26). Rabbi Shimon opened the discussion saying: "Behold, the young woman is with child, and she will bear a son, and shall call his name 'Immanuel' (lit. 'El is with us')" (Yeshayah 7:14). Pregnancy and birth ARE MENTIONED IN THIS VERSE, AND were fulfilled in exiles, bad troubles and evil times, FOR THE VERSE CONTINUES: "FOR BEFORE THE CHILD SHALL KNOW HOW TO REFUSE THE EVIL AND CHOOSE THE GOOD, THE LAND...SHALL BE DESERTED..." (IBID.16). And though THE HOLY ONE, BLESSED BE HE, will be with us DURING THESE YEARS, AS INDICATED BY THE CHILD'S NAME, IMMANU – EL, WHICH IS THE NAME OF THE SHECHINAH, YET The Shechinah trembled and separated from Her husband, ZEIR ANPIN, and stayed with us in exile. THOUGH THE SHECHINAH IS WITH US, SHE SUFFERS PAIN AND EXILE, AND IS ALONE. SO THERE IS PREGNANCY THAT PRECEDES THE BIRTH OF EXILE. "A hundred and ten years old," is the further impression CONSIDERED THE PREGNANCY OF THE EXILE. THE VERSE wishes to point out that of the EGYPTIAN exile, one hundred and ten years passed AS PREGNANCY, WHILE 290 years WERE THE EXILE ITSELF. In all, there are four hundred years WHICH THE HOLY ONE, BLESSED BE HE, SPOKE OF TO ABRAHAM, IN THE DECREE OF 'BETWEEN THE PIECES.' The exile of Jacob started only when Joseph died. In connection to this it was said: "And from the time that the daily sacrifice shall be taken away, and the abomination that makes desolate be set up, there shall be a thousand (Heb. *eleph*) two hundred and ninety days" (Daniel 12:11).

21. וַיִּהְיוּ יְמֵי יַעֲקֹב שְׁנֵי חַיָּיו שֶׁבַע שָׁנִים וְאַרְבָּעִים וּמְאַת שָׁנָה, הָכָא רָזָא בְּגָלוּתָא בְּמִנְיָינָא, תִּקּוּנָתָא יְהוֹן בְּנַיָּיא דְאִתְגַּלְיָין בְּמִכִילְתָא דְדִינָא, תְּלָתָא גַּלְוָון, קַדְמָאָה דְמִצְרָאֵי, דְּאִתְמְתַל בְּשֶׁבַע שְׁנִין. רִבִּי חִיָּיא פָּתַח וְאָמַר, הִשְׁבַּעְתִּי אֶתְכֶם בְּנוֹת יְרוּשָׁלַ͏ִם בִּצְבָאוֹת אוֹ בְּאַיְלוֹת וְגו'.

-13-

21. "So the whole age of Jacob was a hundred and forty seven years" (Beresheet 47:28). THE 147 YEARS OF JACOB'S LIFE CONTAIN the secret of the number of correction by exile the descendants will endure, who were exiled under strict Judgment into three exiles. The first one in Egypt is likened to seven years. Rabbi Chiya opened the discussion saying: "I charge you, O daughters of Jerusalem, by the gazelles, and by the hinds of the fields" (Shir Hashirim 2:7). HERE TOO, THE NUMBER SEVEN (HEB. *SHEVA*), OF JACOB'S LIFE, IS DERIVED FROM THE OATH (HEB. *SHEVUAH*), NOT TO AWAKEN LOVE, UNTIL REDEMPTION PLEASES.

22. ר' שִׁמְעוֹן אָמַר, מֵהָכָא, מֵרָחוֹק ה' נִרְאָה לִי וְאַהֲבַת עוֹלָם אֲהַבְתִּיךְ וְגו', הָכָא רָזָא בְּגָלוּתָא תַּקְנָתָא יְהוֹן בְּנוֹהִי דְיִשְׂרָאֵל, מִשְׁתְּרֵי גַּלְיָיא, וְיִתְרְעֵי לְמֵימַר, יְהוֹן בְּנַיָא קַדִּישָׁא, דְּאִתְגַּלְיָוֹן עַל חוֹבֵיהוֹן בְּדִינָא שְׁנִין סַגִּיאִין יְהֵא, שֶׁבַע כְּחַטֹאתֵיכֶם, כִּי שִׁבְעָתַיִם יֻקַּם קָיִן, בְּגָלוּתָא קַדְמָאָה דְמִצְרָאֵי, דְּהִיא זְעֵירָא.

22. Rabbi Shimon said: From this WE LEARN THE EXPLANATION OF THE NUMBER SEVEN. IT IS WRITTEN, "Hashem appeared to me from afar, saying: I have loved you with an everlasting love" (Yirmeyah 31:3). FROM AFAR, NAMELY, IN EXILE, BECAUSE GREAT LOVE IS REVEALED ONLY BY EXILE. Here lies the secret, that exile is the means of the children of Yisrael to be freed from exile AND THAT HIS LOVE WILL BE REVEALED TO US. Scripture wishes to point out, BY THE NUMBER SEVEN OF JACOB'S LIFE, that the holy children who were exiled for their sins will be sentenced for many years, which will amount to "seven times...according to your sins" (Vayikra 26:21). IT ALSO SAYS, "If Cain shall be avenged sevenfold" (Beresheet 4:24), WHICH NUMBER FIXES THE DAMAGE THEY MADE, AND REVEALS THE LIGHT OF REDEMPTION. THIS IS during the first exile in Egypt, which is the shortest OF THE EXILES.

23. תִּנְיָינָא, גָּלוּתָא דְשׁוֹפְטִים, דְּאִתְמְתַל לְאַרְבָּעִים שְׁנִין, בְּשֶׁבַע דְּאִינְהוּ סַגִּיאֵי מִנֵּיה.

23. The second exile is in Babylon, likened to forty years FROM JACOB'S LIFE IN RELATION TO the seven IN EGYPT, for it is longer than it.

24. תְּלִיתָאֵי, גָּלוּתָא דַאֲנַן בֵּיה, אֲרִיכָא, דְּאִתְמְתַל לְמֵאָה שְׁנִין,

לְאַרְבְּעִין.

24. The third exile is the longest, likened to the hundred years OF JACOB'S LIFE, IN RELATION TO the forty years OF THE BABYLONIAN EXILE.

2. "And the time drew near...and he called his son Joseph"

A Synopsis

Rabbi Chizkiyah begins by explaining that Israel saw the torture of exile upon his descendants, and consequently, his soul began to die. Israel then gathered his exiles and told them that if they wished to be absolved of their sins, they must behave according to truth and justice in the eyes of God. Rabbi Shimon then explains why Israel called only Joseph his son and not all the other exiles. This is because all the children of Yisrael were called Joseph. Rabbi Chizkiyah then refers to the secret of the *Vav* as including Jacob, Joseph, and others, as well as the six Sfirot.

The Relevance of this Passage

Israel's action of talking to the people of the exile is a code for the great Patriarch calling upon all generations, including the readers of this passage, and awakening them to the power of the Light and the path to eternal freedom, fulfillment, and the final redemption. When Yisrael calls only the name Joseph, the Zohar is indicating a direct reference to the Sfirah/dimension of Yesod, the portal and funnel through which the supernal Light flows into our world. The name Joseph refers to the Light that is flowing from Yesod to us – the reader and all the people who remain in exile in our current generation. This Light now becomes part of our being.

25. וַיִּקְרְבוּ יְמֵי יִשְׂרָאֵל לָמוּת. רִבִּי חִזְקִיָּה אָמַר, חֲמָא דָא עַקְתָּא דְגָלוּתָא, דַּהֲוָה עָרְעָן לִבְנוֹהִי, קְרִיבָא אַנְפְּשֵׁיה וּדְחִיקַת לְמִמָת, לָא אִשְׁתְּאַר חַי, כַּד הֲוָה נָחֵית מַדְרְגִין, בְּדִיל חוֹבֵיהוֹן דְּיִשְׂרָאֵל, לָא נָחֵית עִמְּהוֹן בְּגָלוּתָא, זַכָּאָה חוּלְקֵהוֹן, דְּאִי לָא נָחֵית עִמְּהוֹן בְּגָלוּתָא, אִשְׁתְּאָרָן בֵּינֵי עַמְמַיָּא, וְאַתְּ אֲמַרְתְּ מַדּוּעַ בָּאתִי וְאֵין אִישׁ קָרָאתִי וְאֵין עוֹנֶה. וְאֵין עוֹנֶה: דָּא יִשְׂרָאֵל, בָּאתִי וְאֵין אִישׁ: דָּא שְׁכִינָה. הַקָּצוֹר קָצְרָה יָדִי מִפְּדוּת וְאִם אֵין בִּי כֹּחַ לְהַצִּיל הֵן בְּגַעֲרָתִי אַחֲרִיב יָם אָשִׂים נְהָרוֹת מִדְבָּר, קוּדְשָׁא בְּרִיךְ הוּא יְהַב חוּלְקָא לְיִשְׂרָאֵל, דְּלָא יִשְׁלוֹט רַבְרְבָנָא אַחֲרָא בְּהוֹן, נָחֲתוּ לְגָלוּתָא שְׁכִינְתָּא עִמְּהוֹן וְהוּא רָחֵיק מִמַּטְרוֹנִיתָא.

25. "And the time drew near for Israel to die" (Beresheet 47:29). Rabbi Chizkiyah said: He saw this trouble of exile upon his children, and his soul

drew near death. He did not remain alive when he descended his grades because of the sins of Yisrael. YISRAEL, ZEIR ANPIN, did not go into exile with them, LIKE THE SHECHINAH, WHO WENT INTO EXILE WITH THEM. HE ASKS: Happy is the portion OF YISRAEL, for if He, ZEIR ANPIN, would not have gone down with them into exile, they would have remained among the nations WITHOUT BEING ABLE TO ESCAPE. Why then does it say, "Why, when I came, was there no man? when I called, was there none to answer?" (Yeshayah 50:2). "Was there none to answer" alludes to Yisrael, NAMELY ZEIR ANPIN; "when I came, was there no man": This is the Shechinah. "Is my hand shortened at all, that it cannot redeem? or have I no power to deliver? behold, at my rebuke I dry up the sea, I make the rivers a wilderness." SO ZEIR ANPIN DID COME DOWN ALSO WITH THEM INTO EXILE? HE ANSWERS: The Holy One, blessed be He, gave a portion to Yisrael, so that no other minister would rule over them; THUS HE IS WITH THEM IN EXILE. ALSO when they went into exile, the Shechinah is with them, but ZEIR ANPIN is far away from the Shechinah.

26. וַיִּקְרָא לִבְנוֹ לְיוֹסֵף וַיֹּאמֶר לוֹ אִם נָא מָצָאתִי חֵן בְּעֵינֶיךָ, חָקַר יַת בְּנוֹהִי כֻּלְּהוֹן, וַאֲמַר לְהוֹן, עֲקָתָן סַגִּיאִין, בִּישִׁין רַבְרְבִין, חָמֵית לְמֵיעַל לִבְרֵיכוֹן אַשְׁכְּחָן רַחֲמֵי עִלָּאֵי.

26. "And he called his son Joseph, and said to him, if now I have found favor in your sight" (Beresheet 47:29). He examined all his sons and said to them, I see many evil troubles come upon your children, and ONE SHOULD find supernal Mercy.

27. וְאִי אַתּוּן בָּעָאן לְמֵיפַק מִכָּל עֲקָתָא, קַיְימוּ לִי, וַהֲבוּ בֵּינָנָא רִבּוֹן עָלְמָא וְתַעַבְדוּן קְשׁוֹט וְדִינָא, וְתֶהֱווֹ כַּאֲבָהַתְכוֹן, וּפַקִּידֵי בְּכָל דָּר וְדָר דְּיֵיתֵי בַּתְרֵיכוֹן, וְאִי אַתּוּן בָּעָאן לְמֶעְבַּד הָכֵי, תִּפְקוּן מִכָּל עֲקָתָא דְּיֵיתֵי עֲלֵיכוֹן.

27. If you wish to be delivered from all these troubles, swear before me, and we shall have the Master of the universe AS WITNESS between us, that you will conduct yourself according to truth and justice, and behave like your fathers. You shall teach it to every generation that will come after you. If you shall do so, you shall escape all the troubles that will come upon you.

28. רִבִּי שִׁמְעוֹן אָמַר, וְהַצִּיגוּ בַשַּׁעַר מִשְׁפָּט אוּלַי יֶחֱנַן ה' אֱלֹהֵי צְבָאוֹת שְׁאֵרִית יוֹסֵף. דְּאִתְקְרִיאוּ בְּנוֹהִי יִשְׂרָאֵל כֻּלְּהוֹן יוֹסֵף.

28. Rabbi Shimon said: To EXPLAIN AWAY THE DIFFICULTY THAT HE CALLED ONLY JOSEPH HIS SON AND NOT ALL THE TRIBES, THE WORDS OF RABBI SHIMON ARE BROUGHT HERE. "And establish justice in the gate: it may be that Hashem Elohim of Tzeva'ot will be gracious to the remnant of Joseph" (Amos 5:15), for all the children of Yisrael are called Joseph.

29. וְאִי תַעַבְדוּן הָכֵי, לָא תִקְבְּרוּן חַד מִן בְּרִי, אֶלָּא אָתֵי תְּתוּבוּן לְאַרְעֲכוֹן בִּשְׁלָמָא.

29. THE ZOHAR RETURNS TO THE WORDS OF JACOB: 'If you shall do so, you shall bury not one of my children in Egypt, but return safely with me to your land.'

30. הה״ד שִׂים נָא יָדְךָ תַּחַת יְרֵכִי, מַהוּ יָדְךָ. פָּתַח וַאֲמַר חֲגוֹר חַרְבְּךָ עַל יָרֵךְ גִּבּוֹר הוֹדְךָ וַהֲדָרֶךָ, סַיְיפָא דְקָאֵי בָּה חֶסֶד וֶאֱמֶת, תְּרֵין סְפִירָן סְפִירָן, וְלָא שָׁבְקִין דָּא לְדָא, וְעַ״ד אֲמַר חֶסֶד וֶאֱמֶת יְקַדְּמוּ פָנֶיךָ, פְּנֵי ה' חֶלְקָם, וְאִי הֲווֹ טָבָאן בְּנוֹהִי, וַעֲבִידוּ מַה דְּקַיְימוּ, לָא מִית חַד מִבְּנַיְיהוּ בְּמִצְרָאֵי, דְּכָל טַב וְטַב דְּגָזֵיר שְׁמָא דֶאֱלָהָא עַל אֵינָשָׁא, לָא הֲוֵי, אֶלָּא עַל דְּיהוֹן טָבִין, וְאִי לָא, לָא, כְּמָה דַאֲמַר דָּוִד, לְמַעַן יָקִים ה' אֶת דְּבָרוֹ אֲשֶׁר דִּבֶּר עָלַי לֵאמֹר אִם יִשְׁמְרוּ בָנֶיךָ אֶת דַּרְכָּם לָלֶכֶת לְפָנַי בֶּאֱמֶת. וְאִי לָא, לָא מַיְיתֵי בִּרְכָאן דַּאֲמַר עֲלֵיהוֹן.

30. It is written: "Put, I pray you, your hand under my thigh" (Beresheet 47:29). HE ASKS: What is "your hand"? He opened the discussion saying: "Gird your sword upon your thigh, O mighty warrior: your glory and your majesty" (Tehilim 45:4). ALSO "YOUR HAND UNDER MY THIGH" ALLUDES TO A SWORD, WHICH IS a sword of Grace and Truth, the two Sfirot which do not separate from each other; NAMELY YESOD WHICH CONTAINS THE LIGHT OF CHASSADIM AND THE LIGHT OF CHOCHMAH, CALLED TRUTH AND BRIGHTNESS OF COUNTENANCE. Therefore it says, "Love and Truth shall go before you" (Tehilim 89:15), "The anger of Hashem divided them" (Eichah 4:16). And if His children were good and did what they accepted upon them, not one of the children would have died in Egypt, for each kindness that the Holy One blessed be He decrees upon men is on the condition they will be good. As David said: "That Hashem may continue His word which He spoke concerning me, saying: 'If your children take heed to their way, to walk before Me in Truth'" (I Melachim 2:4). But if not, He shall not.

31. תָּא חֲזֵי, כַּמָּה הוּא עָדִיף רוּחָא דְּאַבָּא מֵרוּחָא דִּבְרָא, דְּרוּחָא דְּאַבָּא הוּא רוּחָא דִּבְרָא, רוּחָא מֵרוּחָא סָלְקָא, וְאִי סַיְּיעַת אֲוִירָא אָחֳרָא בְּרוּחָא, לָא נָפֵיק שְׁלִים, דְּהָא חָסֵיר הוּא, בְּהַאי אֲוִירָא, וְהַיְינוּ פֶּרֶה לִמֵּד מִדְבָּר בְּאַוַּת נַפְשָׁהּ שָׁאֲפָה רוּחַ.

31. Come and behold: better is the spirit of the father than the spirit of the son, for the spirit of the father is that of the son, spirit drawn from spirit. THUS WE FIND THE FATHER'S SPIRIT IN RELATION TO HIM IS THAT OF THE ROOT IN RELATION TO ITS BRANCH. But if another air OF THE OTHER SIDE contributes to the spirit of the son, he is not born whole, but rendered defective by that air OF THE OTHER SIDE; NAMELY "a wild donkey used to the wilderness, that snuffs up the wind in her desire" (Yirmeyah 2:24).

32. תָּנָא רַב הַמְנוּנָא סָבָא אֲזַל לְקַפּוֹטְקַיָּיא, עָאל לְקַמַּיְיהוּ, רַב יֵיסָא סָבָא, אָ"ל בְּמַאי עַסְקִיתוּ, וַוי לֵיהּ, וַוי לְנַפְשֵׁיהּ, אִי אִשְׁתְּלַח רוּחָא דִמְסָאֲבָא דְּאִשְׁתַּכַּח עִמֵּיהּ, וְאוֹרֵית לֵיהּ לִבְרֵיהּ, וְהַאי אִיהוּ דְּקוּדְשָׁא בְּרִיךְ הוּא לֵית לֵיהּ חוּלָקָא, שָׁבֵיק לֵיהּ חוּלָקָא שָׁבֵיק לֵיהּ לְשֵׁיצָאָה לֵיהּ לְעָלְמָא דְּאָתֵי, אָ"ל מַנָ"ל הָא, אָ"ל הָכָא אוֹלִיפְנָא, דְּהַאי יְרוּתָא בִישְׁתָּא, אַחֲסְנִין כֻּלְּהוּ בְּנוֹ אִי לָא יְתוּבוּן, דְּהָא לֵית מִלָּה קַיְּימָא קַמֵּי תְּשׁוּבָה. וַאֲנָא הָכֵי אוֹלִיפְנָא, דְּהָא אַסְוָותָא דָּא, יַהֲבוּ לִי זִמְנָא חֲדָא, דַּהֲוֵינָא רְשִׁים בְּאַנְפַּי, וְיוֹמָא חַד הֲוֵינָא אָזִיל בְּאָרְחָא, וְעַרְעָנָא בְּחַד זַכָּאָה, וְעַל יְדוֹי אִתְעֲבַר מִנַּאי, הַהוּא רְשִׁימָא, אָ"ל מַה שְׁמָךְ, אָ"ל אֶלְעָזָר, וְקָרֵינָא לֵיהּ אֶלְעָזָר אָחֳרָא, אָ"ל בְּרִיךְ רַחֲמָנָא דְּחָמֵינָא לָךְ, זַכָּאָה חוּלָקָךְ בְּעָלְמָא דֵין, וּבְעָלְמָא דְּאָתֵי.

32. We learned that Rabbi Hamnuna Saba (the elder) once went to Cappadocia. Going towards him was Rabbi Yisa Saba. According to Rav Ashlag, this paragraph is a later interpolation, which in other versions starts with Rabbi Aba.

33. וַיֹּאמֶר הִשָּׁבְעָה לִי וגו'. רִבִּי חִזְקִיָּה פָּתַח וְאָמַר, נִשְׁבַּע ה' בִּימִינוֹ וּבִזְרוֹעַ עֻזּוֹ, קַיֵּים קוּדְשָׁא בְּרִיךְ הוּא, דְּיִפּוֹק לְיִשְׂרָאֵל מִן גָּלוּתָא דִלְהוֹן, וְדָא קַיָּים לְהוֹן, קַיָּים, דְּלָא יִשְׁבּוֹק לוֹן בְּאַרְעָא שַׂנְאֵיהוֹן.

33. "And he said: 'Swear to me'" (Beresheet 47:31). Rabbi Chizkiyah opened the discussion saying: "Hashem has sworn by His right hand, and by the arm of His strength" (Yeshayah 62:8), WHICH MEANS Hashem swore He would deliver Yisrael from their exile. This is what He swore to them BY THE VERSE: "AND HE SWORE TO HIM" (BERESHEET 47:31) HERE WHICH ALSO REFERS TO THE HOLY ONE, BLESSED BE HE. He swore to them He would not abandon them in the land of their enemies.

34. וַיֹּאמֶר שַׁלְּחֵנִי כִּי עָלָה הַשָּׁחַר וַיֹּאמֶר לֹא אֲשַׁלֵּחֲךָ כִּי אִם בֵּרַכְתָּנִי. מַאן בֵּרַכְתָּנִי. יְהַב לוֹן גָּלוּתָא, וְקַיֵּים לוֹן, דְּיִפְּקוּן מִנֵּיהּ.

34. "And he said: 'Let me go, for the day breaks.' And he said: 'I will not let you go, unless you bless me'" (Beresheet 32:27). What does "bless me" mean; TO WIT, WHAT WAS THE BLESSING HE CONFERRED UPON HIM? HE ANSWERS: he assigned them to exile and swore to them He would deliver them from it.

35. תָּנָא, זַמִּין קוּדְשָׁא בְּרִיךְ הוּא לִבְרֵיהוֹן דְּיִשְׂרָאֵל, דְּיהוֹן כָּל חַד וְחַד תְּחוֹת כָּרְסֵיהּ, וִיהוֹן מַעַלְיָין מִכָּל עִלָּאֵי, בְּגִין דָּא תִּשְׁכַּח וא"ו אֲרִיכָא, קַיָּים קוּדְשָׁא בְּרִיךְ הוּא לִשְׁלֵמוּתָא דו' דר"א וּבְגִין שָׁתָּא וַיִּשְׁתַּחוּ יִשְׂרָאֵל עַל רֹאשׁ הַמִּטָּה, סָגִיד יִשְׂרָאֵל, דְּלֵיתֵי מְשִׁיחָא, בְּסוֹף מִנְיָינָא דָּא, וְתִשְׁרֵי שְׁכִינְתָּא עִמְּהוֹן.

35. We learned that the Holy One, blessed be He, would DO for His children of Yisrael, that they would all dwell under His throne, and excel the high ANGELS. Therefore, one finds a long *Vav* IN THE TORAH, LIKE IN

"WHATEVER GOES ON ITS BELLY (HEB. *GACHON*)" (VAYIKRA 11:42), which is an allusion that the Holy One, blessed be He, swore upon the perfection of the *Vav* (= 6) generations, THE SECRET OF ABRAHAM, ISAAC, JACOB, MOSES, AARON AND JOSEPH, THE SECRET OF THE SIX SFIROT: CHESED, GVURAH, TIFERET, NETZACH, HOD AND YESOD. Because of these six, IT IS WRITTEN: "And Israel bowed himself upon the bed's head" (Beresheet 47:31), YISRAEL BEING THE SECRET OF ZEIR ANPIN, WHICH INCLUDES: CHESED, GVURAH, TIFERET, NETZACH, HOD AND YESOD. The bowing of Israel ALLUDES TO the coming of Messiah at the end of this time; TO WIT, AFTER SIX THOUSAND YEARS, ALLUDING TO THE SIX COMPLETE SFIROT, CHESED, GVURAH, TIFERET, NETZACH, HOD AND YESOD, CLOTHED BY SUPERNAL ABA AND IMA, WHICH SFIROT ARE EACH OF A THOUSAND YEARS. And the Shechinah will dwell among them.

3. "Behold, your father is sick"

A Synopsis

Rabbi Chizkiyah begins by saying that this quotation refers to events at the end of exile, and means, literally, Joseph's father, Yisrael, is "worried and in haste." Rabbi Aba then adds that the name Yud-Hei-Vav יהו would be changed to Yud Hei Vav Hei יהוה to expedite Yisrael doing good for his children, so they would come out of exile. Rabbi Aba then explains Jacob's exposure to truth, and Abraham's to grace.

The Relevance of this Passage

The Hebrew letters Yud Hei Vav Hei יהוה are known as the Tetragrammaton, one of the Holy Names of The Creator. The addition of the final *Hei* ה in the Holy Name corresponds to our physical realm. The other three letters יהו represent the Upper Worlds, specifically four dimensions of Keter, Chochmah, Binah, and Zeir Anpin. Thus, this passage is our connection to the Upper Worlds, via the Tetragrammaton, so that we may brighten our lives and the world with the resplendent Light of The Creator.

36. וַיְהִי אַחַר הַדְּבָרִים הָאֵלֶּה וַיֹּאמֶר לְיוֹסֵף הִנֵּה אָבִיךָ חוֹלֶה וגו'. מַתְנִיתִין, א"ר חִזְקִיָּה, לָא אָתָא קְרָא לְאַשְׁמוּעִינָן דְּעָבַד, אֶלָּא אָתָא קְרָא לְאַתְיָא מַה דִּיהֱוֵי בְּסוֹף גָּלוּתָא, כָּל אִלֵּין מִנְיָינָא דְּאִתְמְנֵי, צָבֵי לְמֵימַר דְּיֵיתֵי מְשִׁיחָא, וְיֵימָא לֵיהּ אָבוּךְ דְּבִשְׁמַיָּא בָּהִיל לְסַבְּר אַפָּךְ, סָפִין לְקָצָא דִּמְשִׁיחָא, יְהֵא רַעֲוָא מִן אֱלָהָא דִּשְׁמַיָא, דְּיֵסַב בְּרֵיהּ דְּאַסְגִּיאוּ בְּגָלוּתָא, וּמִדְּאִתְנְשִׁיאוּ בְּהוֹ, דְּנָשֵׁי יַתְהוֹן קוּדְשָׁא בְּרִיךְ הוּא בְּחוֹבֵיהוֹן בְּקוּשְׁטָא.

36. "And it came to pass after these things that one told Joseph, 'Behold, your father is sick'" (Beresheet 48:1). In the Mishnah Rabbi Chizkiyah said, that the verse does not teach us what JOSEPH did, but brings before us the events at the end of exile, at the end of the set time AT THE END OF THE SIXTH MILLENIUM. THE VERSE says that Messiah, THE SECRET OF JOSEPH, will come and say to him, Your Father in heaven makes haste to welcome you, who looks to the end of Messiah. "YOUR FATHER IS SICK" MEANS, HE IS WORRIED AND IN HASTE. "AND HE TOOK WITH HIM MENASHE AND EPHRAIM" (IBID.) MEANS: May it please Elohim in heaven

to receive His children, who increased and multiplied (Heb. *paru*) in exile, FOR WHICH THEY ARE CALLED EPHRAIM, and THEIR SINS forgotten BECAUSE OF THE EXILE, THE SECRET OF THEIR BEING CALLED MENASHE, WHICH IS DERIVED FROM THE WORD FORGETFULNESS (HEB. *NESHIYAH*). For the Holy One, blessed be He, truly forgot their transgressions.

37. כַּד אָתָא רִבִּי אַבָּא אָמַר, לָאו לְדַרְשָׁא קָא אֲתֵינָא, חֲשׁוֹב רָזָא דְּמִלְּתָא יוֹסֵף ה' לִי בֵּן אַחֵר, כִּדְפָרִישְׁנָא לְעֵיל, הַאי שְׁמֵיהּ קַדִּישָׁא בְּיוֹסֵף, יה"ו יֵאמַר, הָא אֲבוּךְ מָארֵי עַלְמָא דְּאָתֵי, לְמֶעְבַּד טָבָא לִבְרֵיהּ, דְּיִפְקוּן מִן גָּלוּתָא דִּלְהוֹן, וְאִי אַתְּ לָא רָעֵי בְּקוּשְׁטָךְ, רְבוּעָא יְדוּ"ד אֶחָד יַעֲבֵד יָתָךְ, וְיַדְעֵי דְּתֵיתוּב מַטְרוֹנִיתָא לְאַתְרָא.

37. When Rabbi Aba came, he said he came not to discourse ON THE VERSE, BUT TO EXPLAIN ITS MYSTERY. HE SAID: The secret of this matter is very important AS THAT OF THE VERSE, "Hashem shall add (Heb. *Joseph*) to me another son" (Beresheet 30:24). As we explained in relation to that verse, the Holy Name written in Joseph, TO WIT, THAT THE THREE - LETTERED NAME *Yud-Hei-Vav* will say to him, here your Father, the Master over the World to Come, SECRET OF ZEIR ANPIN WITH THE MOCHIN OF SUPERNAL BINAH, CALLED THE WORLD TO COME, wishes to do good for His children, so they may come out of exile. But if you do not favor your Truth BECAUSE YOU FIND THAT THEY DO NOT MERIT IT, here is a four - lettered name Yud Hei Vav Hei to set you right and then will favor it for the Shechinah to return to Her place.

38. דַּאֲבָהָתָנָא אִינּוּן רְתִיכִין דִּלְעֵילָּא, וַיַּעַל אֱלֹקִים מֵעַל אַבְרָהָם, אֲבָהָן שׁוֹקֵי עַלְמָא, תִּתֵּן אֱמֶת לְיַעֲקֹב חֶסֶד לְאַבְרָהָם, תָּנָא דְּיֵיתֵי מְשִׁיחָא.

38. For the fathers are the supernal Chariot FOR THE HOLY NAME on high, as it is written: "And Elohim went up from Abraham" (Beresheet 17:22), WHICH MEANS HE WAS RIDING ON HIM. IT IS ALSO WRITTEN, "You will show Truth to Jacob, Grace (Heb. *chesed*) to Abraham" (Michah 7:20). THUS JACOB WAS A CHARIOT TO TIFERET CALLED TRUTH, AND ABRAHAM A CHARIOT TO CHESED. And we learned that BY THE UNISON OF THE ONE YUD HEI VAV HEI, Messiah will come.

4. "At evening time, there will be light"

A Synopsis
Rabbi Yosi describes how there will be a day without day or night, until the evening, when there will be light, at which time, two evils will befall Jacob's children. But these occur so his children can be taken to "the good land." Rabbi Aba then poses a conundrum: "What is darkness?" The others determine that "darkness is Gehenom."

The Relevance of this Passage
The phrase, "day without day or night," refers to the potential darkness and destruction [God forbid] that may appear before the final redemption of mankind takes place. Two paths to redemption and eternal peace are always available to us, a Light - filled path that embodies mercy and protection, or a darkened path that embodies pain, torment, and suffering. Our egos constantly urge us towards the path of darkness. Through a meditative, intense read of this passage, we can help ourselves, and the world at large, avoid the potential gloom and devastation that attends the path of darkness.

39. רִבִּי יוֹסֵי פְּתַח וַאֲמַר, וְהָיָה יוֹם אֶחָד הוּא יִוָּדַע לַה' לֹא יוֹם וְלֹא לַיְלָה וְהָיָה לְעֵת עֶרֶב יִהְיֶה אוֹר, רוֹצֶה לְמֵימַר, תְּרֵין מְעַרְעֵין בִּישִׁין דְּאָתָן לִבְנוֹהִי לְמֶהֱוֵי בְּגָלוּתָא בְּאַרְעָ שַׂנְאֵיהוֹן, וְלָא יִסְתְּכֵי בְּהוֹן, כַּמָּה שְׁנִין סַגִּיאִין, עַל חוֹבֵיהוֹן בְּקוּשְׁטָא, הָכִי יִזְנַח יַתְהוֹן בְּאַרְעָ שַׂנְאֵיהוֹן. וְיִסַּב בְּנַיְיהוּ דְּאַרְעָ דְּאַרְעָ לְהוֹן בִּישִׁין אִלֵּין, וְיַדְבַּר לְהוֹן לַאֲרַע טַב כְּפֵירוּשָׁא דִּקְרָא.

39. Rabbi Yosi opened the discussion with the verse: "But it shall be one particular day which shall be known as Hashem's, neither day, nor night: but it shall come to pass that at evening time, there will be light" (Zecharyah 14:7). HE STARTED EXPLAINING THE VERSE, "AND HE TOOK... EPHRAIM AND MENASHE" (BERESHEET 48:1), BUT EXPLAINED NO FURTHER. THE ZOHAR EXPLAINS THE WORDS OF RABBI YOSI, SAYING THAT HE wishes to say that two evils will befall the children OF JACOB: 1) they will be in exile in the land of their enemies, THIS BEING THE ASPECT OF EPHRAIM AND MENASHE. 2) He will not look at them many years on account of their sinning against Truth, and so will abandon them in the land of their enemies. Eventually, He would take their children, to whom these TWO evils befell, and conduct them to the good land, as the verse says, "AND HE

-24-

TOOK... MENASHE AND EPHRAIM"; TO WIT, HE WILL TAKE THEM, TO WHOM THE TWO EVILS BEFELL, AND CONDUCT THEM TO THEIR GOOD LAND.

40. וַהֲוָה תְּרֵי רַבְרְבָן סַגִּיאִין מַעֲלְיָיִאן הֲוָה מְטַרְקָן תְּחוֹת כָּרְסֵי יְקָרָא, דְּאַפַּטְרוֹפָא דְּיִשְׂרָאֵל מְכִילָתָא חֲמִישָׁאָה, בְּדִיל דִּיהוֹן בְּגָלוּתָא כָּל עִדָּנָא הָדֵין, וְאַרְע דִּנְשֵׁי יַתְהוֹן בְּאַרַע שַׂנְאֵיהוֹן.

40. There were two great and exalted ministers who were knocking under the Throne of Glory of Yisrael's chieftain, the fifth measure, to cause them to remain in exile for as long AS THEY NEED, FROM THE ASPECT OF EPHRAIM, and worse, that He would forget them in the land of their enemies, WHICH IS THE ASPECT OF MENASHE.

41. וְהוּא תְּרֵין מְכִילָתָן, בִּתְרֵין סְפִין, נָפַק חָדָא וּמַלֵּיל לָקֳבֵל רִבּוֹן עָלְמָא, וְיָהִיב לֵיהּ רְשׁוּ דִּימַלֵּל כָּל מַאן דְּבָעֵי, וְחָזֵי בְּיִשְׂרָאֵל מִן גִּיסָא חָדָא לְמִגְזַר בְּהוֹן בְּיִשְׂרָאֵל, דְּיִפְּקוּן מִן גָּלוּתָא, בְּדִין אֲבָהַתְהוֹן. וּמִן גִּיסָא אַחֲרִינָא, רָעָא לְמִגְזַר עֲלֵיהוֹן, בְּדִיל חוֹבֵיהוֹן, דַּאֲמְרוּ עֲלַיְיהוּ בִּישָׁא סַגִּיאָה הָא ד' מְכִילָתָן, וְלָא הֲוָה בְּהוֹן מְכִילָתָא חֲמִישָׁאָה אַפַּטְרוֹפָא דְּיִשְׂרָאֵל, וּמַלִּילוּ כָּל דִּרְעוּ.

41. These two ministers are two attributes, each containing two aspects; TO WIT, EACH IS DIVIDED INTO TWO ATTRIBUTES. HE EXPLAINS, One ATTRIBUTE came and spoke before the Master of the universe and was given permission to say what it liked. On the one hand, it saw it should be decreed that Yisrael should come out of exile, due to their fathers' merit. On the other hand, it saw they deserve to be sentenced TO REMAIN IN EXILE for their sins, for THE ACCUSERS said great evil things about them. There are four attributes in all. FOR EACH OF THE MINISTERS, THE TWO ATTRIBUTES CONTAINS TWO ASPECTS; TO WIT, ONE FOR AND ONE AGAINST. But they did not have the fifth attribute, Yisrael's chieftain, and they spoke as they pleased. THE TWO MINISTERS SPOKE NOW FOR AND NOW AGAINST, FOR THEY HAD NOT THE FIFTH ATTRIBUTE, WHICH TURNS ALL INTO MERIT.

42. עַד דְּמָטָא לְוָותְהוֹן מְכִילָתָא חֲמִישָׁאָה, וַהֲוָה בְּכָרְסֵי יְקָרָא מִן

שְׁמָא קַדִּישָׁא, וְאָמַר עַל בְּנוֹהִי דְיִשְׂרָאֵל טַב, וְלָא הֲווֹ רַתְיָין תְּרֵין
מְכִילָתָן קַמְיְיתָא לְמַלָּלָא קַמֵּיהּ, בְּדֵין מְכִילְתָּא חֲמִישָׁאָה, דְּאִתְמְתַל
לְלֵילְיָא, וְנָפַק לְנְהוֹרָא דִלְהוֹן, וְעַ״ד פְּתַח, וְהָיָה יוֹם אֶחָד הוּא יִוְּדַע
לַה׳ לֹא יוֹם וְלֹא לַיְלָה וְהָיָה לְעֵת עֶרֶב יִהְיֶה אוֹר.

42. Then the fifth attribute arrived, WHICH WILL BE REVEALED AT THE END OF CORRECTION, to be upon the Throne of Glory of the Holy Name. It would say good things about Yisrael, and the two first measures would no longer be afraid to speak before Him GOOD THINGS ABOUT YISRAEL, AS THEY WERE BEFORE. For the fifth attribute, which was considered the rule of the night, now came out to shine upon them. Therefore RABBI YOSI opened the discussion saying: "But it shall be one particular day which shall be known as Hashem's, neither day, nor night: but it shall come to pass that at evening time, there will be light."

43. תָּנִינָא וַיִּקְרָא אֱלֹקִים לָאוֹר יוֹם וְלַחֹשֶׁךְ קָרָא לַיְלָה, וְהָתָם אָמַר
וְחֹשֶׁךְ עַל פְּנֵי תְהוֹם, וְקַשְׁיָא דִידֵיהּ אֲדִידֵיהּ, אָתָא רַבִּי אֶלְעָזָר לְרִ״שׁ
אֲבוֹי, וְאִ״ל אַבָּא מָארִי, מַאי דָא, אָ״ל, מִבְּרֵאשִׁית עַד וִ׳ דוֹרוֹת בָּרָא
יְדוּ״ד אֶחָד, צָבֵי לְמֵימַר, וִ׳ דִּשְׁמֵיהּ, יָהַב בֵּיהּ רוּחַ חָכְמָה, עַד הָכָא לָא
הֲוָה מִנְדַע מַהוּ חֹשֶׁךְ. קָם רַבִּי אֶלְעָזָר וּנְשַׁק יְדוֹי דַּאֲבוֹי.

43. We have learned that the verse, "And Elohim called the light Day, and the darkness He called Night" (Beresheet 1:5) MEANS THAT THE NUKVA OF ZEIR ANPIN CALLED DARKNESS, AND ALSO CALLED NIGHT, RECEIVES FROM DAY, WHICH IS ZEIR ANPIN. It is also said: "And darkness was on the face of the deep" (Ibid. 2), TO WIT, DARKNESS IS A KLIPAH, NOT PERTAINING TO HOLINESS. The verses contradict each other. Rabbi Elazar came to his father Rabbi Shimon and said to him: My father and master, what is the meaning of this CONTRADICTION? He replied to him, From the beginning, up to the sixth generation, THE SECRET OF CHESED, GVURAH, TIFERET, NETZACH, HOD, AND YESOD OF ZEIR ANPIN, He created one Yud Hei Vav Hei, WHICH IS THE SECRET OF BINAH. He explains, This refers to THE SECRET OF *Vav* of the name YUD HEI VAV HEI, ZEIR ANPIN, upon which BINAH conferred the spirit of Chochmah. THEREFORE, until then, darkness was not known at all. Rabbi Elazar rose and kissed his father's hands.

‏44. קָם ר' אַבָּא וּשְׁאַל, מַאי חֹשֶׁךְ. אִסְתַּחֲרוּ חַבְרַיָּיא וְלָא מָטוֹ מַאי
‏דְּשָׁאֲלוּ, עֲבָדוּ עוֹבָדָא, וּמְטָא קָלָא מִן קֳדָם רִבּוֹן עַלְמָא, בְּהַאי קְרָא,
‏אֶרֶץ עֵיפָתָה וגו' צַלְמָוֶת וְלֹא סְדָרִים, וַתּוֹפַע כְּמוֹ אוֹפֶל, גֵּיהִנֹּם מִקַּמֵּי
‏דְּאִתְבְּרֵי עַלְמָא, הֲוָה גָּנִיז לִרְשִׁיעַיָּא, וַוי לְהוֹן לְחַיָּיבַיָּא, דִּיהוֹן כַּד
‏יַעֲבִיד אֱלָהָא יַת אִלֵּין, כִּי הִנֵּה הַחֹשֶׁךְ יְכַסֶּה אֶרֶץ וַעֲרָפֶל לְאֻמִּים
‏וְעָלַיִךְ יִזְרַח יי' וּכְבוֹדוֹ עָלַיִךְ יֵרָאֶה, זַכָּאָה חוּלְקֵהוֹן דְּיִשְׂרָאֵל, דְּקוּדְשָׁא
‏בְּרִיךְ הוּא לָא בָּרָא לְהוֹן דָּא, אַשְׁרֵי הָעָם שֶׁכָּכָה לוֹ אַשְׁרֵי הָעָם שֶׁיי'
‏אֱלֹהָיו.

44. Rabbi Aba rose and asked: What is darkness? The friends turned around, TO WIT, THEY SOUGHT HARD FOR AN ANSWER, but did not arrive at an answer to his question. They did something, NAMELY A CERTAIN MEDITATION, and a voice from before the Master of the universe resounded this verse, "A land of gloom, as darkness itself; and of the shadow of death, without any order, and where the light is as darkness" (Iyov 10:22). THIS DARKNESS MEANS Gehenom, for even before the world was created, it was stored for the wicked. FROM THIS, THEY UNDERSTOOD THAT DARKNESS IS GEHENOM. Woe to the wicked, who will abide in this darkness, when Elohim will do all this as it says in, "For, behold, the darkness shall cover the earth, and gross darkness the peoples: but Hashem shall arise upon you, and His glory shall be seen upon you" (Yeshayah 60:2). Happy is the portion of Yisrael, that the Holy One, blessed be He, did not create THIS DARKNESS for them. "Happy is that people, that is in such a case: Happy is that people, whose Elohim is Hashem" (Tehilim 144:15).

5. "And one told Jacob"

A Synopsis

Rabbi Yosi explains that the quotation, "And one told Jacob," refers to Jacob being told his children would be redeemed. Through this redemption, Jacob would receive both truth and grace, which are two Sfirot, also contained in two higher Chariots, Abraham and Jacob.

The Relevance of this Passage

To achieve a higher level of spirituality and existence, we sometimes need to "borrow" Light from The Creator in order to use it to awaken and arouse even greater Light in our lives and in this world. This is similar to a businessman borrowing money from a bank for the purpose of building a successful business. In other words, *you need money in order to make money*. Hence, the primary purpose of this passage is to entrust the readers with Light, so that they may use it to for spiritual purposes and the formation of greater Light.

45. וַיַּגֵּד לְיַעֲקֹב וַיֹּאמֶר הִנֵּה בִּנְךָ יוֹסֵף בָּא אֵלֶיךָ. רִבִּי יוֹסֵי אָמַר, מַלְאָכָא הוּא, דַּהֲוָה עָתִיד לְמֵימַר טַב עַל בְּנֵי יִשְׂרָאֵל, כַּד יְתִיבוּן לְקוּדְשָׁא בְּרִיךְ הוּא, בְּכָל עָקָתְהוֹן, כַּד יֵיתֵי קִצָּא דִמְשִׁיחָא, בְּכָל עָקָתָא דְּתֵיתֵי עֲלֵיהוֹן, יֵימְרוּן לִמְכִילְתָּא בְּרִיךְ אָתֵי לְוָתָךְ, וְיִתְפָּרְקוּן טָבָאי.

45. "And one told Jacob, and said: 'Behold, your son Joseph comes to you'" (Beresheet 48:2). Rabbi Yosi said: It was an angel WHO TOLD JACOB that he was about to pronounce good words about the children of Yisrael at the time they would return to the Holy One, blessed be He, with all their troubles, when Messiah's end was to come. And He would say to the attribute, JACOB, THE SECRET OF TIFERET, your children are come to you, and the good ones, THE CHILDREN OF YISRAEL, will be redeemed.

46. זַכָּאָה חוּלְקֵהוֹן דְּיִשְׂרָאֵל, דְּאִתְקְרִיאוּ בְּנוֹי דְּקוּדְשָׁא בְּרִיךְ הוּא, דְּאִינּוּן כְּמַלְאֲכַיָּיא, וַיָרִיעוּ כָּל בְּנֵי אֱלֹקִים, הוי"ה מַאי.

46. Happy is the portion of Yisrael, who are named the children of the Holy One, blessed be He, that are like angels, OF WHOM IT SAYS, "And all the sons of Elohim shouted for joy" (Iyov 38:6). YISRAEL ARE ALSO CALLED

the sons of Hashem, AS IT SAYS, "YOU ARE THE CHILDREN OF HASHEM YOUR ELOHIM" (DEVARIM 14:1).

47. תָּא חֲזֵי, מְנַיִן שְׁקָרָא קוּדְשָׁא בְּרִיךְ הוּא לְיַעֲקֹב אֵ״ל, אַתְּ תְּהֵא בְּתַתָּאָה, וַאֲנָא אֶהֱא אֱלָהָא בְּעֶלְאָה, מַאי קָא מַיְירֵי. וַיַּעַל אֱלֹהִים מֵעַל אַבְרָהָם, אֲבָהָתָן אִינּוּן רְתִיכָאן דְּקוּדְשָׁא בְּרִיךְ הוּא. תָּנָא, תִּתֵּן אֱמֶת לְיַעֲקֹב חֶסֶד לְאַבְרָהָם, הָא תְּרֵין סְפִירָן, בִּתְרֵין רְתִיכִין, רַבְרְבָן עִלָּאִין.

47. Come and behold! Whence do we know that the Holy One, blessed be He, called Jacob, 'El'? He said to him: 'You shall be among the lower beings, and I shall be Elohim among the upper beings'. Whence do we know that? HE ANSWERS: It is written, "And Elohim went up from Abraham" (Beresheet 17:22). Thus the fathers are a Chariot to the Holy One, blessed be He. We learned that "you will show Truth to Jacob, Grace (Heb. *chesed*) to Abraham" (Michah 7:20) has in it two Sfirot, CHESED AND TRUTH WHICH IS TIFERET in two bigger and higher Chariots, ABRAHAM AND JACOB.

48. תְּלִיתָאָה יִצְחָק, מַאי וַיִּשָּׁבַע יַעֲקֹב בְּפַחַד אָבִיו יִצְחָק. וּבְגִין פַּחַד יִצְחָק דַּהֲוָה סְפִירָה, וְקוּדְשָׁא בְּרִיךְ הוּא דְּהוּא כָּרְסֵי יְקָרָא רְתִיכָא עִלָּאָה, וּסְפִירָה דְיִצְחָק הִיא מֵעֶלְאָה, מְפָרְשָׁא יַתִּיר מִכָּל סְפִירָן דַּאֲבָהָתָא, הֲה״ד וַיִּשָּׁבַע יַעֲקֹב בְּפַחַד אָבִיו יִצְחָק.

48. The third one is Isaac, WHO BECAME A CHARIOT TO THE SFIRAH OF GVURAH. Whence DO WE KNOW THAT FROM? FROM THE WORDS "And Jacob swore by the fear of his father Isaac" (Beresheet 31:53). For the fear of Isaac is a Sfirah of the Holy One, blessed be He, NAMELY GVURAH CALLED FEAR, AND BECAME the Throne of Glory, ITS supernal Chariot. Isaac's Sfirah, GVURAH, is more important and explicit than the other Sfirot of the fathers, CHESED AND TIFERET. For that reason it is written, "And Jacob swore by the fear of his father Isaac"; NAMELY BY THE SFIRAH OF GVURAH CALLED FEAR, WHICH IS THE MOST VALUABLE.

49. ר׳ אַבָּא פָּתַח וְאָמַר, אֱלֹהֵי אַבְרָהָם וֵאלֹהֵי נָחוֹר יִשְׁפְּטוּ בֵינֵינוּ אֱלֹהֵי אֲבִיהֶם, וַיִּשָּׁבַע יַעֲקֹב בְּפַחַד אָבִיו יִצְחָק, מֵהַאי קְרָא אֶת יָכִיל

לְמִנְדַע דָא.

49. Rabbi Aba opened the discussion saying: "The Elohim of Abraham, and the Elohim of Nachor, the Elohim of their father, judge between us. And Jacob swore by the fear of his father Isaac." (Beresheet 31:53). From this verse, one may derive THAT ISAAC'S SFIRAH IS MORE VALUABLE THAN THE OTHERS, FOR HE DID NOT SWEAR BY ELOHIM OF ABRAHAM, BUT BY THE FEAR OF ISAAC.

6. "And sat upon the bed"

A Synopsis
Rabbi Shimon explains that chief angel Michael will come to the side of Israel at his time of redemption. Israel will gain strength from this, and will sit on the bed, which is a code alluding to this truth. Rabbi Shimon then explains that "marries the daughter of a strange El" refers to Yisrael, whom, in spite of his sins, would redeem those in exile, and preserve the nations. Rabbi Yosi then describes two angels, Mata and Metatron, as the Shechinah, sent from Binah to protect Yisrael. Rabbi Shimon next explains the meaning of *Rut,* which details the relationship between mercy and judgment. Rabbis Shimon and Aba then begin a discourse on "All the rivers run into the sea; yet the sea is not full."

The Relevance of this Passage
The assistance of the supernal angels, including Michael, who represents the Right Column energy of mercy, and the protective Light of the Shechinah, is drawn into our lives. This Light also helps to accelerate the end of our personal and global exile.

50. וַיִּתְחַזֵּק יִשְׂרָאֵל וַיֵּשֶׁב עַל הַמִּטָּה, וְרָזָא דִקְרָא, בָּעֵת הַהִיא יַעֲמוֹד מִיכָאֵל הַשַּׂר הַגָּדוֹל הָעוֹמֵד עַל בְּנֵי עַמֶּךָ וְהָיְתָה עֵת צָרָה. ר"ש אָמַר, דָּא גְּבוּרַת יְדָא דְמִיכָאֵל רַבְרְבָא. וַיֵּשֶׁב עַל הַמִּטָּה: כַּמָּה לֵיהּ הֲוָה מִקַּדְמַת דְּנָא סָגִיד. לְמַאן הֲוָה סָגִיד, סָגִיד לְעַרְסָא, הֲוָה עַרְסָא פְּתִיחָא מִנֵּיהּ. לְמָהוֹלַתָּא הֲוָה סָגִיד, דְּהָא הֲוַת חֲבִיבָא מִינֵּיהּ.

50. "And Israel strengthened himself, and sat upon the bed." (Beresheet 48:2). The secret of the verse is: "And at that time shall Michael stand up, the great chief angel, who stands for the children of your people: and there shall be a time of trouble" (Daniel 12:1). Rabbi Shimon says, This is the might of the great Michael, WHO WILL STAND UP FOR YISRAEL AT THE TIME OF REDEMPTION, WHICH WILL BE "A TIME OF TROUBLE SUCH AS NEVER WAS SINCE THERE WAS A NATION..." THUS SCRIPTURE CONCLUDES WITH "AND ISRAEL STRENGTHENED." "And sat upon the bed": As before when he bowed upon it, AS IT IS WRITTEN: "AND ISRAEL BOWED HIMSELF UPON THE BED'S HEAD," BUT NOW HE SAT UPON IT. HE ASKS: To whom did Jacob bow? If you say he bowed to the bed, WHICH IS MALCHUT, the bed was ready TO RECEIVE from him, AND THE GIVER

DOES NOT BOW BEFORE THE RECEIVER. HE ANSWERS: He bowed to the circumcision, THE SECRET OF YESOD, of which he was fond.

51. כִּי חִלֵּל יְהוּדָה קֹדֶשׁ ה' אֲשֶׁר אָהֵב וּבָעַל בַּת אֵל נֵכָר, כַּד אִסְתַּלָּק זִיוֵיהּ מִנֵּיהּ עַל חוֹבֵיהוֹן, לָא הֲוָה לֵיהּ לְמֵיקַם קַמֵּיהּ, וְאִתְתָּרְכַת מַטְרוֹנִיתָא מִן מַלְכָּא, בְּדִיל דְּלָא יָכְלָא לְשַׁבְקָא לָהּ לִבְרָהָא בֵּין עַמִּין לְמִקְטַלְהוֹן, וַהֲוָה בְּאַרְעָא קַדִּישָׁא הוּא, בְּהָא דְּיִהוֹן עַמִּין נוּכְרָאִין מִן עַמֵּיהּ. צָבֵי לְמֵימַר, עָאל שְׁכִינְתָּא בֵּינֵיהוֹן בְּגָלוּתָא, וְעִדָּנָא דְּלָא הֲוָה בְּאַרְעָא, וְהִיא בַּאֲרַע עַמְּמִין, בְּזִיוָא דְיִשְׂרָאֵל, אִסְתַּמְּרוּ עַמְמַיָּא דִי בְּסַחֲרָנֵיהוֹן.

51. "For Judah has profaned the holiness of Hashem which he loved, and has married the daughter of a strange El" (Malachi 2:11). HE WAS ASKED A DIFFICULT QUESTION ABOUT THE MEANING OF "MARRIED THE DAUGHTER OF A STRANGE EL." HE SAYS, When the light was gone from ZEIR ANPIN, due to YISRAEL'S sins, THE SHECHINAH could not stand before ZEIR ANPIN and was exiled from the King. TO WIT, SHE WENT TOGETHER WITH YISRAEL INTO EXILE AMONG THE NATIONS, since She could not leave Her children among the nations to be killed. ZEIR ANPIN was in the Holy Land and, by having foreign nations with him, as it says "MARRIED THE DAUGHTER OF A STRANGE EL," it conveys that the Shechinah was going into exile with them among the nations, when She was not in the land of Yisrael but in other lands. Thus, by the light of Yisrael, the nations around them were preserved. THEREFORE, IT SAYS "MARRIED THE DAUGHTER OF A STRANGE EL." (IT LOOKS AS IF IT IS AN INTERPOLATION FROM THE WORDS 'IT CONVEYS.')

52. תָּאנָא, אָמַר רִבִּי יוֹסֵי, תְּרֵין רַבְרְבִין הֲווֹ תְּחוֹת כֻּרְסֵי יְקָרָא קַדִּישָׁא, וְהָא שְׁמֵיהּ חַד מֵאִינוּן, עַרְסָא, דַּהֲוָה שָׁרֵי בְּגַזֵּיהּ דְּהֵיכָלָא. וְהָא אֲנַן בְּגָלוּתָא, לָא אִשְׁתְּאַר בֵּינָנָא אֶלָּא דָא דִזְינֵיהּ, וְהוּא חָתוּם מִן שְׁמֵיהּ דְּקוּדְשָׁא בְּרִיךְ הוּא.

52. We learned, Rabbi Yosi said, that there were two ministers, NAMELY ANGELS, under the Holy Throne of Glory. The one, BY NAME OF MATA, dwells within the treasury of the Temple. And here we are in exile, and

nothing remained to us but him, who is of the nature OF THE HOLY ONE, BLESSED BE HE, and impressed by the Name of the Holy One, blessed be He. THIS IS THE ANGEL METATRON, WHOSE NAME IS AS THE NAME OF HIS MASTER, AS IT IS WRITTEN OF HIM: "FOR MY NAME IS IN HIM" (SHEMOT 23:21).

53. הה״ד הִנֵּה אָנֹכִי שׁוֹלֵחַ מַלְאָךְ לְפָנֶיךָ לִשְׁמָרְךָ וגו׳, לָא לְמַלְלָא הָכִי, אֶלָּא עַלְמָא דְאָתֵי, כַּד פְּרִישְׁנָא בְּאַתְרֵיה וְהִיא צְרָרָא בְּאָרְחָא, אֲנָא שָׁרֵינָא שְׁכִינְתָּא בֵּינַיְכוֹן לְנַטְרָא לְכוֹן בְּגָלוּתָא וְהִיא נָטְרַת יַתְכוֹן, עַד דְּתֵיתֵי יַתְכוֹן לְאַרְעֲכוֹן, כְּמָה דַהֲוֵיתוּן מִקַּדְמַת דְּנָא. אֲשֶׁר הֲכִינוֹתִי, מוֹתְבָן הֲוָה מִקַּדְמַת דְּנָא.

53. It is written: "Behold, I send an angel before you, to keep you" (Shemot 23:20). It is not worthy to speak that way only of the World to Come, NAMELY BINAH, as we explained it to be the protection along the way. TO WIT, THE POWER TO PROTECT COMES FROM BINAH. THEREFORE, IT WAS BINAH WHICH SAID TO YISRAEL, "BEHOLD, I SEND AN ANGEL," NAMELY THE SHECHINAH "TO KEEP YOU," AND NO OTHER GRADE, BECAUSE PROTECTION COMES FROM IT. IT SAID: I cause the Shechinah to dwell among you and She will protect you in exile. She will protect you until bringing you to your country, as you were before. THIS IS WHAT IS WRITTEN, "I HAVE PREPARED" (IBID.), WITH WHICH the verse CONCLUDES "to the place which I have prepared," for THE LAND was their dwelling place even before.

54. דָּא שְׁכִינְתָּא מִן מטטרו״ן. וְאִתְּרְכַת מַטְרוֹנִיתָא מִן מַלְכָּא, עַד דְּתֵיתוּב לְאַתְרָהָא, וְרָזָא כִּי רַק עוֹג מֶלֶךְ הַבָּשָׁן נִשְׁאַר מִיֶּתֶר הָרְפָאִים הִנֵּה עַרְשׂוֹ עֶרֶשׂ בַּרְזֶל הֲלֹא הוּא בְּרַבַּת בְּנֵי עַמּוֹן, כִּדְפָרֵישְׁנָא בְּאַתְרֵיה.

54. THE ANGEL MENTIONED IS the Shechinah, CLOTHED AND WORKING through Metatron. For IN EXILE CALLED 'WAY' the Shechinah was exiled, from the King, ZEIR ANPIN, AND SHE WORKS THROUGH METATRON until THE TIME OF REDEMPTION WHEN She will return to Her place TO ZEIR ANPIN. It is a mystery that: "For only Og, king of Bashan remained of the remnant of the Refaim; behold, his bed is a bed of iron; is it not in Rabba of the children of Amon?" (Devarim 3:11), as we explained elsewhere.

55. וְאָרְחָא, דְּאִתְמְתַל לְגָלוּתָא, נְטַר יַתְהוֹן בְּגָלוּתָא, עַל עַקְתָא דִּתֵתֵי עֲלֵיכוֹן, עַד דְּיֵיתֵי וְיֵיעוֹל יַתְכוֹן לְאַרְעָא, דְקַיֵּים לַאֲבָהַתְכוֹן דְאִתְנַטְרַת.

55. In the way, which is a parable of the exile, THE SHECHINAH will protect you from all the troubles which will come upon you, until He will come and gather you into the land which He promised to your fathers, which is kept FOR YOU.

56. רַבְרְבָא תִּנְיָנָא הוּא, דְּהוּא תְּחוֹת כָּרְסֵי קַדִּישָׁא, דְשָׁרֵי בְּגִזֵּיהּ דְּהֵיכָלָא הוּא נוּרִיאֵל. דְּהָא רַבְרְבָא דְיִשְׂרָאֵל דְּאִתְמַנֵּי עֲלֵיהוֹן, בְּכָל עִידָן דַּהֲוַת מַטְרוֹנִיתָא עִם מַלְכָּא, הֲוָה נָפֵיק וְעָאל קָדְמֵיהוֹן, מְטַטְרוֹ"ן. וְהוּא, קָבֵיל פּוּלְחָנְהוֹן לְקוּדְשָׁא בְּרִיךְ הוּא, כְּנוּרָא. כַּד אִתְבַּטֵּיל נוּרָא וְאִתְגַּלְיָאוּ, אִסְתַּלַּק זִיוָהּ, וְאִסְתַּלְקָא מַטְרוֹנִיתָא מִן מַלְכָּא.

56. The second minister underneath the Holy Throne, which dwells in the treasure of the Temple is Nuriel. For the minister appointed over Yisrael, NAMELY THE FIRST MINISTER UNDER THE HOLY THRONE, Metatron, when the Shechinah was with the King, would come and go before them. THE SECOND MINISTER, NURIEL, would receive the worship of Yisrael to the Holy One, blessed be He, as fire (Aramaic *nura*). And when the fire was no more, because Yisrael were exiled, Her light was gone, and the Shechinah departed from the King.

57. ר' שִׁמְעוֹן פָּתַח וַאֲמַר לִינִי הַלַּיְלָה וְהָיָה בַבֹּקֶר אִם יִגְאָלֵךְ טוֹב יִגְאָל, אֲמַר ר' יוֹסֵי, שַׁלִּיט רַחֲמֵי עַל דִּינָא. וַיַּרְא אֱלֹקִים אֶת הָאוֹר כִּי טוֹב, טוֹב וְאוֹר שָׁוִין, דְּהוּא מַבּוּעוֹי דְּנַחֲלִין, דְּנָפַק מִנְּהוֹן יַמָּא וְנַחֲלָא דִּבְעָלְמָא.

57. Rabbi Shimon opened the discussion saying: "Tarry this night, and it shall be in the morning, that if he will perform to you the part of a kinsman, well (lit. 'good'); let him do the kinsman's part" (Rut 3:13) RUT IS THE SECRET OF MALCHUT, WHICH IS JUDGMENT, AND GOOD IS MERCY.

Rabbi Yosi said: Mercy is more powerful than Judgment. "And Elohim saw the light, that it was good" (Beresheet 1:4). Hence, goodness and light are equal, for it is the source of all the springs, whence the sea and all the rivers in the world come from. THE MEANING OF THE WORDS CONCERNING RUT ARE THAT IF HE WILL DO THE KINSMAN'S PART, GOOD, IS THAT MERCY CALLED GOOD WILL DO THE KINSMAN'S PART BY RUTH AND HAVE CONTROL OVER HER, WHO IS JUDGMENT.

58. תָּנָא אֲמַר ר״ש, זִמְנָא חָדָא סָלִיקְנָא וְנָחֵיתְנָא לְאַנְהָרָא בְּמַבּוּעֵי דְּנַחֲלִין, וְסָלִיק בַּתְרָאי ר׳ אַבָּא, אֲמַר לִי בְּמַאי עַסְקִיתוּ, א״ל בְּהַאי קְרָא דְּכָל הַנְּחָלִים הוֹלְכִים אֶל הַיָּם וְהַיָּם אֵינֶנּוּ מָלֵא, מִזִּיוֵיהּ אִתְבְּרִיאוּ כָּל רַבְרְבַיָּיא דְּמָן עַלְמָא, וּמָן זִיוֵיהּ אִתְנְבִיעוּ כָּל נַחֲלַיָּיא, נַחֲלַיָּיא דְּאִינּוּן בְּהַאי קְרָא, דְּלָא מָלֵא בְּהַאי גָּלוּתָא, דְּהָא חֲשׁוֹכָא וַאֲפֵלָה, חֶבְתָּא דְּאִמָּא עָבֵיד לְהוֹ, וְאִי לָאו, נַחֲלָא לָא עָבֵיד לִבְרַתֵּיהּ. הָא לָא הֲוָה שְׁלִים עַד דְּיֵיתֵי גִּיסָא אָחֳרָא, דְּלָא הֲוָה בְּגָלוּתָא.

58. We learned that Rabbi Shimon said: Once I went up and down to shine at the source of the springs. Rabbi Aba came up after me and said to me, With what are you occupied? I said to him: With the verse, "All the rivers run into the sea; yet the sea is not full" (Kohelet 1:7). From the light OF BINAH were created all the ministers in the world, and from its light flow all the rivers; NAMELY, "the rivers" in the verse, "ALL THE RIVERS RUN INTO THE SEA; YET THE SEA IS NOT FULL." THE SEA, MALCHUT, is not full when in exile, because the darkness and obscurity IN THE EXILE were made by a mother's love, BINAH. And were it not FOR DARKNESS, the river would not have been created which shines unto the daughter, MALCHUT. The sea shall not be filled and made whole until the other side which was not in exile would have come; NAMELY THE RIGHT SIDE, UPON WHICH NO KLIPAH HAS EVER ANY CONTROL. THEN THE SEA, MALCHUT, WILL BE FILLED.

7. The names called hand

A Synopsis

Rabbi Elazar first explains that the hands belong to The Creator, the source of Light for everything, meaning mercy. He then begs Rabbi Shimon to reveal to him the secret of the name "hand." Rabbi Shimon explains that without the "hand," which is mercy, war would prevail, since judgment would be allowed to come before mercy. But the Messiah will come and wage war against Amalek through judgment, and in it, prevail. Rabbi Elazar then explains that the "the great hand" and "the supernal hand" are the same thing. They have the same numerical value and therefore, will be the left and right hands joined together. Even though one is called "great" and the other "strong," and therefore, must be different, they are equal by the name "hand," because of their letters *Yud - Dalet*, and will therefore create the heaven and the earth.

The Relevance of the Passage

Many profound lessons and benefits arise from this passage, including a secret concerning the nation of Amalek. Kabbalists have revealed that the nation of Amalek is a code term that refers to the doubts and uncertainties that dwell within the consciousness of man. Specifically, these doubts concern the following: our recognition of the reality of The Creator; our trust in the spiritual laws of our universe; our willingness to embark on and remain on the correct spiritual path. Whenever we begin to approach these universal truths and come nearer to the Light, doubts automatically set in. Consciously waging war against uncertainty helps to hasten the arrival of our personal Messiah, as well as the global redemption. Moreover, triumphing over our doubt helps to ignite the Light of mercy, which sweetens the Judgments due to us as a result of previous iniquities in this life or past incarnations. Hence, the strength to defeat skepticism is summoned forth herein and the Light of mercy shines brighter in our lives, helping to soften decrees of judgement that might be due us.

59. וּשְׁמָהָן דְּאִתְקְרִיאַת יַד, הִיא מַבּוּעָא לְכֹלָּא, וְתִשְׁכַּח יַד הוי״ה, הֶן לָא קָצְרַת יַד הוי״ה, דְּלָא אִדְכַּר יָדָא אֶלָּא בִּשְׁמָא.

59. The names called 'hand' - NAMELY THE HAND OF HASHEM, THE GREAT HAND, THE STRONG HAND - are the source OF LIGHT for everything. You will find only the hand of Yud Hei Vav Hei, as in the verse "the hand of Hashem is not shortened" (Yeshayah 59:1), since 'hand' is always combined with the name YUD HEI VAV HEI, WHICH IS MERCY.

‏60. אָתָא רִבִּי אֶלְעָזָר, וְשָׁאַל לְרַ״ש אֲבוֹי, וּבְכָה וא״ל, גַּלֵּי לִי הַאי רָזָא‏
‏אַבָּא מָארִי. א״ל בְּהַאי קְרָא אִתְגְּלֵי לָךְ, כִּי יָד עַל כֵּס יָהּ מִלְחָמָה לַיְיָ׳,‏
‏כֵּס בְּגִין הֹוִי״ה, שַׁלִּיט רַחֲמֵי עַל דִּינָא. צָבֵי לְמֵימַר, יְהֵא רַעֲוָא דְּיֶהֵא‏
‏לְעָלְמָא בַּאֲתַר גְּבוּרָה, יַד רַבָּתָא דַּהֲוַת בְּמִצְרַיִם, וְאִי לָאו הֲוֹו בְּדִינֵי.‏

60. Rabbi Elazar came to ask his father Rabbi Shimon. He wept and said to him: Reveal to me this secret, my father and master, OF THE NAME 'HAND'. He said to him: It will be revealed to you through the verse: "Because Hashem has sworn by His throne (lit. 'a hand on the throne of Yah'); that Hashem will have war" (Shemot 17:16), TO WIT, hand on the throne due to Yud Hei Vav Hei, WHICH IS MERCY, Mercy being stronger than Judgment. The verse wishes to say, may there be forever, instead of Gvurah, the great hand which was in Egypt, WHICH IS MERCY; for were it not FOR THE GREAT HAND, WAR would be through Judgment WITHOUT MERCY.

‏61. וְכַד יֵיתֵי מְשִׁיחָא, יֵיתֵי בְּחַדְתּוּ בִּידָא רַבָּתָא, וְיִגַּח קְרָבָא בַּעֲמָלֵק.‏
‏בְּחוֹזֶק יַד הוֹצִיאָךְ ה׳ מִמִּצְרַיִם, וְכַד יֵיתֵי שְׁמָא דְּיַד בְּתוּקְפָּא יְדָא‏
‏לְחוֹדֵיהּ, הוּא בְּדִינָא, דְּיַגִּיחַ קְרָבָא בַּעֲמָלֵק, לֵיתֵי מְשִׁיחָא. ר׳ אֶלְעָזָר‏
‏מְסַיֵּיעַ, וְיָצָא יְיָ׳ וְנִלְחַם בַּגּוֹיִם הָהֵם כְּיוֹם הִלָּחֲמוֹ בְּיוֹם קְרָב.‏

61. When Messiah will come with the renewal of the great hand, he will wage war against Amalek, AND MERCY WILL OVERCOME JUDGMENT LIKE AT THE EXODUS FROM EGYPT, AS IT IS WRITTEN "By strength of hand Hashem brought us out of Egypt" (Shemot 13:14). When the name hand will come with 'strength of hand' alone, NOT WITH HASHEM'S HAND OR THE GREAT HAND, it is then in Judgment; namely war against Amalek will be fought through Judgment, and then Messiah will come. Rabbi Elazar supports his explanation with the verse, "Then shall Hashem go out, and fight against those nations, as when He fought in the day of battle" (Zecharyah 14:3).

‏62. תָּא חֲזֵי כַּמָּה הִיא יְדָא רַבָּתָא דְּמָטָא לְהַאי יְדָא עִלָּאָה, וּבְדָא יְדָא‏
‏נָפְקוּ מִמִּצְרַיִם, בְּגִין דְּמִנְיָנֵיהוֹן שָׁוִין, מַנֵּי י׳ לִי׳, ד׳ לְד׳, שָׁוִין דָּא לְדָא,‏
‏שְׁמָא דִּידָא רַבָּתָא, וּשְׁמָא דִּידָא עִלָּאָה, דְּיִפְקוּן כַּחֲדָא, אִינוּן שָׁוִין‏
‏בְּאַתְוָותְהוֹן דְּמִנְיָינֵיהוֹן כְּמִנְיָינֵיהוֹן, דְּקַבְּלָא תְּרֵי יַד, תְּרֵין כַּחֲדָא.‏

62. Come and see: THE STRENGTH OF the great hand, THE RIGHT HAND, reaches the supernal hand, THE LEFT HAND CALLED THE STRONG HAND. By this hand, they came out of Egypt, AS IT SAYS, "BY STRENGTH OF HAND HASHEM BROUGHT US OUT OF EGYPT." THEY ARE CONNECTED since they have the same numerical value, one *Yud* equals the other *Yud* and one *Dalet* the other (*YUD-DALET* = HAND). The name 'the great hand' and the name 'the supernal hand' are the same, equal in letters and numerical value. UNISON receives two hands together, IN OTHER WORDS, THE RIGHT AND LEFT WERE JOINED TOGETHER.

63. כֵּיצַד לָא אִתְמַנְעוֹ דָּא מִן דָּא, וְלָא שָׁוְיִן. אִתְפְּרַשׁ תְּרֵין אִלֵּין דְּבְאַתְוָותְהוֹן יַד סָיְיעָאן בְּעִנְיָינָא, תְּרֵין לָא בְּעֵינַיְיהוֹן מִתְפְּרַשׁ. מֵאִלֵּין אִתְבְּרִיאוּ שְׁמַיָּא וְאַרְעָא וְדַעְמֵיהּ. (בְּעִגּוּל הָעֶלְיוֹן) י' לְי', ד' לְד'. (בְּעִגּוּל ב' שֶׁבְּתוֹךְ הָעֶלְיוֹן בִּימִין הָעִגּוּל) י' לְי', ו' לְו' ד' לְד'. (וּבִשְׂמֹאלוֹ) לְד' ד', לְל' ל', לְת' ת'. (בְּעִגּוּל ג' שֶׁבְּתוֹךְ הַב' בִּימִין הָעִגּוּל) ד' לְד' ל' לְל' לְת' ת'. (וּבִשְׂמֹאלוֹ) לְל' ל', לְמ' מ', לְד' ד', לְת' ת', לְו' ו'. (בְּמֶרְכַּז אֵלּוּ הָעִגּוּלִים) ו' לְמַעְלָה, (וּמִתַּחְתָּיו) י"ה י"ה (וּמִתַּחְתֵּיהֶם) שַׁדַּי, (וּמִתַּחְתָּיו) מֶרְכָּבָה דַּאֲבָהָן יִשְׂרָאֵל. וְאִינוּן סְפִירָא קַדְמָאָה: דְּהִיא כִּתְרָא עִלָּאָה. תִּנְיָנָא: בְּכָל מָקוֹם עֵינֵי ה' צוֹפוֹת רָעִים וְטוֹבִים. תְּלִיתָאָה: הֵם מְסַיְיעָתָן לִשְׁמָא חַד וְ' דְּעָבַד כַּמָּה אַתְוָון בְּאַרְעָא דְמִצְרַיִם.

63. HE ASKS, Why were their mutual JOINING not withheld, as they are not equal, THE ONE IS CALLED GREAT AND THE OTHER STRONG. HE ANSWERS: The connection of these two was explained BECAUSE their letters, *Yud-Dalet*, are the same, THOUGH they are not exactly of the same content. TO WIT, SINCE THEY ARE EQUAL BY THE NAME HAND, THEY MAY BE JOINED TOGETHER THOUGH THE ONE IS CALLED GREAT AND THE OTHER STRONG. From these TWO HANDS, the heaven and earth were created, and all that is with them. INSIDE THE UPPERMOST CIRCLE: *Yud* to *Yud*, *Dalet* to *Dalet*. INSIDE THE SECOND CIRCLE WITHIN THE UPPERMOST ONE, TO THE RIGHT OF THE CIRCLE: *Yud* to *Yud*, *Vav* to *Vav*, *Dalet* to *Dalet*; AND TO ITS LEFT: *Dalet* to *Dalet*, *Lamed* to *Lamed*, *Tav* to *Tav*. INSIDE THE THIRD CIRCLE, THAT IS WITHIN THE SECOND, TO THE

RIGHT OF THE CIRCLE: *Dalet* to *Dalet, Lamed* to *Lamed, Tav* to *Tav*; AND TO ITS LEFT: *Lamed* to *Lamed, Mem* to *Mem, Dalet* to *Dalet*; *Tav* to *Tav, Vav* to *Vav*. IN THE CENTER OF THESE CIRCLES: *Vav* above; AND BELOW IT *Yud-Hei, Yud-Hei,* BELOW THEM *Shadai,* AND BELOW IT the Chariot of the fathers of Yisrael. They are the first Sfirah, NAMELY THE UPPER CIRCLE, which is sublime Keter, WHERE THE SIMPLE LETTERS ARE, WHICH IS THE SECRET OF KETER. The second CIRCLE IS THE SECRET OF THE VERSE: "The eyes of Hashem are in every place, watching the evil and the good" (Mishlei 15:3); NAMELY THE SFIRAH CHOCHMAH, SINCE EYES ARE THE SECRET OF CHOCHMAH. HENCE, IT CONTAINS THE LETTERS OF THE LETTERS FULLY SPELLED OUT, WHICH IS THE SECRET OF CHOCHMAH. IN the third CIRCLE, THERE IS THE SFIRAH BINAH, SINCE IN IT ARE THE FULLY SPELLED OUT LETTERS OF THE FULLY SPELLED OUT LETTERS. They help AND POUR UPON *Vav* OF THE NAME YUD HEI VAV HEI, WHICH IS ZEIR ANPIN, which performed many miracles in the land of Egypt.

8. "…appeared to me at Luz"

A Synopsis

Rabbi Aba explains that Luz is Jerusalem, namely Binah, which will give a blessing to Jacob and thereby ensure that the land will be given to his children. Rabbi Elazar further describes that the blessing will also ensure a pure land, and happy will be the portion of the land he will keep. Rabbi Elazar comments on circumcision, namely Yud, as being required in order to be called children of The Creator (holy children). Without it, as Rabbis Aba and Yosi point out, they will die without repentance, in this world and in the next.

The Relevance of this Passage

The awesome energy and Light that issues from the land of Yisrael, concentrated in the city of Jerusalem, is bestowed upon the reader. In addition, the power of purification, associated with the mystical Light aroused through circumcision, is imbued within our souls, helping to cleanse iniquities resulting from negative sexual behavior and adulterated thoughts.

64. וַיֹּאמֶר יַעֲקֹב אֶל יוֹסֵף אֵל שַׁדַּי נִרְאָה אֵלַי בְּלוּז בְּאֶרֶץ כְּנָעַן. ר' אַבָּא אָמַר, לוּז דָּא יְרוּשָׁלַם עִלָּאָה, דְּאַשְׁרָאָה שְׁכִינְתָּא בֵּינָתָא, אָמַר יַעֲקֹב עִלָּאָה לְתַתָּא, הַב לִי בִּרְכָתָא דְּהוּא בָּעֵי, לְאַנְפֵּישׁ יַתְכוֹן אֲנָא, וּלְמִיתַּן יַת אַרְעָא לִבְנֵיכוֹן. לוּז זוֹ יְרוּשָׁלַם עִלָּאָה, קוּדְשָׁא בְּרִיךְ הוּא, הַב בִּרְכָתָא דַּהֲווֹין בִּרְכָה דָּא עַל יְדֵיהּ, בְּאַרְעָא קַדִּישָׁא, אֲבָל בְּרָא, לְאַרְעָא אָחֳרָא, לָא יְהֵא בִּרְכָתָא.

64. "And Jacob said to Joseph, 'El Shadai appeared to me at Luz in the land of Canaan'" (Beresheet 48:3). Rabbi Aba said: Luz is the Celestial Jerusalem, NAMELY BINAH, which puts the Shechinah to dwell with us. Supernal Jacob, ZEIR ANPIN, said to the lower JACOB, BINAH blessed me, for it wants to increase you and give the land to your children. Luz, the Celestial Jerusalem, BINAH, WHICH IS the Holy One, blessed be He, gave a blessing which will be fulfilled in the Holy Land, but outside THE LAND, in another land, there shall be no blessing.

65. ר' אֶלְעָזָר פָּתַח וְאָמַר, מְבָרֵךְ רֵעֵהוּ בְּקוֹל גָּדוֹל בַּבֹּקֶר הַשְׁכֵּם קְלָלָה תֵּחָשֶׁב לוֹ, קוּדְשָׁא בְּרִיךְ הוּא קָרָא לְיִשְׂרָאֵל אַחִים וְרֵעִים, מַאי בִּרְכָתָא

יְהַב לוֹן, דִּיהוֹן הַאי עַמָּא דַּכְיָא תְּחוֹת יְדֵיה, וְלִמְהֱוֵי עֲלֵיהוֹן נָטִיר.

65. Rabbi Elazar opened the discussion saying: "He that blesses a friend with a loud voice, rising early in the morning, it shall be counted a curse to him" (Mishlei 27:14). The Holy One, blessed be He, called Yisrael brothers and friends. THE MEANING OF THIS VERSE "THAT BLESSES A FRIEND" REFERS TO THE HOLY ONE, BLESSED BE HE, WHO BLESSES YISRAEL. HE ASKS: What did He bless them? HE REPLIES: That this nation will be pure under Him, and that He will watch over them.

66. זַכָּאָה חוּלָקֵהוֹן דְּהַאי עַמָּא דַכְיָא, דְּהוּא עֲלֵיהוֹן, דְּאִקְרֵי בָּנִים חֲבִיבִים יַתִּיר מֵעֶלָּאָה, כְּתִיב בָּנִים אַתֶּם לַה', כֹּלָּא בְּדִיל דָּא. מַאי הוּא, בְּדִיל דְּאִשְׁתְּלֵים שְׁמָא בְּחוֹתָמָא דִלְהוֹן, דְּאִינוּן גְּזִירִין.

66. Happy is the portion of this pure nation WHICH HE KEEPS, for they are called dear children more than the supernal beings, as it is written: "You are the children of Hashem" (Devarim 14:1), all for that reason. What is this reason? HE REPLIES: That the name SHADAI is completed by their seal, for they are circumcised.

67. תָּא חֲזֵי, בְּאַנְפּוֹי דְּאֵינָשָׁא שְׁמָא דְּקוּדְשָׁא בְּרִיךְ הוּא, וְחַסְרָא יוּ"ד מִנֵּיה, וְלָא אִשְׁתְּלֵים, אָתָא אַבְרָהָם וְחֵבֵב לְקוּדְשָׁא בְּרִיךְ הוּא, וַא"ל בָּךְ אִשְׁתְּלֵים שְׁמָא, וְאִתְגְּזַר, וְאִשְׁתְּלֵים שְׁמָא בְּיוּ"ד דְּמִילָה. בְּאַנְפּוֹי דְּאֵנָשָׁא שִׁי"ן דְּשַׁ"ד"י, וְד', חָסֵר יוּ"ד, אִשְׁתְּלֵים בְּיוּ"ד דְּמִילָה, וּכְדֵין אִקְרוֹן בָּנִים לַה', בְּנִין קַדִּישִׁין.

67. Come and see: The Name of the Holy One, blessed be He, is in a man's face, NAMELY SHIN, but *Yud* is missing and thus it is not complete. When Abraham came and became dear to the Holy One, blessed be He, He said to him: 'In you shall this name be completed. He circumcised himself, and the name became complete through the *Yud* of circumcision. For *Shin* is found in a man's face; NAMELY, THE TWO EYES AND THE NOSE IN THE MIDDLE. IN HIS ARM, you find *Dalet*, and the *Yud* is missing, the which *Yud* of circumcision completes. Then they are called children of Hashem, holy children.

68. וְכַד מְסָאֲבִין לֵיהּ לְהַאי אָת קַיְּימָא קַדִּישָׁא, וְעָאִיל לֵיהּ לִרְשׁוּ אָחֳרָא, סָלִיק מִנֵּיהּ הַאי קְדוּשָׁא דְּחוֹתָמָא, וְהוּא כְּמָה דְּחָרִיב עָלְמָא, וְסָאִיב חוֹתָמָא, דְּאִשְׁתְּלִים בֵּיהּ שְׁמָא דְּקוּדְשָׁא בְּרִיךְ הוּא, וְהָא הוּא חָרִיב עָלְמָא.

68. When the sign of the holy covenant is defiled and put into the dominion of the other, NAMELY BY TRANSGRESSING WITH IT, the holiness of the seal is gone from him, and he is considered as if he ruined the world, for he has defiled the seal upon which the Name of the Holy One, blessed be He, is completed. Thus he ruins the world BY STOPPING THE BOUNTY OF THE HOLY ONE, BLESSED BE HE, FROM THE WORLD.

69. ר' אַבָּא הֲוָה אָזִיל מִקַפּוֹטְקִיָּא, וַהֲוָה עִמֵּיהּ רִבִּי יוֹסֵי, עַד דַּהֲווֹ אָזְלֵי, חָמוּ חַד ב"נ דַּהֲוָה אָתֵי, וּרְשִׁימָא חַד בְּאַנְפּוֹי, אֲבָל וַוי לוֹן לְחַיָּיבַיָא, דִּימוּתוּן בְּלָא תְּשׁוּבָה, דְּלָא יַעֲדֵי מִנֵּיהּ רְשִׁימָא, לָא בְּעָלְמָא דֵין, וְלָא בְּעָלְמָא דְּאָתֵי.

69. Rabbi Aba was walking from Cappadocia with Rabbi Yosi. While they were walking they saw a man there with a mark upon his face. Woe to the wicked, who will die without repentance, and the mark will not disappear, neither in this world nor in the World to Come.

9. "Behold, I will make you fruitful, and multiply you"

A Synopsis
Rabbi Aba first explains that shame will not overcome Jacob, since he will keep his promise to his children, [**Behold, I will make you fruitful and multiply you,**] because to fail would be to invoke shame upon himself. The quotation is a blessing from God, meant to further ensure that Jacob will keep his promise. Rabbi Aba then ends by indicating that at the time of war against Amalek, only The Creator would go to fight.

The Relevance of this Passage
In truth, a man lacks the full power to overthrow the Satan, doubts and internal demons that dwell within him. Nonetheless, when a man willingly overcomes his doubt – known by the code word Amalek, The Creator will fight for him throughout his life, thus assuring a man's victory over the dark side and providing him with a life of fulfillment. This is precisely what occurs herein, as we peruse the letters of this passage with the consciousness and intent to eradicate our doubts and demons and allow The Creator to fight on our behalf.

70. וַיֹּאמֶר אֵלַי הִנְנִי מַפְרְךָ וְהִרְבֵּיתִיךָ. רְבִּי אַבָּא פָּתַח וַאֲמַר, הַאי קְרָא לֹא עַתָּה יֵבוֹשׁ יַעֲקֹב וְלֹא עַתָּה פָּנָיו יֶחֱוָרוּ. וְכִי אֵינִישׁ דַּאֲמַר טַב לְב"ן כַּוָּתֵיהּ. אִי לָא יַשְׁלִים מַה דַּאֲמַר, אַפּוֹהִי מִתְבַּיְישָׁן, עאכ"ו מִן עִלָּאֵי לְב"ן, דְּאִי לָא מַיְיתֵי כָּל טַב דַּאֲמַר עַל בְּנוֹהִי, אַנְפּוֹהִי מִתְבַּיְישָׁן.

70. "...and said to me, 'Behold, I will make you fruitful, and multiply you'" (Beresheet 48:4). Rabbi Aba opened the discussion speaking in relation to the verse: "Jacob shall not now be ashamed, neither shall his face now grow pale" (Yeshayah 29:22). A man who promises good for another man will be ashamed not to keep his promise. How much more so is A PROMISE come to man from above. If He brings not the goodness to his children that he said he would, He will be ashamed.

71. אֲמַר קוּדְשָׁא בְּרִיךְ הוּא לֵיהּ, אֲנָא יִשְׂרָאֵל עִלָּאָה, דַּאֲנָא מַפְשִׁינָךְ וְאַסְגִּינָךְ. הַאי בִּרְכְתָא דְּיָהֵיב לִי, וְאָתֵּן יַת אַרְעָא הָדָא לְבָרְיְכוֹן, לָא הֲוָה בְּאַרְעָא, לָא הֲוָה עִמְּהוֹן. כַּד יֵיתֵי קִיצָא דִּמְשִׁיחָא וְיִשְׁתְּלִים, אֲמַר קוּדְשָׁא בְּרִיךְ הוּא, לֹא עַתָּה יֵבוֹשׁ יַעֲקֹב, כְּעַן אַנְפּוֹי דְּיַעֲקֹב דִּלְעֵילָא,

לָא מִתְבַּיְישָׁן מִדַּאֲמַר לְהוֹן וְנָתַתִּי, אֲרֵי עַד כְּעַן לָא הֲווֹ בִּידֵיה, וַהֲווֹ אַנְפּוֹהִי מִתְבַּיְישָׁן, כְּעַן דִּילֵיה מִסְתַּיֵּיע מִן קָדָם מָארֵי שְׁמַיָּא וְאַרְעָא.

71. The Holy One, blessed be He, said TO JACOB, "Behold, I will make you fruitful, and multiply you" by this blessing given to Me FROM BINAH. And I will give this land to your children'. Yet HIS CHILDREN are not in the land of Yisrael, nor is THE HOLY ONE, BLESSED BE HE, with them. THIS IS SUPPOSEDLY SHAMEFUL THAT HE PROMISES YET DOES NOT KEEP IT. But when Messiah's end will come AND HIS PROMISE will be fulfilled, the Holy One, blessed be He, said: "Jacob shall not now be ashamed." Now the face of supernal Jacob will not be put to shame, because of what he said "and will give THIS LAND TO YOUR SEED AFTER YOU" (Beresheet 48:4). For until now, he had naught in his hand to give them, and he was ashamed. Now his promise was kept before the Master of heaven and earth.

72. כְּמָה דְּאַמְרִינָן, אֲגִחְנָא דַּעֲמָלֵק, כַּד יִשְׁתְּלֵים קִיצָא, לָא יְהֵא אֶלָּא בִּתְקוֹף יְדָא, כְּמָה דַּהֲוֵית בְּיוֹם קְרָב, וְיָצָא ה' וְנִלְחַם בַּגּוֹיִם הָהֵם, דִּידֵיה וְלָא אָחֳרָא.

72. As we said, the war against Amalek will be by strength of hand alone when the end will come, for it is a day for battle, as is written: "Then shall Hashem go out, and fight against those nations, AS WHEN HE FOUGHT IN THE DAY OF BATTLE," He Himself shall go out, and none other.

10. "And now your two sons...who were born to you"

A Synopsis

Rabbi Yosi opens the discussion with the saying that the two sons, Ephraim and Menashe, are born to Israel into 'exile'. *Vav* will help Jacob at the time of redemption, and give his children a portion of the land. The aspect of Ephraim refers to the children who were forgotten, and the aspect of Menashe to those he regards as his own. But Hashem will attend to both aspects and redeem them, taking them out of their land of exile. Rabbi Aba then says that when God executes judgment upon Egypt, Yisrael will be redeemed from exile. Rabbi Shimon next explains that God will make a Chupah (marriage canopy) for every righteous man in Jerusalem, as a means for the giving of the Torah and the building of the Temple. Yisrael will be born after the redemption of the fathers (Chariots). Rabbi Shimon finally explains that all children born in Jerusalem after the redemption, will go to Heaven, will have only Hebrew names, and will inherit the land according to their numbers.

The Relevance of this Passage

The blessings and wisdom contained herein are varied and abounding. Put briefly, we are all children of Jacob and our exile continues to this very day. However, when one earnestly turns to the path of Jacob, the Torah – the Light of the Upper World [the Hebrew letter *Vav]* will assist him in removing the Evil Inclination [Egypt], the underlying cause behind the continued exile. Furthermore, this passage awakens the entire world to the truth of the Torah and the power of Kabbalah and connects the reader to the redemptive Light emanating from the Land of Yisrael. Our personal and global redemption is therefore quickened.

73. וְעַתָּה שְׁנֵי בָנֶיךָ הַנּוֹלָדִים לְךָ, דָא יִשְׂרָאֵל לְתַתָּא, דְּאִתְרַיְיהוּ בְּגָלוּתָא, בְּנוֹי דְּקוּדְשָׁא בְּרִיךְ הוּא, דְּאִתְיְלִידוּ בֵּינֵי עַמְמַיָא. תָּנָא א"ר יוֹסֵי, יִשְׂרָאֵל, כַּד יְהוֹן בְּאַרְעָא קַדִּישָׁא דְיִשְׂרָאֵל, דָּר בְּאַרְעָא, כַּד יֵיתֵי מְשִׁיחָא, יְהוֹן עִם אֲחוּהוֹן דִּילְהוֹן בְּאַתְרַיְיהוּ, דְּלָא אִתְקְרֵי גָּלוּת, אֶלָּא לְמַאן דְּאִיהוּ דָּר בְּאַרְעָא נוּכְרָאָה, אִינוּן אִתְקַרְיָין גָּלְיָין.

73. "And now your two sons...who were born to you" (Beresheet 48:5): These are Yisrael below, who are in exile, the children of the Holy One, blessed be He, who are born among the nations. TO WIT, THE VERSE: "YOUR TWO SONS, EPHRAIM AND MENASHE, WHO WERE BORN TO YOU

IN THE LAND OF EGYPT" REFERS TO YISRAEL WHO ARE IN EXILE AMONG THE NATIONS. FOR EGYPT INCLUDES ALL EXILES. We learned, Rabbi Yosi said, that Yisrael who will be in the Holy Land of Yisrael, dwelling in the land, at the coming of Messiah, will be with their brothers in that place. For exile will be only for those who live in a foreign land, and they are called 'exiles'.

74. וְזָכַרְתִּי אֶת בְּרִיתִי יַעֲקוֹב, וא"ו יְתֵירָה, תֵּיתֵי וא"ו דְּאִסְתַּלְקַת כַּד אִתְחֲרֵיב בֵּיתָא, וּתְהֵא סִיּוּעָא לְיַעֲקֹב, כַּד יְהֵא דָא, וִיהֵא לִבְרָא קַדִּישָׁא אַרְעָא אַחְסָנַת עָלַם, וִיהוֹן בְּנוֹהִי בְּאַרְעֲהוֹן, דְּדָארוּ מִקַּדְמַת דְּנָא, זַכָּאָה חוּלְקֵהוֹן.

74. "I remember my covenant with Jacob" (Vayikra 26:42). The *Vav* OF JACOB is superfluous, WHICH INDICATES that the *Vav* which was gone when the Temple was destroyed will help Jacob at the time OF REDEMPTION, and will be an everlasting possession for the holy son JACOB, whose descendants shall live in the country in which they lived before, happy is their portion.

75. כְּעַן בְּרִיָּא, דַּהֲוָה עַרְעָן לְהוֹן, דְּאִתְגְּלִיאוּ מִן לְבַר לְאַרְעָא וְאִתְנְשִׁיאוּ, וְאִנְפִּישׁוּ, וְיֵימָא יַעֲקֹב עִלָּאָה לְתַתָּא, בְּרֵי דִּילָךְ דְּאִינוּן לְבַר לְאַרְעָא דְּאִתְיְילִידוּ בְּגָלוּתָא, בְּכָל אַרְעָא וְאַרְעָא, עַד דַּאֲנָא אֵיעוֹל לְמִצְרָאֵי, וְאַעֲבֵיד לְהוֹן דִּינָא, לָאו אֲנָא מַסְקִית בְּרָךְ, דְּאִתְבְּרִיאוּ בְּגָלוּתָא, לְבַר לְאַרְעָא בְּאַרְעָא רְחִיקָא, וְאע"ג דְּאִינוּן סַגִּיאִין, וְאִתְנְשִׁיאוּ, דִּילִי אִינוּן, כַּד חֲזֵיתִי דָא גָּלוּתָא דִּלְהוֹן, וְאַסֵּיתִי לְכֵיבֵיהוֹן, וְשַׁמְעִית קֵלֵיהוֹן. רְאוּבֵן: כִּי רָאָה ה' אֶת עָנְיִי. שִׁמְעוֹן: כִּי שָׁמַע ה' כִּי שְׂנוּאָה אָנֹכִי, וְחָשִׁיב בְּלִבָּךְ, כְּאִילוּ יֶהֱוְיָן קַדְמֵי אִינוּן, וּמִדְּנָתוֹב מִמִּצְרָאֵי, מִלְּמֶעְבַּד דִּינָא, נָסֵיק יַתְהוֹן מֵאֲרַע גָּלוּתָא.

75. The children who were exiled out of the Land of Yisrael and were forgotten, THE ASPECT OF MENASHE, and multiplied AND INCREASED ACCORDING TO THE ASPECT OF EPHRAIM: Supernal Jacob, ZEIR ANPIN, said to the one below, 'Your children who are out of the Land of Yisrael, born in exile in other lands, before I came to Egypt and sentenced them for

their sins, I do not consider to be your children those who were born in exile in a foreign land, though they be many, THE ASPECT OF EPHRAIM, and forgotten, THE ASPECT OF MENASHE, they are my own CHILDREN. But when I saw them in this exile, I healed their pains and heard their prayers, for Reuben, "Surely Hashem has looked upon my affliction" (Beresheet 29:32) and for Simeon, "Because Hashem has heard that I was hated" (Ibid. 33)'. THIS IS THE MEANING OF THE VERSE "EPHRAIM AND MENASHE" WHO MULTIPLIED AND WERE FORGOTTEN IN EXILE "AS REUBEN AND SIMEON THEY SHALL BE MINE," TO WIT, HE WILL SEE THEIR POVERTY, HEAR THEIR PRAYER AND REDEEM THEM, ACCORDING TO THE MEANING OF THE NAMES REUBEN AND SIMEON. Think of it as if they were before Me, and when we shall return from Egypt, WHICH INCLUDES ALL THE EXILES, after executing Judgment on them, we shall take them out of the land of their exile'.

76. רִבִּי אַבָּא אֲמַר, מֵהָכָא וְהֵבִיאוּ אֶת כָּל אֲחֵיכֶם מִכָּל הַגּוֹיִם מִנְחָה לַה׳, צָבֵי לְמֵימַר, כַּד יְהֵא קוּדְשָׁא בְּרִיךְ הוּא בְּדִינָא בְּמִצְרָאֵי, בְּעִדָּנָא הַהִיא יֵיתוּן כָּל עַמְמַיָא מִנְחָה, כַּד שָׁמְעוּ שְׁמוּעָה דְקוּדְשָׁא בְּרִיךְ הוּא, הַיְינוּ וְנָהֲרוּ אֵלָיו כָּל הַגּוֹיִם.

76. Rabbi Aba said: From this WE UNDERSTAND THAT AFTER HE WILL EXECUTE JUDGMENT UPON EGYPT, WHICH INCLUDES ALL THE NATIONS, YISRAEL WILL BE REDEEMED FROM EXILE, AS IT IS WRITTEN: "And they shall bring all your brethren out of all the nations for an offering to Hashem" (Yeshayah 66:20). Scripture means that when the Holy One, blessed be He, will execute Judgment upon Egypt; NAMELY UPON ALL THE NATIONS WHICH THE EARLIER VERSE MENTIONED, at that time, all the nations will bring an offering when they hear about the Holy One, blessed be He, "and all the nations shall flow to it" (Yeshayah 2:2).

77. תָּנָא, אֲמַר רִבִּי שִׁמְעוֹן, עָתִיד קוּדְשָׁא בְּרִיךְ הוּא לְמֶיעְבַּד לְכָל זַכָּאָה וְזַכָּאָה, חוּפָּה בִּירוּשְׁלֵם, קוֹל שָׂשׂוֹן וְקוֹל שִׂמְחָה קוֹל חָתָן וְקוֹל כַּלָּה, כַּד תֵּיתוּב מַטְרוֹנִיתָא לְמַלְכָּא, וְעָבֵיד לָה אֵרוּסִין, הה״ד צְאֶינָה וּרְאֶינָה וגו׳ בְּיוֹם חֲתוּנָתוֹ וּבְיוֹם שִׂמְחַת לִבּוֹ. בְּיוֹם חֲתוּנָתוֹ זֶה מַתַּן תּוֹרָה, וּבְיוֹם שִׂמְחַת לִבּוֹ זֶה בִּנְיַן בֵּית הַמִּקְדָּשׁ, שֶׁיִּבָּנֶה בִּמְהֵרָה בְיָמֵינוּ.

77. We learned that Rabbi Shimon said: The Holy One, blessed be He, will make for every righteous man a canopy in Jerusalem. It is written: "the voice of mirth, and the voice of gladness, the voice of the bridegroom, and the voice of the bride" (Yirmeyah 16:9) when the Shechinah will return to the King and He will engage Her, as it is written: "Go forth, O daughters of Zion, and behold...on the day of his wedding, and on the day of the gladness of his heart" (Shir Hashirim 2:11). "The day of his wedding" is the giving of the Torah, and "the day of the gladness of his heart" is the building of the Temple, may it be built soon in our days.

78. וּמוֹלַדְתְּךָ אֲשֶׁר הוֹלַדְתָּ אַחֲרֵיהֶם לְךָ יִהְיוּ, דָּא יִשְׂרָאֵל לְתַתָּא, לַאֲבָהָן, דְּאִינּוּן רְתִיכִין, תְּהֵא שְׁמָהַתְהוֹן בְּרָזָא דְּאִתְיַילִידוּ לְבָתַר דְּנָן, עַל שְׁמָא דַּאֲחֵיהוֹן יְהוֹן אִתְקְרוּן בְּאַחְסָנָא דִּלְהוֹן.

78. "And your offspring, which you beget after them, shall be yours" (Beresheet 48:6). This is Yisrael below, WHO WILL BE BORN AFTER THE REDEMPTION to the fathers, who are Chariots, and their names will be in the secret of those born AFTER REDEMPTION. They will be named after their brothers in their inheritance.

79. תָּאנָא, אָמַר רְבִּי שִׁמְעוֹן, וּמוֹלַדְתְּךָ: דָּא יְרוּשָׁלַם דִּלְתַתָּא, מוֹלֶדֶת בַּיִת בְּפָרָשַׁת עֲרָיוֹת, יְרוּשָׁלַם לְתַתָּא, גּוּבְרִין דְּאִתְיַילִידוּ דָּא יְרוּשְׁלַם, בָּתַר דְּנָא, דְּיִתּוּבוּן עַלְמָא לְמָארֵי שְׁמַיָא בִּירוּשְׁלַם, כַּד אִתְגַּיְירוּ לָא אִתְקְרוּן אֶלָּא עַל שְׁמָהָן, דְּהוּא בַּר יִשְׂרָאֵל, וְלָא יִתְקְרוּן כַּד אֲבָהַתְהוֹן, גִּיּוֹרָא מִקַפּוֹטְקִיָּא, אֶלָּא בִּשְׁמָא יִשְׂרָאֵל.

79. We learned that Rabbi Shimon said: "And your issue (also: 'your homeland')" is Terrestrial Jerusalem, NAMELY YOUR HOMELAND. FOR THE WORDS "born at home" (Vayikra 18:9) in relation to the portion concerning sexual misconduct, refer to the Terrestrial Jerusalem. THE MEANING OF THE VERSE IS that people who will be born in that Jerusalem will not only return to their Master in heaven, but will also convert AFTER REDEMPTION. They will have only names of Yisrael, not according to their father, such as 'the proselyte of Cappadocia,' but a name of Yisrael.

80. לְךָ יִהְיוּ: צָבֵי לְמֵימַר, עַל שְׁמֵיהוֹן דְּיִשְׂרָאֵל יִתְקְרוּן, עַל שֵׁם

אֲחֵיהוֹן יִקְרְאוּ בְּנַחֲלָתָם, וְכַד תָּבוּ יִתְחַסְנוּן אֲלֵין עִם יִשְׂרָאֵל בְּאַרְעָא, וְיִסַּב כָּל שִׁבְטָא וְשִׁבְטָא, דִּידֵיהּ וְגוּבְרִין מִנְּהוֹן, כָּל חֲדָא לְפוּם מִנְיָינֵיהּ.

80. "Shall be your": THE VERSE means that they will have names of Yisrael, after their brothers in their inheritance. And when they return, they will inherit together with Yisrael in the country, and each tribe will take its own, AND ALSO for people of their own, CONVERTS. Each will inherit the land according to its numbers.

11. "Rachel died by me on the way"

A Synopsis

Rabbi Aba begins by explaining the discrepancy in the verb tense in "they have come back," used in The Creator's promise for the future. Rabbi Aba then explains how Rabbi Elazar answers that the Shechinah will think her children have died by judgement. Only then will she return to her husband. "Rachel weeping" refers to the Shechinah being told by her husband that her children have perished. Only then will He tell her that her children have been redeemed. God then tells her that those who have died in the war will be resurrected. Rabbi Shimon tells us that the quotation refers to the Shechinah's children who die in the war, but are resurrected and will return to Efrat, the Land of Yisrael. Rabbi Aba finally explains the meaning of Lechem, derived from Milchamah (war), and "fought" (lacham).

The Relevance of this Passage

Two paths to the final redemption lie before us: a path of destruction – war and death – and a path of mercy that offers us protection, the path of spiritual transformation. We have the free will to choose our fate. In the end, all the souls of mankind will be resurrected and the arrival of the Messiah will bring immortality and endless fulfillment. The Light that radiates from this passage of Zohar awakens the wisdom to walk the path of spiritual transformation. It helps accelerate the arrival of the Resurrection and the Messiah through the path of mercy for all mankind.

81. וַאֲנִי בְּבֹאִי מִפַּדָּן מֵתָה עָלַי רָחֵל בַּדֶּרֶךְ וגו', רבי אבא פָּתַח, כֹּה אָמַר ה' קוֹל בְּרָמָה נִשְׁמָע וגו', מַה כְּתִיב בַּתְרֵיה, כֹּה אָמַר ה' מִנְעִי קוֹלֵךְ מִבֶּכִי וְעֵינַיִךְ מִדִּמְעָה כִּי יֵשׁ שָׂכָר לִפְעֻלָּתֵךְ וגו' וְשָׁבוּ בָנִים לִגְבוּלָם לֹא אָמַר וְיָשׁוּבוּ, אֶלָּא וְשָׁבוּ, כְּבָר שָׁבוּ.

81. "And as for me, when I came from Paddan, Rachel died by me" (Beresheet 48:7). Rabbi Aba opened the discussion, saying: "A voice was heard in Rama" (Yirmeyah 31:14) followed by: "Thus says Hashem; Keep your voice from weeping, and your eyes from tears: for your work shall be rewarded, says Hashem; and they shall (lit. 'they have') come back again to their own border" (Ibid. 15). HE ASKS: It does not say 'They shall come back' IN THE FUTURE TENSE, but that they have come back. YET THIS IS A PROMISE FOR THE FUTURE, AND IT SHOULD HAVE BEEN 'AND THEY SHALL COME BACK.'

82. תָּא חֲזֵי אָמַר רִבִּי אֶלְעָזָר, בְּשַׁעְתָּא דִיהֵא דִינָא עַל טוּרָא, תִּתְעַטָּר מַטְרוֹנִיתָא עַל טוּרָא, וְהִיא סָבְרַת דִּבְנֵיהוֹן אָבְדִין בְּדִינָא, וְרָזָא רְנִי עֲקָרָה לֹא יָלָדָה פִּצְחִי רִנָּה וְצַהֲלִי וגו', תָּנָא, סַגִּיִין יְהוֹן בְּנֵי כָּרְסְיָיא, מִן דִּידָה, הה"ד כִּי רַבִּים בְּנֵי שׁוֹמֵמָה מִבְּנֵי בְעוּלָה, תֵּיתוּב מַטְרוֹנִיתָא לְבַעֲלָה, בַּיּוֹם הַהוּא יִהְיֶה ה' אֶחָד וּשְׁמוֹ אֶחָד.

82. HE ANSWERS: Come and see, Rabbi Elazar said that when there will be justice upon the mountain, and the Shechinah will be adorned on the mountain, She will think her children perished by judgment. The secret is, "Sing, O barren one, you that did not bear; break forth into singing, and cry aloud" (Yeshayah 54:1). We have learned that many children of the throne will be Her own CHILDREN, as it is written: "For more are the children of the desolate than the children of the married wife" (Ibid.). The Shechinah will then return to Her husband. "On that day Hashem shall be one, and His name One" (Zecharyah 14:9).

83. מִן קַדְמַת דְּנָא, תֵּימָא מַטְרוֹנִיתָא לְקוּדְשָׁא בְּרִיךְ הוּא בְּנַיָּיא דִילִי אָן. יֵימָא לָהּ בְּדִינָא. הִיא תִסְבַּר דְּאָבְדִין בְּדִינָא, וּבְכָה עַל דִּינָא לִבְנַיָּא דִידָהּ, כִּי אֲרֵי סַגִּי אִית לָךְ לְמֵיסַב מְנִי בְּדִלְהוֹן, דַּהֲוַת עִמְּהוֹן, וְהָא תָבוּ מֵאַרְעָא דְשַׂנְאָה.

83. Before that, the Shechinah will say to Her husband, Where are my children? He will say to Her that they were judged, and She will think they perished by judgment, and weep for Her children, who perished by justice. THIS IS THE SECRET OF "A VOICE WAS HEARD IN RAMA... RACHEL WEEPING FOR HER CHILDREN," AND HE WILL SAY TO HER, "KEEP YOUR VOICE FROM WEEPING... FOR YOUR WORK SHALL BE REWARDED." For you are to be greatly rewarded by Me for being with them, and the children have already come back from the hated land, FOR THEY HAVE ALREADY BEEN REDEEMED.

84. וְכִי לָא הֲוָה יָדַע יוֹסֵף דְּמֵתָה אִמֵּיהּ, תַּמָּן הֲוָה עִמָּהּ כַּד מֵתָה. אֶלָּא יֵאמַר יִשְׂרָאֵל עִלָּאָה, כַּד נֵיתֵי מִפֻּרְקָנֵיהוֹן דְּיִשְׂרָאֵל, תִּתְעַר מַטְרוֹנִיתָא, וְתִתְעַר כ"י, וְתִתְגַּח קְרָבָא עִם עַמְמִין, וְיִמוּתוּן מִנְּהוֹן,

וְיִתְקָרְבוּן בִּזְעֵיר לְמֵיחֵי אַרְעָא, יֵימַר לָהּ קוּדְשָׁא בְּרִיךְ הוּא, כַּד הִיא בָּכָה, לָא תִדְחֲלִי, אַגְרָא לְהוֹן בְּנַיָּיא דְּמִיתָן עַל שְׁמִי, אָחֳרָנִין הָא תָּבוּ, אִינוּן יְתוּבוּן לְחַיֵּי מֵיתַיָּיא.

84. HE ASKS: Did not Joseph know his mother died? Indeed, he was with her when she died. WHY DID JACOB HAVE TO TELL HIM THAT? HE REPLIES: Supernal Yisrael said that when he prophesied about the redemption of Yisrael, the Shechinah will stir, and the Congregation of Yisrael will stir and wage war against the nations. Some OF YISRAEL will die IN THIS WAR. They will slowly approach the Land of Yisrael. When She weeps FOR HER DEAD SONS, the Holy One, blessed be He, will say to Her, Do not be afraid, there is a reward for the sons who died IN THE WAR for My name's sake. The others, who did not die, have already returned and those who died will live again through the resurrection of the dead.

85. מֵתָה עָלַי רָחֵל, מֵתָה עַל יִיחוּד שְׁמָא דְקוּדְשָׁא בְּרִיךְ הוּא, וְעַ״ד אִתְּמָר בְּעוֹד כִּבְרַת אֶרֶץ לָבֹא, דְּמִיתוּ עַל יִיחוּד שְׁמָא דְקוּדְשָׁא בְּרִיךְ הוּא, לְבַר לְאַרְעָא, בְּאַרְעָא דָּא, לָא יָמוּת חַד מִנְּהוֹן.

85. "Rachel died by me." She died for the unity of the Name of the Holy One, blessed be He, TO WIT, HER SONS WHO WERE KILLED FOR THE SANCTIFICATION OF THE HOLY NAME. THE VERSE says of it: "When yet there was but a little way" (Beresheet 48:7), WHICH MEANS they died for the unity of the Name of the Holy One, blessed be He, outside the land of Yisrael, AT THE WAR FOR THE COMING TO YISRAEL. For in the land of Yisrael, none shall die. THEREFORE SCRIPTURE SAYS, "WHEN YET THERE WAS BUT A LITTLE WAY TO COME TO EFRAT" TO THE LAND OF YISRAEL, FOR AFTER COMING TO THE LAND OF YISRAEL THEY WILL DIE NO MORE.

86. תָּנָא, א״ר אַבָּא, עֲתִידִין יִשְׂרָאֵל לְאַגָּחָא קְרָבָא בְּאַרְחָא דְּאֶפְרָת, וְיָמוּתוּן עַמָּא סַגְיָא מִנְּהוֹן, וּבָתַר כֵּן לְחַיֵּי מֵיתַיָּא יְקוּמוּן, וְיַתִּיר שָׁלְטָנָא יְהֵא לְכוֹן דְּמִיתִין בְּאַרְחָא הָדֵין, מִכָּל דִּיהֵא קַדְמֵיהוֹן בִּירוּשְׁלֵם.

86. We have learned that Rabbi Aba said: Yisrael will be engaged in war on the way to Efrat, and many of them will die. Then they will rise at the resurrection of the dead, and will have more power than those who reached Jerusalem before them, WHO DID NOT DIE IN THE WAR.

‫87. וְלָמָּה אִתְקְרֵי שְׁמָא דְּאַתְרָא קַדִּישָׁא, דְּאַתְרָא הָדֵין לֶחֶם, בְּדִיל‬
‫דְּהוּא מִן שְׁמָא דְּקוּדְשָׁא בְּרִיךְ הוּא בֵּיה, דִּימוּתוּן תַּמָּן עַל שְׁמֵיה, י״ד:‬
‫דִּימוּתוּן תַּמָּן עַל שְׁמֵיה י״ה, לֶחֶם בְּגָלוּתָא, בְּדִיל דְּהוּא מִן שְׁמֵיה‬
‫דְּקוּדְשָׁא בְּרִיךְ הוּא.‬

87. Why is this holy place called '*Lechem*' (Eng. 'bread'), AS IT IS WRITTEN "THAT IS BET LECHEM"? (BERESHEET 48:7) HE ANSWERS: Since it is one of the Names of the Holy One, blessed be He, they will die there IN WAR for sanctifying His name, "hand ON THE THRONE OF YAH...WAR" (SHEMOT 17:16). THIS MEANS they will die there TO MAKE COMPLETE the name *Yah*, WHICH SHALL NOT BE COMPLETE IN YUD HEI VAV HEI UNTIL THE MEMORY OF AMALEK SHALL BE FORGOTTEN. THEREFORE THE PURPOSE OF THIS WAR IS TO COMPLETE THE NAME OF *YUD-HEI* WITH *VAV-HEI*. THUS THE PLACE IS CALLED LECHEM DERIVED FROM *MILCHAMAH* (ENG. 'WAR'), for it fought (Heb. *lacham*) in exile to render complete the Name of the Holy One, blessed be He.

12. "And Israel beheld Joseph's sons"

A Synopsis

Rabbi Aba explains that lower Israel will be joined with the children of Yisrael into a great crowd, at which point they will all be circumcised and converted. Together, they will then return to their country with love for each other, and only then, "The Creator shall be one." Rabbi Shimon next explains that sores on the skin of the people of Yisrael represent the borders that will separate them from the others in their new land.

The Relevance of this Passage

The universal truth of the Torah and the spiritual power of the Zohar are awakened within the souls of all mankind, facilitating the objective of global unity. The purifying Light that shines and cleanses during circumcision helps refine our souls and purge the Evil Inclination, associated negative sexual behavior, from the souls of all mankind. As well, the arrival of the final redemption is accelerated and our commitment to the path of Torah is strengthened.

88. וַיַּרְא יִשְׂרָאֵל אֶת בְּנֵי יוֹסֵף וַיֹּאמֶר מִי אֵלֶּה. רִבִּי אַבָּא פָּתַח וְאָמַרְתְּ בִּלְבָבֵךְ מִי יָלַד לִי אֶת אֵלֶּה, מַאי קָא מַיְירֵי, יִשְׂרָאֵל לְתַתָּא, חָזֵי דְּיֵיתוּן בְּנוֹהִי דְיִשְׂרָאֵל קַדְמֵיה, כַּד יֵיתוּן מֵעֵילָם וּמִשִּׁנְעָר וּמֵחֲמָת וּמֵאִיֵּי הַיָּם וְאִכְּנָשׁוּ כֻּלְּהוּ וְיהוֹן סַגִּיאִין, תֵּימָא שְׁכִינְתָּא מָאן אִינּוּן כֻּלְּהוֹן, וְלָא בְּהוֹן פְּסוּל מִבְּנֵי נוּכְרָאָה, יֵימְרוּן לֵיה, אֲנַחְנָא כֻּלָּנָא מְבָרַךְ, וְלֵית בָּנָא נוּכְרָאָה בַּהֲדָן, דְּיִתְפָּרְשׁוּן דָּא מִן דָּא וְכָרַת לְהוֹן כַּחֲדָא, וְיִתְגַּיְירוּן, יְתוּבוּן גִּיּוּרִין עִם יִשְׂרָאֵל, וְיהוֹן כַּחֲדָא.

88. "And Israel beheld Joseph's sons, and said, 'Who are these?'" (Beresheet 48:8). Rabbi Aba opened the discussion with the verse, "Then shall you say in your heart, 'Who has begotten me these'" (Yeshayah 49:21). HE ASKS: What does scripture mean by that? HE ANSWERS: Lower Israel saw that the children of Yisrael will come before Him, when they will come "from Elam and from Shin'ar and from Chamat and from the islands of the sea" (Yeshayah 11:11), they will all gather into a great number. The Shechinah will say, Who are all these, are there not any who are unfit, of foreign children? They will say to Him, we are all Your children, there is no foreigner among us. For they will be separated the one from the other, THE MOTLEY CROWD WILL BE SEPARATED FROM YISRAEL, and they will be

circumcised together and converted. The proselyte then will return together with Yisrael and they will be together.

אַ8. תָּנָא, קָשִׁים גֵּרִים לְיִשְׂרָאֵל כְּסַפַּחַת בְּעוֹר הַחַי, לְאַרְעֲהוֹן. כְּתִיב כִּי יְרַחֵם ה' אֶת יַעֲקֹב וּבָחַר עוֹד בְּיִשְׂרָאֵל וְנִלְוָה הַגֵּר עֲלֵיהֶם וְנִסְפְּחוּ עַל בֵּית יַעֲקֹב, כַּד יְתוּבוּן לְאַרְעֲהוֹן בְּרַיָּא, וְיֶהֱוְיָין רְחִימוּ בְּהוֹן, יִהְיֶה ה' אֶחָד וּשְׁמוֹ אֶחָד, יִתְלַווּן גִּיּוּרִין עִם יִשְׂרָאֵל וְיֶהֱוְיָין לְהוֹן כְּעוּמְקָא בְּבִשְׂרֵיהוֹן.

89. We have learned that proselytes are as bad to Yisrael as a sore on the skin. It is written, "For Hashem will have Mercy on Jacob, and will yet choose Yisrael, and set them in their own land: and the stranger shall be joined with them, and they shall cleave to the house of Jacob" (Yeshayah 14:1). When the children will return to their country and there will be love among them, then "Hashem shall be one, and His name One" (Zecharyah 14:9). The proselyte will then cleave to the people of Yisrael and will be like a sore on their skin.

אַ9. וְכָל כָּךְ לָמָּה. ת״ש, אָמַר רִבִּי שִׁמְעוֹן, עַל תְּחוּמִין דְּאַרְעָא, דְּכָל חַד יְהֵא רַעֲוָא לְמֵידָר בְּאַרְעָא דְיִשְׂרָאֵל, וְתִסְתָּעַר דִּיּוּרִין. כְּתִיב וִיתֵדוֹתַיִךְ חַזֵּקִי, צָבֵי לְמֵימַר, סִיכְיָא דְּהַוְיָין עִמָּךְ מֵעִקָּרָא, אַתְקִיף יַתְהוֹן, וְסַיַּיע יַתְהוֹן יַתִּיר מִשְּׁאָר עַמְמִין, כִּבְיָכוֹל, דְּאַתְּ סָכֵי לְאִתְתַּקָּפָא יַתְהוֹן, בְּכָל עַמְמַיָּא אָחֳרָא. וִיהוֹן סַגִּיאִין.

90. He asks: Why are they LIKE A SORE ON THE SKIN? He says, come and hearken, Rabbi Shimon said that IT REFERS TO the borders of the country, for every one will want to live in the land of Yisrael, and the people OUTSIDE ITS BORDERS will be afraid. HENCE it is written: "And let them stretch forth the curtains of your habitations" (Yeshayah 54:2). The verse implies that the curtains you had before FROM THE TIME OF EXILE should be stretched and fortified more than those of the other nations so to speak, whom you saw strengthening them, when you were with the other nations, NAMELY IN EXILE AMONG THE NATIONS. AND THE PROSELYTES shall be many.

13. "Whom Hashem has given me"

13. "Whom Hashem has given me"

A Synopsis

Rabbi Shimon first describes how the Torah (*zeh*) is set before the children of Yisrael. Rabbi Rav Nachman then explains the difference between *zeh* and *zot*, pointing out that the Torah is referred to as "Tor," in the feminine, which is a name of a dove – meaning "the time of the singing bird is come," sung by the Levites, which is the secret of the female aspect of the Torah – the turtle being the secret of the male aspect. Rabbi Rav Nachman then explains that *Hei* (holiness) ה is more important than *Aleph* א. Next, Rabbi Aba tells us how the measurement of the span of God is 670 years, from heaven to earth. Rabbi Aba concludes by explaining why the Torah is called *Zeh.*

The Relevance of this Passage

All reality consists of both male and female energies. When these two polar opposites are united, Light flows and shines upon supernal and corporeal worlds. Our physical world of Malchut embodies female energy, while the Upper Realm of Zeir Anpin corresponds to male. This passage enjoins the two worlds, allowing the resplendent Light of The Creator to vanquish all forms of darkness dwelling in our midst.

91. וַיֹּאמֶר יוֹסֵף אֶל אָבִיו בָּנַי הֵם אֲשֶׁר נָתַן לִי אֱלֹקִים בָּזֶה, רִבִּי שִׁמְעוֹן תָּאנֵי, מֵהָכָא, וְזֹאת הַתּוֹרָה אֲשֶׁר שָׂם מֹשֶׁה לִפְנֵי בְּנֵי יִשְׂרָאֵל, יֹאמַר יִשְׂרָאֵל לְתַתָּא, כַּד יִשְׂרָאֵל עֲלֵיהוֹן לְעֵילָא, בָּנַי אִינּוּן, דְּיָהַב לִי ה קוּדְשָׁא בְּרִיךְ הוּא אוֹרַיְיתָא, כַּמָּה יַתְהוֹן וְנִימוּסֵיהוֹן קְשִׁיטִין, בְּנִימוּסֵי אוֹרַיְיתָא דְּאִתְיְהִיבַת לְהוֹן. תָּא חֲזֵי כַּד יְהוֹן יִשְׂרָאֵל תְּחוֹת גַּדְפֵי שְׁכִינְתָּא, אוֹרַיְיתָא דִּלְהוֹן אִתְקְרִיאַת זֶה, הה"ד זֶה אֵלִי וְאַנְוֵהוּ, וּבְכָל עִדָן דְּלָא הֲוָה דָוִד הֲוָה מְמַלֵּל תְּחוֹת גַּדְפֵי שְׁכִינְתָּא דָּא מִלְתָא, אֶלָּא אִתְנַבֵּי מַה דְּלֵיהֱוֵי, אִתְקְרֵינָא זֹאת.

91. "And Joseph said to his father, 'They are my sons, whom Elohim has given me in this here (Heb. *zeh* masc.)'." (Beresheet 48:9) Rabbi Shimon explained in relation to this the verse: "And that (Heb. *zot* fem.) is the Torah which Moses set before the children of Yisrael" (Devarim 4:44). When lower Israel – WHO ARE CALLED JOSEPH – said: When SUPERNAL Israel is high above them, "They are my children," for the Holy One, blessed be He,

gave me the Torah CALLED ZEH (ENG. 'THIS'). THEREFORE SCRIPTURE SAYS "IN THIS (HEB. ZEH)." Behold YISRAEL AND their true laws, according to the laws of the Torah which were given them. Come and see: When Yisrael will shelter under the wings of the Shechinah, the Torah is called 'zeh,' as in "this (zeh) is my El, and I will praise Him" (Shemot 15:2). THIS IS ALSO THE MEANING OF THE VERSE "WHOM ELOHIM HAS GIVEN ME IN THIS," WHICH IS THE TORAH. But as long as David was not speaking from under the wings of the Shechinah, but prophesied that which will be, THE TORAH is called zot (Eng. 'this', fem.), AS IN "AND THAT (HEB. ZOT) IS THE TORAH."

92. רַב נַחְמָן אֲמַר מֵהָכָא, אִם תַּחֲנֶה עָלַי מַחֲנֶה לֹא יִירָא לִבִּי וְגוֹ' בְּזֹאת אֲנִי בּוֹטֵחַ, זֹאת דָּא אוֹרַיְיתָא תְּהֵא לְיֵיתֵי מְשִׁיחָא, וּבְגִ"ד, וְקוֹל הַתּוֹר נִשְׁמַע בְּאַרְצֵנוּ, עַל מָה אִתְמְתְלַת אוֹרַיְיתָא לְגוֹזָלָא, מַה גּוֹזָלָא קָלֵיהּ עָרֵב, אַף פִּתְגְמֵי אוֹרַיְיתָא קָלֵיהּ עָרֵב, וְדָא קָלָא יְהֵא לְיֵיתֵי מְשִׁיחָא, לְיוֹמָא דְּדִינָא.

92. Rav Nachman said: From this, WE UNDERSTAND THE DIFFERENCE BETWEEN 'ZEH' AND 'ZOT', AS IT IS WRITTEN: "Though a host should camp against me, my heart shall not fear: though war should rise against me, even then I will be confident (lit. 'in zot')" (Tehilim 27:4), zot (Eng. 'this') being the Torah when Messiah will come, WHEN THE TORAH SHALL BE REVEALED. It is therefore written: "And the voice of the turtledove (Heb. tor) is heard in our land" (Shir Hashirim 2:12) IN THE MASCULINE, INSTEAD OF TORAH, WHICH IS THE FEMININE. TOR IS A NAME OF A DOVE. Why was Torah likened to a dove? Because its voice is sweet like that of a dove. This voice will resound when Messiah will come at Judgment Day; NAMELY BEFORE REDEMPTION, WHEN MESSIAH WILL EXECUTE JUDGMENT AND WAGE WAR AGAINST THE NATIONS WHICH ENSLAVE YISRAEL. YET IT IS NOT YET THE TIME TO REVEAL THE TORAH. IT IS THEREFORE CALLED 'TOR' IN THE MASCULINE, AND ZEH ('THIS', MASC.).

93. תָּנָא הַנִּצָּנִים נִרְאוּ בָאָרֶץ עֵת הַזָּמִיר הִגִּיעַ וְקוֹל הַתּוֹר נִשְׁמַע בְּאַרְצֵנוּ. הַנִּצָּנִים: דָּא אֲבָהָתָן דְּמֶרְכַּבְתָּא, דְּמִן עָלְמָא יְקוּמוּן וְיִתְחֲזוּ.

93. We learned: "The flowers appear on the earth; the time of the singing bird is come, and the voice of the turtledove is heard in our land" (Ibid.). The flowers are the patriarchs of the Chariot, ABRAHAM, ISAAC AND JACOB, who will rise in the world and will be seen IN THE LAND.

94. עֵת הַזָּמִיר הִגִּיעַ, תּוּשְׁבַּחְתָּא דִּישַׁבְּחוּן לֵיוָאֵי, כַּד יְתוּבוּן לְפוּלְחָנֵיהוֹן כִּדְבְּקַדְמֵיתָא. וְקוֹל הַתּוֹר, אֲשֶׁר נָתַן לִי אֱלֹקִים בָּזֶה, פִּתְגָּמֵי דְּאוֹרַיְיתָא, דְּאִינוּן עֲרֵבִין כְּקָלָא דְּתוֹרָא, דָּא זֶ"ה.

94. "The time of the singing bird is come," that is, the singing that will be sung by the Levites when they return to their worship of yore. "The voice of the turtledove" IS THE SECRET OF THE VERSE "whom Elohim has given me in this (Heb. *zeh*)." THIS REFERS TO THE SECRET OF THE TORAH IN ITS MALE ASPECT, CALLED 'ZEH', WHICH IS ALLUDED TO IN THE VERSE "WHOM ELOHIM HAS GIVEN ME IN THIS (HEB. *BAZEH*)." These are the words of the Torah which are pleasant as the voice of the turtledove, Zeh.

95. מַאי קָא מַיְירֵי, וְרָזָא דְּמִלְּתָא, בְּעִדָּנָא דְּלָא תֶהֱוָיָין תְּחוֹת גַּדְפֵי שְׁכִינְתָּא, א' דִּלְזֹאת נָחִית, וְהוּא מִתְּחוֹת לְכֹלָּא, וּסְלִיקַת ה', דְּזֶה אֵלִי וְאַנְוֵהוּ, מִדְּחָרַב בֵּיתָא, דְּה"א, לָא יָכְלָא לָדוּר וּלְמֶהֱוֵי בֵּין עַמְמִין עכו"ם, ה"א קַדִּישָׁא חַתוּכָא מִן שְׁמָא. כַּד יְתוּבוּן יִשְׂרָאֵל לְאַרְעֲהוֹן, ה"א קַדִּישָׁא דְּהוּא חַתוּכָא מִן שְׁמָא דְּקוּדְשָׁא בְּרִיךְ הוּא, תֵּיתוּב בָּזֶה וְיִפּוֹק מִיּוֹמָא דְּדִינָא, וְהָא' תְּקַבֵּל תַּקַנְתָּא. ה"א אָלֶף: ה"א עֲדִיפַת בִּקְדוּשָׁה, א' עֲדִיפַת לְאַתְוָון.

95. HE ASKS: What does this mean? HE ANSWERS: The secret of this matter is that when Yisrael are not sheltered under the wings of the Shechinah, the *Aleph* of 'zot' descends beneath all THE GRADES, and the *Hei* of "zeh (Eng. 'this') is my El, and I will praise Him" departs. Since the Temple was ruined, the *Hei* could not dwell among the idolatrous nations and the Holy *Hei* was separated from the Name. When Yisrael will return to their country, the Holy *Hei*, which was cut from the Name of the Holy One, blessed be He, shall return to 'zeh' and come out of the Day of Judgment, while the *Aleph* will be mended AND COME BACK TO 'ZOT'. HE ASKS: WHICH IS MORE IMPORTANT, *Hei* or *Aleph*? HE ANSWERS: *Hei* is more important with respect to holiness, and *Aleph* is more important with respect to the letters.

96. ר' אַבָּא פְּתַח וַאֲמַר, מִי מָדַד בְּשָׁעֲלוֹ מַיִם וְשָׁמַיִם בַּזֶּרֶת תִּכֵּן, זֶה תּוֹר: שָׁוִין כְּבִיָכוֹל, ז' לְר', ר' לְת', ת' לְה', ו' לְה', זַרְתָּא דְקוּדְשָׁא בְּרִיךְ הוּא, בְּשִׁית מְאָה וְשִׁבְעִין שְׁנִין, מֵהָכָא מִן שְׁמַיָּא, וְעַד אַרְעָא, כֵּיצַד זְ"ה תּוֹ"ר, זֶרֶת ו"ה ה"ו תר"ז, אִתְקַדְּמַת ה' לְו', וְאִתְקַדְּמַת ו' לְת', ת' לְר', ר' לְז', רָבוֹעַ יִהְיֶה כָּפוּל זֶרֶת אָרְכּוֹ וְזֶרֶת רָחְבּוֹ כָּפוּל.

96. Rabbi Aba opened the discussion with the verse: "Who has measured the waters in the hollow of his hand, and meted out heaven with the span?" (Yeshayah 40:12). '*Zeh* (*Zayin-Hei*)' and the turtledove (*Tav-Vav-Resh*) are supposedly alike; NAMELY, THEY JOIN TOGETHER. *Zayin* OF *ZEH* joins *Resh* OF *TOR*, the *Resh* OF *TOR* joins the *Tav* OF *TOR*, AND FROM THIS COMES THE COMBINATION OF ZERET (ENG. 'SPAN'). Vav OF *TOR* IS ATTACHED to Hei OF *ZEH*, TO FORM *VAV-HEI* OF THE NAME OF YUD HEI VAV HEI; ZEIR ANPIN AND HIS NUKVA. The measurement of the span of the Holy One, blessed be He, is 670 years, from heaven, ZEIR ANPIN, to earth, THE NUKVA. HE ASKS: How can this be? HE SAYS: *Zeh - tor* HAS TWO PERMUTATIONS: 1) *Zeret - Vav-Hei* 2) *Hei-Vav - Terez*, in which *Hei* OF ZEH comes before *Vav* OF TOR. *Hei* OF *ZEH* precedes *Vav* OF *TOR*, THE PRECEDENCE OF *HEI* ALLUDES TO BINAH, WHICH POURS ABUNDANCE UPON ZEIR ANPIN, WHICH IS THE *VAV*. The *Vav* before the *Tav* OF TOR and *Tav* before *Resh* OF TOR and *Resh* OF TOR before *Zayin* OF ZEH: THIS IS THE PERMUTATION OF *HEI-VAV - TEREZ*, THE SECRET OF 670 YEARS FROM HEAVEN TO EARTH. "Foursquare it shall be, being doubled; a span shall be its length, and a span shall be the breadth of it" (Shemot 28:26).

97. וַיֹּאמֶר קָחֶם נָא אֵלַי וַאֲבָרֲכֵם, יֹאמַר מִדַּהֲווֹ בְּפִתְגָּמֵי אוֹרַיְיתָא מִתְעַסְּקִין, וַהֲוָה דָּא מְכִילְתָּא בֵּין חַכִּימַיְהוּ, אֲבָרֲכִינוּן, וְרָזָא וַיֹּאמֶר אֵלָיו מַה שְׁמֶךָ וַיֹּאמֶר יַעֲקֹב. וַיֹּאמֶר לָמָּה זֶה תִּשְׁאַל לִשְׁמִי, מַה עִנְיָינָא דָא, לְעִנְיָינָא קַדְמֵיתָא דִּקַמֵּיהּ, כִּדְפָרֵישְׁנָא בְּאַתְרֵיהּ.

97. "And he said: Bring them, I pray you, to me, and I will bless them" (Beresheet 48:9). He says, Since they study the Torah, AS SAID "WHOM

ELOHIM HAS GIVEN ME IN THIS (HEB. *ZEH*)," WHICH IS THE TORAH, and the attribute ZEH is between them, I will bless them.

98. וְרָזָא אָחֳרָא, וַיִּשְׁאַל יַעֲקֹב וְגוֹ׳ וַיֹּאמֶר לָמָּה זֶּה תִּשְׁאַל לִשְׁמִי וַיְבָרֶךְ אוֹתוֹ שָׁם, הָא לָא עָתִיד, אֶלָּא בִּזְכוּתָא דְּזֶה, לְבָרְכֵהוֹן.

98. This is the secret of the words, "And he said to him, 'What is your name?' And he said: 'Jacob'" (Beresheet 32:28): THE NAME JACOB IS OF SMALLNESS WITHOUT MOCHIN. IT IS THEN WRITTEN, "And he said: 'Why is it that you ask after my name?'" (Ibid. 30). HE SAID TO HIM: What is it, WHY DO YOU ASK FOR MY NAME, A NAME BEING UNDERSTANDING? Yet in the former verse, YOU SAID THAT YOUR NAME IS JACOB, WHICH MEANS A LITTLE IS ENOUGH FOR YOU, AND YOU DO NOT WISH TO ATTAIN AND KNOW THE NAME. Like we explained elsewhere. There is another secret IN THIS VERSE, "And Jacob asked him... And he said: 'Why is it (Heb. *zeh*) that you ask after my name?' And he blessed him there." That is, he said to him that he will bless him due to Zeh.

99. וְרָזָא סַגִּיאָה תִּנְיָנָא, בְּאַתְרָה דְּהַאי קְרָא, אֲבָל לָא אָתֵינָא לְקַמָּךְ, אֶלָּא לְאַשְׁמוֹעִינָן הַאי קְרָא דַּאֲמַרְנָא, מִקַּמֵּיהּ דַּאֲמֵינָא לָךְ דְּאִתְקְרִיאַת אוֹרַיְיתָא זֶה, כְּתִיב זֶה סִינַי מִפְּנֵי ה׳ אֱלֹהֵי יִשְׂרָאֵל, כַּד אִתְיְיהִיבַת אוֹרַיְיתָא עַל יְדָא דְּמֹשֶׁה, כִּי זֶה מֹשֶׁה הָאִישׁ זֶה אֵלִי וְאַנְוֵהוּ, אוֹרַיְיתָא הֲוָה נָחֲתַת, מִן קַמֵּי אֱלָהָא דְיִשְׂרָאֵל.

99. We learned a great mystery from this verse, but I have come before you only to teach you the verse I just spoke of, saying that the Torah is called Zeh. It is also written: "That (Heb. *zeh*) Sinai before Hashem the Elohim of Yisrael" (Shoftim 5:5), SINAI BEING THE TORAH GIVEN ON SINAI. ALSO, when the Torah was given by Moses, IT WAS SAID OF HIM, "This (Heb. *zeh*) man Moses" (Shemot 32:1), and also "this is my El, and I will praise Him," WHICH MEANS the Torah CALLED ZEH descended before the Elohim of Yisrael. THEN THEY SAID: "THIS IS MY EL..."

14. "Now the eyes of Israel were dim from age"

A Synopsis

Rabbi Chizkiyah first explains that this language is from lower Israel, since none of it is found in the Torah. Since the exiles did not follow the rules of the Torah, they became old and weak. Rabbi Chiya then says that when the exiles return to their land, God will invest them with His spirit. Rabbi Aba goes on to explain the meaning of "dim" as referring to the length in which the exiles lived without "light." Rabbi Aba then answers the question of why the Torah speaks in the language and names of men.

The Relevance of this Passage

Here we are connected to the divine language of the Torah, whose letters are the bridge between the Upper and Lower Worlds. The words of the Torah are like cables that carry spiritual current from the supernal realm into the material dimension. The energy that flows between these two worlds helps us expedite the end of both our personal exile and the global one. This Light illuminates for us the importance of spiritual transformation through the path of Torah and strengthens our commitment to it.

100. וְעֵינֵי יִשְׂרָאֵל כָּבְדוּ מִזֹּקֶן וְגו', תָּאנֵי ר' חִזְקִיָּה, דָּא יִשְׂרָאֵל לְתַתָּא, וּבְגִין דָּא, לָא אַתְּ מַשְׁכַּח דְּכַוָותֵיה, וְכַד יְהוֹן בְּגָלוּתָא כָּל זִמְנָא חֲרוּבָא הָדֵין, סִיבוּ, לָא יָכְלִין לְמֶחֱזֵי אַפֵּי שְׁכִינְתָּא, עַד דְּתֵיתֵי רוּחָא אָחֳרָא בְּהוֹן.

100. "Now the eyes of Israel were dim from age" (Beresheet 48:19). Rabbi Chizkiyah taught that this is lower Israel, for such language is not found THROUGH THE WHOLE TORAH. For when YISRAEL will be in exile all the days of destruction, they will become old with age, and will not be able to behold the face of the Shechinah until another spirit will come upon them.

101. מִקַּדְמַת דְּנָא אִסְתָּאִיבוּ בְּאַרְעָא עַמְמַיָא, וְלָא הֲווֹ בְּנִימוּסֵי אוֹרַיְיתָא. כַּמָּה דִּיהוֹן כָּהֵיל לְמֵיהַךְ, וְתָבוּ עִדָּנָא סַגֵּי בֵּינֵי נֻכְרָאִין, דָּרָא בָּתַר דָּרָא, וְאוֹלִיפוּ מִן אָרְחֵיהוֹן, כַּד יְתוּבוּן אַפֵּי שְׁכִינְתָּא לְאַרְעֲהוֹן, בְּקַדְמֵיתָא לָא יָכְלִין לְמֶחֱמֵי אַפֵּי שְׁכִינְתָּא, עַד דְּיָהֵיב קוּדְשָׁא בְּרִיךְ הוּא רוּחָא דִּילֵיה לְהוֹן.

101. HE EXPLAINS FURTHER THAT they were defiled among the nations IN EXILE, and did not follow the laws of the Torah as they should have. They sat a long while among the gentiles, generation after generation, and learned their ways, AS IT IS WRITTEN "BUT WERE MINGLED AMONG THE NATIONS, AND LEARNED THEIR WORKS" (TEHILIM 106:35). When they will return to their land, they will not at first be able to behold the face of the Shechinah until the Holy One, blessed be He, will invest them with His spirit.

102. ר' חִיָּיא פְּתַח, וְאֶת רוּחִי אֶתֵּן בְּקִרְבְּכֶם, לְבָתַר וְעָשִׂיתִי אֶת אֲשֶׁר בְּחוּקַי תֵּלֵכוּ וּמִשְׁפָּטַי תִּשְׁמְרוּ וַעֲשִׂיתֶם, מִן בָּתַר דְּיָהַב רוּחִין בְּכוֹן וּקְדוּשָׁה, בְּנִימוּסַי תֶּהֱכוֹן וְתִתְהֲכוּן.

102. Rabbi Chiya opened the discussion saying: "And I will put My spirit within you" (Yechezkel 36:27). Then it said: "And cause you to follow My statutes, and you shall keep My judgments, and do them" (Ibid.). For after I will put My spirit within you, and holiness, you shall follow My rules and go by them.

103. לֹא יוּכַל לִרְאוֹת, רִבִּי אַבָּא פְּתַח וַאֲמַר, בְּאוֹר פְּנֵי מֶלֶךְ חַיִּים וּרְצוֹנוֹ כְּעָב מַלְקוֹשׁ, כַּד יִסְבְּרוּן אַפֵּי שְׁכִינְתָּא דְּקוּדְשָׁא בְּרִיךְ הוּא, וְיִתְעַסְּקוּן בְּאִינוּן רְתִיכִין דְּמִנְּהוֹן חֵיוָון דְּעָלְמָא.

103. "So that he could not see" (Beresheet 48:10): Rabbi Aba opened the discussion saying: "In the light of the king's countenance is life; and his favor is as a cloud bringing the spring rain" (Mishlei 16:15). For when they will welcome the Shechinah of the Holy One, blessed be He, and be occupied with the Chariots, where the living creatures in the world come from, NAMELY THE LIVING CREATURES WHICH CARRY THE CHARIOT (YECHEZKEL CHAPTER 1), THEN IT WILL BE SAID OF THEM "IN THE LIGHT OF THE KING'S COUNTENANCE IS LIFE..."

104. תָּא חֲזֵי, לָא תִשְׁכַּח בְּהָנֵי קְרָאֵי כֻּלְּהוֹן לִישָׁנָא, אֶלָּא לְאִינִישׁ, וְלָא אַתְּ מַשְׁכַּח בְּהָנֵי קְרָאֵי בְּקוּדְשָׁא בְּרִיךְ הוּא, בְּגִין כַּד יְתוּבוּן לְאַרְעֲהוֹן, וְיָהַב קוּדְשָׁא בְּרִיךְ הוּא רוּחַ חָכְמְתָא בְּהוֹן, לִישָׁנָא דִּלְהוֹן

תֶּהֱוְיָין תָּדִיר בְּקוּדְשָׁא בְּרִיךְ הוּא, גַּם לְשׁוֹנִי כָּל הַיּוֹם תֶּהֱגֶּה צִדְקָתֶךָ.

עַד כָּאן סִתְרֵי תּוֹרָה

104. Come and see: You shall not find in the language of all the verses IN THE PORTION OF VAYECHI UP TO HERE but words which talk of men, and no verses which speak of the Holy One, blessed be He. TO WIT, THOUGH THEY SPEAK OF REDEMPTION, WHEN JACOB IS MENTIONED, IT REFERS TO SUPERNAL JACOB OR SUPERNAL ISRAEL, NAMELY THE HOLY ONE, BLESSED BE HE. WHY DOES SCRIPTURE SPEAK IN THE LANGUAGE AND NAMES OF MEN? HE ANSWERS: For when they will return to their land, and the Holy One, blessed be He, will put upon them the spirit of Wisdom, they will always speak of the Holy One, blessed be He, as it says, "My tongue also shall tell of Your righteousness" (Tehilim 71:24).

End of Sitrei Torah

15. "And Jacob lived," part two

A Synopsis

Rabbi Chiya opens the discussion by saying that God called the children of Yisrael "righteous" and that they will be happy in the World to Come because they cleaved to His body (the Central Column). Rabbi Yitzchak then explains that the land they shall inherit will be supernal, meaning the Malchut. Then, we learn, they will surely inherit the Shechinah, the land of the living. The secret of the Malchut is that the land is one of planting, referring in scripture to God planting when He created the universe. The children of Yisrael will thus inherit the land forever. Rabbi Ya'akov and Rabbi Yehuda next explain why there is no space in the Torah between the portion of Vayigash and the beginning of the portion of Vayechi. Rabbi Shimon tells us that there are no spaces between the two verses separating "And Jacob lived" to indicate that Yisrael and his children lived in luxury like kings. Rabbi Shimon goes on to explain the importance of seventeen years, because Jacob was sorrowful all his life, but the beauty of Joseph upon first seeing him, reminded Jacob of his wife Rachel, and all his sorrow fell away. But when Joseph, being seventeen, was separated from Jacob, we learn, his sorrow returned. Therefore, Jacob lived in Egypt "for seventeen years." Rabbi Elazar next tells us why the word "play" is mentioned three times in the verse; it refers to the three Columns. Rabbi Aba explains the three Columns as south, north, and east. From them come the three worlds: The Right Column is called "south," the Left Column "north," the Central Column "east." Rabbi Shimon concludes by pointing out that "Your fathers" refers to three: Abraham, Isaac and Jacob.

The Relevance of this Passage

The power of the three Column System lies at the heart of this passage. The three Columns refer to the following behavioral traits: Right Column signifies a man's desire to share, the God - like nature of his soul. Left Column refers to the covetous desire of receiving for the self alone, the insatiable impulses of the ego. The crucial Central Column correlates to a man's free will to resist his selfish desires and instead, choose the truthful longings lingering in his soul, which include unconditional sharing. When a man integrates these three Columns into his life in a spiritually balanced way, he creates a circuit of energy igniting profound Light in his life. The patriarchs, Abraham, Isaac and Jacob, were the Vessels and template that established these three Columns in our physical world by virtue of their deeds throughout their lifetimes. Upon their merit and through the mention of their names in this passage, we can draw upon their respective strength and wisdom to manage these three traits in a fashion that will bring forth spiritual luxuries into our own lives.

105. וַיְחִי יַעֲקֹב וגו׳, ר׳ חִיָּיא פָּתַח וַאֲמַר, וְעַמֵּךְ כֻּלָּם צַדִּיקִים לְעוֹלָם יִירְשׁוּ אָרֶץ וגו׳, זַכָּאִין אִינוּן יִשְׂרָאֵל, יַתִּיר מִכָּל עַמִּין עכו״ם, דְּקוּדְשָׁא בְּרִיךְ הוּא קָרָא לוֹן צַדִּיקִים. לְאַחֲסֵין לוֹן יְרוּתַת עָלְמִין בְּעָלְמָא דְּאָתֵי, לְאִתְעַנְּגָא בְּהַהוּא עָלְמָא, כְּמָה דִּכְתִיב אָז תִּתְעַנַּג עַל ה׳. מַאי טַעְמָא. בְּגִין דְּמִתְדַּבְּקִין בְּגוּפָא דְּמַלְכָּא, דִּכְתִיב וְאַתֶּם הַדְּבֵקִים בַּה׳ אֱלֹהֵיכֶם חַיִּים כֻּלְּכֶם הַיּוֹם.

105. "And Jacob lived" (Beresheet 47:28). Rabbi Chiya opened the discussion saying: "Your people also shall be all righteous...they shall inherit the land forever" (Yeshayah 60:21). Happy are Yisrael above all the other idolatrous nations, for the Holy One, blessed be He, called them righteous, so they may receive the inheritance of the World to Come, and delight in that world, as it is written: "Then shall you delight yourself in Hashem" (Yeshayah 58:14). For what reason? Because YISRAEL cleaved to the body of the King; NAMELY THE CENTRAL COLUMN, as it is written "But you that did cleave of Hashem your Elohim are alive every one of you this day" (Devarim 4:4).

106. רִבִּי יִצְחָק פָּתַח וַאֲמַר, וְעַמֵּךְ כֻּלָּם צַדִּיקִים לְעוֹלָם יִירְשׁוּ אָרֶץ, הַאי קָרָא רָזָא עִלָּאָה אִיהוּ, בֵּין מְחַצְדֵי חַקְלָא, דְּהָא בְּרָזָא דְּאַגַּדְתָּא, תָּנֵי רִבִּי שִׁמְעוֹן, דְּאַחֲסָנַת יְרוּתָא עִלָּאָה. דְּהַהִיא אָרֶץ, לֵית מַאן דְּיָרֵית לָהּ, בַּר הַהוּא דְּאִקְרֵי צַדִּיק, דְּהָא מַטְרוֹנִיתָא בֵּיהּ אִתְדַּבְּקַת לְאִתְבַּסְּמָא, וְצַדִּיק יָרֵית לְמַטְרוֹנִיתָא וַדַּאי.

106. Rabbi Yitzchak opened the discussion saying: "Your people also shall be all righteous; they shall inherit the land for ever." This verse is a sublime mystery among the reapers of the field, TO WIT, THOSE WHO MERITED TO RECEIVE THE FRUIT OF THEIR LABOR IN THE SUPERNAL FIELD, THE NUKVA. For we have learned that among the secrets of the Agada, Rabbi Shimon taught about the possession of the supernal inheritance of the land, WHICH IS THE NUKVA. No one inherits it save the one called righteous, for

the Nukva cleaves to him in order to sweeten THE BITTER JUDGMENTS IN HER. The righteous then surely inherits the Shechinah.

107. אוֹף הָכָא, בַּחֲבִיבוּתָא דְּקוּדְשָׁא בְּרִיךְ הוּא לְיִשְׂרָאֵל, אָמַר וְעַמֵּךְ כֻּלָּם צַדִּיקִים, וּבְג״כ לְעוֹלָם יִירְשׁוּ אֶרֶץ, אִתְחֲזוּן לִירִית לְמַטְרוֹנִיתָא, מַאי טַעֲמָא אִקְרוֹן צַדִּיקִים, וּמ״ט יָרְתִין לְמַטְרוֹנִיתָא. בְּגִין דְּאִתְגַּזְרוּ, כְּמָה דְּתָנִינָן, כָּל מַאן דְּאִתְגְּזַר, וְעָיֵיל בְּהַאי אַחְסָנָא, וְנָטִיר לְהַאי בְּרִית, עָאל וְאִתְדְּבַק בְּגוּפָא דְּמַלְכָּא, וְעָאל בְּהַאי צַדִּיק, וּבְגִינֵי כָּךְ אִקְרוֹן צַדִּיקִים, וְעַל דָּא לְעוֹלָם יִירְשׁוּ אֶרֶץ. מַאי אֶרֶץ. דָּא אֶרֶץ הַחַיִּים.

107. Here too, in His love for Yisrael, the Holy One, blessed be He, said: "Your people also shall be all righteous," for which reason "they shall inherit the land for ever." For they are worthy of inheriting the Shechinah, AS THE RIGHTEOUS INHERITS THE SHECHINAH. Wherefore are Yisrael called righteous, and wherefore do they inherit the Shechinah? Because they are circumcised, and as we learned, whoever is circumcised and enters this possession, NAMELY THE SHECHINAH, whoever keeps the covenant, enters and cleaves to the body of the King, HE BECOMES A CHARIOT TO ZEIR ANPIN, and enters the righteous, BY BECOMING A CHARIOT TO YESOD. Hence, Yisrael are called righteous and "they shall inherit the land for ever." What is this land? It is the land of the living, NAMELY THE SHECHINAH.

108. אַהֲדַר וְאָמַר, נֵצֶר מַטָּעַי מַעֲשֵׂה יָדַי לְהִתְפָּאֵר. נֵצֶר מַטָּעַי: עֲנָפָא מֵאִינוּן עֲנָפִין, דְּנָטַע קוּדְשָׁא בְּרִיךְ הוּא, כַּד בָּרָא עַלְמָא, דִּכְתִיב וַיִּטַּע ה' אֱלֹקִים גַּן בְּעֵדֶן מִקֶּדֶם, וְהַאי אֶרֶץ חַד מִנַּיְיהוּ, בְּגִינֵי כָּךְ נֵצֶר מַטָּעַי מַעֲשֵׂה יָדַי לְהִתְפָּאֵר.

108. Scripture repeats, "The branch of My planting, the work of My hands, that I may be glorified" (Yeshayah 60:21). "The branch of my planting" is one of the branches the Holy One, blessed be He, planted when He created the universe, as it is written: "And Hashem Elohim planted a garden eastward in Eden" (Beresheet 2:8). This land is one of the planting, THE SECRET OF THE NUKVA. Therefore SCRIPTURE SAYS, "The branch of My planting, the work of My hands, that I may be glorified."

109. ד״א וְעַמֵּךְ כֻּלָּם צַדִּיקִים, דָּא יַעֲקֹב וּבְנוֹי, דְּנָחֲתוּ לְמִצְרַיִם בֵּין עַם קְשֵׁי קְדַל, וְאִשְׁתַּכָּחוּ כֻּלְּהוּ זַכָּאִין, וּבְג״כ כְּתִיב, לְעוֹלָם יִירְשׁוּ אָרֶץ דְּמִתַּמָּן סְלִיקוּ לְיָרְתִית אַרְעָא קַדִּישָׁא.

109. According to another explanation, "Your people also shall be all righteous": are Jacob and his children, who went down to Egypt among a stiff-necked nation, and they all remained righteous. Therefore scripture says OF THEM that "they shall inherit the land for ever" because they went up FROM EGYPT to inherit the Holy Land.

110. וַיְחִי יַעֲקֹב בְּאֶרֶץ מִצְרַיִם, אֲמַאי פַּרְשָׁתָא דָּא סְתִימָא. רִבִּי יַעֲקֹב אֲמַר, בְּשַׁעְתָא דְּמִית יַעֲקֹב, אִסְתִּימוּ עֵינֵיהוֹן דְּיִשְׂרָאֵל. רִבִּי יְהוּדָה אֲמַר, דִּכְדֵין נָחֲתוּ לְגָלוּתָא, וְאִשְׁתַּעְבִּידוּ בְּהוֹן.

110. "And Jacob lived in the land of Egypt." HE ASKS: Why is this portion closed, THERE BEING NO SPACE AT ALL IN THE TORAH BETWEEN THE END OF VAYIGASH AND THE BEGINNING OF THE PORTION OF VAYECHI? Rabbi Jacob said: When Jacob died, Israel's eyes were closed. Rabbi Yehuda said: Then, AFTER THE DEATH OF JACOB, they descended into exile, and THE EGYPTIANS enslaved YISRAEL.

111. רִבִּי שִׁמְעוֹן אֲמַר, מַה כְּתִיב לְעֵילָּא, וַיֵּשֶׁב יִשְׂרָאֵל בְּאֶרֶץ מִצְרַיִם בְּאֶרֶץ גֹּשֶׁן וַיֵּאָחֲזוּ בָהּ וַיִּפְרוּ וַיִּרְבּוּ מְאֹד. וּכְתִיב וַיְחִי יַעֲקֹב, דְּלָא אִתְחֲזֵי לְאַפְרָשָׁא בֵּין דָּא לְדָא, מָה אִינּוּן קַיְימֵי בְּתַפְנוּקִין דְּמַלְכִין, וְקַבִּילוּ עֲנוּגָא וְכִסּוּפִין לְגַרְמַיְיהוּ, אוֹף יַעֲקֹב נָמֵי, קַיָּים בְּתַפְנוּקֵי מַלְכִין, בְּעֲנוּגָא וְכִסּוּפָא לְגַרְמֵיהּ, לָא אִתְפְּרַשׁ דָּא מִן דָּא.

111. Rabbi Shimon said: It is written above, "And Yisrael dwelt in the land of Egypt in the country of Goshen; and they took possession of it, and grew, and multiplied exceedingly" (Beresheet 47:27), WHICH MEANS THEY LIVED IN LUXURY LIKE KINGS. THE VERSE IS FOLLOWED BY, "And Jacob lived," WITHOUT ANY SPACE BETWEEN THE VERSES. THIS INDICATES that we should not separate the two VERSES. As ISRAEL lived in luxury and had pleasures and were short of nothing, so did Jacob live in luxury and pleasure. Therefore, THE VERSES are not separated.

112. וְהָכָא אִקְרֵי וַיְחִי. דְּהָא כָּל יוֹמוֹי לָא אִקְרֵי וַיְחִי, בְּגִין דְּכָל יוֹמוֹי בְּצַעֲרָא הֲווֹ, בְּצַעֲרָא אִשְׁתַּכְּחָן, עֲלֵיהּ כְּתִיב, לֹא שָׁלַוְתִּי וְלֹא שָׁקַטְתִּי וְלֹא נָחְתִּי וַיָּבֹא רֹגֶז. בָּתַר דְּנָחַת לְמִצְרַיִם, אִקְרֵי וַיְחִי: חָמָא לִבְרֵיהּ מַלְכָּא, חָמָא לְכָל בְּנוֹי זַכָּאִין צַדִּיקִין, וְכֻלְּהוּ בְּתַעֲנוּגֵי וְתַפְנוּקֵי עַלְמָא, וְהוּא יָתֵיב בֵּינַיְהוּ כַּחֲמַר טַב דְּיָתֵיב עַל דּוּרְדַּיֵּיהּ, כְּדֵין אִקְרֵי וַיְחִי יַעֲקֹב, וְלָא פְּרֵישׁ בֵּין וַיִּפְרוּ וַיִּרְבּוּ מְאֹד לְוַיְחִי יַעֲקֹב וְהָכֵי אִתְחֲזֵי.

112. Here IN EGYPT, it is considered that "Jacob lived" FOR IT WAS CONSIDERED LIFE FOR HIM. It was not said of him: 'Jacob lived' all his life, for his life was that of sorrow. Of him it is written, "I had no repose" IN LABAN'S HOUSE, "nor had I rest" FROM ESAU, "nor was I quiet" BECAUSE OF DINAH AND SHCHEM; "yet trouble came" OF SELLING JOSEPH (Iyov 3:26). But after he went down to Egypt, it is said of him "And Jacob lived." He saw his son a king, he saw all his sons pure and righteous, living in pleasure and luxury, and he dwelling in their midst as good wine resting on its lees. Then it is said: "And Jacob lived." THEREFORE, there is no separation, NO SPACE, between "And grew and multiplies exceedingly" and "And Jacob lived," and so it should be, THE ONE BEING THE CONTINUANCE OF THE OTHER.

113. שְׁבַע עֶשְׂרֵה שָׁנָה, מַאי טַעֲמָא שְׁבַע עֶשְׂרֵה שָׁנָה. אֶלָּא אר"שׁ, כָּל יוֹמוֹי דְּיַעֲקֹב בְּצַעֲרָא הֲווֹ, בְּצַעֲרָא אַעֲבַר לוֹן בְּקַדְמֵיתָא, כֵּיוָן דְּחָמָא לְיוֹסֵף, וַהֲוָה קָאִים קַמֵּיהּ, כַּד יַעֲקֹב מִסְתַּכֵּל בְּיוֹסֵף, הֲוָה אִשְׁתְּלִים בְּנַפְשֵׁיהּ, כְּאִילּוּ חָמָא לְאִמֵּיהּ דְּיוֹסֵף, דְּשַׁפִּירוּ דְּיוֹסֵף דָּמֵי לְשַׁפִּירוּ דְּרָחֵל, וַהֲוָה דָּמֵי בְּגַרְמֵיהּ, כְּמָה דְּלָא אַעֲבַר עֲלֵיהּ צַעֲרָא בְּיוֹמוֹי.

113. "Seventeen years": HE ASKS: Why seventeen years? HE ANSWERS: Rabbi Shimon said that Jacob was sorrowful all his life, and his days passed in sorrow in the beginning. When he saw Joseph standing before him, Jacob looked at Joseph and his soul was made whole as if he saw Joseph's mother. For the beauty of Joseph resembled that of Rachel, and it seemed to him as if he had never known sorrow.

114. וְכַד יוֹסֵף אִתְפְּרַשׁ מִנֵּיהּ, כְּדֵין אִתְקַיַּים, לֹא שָׁלַוְתִּי וְלֹא שָׁקַטְתִּי

וְלָא נָחְתִּי וַיָּבֹא רֹגֶז, דְּדָא קַשְׁיָא לֵיהּ לְיַעֲקֹב מִכָּל מַה דַּעֲבַר, וּבְזִמְנָא דְּאִתְפְּרַשׁ יוֹסֵף מִנֵּיהּ, מַה כְּתִיב, יוֹסֵף בֶּן שְׁבַע עֶשְׂרֵה שָׁנָה הָיָה רוֹעֶה וְגוֹ', וְכָל יוֹמִין דְּיַעֲקֹב, לָא הֲוָה לֵיהּ צַעֲרָא כְּהַאי, וַהֲוָה בָּכֵי כָּל יוֹמָא, לְאִינּוּן שְׁבַע עֶשְׂרֵה שָׁנָה דְּיוֹסֵף.

114. When Joseph departed from him, it came to pass that "I had no repose, nor had I rest, nor was I quiet; yet trouble came." For this trouble was harder to Jacob than everything that came over him. When Joseph was separated from him, it is said: "Joseph being seventeen years old, was feeding the flock" (Beresheet 37:2). All his days, Jacob had no such sorrow. He used to weep every day for the seventeen years of Joseph.

115. מַאי קָאֲתִיבוּ לֵיהּ, וְיוֹסֵף יָשִׁית יָדוֹ עַל עֵינֶיךָ, הָא לְךָ שְׁבַע עֶשְׂרֵה שָׁנָה אָחֳרָנִין, בְּעִנּוּגִין וְתַפְנוּקִין וַהֲנָאוֹת וְכִסּוּפִין, הה"ד וַיְחִי יַעֲקֹב בְּאֶרֶץ מִצְרַיִם שְׁבַע עֶשְׂרֵה שָׁנָה וְגוֹ'. תָּנָא כָּל אִינּוּן שְׁנִין, שְׁכִינְתָּא יְקָרָא דְּקוּדְשָׁא בְּרִיךְ הוּא, עִמֵּיהּ אִשְׁתַּכְּחָא, וּבְגִין כָּךְ חַיִּים אִקְרוּן.

115. They replied to him FROM HEAVEN, "And Joseph shall put his hand on your eyes" (Beresheet 46:4). Here are other seventeen years for you: in pleasure and delight, luxury and lack for nothing. This is the meaning of: "And Jacob lived in the land of Egypt for seventeen years" (Beresheet 47:28). Come and see: The Shechinah of the glory of the Holy One, blessed be He, was with him all those years, for which reason ALL THOSE YEARS IN EGYPT are called 'Life'.

116. תָּא חֲזֵי, כְּתִיב וַתְּחִי רוּחַ יַעֲקֹב אֲבִיהֶם, אִתְחֲזֵי דְּהָא בְּקַדְמֵיתָא מִית הֲוָה הַהוּא רוּחָא דִּילֵיהּ, וְלָא הֲוָה מִתְכַּוֵּין לְקַבְּלָא רוּחָא אָחֳרָא, דְּהָא רוּחָא דִּלְעֵילָּא, לָא שַׁרְיָא בְּרֵיקַנְיָא. אָמַר רִבִּי יוֹסֵי, שְׁכִינְתָּא לָא שַׁרְיָא, אֶלָּא בַּאֲתַר שְׁלִים, וְלָא בַּאֲתַר חָסֵר, וְלָא בַּאֲתַר פָּגִים, וְלָא בַּאֲתַר עָצִיב, אֶלָּא בַּאֲתַר דְּאִתְכַּוֵּון, בַּאֲתַר חֶדוּ, וּבְג"כ, כָּל אִינּוּן שְׁנִין דְּיוֹסֵף אִתְפְּרַשׁ מֵאֲבוֹי, וְיַעֲקֹב הֲוָה עָצִיב, לָא שַׁרְיָא בֵּיהּ שְׁכִינְתָּא.

116. Come and see, it is written: "The spirit of Jacob their father revived." From this we understand that his spirit was dead earlier, and also he had no intention of drawing and receiving another spirit, as the Supernal Spirit does not dwell on an empty place. Rabbi Yosi said: The Shechinah dwells only in a whole spot, not in a place of deficiency or sadness, but a proper place, a place of joy. Therefore, the Shechinah did not rest upon him for all the years that Joseph had been separated from his father and Jacob was in sadness.

117. תָּנָא אָמַר רַבִּי אֶלְעָזָר, אָמַר רַבִּי אַבָּא, כְּתִיב עִבְדוּ אֶת ה' בְּשִׂמְחָה בֹּאוּ לְפָנָיו בִּרְנָנָה, לְאַפָּקָא, דְּלֵית פּוּלְחָנָא דְּקוּדְשָׁא בְּרִיךְ הוּא, אֶלָּא מִגּוֹ חֶדְוָה. דַּאֲמַר רַבִּי אֶלְעָזָר לֵית שְׁכִינְתָּא שַׁרְיָא, מִגּוֹ עַצְבוּת, דִּכְתִיב וְעַתָּה קְחוּ לִי מְנַגֵּן וְהָיָה כְּנַגֵּן הַמְנַגֵּן, מְנַגֵּן מְנַגֵּן תְּלַת זִימְנֵי אֲמַאי. בְּגִין לְאִתְעָרָא רוּחָא מִשְׁלִימוּתָא דְכֹלָּא, דְּהוּא רוּחַ שְׁלֵימָא.

117. We learned that Rabbi Elazar said that Rabbi Aba said: It is written, "Serve Hashem with gladness; come before His presence with singing" (Tehilim 100:2). The verse teaches us that the service of the Holy One, blessed be He, should only be performed through joyfulness, as said Rabbi Elazar, that the Shechinah does not dwell upon sadness. It is written, "But now bring me a minstrel (player). And it came to pass, when the minstrel (player) played" (II Melachim 3:15): HE ASKS: For what reason is the word 'play' mentioned three times IN THIS VERSE? HE ANSWERS: In order to awaken the spirit from the source of wholeness, ZEIR ANPIN WHICH INCLUDES THE THREE COLUMNS, the whole spirit. THREE TIMES 'PLAY' CORRESPONDS TO ITS THREE COLUMNS.

118. אָמַר רַבִּי אַבָּא, תַּמָּן תָּנִינָן, מֵאַרְבַּע סִטְרִין כֹּלָּא אִשְׁתַּכַּח, וְכָל שָׁרְשִׁין דְּעֶלְאִין וְתַתָּאִין בְּהוֹ אֲחִידָן, וְתָנָא, דָּא עָיֵיל, וְדָא נָפִיק, דָּא סָתִים, וְדָא פָּרֵישׁ, אִתְאָחַד חַד בַּחֲבֶרְתֵּהּ, וְאִינוּן אֲבָהָן דְּכֹלָּא.

118. Rabbi Aba said: We have learned that everything is to be found in the four winds: THE THREE COLUMNS OF ZEIR ANPIN, CALLED SOUTH, NORTH, EAST; AND THE SHECHINAH WHICH RECEIVES THE THREE COLUMNS IS THE SECRET OF THE WEST WIND. FROM THEM COME OUT THE THREE WORLDS: BRIYAH, YETZIRAH, ASIYAH AND EVERYTHING THAT IS IN THEM. All the roots of the upper and lower worlds hold on to

them. We have learned that the one enters AND SHINES, NAMELY THE RIGHT COLUMN CALLED SOUTH, and the other comes out BUT DOES NOT SHINE; NAMELY THE LEFT COLUMN CALLED NORTH, WHICH DOES NOT SHINE WITHOUT THE RIGHT COLUMN. Another one is closed, TO WIT, THE CENTRAL COLUMN CALLED EAST, WHICH SHINES ONLY BY COVERED CHASSADIM, BEFORE ITS MATING WITH THE NUKVA, and the other one revealed, NAMELY THE NUKVA, WHICH SHINES BY UNCOVERED CHASSADIM AT THE TIME OF UNION WITH ZEIR ANPIN. SHE IS CALLED THE WEST WIND. All THE WINDS join one another; NAMELY THEY ARE INCLUDED BY ONE ANOTHER, THEN they become the fathers of everything FOR ALL REALITY – NAMELY BRIYAH, YETZIRAH AND ASIYAH, IS DRAWN AND BORN OF THEM.

119. ר"ש אָמַר, רַק בַּאֲבוֹתֶיךָ חָשַׁק ה', כְּתִיב בַּאֲבוֹתֶיךָ, מַמָּשׁ תְּלָתָא, וּמַשְׁמַע דִּכְתִיב רַק, רַק מַמָּשׁ, וּמֵאִלֵּין מִתְפָּרְשָׁן וּמִתְאַחֲדָן כָּל שְׁאָר אָחֳרָנִין, וְסָלְקִין שְׁמָא לְאִתְעַטְּרָא.

119. Rabbi Shimon said: "Hashem took delight only in your fathers" (Devarim 10:15). "Your fathers" are exactly three, NAMELY ABRAHAM, ISAAC AND JACOB. It is written "only" MEANING THERE IS NO MORE THAN THESE THREE. From them are branched out and cleave to them all the others, THE GRADES OF BRIYAH, YETZIRAH AND ASIYAH, who go up TO MAYIN NUKVIN, TO MALE AND FEMALE, to adorn the name, NAMELY TO DRAW NEW MOCHIN UPON THE NUKVA, WHICH IS CALLED NAME.

16. Two camels

A Synopsis

Rabbi Yosi starts by saying that the springs of wisdom were stopped when Rabbi Shimon died. He then explains how Rabbi Yehuda failed to fulfill the words of the verse when he came upon bundles of woolen clothes, which had fallen off two camels and were being attacked by birds. A man walks by and points out his failure to drive the birds away. Rabbi Yosi then explains Rabbi Yehuda's subsequent dream, and that when he woke up, he knew Rabbi Shimon's death caused wisdom to depart from the earth. Rabbi Aba then reveals that manna is the secrets of the Torah, but they are "to be kept," which means hidden.

The Relevance of this Passage

When a great soul departs this physical existence, the full measure of spiritual Light revealed though his lifelong deeds, is awakened each year on the day of his passing. Rabbi Shimon's deeds included the revelation of the Zohar, the mystical secrets of the Torah and soul of the universe. Thus, the brightest of all Lights shines forth in this passage at the mention of Rabbi Shimon's leaving this world. This Light helps to strengthen our connection to the Zohar, Rabbi Shimon, and the hidden Light of the Torah.

120. תָּנָא אֲמַר ר' יוֹסֵי, מִן יוֹמָא דְּאִסְתַּלֵּיק ר"ש מִן מְעַרְתָּא, מִלִּין לָא אִתְכַּסְיָין מִן חַבְרַיָּא, וְרָזִין עִלָּאִין הֲווֹ מִסְתַּכְּלָן, וְאִתְגַּלְיָין מִבֵּינַיְיהוּ, כְּאִלּוּ אִתְיְיהִיבוּ הַהִיא שַׁעֲתָא בְּטוּרָא דְּסִינַי, בָּתַר דְּשָׁכֵיב כְּתִיב, וַיִּסָּכְרוּ מַעְיְינוֹת תְּהוֹם וַאֲרֻבּוֹת הַשָּׁמַיִם, וַהֲווֹ חַבְרַיָּיא מְרַחֲשָׁן מִלֵּי, וְלָא מִתְקַיְימֵי בְּהוּ.

120. We learned that Rabbi Yosi said: Since Rabbi Shimon left the cave, nothing was concealed from the friends. They would behold supernal mysteries, which were revealed to them, as if they were given on Mount Sinai at that hour. After RABBI SHIMON died, it is written: "The fountains also of the deep and the windows of heaven were stopped" (Beresheet 8:2). TO WIT, THE SPRINGS OF WISDOM WERE STOPPED. The friends contemplated these matters but did not understand their secrets.

121. בְּיוֹמָא חַד הֲוָה יָתֵיב ר' יְהוּדָה, אֲפִתְחָא דִטְבֶרְיָה, וְחָמָא תְּרֵי

גְּמַלֵּי, דְּסָלְקֵי קַטְפִּירָא מֵעֲלֹוי דְכִתְפִין, נָפַל מָטוֹלָא דְּקַטְפִּירָא, וַאֲתוּ
צִפֲּרֵי וְעַד לָא מָטוּ עֲלַיְיהוּ, אִתְבַּקָעוּ.

121. For one day, Rabbi Yehuda sat at the gate of Tiberias. He saw two camels laden with BUNDLES OF expensive woolen clothes. The load fell, and birds came TO WHERE IT WOULD FALL. But the birds were torn before the clothes reached it.

122. לְבָתַר אֲתוֹ כַּמָה צִפֲּרִין, וַהֲוֹו אָזְלֵי עֲלַיְיהוּ, וְשָׁרוּ לוֹן בְּטַרְטִישָׁא, וְלָא מִתְבַּקְעִין, וַהֲוֹו צָוְוחִין לוֹן, וְלָא הֲוֹו מִתְפָּרְשָׁן, שָׁמְעוּ חַד קָלָא, עִטְרָא דְעִטְרִין בְּקַדְרִין שַׁרְיָא, וּמָרֵיהּ לְבַר.

122. After that, other birds came on THE TORN BIRDS. They sat upon the rock and were not torn. They shouted AT THE BIRDS, TO REMOVE THEM FROM THE TORN BIRDS, but they would not go. They heard a voice saying that the crown upon the crowns dwells in darkness, and its master is outside.

123. עַד דַּהֲוָה יָתֵיב, עֲבַר חַד גַּבְרָא, אַשְׁגַּח בְּהוֹ, אָמַר, לָא קַיָּים דָּא, הָא דִכְתִיב וַיֵּרֶד הָעַיְט עַל הַפְּגָרִים וַיַּשֵּׁב אוֹתָם אַבְרָם. אָמַר רִבִּי יְהוּדָה, וְהָא עֲבִידְנָא וְלָא אִתְפָּרְשָׁן, אַהֲדַר רֵישֵׁיהּ הַהוּא גַּבְרָא וַאֲמַר, עַד לָא מָרִיט דָּא, רֵישֵׁיהּ דְּמָרֵיהּ, וְעַד לָא גָּלֵישׁ לְמַטְרוֹנִיתָא. רְהַט אֲבַתְרֵיהּ תְּלַת מִלִין, וְלָא אֲמַר לֵיהּ, חָלַשׁ דַּעְתֵּיהּ דְּרִבִּי יְהוּדָה.

123. While RABBI YEHUDA was sitting, a man passed by and looked AT THE BIRDS. He said: This man did not fulfill the words of the verse: "And the birds of prey came down upon the carcasses, and Abram drove them away" (Beresheet 15:11). Rabbi Yehuda said: But I tried TO MAKE THE BIRDS GO AWAY FROM THEM BY SHOUTING AT THEM, but they would not go. The man turned his head TO RABBI YEHUDA and said: He did not yet pluck the hair of his master, nor did he shear the lady. RABBI YEHUDA DID NOT UNDERSTAND WHAT HE MEANT. He ran after him three miles AND BEGGED HIM TO EXPLAIN WHAT HE SAID, but he did not. Rabbi Yehuda was grieved.

124. יוֹמָא חַד, אִדְמוּךְ תְּחוֹת אִילָנָא, וְחָמָא בְּחֶלְמֵיה, ד׳ גַּדְפִין מִתְתַּקְּנָן, וְסָלֵיק רִבִּי שִׁמְעוֹן עֲלַיְיהוּ, וְס״ת עִמֵּיה, וְלָא שָׁבֵיק כָּל סִפְרֵי רָזִין עִלָּאִין וְאַגַּדְתָּא, דְּלָא סָלֵיק לוֹן בַּהֲדֵיה, וְסָלֵיק לְהוֹן לִרְקִיעָא, וְחָמָא דְּמִתְכַּסְיָא מֵעֵינָא, וְלָא אִתְגַּלְיָא.

124. One day RABBI YEHUDA slept under a tree. In his dream he saw four wings prepared and Rabbi Shimon mounting upon them with a book of the Torah. He left no book of sublime mysteries and Agadah, but took all with him to heaven. He saw them hidden from his eyes, never to be revealed again.

125. כַּד אִתְּעַר, אָמַר, וַדַּאי מִדְּשָׁכֵיב ר׳ שִׁמְעוֹן, חָכְמְתָא אִסְתַּלְּקַת מֵאַרְעָא, וַוי לְדָרָא, דְּהַאי אַבְנָא טָבָא, דַּהֲווֹ מִתְחַזָּן מִנֵּיה, וְסָמְכִין עֲלֵיה עִלָּאִין וְתַתָּאִין, אִתְאֲבֵיד מִנַּיְיהוּ.

125. When he woke up he said: Assuredly, when Rabbi Shimon died, Wisdom departed from the earth. Woe to the generation, from which the precious stone they held on to, which was the support of the upper and the lower, was gone.

126. אָתָא לְגַבֵּיה דְּר׳ אַבָּא, סָח לֵיה, סָלֵיק רִבִּי אַבָּא יְדוֹי עַל רֵישֵׁיה, וּבְכָה וַאֲמַר, ר״ש רֵיחַיָּיא דְּטַחֲנִין מִנֵּיה מַנָּא טָבָא כָּל יוֹמָא, וְלָקְטִין לֵיה, כְּמָה דִכְתִיב, הַמַּמְעִיט אָסַף עֲשָׂרָה חֳמָרִים, וְהַשְׁתָּא רֵיחַיָּיא וּמַנָּא אִסְתַּלְּקוּ וְלָא אִשְׁתָּאַר בְּעָלְמָא מִינֵּיה, בַּר כְּמָה דִכְתִיב, קַח צִנְצֶנֶת אַחַת וְתֶן שָׁמָּה מְלֹא הָעוֹמֶר מָן וְהַנַּח אוֹתוֹ לִפְנֵי ה׳ לְמִשְׁמָרֶת. וְאִלּוּ בְּאִתְגַּלְיָיא לָא כְּתִיב, אֶלָּא לְמִשְׁמָרֶת: לְאִצְנָעוּתָא. הַשְׁתָּא מַאן יָכֵיל לְגַלָּאָה רָזִין, וּמַאן יִנְדַע לוֹן.

126. He came before Rabbi Aba and told him. Rabbi Aba raised his hands to his head and wept. He said: A mill to grind good manna every day; NAMELY REVEALING THE SECRETS OF THE TORAH, CALLED MANNA. It is gathered, as it is written: "He that gathered least gathered a quantity of ten homers" (Bemidbar 11:32). Now the mill and the manna are gone, and nothing remained of it in the world, save as it is written: "Take a jar, and put an

omer full of manna in it, and lay it up before Hashem, to be kept for your generations" (Shemot 16:33). It does not say 'in an open place' but "to be kept," which means to be put in a hidden place. Who could now reveal secrets? Who even knows them?

127. לָחֲשִׁישׁ לֵיהּ לְרִבִּי יְהוּדָה בִּלְחִישׁוּ, וְדַאי הַהוּא גַּבְרָא דְּחָמִית, אֵלִיָּהוּ הֲוָה, וְלָא בָּעָא לְגַלָּאָה רָזִין, בְּגִין דְּתִנְדַּע שִׁבְחָא דְר״שׁ, דַּהֲוָה בְּיוֹמוֹי, וְיִבְכּוּן דָּרָא עֲלוֹי. אָ״ל, דִּי לְמִבְכֵּי בְּכִיָּה עֲלֵיהּ.

127. RABBI ABA whispered to Rabbi Yehuda, saying: Surely the man you saw was Elijah. He did not agree to reveal secrets to you, so that you may realize the worth of Rabbi Shimon, who lived in your days, and the generation will weep for him. RABBI ABA said to him: We should indeed mourn him.

128. ר׳ יְהוּדָה, הֲוָה בָּכֵי כָּל יוֹמָא עֲלוֹי, דְּהָא אַעֲרַע עִמֵּיהּ בְּאִדְרָא קַדִּישָׁא דְר״שׁ, וּשְׁאָר חַבְרַיָּיא, אָ״ל וַוי דְּלָא אִסְתַּלְּקְנָא הַהוּא יוֹמָא עִם אִינוּן תְּלָתָא דְּאִסְתַּלָּקוּ, וְלָא לְחֱמֵי דָּרָא דָא, דְּהָא אִתְהַפַּךְ.

128. Rabbi Yehuda wept for him every day, for he was with him, RABBI SHIMON, at the holy assembly of Rabbi Shimon with the other friends. He said TO RABBI ABA, Woe is me that I was not gone at the holy assembly that day with the three who were gone, RABBI YOSI THE SON OF RABBI YA'AKOV, RABBI CHIZKIYAH, AND RABBI YISA, instead of beholding this generation that is changed.

17. "The silver is Mine, and the gold is Mine"

A Synopsis

Rabbi Yehuda begins by explaining to Rabbi Aba that the verse, "The silver is mine, and the gold is mine," means, in other words, that "the heavens are the heavens of The Creator." He then explains the importance of the holy garments, which are Aba and Ima. The High Priest above is Aba, and the one below, Ima. They are the secret of the Malchut of Zeir Anpin.

The Relevance of this Passage

When the energies of male and female unite, spiritual energy is free to flow throughout all the worlds. By revealing the secrets of the holy garments which are Aba [Male] and Ima [Female], the Zohar, is in effect, linking the Upper [Male] and Lower [Female] Worlds. Thus, the dazzling heavenly Light of The Creator gleams throughout our world, removing all forms of darkness from our lives. This splendid occurrence takes place the moment our eyes fall upon the mystical texts that reveal these supernal secrets.

129. א"ל, רִבִּי אֵימָא לִי, כְּתִיב וְהֵם יִקְחוּ אֶת הַזָּהָב וְאֶת הַתְּכֵלֶת וְאֶת הָאַרְגָּמָן וְאֶת תּוֹלַעַת הַשָּׁנִי וְאֶת הַשֵּׁשׁ, וְאִילוּ כֶּסֶף לָא כְּתִיב, וְהָא כְּתִיב זָהָב וָכֶסֶף, א"ל וְהָא נָמֵי נְחֹשֶׁת, דְּכֶסֶף וּנְחֹשֶׁת בְּחֻשְׁבְּנָא הֲוֹוֹ, וְהָכָא לָא. אֶלָּא אִי לָא דְּגַלֵּי בּוֹצִינָא קַדִּישָׁא בְּאַתְרֵיהּ, לָא אִצְטְרִיכְנָא לְגַלָּאָה.

129. RABBI YEHUDA said to RABBI ABA, Tell me Rabbi, it is written: "And they shall take gold, and blue, and purple, and scarlet, and fine linen" (Shemot 28:5), yet silver is not mentioned. But AT THE OFFERING FOR THE TABERNACLE it says "gold and silver" (Shemot 25:3). He said, brass too is not mentioned, though both silver and brass were counted AS AN OFFERING FOR THE TABERNACLE. Here, IN RELATION TO THE VESTMENTS OF THE HIGH PRIEST they are not mentioned. But if the Holy Luminary, NAMELY RABBI SHIMON, did not reveal this mystery when it was discussed, I MYSELF should not reveal it either.

130. פָּתַח וְאָמַר, לִי הַכֶּסֶף וְלִי הַזָּהָב נְאֻם ה', הַיְינוּ דִכְתִיב הַשָּׁמַיִם שָׁמַיִם לַה'.

130. RABBI ABA opened with: "The silver is Mine, and the gold is Mine,' says Hashem" (Chagai 2:8) as it says in the verse, "The heavens are the heavens of Hashem" (Tehilim 115:16).

131. בְּכַמָּה אֲתָר אִסְתַּכַּלְנָא בְּאִלֵּין מָאנֵי דְּקוּדְשָׁא, דִּכְתִיב בְּגִדֵי קֹדֶשׁ הֵם, וּכְתִיב וְעָשׂוּ בִּגְדֵי קֹדֶשׁ, מַאי קְדוּשָׁה הָכָא, אֶלָּא הָכִי תָּנִינָן, קְדוּשָׁה אִינּוּן בְּכָל אֲתַר. וּכְתִיב בִּגְדֵי קֹדֶשׁ הֵם. וְעָשִׂיתָ בִּגְדֵי קֹדֶשׁ, כְּגַוְונָא דִּלְעֵילָּא.

131. I have looked at the vessels of the sanctuary in several places; NAMELY THE RAIMENTS OF THE HIGH PRIEST, as it is written: "These are holy garments" (Vayikra 16:4) "and they shall make holy garments" (Shemot 28:4). HE ASKS: What holiness is there TO THE GARMENTS OF THE HIGH PRIEST? HE SAYS, We have learned that in all of these places THAT ARE MENTIONED there is holiness. NAMELY, "these are holy garments," "and they shall make holy garments," WHICH MEAN they resemble the ones above; TO WIT, ABA AND IMA WHICH ARE CALLED HOLY, FOR THE HIGH PRIEST CORRESPONDS TO SUPERNAL ABA, AND HIS GARMENTS ARE THEREFORE CALLED HOLY GARMENTS, AS WAS SAID.

132. דְּתָנֵינָא כֹּהֵן גָּדוֹל לְעֵילָּא, כֹּהֵן גָּדוֹל לְתַתָּא, לְבוּשִׁין דִּיקָר לְעֵילָּא, לְבוּשִׁין דִּיקָר לְתַתָּא, וּמַה דְּלָא אֲמַר כֶּסֶף וּנְחֹשֶׁת, לַאֲתַר אָחֳרָא אִסְתַּלִּיקוּ, דִּכְתִיב כָּל עַמּוּדֵי הֶחָצֵר סָבִיב מְחוּשָׁקִים כֶּסֶף וְגו', וּכְתִיב וְאַדְנֵיהֶם נְחֹשֶׁת, דְּאִינּוּן מָאנֵי שִׁמּוּשָׁא, לְאִשְׁתַּמְּשָׁא מַשְׁכְּנָא בְּהוּ.

132. For we have learned that there is a High Priest above, ABA, and a High Priest below, WHO CORRESPONDS TO HIM. Therefore, the holy raiments OF ABA above CORRESPOND TO the holy raiment OF THE HIGH PRIEST below. HENCE, AS ABA IS THE SECRET OF HOLINESS SO IS THE HIGH PRIEST HOLY; AS THE RAIMENTS OF HONOR OF ABA ARE HOLY GARMENTS SO ARE THE GARMENTS OF THE HIGH PRIEST. Thus, the verse does not mention silver or brass because they are assigned to another place, NOT CORRESPONDING TO THE SUPERNAL ABA AND IMA, as it is written: "All the pillars round about the court shall be bound with silver...and their sockets of brass" (Shemot 27:17). They are the instruments of service of the tabernacle, THE SECRET OF THE NUKVA OF ZEIR ANPIN.

133. אֲבָל הָכָא בְּאִלֵּין לְבוּשִׁין דִּיקָר, לָא בָּעֵי לְאִשְׁתַּמְּשָׁא בְּהוֹ ב״נ אַחֲרָא, בַּר מְכַּהֲנָא רַבָּא, דִּרְבוּ מְשַׁח קוּדְשָׁא עַל רֵישֵׁיהּ, דִּכְתִיב וְעָשִׂיתָ בִגְדֵי קֹדֶשׁ לְאַהֲרֹן אָחִיךָ לְכָבוֹד וּלְתִפְאָרֶת, דִּבְאִינּוּן לְבוּשִׁין דָּמֵי לְגַוְונָא דִלְעֵילָא.

133. But no one is allowed to use the garment of honor OF THE HIGH PRIEST only the High Priest, who is anointed with the oil of holy ointment upon his head, as it is written: "And you shall make holy garments for Aaron your brother for honor and for beauty" (Shemot 28:2). For in these garments, he resembles ABA above.

18. "And the time drew near for Israel to die," part two

A Synopsis

Rabbi Yehuda opens the discussion by describing that every day a herald resounded in 250 worlds, in which two birds, one going to the north and the other to the south, would return to report the trembling of the world. When a man's end draws near, his legs, like the birds upon their return, become trapped, called "the day of Hashem." A man's spirit must be righteous in order to have it sucked from him by God. Rabbi Yosi further explains that when a man is about to die, if he is righteous, it is proclaimed for thirty days by those in the Garden of Eden.

The Relevance of this Passage

Here, the purifying Light of The Creator cleanses our soul and awakens us to the value and importance of spiritual growth, so that we will merit a high place in the World to Come. The World to Come refers to both the Garden of Eden and to our present lifetime in this material realm. A man's end can refer to both his demise in this physical world, and to the end of his negative and wicked ways in this current life.

134. תַּנְיָא, וַיִּקְרְבוּ יְמֵי יִשְׂרָאֵל לָמוּת א״ר יְהוּדָה, וַוי לְעָלְמָא, דְּהָא בְּנֵי נָשָׁא לָא חָמָאן וְלָא שָׁמְעָן, וְלָא יָדְעִין דְּהָא כָּל יוֹמָא וְיוֹמָא, קָלָא דִּכְרוֹזָא אִשְׁתְּמַע, בְּמָאתָן וְחַמְשִׁין עָלְמִין.

134. We learned "And the time drew near for Israel to die" (Beresheet 47:29). Rabbi Yehuda said: Woe to the world, who do not see, nor hear or know that on each and every day, a herald resounds in 250 worlds.

135. תָּנָא, עָלְמָא חֲדָא, אִשְׁתְּמוֹדַע לְעֵילָא, וְכַד כָּרוֹזָא נָפֵיק, הַהוּא עָלְמָא מִזְדַּעְזְעָא וּמִתְחַלְחֲלָא, נָפְקֵי תְּרֵין צִפֳּרִין, דְּאִסְתַּלָּקוּ מֵהַהוּא עָלְמָא, דְּמָדוֹרֵיהוֹן תְּחוֹת אִילָנָא דְּחֵיזוּ דְחַיֵּי וּמוֹתָא בֵּיה.

135. We learned about a certain world above, THE NUKVA. When the herald goes forth AND MAKES IT WHOLE, the world shudders and trembles. Two birds come out from that world, that live under the tree in which is the appearance of life and death.

136. נָפְקָא חַד צִפּוֹרָא לִסְטַר דָּרוֹמָא, וְחַד צִפּוֹרָא לִסְטַר צָפוֹנָא, וְחַד צִפּוֹרָא כַּד נָהֵיר יְמָמָא, וְחַד כַּד אִתְחֲשַׁךְ יְמָמָא, כָּל חַד וְחַד קָרֵי וּמַכְרְזָא, מַה דִּשְׁמָעִין מֵהַהוּא כָּרוֹזָא.

136. One bird goes to the south side, and the other bird to the north side; the one goes with daybreak and the other when the day darkens. Each cries out what it heard from the herald.

137. לְבָתַר בָּעוּ לְאִסְתַּלָּקָא לְאַתְרַיְיהוּ, וּמִשְׁתַּמְּטֵי רַגְלַיְיהוּ, בְּנוּקְבָא דִּתְהוֹמָא רַבָּא, וּמִתְלַכְּדָן בְּגַוֵּיהּ, עַד דְּאִתְפְּלִיג לֵילְיָא. כַּד אִתְפְּלִיג לֵילְיָא, כָּרוֹזָא קָרֵי, וְכַצִּפֳּרִים הָאֲחֻזוֹת בַּפָּח כָּהֵם יוּקָשִׁים בְּנֵי הָאָדָם.

137. Later, they wish to return to their place but their legs stumble on a hollow in the great abyss and they are trapped there until midnight, when the herald proclaims, "And like the birds that are caught in the snare; so are the sons of men snared" (Kohelet 9:12).

138. א"ר יְהוּדָה, בְּשַׁעְתָּא דְּמִתְלַכְּדָן רַגְלוֹי דִּבְנֵי נָשָׁא, וְיוֹמוֹי אִתְקְרִיבוּ, הַהוּא יוֹמָא, אִתְקְרֵי יוֹם ה', לְאַתָּבָא רוּחֵיהּ לֵיהּ. תָּנָא בְּהַהִיא שַׁעְתָּא, פַּקְדָּא הַהוּא כִּתְרָא קַדִּישָׁא, עַל רוּחֵיהּ, וּמַאן אִיהוּ, דִּכְתִיב יְמֵי שְׁנוֹתֵינוּ בָהֶם שִׁבְעִים שָׁנָה. וְהִיא כִּתְרָא שְׁבִיעָאָה דְּכֹלָּא.

138. Rabbi Yehuda said: When man's legs are trapped and his time draws near, that day is called "the day of Hashem" when he returns the spirit to Him. We have learned that at that time, the holy crown visits the spirit OF THAT MAN. What is it? According to the verse, "The days of our years are seventy" (Tehilim 90:10) it is the seventh crown of all, NAMELY THE NUKVA, WHICH IS THE SEVENTH, FINAL, SFIRAH.

139. וְאִם מִסִּטְרָא דִּגְבוּרָה קָאָתֵי, כְּתִיב, וְאִם בִּגְבוּרוֹת שְׁמֹנִים שָׁנָה, דְּכִתְרָא דִּגְבוּרָה תְּמִינָאָה הֲוֵי, מִכָּאן וּלְהָלְאָה, לֵית אֲתַר לְאִתְמְשַׁךְ, כְּמָה דְאַתְּ אָמֵר, וְרָהְבָּם עָמָל וָאָוֶן, בַּאֲתַר דְּלָא הֲוֵי יְסוֹדָא, בִּנְיָינָא לָא אִתְקַיַּים.

-80-

139. If THE NUKVA comes TO MAN from the side of Gvurah, NAMELY BINAH ABOVE THE SEVEN SFIROT CHESED, GVURAH, TIFERET, NETZACH, HOD, YESOD AND MALCHUT, it is written: "Or if by special strength (Heb. *gvurot*), eighty years" (Tehilim 90:10) since the crown of Gvurah is the eighth. From that time onward, life cannot be prolonged, as it says, "Yet their pride is but trouble and wretchedness" (Ibid.), for when there is no foundation, the building will not endure.

140. א"ר יְהוּדָה, זַכָּאִין אִינּוּן צַדִּיקַיָּא, כַּד קוּדְשָׁא בְּרִיךְ הוּא בָּעָא לְאַתָּבָא רוּחֵיהּ לֵיהּ, וּלְשָׁאֲבָא הַהוּא רוּחָא בְּגַוֵּויהּ. דְּתָנֵינָא, בְּשַׁעְתָּא דְּקוּדְשָׁא בְּרִיךְ הוּא בָּעָא לַאֲתָבָא רוּחֵיהּ לֵיהּ, אִי זַכָּאָה הוּא הַהוּא רוּחָא, מַה כְּתִיב, וְהָרוּחַ תָּשׁוּב אֶל הָאֱלֹקִים אֲשֶׁר נְתָנָהּ.

140. Rabbi Yehuda said: Happy are the righteous when the Holy One, blessed be He, wishes to take back their spirits to Himself and suck their spirits from within them. For we have learned that when the Holy One, blessed be He, desires to recall the spirit, if it be a righteous spirit, it is written: "And the spirit returns to the Elohim who gave it" (Tehilim 12:7).

141. וְאִי לָא אִשְׁתְּכַּח זַכָּאָה, וַוי לְהַהוּא רוּחָא, דְּבָעֵי לְאִסְתַּחְאָה בְּנוּרָא דְּדָלֵיק, וּלְאִתְתַּקָּנָא בְּגִין לְאִשְׁתָּאֲבָא בְּגוּפָא דְּמַלְכָּא, וְאִי לָא אִתְתַּקָּנַת, וַוי לְהַהוּא רוּחָא, דְּמִתְגַּלְגְּלָא כְּאַבְנָא בְּקוּסְפֵּיתָא, דִּכְתִיב וְאֶת נֶפֶשׁ אֹיְבֶיךָ יְקַלְעֶנָּה בְּתוֹךְ כַּף הַקָּלַע. תָּנֵינָא, אִי הַהוּא רוּחָא זָכֵי, כַּמָּה טָבִין גְּנִיזִין לֵיהּ בְּהַהוּא עָלְמָא, דִּכְתִיב עַיִן לֹא רָאָתָה אֱלֹקִים זוּלָתְךָ יַעֲשֶׂה לִמְחַכֵּה לוֹ.

141. If it is not found to be righteous, woe to that spirit, which must bathe in the burning fire and be purified in order to be sucked into the body of the King, NAMELY THE HOLY ONE, BLESSED BE HE. If it is not corrected, woe to that spirit, which rolls like a stone in the hollow of the sling, as it is written: "And the souls of your enemies, them shall he sling out, as out of the hollow of a sling" (I Shmuel 25:29). We learned that if the spirit is worthy, much good is stored for it in that world, as it is written: "Neither has the eye seen, that an Elohim, beside You, should do such a thing for he that waits for Him" (Yeshayah 64:3).

142. א״ר יוֹסֵי, כַּד הַהוּא בַּר נָשׁ אִתְקְרִיבוּ יוֹמוֹי, תְּלָתִין יוֹמִין מַכְרִיזֵי עֲלוֹי בְּעַלְמָא וַאֲפִילוּ צִפֳּרֵי שְׁמַיָּא מַכְרִיזִין עֲלוֹי, וְאִי זַכָּאָה הוּא, תְּלָתִין יוֹמִין מַכְרִיזִין עֲלוֹי בֵּין צַדִּיקַיָּא, בְּגִינְתָּא דְעֵדֶן.

142. Rabbi Yosi said: When the time approaches for a man TO DIE, it is proclaimed in the world for thirty days THAT HIS TIME HAS COME TO DIE. Even the birds in the sky proclaim it, and if he is righteous, it is proclaimed for thirty days among the righteous in the Garden of Eden.

143. תָּנָא, כָּל אִינּוּן תְּלָתִין יוֹמִין, נִשְׁמָתֵיהּ נָפְקַת מִנֵּיהּ בְּכָל לֵילְיָא, וְסָלְקַת וְחָמָאת דּוּכְתָּהּ בְּהַהוּא עַלְמָא, וְהַהוּא ב״נ לָא יָדַע, וְלָא אַשְׁגַּח, וְלָא שַׁלִּיט בְּנִשְׁמָתֵיהּ, כָּל אִינּוּן תְּלָתִין יוֹמִין, כְּמָה דַהֲוָה בְּקַדְמֵיתָא, דִּכְתִיב אֵין אָדָם שַׁלִּיט בָּרוּחַ לִכְלֹא אֶת הָרוּחַ וגו'. א״ר יְהוּדָה, מִכַּד שָׁרָאן אִינּוּן תְּלָתִין יוֹמִין, צַלְמָא דְב״נ אִתְחֲשַׁךְ, וּדְיוֹקְנָא דְאִתְחֲזֵי בְּאַרְעָא אִתְמְנָעַת.

143. We have learned that all these thirty days, the soul ascends from him each night to go up and look at its place in that world, yet the man does not know ABOUT THIS, nor care, nor have control over his soul during these thirty days like before, as it is written: "There is no man who has power over the spirit to retain the spirit" (Kohelet 8:8). Rabbi Yehuda said: At the beginning of the thirty days, the man's shadow is darkened, and the shape OF THE SHADOW is not seen upon the ground.

19. Rabbi Yitzchak sat sadly

A Synopsis

Rabbi Yitzchak asks Rabbi Yehuda for three things that were troubling him. Rabbi Yehuda then asks him why he thinks he is going to die. Rabbi Yitzchak explains that he no longer sees his shadow. They go to see Rabbi Shimon, who protects them from the Angel of Death. Rabbi Shimon asks Rabbi Yitzchak if he has seen his father today, for if so, that means he will die. Rabbi Shimon summons God to prepare to take Rabbi Yehuda away. Rabbi Yitzchak then sleeps and sees his father in his dream, who tells him that they are preparing his chamber in Heaven. Next, Rabbi Shimon asks God that Rabbi Yitzchak will not die, and the wish is granted. Not only that, Rabbi Yitzchak is given seventy places with doors to seventy worlds. Rabbi Yitzchak is then told that he will discover the secrets with Rabbi Shimon upon his death.

The Relevance of this Passage

The profound greatness of Rabbi Shimon is made evident here through his influence and connection to The Creator that allows him to turn aside the Angel of Death on behalf of a fellow rabbi, reversing a decree of death. Moreover, great spiritual worlds and treasures await the rabbi in the World to Come, by virtue of his association to Rabbi Shimon. In effect, this ancient passage is telling us that anyone who truthfully embraces the path of Rabbi Shimon and connects deeply to the Zohar and its wisdom, will have the power to stop the Angel of Death in its tracks and secure a place high in the heavens in the World to Come. The Light emitted here helps to facilitate our connection to the path of the Zohar and deepens our relationship with the giant of all Kabbalists, the master Rabbi Shimon bar Yochai.

144. ר' יִצְחָק, הֲוָה יָתֵיב יוֹמָא חַד, אֲפִּתְחָא דְר' יְהוּדָה, וַהֲוָה עָצִיב, נָפִיק ר' יְהוּדָה, אַשְׁכְּחֵיה לְתַרְעֵיה, דַּהֲוָה יָתֵיב וְעָצִיב, א"ל מַאן יוֹמָא דֵין מִשְׁאָר יוֹמִין.

144. Rabbi Yitzchak was sitting sadly one day by the door of Rabbi Yehuda. Rabbi Yehuda came out and found him sitting sadly at his door. He said to him: What is the matter today?

145. א"ל, אָתֵינָא לְגַבָּךְ, לְמִבְעֵי מִינָךְ תְּלַת מִלִּין: חַד, דְּכַד תֵּימָא מִלֵּי

דְאוֹרַיְיתָא, וְתִדְכַּר מֵאִינוּן מִלִּין דַּאֲנָא אֲמֵינָא, דְּתֵימָא לוֹן מִשְּׁמִי, בְּגִין לְאַדְכָּרָא שְׁמִי. וְחַד דְּתִזְכֵּי לְיוֹסֵף בְּרִי בְּאוֹרַיְיתָא. וְחַד, דְּתֵיזֵיל לְקִבְרִי כָּל ז' יוֹמִין, וְתִבְעֵי בָּעוּתִיךְ עָלֵי.

145. He said to him: I come to you to ask you three things. The first is that when you say words of the Torah, and you shall say the things that I said, say them in my name so as to mention my name. Also, that you shall teach my son, Joseph, the Torah and that you shall go to my grave all the seven days OF MOURNING and pray for me.

146. א"ל מְנַיִן לָךְ. א"ל, הָא נִשְׁמָתִי אִסְתַּלְּקַת מֵינִי בְּכָל לֵילְיָא, וְלָא אַנְהִיר לִי בְּחֶלְמָא, כְּמָה דַּהֲוָה בְּקַדְמֵיתָא, וְעוֹד דְּכַד אֲנָא מַצְלֵינָא, וּמָטֵינָא לְשׁוֹמֵעַ תְּפִלָּה, אַשְׁגַּחְנָא בְּצוּלְמִי דִילִי בְּכוֹתְלָא, וְלָא חָמֵינָא לֵיהּ, וַאֲמֵינָא דְּהוֹאִיל וְצוּלְמָא אִתְעֲבַר וְלָא אִתְחֲזֵי, דְּהָא כָּרוֹזָא נָפֵיק וְכָרֵיז, דִּכְתִיב אַךְ בְּצֶלֶם יִתְהַלֶּךְ אִישׁ, כָּל זִמְנָא דְּצוּלְמָא דְּבַר נָשׁ לָא יִתְעֲבַר מִנֵּיהּ, יִתְהַלֶּךְ אִישׁ, וְרוּחֵיהּ אִתְקַיְּימָא בְּגַוֵּיהּ, אִתְעֲבַר צוּלְמָא דְּבַר נָשׁ וְלָא אִתְחֲזֵי, אִתְעֲבַר מֵהַאי עָלְמָא.

146. He said to him: How do you know YOU ARE GOING TO DIE? Rabbi Yitzchak said to him: My soul departs from me every night, but it does not enlighten me with dreams as before. Moreover, when I pray and reach the part of 'who hears prayer', I look at my shadow upon the wall but do not see it. I think I SHALL DIE since the shadow is gone from me and cannot be seen. For a herald comes forth and proclaims, as it is written: "Surely every man walks in a shadow" (Tehilim 39:7). As long as his shadow has not gone from him, "every man walks" and his spirit within him. Once a man's shadow is no longer seen, he passes away from this world.

147. א"ל וּמֵהֲכָא, דִּכְתִיב כִּי צֵל יָמֵינוּ עֲלֵי אָרֶץ. א"ל, כָּל אִלֵּין מִלִּין דְּאַתְּ בָּעֵי עֲבִידְנָא, אֲבָל בָּעֵינָא מִינָךְ דִּבְהַהוּא עָלְמָא תְּבָרֵיר דּוּכְתָּאי גַּבָּךְ, כְּמָה דַּהֲוֵינָא בְּהַאי עָלְמָא. בָּכָה רִבִּי יִצְחָק וַאֲמַר, בְּמָטוּ מִינָךְ, דְּלָא תִתְפָּרֵשׁ מִנָּאי כָּל אִלֵּין יוֹמִין.

147. RABBI YEHUDA said to him: It is also derived from the verse, "Because our days upon earth are a shadow" (Iyov 8:9). RABBI YEHUDA said to him: I shall carry out your requests. But I also ask that you shall reserve a place for me by you in the other world, as I was by your side in this world. Rabbi Yitzchak wept and said: Please do not go away from me all these days.

148. אֲזָלוּ לְגַבֵּיהּ דְּרִבִּי שִׁמְעוֹן, אַשְׁכְּחוּהוּ דַּהֲוָה לָעֵי בְּאוֹרַיְיתָא, זָקִיף עֵינוֹי ר"ש, וְחָמָא לְרִבִּי יִצְחָק, וְחָמָא לְמַלְאַךְ הַמָּוֶת דְּרָהֵיט קַמֵּיהּ, וְרָקִיד קַמֵּיהּ. קָם רִבִּי שִׁמְעוֹן, אָחִיד בִּידֵיהּ דְּרִבִּי יִצְחָק, אָמַר, גּוֹזַרְנָא, מַאן דְּרָגִיל לְמֵיעַל, יֵיעוֹל. וּמַאן דְּלָא רָגִיל לְמֵיעָאל, לָא יֵיעוֹל. עָאלוּ רִבִּי יִצְחָק וְרִבִּי יְהוּדָה, קָטִיר מַלְאַךְ הַמָּוֶת לְבַר.

148. They went to Rabbi Shimon and found him occupied with the Torah. Rabbi Shimon lifted up his eyes and saw the Angel of Death running and dancing before Rabbi Yitzchak. Rabbi Shimon stood up, held Rabbi Yitzchak by the hand and said: I decree that whoever is wont to come to me shall enter, and he who is not wont shall not come. Rabbi Yitzchak and Rabbi Yehuda came in. And he thus kept the Angel of Death remaining outside, UNABLE TO COME IN.

149. אַשְׁגַּח ר"ש, וְחָמָא, דְּעַד כְּעַן לָא מָטָא עִדָּנָא, דְּהָא עַד תְּמַנְיָא שַׁעֲתֵי דְּיוֹמָא הֲוָה זִמְנָא, אוֹתְבֵיהּ קַמֵּי ר"ש, וַהֲוָה לָעֵי לֵיהּ בְּאוֹרַיְיתָא. אר"ש לְרִבִּי אֶלְעָזָר בְּרֵיהּ, תִּיב אֲפִתְחָא וּמַה דְּתֶחֱמֵי, לָא תִשְׁתָּעֵי בַּהֲדֵיהּ, וְאִי יִבְעֵי לְמֵיעָאל הָכָא, אוֹמֵי אוֹמָאָה דְּלָא לֵיעוֹל.

149. Rabbi Shimon looked and saw that his time had not yet come TO DIE, until the eighth hour of the day. Rabbi Shimon placed him before him and studied the Torah with him. Rabbi Shimon said to his son Rabbi Elazar, Sit at the door, and whoever you see do not speak with him; if he shall want to enter, swear he may not enter.

150. אָמַר ר"ש לְרִבִּי יִצְחָק, חָמֵית דְּיוֹקְנָא דַּאֲבוּךְ יוֹמָא דָא, אוֹ לָא. דְּהָא, תָּנִינָן, בְּשַׁעְתָּא דְּבַר נָשׁ אִסְתַּלַּק מֵעַלְמָא, אֲבוֹי וְקַרִיבוֹי מִשְׁתַּכְּחִין תַּמָּן עִמֵּיהּ, וְחָמָא לוֹן וְאִשְׁתְּמוֹדַע לוֹן, וְכָל אִינּוּן דַּהֲוָה מְדוֹרֵיהּ גַּבַּיְיהוּ בְּהַהוּא עַלְמָא בְּדַרְגָּא חַד, כֻּלְּהוּ מִתְכַּנְּשֵׁי וּמִשְׁתַּכְּחֵי

עֲמֵיהּ, וְאָזְלִין עִם נִשְׁמָתֵיהּ, עַד אֲתַר דְּתִשְׁרֵי בְּאַתְרֵיהּ. אֲמַר, עַד כְּעָן לָא חָמֵינָא.

150. Rabbi Shimon said to Rabbi Yitzchak, Have you seen your father's image today, or have you not? For we have learned that when a man departs from the world, his father and relatives are there with him, and he sees and recognizes them. And all those with whom he will dwell in the other world in the same grade, all gather to be with him, and accompany his soul to its dwelling place. RABBI YITZCHAK said: Until now I have not seen THE IMAGE OF MY FATHER.

151. אַדְּהָכִי קָם ר' שִׁמְעוֹן וַאֲמַר, מָארֵי דְעָלְמָא, אִשְׁתְּמוֹדַע רַבִּי יִצְחָק לְגַבָּן, וּמֵאנּוּן שִׁבְעָה עַיְינִין דְּהָכָא הוּא, הָא אֲחִידְנָא בֵּיהּ, וְהַב לִי. נָפַק קָלָא וַאֲמַר, כּוּרְסַיָּיא דְמָארֵיהּ קְרִיבָא בְּגַדְפוֹי דְּר' שִׁמְעוֹן, הָא דִידָךְ הוּא, וְעִמָּךְ תֵּיתֵיהּ, בְּזִמְנָא דְּתֵיעוֹל לְמִשְׁרֵי בְּכוּרְסִיָּךְ. אֲמַר ר"ש וַדַּאי.

151. Rabbi Shimon stood up and said: Master of the universe, we have a certain Rabbi Yitzchak with us, one of the seven eyes here; TO WIT, ONE OF THE SEVEN STUDENTS WHO REMAINED ALIVE WHEN THEY WENT OUT OF THE HOLY ASSEMBLY. Behold, I hold him, give Him to me! A voice resounded saying: the throne of His Master, NAMELY THE NUKVA, has approached UNION through the wings of Rabbi Shimon. Behold, Rabbi Yitzchak is yours, and you shall come with him when you shall sit in your throne AT THE TIME RABBI SHIMON WILL PART FROM THE WORLD. Rabbi Shimon said: Certainly, I SHALL DO SO AND BRING HIM WITH ME WHEN I WILL DEPART FROM THE WORLD.

152. אַדְּהָכִי, חָמָא רַבִּי אֶלְעָזָר, דַּהֲוָה אִסְתַּלִּיק מַלְאַךְ הַמָּוֶת, וַאֲמַר, לֵית קוּפְטְרָא דְטִיפְסָא, בַּאֲתַר דְּרַבִּי שִׁמְעוֹן בֶּן יוֹחַאי שְׁכִיחַ. אֲמַר רַבִּי שִׁמְעוֹן לְרַבִּי אֶלְעָזָר בְּרֵיהּ, עוֹל הָכָא, וְאָחֵיד בֵּיהּ בְּרַבִּי יִצְחָק, דְּהָא חָמֵינָא בֵּיהּ דְּמִסְתָּפֵי, עָאל רַבִּי אֶלְעָזָר, וְאָחֵיד בֵּיהּ. וְרַבִּי שִׁמְעוֹן אַהֲדַר אַנְפֵּיהּ וְלָעֵי בְּאוֹרַיְיתָא.

152. While he was speaking, Rabbi Elazar saw the Angel of Death departing. He said: No sentence stands at the place of Rabbi Shimon. Rabbi Shimon said to his son Rabbi Elazar, Come here and hold Rabbi Yitzchak, for I see he is afraid. Rabbi Elazar entered and held him, and Rabbi Shimon turned to study the Torah.

153. נַיִּים רְבִּי יִצְחָק, וְחָמָא לַאֲבוֹי, א״ל בְּרִי, זַכָּאָה חוּלָקָךְ, בְּעַלְמָא דֵין, וּבְעַלְמָא דְאָתֵי, דְּהָא בֵּין טַרְפֵּי אִילָנָא דְחַיֵּי דְּגִנְתָּא דְעֵדֶן, אִתְיְהִיב אִילָנָא רַבָּא וְתַקִּיף בִּתְרֵין עָלְמִין, ר״ש בֶּן יוֹחָאי הוּא, דְּהָא הוּא אָחִיד לָךְ בְּעַנְפוֹי, זַכָּאָה חוּלָקָךְ בְּרִי.

153. Rabbi Yitzchak slept and saw his father. HIS FATHER said to him: Son, happy is your portion in this world and in the World to Come, for you sit among the leaves of the Tree of Life in the Garden of Eden. A great and strong tree in both worlds is Rabbi Shimon, who holds you in his boughs. Happy is your portion, my son.

154. אֲמַר לֵיהּ אַבָּא, וּמָה אֲנָא הָתָם, אֲמַר לֵיהּ תְּלַת יוֹמִין הֲווֹ דְּחָפוּ אִדְרָא דְּמִשְׁכְּבָךְ, וְתַקִּינוּ לָךְ כֵּיוָן פְּתִיחָן, לְאַנְהָרָא לָךְ מֵאַרְבַּע סִטְרִין דְּעַלְמָא, וַאֲנָא חָמֵינָא דּוּכְתֵּיךְ וְחָדֵינָא, דַּאֲמֵינָא זַכָּאָה חוּלָקָךְ בְּרִי. בַּר דְּעַד כְּעָן, בְּרָךְ לָא זָכֵי בְּאוֹרַיְיתָא.

154. He said to him: Father, what am I there, IN THE WORLD OF TRUTH? He said to him: For three days they have been hastily preparing your chamber with open windows to shine upon you from the four directions of the world. I have seen your place, rejoiced and said: Happy is your portion, son. Only your son has not yet studied the Torah AND I WAS SORRY FOR THIS.

155. וְהָא הַשְׁתָּא הֲוֵי זְמִינִין לְמֵיתֵי גַּבָּךְ, תְּרֵיסַר צַדִּיקַיָּא דְחַבְרַיָּיא, וְעַד דַּהֲוֵינָא נָפְקֵי, אִתְעַר קָלָא בְּכֻלְּהוּ עָלְמִין, מַאן חַבְרִין דְּקַיְימִין הָכָא, אִתְעֲטָרוּ, בְּגִינֵיהּ דְּרְבִּי שִׁמְעוֹן, שְׁאֶלְתָּא שָׁאִיל, וְאִתְיְיהֵיב לֵיהּ.

155. Even now, twelve righteous men from among the friends were preparing to come to you. As they were going, a sound went forth in all the worlds: Friends who stand here, bedeck yourself for Rabbi Shimon who has asked a request OF THE HOLY ONE, BLESSED BE HE, THAT RABBI YITZCHAK SHALL NOT DIE, and it was granted him.

156. וְלָא דָא בִּלְחוֹדוֹי, דְּהָא שַׁבְעִין דּוּכְתֵּי מִתְעַטְּרָן הָכָא דִילֵיהּ. וְכָל דּוּכְתָּא וְדוּכְתָּא, פְּתִיחִין פְּתִיחָן לְשַׁבְעִין עָלְמִין, וְכָל עָלְמָא וְעָלְמָא, אִתְפַּתַּח לְעֵ' רְהִיטִין, וְכָל רְהִיטָא וּרְהִיטָא, אִתְפַּתַּח לְשַׁבְעִין כִּתְרִין עִלָּאִין, וּמִתַּמָּן אִתְפַּתְּחוּ אָרְחִין לְעַתִּיקָא, סְתִימָאָה דְכֹלָּא, לְמֶחֱמֵי בְּהַהוּא נְעִימוּתָא עִלָּאָה דְּנָהֲרָא, וּמְהַנְיָא לְכֹלָּא, כְּמָה דְאַתְּ אָמַר, לַחֲזוֹת בְּנֹעַם ה' וּלְבַקֵּר בְּהֵיכָלוֹ, מַהוּ וּלְבַקֵּר בְּהֵיכָלוֹ, הַיְינוּ דִכְתִיב בְּכָל בֵּיתִי נֶאֱמָן הוּא.

156. Not only this, but seventy places are adorned for him here. Each place has doors opening to seventy worlds, each world opening to seventy channels, each opened for seventy supernal crowns, where there are ways leading to Atika, the most concealed of all, to see the highest pleasantness which delights and shines upon all, as it says "to behold the pleasantness of Hashem, and to inquire in His temple" (Tehilim 27:4). "To inquire in His temple" as it is written: "For he is the trusted one in all My house" (Bemidbar 12:7).

157. אֲמַר לֵיהּ אַבָּא, כַּמָּה זִמְנָא יְהִיבוּ לִי בְּהַאי עַלְמָא, א"ל לֵית לִי רְשׁוּתָא, וְלָא מוֹדְעֵי לֵיהּ לְבַר נָשׁ, אֲבָל בְּהִלוּלָא רַבָּא דְר' שִׁמְעוֹן, תְּהֵא מְתַקֵּן פָּתוֹרֵיהּ, כְּד"א צְאֶינָה וּרְאֶינָה בְּנוֹת צִיּוֹן בַּמֶּלֶךְ שְׁלֹמֹה בָּעֲטָרָה שֶׁעִטְּרָה לוֹ אִמּוֹ בְּיוֹם חֲתֻנָתוֹ וּבְיוֹם שִׂמְחַת לִבּוֹ.

157. He said to him: Father, how long am I given to live in this world? He said to him: I was not given permission to tell you this, and man is not made to know. But at the feast for Rabbi Shimon, NAMELY ON HIS DAY OF DEPARTURE, WHEN THERE WILL BE GREAT JOY IN ALL THE WORLDS FOR ALL THE SECRETS HE REVEALED, AS MENTIONED IN THE SMALL ASSEMBLY, you shall be there to set his table TO REVEAL MYSTERIES WITH HIM. As it says, "Go forth, O daughters of Zion, and behold King Solomon with the crown with which his mother crowned him on the day of his wedding, and on the day of the gladness of his heart" (Shir Hashirim 3:11).

158. אַדְהָכֵי אִתְעַר רַבִּי יִצְחָק, וַהֲוָה חָיֵיךְ, וְאַנְפּוֹי נְהִירִין, חָמָא רַבִּי שִׁמְעוֹן, וְאִסְתָּכֵּל בְּאַנְפּוֹי, א״ל מִלָּה חַדְתָּא שְׁמַעְתָּא, אֲמַר לֵיה וַדַּאי, סָח לֵיה, אִשְׁתְּטַח קַמֵּיה דְּרִבִּי שִׁמְעוֹן.

158. Rabbi Yitzchak then awoke and laughed and his face shone. Rabbi Shimon looked at his face and said to him: You have heard something new. RABBI YITZCHAK said to him: Surely I HAVE HEARD; He told him WHAT HE SAW IN HIS DREAM. RABBI YITZCHAK prostrated himself ON THE GROUND before Rabbi Shimon.

159. תָּאנָא, מֵהַהוּא יוֹמָא, הֲוָה רַבִּי יִצְחָק אָחֵיד לִבְרֵיה בִּידֵיה, וְלָעֵי לֵיה בְּאוֹרַיְיתָא, וְלָא הֲוָה שַׁבְקֵיה. כַּד הֲוָה עָאל קַמֵּיה דְּרִבִּי שִׁמְעוֹן, אוֹתְבֵיה לִבְרֵיה לְבַר, וְיָתֵיב קַמֵּיה דְּרִבִּי שִׁמְעוֹן, וַהֲוָה קָרֵי קַמֵּיה ה׳ עָשְׁקָה לִי עָרְבֵנִי.

159. We have learned from that day onward that Rabbi Yitzchak would hold his son in his hand. He studied the Torah with him, and never left him. When he came before Rabbi Shimon, he made his son sit outside. He used to come in and sit before Rabbi Shimon and call before him, "O Hashem, I am oppressed, be You my security" (Yeshayah 38:14).

20. When it is time for a man to depart from the world

A Synopsis

This section starts by saying that when a man dies, Four Judgments arise from four winds of the world. The four elements in man – earth, air, fire, water – attach and fight with each other. They are then separated upon his death. The herald next explains that man is evil if he has no merit, and his soul will burn in the Dinur River (Eng. 'river of fire'). At this time, he confesses his deeds. Rabbi Yehuda then explains to Rabbi Yosi the reason for "a black cock," black being the color of judgment. When judgment comes upon man, the black cock starts crowing, then a second Supernal Spirit is added to him, so that he may see what he never saw in his days. If he is righteous, he goes to heaven; if not, his spirit stays in this world, and eventually ends up in Gehenom. Rabbi Yehuda then explains the triple - colored pillar in the lower Garden of Eden, meaning the three colors of the rainbow. The soul ascends through the pillar into righteousness, and so on towards God, if he is worthy.

The Relevance of this Passage

The power to cleanse the evil from our nature and purify our souls from the iniquities we knowingly or unknowingly committed in life, is bestowed upon us, provided we connect to this passage with an atoning heart. This Light sweetens judgments and helps us recognize the foolishness and dangers of self - centered behavior. We are inspired to travel the path of righteousness.

160. תָּנָא, בְּהַהוּא יוֹמָא תַּקִּיפָא וּדְחִילוּ דְּבַר נָשׁ, כַּד מָטֵי זִמְנֵיהּ לְאִסְתַּלְּקָא מֵעַלְמָא, אַרְבַּע סִטְרִין דְּעַלְמָא קָיְימִין בְּדִינָא תַּקִּיפָא, וּמִתְעָרִין דִּינִין מֵאַרְבַּע סִטְרֵי עָלְמָא. וְאַרְבַּע קִשּׁוּרִין נָצָאן, וּקְטָטוּתָא אִשְׁתַּכַּח בֵּינַיְיהוּ, וּבָעְיָין לְאִתְפָּרְשָׁא כָּל חַד לְסִטְרוֹי.

160. We have learned that on that hard and terrible day, when it is time for a man to depart from the world, the four winds of the world, CHESED, GVURAH, TIFERET AND MALCHUT, sentence the world with severe Judgment. Four Judgments arise from the four winds of the world. The four ELEMENTS IN MAN, FIRE, AIR, WATER AND EARTH that are attached to each other, fight and quarrel between them and wish to depart each to its own side, THE ELEMENT OF FIRE WITHIN MAN TO THE GENERAL ELEMENT OF FIRE, THE ELEMENT OF WATER WITHIN MAN INTO THE ELEMENT OF

WATER IN THE WORLD, AND SO ON. FOR THE ELEMENTS WITHIN MAN ARE SEPARATED IN HIS DEATH.

161. כָּרוֹזָא נָפֵיק וּמַכְרְזָא בְּהַהוּא עָלְמָא, וְאִשְׁתְּמַע בְּמָאתָן וְשַׁבְעִין עָלְמִין, אִי זַכָּאָה הוּא, כֻּלְּהוּ עָלְמִין חָדָאן לְקָדְמוּתֵיה, וְאִי לָאו וַוי לְהַהוּא בַּר נָשׁ, וּלְחוּלָקֵיה.

161. The herald, THE SECRET OF THE ILLUMINATION OF CHOCHMAH FROM THE UNION ON THE LEFT, comes forth. He proclaims in the supernal world TEVUNAH and is heard in 270 worlds. If he is righteous, all the worlds welcome him with joy, FOR IF HE HAS MERIT, HE IS GOOD. But if he is not righteous, woe to this man and his portion, FOR IF HE HAS NO MERIT HE IS EVIL.

162. תָּנָא, בְּהַהוּא זִמְנָא דְּכָרוֹזָא כָּרֵיז, כְּדֵין נָפַק חַד שַׁלְהוֹבָא מִסְטַר צָפוֹן, וְאָזְלָא וְאִתּוֹקַד בִּנְהַר דִּינוּר, וּמִתְפָּרְשָׁא לְאַרְבַּע סִטְרֵי עָלְמָא, וְאוֹקֵיד נִשְׁמַתְהוֹן דְּחַיָּיבַיָּא.

162. HE EXPLAINS WHY HE IS EVIL IF HE HAS NO MERIT. HE SAYS, We have learned that when the crier makes his proclamation, a flame comes out from the north side, and goes to be burned in the River of Fire (Nahar Dinur), MENTIONED AS "A FIERY STREAM ISSUED AND CAME FORTH FROM BEFORE HIM" (DANIEL 7:10). It expands to the four directions of the world and burns the souls of the wicked.

163. וְנָפַק הַהוּא שַׁלְהוֹבָא, וְסַלְקָא וְנָחֲתָא בְּעַלְמָא, וְהַהוּא שַׁלְהוֹבָא מָטָא בְּגַדְפוֹי דְּתַרְנְגוֹלָא אוּכְמָא, וּבָטַשׁ בְּגַדְפוֹי, וְקָרֵי, בְּפִתְחָא בֵּין תַּרְעֵי.

163. The flame, THE JUDGMENT OF MALCHUT, WHICH IS REVEALED BY THE SECRET OF 'IF HE HAS NO MERIT, HE IS EVIL' ascends TO BINAH, and descends back into the world, BACK TO MALCHUT. The flame alights beneath the wings of a black cock, which flaps its wings and crows at the opening between the gates.

164. זִמְנָא קַדְמָאָה קָרֵי וַאֲמַר, הִנֵּה יוֹם ה' בָּא בּוֹעֵר כַּתַּנּוּר וְגו'. זִמְנָא תִּנְיָינָא קָרֵי וַאֲמַר, כִּי הִנֵּה יוֹצֵר הָרִים וּבוֹרֵא רוּחַ וּמַגִּיד לְאָדָם מַה שֶּׂחוֹ. וְהַהִיא שַׁעְתָּא, יָתִיב בַּר נָשׁ בְּעוֹבָדוֹי, דְּסָהֲדִין קַמֵּיהּ, וְהוּא אוֹדֵי עֲלַיְיהוּ. זִמְנָא תְּלִיתָאָה, כַּד בָּעְיָין לְאַפָּקָא נִשְׁמָתֵיהּ מִנֵּיהּ, קָרֵי תַרְנְגוֹלָא וַאֲמַר, מִי לֹא יִירָאֲךָ מֶלֶךְ הַגּוֹיִם כִּי לְךָ יָאָתָה וְגו'.

164. At the first time, it crows, saying "For, behold, that day is coming: it burns like a furnace..." (Malachi 3:19). On the second time, it crows and says, "For, lo, He that forms the mountains, and creates the wind, and declares to man what is his thought" (Amos 4:13). At that time, man sits AND HEARS THE WITNESSES give testimony on his deeds before him, and he confesses them. On the third time, when they want to take his soul from him, the cock crows, saying: "Who would not fear You, O King of the nations? for to You it is fitting" (Yirmeyah 10:7).

165. אָמַר רַבִּי יוֹסֵי, תַּרְנְגוֹלָא אוּכְמָא לְמַאי נַפְקָא. אָמַר לֵיהּ רַבִּי יְהוּדָה, כָּל מַה דַּעֲבַד קוּדְשָׁא בְּרִיךְ הוּא בְּאַרְעָא, כֻּלְּהוּ רָמִיז בְּחָכְמָה, בַּר דִּבְנֵי נָשָׁא לָא יָדְעֵי, הֲה"ד מָה רַבּוּ מַעֲשֶׂיךָ ה' כֻּלָּם בְּחָכְמָה עָשִׂיתָ מָלְאָה הָאָרֶץ קִנְיָנֶךָ, וּמִשּׁוּם דְּאִתְעֲבִידוּ בְּחָכְמָה, כֻּלְּהוּ רְמִיזִין בְּחָכְמָה.

165. Rabbi Yosi said: Why a black cock? Rabbi Yehuda said to him: Everything that the Holy One, blessed be He, created upon earth alludes to Wisdom, only men do not know. This is the meaning of the words "O Hashem, how manifold are Your works! in Wisdom have You made them all. The earth is full of Your creatures" (Tehilim 104:24), for they have been made in Wisdom and allude to Wisdom.

166. וְתַרְנְגוֹלָא אוּכְמָא, תָּנֵינָן, לֵית דִּינָא שַׁרְיָא, אֶלָּא בַּאֲתַר דְּהוּא זִינֵיהּ, וְאוּכְמָא מִסִּטְרָא דְּדִינָא קָאָתֵי, וּבְגִין כָּךְ, בְּפַלְגוּת לֵילְיָא מַמָּשׁ, כַּד רוּחָא דְסִטְרָא דְּצָפוֹן אִתְעַר, חַד שַׁלְהוֹבָא נָפֵיק, וּבָטַשׁ תְּחוֹת גַּדְפוֹי דְּתַרְנְגוֹלָא, וְקָרֵי. וְכ"שׁ בְּתַרְנְגוֹלָא אוּכְמָא, דְּאִתְכַּוֵּון יַתִּיר מֵאַחֲרָא.

166. We have learned IN THE MATTER of the black cock that Judgment abides only in a place of its own kind, and black pertains to the side of Judgment, SINCE THE BLACK COLOR ALLUDES TO MALCHUT, THE ATTRIBUTE OF JUDGMENT. Therefore at midnight exactly, when the north wind, THE LEFT COLUMN, stirs, a flame comes out and strikes under the wings of the cock, and it crows. The cock is black, BEING OF THE ATTRIBUTE OF JUDGMENT, and thus is more appropriate than A COCK OF a different COLOR.

167. אוֹף הָכָא, בְּשַׁעְתָּא דְּדִינָא דְּבַר נָשׁ יִתְעַר, שָׁארֵי וְקָרֵי לֵיהּ, וְלֵית דְּיָדַע לֵיהּ, בַּר הַהוּא בַּר נָשׁ דְּשָׁכִיב, דְּתָנִינָן בְּשַׁעְתָּא דְּבַר נָשׁ שָׁכִיב, וְדִינָא שַׁרְיָא עֲלֵיהּ, לְנַפְקָא מֵהַאי עָלְמָא, אִתּוֹסַף רוּחָא עִלָּאָה בֵּיהּ, מַה דְּלָא הֲוָה בְּיוֹמוֹי, וְכֵיוָן דְּשַׁרְיָא עֲלוֹי וְאִתְדַּבַּק בֵּיהּ, חָמֵי מַה דְּלָא זָכָה בְּיוֹמוֹי, מִשּׁוּם דְּאִתּוֹסַף בֵּיהּ הַהוּא רוּחָא, וְכַד אִתּוֹסַף בֵּיהּ וְחָמָא, כְּדֵין נָפֵיק מֵהַאי עָלְמָא, הה"ד תּוֹסֵף רוּחָם יִגְוָעוּן וְאֶל עֲפָרָם יְשׁוּבוּן. כְּדֵין כְּתִיב, כִּי לֹא יִרְאַנִי הָאָדָם וָחָי, בְּחַיֵּיהוֹן לָא זָכָאן, בְּמִיתַתְהוֹן זָכָאן.

167. Here too, when Judgment is aroused upon man, THE BLACK COCK starts crowing. No one knows it save the man who is about to die. For we have learned that when a man is about to die, and Judgment hovers about him so he would depart from the world, another Supernal Spirit is added to him which he had not before during his lifetime. When it hovers about him and cleaves to him, he is able to see what he never saw in his life, due to the additional spirit in him. When the spirit is added to him, he sees and then departs from this world. This is the meaning of the verse, "You take away their breath (lit. 'you shall add their spirit'), they die, and return to their dust" (Tehilim 104:29). Then it is written: "For no man shall see Me, and live" (Shemot 33:20), WHICH MEANS THAT when they are alive they cannot see, but they do when they die.

168. תָּאנָא, בְּשַׁעְתָּא דְּבַר נָשׁ מִית, אִתְיְהִיב לֵיהּ רְשׁוּתָא לְמֶחֱמֵי, וְחָמֵי גַּבֵּיהּ, קְרִיבוֹי וְחַבְרוֹי מֵהַהוּא עָלְמָא, וְאִשְׁתְּמוֹדַע לְהוֹ, וְכֻלְּהוּ גְּלִיפִין בִּדְיוֹקְנַיְיהוּ, כְּמָה דַּהֲווֹ בְּהַאי עָלְמָא, אִי זַכָּאָה הַהוּא בַּר נָשׁ, כֻּלְּהוּ חַדָּאן קַמֵּיהּ, וּמַקְדְּמֵי לֵיהּ שְׁלָם.

-93-

168. We have learned that when a man dies, he is given permission to see, and he sees about him his relatives and friends from the world of Truth. They all have their forms engraved upon them like they were in this world. If the man is righteous, they are all happy to see him and greet him.

169. וְאִי זַכָּאָה לָא הֲוֵי, לָא אִשְׁתְּמוֹדְעָן גַּבֵּיהּ, בַּר מֵאִינּוּן חַיָּיבַיָא, דְּטָרְדִין לוֹן בְּכָל יוֹמָא בַּגֵּיהִנֹּם, וְכֻלְּהוּ עֲצִיבִין, וּפָתְחִין בְּוַוי, וּמְסַיְּימִין בְּוַוי, וְסָלֵיק עֵינוֹי, וְחָמָא לוֹן כְּטִיסָא דְּמִסְתַּלְּקָא מִן נוּרָא, אוֹף הָכֵי הוּא פָּתַח וַוי.

169. If he is not righteous, they do not recognize him but only the wicked, who are smitten daily in Gehenom. They are all sad, they open their speech with 'woe' and end with 'woe'. The man lifts up his eyes and sees them as something burnt rising from the fire. He too opens AND SAYS OF THEM 'woe'.

170. תַּנְיָא, בְּשַׁעְתָּא דְּנָפַק נִשְׁמָתֵיהּ דְּבַר נָשׁ, אָזְלִין כֻּלְּהוּ קְרִיבוֹי וְחַבְרוֹי דְּהַהוּא עַלְמָא עִם נִשְׁמָתֵיהּ, וּמַחֲזְיָין לֵיהּ אַתְרָא דְעֶדוּנָא, וְאַתְרָא דְעוֹנָשָׁא, אִי זַכָּאָה הֲוֵי, חָמֵי דוּכְתֵּיהּ, וְסָלֵיק וְיָתֵיב, וְאִתְעַדָּן בְּעֶדוּנָא עִלָּאָה דְּהַהוּא עַלְמָא. וְאִי לָא הֲוֵי זַכָּאָה, אִשְׁתְּאָרַת הַהִיא נִשְׁמָתָא בְּהַאי עַלְמָא, עַד דְּאִתְטְמֵיר גּוּפָא בְּאַרְעָא. כֵּיוָן דְּאִתְטְמַר, כַּמָּה גַּרְדִינִין דְּנִמּוּסִין אַחֲדָן בֵּיהּ, עַד דְּמָטָא לְדוּמָ"ה, וְעָאלִין לֵיהּ בְּמָדוֹרוֹי דְּגֵיהִנֹּם.

170. We have learned that when a man's soul departs, all his relatives and friends in the world of Truth accompany his soul and show it the place of delight and place of punishment. If he is righteous, he sees his place, and goes up to sit and take delight in the lofty pleasure of that world. If he is not righteous, the soul remains in this world, until the body is buried in the ground. Once it is buried, numerous executioners grab it until it reaches Dumah, and is put in the stories of Gehenom.

171. אָמַר רִ' יְהוּדָה, כָּל ז' יוֹמִין, נִשְׁמָתָא אָזְלָא מִבֵּיתֵיהּ לְקִבְרֵיהּ, וּמִקִּבְרֵיהּ לְבֵיתֵיהּ, וְאִתְאַבָּלַת עֲלוֹי דְּגוּפָא, דִּכְתִיב אַךְ בְּשָׂרוֹ עָלָיו

יִכְאָב וְנַפְשׁוֹ עָלָיו תֶּאֱבָל. אָזְלָא וְיָתְבָא בְּבֵיתֵיהּ, חָמֵי לְכֻלְּהוּ עֲצִיבִין וּמִתְאַבְּלָא.

171. Rabbi Yehuda said: All the seven days OF MOURNING the soul goes from the house to the grave and from the grave BACK to the house and mourns for the body, as it is written: "His flesh shall suffer pain for him, and his soul shall mourn for it" (Iyov 14:22). It goes to sit in the house, and when it sees everybody sad, it mourns TOO.

172. תָּנָא, בָּתַר ז' יוֹמִין, גּוּפָא הֲוֵי כְּמָה דַּהֲוָה, וְנִשְׁמָתֵיהּ עָאלַת לְדוּכְתָּא, עָאלַת לִמְעַרְתָּא דְכָפֶלְתָּא, חָמַאת מַה דְּחָמַאת, וְעָאלַת לַאֲתַר דְּעָאלַת, עַד דְּמָטַת לְגֵ״ע, וְעָרְעַת לִכְרוּבִים, וְשָׁנַן דְּחַרְבָּא, דִּי בְגֵ״ע דִּלְתַתָּא. אִי זַכָּאָה הוּא דְּתֵיעוֹל, עָאלַת.

172. We have learned that after seven days the body becomes whatever it turns into, and the soul goes into its place. It enters the cave of the Machpelah. It sees whatever it sees, and enters wherever it enters until arriving at the Garden of Eden, it meets the Cherubs and the flash of the turning sword in the Garden of Eden. If it is worthy of entering, it enters.

173. תָּאנָא, אַרְבַּע סַמְכִין זְמִינִין, וְחַד דְּיוֹקְנָא דְגוּפָא בִּידַיְיהוּ, מִתְלַבְּשָׁא בֵּיהּ בְּחֶדְוָותָא וְיָתִיבַת בְּהַהוּא מָדוֹרָא דְג״ע דִּלְתַתָּא, עַד זִמְנָא דְּאִתְגְּזַר עֲלָהּ, לְבָתַר כָּרוֹזָא קָרֵי.

173. We have learned that four pillars, THE FOUR ANGELS COMING FROM THE FOUR SPIRITUAL ELEMENTS CHOCHMAH AND BINAH, TIFERET AND MALCHUT, are appointed OVER THE SOUL. They have a bodily form in their hands, and it gleefully dons it, and sits in a story in the lower Garden of Eden for the period of time allotted for it TO SIT THERE.

174. וְעַמּוּדָא דִתְלַת גַּוְונֵי אִזְדַּמַּן, וְהַהוּא עַמּוּדָא אִתְקְרֵי, מְכוֹן הַר צִיּוֹן דִּכְתִיב וּבָרָא ה' עַל מְכוֹן הַר צִיּוֹן וְעַל מִקְרָאֶיהָ עָנָן יוֹמָם וְעָשָׁן וְגו'. סָלְקָא בְּהַהוּא עַמּוּדָא, לְפִתְחָא דְצֶדֶק, דְּצִיּוֹן וִירוּשָׁלַם בֵּיהּ.

174. A triple - colored pillar stands there IN THE LOWER GARDEN OF EDEN, THE SECRET OF THE THREE COLORS OF THE RAINBOW. This pillar is called the "dwelling place of Mount Zion" (Yeshayah 4:5), as it is written "And Hashem will create upon every dwelling place of Mount Zion, and upon her assemblies, a cloud and smoke by day..." THE SOUL ascends through that pillar into the opening of righteousness, where Zion and Jerusalem are, YESOD AND MALCHUT OF THE NUKVA OF ZEIR ANPIN CALLED RIGHTEOUSNESS.

175. אִי זָכֵי לְסַלְקָא יַתִּיר, טַב חוּלָקֵיהּ וְעַדְבֵיהּ, לְאִתְדַּבְּקָא בְּגוֹ גוּפָא דְמַלְכָּא, וְאִי לָא זָכֵי לְסַלְקָא יַתִּיר, כְּתִיב וְהָיָה הַנִּשְׁאָר בְּצִיּוֹן וְהַנּוֹתָר בִּירוּשָׁלַם קָדוֹשׁ יֵאָמֶר לוֹ, וְאִי זָכֵי לְסַלְקָא יַתִּיר, זַכָּאָה הוּא, דְּזָכֵי לִיקָרָא דְמַלְכָּא, וּלְאִתְעַדְּנָא בְּעִדּוּנָא עִלָּאָה, דִּלְעֵילָא מֵאֲתַר דְּאִקְרֵי שָׁמַיִם, דִּכְתִיב אָז תִּתְעַנַּג עַל ה', עַל ה' דַּיְיקָא. זַכָּאָה חוּלָקֵיהּ דְּמַאן דְּזָכֵי לְחֶסֶד דָּא, דִּכְתִיב כִּי גָדוֹל מֵעַל שָׁמַיִם חַסְדֶּךָ.

175. If it is worthy of ascending further than that, happy is its lot and portion which cleaves to the body of the King; NAMELY TO ZEIR ANPIN, FOR IT ALREADY MERITED TO ASCEND TO ZION AND JERUSALEM, THE SECRET OF THE NUKVA. THE NEXT GRADE IS THE BODY OF THE KING, ZEIR ANPIN. If it is not worthy of going further up, it is written OF IT: "And it shall come to pass, that he that is left in Zion, and he that remains in Jerusalem (THE SECRET OF THE NUKVA), shall be called holy" (Ibid. 3). But if he is worthy of going further up, happy is he to attain the glory of the King, NAMELY ZEIR ANPIN, and to be delighted in the supernal Eden above the place called heaven, NAMELY ZEIR ANPIN, as it is written: "Then shall you delight yourself in (lit. 'alone') Hashem" (Ibid. 58:14). "Above Hashem" is precise ZEIR ANPIN CALLED YUD HEI VAV HEI. Happy is the portion of him who is worthy of this Chesed, as it is written: "For Your steadfast love (Heb. *chesed*) is great above the heavens" (Tehilim 108:5).

176. וְכִי עַל הַשָּׁמַיִם הוּא, וְהָא כְּתִיב כִּי גָדוֹל עַד שָׁמַיִם חַסְדֶּךָ. אָמַר ר' יוֹסֵי, אִית חֶסֶד, וְאִית חֶסֶד, חֶסֶד עִלָּאָה, וְחֶסֶד תַּתָּאָה, חֶסֶד עִלָּאָה מֵעַל שָׁמַיִם הוּא. חֶסֶד תַּתָּאָה, הוּא דִכְתִיב, חַסְדֵי דָוִד הַנֶּאֱמָנִים, וּבְהַנֵּי כְּתִיב עַד שָׁמַיִם.

176. HE ASKS: Is Chesed above the heavens? It is written: "For Your Chesed is great unto the heavens" (Tehilim 57:11), WHICH MEANS THAT CHESED IS UNDER THE HEAVENS. HE ANSWERS: There is Chesed and Chesed, an upper Chesed and a lower. The upper Chesed, CHESED OF ZEIR ANPIN ITSELF, is above the heavens, AS HEAVEN IS TIFERET AND CHESED PRECEDES TIFERET. THEREFORE, SCRIPTURE SAYS, "FOR YOUR CHESED IS GREAT ABOVE THE HEAVENS." The lower Chesed, CHESED OF ZEIR ANPIN CLOTHED BY THE NUKVA THROUGH NETZACH HOD OF ZEIR ANPIN is like "the sure Chassadim of David" (Yeshayah 55:3), CALLED DAVID AFTER THE NUKVA, of which it says, "FOR YOUR CHESED is great unto the heavens" SINCE THEY ARE BELOW THE HEAVENS, TIFERET OF ZEIR ANPIN.

21. "A joyful mother of children"

A Synopsis
Rabbi Yitzchak begins by saying the mother is Binah. Rabbi Shimon adds that there are two children: one male, who went to Jacob, and one female, who went to Abraham. He continues by saying that the quotation is a warning to men not to sin, for it may cause Binah to depart from the children, Zeir Anpin and Nukva. When the inhabitants perform good deeds, Binah returns to her young. Rabbi Shimon concludes by saying that happy is the portion for those who "behold the pleasantness of Hashem" and desire righteousness.

The Relevance of this Passage
The Light of The Creator is endless, ever present, and it never changes. Darkness only exists when our Lower World disconnects from the Upper World. Disconnection occurs each time we succumb to the will of our ego and treat others with anything less than human dignity. Connection to the Upper World takes place when a man masters the drives of his ego and yields to the longings of his soul. Here we are stimulated to perform positive deeds and we strengthen our connection to the Upper World, the realm of Binah.

177. תַּנְיָא, אָמַר ר' יִצְחָק, כְּתִיב אֵם הַבָּנִים שְׂמֵחָה הַלְלוּיָה, אִמָּא יְדִיעָא, הַבָּנִים מַאן אִינוּן. אָמַר ר"ש, הָא תָּנִינָן, תְּרֵין בְּנִין אִית לְקוּדְשָׁא בְּרִיךְ הוּא, חַד דְּכַר וְחַד נוּקְבָא. דְּכַר, יַהֲבֵיהּ לְיַעֲקֹב, דִּכְתִיב בְּנִי בְכוֹרִי יִשְׂרָאֵל, וּכְתִיב, יִשְׂרָאֵל אֲשֶׁר בְּךָ אֶתְפָּאָר. בַּת, יַהֲבָהּ לְאַבְרָהָם, דִּכְתִיב, וַה' בֵּרַךְ אֶת אַבְרָהָם בַּכֹּל, בַּת הָיְתָה לוֹ לְאַבְרָהָם, וּבַכֹּל שְׁמָהּ.

177. We learned that Rabbi Yitzchak said: "A joyful mother of children. Haleluyah" (Tehilim 113:9). We know who the mother is, SHE IS BINAH, but who are the children? Rabbi Shimon said: We have learned that the Holy One, blessed be He, BINAH, has two children, one male and one female. The male He gave to Jacob, as it is written: "Yisrael is My son, my firstborn" (Shemot 4:22) and "Yisrael, in whom I will be glorified" (Yeshayah 49:3), and the girl He gave to Abraham, as it is written: "And Hashem had blessed Abraham in all things (Heb. bakol)" (Beresheet 24:1). Abraham had a daughter named Bakol.

178. וְאִמָּא רְבִיעָא עֲלַיְיהוּ, דְּיָנְקָא לְהוּ, וְעַל הַאי כְּתִיב, לֹא תִקַּח הָאֵם עַל הַבָּנִים. וְתָנֵינָן, לָא יַסְגֵּי ב"נ חוֹבוֹי לְתַתָּא, בְּגִין דְּיִסְתַּלַּק אִמָּא מֵעַל בְּנִין, וּכְתִיב, אִמְּךָ הִיא לֹא תְגַלֶּה עֶרְוָתָהּ, וַוי לְמַאן דְּגָלֵי עֶרְיָיתָא.

178. The mother, BINAH, sits on them, MALE AND FEMALE and suckles them. Hence it is written: "You shall not take the mother together with the young" (Devarim 22:6). We learned ITS MEANING that a man should beware of sinning below, IN THIS WORLD, for it might cause the mother, BINAH, to depart from the children, MALE AND FEMALE. It is also written, "She is your mother; you shall not uncover her nakedness" (Vayikra 18:7); TO WIT, NOT TO CAUSE HER TO LEAVE THE YOUNG. Woe to him who indulges in incest, WHO CAUSES THE MOTHER TO DEPART FROM THE YOUNG.

179. וְכַד תָּיְיבִין בְּנֵי עַלְמָא, וְאַסְגִּין בִּזְכוּתָא קַמֵּי קוּדְשָׁא בְּרִיךְ הוּא, וְאִמָּא תָבַת וְכַסְיָא עַל בְּנִין, כְּדֵין אִתְקְרֵי תְּשׁוּבָה. מַאי תְּשׁוּבָה. דָּא תְּשׁוּבָה דְּאִמָּא, דְּתָבַת בְּקִיּוּמָהָא, וּכְדֵין כְּתִיב אֵם הַבָּנִים שְׂמֵחָה, אֵם הַבָּנִים וַדַּאי. וְע"ד, לָא לְפָטַר אִינִישׁ מִפִּרְיָה וּרְבִיָּה, עַד דְּאוֹלִיד בֵּן וּבַת.

179. When the inhabitants of the world repent and do many good deeds before the Holy One, blessed be He, and the mother, BINAH, returns to cover the young, MALE AND FEMALE, BINAH is then called repentance (lit. 'returning'). HE ASKS: Why is it called returning? HE REPLIES: For she returns to her sustenance; TO WIT, BINAH RETURNS TO COVER THE CHILDREN, MALE AND FEMALE, AND GIVES THEM SUCK AS BEFORE. It is then written, "a joyful mother of children." The "joyful mother" is surely BINAH, and hence a man should continue multiplying until he begets a boy and a girl, TO CORRESPOND TO MALE AND FEMALE, THE CHILDREN OF BINAH.

180. תַּנְיָא אָמַר ר' יִצְחָק, כְּתִיב לַחֲזוֹת בְּנֹעַם ה' וּלְבַקֵּר בְּהֵיכָלוֹ, תֵּיאוּבְתָּא דְצַדִּיקַיָּא לְמֶחֱמֵי דָא, וְאַתְּ אֲמַרְתְּ עַל ה'. אָמַר ר"ש, כֹּלָּא חַד, מַשְׁמַע דִּכְתִיב נֹעַם ה', דְּאַתְיָא מֵעַתִּיקָא קַדִּישָׁא לְהַאי שָׁמַיִם,

וְתֵיאוּבְתָּא דְצַדִיקַיָא כָּךְ הוּא וַדַאי, וְעַל הַשָּׁמַיִם כְּתִיב, אָז תִּתְעַנֵּג עַל
ה'. זַכָּאָה חוּלָקֵיה מַאן דְזָכֵי. וַדַאי זְעֵירִין אִינוּן.

180. Rabbi Yitzchak said: It is written: "To behold the pleasantness of Hashem, and to inquire in His temple" (Tehilim 27:4). We understand from this that the desire of the righteous is to behold THE PLEASANTNESS OF HASHEM, THE PLEASANT MOCHIN OF ZEIR ANPIN. How can you say 'above Hashem'? Rabbi Shimon said: All is one, because we understand from the words "the pleasantness of Hashem" that it comes from Atika Kadisha to heaven, TO WIT, ZEIR ANPIN RECEIVES MOCHIN FROM ABOVE HIM. The desire of the righteous is assuredly ONLY TO ATTAIN THESE MOCHIN OF ZEIR ANPIN AND NOT ABOVE HIM, FOR THERE IS NO CONCEPTION OF THE FIRST THREE SFIROT. It is written of them: "Great above the heavens" (Tehilim 108:5), BECAUSE THEY COME FROM ABOVE ZEIR ANPIN. FOR THE SAME REASON, it is also written: "Then shall you delight yourself in (lit. 'above') Hashem" (Yeshayah 58:14) WHEN THEY ARE CLOTHED IN ZEIR ANPIN AND NAMED "THE PLEASANTNESS OF HASHEM." BUT BEFORE THAT PLEASANTESS IS CLOTHED IN ZEIR ANPIN, IT CANNOT BE CONCEIVED. Happy is the portion of him, who merit this. They must be few.

22. "My mother's children were angry with me"

A Synopsis

Rabbi Shimon describes this quotation as the one that explains the exile of Yisrael's children, when God decided he wanted to destroy His lower house. By exiling the children, he remained "aloof" from Malchut (earth). So "my mother's children" refers to Malchut and Zeir Anpin, Binah the mother. Then Rabbi Yosi describes how he was walking with Rabbi Chiya when they spotted a man in the river who said "Crown, crown," referring to the crowns Malchut and Zeir Anpin. Then "a flame came and consumed the bird" on the man's head, referring to Malchon, a button.

The Relevance of this Passage

In reality, The Creator does not choose to destroy or reward his Creation. The Light of The Creator is a constant expanding force of goodness, positivity, and fulfillment. It is man's free - willed choice as to whether he connects to this divine force of Energy [reward] or disconnects from the Light [destruction]. The entire structure of the Upper and Lower Worlds can be simplified and understood by the following analogy. The electrical current flowing through a home is always available for use. If a room is in darkness and we mistakenly [or purposely] fail to plug a lamp into the wall socket, the room remains darkened. The electrical current, however, never changed. It is not logical to conclude that the electricity decided to withhold its energy, keeping the room darkened. It is our own actions or lack of actions that determine whether we live in darkness or light. Kabbalah is the blueprint of the universe, providing man with the tools and methods for connecting to spiritual Light. The verses appearing in this passage are one such tool. We connect ourselves to the mother, Binah, the source and fountainhead of the Light that shines in this world.

181. תָּנִינָן, אר"ש, כְּתִיב בְּנֵי אִמִּי נִחֲרוּ בִי שָׂמוּנִי נוֹטֵרָה אֶת הַכְּרָמִים, בְּנֵי אִמִּי, כְּמָה דִכְתִיב, הַשְׁלִיךְ מִשָּׁמַיִם אֶרֶץ, דְּכַד בָּעָא קוּדְשָׁא בְּרִיךְ הוּא לְמֶחֱרָבָא בֵּיתֵיה דִלְתַתָּא, וּלְאַגְלָאָה יִשְׂרָאֵל בֵּינֵי עַמְמַיָּא, אַעֲבַר קוּדְשָׁא בְּרִיךְ הוּא מִקַּמֵּיה לְהַאי אֶרֶץ, וְאִתְרַחֲקָא מִנֵּיה, כְּדִכְתִיב וַתִּתְצַב אֲחוֹתוֹ מֵרָחוֹק. וְכַד הַאי אֶרֶץ אִתְרַחֲקָא מִשָּׁמַיִם דִּלְעֵילָא, הַאי אֶרֶץ דִלְתַתָּא אִתְחָרְבָא, וְיִשְׂרָאֵל אִתְפַּזְּרוּ בֵּינֵי עַמְמַיָּא, אָמְרָה כ"י, מַאן גָּרֵים לִי הַאי, וּמַאן עָבֵיד לִי הַאי, בְּנֵי אִמִּי דְּנִחֲרוּ בִי, וְאִתְרַחֲקוּ מִנִּי, בְּנֵי אִמִּי וַדַּאי.

181. We learned that Rabbi Shimon said: It is written, "My mother's children were angry with me; they made me the keeper of the vineyards" (Shir Hashirim 1:6). "My mother's children" are as in the verse: "Cast down from heaven to (or: 'the') earth" (Eichah 2:1), THE EARTH BEING THE NUKVA. For when the Holy One, blessed be He, wanted to destroy His lower house, NAMELY THE TEMPLE, and exile Yisrael among the nations, He removed the earth, THE NUKVA, from before Him, and remained aloof from it: "And his sister stood afar off" (Shemot 2:4). And when the earth was afar from the heaven above, ZEIR ANPIN, the lower earth, NAMELY THE TEMPLE, was destroyed and Yisrael were dispersed among the nations. The Congregation of Yisrael said: Who has done this to me, who caused this? "My mother's children," ZEIR ANPIN AND THE NUKVA, who "were angry with me" and kept away from me. Assuredly they are "my mother's children," ZEIR ANPIN AND NUKVA BEING THE CHILDREN OF BINAH, THE MOTHER.

182. רִבִּי יוֹסֵי הֲוָה אָזֵיל בְּאָרְחָא, וַהֲוָה עִמֵּיה רִבִּי חִיָּיא בַּר רַב, עַד דַּהֲווֹ אָזְלֵי, אָמַר רִבִּי יוֹסֵי לְרִבִּי חִיָּיא, חֲמֵיתָא מַה דַּאֲנָא חָמֵית. אָמַר לֵיה, חָמֵינָא גַבְרָא חַד בְּנַהֲרָא, וְצִפְרָא חַד עַל רֵישֵׁיה, וְעַלְעָא בְּפוּמֵיה דְּצִפֹּורָא, וְאָכְלָא וְרָפְסָא בְּרַגְלוֹי, וְהַהוּא גְּבַר רָמֵי קָלִין וְצָוַוח, וְלָא יָדַעְנָא מַאי קָאֲמַר.

182. Rabbi Yosi went on the road with Rabbi Chiya bar Rav. While they were walking, Rabbi Yosi said to Rabbi Chiya, Do you see what I see? He said to him: I see a man in the river, and a bird on his head with teeth in her mouth. It is eating and tearing with its claws. The man raises his voice and shouts, but I do not know what he says.

183. אֲמַר, נִקְרַב גַּבֵּיה, וְנִשְׁמַע. אָמַר מִסְתְּפֵינָא לְמִקְרַב. א״ל, וְכִי ב״נ הוּא בַּאֲתַר דָּא, אֶלָּא רְמִיזָא דְּחָכְמְתָא, דְּרָמִיז לָן קוּדְשָׁא בְּרִיךְ הוּא. קְרִיבוּ גַבֵּיה, שָׁמְעוּ דַּהֲוָה אָמַר, עוֹטְרָא עוֹטְרָא, תְּרֵין בְּנִין שַׁרְיָין לְבַר, לָא נָח וְלָא נַיְיחָא, עַד דְּצַפְרָא בְּקֵיסָרָא רָמִיו.

183. RABBI YOSI said: Let us approach the man and hear what he says. Rabbi Chiya said: I am afraid to come near. He said to him: Is this a man in that place? The Holy One, blessed be He, gave us a hint of Wisdom. They came near him and heard him say, Crown, crown, NAMELY, ZEIR ANPIN AND NUKVA CALLED CROWNS, two children OF BINAH dwell outside THEIR PLACE. ZEIR ANPIN does not have rest, nor is there respite FOR THE NUKVA, until the bird will be cast away TORN to pieces in Caesarea.

184. בָּכָה ר׳ יוֹסֵי וַאֲמַר, הַיְינוּ דְּתָנִינָן, בְּנֵי אִמִּי נִחֲרוּ בִי וְגוֹ׳, מ״ט. בְּגִין דְּכַרְמִי שֶׁלִּי לֹא נָטָרְתִּי.

184. Rabbi Yosi wept and said: This is what we learned in relation to the verse: "My mother's children were angry with me," WHICH ALLUDES TO MALE AND FEMALE. Why? Because "my own vineyard I have not kept" (Shir Hashirim 1:6).

185. אֲמַר וַדַּאי גָּלוּתָא אִתְמְשַׁךְ, וְעַל דָּא צִפֲּרֵי שְׁמַיָּא לָא אַעֲדִיוּ, עַד דִּי שָׁלְטָנוּתָא דְּעַמִּין עכו״ם אַעֲדִיאוּ מִן עַלְמָא, וְאֵימָתַי. עַד דְּיִמְטֵי יוֹמָא, דְּקוּדְשָׁא בְּרִיךְ הוּא אִתְעַר הוּא דִּינוֹי בְּעַלְמָא, דִּכְתִיב וְהָיָה יוֹם אֶחָד הוּא יִוָּדַע לַה׳ לֹא יוֹם וְלֹא לָיְלָה.

185. He said: Assuredly the exile will continue, and therefore the birds in the sky, THE MINISTERS OF THE NATIONS, will be in power until the government of the idolatrous nations will pass away from the world. When will that be? When the day of the Holy One, blessed be He, will come and His Judgment will be set upon the world, as it is written: "But it shall be one particular day which shall be known as Hashem's, neither day, nor night" (Zecharyah 14:7).

186. עַד דַּהֲווֹ אָזְלִין, שָׁמְעוּ חַד קָלָא דַּהֲוָה אָמַר, אוֹקִידָא דְּקוּפְטִירָא מָטָא בְּדִינוֹי, נָפַק חַד שַׁלְהוֹבָא, וְאוֹקִיד לְהַהוּא צִפּוֹרָא. אָמַר וַדַּאי, כְּמָה דִכְתִיב, וִיהִיבַת לִיקֵדַת אֶשָּׁא.

186. While they were walking, they heard a voice saying: 'The flame of the button has come with its judgment'; TO WIT, OF MALCHUT CALLED BUTTON. A flame came and consumed the bird. Rabbi Yosi said: Surely, it happened as in the verse, "And given to the burning flame" (Daniel 7:11).

23. "And your covenant with death shall be annulled"

A Synopsis

Rabbi Yosi begins the discussion by saying that God exiled Yisrael only after His children lost Faith, which is the secret of the Shechinah. Then the Shechinah is separated, or "annulled" from Zeir Anpin. Death, we learn, will be destroyed from the world only when the children of Yisrael "cleave to the right" of God.

The Relevance of this Passage

At the moment of creation, the souls of mankind sought the opportunity to create their own Light through their effort towards spiritual transformation. For this reason, our physical world, and all the supernal worlds above, was created. We create our own Light when we overcome our doubts concerning the reality of The Creator and when we triumph over our Evil Inclinations. When we experience doubt or succumb to the selfish impulses of our nature, we disconnect from the Light and our exile continues. These negative attributes are associated with the Left Column energy. However, when a man "cleaves to the right" of God, it means he is becoming a more sharing and tolerant person, the attributes associated with Right Column energy. Thus, one purpose behind this passage is to ignite the power of Right Column energy within us, so that we overcome our dark side and attract the Light of the Shechinah into our lives. In addition, the mere act of reading the words contained herein strengthens our faith, arouses the Light of the Shechinah and helps to remove the force of the death from this universe.

187. א״ר יוֹסֵי, לָא אַגְלֵי קוּדְשָׁא בְּרִיךְ הוּא לְיִשְׂרָאֵל, אֶלָּא בְּזִמְנָא דְּלָא אִשְׁתְּכַח מְהֵימְנוּתָא בֵּינַיְיהוּ, כַּד אִתְמְנַע מְהֵימְנוּתָא בֵּינַיְיהוּ, כִּבְיָכוֹל, הָכֵי אִשְׁתְּכַח בְּכֹלָּא, דִּכְתִיב וְכֻפַּר בְּרִיתְכֶם אֶת מָוֶת.

187. Rabbi Yosi said: The Holy One, blessed be He, exiled Yisrael only when there was no faith among them, WHICH IS THE SECRET OF THE SHECHINAH CALLED FAITH, FOR SINCE THEY HAVE IMPAIRED THEIR COVENANT, THE SHECHINAH WAS GONE FROM THEM. For when faith is withheld from them, it is so in everything, NAMELY, ALSO ABOVE, THE SHECHINAH IS SEPARATED FROM ZEIR ANPIN, as it is written: "And your covenant with death shall be annulled" (Yeshayah 28:18), WHICH MEANS THAT KEEPING THE COVENANT ATONES FROM DEATH, AND IT ATONED FOR THEM TOO, SO THEY WOULD NOT GO INTO EXILE. BUT THEY DID

IMPAIR THE COVENANT AND THUS THE SHECHINAH DEPARTED FROM THEM.

188. א"ר חִיָּיא, מַאי דִּכְתִּיב, בִּלַּע הַמָּוֶת לָנֶצַח. א"ל, כַּד יִתְּעַר קוּדְשָׁא בְּרִיךְ הוּא יְמִינָא דִּילֵיהּ, אִתְמְנַע מוֹתָא מִן עַלְמָא, וְלָא יִתְּעַר הַאי יְמִינָא, אֶלָּא כַּד יִתְעָרוּן יִשְׂרָאֵל בִּימִינָא דְּקוּדְשָׁא בְּרִיךְ הוּא, וּמַאי נִיהוּ תּוֹרָה, דִּכְתִּיב בָּהּ, מִימִינוֹ אֵשׁ דָּת לָמוֹ, בְּהַהוּא זִמְנָא, יְמִין ה' עוֹשָׂה חָיִל וְגו', לֹא אָמוּת כִּי אֶחְיֶה וַאֲסַפֵּר מַעֲשֵׂי יָהּ.

188. Rabbi Chiya said: This is the meaning of, "He will destroy death for ever" (Yeshayah 25:8). RABBI YOSI said to him: When the Holy One, blessed be He, will awaken His right, death will be destroyed forever from the world. But the right will not stir until Yisrael will arise and cleave to the right of the Holy One, blessed be He. What is "THE RIGHT" OF THE HOLY ONE, BLESSED BE HE? It is the Torah, as is written: "From His right hand went a fiery law for them" (Devarim 33:2). At that time, "the right hand of Hashem does valiantly" (Tehilim 118:16) followed by, "I shall not die, but live, and declare the works of Hashem" (Ibid. 17), AS THE RIGHT ANNULS DEATH.

189. תָּנָא, הַהוּא זַכָּאָה דְּקוּדְשָׁא בְּרִיךְ הוּא אִתְרְעֵי בֵּיהּ, וְכָרוֹזָא קָרֵי עֲלֵיהּ, ל' יוֹמִין, בֵּינֵי צַדִּיקַיָּיא בְּגִנְתָּא דְּעֵדֶן, כֻּלְּהוּ צַדִּיקַיָּיא חָדָאן, כֻּלְּהוּ צַדִּיקַיָּיא אַתְיָין, וּמְעַטְּרָן דּוּכְתֵּיהּ דְּהַהוּא צַדִּיקָא, עַד דְּיֵיתֵי לְמֵידַר דִּיּוּרֵיהּ בֵּינַיְיהוּ.

189. We have learned that a righteous man, with whom the Holy One, blessed be He, is delighted, is proclaimed by a herald for thirty days among the righteous in the Garden of Eden, and all the righteous rejoice. They all come to decorate his place until he will come to be seated among them.

24. "Woe to the wicked, it shall be ill"

A Synopsis

This section opens by stating that all wicked men are sad and that they say, "Woe." The wicked, as Rabbi Yitzchak points out, are those who spill their "semen in vain." Those who do this are called *ra* (evil), and it is the worst transgression. They never escape from Gehenom. Rabbi Yehuda further adds that it is the only sin for which one cannot atone.

The Relevance of this Passage

The entire physical world is a shadow, a reflection of the Upper World. Everything on this physical plane has a corresponding counterpart in the supernal realm. Semen is the substance most reflective of the Light of The Creator. Hence, as raw naked energy must be concealed in high voltage cables in order to harness its power, semen must remain concealed in this physical world. When it is wasted in vain, through selfish gratification, and not used for the divine purpose of creating life and/or sharing pleasure with one's spouse, negative forces that dwell among us are free to use this energy for destructive purposes. This passage helps us cleanse sexual iniquities from the world and gives us the strength to direct our urges in a positive and sharing way.

190. וְאִי חַיָּיבָא הוּא, כָּרוֹזָא קָרֵי עֲלֵיה בַּגֵּיהִנֹּם תְּלָתִין יוֹמִין, וְכֻלְּהוּ חַיָּיבַיָא, כֻּלְּהוּ עֲצִיבִין.

190. If he be evil, a herald announces him in Gehenom for thirty days. All the wicked men are sad and open AND SAY, 'Woe'. For a new Judgment is awakened because of a certain person, and numerous accusers await him to welcome him AND SAY TO HIM, 'Woe.' Woe unto the wicked, woe unto his neighbor.

191. כֻּלְּהוּ פָּתְחִין וַוי, דְּהָא דִּינָא חַדְתָּא אִתְעַר הַשְׁתָּא, בְּגִינֵיה דִּפְלַנְיָא כַּמָּה גַּרְדִּינִין דְּנִמּוּסִין מְזַדַּמְּנִין לְקַבְּלֵיהּ, וּלְאַקְדְּמָא לֵיהּ וַוי, אוֹי לָרָשָׁע אוֹי לִשְׁכֵנוֹ, וְכֻלְּהוּ פָּתְחִין וְאָמְרִין, אוֹי לְרָשָׁע רָע כִּי גְמוּל יָדָיו יֵעָשֶׂה לּוֹ. מַאי גְּמוּל יָדָיו. אָמַר ר' יִצְחָק. לְאַכְלְלָא, מָאן דְּזָנֵי בִּידוֹי, לְאַפָּקָא וּלְחַבְּלָא זַרְעֵיהּ בְּרֵיקַנְיָא.

191. They all open and say, "Woe to the wicked, it shall be ill with him, for according to the deserving of his hands shall be done to him" (Yeshayah 3:11). What is "the deserving of his hands"? Rabbi Yitzchak said: It includes him who defiles with his hands by spilling his semen in vain.

192. דְּהָא תָּנִינָן, כָּל מַאן דְּאַפֵּיק זַרְעֵיהּ בְּרֵיקַנְיָא, אִקְרֵי רָע, וְלָא חָמֵי אַפֵּי שְׁכִינְתָּא, דִּכְתִיב כִּי לֹא אֵל חָפֵץ רֶשַׁע אַתָּה לֹא יְגוּרְךָ רָע, וּכְתִיב וַיְהִי עֵר בְּכוֹר יְהוּדָה רָע, אוּף הָכָא, אוֹי לְרָשָׁע רָע, וַוי לְהַהוּא חַיָּיבָא דְּאִיהוּ רָע, דַּעֲבַד גַּרְמֵיהּ רָע, כִּי גְמוּל יָדָיו יֵעָשֶׂה לוֹ, לְאַכְלְלָא, מַאן דְּזָנֵי בִּידוֹי, לְאַפָּקָא וּלְחַבְּלָא זַרְעֵיהּ בְּרֵיקַנְיָא, וּלְהַאי טַרְדִין בְּהַהוּא עָלְמָא יַתִּיר מִכֹּלָּא.

192. For we have learned that he who spills his semen in vain is called evil (Heb. *ra*), and cannot behold the face of the Shechinah, as it is written: "For You are not an El that has pleasure in wickedness: nor shall evil dwell with You" (Tehilim 5:5) and also "And Er, Yehuda's firstborn, was evil (Heb. *ra*)" (Beresheet 38:7). Here too, "Woe to the wicked...ill (Heb. *ra*)" ALLUDES TO HIM WHO SPILLS HIS SEMEN IN VAIN. Woe to the wicked who is evil and made himself evil (Heb. *ra*), "for according to the deserving of his hands shall be done to him." This means that whoever whores himself by letting his semen spill in vain is punished in the world of truth more than any OTHER TRANSGRESSION.

193. תָּא חֲזֵי, דְּהָא כְתִיב אוֹי לְרָשָׁע, כֵּיוָן דִּכְתִיב אוֹי לְרָשָׁע, אַמַּאי רָע. אֶלָּא כְּמָה דַאֲמֵינָא, דַּעֲבַד גַּרְמֵיהּ רָע. וּכְתִיב לֹא יְגוּרְךָ רָע. וְכֻלְּהוּ סַלְקִין, וְהַאי לָא סָלֵיק, וְאִי תֵימָא שְׁאָר חַיָּיבִין דְּקַטְלוּ בְּנֵי נָשָׁא. תָּא חֲזֵי, כֻּלְּהוּ סַלְקִין, וְהוּא לָא סָלֵיק, מ"ט, אִינוּן קְטִילוּ בְּנֵי נָשָׁא אָחֳרָא, וְהַאי קָטֵיל בְּנוֹי מַמָּשׁ, אוֹשִׁיד דָּמִין סַגִּיאִין. תָּא חֲזֵי, בִּשְׁאָר חַיָּיבֵי עָלְמָא, לָא כְּתִיב וַיֵּרַע בְּעֵינֵי ה', וְכָאן כְּתִיב, וַיֵּרַע בְּעֵינֵי ה' אֲשֶׁר עָשָׂה. מ"ט, מִשּׁוּם דִּכְתִיב וְשִׁחֵת אַרְצָה.

193. Come and see it is written: "Woe to the wicked." Since it says, "Woe to the wicked (Heb. *rasha*)," why add 'evil (ra)' SEEING THAT THE WICKED IS EVIL? This is as I said: that he has made himself evil, ESPECIALLY HE

WHO SPILLED HIS SEMEN IN VAIN. ALSO: "...nor shall evil dwell with You." Everyone ascends FROM GEHENOM save this one, who does not. HE ASKS: Would you say that other evil - doers who killed people ARE BETTER THAN HE, AND WILL ASCEND WHILE HE SHALL NOT? HE ANSWERS, Come and behold: everyone rises but he does not, because they killed other people, yet he killed his own children, and spilled much blood. Come and behold: it is not written of any other wicked man in the world that he "displeased Hashem" (Beresheet 38:10), only in this case where it says, "And the thing which he did displeased Hashem." Why? Because, the verse says, "He spilled it on the ground" (Ibid. 9).

194. תְּנַן, אֲמַר ר' יְהוּדָה, לֵית לָךְ חוֹבָא בְּעַלְמָא דְּלָא אִית לֵיהּ תְּשׁוּבָה, בַּר מֵהַאי, וְלֵית לָךְ חַיָּיבַיָּא דְּלָא חָמָאן אַפֵּי שְׁכִינְתָּא, בַּר מֵהַאי, דִּכְתִיב לֹא יְגוּרְךָ רָע כְּלָל. א"ר יִצְחָק, זַכָּאִין אִינּוּן צַדִּיקַיָּיא, בְּעַלְמָא דֵין, וּבְעַלְמָא דְּאָתֵי, עֲלַיְיהוּ כְּתִיב, וְעַמֵּךְ כֻּלָּם צַדִּיקִים לְעוֹלָם יִירְשׁוּ אָרֶץ. מַאי לְעוֹלָם יִירְשׁוּ אָרֶץ, א"ר יְהוּדָה, כְּמָה דִכְתִיב אֶתְהַלֵּךְ לִפְנֵי ה' בְּאַרְצוֹת הַחַיִּים.

194. We learned that Rabbi Yehuda said: There is no sin in the world for that one cannot repent other than the one OF SPILLING ONE'S SEMEN IN VAIN. There are no wicked men who shall not behold the face of the Shechinah IN THEIR DEATH, save him of whom it says "nor shall evil dwell with You" at all. Rabbi Yitzchak said: Happy are the righteous in this world and in the World to Come, of whom scripture says, "Your people also shall be all righteous: they shall inherit the land for ever" (Yeshayah 60:21). Rabbi Yehuda said: It is also said in "I will walk before Hashem in the land of the living" (Tehilim 116:9), WHICH IS THE SHECHINAH, CALLED LAND; THE LAND HERE ALLUDES TO THE SHECHINAH.

195. וַיְחִי יַעֲקֹב בְּגַוְויְיהוּ. ע"ד לְבָעֵי לֵיהּ לְבַר נָשׁ דְּלָא לְאִתְעָרְבָא צוּלְמָא דִילֵיהּ בְּצוּלְמָא דְעכו"ם, בְּגִין דְּהַאי קַדִּישָׁא, וְהַאי מְסָאֲבָא.

195. "And Jacob lived" (Beresheet 47:28) among them: Another explanation for this is that a man should not mingle his image with that of the idolatrous nations, for the one is holy and the other defiled.

25. The image

A Synopsis

This section begins by describing the difference between what happens when a person dies to the body of a man of Yisrael, and to the body of an idolatrous heathen. Unlike Yisrael, a heathen's impurities cannot be defiled. Each Israelite contains two shadows (*tzelamim,*) the ordinary and the holy shadow. As he approaches death, both shadows depart, since they are joined together. He must write letters and put them in a bag, and then on Yom Kippur (Day of Atonement), he must repent. If he attains repentance, the letters are torn; if not, they are read in consideration for judgment. Then, there follows a description of the significance of various parts of a man's shadow, and what it means if one or many of them are missing. Everything in the Lower World has its root in higher worlds. When one stirs, so does the other.

The Relevance of this Passage

The Light to cleanse ourselves from sin and wrongdoing is bestowed upon readers of this passage. The importance of repentance is awakened within us and we remove judgments decreed against us in the Upper Worlds. Our shadow is the link between the body and soul, and when a person is about to leave this world, the shadow becomes dimmer. This section helps strengthen our shadow, removing the force of death from life.

196. תָּא חֲזֵי, מַה בֵּין יִשְׂרָאֵל לְעַמִּין עכו"ם, דְּיִשְׂרָאֵל כַּד אִשְׁתְּכַּח ב"נ מִית הוּא מְסָאַב לְכָל גּוּפָא, וּבֵיתָא מְסָאֲבָא, וְגוּפָא דְעכו"ם, לָא מַסְאִיב לְאָחֳרָא, וְגוּפֵיה לָא מְסָאֲבָא כַּד אִיהוּ מִית, מ"ט.

196. Come and see the difference between Yisrael and the idolatrous nations. When a man of Yisrael dies, he defiles the body and the house. But the body of a heathen man does not defile and his body is not defiled in his death. Why is it so?

197. יִשְׂרָאֵל בְּשַׁעְתָּא דְאִיהוּ מִית כָּל קְדּוּשֵׁי דְמָארֵיה מִתְעַבְּרָן מִנֵּיה, אִתְעֲבַר מִנֵּיה הַאי צוּלְמָא קַדִּישָׁא, וְאִתְעֲבַר מִנֵּיה הַאי רוּחַ קוּדְשָׁא, אִשְׁתְּאַר גּוּפָא מְסָאֲבָא.

197. HE ANSWERS: When a man from Yisrael dies, all the holiness of his Master is removed from him, the holy image and the Holy Spirit is gone from him and leave his body defiled.

198. אֲבָל עכו"ם עוֹבֵד ע"ז, לֵית הָכֵי, דִּבְחַיֵּי מִסָאַב בְּכָל סִטְרִין, צוּלְמָא דִּילֵיהּ מִסָאֲבָא, וְרוּחָא דִּילֵיהּ מִסָאֲבָא, וּבְגִין דְּסוֹאֲבוּתֵי אָלֵין שַׁרְיָין בְּגַוֵּיהּ, אָסִיר לְמִקְרַב לְגַבֵּיהּ, כֵּיוָן דְּמִית, נָפְקֵי כָּל אָלֵין מִסָאֲבוּתָא וְאִשְׁתְּאַר גּוּפָא בְּלָא מִסָאֲבוּתָא לְסוֹאֲבָא.

198. But this is not so for an idolatrous heathen. For during his lifetime he is impure on all sides, his image is impure and his spirit is impure. Since impurities lie within him, it is forbidden to come near him. Once he dies, all the impurities depart from him and the body is left without defiling impurity.

199. וְאע"ג דְּגוּפָא דִּלְהוֹן מִסָאַב, בֵּין בְּחַיֵּיהוֹן וּבֵין בְּמִיתַתְהוֹן, אֲבָל בְּחַיֵּיהוֹן דְּכָל אִינוּן מִסָאֲבִין אִשְׁתַּכְּחֵי לְגַבַּיְיהוּ, אִית לוֹן חֵילָא לְסוֹאֲבָא לְאַחֲרִינֵי, בְּמִיתַתְהוֹן דְּנָפְקֵי כָּל אִינוּן מִסָאֲבִין מִנַּיְיהוּ, לָא יַכְלִין לְסָאֲבָא. וּדְיִשְׂרָאֵל, יָכִיל לְסָאֲבָא לְאַחֲרִינֵי, בְּגִין דְּכָל קַדִּישִׁין נָפְקִין מִנֵּיהּ וְשָׁרָא עֲלֵיהּ סִטְרָא אָחֳרָא.

199. Though their bodies are defiled both during their life and in their deaths, yet when they are alive all the impurities within them have the power to defile others. In their deaths, when impurities leave them, they cannot defile. A BODY OF an Yisrael AFTER DEATH can defile others, since all that is holy has left him and the Other Side dwells upon him.

200. תָּא חֲזֵי, הַאי צֶלֶם קַדִּישָׁא, כַּד אָזִיל ב"נ וְאִתְרַבֵּי, וְאִתְעֲבֵיד מֵהַאי פַּרְצוּפָא דְּיוֹקְנָה דִּילֵיהּ, אִתְעֲבֵיד צוּלְמָא אָחֳרָא, וּמִתְחַבְּרָן כַּחֲדָא, וְדָא נָטִיל לְדָא, בְּשַׁעְתָּא דְּאִשְׁתַּכְּחוּ תְּרֵין צוּלְמִין, נָטִיר הוּא ב"נ, וְגוּפָא דִּילֵיהּ בְּקִיּוּמָא, וְרוּחֵיהּ שַׁרְיָא בְּגַוֵּיהּ.

200. Come and see this holy image. When a man grows and his shape is made AND COMPLETED by a face, another image is made and joins THE

FIRST ONE, each embracing the other. When a man has two images, he is protected and his body lives with a spirit abiding within it.

201. בְּשַׁעְתָּא דְּקָרִיבוּ יוֹמוֹי, מִתְעַבְרָן מִנֵּיהּ, וְדָא סָלִיק לְדָא, וְאִשְׁתְּאַר בַּר נָשׁ בְּלָא נְטִירוּ, כְּדֵין עַד שֶׁיָּפוּחַ הַיּוֹם וְנָסוּ הַצְּלָלִים: תְּרֵי.

201. When his time draws near for him to die, the images (Heb. *tzelamim*) depart from him, the one causes the other to depart SINCE THEY ARE JOINED TOGETHER. The man remains without protection, in accordance with the verse: "Before the day cools, and the images (Heb. *tzelalim*) flee away" (Shir Hashirim 2:17), NOT SAYING 'SHADOW' BUT 'SHADOWS,' NAMELY two – AS WE SAID.

202. תָּא חֲזֵי, כַּד אִתְּעַר דִּינָא בְּעָלְמָא, דְּקוּדְשָׁא בְּרִיךְ הוּא יָתֵיב עַל כָּרְסֵי דְדִינָא לְמֵידַן עָלְמָא, בָּעֵי ב״נ לְאִתְעָרָא תְּשׁוּבָה, דְּיֵיתוּב מֵחִיּוּבָא, דְּהָא הַהוּא יוֹמָא, פִּתְקִין כְּתִיבוּ, וּמִשְׁתַּכְּחֵי כֻּלְּהוּ בְּאַחְמָתָא הָא כְּתִיבִין, אִי זָכֵי ב״נ דְּיֵיתוּב קַמֵּי מָארֵיהּ, קָרְעִין פִּתְקִין דַּעֲלֵיהּ.

202. Come and see: When Judgment awakens in the world and the Holy One, blessed be He, sits on His throne of justice to sentence the world ON ROSH HASHANAH (THE JEWICH NEW YEAR), a man should awaken to repent his sins. For on that day, letters are written and put in a bag all written down. If a man succeeded and returned IN REPENTANCE before his Master, the letters concerning him are torn.

203. לְבָתַר קוּדְשָׁא בְּרִיךְ הוּא זַמִּין קַמֵּיהּ דב״נ, יוֹמָא דְכִפּוּרֵי יוֹמָא דִּתְשׁוּבָה, אִי תָב מֵחֲטָאוֹי טַב. וְאִי לָא, פַּקִּיד מַלְכָּא לְמִחְתַּם פִּתְקִין, וַוי דְּהָא תְּשׁוּבָה בַּעְיָא לְאִסְתַּלָּקָא מִנֵּיהּ.

203. After that, the Holy One, blessed be He, prepared Yom Kippur for man. If he repents his sins, it is well. If not, the King commands to seal the letters. Woe to him, for repentance is about to depart from him.

204. אִי זָכֵי בִּתְשׁוּבָה, וְלָא שְׁלֵימָתָא כְּדְקָא יָאוֹת, תַּלְיָין לֵיהּ עַד

הַהוּא יוֹמָא בַּתְרָאָה דַּעֲצֶרֶת, דְּהוּא תְּמִינָאָה לְחַג, וְאִי עֲבַד תְּשׁוּבָה
שְׁלִימָתָא לְקַמֵּי מָארֵיה, אִתְקְרָעוּ. וְאִי לָא זָכֵי, אִינּוּן פִּתְקִין נָפְקִין מִבֵּי
מַלְכָּא, וְאִתְמַסְּרָן בִּידוֹי דְּסַנְטֵירָא, וְדִינָא מִתְעֲבֵיד, וּפִתְקִין לָא מְהַדְרָן
תּוּ לְבֵי מַלְכָּא.

204. If he attains repentance, yet it is not whole, the letter is withheld until the last day called Atzeret (Eng. 'gathering'), which is the eighth day of Sukkot (Holiday of the Booths). If he wholly repented before his Master, the letters are torn; if he has not, the letters are sent from the King's house and given to the punishing angel for the judgment to be executed. After the letters are handed out, they return no more to the King's house, AND THE JUDGMENT WRITTEN IN THEM MUST BE EXECUTED.

205. כְּדֵין צוּלְמִין אִתְעֲבָרוּ מִנֵּיה, וְלָא מִשְׁתַּכְּחִין עִמֵּיה, כֵּיוָן
דְּמִתְעַבְרָן מִנֵּיה, הָא וַדַּאי טוּפְסְקָא דְּמַלְכָּא יַעֲבַר עֲלֵיה, וְיִטְעוֹם כַּסָּא
דְּמוֹתָא. וּבְהַהוּא לֵילְיָא דְּחַגָּא בַּתְרָאָה, סַנְטֵירִין זְמִינִין, וּפִתְקִין נָטְלִין,
בָּתַר דְּנַטְלֵי לוֹן, צוּלְמִין מִתְעַבְרָן, וְלָא מִשְׁתַּכְּחִין בְּהוּ יָדֵי, וְאִי
מִשְׁתַּכְּחִין בְּהוּ יָדֵי, דִּינָא גְּרִיעָא, אוֹ יַעֲבַר עֲלוֹי דִּינָא מַרְעִין בִּישִׁין,
בִּגְרִיעוּתָא דִּלְהוֹן, וְהָא אוֹקִימְנָא לְהָא.

205. Then, the images are gone and do not abide with him. Once they are gone from him, the King's punishment comes upon him, and he tastes the cup of death. On the night of the last festival, THE EIGHTH DAY OF SUKKOT, the executioners are ready and receive the letters. After they do, the images are gone and cannot be with them. If THE SHADOWS are with him, no judgment comes upon him, nor evil illnesses THAT COME when the shadows are flawed, as we already explained elsewhere.

206. וּבְסִפְרֵי קַדְמָאֵי אַמְרֵי יַתִּיר, כַּד רֵישָׁא אִגְרַע, וְיִשְׁתַּכַּח גּוּפָא,
בְּרֵיה, אוֹ אַנְתְּתֵיה, יִשְׁתַּכְּחוּ, וְהוּא יִסְתַּלֵּק. וְה"מ, כַּד לָא אַהֲדַר כָּל
הַהוּא זִמְנָא בִּתְיוּבְתָּא, אֲבָל אִי אַהֲדַר, טַעֲמָא דְּמוֹתָא יִטְעַם, וְיִתְּסֵי.

206. In ancient books, this is explained further: When the head of his shadow is missing but the body is not, it indicates that his child or wife will survive but he will pass away. This is true as long as he does not repent. If he does, he will only taste death and recover from his illness.

207. וְאִי גוּפָא לָא אִתְחֲזֵי, וְיִשְׁתַּכַּח רֵישָׁא, אִינּוּן סָלְקִין, וְהוּא אִתְקַיֵּים. וְה"מ, כַּד בְּרֵיה זְעֵירָא בִּרְשׁוּתֵיה.

207. If the body OF HIS SHADOW will not be seen, but only the head, HIS FAMILY WILL DIE and he will stay alive. This is true as long as he is responsible for his small child.

208. וְאִי יְדוֹי פְּגִימוּ, עֲבִידְתָּא דִידוֹי פְּגִימִין. רַגְלוֹי, מַרְעִין רָדְפִין עֲלֵיה. עָרַק צוֹלְמָא וְאַהֲדַר, עָרַק וְאַהֲדַר, עֲלֵיה כְּתִיב, בַּבֹּקֶר תֹּאמַר מִי יִתֵּן עֶרֶב, וְהַאי כַּד נָהֲרָא סִיהֲרָא, וְלֵילְיָא אִתְתַּקַּן בִּנְהוֹרָא.

208. If the hands OF THE SHADOW are flawed, IT IS AN INDICATION THAT the works of his hands will deteriorate, and if his legs ARE FLAWED, IT IS AN INDICATION THAT illnesses pursue him. If the shadow flees and returns, then flees and returns again, it is said of him, "In the morning you shall say, 'Would it were evening'" (Devarim 28:67). This is true only when the moon shines and the night is diffused with her light, WHEN HE CHECKS HIS SHADOW.

209. אֲבָל זַכָּאֵי חֲסִידֵי, בְּכָל יוֹמָא וְיוֹמָא מִסְתַּכְּלֵי בְּלִבַּיְיהוּ, כְּאִלּוּ הַהוּא יוֹמָא מִסְתַּלְּקֵי מֵעַלְמָא, וְעַבְדִין תְּיוּבְתָּא שְׁלֵימָתָא קַמֵּי מָארֵיהוֹן, וְלָא יִצְטָרְכוּן לְמִלָּה אָחֳרָא, זַכָּאָה חוּלְקָהוֹן, בְּעַלְמָא דֵין, וּבְעַלְמָא דְּאָתֵי.

209. But the righteous and the pious search in their hearts every day as if on this very day they are to pass away from the world, and they repent wholly before their Master. They have need of nothing else, NAMELY CHECKING THEIR SHADOW OR THE LIKE OF IT. Happy is their portion in this world and in the World to Come.

210. תָּא חֲזֵי כָּל הַנִּקְרָא בִשְׁמִי, כַּמָּה עִלָּאִין עוֹבָדֵי מַלְכָּא קַדִּישָׁא,

דְּהָא בְּאִינּוּן עוֹבָדֵי דְּאִיהוּ עָבֵיד לְתַתָּא, קָטֵיר לוֹן בְּמִלִּין עִלָּאִין
דִּלְעֵילָא, וְכַד נָטְלִין לוֹן לְתַתָּא, וְעָבְדֵי בְּהוֹ עוֹבָדָא, אִתְּעַר הַהוּא
עוֹבָדָא דִּלְעֵילָא דְּקָטֵיר בַּהּ, כְּגוֹן אֵזוֹבָא, עֵץ אֶרֶז, וְהָא אוֹקִימְנָא מִלֵּי.

210. Come and see "every one that is called by My name" (Yeshayah 43:7). How exalted are the worshipers of the Holy King, for their actions below connect them to the higher things above, TO WIT, TO THEIR ROOTS. FOR EACH THING BELOW IN THE WORLD HAS A ROOT ABOVE IN HIGHER WORLDS. When they are taken down and act by them, the action above, THEIR ROOT IN HIGHER WORLDS, AWAKENS in accordance with it. This is like the hyssop and the cedar wood THE TORAH COMMANDS HIM WHO IS PURIFIED TO USE, as we already explained.

26. The four kinds

A Synopsis

This further describes the importance of the root connection between aspects of the lower and higher worlds. There are four things to cleave to: the Lulav, Etrog (citron), myrtle, and willow. Then, we learn of the significance of "the fifteenth day," the first of the three travelling Columns. Next, we are told that Yom Kippur is the secret of Ima, the day in which Binah sets the prisoners free, who name that day "the first day," and ask Binah for water. It is either the beginning of "Clouds of Glory" or of "Living Water."

The Relevance of this Passage

Here we connect ourselves to the internal spiritual forces associated with the Lulav, Etrog, myrtle branch, and willow. These physical items work like an antenna. They have powerful spiritual counterparts in the Upper World which help us draw the Light of protection to our lives. We also destroy any judgments that might be pending in the Upper Courts, provided our hearts are filled with repentance.

211. וְאִית מִנַּיְיהוּ דַּאֲחִידָן בִּשְׁמָא קַדִּישָׁא, כְּגוֹן לוּלָב, וְאֶתְרוֹג, הֲדַס, וַעֲרָבָה, דְּכֻלְּהוּ אֲחִידָן בִּשְׁמָא קַדִּישָׁא, לְעֵילָא. וְעַל דָּא תָּנִינָן, לְאַחֲדָא לוֹן, וּלְמֶעְבַּד בְּהוּ עוֹבָדָא, בְּגִין לְאִתְעָרָא הַהוּא חֶדְוָה דְּאָחִיד בֵּיהּ. וְעַל דָּא תָּנִינָן, בְּמִלִּין וְעוֹבָדָא בָּעְיָין לְאַחֲזָאָה מִלָּה, בְּגִין לְאִתְעָרָא מִלָּה אָחֳרָא.

211. Some of them cleave to the Holy Name above, like the Lulav, Etrog (citron), myrtle and willow. In relation to them, we learned that we should unite them; NAMELY TO BIND THEM TOGETHER and perform an action with them; NAMELY TO SHAKE THEM, in order to arouse joy in the root to which it cleaves above. We have learned that by speech, THE BENEDICTION OF THE PRECEPTS, and by deed, THE PRECEPT, we should exhibit it BELOW in order to awaken that WHICH IS ABOVE; NAMELY ITS SUPERNAL ROOT.

212. הה״ד כָּל הַנִּקְרָא בִשְׁמִי וְלִכְבוֹדִי: לְאִתְעָרָא יְקָרִי, בְּרָאתִיו: לְיַיחֲדָא לִי. יְצַרְתִּיו: לְמֶעְבַּד בֵּיהּ עוֹבָדָא. אַף עֲשִׂיתִיו: לְאִתְעָרָא בֵּיהּ חֵילָא דִּלְעֵילָא.

212. This is the meaning of the words: "Every one that is called by My Name: for My Glory" (Ibid.) namely, so it would glorify Me; "I have created him" so he would declare My unity; "I have formed him" so he would perform good deeds for My sake; "I have made him" so that through him the supernal force will awaken.

213. ד"א, כָּל הַנִּקְרָא בִּשְׁמִי: הַיְינוּ דִּכְתִיב פְּרִי עֵץ הָדָר. וְלִכְבוֹדִי בְּרָאתִיו: הַיְינוּ כַּפּוֹת תְּמָרִים. יְצַרְתִּיו: הַיְינוּ וַעֲנַף עֵץ עָבוֹת. אַף עֲשִׂיתִיו: הַיְינוּ וְעַרְבֵי נָחַל.

213. Another explanation: "Every one that is called by My Name" (Ibid.) as it is written "the fruit of the tree Hadar (citrus)" (Vayikra 23:40); "For My glory I have created him" namely, the "branches of palm trees;" "I have formed him," "the boughs of thick leaved tree;" "I have made him," the "willow of the brook."

214. וְתִקּוּנָא דְּהַאי דְּאָמַר קְרָא, וּלְקַחְתֶּם לָכֶם בַּיּוֹם הָרִאשׁוֹן, דַּיְיקָא דְּהוּא חֲמִישָׁאָה עַל עָשׂוֹר.

214. They are to be used, as it says, "And you shall take for yourselves on the first day" (Ibid.), which is the fifteenth.

215. אֲבָל בַּיּוֹם הָרִאשׁוֹן, הַהוּא יוֹם רִאשׁוֹן מַאן הוּא. אֶלָּא יוֹם דְּנָפֵיק רִאשׁוֹן, לְנַטְלָא בְּמַבּוּעוֹי דְּמַיִין נְבִיעִין, וַאֲנַן בָּעְיָין לְאַמְשָׁכָא לֵיהּ לְעָלְמָא.

215. But what is the first day SCRIPTURE MENTIONS, WHAT DOES IT ALLUDE TO? HE REPLIES: It is the first to travel by the sources of living water, BEING THE FIRST COLUMN OF THE THREE TRAVELING COLUMNS, THROUGH WHICH TRAVEL CHASSADIM BECOME REVEALED BY CHOCHMAH CALLED LIVING WATER. FOR THE RIGHT COLUMN, CHESED, TRAVELS FIRST, and we should draw it into the world. FOR IN SUKKOT, IT IS TIME FOR DRAWING CHASSADIM, ACCORDING TO THE SECRET OF "HIS RIGHT HAND EMBRACES ME" (SHIR HASHIRIM 8:3).

216. מָתָל לְמַלְכָּא דְּקָטַר בְּנֵי נָשָׁא בְּקִטְרוֹי, אֲמֵיהּ מַטְרוֹנִיתָא אֲתַת,

וְאַפֵּיקַת לוֹן לְחֵירוּת, וּמַלְכָּא אַשְׁגַּח לִיקָרָא דִילָהּ, וְיָהַב לוֹן בִּידָהָא. אַשְׁכְּחַת לוֹן כַּיְיפִין וְצַחִין, אָמַרְתְּ, הָא אַפֵּיקַת לוֹן לְחֵירוּ, אַיְיתֵי לוֹן מֵיכְלָא וּמִשְׁתַּיָּא.

216. This is like the story of a king who put people into his prison. The lady, his mother, came and set them free. The king, mindful of her honor, put them under her authority. She found them hungry and thirsty and said TO HER SON THE KING, now that I set them free, give them food and drink.

217. כָּךְ, הָא יוה״כ אַפֵּיק לְכֹלָּא לְחֵירוּ, וַאֲנַן כַּפְנֵי מְזוֹנָא קָאִימְנָא, וְצַחִינָן לְמִשְׁתַּיָּא, הִיא אַעֲטָרַת לְמַלְכָּא בְּעִטְרוֹי. בְּהַאי יוֹמָא יָדְעָנָא, דְּהָא מַיִין נְבִיעִין עִמֵּהּ שַׁרְיָין, שָׁאִילְנָא לְמִשְׁתַּיָּא, לְמַאן דְּאַפֵּיק לוֹן לְחֵירוּ, וְעַל דָּא קָרֵינָן לֵיהּ יוֹם רִאשׁוֹן.

217. Thus Yom Kippur, WHICH IS THE SECRET OF IMA, BINAH sets them free. We are hungry for nourishment and thirsty for a drink, FOR NO PHYSICAL FOOD AND DRINK IS DRAWN FROM BINAH, FOR WHICH REASON WE FAST AND AFFLICT OUR SOULS ON THE DAY OF ATONEMENT. She therefore adorns THE KING, ZEIR ANPIN, THE SON OF BINAH, with his crown, MOCHIN OF CHASSADIM on this day, THE FIRST OF SUKKOT. We know that there is living water there, and we ask for water from the one who set us free, SO SHE WOULD GIVE CHASSADIM TO ZEIR ANPIN FOR US, AFTER WE ATTAINED MOCHIN OF CHOCHMAH FROM HER ON YOM KIPPUR, THE SECRET OF FREEDOM. We therefore name this day 'the first day'.

218. דָּא בְּסִפְרָא דְּאַגַּדְתָּא וְשַׁפִּיר הוּא. אֲבָל בְּהַאי יוֹמָא, לְאַבְרָהָם שֵׁירוּתָא דְּכֹלָּא, אִי בַּעֲנָנֵי יְקַר הוּא שֵׁירוּתָא, אִי בְּמַיָּא הוּא שֵׁירוּתָא, דְּאַבְרָהָם שָׁארֵי לְמֶחְפְּרֵי בֵּירֵי דְמַיָּא.

218. All this is written in the book of Agadah, and is correct. But BESIDES WHAT WAS SAID, this day THAT ALLUDES TO Abraham, THE SECRET OF THE SFIRAH OF CHESED, is the starting point of everything - whether it is the beginning of the clouds of glory THAT ARE THE SECRET OF THE SURROUNDING LIGHTS, IT IS THE BEGINNING AS THE FIRST SURROUNDING

LIGHT IS CHESED, or the beginning of water, THE SECRET OF INTERNAL
LIGHT, AS FOR THE FIRST SURROUNDING LIGHT IS CHESED, THE FIRST
INTERNAL LIGHT IS CHESED. THIS IS THE SECRET MEANING OF Abraham
starting to dig wells of water.

219. פְּרִי עֵץ הָדָר: דָּא בֵּירָא דְּיִצְחָק, דְּיִצְחָק אַהֲדַר לֵיהּ לְקוּדְשָׁא
בְּרִיךְ הוּא וְקָרָא לֵיהּ עֵץ הָדָר, פְּרִי דְּהַאי עֵץ הָדָר יְדִיעָא. כַּפּוֹת
תְּמָרִים: דִּכְתִיב, צַדִּיק כַּתָּמָר יִפְרָח, וְלָא אִשְׁתְּכַּח בֵּינַיְיהוּ פֵּרוּדָא,
וְע"ד לָא כְּתִיב וְכַפּוֹת, אֶלָּא כַּפּוֹת, בְּגִין דְּלָא סָלֵיק דָּא בְּלָא דָא,
וּבְהַאי אִתְמַלְיָא הַאי בְּאֵר, מִבְּאֵר מַיִם עִלָּאִין נְבִיעִין, הַהוּא אִתְמַלֵּי
בְּקַדְמֵיתָא, וּמִנֵּיהּ אִתְמַלְיָיא בֵּירָא, עַד דְּאִיהוּ נְבִיעוּ לְכֹלָּא.

219. "The fruit of the tree Hadar" is the well of Isaac; NAMELY THE NUKVA
CALLED WELL WHEN RECEIVING CHOCHMAH FROM THE LEFT COLUMN
OF ZEIR ANPIN CALLED ISAAC. For Isaac glorified (Heb. *hider*) the Holy
One, blessed be He, and called Him "the tree Hadar," THE NUKVA BEING
the fruit of this particular tree. "Branches of palm trees" are as it is written:
"The righteous man flourishes like the palm tree" (Tehilim 92:13), NAMELY
THE RIGHTEOUS YESOD. There is no dividing between YESOD AND THE
NUKVA, for which reason it does not say "and branches" but just "branches
(Heb. *kapot*)," WHICH IS AN INDICATION OF BINDING (HEB. *KAPHUT*) AND
UNITY. For they cannot exist without each other, BUT ARE ALWAYS BOUND
TOGETHER. Through this the well, THE NUKVA, is filled from the well of
supernal living water, BINAH, for YESOD is filled first FROM TIFERET AND
TIFERET FROM BINAH, and from it, the well is filled until it BECOMES a
gushing spring for everyone.

220. וַעֲנַף עֵץ עָבוֹת: דָּא עֲנָפָא דְּאִילָנָא רַבְרְבָא, דְּאִתְקַיַּף וְאִשְׁתָּרְשָׁא
בְּשָׁרְשׁוֹי, אִתְעֲבֵיד אִילָנָא עִלָּאָה עַל כֹּלָּא, דְּאָחֵיד בְּכָל סִטְרֵיהּ, עָנָף
דְּאִיהוּ עֵץ עָבוֹת, עֵץ דְּאָחֵיד לְעָבוֹת, דְּהָא מֵהַאי נָטַל יְסוֹדָא דְּעָלְמָא,
וְאִתְמַלְיָא לַאֲרָקָא בְּבֵירָא, הַאי הוּא עַלְמָא אֲרָקָא דְּשַׁקְיוּתָא.

220. "The bough of thick leaved tree": This is the bough of the great tree
TIFERET, which was strengthened, struck root and became the highest tree,
connected on every side; NAMELY TIFERET WHICH INCLUDES THE SIX
SFIROT CHESED, GVURAH, TIFERET, NETZACH, HOD AND YESOD

WHICH HOLD TO IT ON EVERY SIDE. This bough is a thick tree (Heb. *avot*, with *Ayin*), holding on to the patriarchs (Heb. *avot*, with *Aleph*). FOR IT IS THE CENTRAL COLUMN THAT COMPRISES RIGHT AND LEFT, CHESED AND GVURAH, CALLED ABRAHAM AND ISAAC. THE *ALEPH* OF *AVOT* (ENG. 'FATHERS') AND THE *AYIN* OF *AVOT*, THICK TREES ARE INTERCHANGEABLE. For from TIFERET, the foundation (Yesod) of the world receives and is filled and pours unto the well, THE NUKVA, which is the land that is all water, WHEN RECEIVING FROM YESOD.

221. וְעַרְבֵי נַחַל: תְּרֵי אִינוּן, תְּרֵין נַחֲלִין דְּמַיָּא אִתְכְּנֵישׁ בְּהוּ, לַאֲרָקָא לַצַּדִּיק. ד״א, וְעַרְבֵי נַחַל: אִלֵּין אִינוּן גְּבוּרָן, דַּאֲחִידָן בֵּיהּ בְּיִצְחָק, דְּאַתְיָין מִסִּטְרָא דְּהַהוּא נַחַל עִלָּאָה, וְלָא מִסִּטְרָא דְּאַבָּא. בְּג״כ, כֻּלָּא יָאֵי, וְלָא בְּסִימָא לְפֵירִין, וְלָא עָבֵיד פֵּירִין.

221. There are two "willows of the brook," ALLUDING TO the two brooks of water, THE TWO SFIROT, NETZACH AND HOD, where the water gathers to pour upon the Righteous, YESOD WHICH RECEIVES FROM NETZACH AND HOD. Another explanation: The "willows of the brook" are the Gvurot which hold fast to Isaac, THE LEFT COLUMN. They come from the supernal brook, IMA, and not from the side of Aba, THE RIGHT COLUMN, and this is why the willows are all handsome but not sweet like fruit and do not produce fruit.

222. וְעַרְבֵי נַחַל: תְּרֵין קַיָּימִין, דְּגוּפָא קַיְימָא עֲלַיְיהוּ, אֲבָל וְעַרְבֵי נַחַל וַדַּאי, כְּמָה דְּאִתְּמַר, וְאִלֵּין אִינוּן כֻּלְּהוּ לַאֲרָקָא מַיָּיא לְבֵירָא.

222. The "willows of the brook" are the two pillars, NETZACH AND HOD, which support the body, yet the "willows of the brook," as was explained, all pour water to the well TO GIVE TO THE NUKVA.

223. ד״א, וּלְקַחְתֶּם לָכֶם בַּיּוֹם הָרִאשׁוֹן פְּרִי עֵץ הָדָר: דָּא אַבְרָהָם. כַּפֹּת תְּמָרִים: דָּא יִצְחָק. וַעֲנַף עֵץ עָבוֹת: דָּא יַעֲקֹב. וְעַרְבֵי נַחַל: אִלֵּין אִינוּן תְּרֵין דַּרְגִּין דַּאֲמָרָן.

223. Another explanation for: "And you shall take for yourselves on the first day the fruit of the tree Hadar" is that it is Abraham; NAMELY CHESED.

"Branches of palm tree" is Isaac, NAMELY GVURAH; "the bough of thick leaved tree" is Jacob, NAMELY TIFERET; and the "willows of the brook" are the two grades we mentioned, NETZACH AND HOD.

224. וּמַאן דְּמַתְנֵי הַאי, בְּגִין דְּעֵץ עָבוֹת דָּא יַעֲקֹב, דְּאָחִיד לְכֻלְּהוּ חֲלָקִין, וַדַּאי דָּא יַעֲקֹב. אֲבָל הָא אוּקִימְנָא, פְּרִי עֵץ הָדָר, דָּא בֵּירָא דְּיִצְחָק, דָּא גְּבוּרָה תַּתָּאָה. כַּפֹּת תְּמָרִים. כַּפֹּת חָסֵר, קְשׁוּרָא דְּאִתְקְשַׁר בְּבֵירָא, כְּד"א כְּפִיתוּ בְּסַרְבָּלֵיהוֹן, בְּגִין דְּאִלֵּין לָא סָלְקִין דָּא בְּלָא דָּא. וַעֲנַף עֵץ עָבוֹת, עֲנָפָא הוּא עִלָּאָה, דְּאִתְעֲבֵיד עֵץ עָבוֹת, וְאָחִיד לְכָל סִטְרָא, כְּמָה דְּאִתְּמַר. עַרְבֵי נַחַל דָּא יִצְחָק, בְּכָל סִטְרֵי, דַּאֲחִידָן בְּסִטְרָא דְּנַחֲלָא, וְלָא בְּסִטְרָא דְּאַבָּא. דִּתְנִינָן, אע"ג דִּבְהַאי נַחַל דִּינָא לָא אִשְׁתַּכַּח בֵּיהּ, דִּינִין מִתְעָרִין מִנֵּיהּ.

224. We learn that THE FRUIT OF THE HADAR TREE IS ABRAHAM AND THE BRANCHES OF PALM TREES ARE ISAAC because the thick tree is Jacob, who holds all the parts, THE SIX ENDS CHESED, GVURAH, TIFERET, NETZACH, HOD AND YESOD, WHICH ARE INCLUDED WITHIN HIM, FOR WHICH REASON HE IS CALLED A THICK TREE. Assuredly, we have shown that "the fruit of the tree Hadar" is the well of Isaac, the lower Gvurah; NAMELY THE NUKVA. In "branches (Heb. *kapot*) of palm trees," 'kapot' is spelled without *VAV*, WHICH MEANS IT IS TIED; NAMELY a tie upon the well, as it is written "bound (Aramaic *kephitu*) in their mantles" (Daniel 3:21), NAMELY YESOD AND NUKVA, which do not exist without one another, AS IF THEY ARE BOUND. "The bough of thick leaved tree" is the supernal bough turned into a thick tree cleaving to every side; NAMELY CHESED, GVURAH, TIFERET, NETZACH, HOD AND YESOD, FOR TIFERET IS THE TORSO, CHESED - GVURAH THE ARMS, NETZACH - HOD THE LEGS, AND YESOD THE HOLY COVENANT, as we explained. The "willows of the brook" is Isaac, for on all sides they hold to the side of the brook, IMA, instead of the side of Aba. As we learned, though there are no Judgments in this brook, BINAH, yet all Judgments are awakened thence.

225. וְרַב הַמְנוּנָא סָבָא פָּרֵישׁ, וְעַרְבֵי נַחַל, אִינּוּן תְּרֵין קַיְּימִין דְּקָאֲמָרָן, דְּמַיָּיא נָפְקֵי מִנַּיְיהוּ, וְשַׁפִּיר. אֲבָל תָּא חֲזֵי, הָא חֲזִינָן דִּתְרֵין דַּרְגִּין אִלֵּין דְּקַיְּימֵי עַל דַּרְגָּא דְּצַדִּיק, אִיבָּא וּכְנִישׁוּ דְּבִרְכָאן נָפְקֵי

מִנַּיְיהוּ, וְעַרְבֵי נַחַל לָא נָפְקֵי מִנַּיְיהוּ, אִיבָּא, וְלָא טַעְמָא, וְלָא רֵיחָא, וְהָא אוֹקִימְנָא וְכֹלָּא שַׁפִּיר.

225. Rabbi Hamnuna Saba (the elder) explained that "willows of the brook" are the two pillars we mentioned, NETZACH AND HOD, from which water comes out. THE EXPLANATION is well, yet come and behold: we see that these two grades, NETZACH AND HOD, stand on the grade of the Righteous, YESOD. Fruits and gathered blessings are issued from them; but from the willows of the brook, WHICH ALSO ALLUDE TO NETZACH AND HOD, no fruits are produced, nor taste or smell, as we already explained. And all is well.

226. וְעַל דָּא אֶתְרוֹג בִּשְׂמָאלָא, לָקֳבֵיל לִבָּא, לוּלָב בִּימִינָא, כַּפֵּת בְּכֹלָּא, וְקָטֵיר בְּכֹלָּא, דְּהָא צַדִּיק כָּפוֹת הוּא בְּכָל סְטְרִין, וְקָטֵיר בְּכֹלָּא. וְדָא הוּא קְשׁוּרָא דִּמְהֵימְנוּתָא.

226. Therefore WE HOLD the Etrog with the left hand against the heart, while Lulav is held by the right together with the other kinds all tied. For the Righteous, YESOD, is united with all THE SFIROT, and bound to them all. This is the bond of faith, SHINING UPON THE NUKVA CALLED FAITH.

227. וּבְסִפְרָא דְּאַגַּדְתָּא שַׁפִּיר קָאֲמַר, דְּכָל אִלֵּין אִינוּן אוּשְׁפִּיזִין, דְּזַמִּינִין עַמָּא קַדִּישָׁא בְּהַאי יוֹמָא, דְּבָעְיָין לְאַשְׁכָּחָא לְהוֹ, כֵּיוָן דְּזַמִּין לוֹן, וּבְהוֹ בָּעֵי ב"נ לְמַלְכָּא בְּעוּתֵיהּ, זַכָּאִין אִינוּן יִשְׂרָאֵל דְּיָדְעִין אָרְחוֹי דְּמַלְכָּא קַדִּישָׁא, וְיָדְעִין אָרְחוֹי דְּאוֹרַיְיתָא, לְמֵהַךְ בְּאוֹרַח קְשׁוֹט, לְמִזְכֵּי בְּהוֹ בְּעָלְמָא דֵּין וּבְעָלְמָא דְּאָתֵי.

227. In the book of Agada it is well versed that all THE FOUR KINDS are the guests, THE SECRET OF THE SEVEN SFIROT CHESED, GVURAH, TIFERET, NETZACH, HOD, YESOD AND MALCHUT, who were invited by the holy people on this day, BY PRAYING ON THE DAYS OF SUKKOT BEFORE THE MEAL AND INVITING THE SUPERNAL GUESTS. They should be there, since they were invited, and man uses them in his prayer to the King. BY THE FOUR KINDS, WHICH ALLUDE TO THESE SFIROT, ONE ATTAINS THEM. Happy are Yisrael who know the ways of the Holy King, and know the ways of the Torah, with which to walk the path of Truth and merit this world and the World to Come.

228. בְּיוֹמָא דָא נָפְקֵי יִשְׂרָאֵל, בְּסִימָנִין רְשִׁימִין מִגּוֹ מַלְכָּא, בְּגִין דְּאִינוּן נָצְחִין דִּינָא, וּמַאי סִימָנִין אִינוּן, סִימָנֵי מְהֵימְנוּתָא, חוֹתָמָא דְמַלְכָּא עִלָּאָה. לִתְרֵי בְּנֵי נָשָׁא, דְּעָאלוּ קָדָם מַלְכָּא לְדִינָא וְלָא יָדְעֵי עַלְמָא מַאן מִנַּיְיהוּ נָצַח, נָפַק חַד לִגְיוֹן מִבֵּי מַלְכָּא, שָׁאִילוּ לוֹ, אָמַר לוֹן, מַאן דְּיִפּוֹק וּבִידוֹי סִימָנִין דְּמַלְכָּא, הוּא נָצַח.

228. On that day, Yisrael come out from before the King with certain signs; NAMELY THE FOUR KINDS, for they received a favorable judgment. What are these signs? The signs of the faith, THE SHECHINAH, the seal of the most high King, ZEIR ANPIN. It is like two men come before the king to be judged. The people in the world did not know who won. A minister came from the king's house and they asked him. He said to them, Whoever leaves THE KING'S HOUSE with the king's signs in his hands, he is the winner.

229. כָּךְ, כּוּלֵי עַלְמָא עָאלִין לְדִינָא, קָדַם מַלְכָּא עִלָּאָה, וְדָאִין לוֹן מִיּוֹמָא דר״ה וְיוֹם הַכִּפּוּרִים, עַד חֲמֵשׁ סְרֵי יוֹמִין לְיַרְחָא, וּבֵין כָּךְ אִשְׁתַּכָחוּ יִשְׂרָאֵל זַכָּאִין כֻּלְּהוּ בִּתְיוּבְתָּא, טָרְחִין בְּסֻכָּה וְלוּלָב וְאֶתְרוֹג, וְלָא יָדְעֵי מַאן נָצַח דִּינָא, מַלְאֲכֵי עִלָּאֵי שָׁאֲלוּ מַאן נָצַח דִּינָא. קוּדְשָׁא בְּרִיךְ הוּא א״ל, אִינּוּן דְּמַפְּקֵי בִּידַיְיהוּ סִימָנִין דִּילִי, אִינּוּן נָצְחִין דִּינָא.

229. All the people in the world come to be judged before the most high King and He judges them on Rosh Hashanah and on Yom Kippur until the fifteenth day of the month. Thus, it was found out that Yisrael had all succeeded in repenting, and work hard in building the Sukkah and acquiring a Lulav and Etrog. It is not known who won the judgment. The supernal angels ask who has won, and the Holy One, blessed be He, says 'they who hold My signs in their hands, THE FOUR KINDS, have received a favorable judgment'.

230. בְּהַאי יוֹמָא, נָפְקֵי יִשְׂרָאֵל בִּרְשִׁימוּ דְּמַלְכָּא, בְּתוּשְׁבַּחְתָּא

דְּהַלֵּילָא, עָאלִין בַּסֻּכָּה, אֶתְרוֹג בִּשְׂמָאלָא, לוּלָב בִּימִינָא, חָמָאן כָּלְהוּ, דְּיִשְׂרָאֵל רְשִׁימִין בִּרְשִׁימִין דְּמַלְכָּא קַדִּישָׁא, פָּתְחֵי וְאָמְרֵי, אַשְׁרֵי הָעָם שֶׁכָּכָה לּוֹ אַשְׁרֵי הָעָם שֶׁה' אֱלֹהָיו.

230. On that day, Yisrael leave with a mark from the King with a song of glory and enter the Sukkah, Etrog in their left hand, a Lulav in their right. Every one sees that Yisrael are written in the King's list, and open and say, "Happy is that people, that is in such a case: happy is that people, whose Elohim is Hashem" (Tehilim 144:15).

231. עַד כָּאן חֶדְוָותָא דְּכֹלָּא, חֶדְוָותָא דְּאוּשְׁפִּיזִין, וַאֲפִילוּ אוּמוֹת הָעוֹלָם חָדָאן בְּחֶדְוָותָא, וּמִתְבָּרְכִין מִנָּה, וְעַל דָּא קָרְבְּנִין בְּכָל יוֹמָא עֲלַיְיהוּ, לְאַטְלָא עֲלַיְיהוּ שְׁלָם, וְיִתְבָּרְכוּן מִינָן. מִכָּאן וּלְהָלְאָה, יוֹמָא חַד, דְּמַלְכָּא עִלָּאָה, דְּחָדֵי בְּהוֹ בְּיִשְׂרָאֵל, דִּכְתִיב בַּיּוֹם הַשְּׁמִינִי עֲצֶרֶת תִּהְיֶה לָכֶם, דְּהָא יוֹמָא דָא מִן מַלְכָּא בִּלְחוֹדוֹי, חֶדְוָותָא דִּילֵיהּ בְּיִשְׂרָאֵל, לְמַלְכָּא דְּזַמִּין אוּשְׁפִּיזִין וְכוּ'.

231. Now all rejoice, and the guests rejoice. Even the nations of the world participate in that joy and are blessed by it. Hence sacrifices are offered for them in every day, so there will be peace upon them, and they will be blessed by it. From now on, there is one day in which the highest King rejoices with the people of Yisrael, as it is written: "On the eighth day you shall have a solemn assembly" (Bemidbar 29:35). This day comes solely from the King, who delights in Yisrael as a king who has invited guests.

27. The tulip and the lily

A Synopsis

Rabbi Shimon begins the discussion by providing two explanations for this title verse. He reveals that the "tulip of Sharon" signifies both the Congregation of Yisrael and the Malchut. Rabbi Shimon continues by explaining that the Malchut is called "Sharon" and that it thirsts for the water of Binah. The tulip, we are told, is also called "the lily of the valley," since it changes hues when she unites with the King. This change, we learn, indicates an alignment with mercy or judgment. Rabbi Shimon next proceeds by providing a description of Adam's mortal sin, the crime by which he brought punishment upon all people. We are told that in fact it was Eve who led Adam to sin and thereby, brought death to all. As punishment for this sin, both Adam and Eve, as well as the rest of humanity, became subject to constant change and eventual death.

The Relevance of this Passage

The Light of Binah flows into our world as we peruse this passage with a pure heart. This Light brings mercy into our lives, softening judgments. This energy of purification also helps to correct the original sin of Adam, and assists in the removal of death from the landscape of human existence.

232. ר"ש פָּתַח וַאֲמַר, אֲנִי חֲבַצֶּלֶת הַשָּׁרוֹן שׁוֹשַׁנַּת הָעֲמָקִים, כַּמָּה חֲבִיבָה כְּנֶסֶת יִשְׂרָאֵל קַמֵּי קוּדְשָׁא בְּרִיךְ הוּא, דְּקוּדְשָׁא בְּרִיךְ הוּא מְשַׁבַּח לָהּ, וְהִיא מְשַׁבַּחַת לֵיהּ תָּדִיר, וְכַמָּה מְשַׁבְּחִין וּמְזַמְּרִין אַזְמֵינַת לֵיהּ תָּדִיר לְקוּדְשָׁא בְּרִיךְ הוּא, זַכָּאָה חוּלָקְהוֹן דְּיִשְׂרָאֵל, דַּאֲחִידָן בֵּיהּ בְּעַדְבָּא דְחוּלָקָא קַדִּישָׁא, כְּמָה דִכְתִיב כִּי חֵלֶק ה' עַמּוֹ וְגוֹ'.

232. Rabbi Shimon opened the discussion saying: "I am the tulip of the Sharon; the lily of the valleys" (Shir Hashirim 2:1). How fond is the Holy One, blessed be He, of the Congregation of Yisrael. He always praises it, and she always praises the Holy One, blessed be He, as said in Shir Hashirim. How many poets and singers it summons before the Holy One, blessed be He. Happy is the portion of Yisrael, who cleave to the lot of the holy portion, as it says, "For Hashem's portion is His people..." (Devarim 32:9).

233. אֲנִי חֲבַצֶּלֶת הַשָּׁרוֹן, דָּא כְּנֶסֶת יִשְׂרָאֵל, דְּקַיְּימָא בְּשַׁפִּירוּ דְּנוֹי בְּגִנְתָּא דְעֵדֶן. הַשָּׁרוֹן: דְּהִיא שָׁרָה וּמְשַׁבַּחַת לְמַלְכָּא עִלָּאָה.

233. "I am the tulip of the Sharon." This is the Congregation of Yisrael, NAMELY THE NUKVA, which stands in the Garden of Eden in the magnificence of her beauty. She is called Sharon, because she sings (Heb. *sharah*) and praises before the most high King.

234. ד״א אֲנִי חֲבַצֶּלֶת הַשָׁרוֹן, דְּבָעְיָא לְאַשְׁקָאָה מַשְׁקְיוּ דְּנַחֲלָא עֲמִיקָא, מַבּוּעָא דְּנַחֲלִין, כְּד״א וְהָיָה הַשָׁרָב לַאֲגַם. שׁוֹשַׁנַּת הָעֲמָקִים דְּקָיְימָא בַּעֲמִיקְתָּא דְּכֹלָּא. מַאן אִינוּן עֲמָקִים. כְּד״א מִמַּעֲמַקִים קְרָאתִיךָ ה׳. חֲבַצֶּלֶת הַשָׁרוֹן. חֲבַצֶּלֶת, מֵהַהוּא אֲתַר, דְּשַׁקְיוּ דְּנַחֲלִין נָפְקִין, וְלָא פָּסְקִין לְעָלְמִין. שׁוֹשַׁנַּת הָעֲמָקִים: שׁוֹשַׁנָּה מֵהַהוּא אֲתַר דְּאִקְרֵי עֲמִיקָא דְּכֹלָּא, סָתִים מִכָּל סִטְרִין.

234. Another explanation is that "I am the tulip of the Sharon" in need of watering from the deep river, the source of all springs; NAMELY BINAH, as it says, "And the parched ground (Heb. *sharav*) shall become a pool" (Yeshayah 35:7). HENCE THE NUKVA IS CALLED SHARON, DERIVED FROM SHARAV, FOR SHE IS THIRSTY FOR THE WATER OF BINAH. She is called "the lily of the valley (also: 'the deeps')" since she is to be found very deep. The deeps are those in the verse, "Out of the depths I have cried to you, O Hashem" (Tehilim 130:1). "The tulip of the Sharon" comes from the place where the waters of the springs come and never stop flowing. "The lily of the valley" is from the place called the depth of all, closed on all sides.

235. תָּא חֲזֵי בְּקַדְמֵיתָא יְרוּקָא כַּחֲבַצֶּלֶת, דְּטַרְפִּין דִּילָהּ יְרוֹקִין, לְבָתַר שׁוֹשַׁנַּת סוּמְקָא בִּגְוָונִין חִוָּורִין. שׁוֹשַׁנָּה בְּשִׁית טַרְפִּין, שֹׁשַׁנַּת: דְּאִשְׁתְּנִיאַת מִגְּוָונָא לִגְוָונָא, וְשַׁנִּיאַת גְּוָונָהָא.

235. Come and see: In the beginning, she is green as a tulip, which has leaves of green. Then, she is red as a lily with white shades, a lily (Heb. *shoshana*) of six leaves. THE WORD IS DERIVED FROM CHANGE (HEB. SHINUY), for she changes hues, changes from one color to another.

236. שֹׁשַׁנַּת: בְּקַדְמֵיתָא חֲבַצֶּלֶת, בְּעִדָּנָא דְּבָעְיָא לְאִזְדַּוְּוגָא בֵּיהּ בְּמַלְכָּא, אִקְרֵי חֲבַצֶּלֶת, בָּתַר דְּאִתְדַּבְּקַת בֵּיהּ בְּמַלְכָּא בְּאִינוּן נְשִׁיקִין,

אִקְרֵי שֹׁשַׁנַּת, בְּגִין דִּכְתִיב שִׂפְתוֹתָיו שׁוֹשַׁנִּים. שֹׁשַׁנַּת הָעֲמָקִים דְּהִיא מְשַׁנְיָיא גְּוָונָהָא, זִמְנִין לְטַב, וְזִמְנִין לְבִישׁ, זִמְנִין לְרַחֲמֵי, זִמְנָא לְדִינָא.

236. SHE IS CALLED a lily, THOUGH at first she was a tulip. WHEN she desired to be united with the King, she was called a tulip. Now that she is joined to the King in kisses, she is called a lily, since it is written: "His lips are lilies" (Shir Hashirim 5:13). She is called "the lily of the valley," for she changes colors, now for better now for worse, now for Mercy now for Judgment.

237. וַתֵּרֶא הָאִשָּׁה כִּי טוֹב הָעֵץ לְמַאֲכָל וְכִי תַאֲוָה הוּא לָעֵינַיִם. תָּא חֲזֵי, דְּהָא בְּנֵי נָשָׁא לָא מִסְתַּכְּלִין, וְלָא יָדְעִין, וְלָא מַשְׁגִּיחִין, בְּשַׁעְתָּא דִּבְרָא קוּדְשָׁא בְּרִיךְ הוּא לְאָדָם, וְאוֹקִיר לֵיהּ בִּיקִירוּ עִלָּאָה, בָּעָא מִנֵּיהּ לְאִתְדַּבְּקָא בֵּיהּ בְּגִין דְּיִשְׁתַּכַּח יְחִידָאי, וּבְלִבָּא יְחִידָאי, וּבַאֲתַר דִּדְבֵקוּתָא יְחִידָאי, דְּלָא אִשְׁתַּנֵּי, וְלָא מִתְהַפֵּךְ לְעָלְמִין, בְּהַהוּא קְשׁוּרָא יְחִידָא, דְּכֹלָּא בֵּיהּ אִתְקַשַּׁר, הֲדָא הוּא דִכְתִיב וְעֵץ הַחַיִּים בְּתוֹךְ הַגָּן.

237. "And when the woman saw that the tree was good for food, and that it was a delight to the eyes" (Beresheet 3:6). Come and see: Men do not behold, nor do they know or care, that when the Holy One, blessed be He, created Adam, He donned him with what is most dear, THE SUPERNAL MOCHIN, and asked Adam to cleave to Him, so he will be the only one, of one heart, to cling to the place of one never - changing clinging; NAMELY ZEIR ANPIN, OF WHICH IT SAYS, "FOR I AM HASHEM, I DO NOT CHANGE" (MALACHI 3:6), which never alters, the knot to which the all embracing unison is tied. This is the meaning of "The Tree of Life in the midst of the garden" (Beresheet 2:10), NAMELY ZEIR ANPIN.

238. לְבָתַר סָטוֹ מֵאָרְחָא דִמְהֵימְנוּתָא, וְשָׁבְקוּ אִילָנָא יְחִידָאי, עִלָּאָה מִכָּל אִילָנִין, וְאָתוּ לְאִתְדַּבְּקָא, בַּאֲתַר דְּמִשְׁתַּנֵּי, וּמִתְהַפֵּךְ מִגַּוְונָא לְגַוְונָא וּמִטַּב לְבִישׁ וּמִבִּישׁ לְטַב, וְנַחֲתֵי מֵעֵילָא לְתַתָּא, וְאִתְדַּבְּקוּ לְתַתָּא, בְּשִׁנּוּיִין סַגִּיאִין, וְשָׁבְקוּ אִילָנָא יְחִידָאָה, עִלָּאָה מִכָּל אִילָנִין, הה"ד אֲשֶׁר עָשָׂה הָאֱלֹקִים אֶת הָאָדָם יָשָׁר וְגוֹ'.

238. Later, they turned from the path of faith, and left the only supernal tree among the trees, NAMELY ZEIR ANPIN, and alighted upon the place which changes colors, and changes from good to evil and from evil to good, TO WIT, THE NUKVA WHEN NOT WITH ZEIR ANPIN, BUT SUCKING FROM THE LEFT ALONE. They descended downward from above, and were greatly changed. They left the only tree, the highest among the trees, as it is written: "That the Elohim has made man upright; but they have sought out many inventions" (Kohelet 7:29).

239. וַדַּאי כְּדֵין אִתְהַפַּךְ לִבַּיְיהוּ, בְּהַהוּא סִטְרָא מַמָּשׁ, זִמְנִין לְטַב, זִמְנִין לְבִישׁ, זִמְנִין לְרַחֲמֵי, זִמְנִין לְדִינָא, בְּהַאי מִלָּה דְּאִתְדַּבְּקוּ בָּהּ וַדַּאי, בְּקֵשׁוּ חֻשְׁבּוֹנוֹת רַבִּים, וְאִתְדַּבָּקוּ בְּהוֹ.

239. Surely then their heart was changed on that very side, FOR THEY UNDERWENT MANY CHANGES, now for good now for evil, now for Mercy now for Judgment. They clung to THE LEFT, surely seeking many inventions there, NAMELY NAMELY CHANGES, and cleaved to them.

240. א״ל קוּדְשָׁא בְּרִיךְ הוּא, אָדָם, שָׁבַקְתְּ חַיֵּי וְאִתְדַּבַּקְתְּ בְּמוֹתָא. חַיֵּי: דִּכְתִיב וְעֵץ הַחַיִּים בְּתוֹךְ הַגָּן, דְּאִקְרֵי חַיִּים, דְּמַאן דְּאָחִיד בֵּיהּ, לָא טָעִים מוֹתָא לְעָלְמִין. אִתְדַּבַּקְתְּ בְּאִילָנָא אָחֳרָא, הָא וַדַּאי מוֹתָא הוּא לְקַבְלָךְ, הה״ד רַגְלֶיהָ יוֹרְדוֹת מָוֶת, וּכְתִיב וּמוֹצֵא אֲנִי מַר מִמָּוֶת אֶת הָאִשָּׁה, וַדַּאי בַּאֲתַר דְּמוֹתָא אִתְדַּבַּק, וּשְׁבַק אֲתַר דְּחַיֵּי, בְּגִין כָּךְ אִתְגְּזַר עֲלֵיהּ, וְעַל כָּל עָלְמָא, מוֹתָא.

240. The Holy One, blessed be He, said to him: 'Adam, you have abandoned life and clung to death. Life is, as it is written: "The Tree of Life in the midst of the garden," NAMELY ZEIR ANPIN called life, for whoever cleaves to it shall never taste death. Yet you clung to another tree, THE NUKVA WHEN NOT UNITED WITH ZEIR ANPIN. Now surely death awaits you', as it is written: "Her feet go down to death" (Mishlei 5:5), FOR WHOEVER HAS NO MERIT IS EVIL. It is also written: "And I find more bitter than death the woman" (Kohelet 7:26), THE SECRET OF THE NUKVA WHEN NOT UNITED WITH ZEIR ANPIN. Surely he clung to the place of death and abandoned the place of living and was therefore doomed to death together with the rest of the world.

241. אִי הוּא חָטָא, כָּל עָלְמָא מַה חָטוּ. אִי תֵימָא, דְּכָל עָלְמָא אָכְלֵי
מֵאִילָנָא דָא, וְאִתְרְמֵי לְכֹלָּא. לָאו הָכֵי. אֶלָּא בְּשַׁעְתָּא דְּאָדָם קָאִים עַל
רַגְלוֹי, חָמֵי לֵיהּ בִּרְיָין כֻּלְּהוּ, וּדְחִילוּ מִקַּמֵּיהּ, וַהֲווֹ נַטְלִין אֲבַתְרֵיהּ,
כְּעַבְדִּין בָּתַר מַלְכָּא, וְהוּא אֲמַר לוֹן, אֲנָא וְאַתּוּן, בֹּאוּ נִשְׁתַּחֲוֶה
וְנִכְרָעָה וְגוֹ'. וַאֲזָלוּ כֻּלְּהוּ אֲבַתְרֵיהּ, כֵּיוָן דְּחָזוּ דְּאָדָם סָגִיד לְהַאי אֲתַר,
וְאִתְדַּבַּק בֵּיהּ, כֻּלְּהוּ אִתְמַשְּׁכוּ אֲבַתְרֵיהּ וְגָרִים מוֹתָא לְכָל עָלְמָא.

241. HE ASKS: If he sinned, what was the sin of the whole world, WHY WAS IT DECREED THAT THE REST OF THE WORLD WOULD DIE? If, you might say, it is because the whole world ate of this tree, and therefore were all sentenced to death, this is not so. HE ANSWERS: When Adam WAS CREATED AND stood upon his feet, all the creatures saw and feared him, and followed him like servants after the king. But he said to them, "O come, let us worship and bow down" (Tehilim 95:6), you and I. When they saw Adam bowing before that place, THE LEFT SIDE, and cleaving to it, they all followed him. Thus, he brought death upon the whole world.

242. וּכְדֵין אִשְׁתַּנֵּי אָדָם לְכַמָּה גְּוָונִין, זִמְנִין דִּינָא, זִמְנִין רַחֲמֵי זִמְנִין
מוֹתָא, זִמְנִין חַיֵּי, וְלָא קָאִים בְּקִיּוּמָא תָּדִיר בְּחַד מִנַּיְיהוּ, בְּגִין דְּהַהוּא
אֲתַר גָּרִים לֵיהּ. וְעַל דָּא אִקְרֵי, חֶרֶב הַמִּתְהַפֶּכֶת: הַמִּתְהַפֶּכֶת מִסִּטְרָא
דָא, לְסִטְרָא דָא, מִטַּב לְבִישׁ, מֵרַחֲמֵי לְדִינָא, מִשְּׁלָם לִקְרָבָא,
מִתְהַפֶּכֶת הִיא בְּכֹלָּא, טַב וְרַע דִּכְתִיב וְעֵץ הַדַּעַת טוֹב וָרָע.

242. Then was Adam changed in several ways, now Judgment, now Mercy, now to death and now to life. He never stood still in one of them, because of the nature of that place which was therefore called the revolving sword, which revolves from this to that side, from good to evil, from Mercy to Judgment, from peace to war. Usually it turns from good to evil, as it is written: "The Tree of Knowledge of Good and Evil" (Beresheet 2:9).

243. וּמַלְכָּא עִלָּאָה, לְרַחֲמָא עַל עוֹבָדוֹי, אוֹכַח לֵיהּ, וא"ל, וּמֵעֵץ
הַדַּעַת טוֹב וָרָע לֹא תֹאכַל מִמֶּנּוּ וְגוֹ', וְהוּא לָא קַבִּיל מִנֵּיהּ, וְאִתְמְשַׁךְ
בָּתַר אִתְּתֵיהּ, וְאִתְתְּרַךְ לְעָלְמִין, דְּהָא אִתְּתָא לְאַתְרָא סַלְקָא וְלָא יַתִּיר,

וְאִתְּתָא גָּרֵים מוֹתָא לְכֹלָּא.

243. The most high King, in His love for His creatures, rebuked him saying: "But from the Tree of Knowledge of Good and Evil, you shall not eat of it..." (Ibid. 17), but he did not accept it and was drawn after his wife and was expelled FROM THE GARDEN OF EDEN for ever, for the woman ascended to the place OF THE REVERSAL BETWEEN LIFE AND DEATH and no more. THUS the woman brought death to all.

244. תָּא חֲזֵי, לְעָלְמָא דְאָתֵי כְּתִיב, כִּי כִימֵי הָעֵץ יְמֵי עַמִּי, כִּימֵי הָעֵץ, הַהוּא דְאִשְׁתְּמוֹדְעָא, בֵּיה זִמְנָא, כְּתִיב, בִּלַּע הַמָּוֶת לָנֶצַח וּמָחָה ה' אֱלֹהִים דִּמְעָה מֵעַל כָּל פָּנִים וְחֶרְפַּת עַמּוֹ יָסִיר מֵעַל כָּל הָאָרֶץ וגו'.

244. Come and see: It is written of the World to Come: "For as the days of a tree shall the days of My people be" (Yeshayah 65:22). "The days of a tree" refer to the well known TREE OF LIFE, of which it says "He will destroy death for ever; and Hashem Elohim will wipe away tears from off all faces; and the insult of His people shall He take away from off all the earth" (Yeshayah 25:8), FOR THERE ARE NO CHANGES OR DEATH IN THE TREE OF LIFE.

28. "And the days drew near for Israel to die," part three

A Synopsis

Rabbi Chiya explains to Rabbi Yosi that when the Holy One wishes to take back a man's spirit, the days that man has lived are enumerated before Him. If this man is righteous, all the days will draw near Him without reproach. The wicked, however, cannot draw near Him since they are consumed by darkness. The name "Israel" is more complete than, and superior to, the name Jacob, we are told. This is why we find Israel rather than Jacob written in the title quotation.

The Relevance of this Passage

A rare opportunity is afforded to the readers of this mystical passage. Through the spiritual power ingrained into the name Israel, we receive the Light of the great Patriarch, which helps merit closeness to The Creator in this world and the next, by removing the darkness created by our misdeeds and selfish actions. Moreover, we are inspired to seek higher levels of spirituality, so that we, too, can elevate from the realm of "Jacob" to "Israel" over the course of our lives.

245. וַיִּקְרְבוּ יְמֵי יִשְׂרָאֵל לָמוּת. תָּאנָא, א"ר חִיָּיא, כְּתִיב וַיְחִי יַעֲקֹב בְּאֶרֶץ מִצְרַיִם שְׁבַע עֶשְׂרֵה שָׁנָה, הָתָם בְּקִיּוּמֵיה יַעֲקֹב, וְהָכָא בְּמִיתָתֵיה יִשְׂרָאֵל, דִּכְתִיב וַיִּקְרְבוּ יְמֵי יִשְׂרָאֵל לָמוּת. א"ר יוֹסֵי, הָכֵי הוּא וַדַּאי, דְּהָא לָא כְּתִיב וַיִּקְרַב יוֹם יִשְׂרָאֵל לָמוּת, אֶלָּא יְמֵי, וְכִי בְּכַמָּה יוֹמֵי מִית ב"נ, וְהָא בְּשַׁעְתָּא חֲדָא, בְּרִגְעָא חֲדָא, מִית וְנָפֵיק מֵעַלְמָא.

245. "And the days drew near for Israel to die" (Beresheet 47:29). We learned that Rabbi Chiya said: It is written, "And Jacob lived in the land of Egypt seventeen years." In his life, it is written Jacob and in his death, it says Israel. YET THE NAME ISRAEL IS MORE ELEVATED THAN THE NAME JACOB. Rabbi Yosi said: Surely IT SHOULD HAVE BEEN SAID HERE ISRAEL, for it does not say, 'The day drew near,' but "the days." THIS IS DIFFICULT TO UNDERSTAND, for a man does not die in several days; within one hour, one moment, he dies and passes away from the world.

246. אֶלָּא הָכֵי תָּאנָא, כַּד קוּדְשָׁא בְּרִיךְ הוּא בָּעֵי לְאַתָּבָא רוּחֵיה לֵיה, כָּל אִינּוּן יוֹמִין דְּקָאֵים ב"נ בְּהַאי עַלְמָא, אִתְפַּקְדָן קַמֵּיה, וְעָאלִין בְּחוּשְׁבָּנָא, וְכַד אִתְקְרִיבוּ קַמֵּיה לְמֵיעַל בְּחוּשְׁבָּנָא, מִית ב"נ, וְאָתֵיב

קוּדְשָׁא בְּרִיךְ הוּא רוּחֵיהּ לֵיהּ, הַהוּא הֶבֶל דְּאַפֵּיק וְנָפַח בֵּיהּ, אוֹתְבֵיהּ לְגַבֵּיהּ.

246. HE ANSWERS: We have so learned that when the Holy One, blessed be He, wishes to take back to Him the spirit of man, all the days the man lived come before Him and are counted. When the days draw near him to be reckoned, the man dies, and the Holy One, blessed be He, takes back to Himself the spirit of man, that breath which the man breathes in and out.

247. זַכָּאָה חוּלָקֵיהּ דְּהַהוּא ב"נ, דְּיוֹמוֹי אִתְקְרִיבוּ גַּבֵּי מַלְכָּא. בְּלָא כְּסוּפָא, וְלָא דָחֵי יוֹמָא מִנַּיְיהוּ לְבַר, דְּיִשְׁכַּח בְּהַהוּא יוֹמָא, דְּאִתְעֲבֵיד בֵּיהּ חוֹבָא, בְּגִין כָּךְ, כְּתִיב בְּצַדִּיקַיָּא קְרִיבָה, מִשּׁוּם דְּקָרִיבוּ יוֹמוֹי קַמֵּי מַלְכָּא, בְּלָא כְּסוּפָא.

247. Happy is the portion of the man, whose days draw near the King without reproach, and none is pushed out for containing a transgression committed in it. The reason the words 'drawing near' are used in relation to the righteous is that the days draw near the King without reproach.

248. וַוי לְרַשִׁיעַיָּא, דְּלָא כְּתִיב בְּהוּ קְרִיבָה, וְהֵיךְ יִקְרְבוּן יוֹמֵי קַמֵּי מַלְכָּא, דְּהָא כָּל יוֹמוֹי בְּחוֹבֵי עַלְמָא אִשְׁתַּכָּחוּ, וּבְגִינֵי כָּךְ לָא יִקְרְבוּן קַמֵּי מַלְכָּא, וְלָא יִתְמַנּוּן קַמֵּיהּ, וְלָא יִדְכְּרוּ לְעֵילָא, אֶלָּא אִינּוּן שְׁצִיאָן מִגַּוְויְיהוּ, עֲלַיְיהוּ כְּתִיב, דֶּרֶךְ רְשָׁעִים כָּאֲפֵלָה לֹא יָדְעוּ בַּמֶּה יִכָּשֵׁלוּ.

248. Woe to the wicked of whom it does not say 'drawing near'. For how could their days draw near the King, when all the crimes of the world are found in them? Hence they do not draw near the King, nor come before Him nor are they recorded above, but are consumed of themselves, as is said of them, "The way of the wicked is like darkness: they know not at what they stumble" (Mishlei 4:19).

249. וְהָכָא וַיִּקְרְבוּ יְמֵי יִשְׂרָאֵל וַדַּאי, בְּלָא כְּסוּפָא, בִּשְׁלֵימוּתָא, בְּחֶדְוָותָא שְׁלִים, וּבְגִינֵי כָּךְ, יְמֵי יִשְׂרָאֵל, דַּהֲוָה שְׁלִים יַתִּיר יִשְׂרָאֵל מִיַּעֲקֹב. וְאִי תֵימָא, וְהָא כְּתִיב וְיַעֲקֹב אִישׁ תָּם: שָׁלִים הֲוָה, וְלָא

שְׁלִים בְּדַרְגָּא עִלָּאָה כְּיִשְׂרָאֵל.

249. And here it says, "And the days drew near for Israel to die," for assuredly they drew near without shame, in complete joy. This is why it says (lit.) "the days of Israel," AND NOT "THE DAYS OF JACOB," as the name Yisrael is more complete than that of Jacob. You might say that it is written "and Jacob was a plain (lit. 'whole') man" (Beresheet 25:27), indicating that the name Jacob too is whole. HE ANSWERS: THE NAME JACOB IS ALSO WHOLE, but not whole on a superior grade like Israel is.

250. תַּנְיָא, אָמַר רִבִּי יוֹסֵי, בְּשַׁעְתָּא דְיוֹמוֹי דְּבַר נָשׁ אִתְפָּקִידָן קַמֵּי מַלְכָּא, אִית זַכָּאָה דְּאִתְפַּקְּדָן יוֹמוֹי, וּרְחִיקִין מִקַּמֵּי מַלְכָּא, וְאִית זַכָּאָה, דְּכַד מִתְפַּקְּדָן יוֹמוֹי, קְרִיבִין וּסְמִיכִין לְמַלְכָּא, וְלָא מִתְרַחֲקִין, בְּלָא כִסוּפָא עָאלִין, וְקָרֵיבִין לְמַלְכָּא, זַכָּאָה חוּלָקֵהוֹן, הה״ד וַיִּקְרְבוּ יְמֵי יִשְׂרָאֵל לָמוּת.

250. We have learned that Rabbi Yosi said: When a man's days are enumerated before the King, those of a certain righteous are enumerated far from the King, and the days of another righteous are counted close to the King. They do not stand at a distance but come in without shame and draw near the King. Happy is their portion. This is the meaning of the verse, "And the days drew near for Israel to die."

29. "And he called his son Joseph"

A Synopsis

Through a discussion of the title verse, the rabbis reveal the special connection that exists between Joseph and his father Jacob. Not only were the two very similar in appearance, but Jacob also recognized Joseph's holiness and knew that he would one day be a great man. We also learn that Jacob was afraid to go to Egypt because he feared that in the future his children would be made slaves, that the Shechinah would leave him, and that he would be buried among the wicked. However, the Lord assured him that he would be buried in the grave of his forefathers, and Jacob saw that the Shechinah would dwell with Yisrael in exile.

Rabbi Shimon then addresses the topic of Jacob's relationship with Leah and Rachel. The deception that was played out by Leah, posing as Rachel, leads to the transference of the birthright from Reuben to Joseph. This also relates to the significance of the name Reuben (lit. 'see, a son').

Rabbi Shimon then explains the holy significance of the verse, "Put, I please you, your hand under my thigh." Written in connection with Abraham, Jacob, and Joseph, this verse alludes to the place that emits the holy seed.

Finally, Rabbi Yehuda explains why Jacob was buried with Leah rather than Rachel. The reasons, we're told, are that Leah stood by the roadside day after day, weeping and praying that Jacob would marry her. Furthermore, she bore six holy tribes into the world and therefore, deserved this privilege more than Rachel.

The Relevance of this Passage

The story of Jacob entering into the land of Egypt is synonymous with the men of all generation confronting their own personal demons when they fall into negativity. As the Shechinah dwelled in the presence of Jacob during his sojourn in Egypt, the Light of The Creator can illuminate our lives when we fall into negativity and find ourselves enslaved to dark forces. This passage is our connection to this Light. Moreover, we can share this Light with all the world and help bring about the end of the exile.

The discourse concerning Jacob's relationship with Leah and Rachel shows us that everything that takes place within the drama of human existence has underlying meaning and that all events that transpire are necessary in the course of mankind's spiritual development. Thus, this verse instills wisdom within us to accept the things we might not

understand at the present moment. It ensures that order will emerge
from chaos. The Light that shines from the story concerning Leah's
burial with Jacob inspires us to weep and yearn for the Light of The
Creator, for the tears of man cause great stirrings above.

251. וַיִּקְרָא לִבְנוֹ לְיוֹסֵף, אָמַר רִבִּי יִצְחָק, וְכִי שְׁאָר שִׁבְטִין לָאו בְּנוֹי
אִינוּן. אֶלָּא אָמַר רִבִּי אַבָּא, יוֹסֵף בְּנוֹ הֲוָה יַתִּיר מִכֻּלְּהוּ, דְּתָנִינָן
בְּשַׁעְתָּא דְּאִנְתְּתֵיהּ דְּפוֹטִיפַר דְּחָקַת לֵיהּ לְיוֹסֵף, מַה כְּתִיב, וַיָּבֹא
הַבַּיְתָה לַעֲשׂוֹת מְלַאכְתּוֹ וְאֵין אִישׁ מֵאַנְשֵׁי הַבָּיִת. הַאי קְרָא הָכִי מִבָּעֵי
לֵיהּ, וְאֵין אִישׁ בַּבַּיִת מַהוּ מֵאַנְשֵׁי הַבָּיִת. אֶלָּא לְאַכְלְלָא דְּיוֹקְנָא
דְּיַעֲקֹב, דַּהֲוָה תַּמָּן, וְאִשְׁתְּכַח תַּמָּן, וּבְגִינֵי כָּךְ מֵאַנְשֵׁי הַבָּיִת, אֲבָל אִישׁ
אָחֳרָא הֲוָה תַּמָּן. כֵּיוָן דְּסָלֵיק יוֹסֵף עֵינוֹי, וַחֲמָא דְּיוֹקְנָא דַּאֲבוּי, יְתִיב
בְּקִיּוּמֵיהּ, וְתָב לַאֲחוֹרָא.

251. "And he called his son Joseph" (Beresheet 47:29). Rabbi Yitzchak
said: Are the other tribes not his sons? WHY DID HE CALL JOSEPH ALONE?
HE REPLIES: Rabbi Aba said that Joseph was his son more than the others.
We have learned that when Potifar's wife begged Joseph, it is written:
"Joseph went into the house to do his work; and there was none (lit. 'no
man') of the men of the house there within" (Beresheet 39:11). This verse
should have said 'there was no man in the house', but why add "of the men
of the house"? HE ANSWERS: This indicates the image of Jacob which was
there. It says "the men of the house" to show us there was another man, NOT
OF THE MEN OF THE HOUSE; NAMELY JACOB. Once Joseph lifted up his
eyes and saw the image of his father, his mind was settled and he withdrew.

252. תָּא חֲזֵי, מַה כְּתִיב, וַיְמָאֵן וַיֹּאמֶר אֶל אֵשֶׁת אֲדֹנָיו. א"ל קוּדְשָׁא
בְּרִיךְ הוּא אַתְּ אַמְרַתְּ וַיְמָאֵן וַיֹּאמֶר. חַיֶּיךָ, וַיְמָאֵן וַיֹּאמֶר אָחֳרָא, יֵיתֵי
לְבָרְכָא לִבְנָךְ, וְיִתְבָּרְכוּן בֵּיהּ, הֲדָא הוּא דִּכְתִיב וַיְמָאֵן אָבִיו וַיֹּאמֶר
יָדַעְתִּי בְנִי יָדַעְתִּי.

252. Come and see the verse: "But he refused, and said to his master's
wife..." (Beresheet 39:8). The Holy One, blessed be He, said to him, 'Upon
your life, another will say "I refuse" when he will come to bless your sons,
who will be blessed by him'. This is why it says, "And his father refused,
and said, 'I know it, my son, I know it'" (Beresheet 48:19).

253. כֵּיוָן דַּאֲמַר יָדַעְתִּי בְּנִי, אַמַּאי אֲמַר יָדַעְתִּי אָחֳרָא. אֶלָּא, אֲמַר יָדַעְתִּי בְּנִי, בְּזִמְנָא דְּקָיְימַת בְּגוּפָךְ דְּאַתְּ בָּרִי, כַּד חָמֵית דְּיוֹקְנָא דִילִי, וְתָבַת בְּקִיּוּמָךְ, וּבְגִינֵי כָּךְ כְּתִיב, יָדַעְתִּי בְּנִי, יָדַעְתִּי, עַל מַה דַּאֲמַרְתְּ דְּדָא הוּא בּוּכְרָא, גַּם הוּא יִהְיֶה לְעָם וְגַם הוּא יִגְדָּל, וְהָכָא בְּגִין כָּךְ כְּתִיב, וַיִּקְרָא לִבְנוֹ לְיוֹסֵף, לִבְנוֹ לְיוֹסֵף מַמָּשׁ.

253. HE ASKS: Since he said, "I know it, my son," why did he say again, "I know it"? HE ANSWERS: He said, "I know it, my son" meaning 'you showed through your body that you are my son, when you saw my image and returned to your covenant AND DID NOT DESECRATE IT'. This is why it is written: "I know it, my son." THE SECOND TIME IT IS WRITTEN "I know it" is what you said about this one being the firstborn, TO WHICH HE ANSWERED BY "He also shall become a people, and he also shall be great" (Beresheet 48:19). This is why it says here: "And he called his son Joseph" (Beresheet 47:29), his very son Joseph SINCE HE PROVED IT BY HIS BODY, AS EXPLAINED.

254. ד"א וַיִּקְרָא לִבְנוֹ לְיוֹסֵף, דְּבִדְיוֹקְנָא חַד הֲווֹ מִתְחַזְיָין, דְּכָל מַאן דְּחָמֵי לְיוֹסֵף, הֲוָה אַסְהִיד דִּבְרֵיהּ דְּיַעֲקֹב הֲוָה. רִבִּי יוֹסֵי אֲמַר, כֹּלָּא הָכֵי הוּא. וְעוֹד דְּיוֹסֵף זָן לֵיהּ וְלִבְנוֹי בְּסֵבוּתֵיהּ, וּבְגִינֵי כָּךְ בְּנוֹ מַמָּשׁ, יַתִּיר מִכֻּלְּהוּ. וַיִּקְרָא לִבְנוֹ לְיוֹסֵף אַמַּאי לְיוֹסֵף, וְלָא לְאָחֳרָא. מִשּׁוּם דִּרְשׁוּתָא הֲוָה בִּידֵיהּ לְסַלְּקֵיהּ מִתַּמָּן.

254. Another explanation for: "And he called his son Joseph." They looked the same, and whoever saw Joseph said he was Jacob's son. Rabbi Yosi said: This is exactly so, THAT HE CALLED HIM HIS SON SINCE THEY LOOKED THE SAME. Moreover, Joseph gave food for him and his sons in his old age, for which reason he was his own son more than everyone else. "And he called his son Joseph": HE ASKS: Why did he call Joseph and not another one? HE ANSWERS: Because he could take him from there TO THE CAVE OF THE MACHPELAH SINCE HE WAS A KING, BUT NO ONE ELSE HAD THE AUTHORITY.

255. רִבִּי יוֹסֵי אֲמַר, כֵּיוָן דְּיַעֲקֹב הֲוָה יָדַע דִּבְנוֹי יִשְׁתַּעְבְּדוּן בְּגָלוּתָא תַּמָּן בְּמִצְרַיִם, אַמַּאי לָא אִתְקַבַּר תַּמָּן, בְּגִין דִּיגֵין זְכוּתֵיהּ עַל בְּנוֹי,

אַמַּאי בָּעָא לְאִסְתַּלְּקָא מִתַּמָּן, וְהָא כְּתִיב כְּרַחֵם אָב עַל בָּנִים, אָן הוּא רַחֲמָנוּתָא.

255. Rabbi Yosi said: Since Jacob knew his descendants would become slaves in Egypt, why was he not buried there, so that his merit would protect his children? Why did he wish to go up from there? When it says, "As a father pities his children" (Tehilim 103:13), where is pity then?

256. אֶלָּא, הָכֵי תָּאנָא, בְּשַׁעְתָּא דַּהֲוָה נָחִית יַעֲקֹב לְמִצְרַיִם, הֲוָה דָּחֵיל, הֲוָה אָמַר, דִּילְמָא ח״ו יִשְׁתֵּצוּן בָּנַי בֵּינֵי עַמְמַיָא, וְדִילְמָא קוּדְשָׁא בְּרִיךְ הוּא יְסַלֵּק שְׁכִינְתֵּיהּ מִינִי כְּקַדְמֵיתָא, מַה כְּתִיב וַיֵּרָא אֱלֹקִים אֶל יַעֲקֹב וְגוּ'. אַל תִּירָא מֵרְדָה מִצְרַיְמָה כִּי לְגוֹי גָּדוֹל אֲשִׂימְךָ שָׁם. וּמַה דַּאֲמַרְתְּ דִּילְמָא אֲסַלֵּק שְׁכִינָתִי מִבֵּינָךְ, אָנֹכִי אֵרֵד עִמְּךָ מִצְרַיְמָה.

256. HE REPLIES: We have so learned that when Jacob went down to Egypt, he was afraid. He said: Might it come to that, heaven forbid, that my children will perish among the nations, or that the Holy One, blessed be He, will remove the Shechinah from me as before? It is written, "And Elohim appeared to Jacob" (Beresheet 35:9). "Fear not to go down to Egypt; for I will there make of you a great nation" (Beresheet 46:3). As for what you said, that I might remove My Shechinah from you, "I will go down with you into Egypt" (Ibid. 4).

257. אָמַר עוֹד, דָּחֵילְנָא דִּילְמָא אִתְקַבַּר תַּמָּן, וְלָא אֶזְכֶּה עִם אֲבָהָתַי, א״ל וְאָנֹכִי אַעַלְךָ גַם עָלֹה. אַעַלְךָ: מִמִּצְרַיִם. גַם עָלֹה: לְאִתְקַבְּרָאָה בְּקִבְרָא דַּאֲבָהָתָךְ.

257. He also said: I am afraid lest I shall be buried there and will not merit to be buried with my fathers. He answered him, "And I will also surely bring you up again" (Ibid.), to be buried in the grave of your fathers.

258. בְּגִינֵי כָּךְ, בָּעָא לְסַלְּקָא גַרְמֵיהּ מִמִּצְרַיִם, חַד, דְּלָא יַעַבְדוּן מִנֵּיהּ דַּחֲלָא, דְּהָא חָמָא דְקוּדְשָׁא בְּרִיךְ הוּא זַמִּין לְאִתְפָּרְעָא מִדַּחֲלֵיהוֹן.

וְחַד, דְּחָמָא דִּשְׁכִינְתָּא וְשַׁוֵּי מְדוֹרֵיהּ בֵּין בְּנוֹי בְּגָלוּתָא, וְחַד, בְּגִין דְּיהֵא גוּפֵיהּ דַּיָּיר בֵּין גּוּפַיְיהוּ דַּאֲבָהָתוֹי לְאִתְכְּלָלָא בֵּינַיְיהוּ, וְלָא יִתְמַנֵּי עִם חַיָּיבַיָּא דְּמִצְרָאֵי.

258. This is why he wanted to be taken up from Egypt. Another reason is not to be made godlike, for he saw that the Holy One, blessed be He, would take vengeance upon the deities of Egypt. He also saw that the Shechinah would dwell among his children in exile, AND THAT HE NEED NOT BE BURIED IN EGYPT TO PROTECT THEM. Another reason is that he wanted his body to dwell among the bodies of his fathers, to be with them and not with the wicked in Egypt.

259. וְתָנֵינָן, גּוּפָא דְיַעֲקֹב, אִתְמְשִׁיךְ מִשּׁוּפְרוֹי דְּאָדָם הָרִאשׁוֹן, וַהֲוָה דְיוֹקְנֵיהּ דְּיַעֲקֹב, דְּיוֹקְנָא עִלָּאָה קַדִּישָׁא, דְּיוֹקְנָא דְּכוּרְסְיָא קַדִּישָׁא, וְלָא בָּעָא לְאִתְקְבְּרָא בֵּינֵי חַיָּיבַיָּא, וְרָזָא דְּמִלָּה, דְּבַאֲבָהָן לֵית פֵּרוּדָא כְּלָל, וְעַל דָּא כְּתִיב וְשָׁכַבְתִּי עִם אֲבוֹתַי.

259. We learned that the body of Jacob had its beauty from Adam, and the image of Jacob was of the supernal holy form, the form of the Holy Throne. Thus he did not want to be buried among the wicked. The secret of this matter is that there is no separating the patriarchs, AND THEY ARE ALWAYS TOGETHER. It is therefore written, "I will lie with my fathers" (Beresheet 47:30).

260. וַיִּקְרָא לִבְנוֹ לְיוֹסֵף, בְּנוֹ: בְּחַד דְּיוֹקְנָא דְּאַנְפִּין, בְּגִין דְּבִרְעוּתָא דְּרוּחָא וְלִבָּא, אוֹלִיד לֵיהּ יַתִּיר מִכֻּלְּהוּ. תָּא חֲזֵי, מַה כְּתִיב הַמְעַט קַחְתֵּךְ אֶת אִישִׁי, דְּכָל רְעוּתָא דְיַעֲקֹב בְּרָחֵל הֲוָה, וּבְגִין כָּךְ וַיִּקְרָא לִבְנוֹ לְיוֹסֵף.

260. "And he called his son Joseph." SCRIPTURE SAYS his son BECAUSE they had the same countenance, and also because he begot him more willingly than any other TRIBE. Come and see: It is written: "Is it a small matter that you have taken my husband?" (Beresheet 30:15), for Jacob's whole desire was for Rachel. Hence it says, "and he called his son Joseph."

261. תָּאנָא, ר' שִׁמְעוֹן פָּתַח וַאֲמַר, הַנִּסְתָּרֹת לַה' אֱלֹקֵינוּ וגו'. הַנִּסְתָּרֹת לַה' אֱלֹקֵינוּ, תָּא חֲזֵי, כַּמָּה אִית לֵיהּ לְבַר נָשׁ, לְאִזְדַּהֲרָא מֵחוֹבוֹי, וּלְאִסְתַּכְּלָא דְּלָא יַעֲבָר עַל רְעוּתֵיהּ דְּמָארֵיהּ, דְּתָנִינָן, כָּל מַה דְּבַר נָשׁ עָבֵיד בְּהַאי עָלְמָא, בְּסִפְרָא כְּתִיבוּ אִינוּן עוֹבָדִין, וְעָאלִין בְּחוּשְׁבְּנָא קַמֵּי מַלְכָּא קַדִּישָׁא, וְכֹלָּא אִתְגַּלְיָיא קַמֵּיהּ, הה"ד אִם יִסָּתֵר אִישׁ בַּמִּסְתָּרִים וַאֲנִי לֹא אֶרְאֶנּוּ נְאֻם ה'. אִי הָכִי, אֵיךְ לָא יִסְתַּמַּר בַּר נָשׁ מִלְמֶחֱדַב קַמֵּיהּ דְּמָארֵיהּ, וְתָנִינָן, אֲפִילוּ הַהוּא מַה דְּחָשֵׁיב בַּר נָשׁ וְאִסְתַּלַּק בִּרְעוּתֵיהּ, כֹּלָּא אִשְׁתְּכַח קַמֵּי קוּדְשָׁא בְּרִיךְ הוּא, וְלָא אִתְאֲבֵיד מִנֵּיהּ.

261. We learned: Rabbi Shimon opened the discussion saying: "The secret things belong to Hashem our Elohim..." (Devarim 29:28). Come and see how a man should beware sins, and be watchful lest he would transgress his Master's wishes. For we have learned that every thing a man does in this world is written in a book and reckoned before the Holy King. All is known before Him, as it is written: "'Can any hide himself in secret places that I shall not see him?' says Hashem" (Yirmeyah 23:24). How can a man not guard himself from sinning before his Master? We learned that even a man's thoughts and plans are all placed before the Holy One, blessed be He, and are not lost before Him.

262. תָּא חֲזֵי, בְּהַהוּא לֵילְיָא דְּעָאלַת לֵאָה לְגַבֵּיהּ דְּיַעֲקֹב, וְיָהֲבַת לֵיהּ אִינוּן סִימָנִין, דִּיהַב יַעֲקֹב לְרָחֵל, סָלִיק בִּרְעוּתֵיהּ דְּאִיהִי רָחֵל, וְשַׁמָּשׁ שִׁמּוּשָׁא בָּהּ, וְהַהִיא טִפָּה קַדְמֵיתָא דְּיַעֲקֹב הֲוַת, דִּכְתִיב כֹּחִי וְרֵאשִׁית אוֹנִי, וְסָבַר דְּאִיהִי רָחֵל. קוּדְשָׁא בְּרִיךְ הוּא דְּאִיהוּ גָּלֵי עֲמִיקְתָּא וּמְסַתְּרָתָא, וְיָדַע מַה בַּחֲשׁוֹכָא, סָלִיק הַהוּא רְעוּתָא לְאַתְרֵיהּ, וּבְכֵירוּתָא דִּרְאוּבֵן אִסְתַּלַּק לְיוֹסֵף. מַאי טַעְמָא, מִשּׁוּם דְּהָא דְּרָחֵל הֲוַת, הַהִיא טִפָּה קַדְמֵיתָא דְּנָפְקַת מִיַּעֲקֹב, וּבְגִין דַּהֲוַת דִּילָהּ, הַהוּא בְּכֵירוּתָא מַמָּשׁ דִּרְאוּבֵן, יָרֵית יוֹסֵף, וְרָחֵל יָרְתָה לְהַהוּא דִּילָהּ.

262. Come and see: on the night Leah came to Jacob, she gave him the tokens he gave Rachel, LEST HER FATHER SHOULD REPLACE HER WITH ANOTHER. WHEN RACHEL SAW THAT HIS FATHER GIVES LEAH IN HER

-138-

PLACE, AND THAT SHE DOES NOT KNOW OF THE TOKEN AND MIGHT BE PUT TO SHAME, SHE GAVE HER THE TOKENS. He thought he was with Rachel, when he had intercourse with her. It was his first drop, as it is written: "My might and the beginning of my strength" (Beresheet 49:3), and he thought it was Rachel. The Holy One, blessed be He, who reveals depths and mysteries, who knows what lies in the dark, brought up the desire to its place, and the birthright was gone from Reuben AND GIVEN to Joseph. Why? Because the first drop that came from Jacob belonged to Rachel. Since the actual birthright of Reuben belonged to her, Joseph inherited it and Rachel came into her own inheritance.

263. וּבְגִין כָּךְ, רָזָא דְמִלָּה, לָא אִסְתַּלַּק רְאוּבֵן בִּשְׁמָא כִּשְׁאָר שִׁבְטִין, אֶלָּא רְאוּבֵן, כְּלוֹמַר חֲמוּ בַּר: רְאוּ בֵּן סְתָם, וְהַאי בֵּן לָא אִתְיְדַע שְׁמֵיהּ, וְעַל דָּא לָא קַרְיָא לֵאָה בְּהַאי שְׁמָא, וְלָא אִקְרֵי רְאוּ בְּנִי, דְּהָא לֵאָה יָדְעַת עוֹבָדָא.

263. This is the secret reason why Reuben did not receive a name like the other sons but simply Reuben, namely *Reu ben* (Eng. 'see', 'a son'), a son, not known by name. Leah therefore did not call him 'my son', naming him '*Reu beni*' (Eng. 'see', 'my son'), for she knew what had happened, THAT JACOB'S THOUGHTS WERE WITH RACHEL AND NOT WITH HER.

264. וְתָנֵינָן, גָּלֵי קַמֵּי קוּדְשָׁא בְּרִיךְ הוּא, דְּיַעֲקֹב לָאו רְעוּתֵיהּ לְמֶיחַב קַמֵּיהּ בְּהַאי, וְלָא אִסְתַּכַּל בִּרְעוּתָא בְּאִתְּתָא אַחֲרָא בְּהַהִיא שַׁעְתָּא, כִּשְׁאָר חַיָּיבֵי עַלְמָא, וְעַל כָּךְ כְּתִיב וַיִּהְיוּ בְנֵי יַעֲקֹב שְׁנֵים עָשָׂר, דְּהָא בְּנַיְיהוּ דִּשְׁאָר חַיָּיבֵי עַלְמָא, דְּעָבְדִין הַהוּא עוֹבָדָא, בִּשְׁמָא אַחֲרָא אִקְרוּן. וְהָא יְדִיעָא מִלָּה דָּא לְגַבֵּי חַבְרַיָּא, וּבְגִינֵי כָּךְ וַיִּקְרָא לִבְנוֹ לְיוֹסֵף, בְּנוֹ מַמָּשׁ, מִשֵּׁירוּתָא וְסִיּוּמָא בְּנוֹ הֲוָה.

264. We learned it is known to the Holy One, blessed be He, that Jacob did not mean to sin by COMING INTO LEAH AND THINKING OF RACHEL, and that he never knowingly thought of another woman at that time, like the wicked men in the world. It is therefore written, "Now the sons of Jacob were twelve" (Beresheet 35:23), for the sons of the other wicked men in the world, who act in this way, are called by another name, NAMELY CHANGED

CHILDREN, which is known to the friends. He therefore "called his son Joseph," his own son from the beginning, REUBEN'S BIRTH, and his son in the end.

265. תָּאנָא, א״ר יוֹסֵי, בַּמֶּה אוֹמֵי לֵיה יַעֲקֹב לְיוֹסֵף, דִּכְתִיב שִׂים נָא יָדְךָ תַּחַת יְרֵכִי. אֶלָּא בְּהַהוּא אָת קַיָּימָא, דַּהֲוָה רָשִׁים בְּבִשְׂרֵיה, דְּדָא חֲשִׁיבוּתָא דַּאֲבָהָן יַתִּיר מִכֹּלָּא, וְהַאי בְּרִית, רָזָא דְיוֹסֵף אִיהוּ.

265. We learned that Rabbi Yosi said: What did Jacob use to make Joseph swear? It is written "Put, I pray you, your hand under my thigh" (Beresheet 47:29). HE ANSWERS: HE MADE HIM SWEAR by the sign of the covenant, which was stamped upon his flesh, for the patriarchs assigned it more importance than everything else, and the covenant is the secret of Joseph. TO WIT, JOSEPH IS THE SECRET OF THE ATTRIBUTE OF THE RIGHTEOUS YESOD, OF WHICH HE IS A CHARIOT.

266. אר״ש, בְּאַבְרָהָם וּבְיַעֲקֹב, כְּתִיב, שִׂים נָא יָדְךָ תַּחַת יְרֵכִי, תְּחוֹת יְרֵכִי, כְּלוֹמַר, בְּהַהוּא אֲתָר דִּרְמִיזָא בִּשְׁמָא קַדִּישָׁא, וְאַפֵּיק זַרְעָא קַדִּישָׁא מְהֵימָנָא לְעַלְמָא. בְּיִצְחָק לֹא כְּתִיב, בְּגִין דְּנָפֵיק מִנֵּיה עֵשָׂו.

266. Rabbi Shimon said: It is written of Abraham and Jacob, "Put, I pray you, your hand under my thigh," in the place alluded to by the Holy Name, which emits holy seed, THE SEED of faith, into the world. It is not written in connection to Isaac: "PUT, I PRAY YOU, YOUR HAND UNDER MY THIGH," since Esau issued from him.

267. תּוּ, מ״ט הָכָא, שִׂים נָא יָדְךָ תַּחַת יְרֵכִי אַל נָא תִקְבְּרֵנִי בְּמִצְרָיִם. אֶלָּא אָמַר לֵיה יַעֲקֹב לְיוֹסֵף, בְּהַאי רְשִׁימָא קַדִּישָׁא אוֹמֵי לִי, דְּאַפֵּיק זַרְעָא קַדִּישָׁא מְהֵימָנָא לְעַלְמָא, וְאִתְנְטֵיר, וְלָא אִסְתָּאַב לְעָלְמִין, דְּלָא יִתְקַבַּר בֵּין אִינוּן מְסָאֲבִין, דְּלָא נָטְרוּ לֵיה לְעָלְמִין, דִּכְתִיב בְּהוֹ, אֲשֶׁר בְּשַׂר חֲמוֹרִים בְּשָׂרָם וְזִרְמַת סוּסִים זִרְמָתָם.

267. Another reason it is written: "Put, I pray you, your hand under my thigh...bury me not, I pray you, in Egypt." Jacob said to Joseph, Swear to me by this holy impression, which emitted holy and faithful seed into the

world and was always kept from being defiled, that it will never be buried among the unholy who did never keep it, of whom it says, "Whose flesh is the flesh of donkeys, and whose issue is the issue of horses" (Yechezkel 23:20).

268. וְאִי תֵימָא, הָא יוֹסֵף דְּנָטִיר לֵיהּ עַל כֹּלָּא, אֲמַאי אִתְקַבַּר בֵּינַיְיהוּ. אֶלָּא תָּנִינָן, כְּתִיב הָיֹה הָיָה דְּבַר ה' אֶל יְחֶזְקֵאל בֶּן בּוּזִי הַכֹּהֵן בְּאֶרֶץ כַּשְׂדִּים עַל נְהַר כְּבָר, וְהָא תָּנִינָן, דִּשְׁכִינְתָּא לָא שַׁרְיָא אֶלָּא בְּאַרְעָא דְיִשְׂרָאֵל, אֲמַאי הָכָא שְׁכִינְתָּא. אֶלָּא עַל נְהַר כְּבָר כְּתִיב, וּכְתִיב וַתְּהִי עָלָיו שָׁם יַד ה'. אוֹף הָכָא, יוֹסֵף בְּמַיָּא אִתְרְמֵי אֲרוֹנָא דִילֵיהּ, אֲמַר קוּדְשָׁא בְּרִיךְ הוּא, אִי יוֹסֵף אִסְתַּלַּק מֵהָכָא, גָּלוּתָא לָא אִתְקַיַּים, אֶלָּא תְּהֵא קְבוּרְתֵּיהּ בַּאֲתַר דְּלָא יִסְתָּאַב, וְיִסְבְּלוּן בְּנֵי יִשְׂרָאֵל גָּלוּתָא.

268. It may be said that Joseph guarded his covenant more than everyone else, but why was he buried among them IN EGYPT? HE REPLIES: We have learned that it is written, "The word of Hashem came to Ezekiel the priest, the son of Buzi, in the land of Chaldeans by the river K'var" (Yechezkel 1:3). Yet we learned that the Shechinah does not dwell outside the land of Yisrael. Why was She revealed there? HE ANSWERS: It is written "by the river K'var," FOR WATER CANNOT BE DEFILED, UNLIKE THE LAND OF NATIONS. It is also written: "And the hand of Hashem was there upon him" (Ibid.), WHICH IS THE SHECHINAH. Here too, Joseph's coffin was thrown into the water. The Holy One, blessed be He, said: If Joseph will be gone from here, the exile will not be carried out, FOR YISRAEL WILL NOT BE ABLE TO TOLERATE IT. His burial place will then be in an undefiled place, and the children of Yisrael will endure the exile.

269. תָּאנָא, אֲמַר רִבִּי יוֹסֵי, חָמָא יַעֲקֹב, דְּהָא בְּכֹלָּא אִתְתַּקַּן לְכָרְסְיָא קַדִּישָׁא בַּאֲבָהָן, אֲמַר, אִי הָכֵי יִתְקַבַּר, הֵיךְ גּוּפָא דָא אֲחִידָא בַּאֲבָהָתָא, וַאֲפִילוּ מְעַרְתָּא דְּאִתְקַבַּר תַּמָּן אִקְרֵי כָּפֵילְתָּא, בְּגִין דְּכָל מִלָּה דִכְפֵילְתָּא הוּא תְּרֵין וְחַד, אוֹף מְעַרְתָּא תְּרֵין וְחַד.

269. We learned that Rabbi Yosi said: Jacob saw that the Holy Throne was fitted in every way by the patriarchs, ABRAHAM AND ISAAC ON RIGHT AND

LEFT, AND HE IN THE CENTER. JACOB said to himself, If he is to be buried here IN EGYPT, how will the body be attached to the patriarchs? Even the cave where he was to be buried is called Machpelah (from the term for 'double'), for in every thing it is double, TO THE RIGHT AND TO THE LEFT, both double and single. TO WIT, THEY ARE IN NEED OF A THIRD ONE TO RECONCILE THEM. The cave too is both double and single, ABRAHAM AND ISAAC BEING ON THE RIGHT AND LEFT, AND JACOB BETWEEN THEM.

270. וְתָא חֲזֵי אַבְהָתָא זָכוֹ לְאִתְקַבְּרָא תַּמָּן, אִינוּן וְזִווּגַיְיהוּ. יַעֲקֹב הוּא וְלֵאָה, מ״ט רָחֵל לָא, וְהָא כְּתִיב וְרָחֵל עֲקָרָה, דְּאִיהִי עִקָּרָא דְּבֵיתָא. אֶלָּא, לֵאָה זָכְתָה בֵּיה, לְאַפָּקָא שִׁית שִׁבְטִין, מִגִּזְעָא קַדִּישָׁא בְּעַלְמָא יַתִּיר, וּבְגִינֵי כָּךְ, אִתְיְיהִבַת עִמֵּיה לְזִווּגָא בִּמְעַרְתָּא.

270. Come and see: The patriarchs merited to be buried in the cave of the Machpelah together with their spouses, Jacob was buried with Leah. Why was Rachel not buried with him, especially when it says, "And Rachel was barren (Heb. *akarah*)" (Beresheet 29:31), which is an indication that she was the foundation (Heb. *akarah*) of the house? HE ANSWERS: Leah had more worthy OF JACOB since she bore six tribes into the world from the holy stock. Thus, she was given to him as his spouse in the cave.

271. א״ר יְהוּדָה לֵאָה כָּל יוֹמָהָא, הֲוַת בְּפָרָשַׁת אוֹרְחִין קַיְימָא, וּבָכַת בְּגִינֵיה דְּיַעֲקֹב, כַּד שְׁמַעַת דְּאִיהוּ צַדִּיקָא, וּצְלוֹתָא אַקְדָּמַת לֵיה, וְהַיְינוּ דִּכְתִיב וְעֵינֵי לֵאָה רַכּוֹת, כְּמָה דְּאוֹקִימְנָא, דְּמְקְדְּמַת וְיָתְבַת בְּפָרָשַׁת אוֹרְחִין לְמִשְׁאַל.

271. Rabbi Yehuda said: Leah used to stand every day by the highway and weep for Jacob, THAT HE WOULD MARRY HER, for she heard he was righteous. She thus prepared herself through prayer. It says, "And Leah's eyes were weak" (Beresheet 29:16), since she rose early and sat by the highway to pray.

272. רָחֵל לָא נָפְקַת לְאוֹרְחִין לְעָלְמָא. בְּגִינֵי כָּךְ זָכְתָה לֵאָה לְאִתְקַבְּרָא עִמֵּיה. וְרָחֵל קַיְימֶת קְבוּרָתָה בְּפָרָשַׁת אוֹרְחִין וְאִתְקְבָרַת תַּמָּן, הה״ד וַאֲנִי בְּבֹאִי מִפַּדָּן מֵתָה עָלַי רָחֵל, מַהוּ עָלַי. עָלַי וַדַּאי,

כְּלוֹמַר בְּגִינִי, בְּאֶרֶץ כְּנָעַן בַּדֶּרֶך: בְּגִינִי מִיתַת בַּדֶּרֶך, דְּלָא נָפְקַת בְּגִינִי לְעָלְמִין כַּאֲחָתָה.

272. Rachel never went to the highway TO ASK TO BE MARRIED TO JACOB, LIKE LEAH DID. For this Leah was privileged to be buried with him, and Rachel is by the highway, buried there. This is the meaning of the words "And as for me, when I came from Paddan, Rachel died by me" (Beresheet 48:7). What is "by me"? It means "because of me in the land of Canaan on the way." Because of me, she died on the way, for she never went out for my sake TO PRAY like her sister.

273. בג״כ, לֵאָה דְּנָפְקַת וּבָכַת בְּפָרָשַׁת אוֹרְחִין בְּגִינֵיה דְּיַעֲקֹב, זָכְתָה לְאִתְקַבְּרָא עִמֵּיה. רָחֵל דְּלָא בָּעָאת לְמֵיפַק וּלְמִשְׁאַל בַּהֲדֵיה, בג״כ קְבוּרְתָה בְּפָרָשַׁת אוֹרְחִין. וְרָזָא דְמִלָּה, הָא אוֹקִימְנָא וְאִתְּמַר, דָּא בְּאִתְגַּלְיָא, וְדָא בְּאִתְכַּסְיָא.

273. Since Leah went and wept by the highway for Jacob, she merited to be buried with him. Rachel, who did not want to go out to pray for him, was therefore buried by the highway. The secret of this matter is that the one is disclosed and the other undisclosed.

274. וְתָא חֲזֵי , דְּתַנְיָא, דְּמַעְיָן סַגִּיאִין שָׁדִיאַת הַהִיא צַדֶּקֶת לֵאָה, בְּגִין לְמֶהֱוֵי חוּלְקֵיה דְּיַעֲקֹב, וְלָא בְּהַהוּא רָשָׁע דְּעֵשָׂו, וְהַיְינוּ דְּתָנִינָן, כָּל בַּר נָשׁ, דְּאוֹשִׁיד דִּמְעִין קַמֵּיה דְּקוּדְשָׁא בְּרִיך הוּא, אע״ג דְּאִתְגְּזַר עֲלֵיה עוֹנָשָׁא, יִתְקְרַע, וְלָא יָכִיל הַהוּא עוֹנָשָׁא לְשַׁלְטָאָה בֵּיה. מְנָלָן, מִלֵּאָה, דְּהָא לֵאָה אִתְגְּזַר לְמֶהֱוֵי חוּלְקָא דְעֵשָׂו, וְהִיא בִּבְעוּתָא אַקְדִּימַת לֵיה לְיַעֲקֹב, וְלָא אִתְיְיהִיבַת לֵיה לְעֵשָׂו.

274. Come and see: The righteous Leah shed many tears in order to be the portion of Jacob instead of that of the evil Esau. Hence, we learned that any man who sheds tears before the Holy One, blessed be He, even if punishment was already given, will have the verdict annulled, and the punishment will not have any effect upon him. Whence do we know that? From Leah, for it was decreed that Leah would be in the portion of Esau, but through her prayer she was married to Jacob, and not to Esau.

30. And the Wisdom of Solomon excelled

A Synopsis

Here we learn that during the days of King Solomon, the Malchut grew, was blessed, and attained fullness. Consequently, the wisdom of Solomon excelled that of the children of the east, who inherited their wisdom from Abraham, derived from the lower Crowns. Hadar was the only king of the east country who endured because he was composed of both male and female and he maintained the Malchut. There follows a description of the awesome form of Malchut [Female Principle] and her son Metatron, the son of Yered. We learn that the comets fastened to the hairs of the moon are the scourge by which the world is sentenced, and the nails of the Female Principle write and record the transgressions of men under strict judgment. Finally, Rabbi Chiya comments on the verse, "What profit has a man of all his labor"

The Relevance of this Passage

The wisdom of King Solomon shines into our physical world [Malchut], helping mankind achieve its final correction. Solomon's wisdom is founded upon the Three Column System, whereas the spiritual teachings of the East are based upon Two Column System, such as Yin and Yang. The third and Central Column creates resistance between the two positive and negative columns of energy, like a filament in a light bulb – that generates spiritual Light for the entire planet. This Light shines forth in this passage and helps sweeten judgments decreed against mankind.

275. אָמַר רִבִּי חִיָּיא, וְשָׁכַבְתִּי עִם אֲבוֹתַי וגו'. רִבִּי יִצְחָק פָּתַח וַאֲמַר, מַה יִּתְרוֹן לָאָדָם בְּכָל עֲמָלוֹ שֶׁיַּעֲמֹל תַּחַת הַשָּׁמֶשׁ. בְּכַמָּה אֲתַר אִתְּמָר דְּאִסְתַּכַּלְנָא בְּמִלּוֹי דִּשְׁלֹמֹה וְאִתְחֲזֵי מִלּוֹי סְתִימִין, אֲבָל כֻּלְּהוּ מִלֵּי דִשְׁלֹמֹה, כֻּלְּהוּ אִקְרוּן בְּחָכְמְתָא.

275. Rabbi Chiya said: "And I will lie with my fathers..." Rabbi Yitzchak opened the discussion with the verse, "What profit has a man of all his labor wherein he labors under the sun?" (Kohelet 1:3). We have studied several times the words of Solomon, and they do not seem to be understood, for all his words should be read with wisdom.

276. דְּתַנְיָא כְּתִיב, וַתֵּרֶב חָכְמַת שְׁלֹמֹה, בְּיוֹמוֹי דִשְׁלֹמֹה מַלְכָּא, קַיְימָא סִיהֲרָא בְּאַשְׁלָמוּתָא, וְהַיְינוּ דִכְתִיב, וַתֵּרֶב חָכְמַת שְׁלֹמֹה

מֵחָכְמַת כָּל בְּנֵי קֶדֶם, תַּמָּן תָּנִינָן, מַאן אִינוּן בְּנֵי קֶדֶם, הָא אוֹקְמוּהָ, אֲבָל חָכְמַת בְּנֵי קֶדֶם, הִיא חָכְמְתָא דְּיָרְתוּ מֵאַבְרָהָם.

276. We studied the verse, "And Solomon's Wisdom excelled" (I Melachim 5:10). During the days of King Solomon, the moon, NAMELY THE NUKVA, was in her fullness. Hence it is written, "And Solomon's Wisdom excelled the Wisdom of all the children of the east country." Regarding this, we learned who the children of the east were. It has already been explained. Nevertheless, the wisdom of the children of the east is the Wisdom they inherited from Abraham.

277. דְּתָנֵינָא כְּתִיב, וַיִּתֵּן אַבְרָהָם אֶת כָּל אֲשֶׁר לוֹ לְיִצְחָק. מַאי אֶת כָּל אֲשֶׁר לוֹ. דָּא חָכְמְתָא עִלָּאָה דַּהֲוָה יָדַע בִּשְׁמָא קַדִּישָׁא דְּקוּדְשָׁא בְּרִיךְ הוּא, וּמַשְׁמַע אֶת אֶת כָּל אֲשֶׁר לוֹ, דַּהֲוָה דִּילֵיהּ. כִּדְתָנֵינָן בְּהַהִיא בַּת דַּהֲוַת לֵיהּ לְאַבְרָהָם, וּבַכֹּל שְׁמָהּ.

277. We learned: It is written, "And Abraham gave all that he had to Isaac" (Beresheet 35:5). HE ASKS: What was "all that he had" WHICH HE GAVE TO ISAAC? HE ANSWERS: It is supernal Wisdom, for he knew the name of the Holy One, blessed be He. This may be understood from the verse: "All that he had," for the supernal Wisdom is his, in the same way we learned of the daughter he had named *Bakol* (lit. 'in everything'), THE SECRET OF THE NUKVA.

278. וְלִבְנֵי הַפִּילַגְשִׁים אֲשֶׁר לְאַבְרָהָם נָתַן אַבְרָהָם מַתָּנוֹת וגו'. דְּיַהַב לְהוּ. מִילִין יְדִיעָאן, בְּכִתְרִין תַּתָּאִין, וּבְכַאן אֲתָר אַשְׁרֵי לוֹן, אֶל אֶרֶץ קֶדֶם. וּמִתַּמָּן יָרִיתוּ בְּנֵי קֶדֶם חָכְמְתָא, וְהַיְינוּ דִכְתִיב מֵחָכְמַת כָּל בְּנֵי קֶדֶם.

278. "But to the sons of the concubines, which Abraham had, Abraham gave gifts" (Beresheet 35:6). He gave them certain knowledge from the lower crowns and settled them in the east country. From this, the children of the east country inherited Wisdom, NAMELY FROM THE LOWER CROWNS, as it is written: "The wisdom of all the children of the east country."

279. תָּאנָא יוֹמָא חַד הֲוָה אָתֵי רְבִּי שִׁמְעוֹן מִקַפּוֹטְקַיָא לְלוֹד, וַהֲוָה עִמֵיה ר׳ אַבָּא, וְר׳ יְהוּדָה, ר׳ אַבָּא הֲוָה לָאֵי, וַהֲוָה רָהִיט אֲבַתְרֵיה דְּר׳ שִׁמְעוֹן, דַּהֲוָה רָכֵיב, אֲמַר רְבִּי אַבָּא, וַדַּאי אַחֲרֵי ה׳ יֵלְכוּ כְּאַרְיֵה יִשְׁאָג.

279. We learned that one day Rabbi Shimon came from Cappadocia to Lod. Rabbi Aba and Rabbi Yehuda came with him. Rabbi Aba was tired running after Rabbi Shimon who was mounted. He said: "They shall walk after Hashem, who shall roar like a lion" (Hoshea 11:10).

280. נָחַת ר׳ שִׁמְעוֹן, א״ל, וַדַּאי כְּתִיב, וָאֵשֵׁב בָּהָר אַרְבָּעִים יוֹם וְאַרְבָּעִים לַיְלָה, וַדַּאי חָכְמְתָא לָא מִתְיַישְׁבָא, אֶלָּא כַּד ב״נ יָתֵיב, וְלָא אָזֵיל, אֶלָּא קָאֵים בְּקִיּוּמֵיה. וְהָא אוֹקִימְנָא מִלֵּי עַל מַה כְּתִיב וָאֵשֵׁב. הַשְׁתָּא בְּנַייחָא תַּלְיָיא מִילְתָא. יָתְבוּ.

280. Rabbi Shimon dismounted and said to him: Indeed it is written, "Then I abode in the mountain forty days and forty nights" (Devarim 9:9). Surely wisdom does not settle upon man when he walks but when he just sits down. We have already explained why it says, "I abode (or: 'sat')" and now we should rest. They sat down.

281. אֲמַר רְבִּי אַבָּא, כְּתִיב וַתֵּרֶב חָכְמַת שְׁלֹמֹה מֵחָכְמַת כָּל בְּנֵי קֶדֶם וּמִכָּל חָכְמַת מִצְרָיִם. מַאי הִיא חָכְמַת שְׁלֹמֹה. וּמַאי הִיא חָכְמַת מִצְרָיִם. וּמַאי הִיא חָכְמַת כָּל בְּנֵי קֶדֶם. א״ל תָּא חֲזֵי בְּכַמָּה אֲתַר אוֹקְמוּהָ בְּהַהוּא שְׁמָא, דְּסִיהֲרָא כַּד אִתְבָּרְכָא מִכֹּלָּא, כְּתִיב וַתֵּרֶב. בְּיוֹמוֹי דִשְׁלֹמֹה, דְּאִתְרְבִיאַת וְאִתְבָּרְכַת וְקַיְימָא בְּאַשְׁלָמוּתָא.

281. Rabbi Aba said: It is written: "And Solomon's Wisdom excelled the Wisdom of all the children of the east country and all the Wisdom of Egypt." What is the Wisdom of Solomon, the Wisdom of Egypt and the Wisdom of the east country? He said to him, Come and behold: we have explained in several places in regard to the name of the moon, NAMELY THE NUKVA. When She is blessed by all THE SFIROT, it is written "excelled." THIS WAS SAID in the days of Solomon, THE NUKVA grew and was blessed and reached her fullness.

282. וְתָנֵינָן, אֶלֶף טוּרִין מִתְרַבְרְבִין קַמָּהּ, וְכֻלְּהוּ נְשִׁיבָא חַד הֲוִוֹ לְקַמָּהּ. אֶלֶף נַהֲרִין סַגִּיאִין לָהּ, וּבִגְמִיעָא חֲדָא גָּמְעָא לוֹן.

282. We have learned that a thousand mountains grow GRASS before her, and she swallows them in one bite; a thousand great rivers she has, which she swallows in one gulp.

283. טוּפְרָהָא מֵאַחֲדָא לְאֶלֶף וְשַׁבְעִין עֵיבַר. יְדָהָא אֲחִידָן, לְאַרְבַּע וְעֶשְׂרִין אֶלֶף עֵיבַר, לֵית דְּנָפֵיק מִנָּה לְסִטַר הַאי, וְלֵית דְּנָפֵיק מִנָּה לְסִטַר אָחֳרָא. כַּמָּה וְכַמָּה אֶלֶף תְּרֵיסִין, מִתְאַחֲדִין בְּשַׂעֲרָהָא.

283. Her nails reach 1,070 directions, her hands hold four and twenty directions. None escapes her to the RIGHT side and none escapes her to the LEFT side, BUT THROUGH THE MIDDLE. Many thousands of shields cling to her hairs.

284. עוּלֵימָא, דְּאוֹרְכֵּיה מֵרֵישָׁא דְעָלְמָא, לְסֵיְיפֵי דְעָלְמָא, נָפֵיק בֵּין רַגְלָהָא, בְּשִׁתִּין פּוּלְסֵי דְנוּרָא מִתְלַבֵּשׁ, בְּגַוְוֹנֵי דָא אִתְמַנָּא עַל תַּתָּאֵי מֵאַרְבַּע סִטְרָהָא. דָּא אִיהוּ נַעַר, דְּאָחֵיד שִׁית מְאָה וּתְלַת עֲשַׂר מַפְתְּחָן עִלָּאִין, מִסִּטְרָא דְאִמָּא, וְכֻלְּהוּ מַפְתְּחָן עִלָּאִין, בְּשִׁנָּנָא דְחַרְבָּא דַחֲגֵיר בְּחַרְצֵיה תַּלְיָין.

284. A youth, whose height is from the top of the world to its bottom, NAMELY METATRON, WHOSE HEIGHT IS FROM THE HEAD OF BRIYAH TO THE BOTTOM OF ASIYAH, comes from between her legs, NETZACH AND HOD OF THE NUKVA, clothed in sixty clubs of fire, BY WHICH HE DRIVES AWAY THE EXTERNAL FORCES SO THEY WOULD NOT CLING TO THE LEGS OF THE NUKVA. In this way, he is in charge over the lower beings of the four sides. This is the youth, who holds 613 upper keys on the side of Ima. All the supernal keys dangle from the sharp sword girded about his waist.

285. הַהוּא נַעַר, קָרוֹן לֵיה חֲנוֹךְ בֶּן יֶרֶד, בְּאִינוּן בְּרַיְיתֵי, דִּכְתִיב חֲנוֹךְ לַנַּעַר עַל פִּי דַרְכּוֹ. וְאִי תֵימָא מַתְנִיתִין הִיא, וְלָא בְּרַיְיתָא, בְּמַתְנִיתָא

דִּילָן אוֹקִימְנָא מִילֵי, וְהָא אִתְּמָר, וְכֹלָּא מִלְּתָא חֲדָא אִסְתַּכָּלוּ. תְּחוֹתֵיה תִּטְלַל חֵיוַת בְּרָא, דְּתַנְיָא, כְּמָה דְיִשְׂרָאֵל קַדִּישָׁא עִלָּאָה, אִקְרֵי בֵּן לְאִמֵּיה, דִּכְתִיב כִּי בֵן הָיִיתִי לְאָבִי רַךְ וְיָחִיד לִפְנֵי אִמִּי, וּכְתִיב בְּנִי בְכוֹרִי יִשְׂרָאֵל, הָכֵי נָמֵי לְתַתָּא, דָּא אִקְרֵי נַעַר לְאִמֵּיה, דִּכְתִיב כִּי נַעַר יִשְׂרָאֵל וָאוֹהֲבֵהוּ. וּבְכַמָּה גְוָונִין אִקְרֵי בֶּן יָרֶד, וְהָא אוֹקִימְנָא. אֲבָל תָּא חֲזֵי בֶּן יֶרֶד מַמָּשׁ, דְּתָנִינָן, עֶשֶׂר יְרִידוֹת יָרְדָה שְׁכִינָה לְאַרְעָא, וְכֻלְּהוּ אוֹקִמוּהָ חַבְרַיָּיא וְאִתְּמָר. וּתְחוֹת הַאי, כְּמָה חֵיוָתָא קָיְימִין, דְּאִקְרוּן חֵיוַת בְּרָא מַמָּשׁ.

285. This youth is called Chanoch the son of Yered in the Baraita, as it is written: "Train up (Heb. *chanoch*) a youth in the way he should go" (Mishlei 22:6). It may be said it is written in the Mishnah, not in the Baraita. Yet we explained it when studying the Mishnah, and this has been explained. They all looked into the same thing. Under HIS SHADE, the beasts of the field shall find shelter; NAMELY THE ANGELS OF YETZIRAH we learned of, like Supernal Holy Yisrael - NAMELY ZEIR ANPIN, called 'the son of his mother', BINAH. It is written, "For I was my father's son, tender and the only one in the sight of my mother" (Mishlei 4:3), and "Yisrael is My son, My firstborn" (Shemot 4:22), WHICH REFERS TO ZEIR ANPIN. Underneath ATZILUT, METATRON too is called the son of his mother, THE NUKVA, as it is written "Yisrael was a youth, then I loved him" (Hoshea 11:1), WHICH REFERS TO METATRON. He was named the son of Yered for several reasons, NAMELY, NOW TO SHAME HIM AND NOW TO RECOMMEND, as we have already explained. Yet come and behold: HERE WE SPEAK OF the very son of Yered (lit. 'descent'), for we have learned that the Shechinah descended to the earth by ten steps (Heb. *yeridot*), all of them explained by the friends. Underneath, several living creatures are standing; NAMELY THE ANGELS OF YETZIRAH, which are called the very beasts of the field.

286. תְּחוֹת אִינוּן חֵיוָותָא, מִתְאַחֲדָן שַׁעֲרָתָא דְּסִיהֲרָא, דְּאִקְרוּן כְּכָבַיָּא דְּשַׁרְבִיטָא, דְּשַׁרְבִיט מַמָּשׁ, מָארֵי דְּמָדִין, מָארֵי דְּמַתְקְלָא, מָארֵי דְּקַשְׁיוּ, מָארֵי דְחוּצְפָּא. וְכֻלְּהוּ אִקְרוּן מָארֵי דְאַרְגְּוָונָא, יְדָהָא וְרַגְלָהָא אֲחִידָן בְּהַאי, כְּאַרְיֵה תַּקִּיפָא דְּאָחִיד עַל טַרְפֵּיה, וְעַ״ד כְּתִיב וְטָרַף וְאֵין מַצִּיל.

286. Under these living creatures are fastened the hairs of the moon, THE
NUKVA, called the comets (Heb. *shevet*), a very scourge (Heb. *shevet*); TO
WIT, THEY ARE CONSIDERED THE SCOURGE WITH WHICH THE WORLD IS
SENTENCED. THEY ARE DIVIDED INTO the accusers, the weighty, those of
strict JUDGMENT, and the impudent. They are all called hairy. Her hands
and feet hold on to it like a mighty lion holding its prey, of which it says
"and tears in pieces, and none can deliver" (Michah 5:7).

287. טוּפְרָהָא: כָּל אִינוּן דְּאַדְכְּרִין חוֹבֵי בְּנֵי נָשָׁא, וְכָתְבִין וְרָשְׁמִין
חוֹבַיְיהוּ, בִּתְקִיפוּ דְּדִינָא קַשְׁיָא, וְעַ"ד כְּתִיב חַטַּאת יְהוּדָה כְּתוּבָה בְּעֵט
בַּרְזֶל בְּצִפּוֹרֶן שָׁמִיר. מַהוּ שָׁמִיר. הַהוּא דְּרָשִׁים וְנָקִיב אַבְנָא, וּפָסֵיק לָה
לְכָל סִטְרָא.

287. Her nails are the ones who call to mind the sins of men, who write and
record their transgression under strict judgment. Of this says the verse: "The
sin of Judah is written with a pen of iron, and with the point of a diamond"
(Yirmeyah 17:1). What is the diamond? HE ANSWERS: That which imprints
and carves the stone, and hews in it on all sides.

288. זוּהֲמָא דְּטוֹפְרָהָא: כָּל אִינוּן דְּלָא מִתְדַּבְּקִין בְּגוּפָא דְּמַלְכָּא,
וְיָנְקִין מִסִּטְרָא דִּמְסָאֲבוּתָא, כַּד שָׁאֲרֵי סִיהֲרָא בִּפְגִימוּ.

288. The filth of the nails REFERS TO those who do not cleave to the body
of the King, THE CENTRAL COLUMN, BUT CLEAVE TO THE LEFT and suck
from the side of defilement when the moon is diminished, TO WIT, WHEN
THE ABUNDANCE THEN DRAWN FROM THE NAILS PASSES TO THE SIDE OF
DEFILEMENT, AND CONSIDERED THE FILTH OF THE NAILS.

289. וּבְגִין דִּשְׁלֹמֹה מַלְכָּא יָרְתָא לְסִיהֲרָא בִּשְׁלֵימוּתָא, בָּעֵי לְיָרְתָא לָה
בִּפְגִימוּתָא, וְעַ"ד אִשְׁתַּדַּל לְמֵידַע, בְּדַעְתָּא דְּרוּחִין וְשֵׁדִין, לְמֵירַת
סִיהֲרָא בְּכָל סִטְרָא.

289. Since King Solomon inherited the moon at her fullness, THE NUKVA IN
GREATNESS, he ought to inherit her when she is defective. He therefore
strove to know about the spirits and demons, in order to receive the moon,
THE NUKVA, in all her aspects.

290. וּבְיוֹמוֹי דִשְׁלֹמֹה מַלְכָּא, בְּכֹלָּא אִתְנְהֵיר סִיהֲרָא, הה״ד וַתֵּרֶב חָכְמַת שְׁלֹמֹה, וַתֶּרֶב דַּיְיקָא. מֵחָכְמַת כָּל בְּנֵי קֶדֶם, רָזָא עִלָּאָה הוּא, כְּמָה דִכְתִיב, וְאֵלֶּה הַמְּלָכִים אֲשֶׁר מָלְכוּ בְּאֶרֶץ אֱדוֹם וְגוֹ'. וְאִלֵּין אִקְרוּן בְּנֵי קֶדֶם, דְּכֻלְּהוּ לָא אִתְקַיְימוּ, בַּר מֵהַאי דִכְלִילָא דְּכַר וְנוּקְבָא, דְּאִקְרֵי הֲדַר, דִּכְתִיב וַיִּמְלֹךְ תַּחְתָּיו הֲדַר וְגו'.

290. In the days of King Solomon, the moon shone from all the grades, as it is written: "And Solomon's Wisdom excelled (also: 'increased')," meaning that it was greater than the Wisdom of all the children of the east country SINCE IT WAS INCLUDED WITHIN THE NUKVA, AND ALSO THE WISDOM OF EGYPT WAS COMPRISED IN IT AND THE WISDOM OF THE CHILDREN OF THE EAST. This is a supernal secret, in accordance with the verse, "And these are the kings that reigned in the land of Edom" (Beresheet 36:31). They were all called the children of the east country. None of them endured except he who was comprised of male and female, who was called Hadar. For it says, "And Hadar reigned in his place...AND HIS WIFE'S NAME..." (Ibid. 39). BUT NO WOMAN WAS MENTIONED IN RELATION TO THE OTHER KINGS.

291. וְתָאנָא, דְּאע״ג דְּאִתְקַיְּימַת, לָא אִתְנְהֵירַת בְּאַשְׁלָמוּתָא, עַד דַּאֲתָא שְׁלֹמֹה, דְּאִתְחֲזֵי לְקַבְלָהָא, כְּמָה דְּאוֹקִימְנָא, דְּבג״כ אִמֵּיהּ בַּת שֶׁבַע הֲוַת.

291. We have learned that though the Nukva was maintained BY KING HADAR, she nevertheless did not illuminate wholly until the time of King Solomon, who was worthy of her, as we explained, for his mother was Bathsheba (lit. 'daughter of seven,') TO WIT, THE NUKVA WAS CALLED IN HER GREATNESS DAUGHTER OF SEVEN, SINCE SHE INCLUDES CHESED, GVURAH, TIFERET, NETZACH, HOD, YESOD AND MALCHUT OF ZEIR ANPIN, BEING HIS MOTHER. HE WAS THEREFORE WORTHY OF INHERITING HER IN HER DAYS OF GREATNESS.

292. וּמִכָּל חָכְמַת מִצְרָיִם: דָּא חָכְמָה תַּתָּאָה, דְּאִקְרֵי שֶׁפְחָה דְּבָתַר רֵיחַיָא, וְכֹלָּא אִתְכְּלִילַת הַאי חָכְמָה דִשְׁלֹמֹה, חָכְמַת בְּנֵי קֶדֶם, וְחָכְמַת מִצְרָיִם. א״ר אַבָּא, בְּרִיךְ רַחֲמָנָא, דְּשָׁאֵילְנָא קַמָּךְ מִלָּה דָא, דְּהָא בְּכָל הַנֵּי מִילֵי זָכֵינָא. אֲמַר ר״ש, מִלִּין אִלֵּין, הָא אוֹקִימְנָא לוֹן, וְהָא אִתְּמָרוּ.

292. "And all the Wisdom of Egypt." This is the lower Wisdom called 'the maid behind the millstones.' The Wisdom of Solomon included everything, the Wisdom of the children of the east country together with the Wisdom of Egypt. Rabbi Aba said: Blessed be the Merciful One, that I have asked about it, and so merited all these words. Rabbi Shimon said: I have explained this subject, and we already interpreted it.

293. תָּאנָא, מַה יִּתְרוֹן לְאָדָם בְּכָל עֲמָלוֹ, יָכוֹל אַף עֲמָלָה דְאוֹרַיְיתָא, ת"ל שֶׁיַּעֲמוֹל תַּחַת הַשֶּׁמֶשׁ. שָׁאנֵי עֲמָלָה דְאוֹרַיְיתָא, דְּלְעֵילָא מִן שִׁמְשָׁא הוּא. רִבִּי חִיָּיא אָמַר, אַף עֲמָלָה דְאוֹרַיְיתָא, דְּאִיהוּ עָמָל בְּגִינֵיהוֹן דִּבְנֵי נָשָׁא, אוֹ בְּגִין יְקָרָא דִילֵיה, הַאי תַּחַת הַשֶּׁמֶשׁ כְּתִיב, דְּהָא לָא סָלֵיק לְעֵילָא. תַּנְיָא אָמַר ר' אֶלְעָזָר, אֲפִילוּ אִי ב"נ קַיָּים אֶלֶף שְׁנִין, הַהוּא יוֹמָא דְאִסְתַּלַּק מֵעַלְמָא, דָּמֵי לֵיה כְּאִילוּ לָא אִתְקַיַּים בַּר יוֹמָא חַד.

293. We learned: "What profit has a man of all his labor wherein he labors" (Kohelet 1:3). One may say that this is true also for laboring in the Torah. Yet it is said "wherein he labors under the sun," and the labor in the Torah is different by being above the sun, OF THE SUPERNAL ONES. Rabbi Chiya said: This is true also for the Torah, THE WORDS "WHAT PROFIT…" if it is done for the sake of people or to gain respect. Of this, it is said "under the sun," for this study of the Torah does not ascend. We learned that Rabbi Elazar said: Even if a man lives to a thousand years, on the day he departs from the world, it would seem to him as if he lived but one day.

31. "And I will lie with my fathers"

A Synopsis

Rabbi Yehuda begins by explaining the significance of each day with or without sin for the individual. We learn that if man sins and repents, that day returns to its place. However, if he does not repent, that day ascends to bear testimony to this sin, then descends, joins with the spirit outside, and brings evil to that man. At the end of his days, man's soul is clothed with the days in which he did not sin. If there are none, he is sentenced to Gehenom, wherein he is punished two days for each day of sin.

We learn that Adam repented for his great sin, although he did not completely repair the damage his sin caused. Therefore, the Lord accepted his repentance and clothed him with garments that were not made from his days. In contrast, Abraham wore a complete raiment of glory when he departed this world, since he merited it. Jacob also merited to be clothed in his own days. Indeed, his garments were scented with the perfume of the Female Principle, as signified by the verse, "And he smelled the smell of his garments" Rabbi Elazar then explains to Rabbi Yehuda that three garments are made for man from his days. These are worn by the Ruach, the Neshamah, and the Nefesh. Rabbi Elazar explains the relationship between, and the significance of, these bodies.

Rabbi Shimon directs the final portion of the discussion. He says that the companions of Babylon listen and learn from him, but do not share these matters with others. The reason for this, we are told, is that they are outside the Holy Land and do not draw from Holiness. Rabbi Shimon then warns us of the time when people abandon the study of the Torah and the scrolls are moved. Without the wisdom of the scholars and without the righteous to arouse the souls to pray for the living, the people of the world will be punished by the accusers – unless all people do penance for their sins. Rabbi Yehuda explains that when the world is in distress and is in need of mercy, the scroll of the Torah must be stirred. Then, the Nefesh informs the Ruach, the Ruach the Neshamah, and lastly, the Neshamah informs the Holy One. The Lord then draws the crystal dew to flow upon the sleeping patriarchs who join in and pray for the world. Only then does the Lord have mercy on the world.

The Relevance of this Passage

Each day in our lives presents us with opportunities to fulfill our personal spiritual mission in life and complete our transformation. Unfortunately, most people fail to realize the meaning of life and the purpose of their existence. Each lost opportunity creates a negative blockage that diminishes and dims the Light of The Creator in our lives. It is within this expanding darkness that turmoil, hardship, pain, and suffering are born. Thus, it behooves a man to awaken to the spiritual truths of his existence, so that he may develop himself spiritually. This passage ignites that awareness in our consciousness. It helps to remove the negative blockages and darkness created by our lack of action in previous times, while arousing penitence in our hearts for our unkind behavior. Moreover, the Light of the Torah is set aflame, drawing to us both mercy and protection.

294. וְשָׁכַבְתִּי עִם אֲבֹתַי, זַכָּאָה חוּלְקֵהוֹן דַּאֲבָהָתָא, דְּקוּדְשָׁא בְּרִיךְ הוּא עָבֵיד לוֹן רְתִיכָא קַדִּישָׁא לְעֵילָּא, וְאִתְרְעֵי בְהוּ, לְאִתְעַטְּרָא עִמְּהוֹן, הֲהָ"ד רַק בַּאֲבוֹתֶיךָ חָשַׁק ה' וְגוֹ'. א"ר אֶלְעָזָר, יַעֲקֹב הֲוָה יָדַע, דְּהָא עִטּוּרָא דִּילֵיהּ בַּאֲבָהָתֵיהּ הוּא, דְּהָא עִטּוּרָא דַאֲבָהָן עִמֵּיהּ הוּא, וְהוּא עִמְּהוֹן. וְעַל דָּא בְּאַתְוָון גְּלִיפִין תָּנֵינָן, תְּלַת קִשְׁרִין, תְּרֵין קִשְׁרִין חַד מֵהַאי סִטְרָא, וְחַד מֵהַאי סִטְרָא, וְחַד דְּכָלֵיל לוֹן. וְדָא הוּא דְּתָנֵינָן, וְהַבְּרִיחַ הַתִּיכוֹן בְּתוֹךְ הַקְּרָשִׁים מַבְרִיחַ מִן הַקָּצֶה אֶל הַקָּצֶה, וְהַהוּא קִשְׁרָא דִּבְאֶמְצָעִיתָא, אָחִיד לְהַאי סִטְרָא, וּלְהַאי סִטְרָא. וְעַל הַאי כְּתִיב, וְשָׁכַבְתִּי עִם אֲבֹתַי וַדַּאי.

294. "And I will lie with my fathers" (Beresheet 47:30). Happy is the portion of the patriarchs, for the Holy One, blessed be He, made them into a Holy Chariot, and desired to be crowned with them. Hence it is written, "Only in your fathers Hashem took delight..." (Devarim 10:15). Rabbi Elazar said: Jacob knew that he was to be crowned by his fathers for they would be crowned with him, and he with them. We learned regarding the engraved letters THAT SHIN HAS three knots, two knots on both sides, RIGHT AND LEFT, and one knot that binds them together, THE MIDDLE ONE. This we learned from the verse: "And the middle bar in the midst of the boards shall reach from end to end" (Shemot 26:28), that the knot in the middle is attached to the RIGHT side and the LEFT side. Hence it says, "And I will lie with my fathers."

295. וְשָׁכַבְתִּי עִם אֲבֹתַי וְגוֹ', רִבִּי יְהוּדָה פָּתַח וַאֲמַר, הַחֵרְשִׁים שְׁמָעוּ וְהַעִוְרִים הַבִּיטוּ לִרְאוֹת. הַחֵרְשִׁים שְׁמָעוּ, אִלֵּין בְּנֵי נָשָׁא, דְּלָא צַיְיתִין

לְמִלּוּלֵי אוֹרַיְיתָא, וְלָא פָּקְחִין אוּדְנַיְיהוּ, לְמִשְׁמַע לְפִקּוּדֵי דְמָארֵיהוֹן. וְהָעִוְרִים: דְּלָא מִסְתַּכְּלִין לְמִנְדַע עַל מָה אִינוּן קַיְימִין, דְּהָא בְּכָל יוֹמָא וְיוֹמָא כָּרוֹזָא נָפֵיק וְקָרֵי, וְלֵית מַאן דְּיַשְׁגַּח.

295. "And I will lie with my fathers." Rabbi Yehuda opened the discussion with the verse, "Hear, O deaf; and look, O blind, that you may see" (Yeshayah 42:18). "Hear, O deaf" refers to the men who neither listen to the words of the Torah, nor open their ears to hearken the precepts of their Master. The blind are those who do not look to know wherefore they live. For every day, a crier comes and proclaims, yet no one pays attention.

296. דְּתַנְיָא, אִינוּן יוֹמִין דְּב״נ כַּד אִתְבְּרֵי, בְּהַהוּא יוֹמָא דְּנָפַק לְעַלְמָא, כֻּלְּהוּ קַיְימִין בְּקִיּוּמַיְיהוּ, וְאָזְלִין וְטָאסִין בְּעַלְמָא, נָחֲתִין וְאַזְהֲרָן לב״נ, כָּל יוֹמָא וְיוֹמָא בִּלְחוֹדוֹי, וְכַד הַהוּא יוֹמָא אָתֵי, וְאַזְהַר לֵיהּ, וּבַר נָשׁ עָבֵיד בְּהַהוּא יוֹמָא, חוֹבָא קַמֵּי מָארֵיהּ, הַהוּא יוֹמָא סָלֵיק בְּכִסּוּפָא, וְאַסְהֵיד סַהֲדוּתָא, וְקָאִים בִּלְחוֹדוֹי לְבַר.

296. We have learned that those days already exist from the day man was born into the world, FOR THEY ARE REAL ILLUMINATIONS, FROM WHICH MAN'S DAYS ARE DRAWN. They go about the world and descend to warn man, each day in its turn. When the day comes to warn the man, yet the man commits a sin on that day before his Master, it ascends shamefacedly and bears testimony on him, and stands outside alone.

297. וְתָאנָא, בָּתַר דְּקָאִים בִּלְחוֹדוֹי, יָתֵיב, עַד דְּבַר נָשׁ עָבֵיד מִנֵּיהּ תְּשׁוּבָה. זָכָה, תָּב הַהוּא יוֹמָא לְאַתְרֵיהּ. לָא זָכָה, הַהוּא יוֹמָא נָחֵית, וְאִשְׁתַּתַּף בְּהַהוּא רוּחָא דִּלְבַר, וְתָב לְבֵיתֵיהּ, וְאִתְתַּקַּן בְּדִיּוּקְנֵיהּ דְּהַהוּא בַּר נָשׁ מַמָּשׁ, בְּגִין לְאַבְאָשָׁא לֵיהּ, וְדַיָּיר עִמֵּיהּ בְּבֵיתָא. וְאִית דִּדִיּוּרָא לְטַב אִי הוּא זָכֵי. וְאִי לָאו, דִּיּוּרֵיהּ עִמֵּיהּ לְבִישׁ.

297. We have learned that after it was put to stand alone OUTSIDE, it sits and waits for the man to repent HIS SIN. If the man repented, the day returns to its place; but if he did not merit AND ATONES, the day descends, joins the spirit outside and comes back to his house, putting on the same appearance as the man to bring evil upon him. THE DAY sits with him in his house, and if he has the merit TO REPENT, it brings him good, but if not, it brings him evil.

298. בֵּין כָּךְ וּבֵין כָּךְ, אִתְפַּקְדָן אִינּוּן יוֹמִין וַחֲסֵרִים, וְלָא עָאלִין בְּמִנְיָינָא דְּאִינּוּן דְּאִשְׁתְּאָרוּ. וַוי לְהַהוּא בַּר נָשׁ, דְּגָרַע יוֹמוֹי קַמֵּי מַלְכָּא קַדִּישָׁא, וְלָא שָׁבֵיק לְעֵילָּא יוֹמִין, לְאִתְעַטְּרָא בְּהוֹ בְּהַהוּא עָלְמָא, וּלְאִתְקָרְבָא בַּהֲדַיְיהוּ קַמֵּי מַלְכָּא קַדִּישָׁא.

298. In either case, when that man's days are accounted they are in want, and those are not numbered because of the sins. Woe to the man who diminished the number of his days before the Holy King, and has no days above with which to be crowned in that world, to approach the Holy King.

299. תָּא חֲזֵי, כַּד קְרִיבוּ אִינּוּן יוֹמִין קַמֵּי מַלְכָּא קַדִּישָׁא, אִי הוּא זַכָּאָה, הַאי, בַּר נָשׁ דְּנָפֵיק מֵעַלְמָא, סָלֵיק וְעָאל בְּאִינּוּן יוֹמִין, וְאִינּוּן לְבוּשֵׁי יְקָר, דְּמִתְלַבְּשָׁא בֵּיהּ נִשְׁמָתֵיהּ. וְאִינּוּן יוֹמִין הֲווֹ, דְּזָכָה בְּהוֹ, וְלָא חָב בְּהוּ.

299. Come and see: When those days come before the Holy King, if the man who passed away from the world be righteous, he ascends and comes in with these days that are the raiments of glory in which his soul is clothed. For he merited these days, by not committing any sin therein.

300. וַוי לְהַהוּא דְּגָרַע יוֹמוֹי לְעֵילָּא, דְּכַד בָּעָאן לְאַלְבָּשָׁא לֵיהּ בְּיוֹמוֹי, אִינּוּן יוֹמִין דְּפָגֵים אִיהוּ בְּחוֹבוֹי, חָסְרִין מֵהַהוּא לְבוּשָׁא, וְאִתְלַבַּשׁ בְּמָנָא חֲסֵרָא. כ״שׁ אִי סַגִּיאִין אִינּוּן, וְלָא לְהֱוֵי לֵיהּ לְב״נ בַּמֶּה דְּאִתְלַבַּשׁ בְּהַהוּא עָלְמָא, כְּדֵין וַוי לֵיהּ, וַוי לְנַפְשֵׁיהּ, דְּדַיְיְנִין לֵיהּ בְּגֵיהִנֹּם, עַל אִינּוּן יוֹמִין, יוֹמִין עַל יוֹמִין, יוֹמִין עַל חַד תְּרֵין. דְּכַד נָפֵיק מֵהַאי עָלְמָא, לָא אַשְׁכַּח יוֹמִין דְּאִתְלַבַּשׁ בְּהוֹ, וְלָא הֲוֵי לֵיהּ לְבוּשָׁא בַּמֶּה דְּאִתְכַּסֵּי. זַכָּאִין אִינּוּן צַדִּיקַיָּא, דְּיוֹמֵיהוֹן כֻּלְּהוֹן טְמִירִין אִינּוּן לְגַבֵּיהּ דְּמַלְכָּא קַדִּישָׁא, וְאִתְעֲבֵיד מִנַּיְיהוּ לְבוּשֵׁי יְקָר, לְאִתְלַבְּשָׁא בְּהוֹ,

בְּעַלְמָא דְּאָתֵי.

300. Woe to the man who reduced the number of his days above. For when he is to don his days, the days he spoilt by his sins are missing from that garment, and he wears a defective costume. All the more so if they are many, THE DAYS WHICH WERE SPOILT, and that man has nothing to be clad in that world. Woe to him, woe to his soul, for he is sentenced to Gehenom on account of these days, days upon days; HE IS PUNISHED TWO days for every SINGLE day. When he departs from the world he finds no day in which to be clad, and has no garment or covering. Happy are the righteous, whose days are all stored with the Holy King, and made into raiments of glory to don in the World to Come.

301. תָּנִינָן בְּרָזָא דְּמַתְנִיתִין, מַאי דִּכְתִיב, וַיֵּדְעוּ כִּי עֵרוּמִּים הֵם, יְדִיעָה יָדְעֵי מַמָּשׁ, דְּהַהוּא לְבוּשָׁא דִּיקָר, דְּאִתְעֲבֵיד מֵאִינּוּן יוֹמִין, גָּרַע מִנַּיְיהוּ, וְלָא אִשְׁתְּאַר יוֹמָא מֵאִינּוּן יוֹמִין לְאִתְלַבְּשָׁא בֵּיהּ. הה"ד גָּלְמִי רָאוּ עֵינֶיךָ וְעַל סִפְרְךָ כֻּלָּם יִכָּתֵבוּ. יָמִים יוּצָרוּ. יָמִים יוּצָרוּ וַדַּאי, וְלֹא אֶחָד בָּהֶם, דְּהָא לָא אִשְׁתְּאַר חַד מִנַּיְיהוּ לְאִתְלַבְּשָׁא בְּהוֹ. עַד דְּאִשְׁתַּדַּל אָדָם, וְעָבַד תְּשׁוּבָה, וְקוּדְשָׁא בְּרִיךְ הוּא קַבִּיל לֵיהּ, וְעָבֵיד לֵיהּ מָאנָא לְבוּשָׁא אָחֳרָנִין, וְלָא מִן יוֹמוֹי, הה"ד וַיַּעַשׂ ה' אֱלֹקִים לְאָדָם וּלְאִשְׁתּוֹ כָּתְנוֹת עוֹר וַיַּלְבִּישֵׁם.

301. We have studied according to the secret of the Mishnah, the words, "And they knew that they were naked" (Beresheet 3:7). They knew exactly that the raiment of glory made of the days was impaired, and no day was left in which to be clad. Hence it says, "Your eyes did see my unshaped flesh; for in Your book all things are written, the days also in which they are to be fashioned" (Tehilim 139:16), WHICH ALLUDES TO ADAM. "The days...to be fashioned" FOR HIM TO WEAR, "and for it too there was one of them" (Ibid.), for he had none left in which to be clad. Then, Adam strove to repent and the Holy One, blessed be He, accepted his repentance and formed for him another vessel and garment, not made from his days BECAUSE HE DID NOT COMPLETELY REPAIR BY HIS ATONEMENT THE SIN OF THE TREE OF KNOWLEDGE OF GOOD AND EVIL. Hence it says, "For the man also and for his wife did Hashem Elohim make coats of skins, and clothed them" (Beresheet 3:21).

302. תָּא חֲזֵי, בְּאַבְרָהָם דִּזְכָה, מַה כְּתִיב בָּא בַּיָּמִים, מִשּׁוּם דִּזְכָה. כַּד אִסְתַּלַּק מֵהַאי עָלְמָא, בְּאִינּוּן יוֹמִין מַמָּשׁ דִּילֵיהּ, עָאל וְאִתְלַבַּשׁ בְּהוּ, וְלָא גָּרַע מֵהַהוּא לְבוּשׁ יְקָר כְּלוּם, דִּכְתִיב בָּא בַּיָּמִים. בְּאִיּוֹב מַה כְּתִיב, וַיֹּאמֶר עָרֹם יָצָאתִי מִבֶּטֶן אִמִּי וְעָרֹם אָשׁוּב שָׁמָּה, דְּהָא לָא אִשְׁתְּאַר לְבוּשָׁא לְאִתְלַבְּשָׁא בֵּיהּ.

302. Come and see the merit of Abraham. It is written, "And Abraham... came with days" (Beresheet 24:1). Since he had the merit, when he departed from this world, he came with his own days and wore them. Nothing was lacking in that raiment of glory, as it says "came with days." Of Job it says, "Naked I came out of my mother's womb and naked I shall return there" (Iyov 1:21), for nothing was left for him to wear.

303. תָּנָא, זַכָּאִין אִינּוּן צַדִּיקַיָּא, דְּיוֹמֵיהוֹן זַכָּאִין, וְאִשְׁתְּאָרוּ לְעָלְמָא דְּאָתֵי, וְכַד נָפְקִין, מִתְחַבְּרָן כֻּלְּהוּ, וְאִתְעֲבִידוּ לְבוּשֵׁי יְקָר, לְאִתְלַבְּשָׁא בֵּיהּ, וּבְהַהוּא לְבוּשָׁא, זַכָּאן לְאִתְעַנְּגָא מֵעֲנוּגָא דְּעָלְמָא דְּאָתֵי, וּבְהַהוּא לְבוּשָׁא, זְמִינִין לְאַחֲיָיא וּלְמֵיקַם. וְכָל אִינּוּן דְּאִית לְהוּ לְבוּשָׁא יְקוּמוּן, הה"ד וַיִּתְיַצְבוּ כְּמוֹ לְבוּשׁ. וַוי לְאִינּוּן חַיָּיבֵי עָלְמָא, דְּיוֹמֵיהוֹן בְּחוֹבֵיהוֹן חַסְרִין, וְלָא אִשְׁתְּאַר מִנַּיְיהוּ, בַּמֶּה דְּאִתְכַּסְיָין, כַּד יִפְקוּן מֵעַלְמָא.

303. We learned that happy are the righteous, whose days are clean FROM SINS and remain for the World to Come. Upon leaving THIS WORLD, they all join together and turn into a raiment of glory to be clothed in. In this raiment, they can be delighted with the pleasure of the World to Come. Through the garment, they will rise into the world AT THE RESURRECTION FROM THE DEAD. All those with a raiment will rise, as it says, "And they stand as a garment" (Iyov 38:14). Woe to the wicked in the world, whose days were diminished through sins, and nothing is left from them to be covered with when they leave this world.

304. תָּאנָא, כָּל אִינוּן זַכָּאִין, דְּזָכוּ לְאִתְלַבְּשָׁא בִּלְבוּשׁ יְקָר בְּיוֹמֵיהוֹן, מִתְעַטְּרָן בְּהַהוּא עָלְמָא, מֵעַטּוּרֵי דְּמִתְעַטְּרֵי בְּהוּ אֲבָהָן, מֵהַהוּא נַחַל דְּנָגֵיד וְנָפֵיק לְגִנְתָא דְּעֵדֶן, הה"ד וְנָחֲךָ ה' תָּמִיד וְהִשְׂבִּיעַ בְּצַחְצָחוֹת

נַפְשֶׁךָ וְגוֹ'. וְאִינוּן חַיָּיבֵי עָלְמָא, דְּלָא זָכוּ לְאִתְלַבְּשָׁא בִּלְבוּשָׁא
דִיוֹמֵיהוֹן, עֲלַיְיהוּ כְּתִיב וְהָיָה כְּעַרְעָר בָּעֲרָבָה וְלֹא יִרְאֶה כִּי יָבֹא טוֹב
וְשָׁכַן חֲרֵרִים בַּמִּדְבָּר.

304. We learned that the righteous who were privileged to don the raiment of glory made of their days, are crowned in that world by the same crowns the fathers were adorned with, from the river that flows and comes into the Garden of Eden. This is the meaning of the words: "And Hashem shall guide you continually, and satisfy your soul in drought" (Yeshayah 58:11). But of the wicked men in the world, who had not the merit to be dressed with the garment from their days, it says, "For he shall be like the juniper tree in the desert, and shall not see when good comes; but shall inhabit the parched places in the wilderness" (Yirmeyah 17:6).

305. אָמַר רַבִּי יִצְחָק, זַכָּאָה חוּלָקֵיה דְּיַעֲקֹב, דִּרְחַצָנוּ יַתִּיר הֲוָה לֵיה,
דִּכְתִיב וְשָׁכַבְתִּי עִם אֲבוֹתַי. דְּאָזְכֵּי בְּהוֹ וְלָא בְּאָחֳרָא. דְּאָזְכֵּי בְּהוֹ,
לְאִתְלַבְּשָׁא בְּיוֹמִין דִּילֵיה, וּבְיוֹמִין דִּלְהוֹן.

305. Rabbi Yitzchak said: Happy is the portion of Jacob, who had the greatest faith, as it is written: "And I will lie with my fathers," for he deserved them, not another, to be clad in his own days and theirs.

306. רַבִּי יְהוּדָה אָמַר, כְּתִיב וַיָּרַח אֶת רֵיחַ בְּגָדָיו וַיְבָרֲכֵהוּ. בְּגָדָיו.
בְּגְדֵי עֵשָׂו מִבָּעֵי לֵיה. דְּהָא לָאו דִּידֵיה הֲווֹ, אֶלָּא דְּעֵשָׂו הֲווֹ הַנְהוּ
בְּגָדִים, דִּכְתִיב וַתִּקַּח רִבְקָה אֶת בִּגְדֵי עֵשָׂו בְּנָה הַגָּדוֹל הַחֲמוּדוֹת, בִּגְדֵי
עֵשָׂו כְּתִיב, וְהָכָא רֵיחַ בְּגָדָיו, דְּיַעֲקֹב מַשְׁמַע.

306. Rabbi Yehuda said: It is written, "And he smelt the smell of his garments, and blessed him" (Beresheet 27:27). HE ASKS: It says "his garments" while it should have been 'Esau's garments,' for the garments were not his but Esau's, as it is written: "And Rivkah took the best clothes of her eldest son, Esau" (Ibid. 15). Yet here it says "the smell of his garments," which means Jacob's.

307. אֶלָּא, הָכֵי אוֹקִימְנָא, וַיָּרַח: כְּלוֹמַר, אִסְתַּכֵּל לְהָלְאָה, וְאָרַח רֵיחָא

דִּלְבוּשׁוֹי דְּהַהוּא עַלְמָא, כְּדֵין בָּרְכֵיהּ. וְעַל דָּא כְּתִיב, רְאֵה רֵיחַ בְּנִי
כְּרֵיחַ שָׂדֶה, דָּא הוּא חֲקַל דְּתַפּוּחִין קַדִּישִׁין, אָמַר, הוֹאִיל וְזָכִיתָ בְּאִינּוּן
לְבוּשֵׁי יְקָר, וְיִתֶּן לְךָ הָאֱלֹקִים מִטַּל הַשָּׁמַיִם, מַאי מַשְׁמַע, בְּגִין
דִּבְהַהוּא חֲקַל דְּתַפּוּחִין קַדִּישִׁין, נָטֵיל טַלָּא כָּל יוֹמָא, מֵהַהוּא אֲתַר
דְּאִקְרֵי שָׁמַיִם, דִּכְתִיב מִטַּל הַשָּׁמַיִם.

307. HE ANSWERS: We have explained that "he smelt" means that he looked further and smelt the smell of his garments in the world of Truth, and then blessed him. Therefore it is written, "See, the smell of my son is like the smell of a field" (Beresheet 27:27), the field of holy apple trees, THE NUKVA OF ZEIR ANPIN. He was saying: Since you deserve to wear these raiments of glory, "therefore the Elohim give you of the dew of heaven" (Ibid. 28). HE ASKS: Does this mean THAT THE DEW OF HEAVEN DEPENDS UPON THE RAIMENTS OF GLORY? HE REPLIES: Since the field of apple trees, WHICH RESEMBLES THE RAIMENTS OF GLORY IN SMELL, receives dew everyday from the place called heaven, ZEIR ANPIN, as it is written "the dew of heaven." HE THEREFORE SAID: SINCE YOU ARE WORTHY OF DONNING THE RAIMENTS OF GLORY, "ELOHIM GIVE YOU OF THE DEW OF HEAVEN."

308. אָמַר רִבִּי יוֹסֵי, בְּכֹלָּא בָּרְכֵיהּ, מִטַּל הַשָּׁמַיִם וּמִשְׁמַנֵּי הָאָרֶץ. מ"ט,
בְּגִין דְּוַיָּרַח אֶת רֵיחַ בְּגָדָיו. בְּגָדָיו מַמָּשׁ, כְּמָה דְּאוֹקִימְנָא. תָּנָא, אֶלֶף
וַחֲמֵשׁ מְאָה רֵיחִין, סַלְּקִין בְּכָל יוֹמָא מִג"ע, דְּמִתְבַּסְּמֵי בְּהוּ אִינּוּן
לְבוּשִׁין דִּיקָר דְּהַהוּא עַלְמָא, דְּמִתְעַטְּרָן מִן יוֹמוֹי דְּבַר נָשׁ.

308. Rabbi Yosi said: He blessed him in everything, "of the dew of heaven, and the fatness of the earth," TO WIT, ALSO FROM THE ABUNDANCE OF THE NUKVA CALLED EARTH. What was the reason for that? Because "he smelt the smell of his garments," his own garments as we explained, AND THESE GARMENTS RECEIVE ALSO FROM THE NUKVA. We learned that 1,500 odors rise every day from the Garden of Eden, THE NUKVA, and perfume the raiments of glory, which are crowned with the man's days in that world, SINCE THE GARMENTS RECEIVE ALSO FROM THE NUKVA.

309. אָמַר רִבִּי יְהוּדָה, כַּמָּה לְבוּשִׁין אִינּוּן. אָמַר רִבִּי אֶלְעָזָר, טוּרֵי

דְּעָלְמָא, עַל דָּא פְּלִיגוּ, אֲבָל תְּלָתָא אִינּוּן. חַד דְּמִתְלַבְּשֵׁי בְּהַהוּא
לְבוּשָׁא, רוּחָא דִּבְגִנְתָּא דְּעֵדֶן דְּאַרְעָא. וְחַד יְקָרָא מִכּלָּא, דְּמִתְלַבְּשָׁא
בֵּיהּ נִשְׁמָתָא בְּגוֹ צְרוֹרָא דְּחַיֵּי, בֵּין פּוּרְפִּירָא דְּמַלְכָּא. וְחַד לְבוּשָׁא
דִּלְבַר, דְּקָאִים וְלָא קָאִים, אִתְחֲזֵי וְלָא אִתְחֲזֵי, בְּהַאי מִתְלַבְּשָׁא בֵּיהּ
נַפְשָׁא, וְאָזְלָא וְשָׁטָא בְּעָלְמָא.

309. Rabbi Yehuda said: How many garments are MADE FOR MAN FROM HIS DAYS? Rabbi Elazar said: There is a controversy over this point, but there are three. The first is the garments the Ruach dons in the terrestrial Garden of Eden. The Neshamah is clothed in another, the most precious, WHICH LIVES inside the bundle of life, NAMELY THE NUKVA amidst the purple cloak of the King. The last one is the external garment, which exists and exists not, seen yet not seen, FOR BEING EXTERNAL IT HAS NO CONTINUOUS EXISTENCE, BUT NOW IT IS SEEN AND NOW IT IS NOT. The Nefesh wears this garment when it goes and hovers about the world.

310. וּבְכָל רֵישׁ יַרְחֵי וְשַׁבַּתָּא, אָזְלַת וְאִתְקַשְּׁרַת בְּרוּחָא דִּבְגִנְתָּא דְּעֵדֶן
דְּאַרְעָא, דְּקַיְּימָא בֵּין פַּרְגּוֹדָא יַקִּירָא, וּמִנֵּיהּ אוֹלִיף וְיָדַע מַה דְּיָדַע,
וְשָׁט וְאוֹדַע לֵיהּ בְּעָלְמָא.

310. In every new moon and Shabbat, THE NEFESH goes to be attached to the Ruach in the terrestrial Garden of Eden, which stands in the midst of the precious curtain. From it, THE NEFESH studies and receives its knowledge, and then it hovers and announces it to the world.

311. תָּנָא, בִּתְרֵין קְשׁוּרִין אִתְקַשַּׁר נַפְשָׁא, בְּכָל רֵישׁ יַרְחָא וְשַׁבַּתָּא,
בְּקִשּׁוּרָא דְּרוּחָא, דִּי בֵּין רֵיחֵי בּוּסְמִין דִּבְגִנְתָּא דְּעֵדֶן דְּאַרְעָא, וּמִתַּמָּן
אָזִיל וְשָׁאט, וְאִתְקַשַּׁר עִם רוּחָא בְּנִשְׁמָתָא דִּצְרִירָא בִּצְרוֹרָא דְּחַיֵּי,
וּמִתְרַוְיָא וּמִתְזָנַת מֵאִינּוּן זִיוִין יְקָרִין, דְּהַאי סִטְרָא, וּדְהַאי סִטְרָא,
הה"ד וְנָחַךְ ה' תָּמִיד דַּיְיקָא.

311. We learned that the Nefesh is attached by two knots on every new moon and Shabbat: 1) to the Ruach amidst the odors of perfumes in the terrestrial Garden of Eden; 2) from there, THE NEFESH roams and goes to attach itself with the Ruach in the Neshamah, which is bound in the bundle of life. There it slakes its thirst and eats of the precious lights on this and that side, RIGHT AND LEFT. This is written in the verse: "And Hashem shall guide you continually" (Yeshayah 58:11). "Continually" is precise, INDICATING THAT IT RECEIVES FROM ALL SIDES CONTINUOUSLY.

312. וְהִשְׂבִּיעַ בְּצַחְצָחוֹת נַפְשֶׁךָ. מַהוּ בְּצַחְצָחוֹת. אֶלָּא צַחוּתָא חַד, כַּד אִתְקַשַּׁר בְּרוּחָא דִּבְגִנְתָּא דִלְתַתָּא, צַחוּתָא דִּלְגוֹ מִן צַחוּתָא, כַּד מִתְקַשְּׁרָן בְּנִשְׁמָתָא דִּלְעֵילָּא, בִּצְרוֹרָא דְּחַיֵּי, וְהַיְינוּ בְּצַח חַד, צַחוּת תְּרֵין, דְּאִינוּן לְעֵילָּא לְעֵילָּא, בִּיקִירוּ דְּנִשְׁמָתָא וַדַּאי, כְּלוֹמַר צַחְצָחוֹת, מַאן יָרֵית דָּא, נַפְשֶׁךָ. נַפְשֶׁךָ מַמָּשׁ. זַכָּאָה חוּלָקֵהוֹן דְּצַדִּיקַיָּיא.

312. "And satisfy your soul (Nefesh) in drought (Heb. *tzachtzachot*)." HE ASKS: What is "tzachtzachot"? HE ANSWERS: One *tzach* (Eng. 'bright') it receives while attached to the Ruach in the terrestrial Garden of Eden; it receives the tzach inside tzach, when attached to the Neshamah above in the bundle of life. This is the meaning of tzachtzachot: tzach is singular, and tzachot dual. They are high above, in the preciousness of the Neshamah. Who will inherit the tzachtzachot? SCRIPTURE SAYS "your soul (Nefesh)." Your Nefesh indeed INHERITS THEM FROM THE NESHAMAH. Happy is the portion of the righteous.

313. אר"ש, כַּד אֲנָא בֵּין אִינוּן חַבְרַיָּיא דְּבָבֶל, מִתְכַּנְּשֵׁי גַבַּאי, וְאוֹלְפֵי מִלֵּי בְּאִתְגַּלְיָיא, וְאִינוּן עַיְילֵי לוֹן בְּגוּשְׁפַנְקָא דְּפַרְזְלָא תַּקִּיפָא, סְתִימָא מִכָּל סִטְרִין. כַּמָּה זִמְנִין אוֹלִיפְנָא לוֹן אָרְחוֹי דְּגִנְתָּא דְמַלְכָּא, אוֹרְחוֹי דְמַלְכָּא.

313. Rabbi Shimon said: When I am with the friends of Babylon, they gather round me and learn things openly, but they put them (these matters) in a sealed iron box, closed on all sides – IN OTHER WORDS, THEY CONCEAL THEM SO NO ONE WOULD KNOW.

314. כַּמָּה זִמְנִין אוֹלִיפְנָא לוֹן, כָּל אִנּוּן דַּרְגִּין דְּצַדִּיקַיָּא, דִּבְהַהוּא עָלְמָא, וְכֻלְּהוּ מִסְתָּפֵי לְמֵימַר מִלִּין אִלֵּין, אֶלָּא לָעָאן בְּגִמְגּוּמָא, בְּגִינֵי

כָּךְ פְּסִילוּסִין אִקְרוּן, כְּהַהוּא פְּסִילוּתָא דִמְגַמְגֵם בְּפוּמֵיה.

314. How many times did I teach them the ways of the King's Garden, THE NUKVA, and the ways of the King, ZEIR ANPIN? How many times did I teach them about the grades of the righteous in that world? They are all fearful of talking of these matters, but mumble instead. They are therefore called mumblers, NAMELY SLOW OF SPEECH, for they mumble as stammerers.

315. אֲבָל לִזְכוּתָא דְּאִינָּנָא לְהוּ, הוֹאִיל וּמִסְתָּפֵי, דְּהָא אֲוִירָא קַדִּישָׁא, וְרוּחָא קַדִּישָׁא, אִתְעֲדֵי מִנַּיְיהוּ, וְיָנְקֵי מֵאֲוִירָא וְרוּחָא דִרְשׁוּתָא אַחֲרָא. וְלָא עוֹד אֶלָּא דְּקֶשֶׁת אִתְחֲזֵי עֲלַיְיהוּ, וְלָאו אִינּוּן כְּדַאי לְמֶחֱמֵי סְבַר אַנְפּוֹי דְּאֵלִיָּהוּ, כָּל שֶׁכֵּן סְבַר אַנְפִּין אַחֲרָנִין.

315. But I see it in a favorable light, for they are afraid because the holy air and the Holy Spirit are gone for them, SINCE THEY ARE OUTSIDE THE LAND OF YISRAEL. And they breathe in the air and spirit of another region THAN THAT OF HOLINESS. Moreover, the rainbow is seen above them, WHICH IS A SIGN THEY ARE UNDER JUDGMENT AND ARE IN NEED OF MERCY, AS IT IS WRITTEN: "I HAVE SET MY BOW...AND I WILL LOOK UPON IT, THAT I MAY REMEMBER THE EVERLASTING COVENANT" (BERESHEET 9:13-16). They are then not deemed worthy of receiving Elijah, let alone someone else.

316. אֲבָל דָּא מְהַנְיָא לְהוּ, דַּאֲנָא שְׁכִיחַ בְּעָלְמָא וַאֲנָא סָמְכָא בְּעָלְמָא, דְּהָא בְּחַיַּי לָא יָתֵיב עָלְמָא בְּצַעֲרָא, וְלָא אִתְדָּן בְּדִינָא דִלְעֵילָא, בַּתְרַאי לָא יָקוּם דָּרָא כְּדָרָא דָא. וְזַמִּין עָלְמָא דְּלָא יִשְׁתַּכַּח מַאן דְּיָגֵין עֲלַיְיהוּ, וְכָל אַנְפִּין חֲצִיפִין יִשְׁתַּכְחוּן בֵּין לְעֵילָא בֵּין לְתַתָּא: לְעֵילָא: בְּחוֹבַיְיהוּ דִלְתַתָּא, וַחֲצִיפוּתָא דִלְהוֹן.

316. But it is beneficent to them that I live in the world and support it, for during my lifetime the world will not be sorrowful, nor suffer Judgment from above. After me, there will never be such a generation as this. The world will be such that there will be no one to protect them, and there will be impudence both above and below. Above ALSO THERE WILL BE

IMPUDENT COUNTENANCES, WHICH ARE THE ACCUSATIONS OF THE KLIPOT, because of the transgressions below and their impudence.

317. וּזְמִינִין בְּנֵי עַלְמָא, דְּצַוְוחִין, וְלֵית מַאן דְּיַשְׁגַּח עֲלַיְיהוּ, יְהַדְרוּן רֵישָׁא לְכָל סִטְרֵי עַלְמָא, וְלָא יְתוּבוּן בְּאַסְוָותָא. אֲבָל חַד אָסוּתָא אַשְׁכַּחְנָא לְהוּ בְּעַלְמָא, וְלָא יַתִּיר, בְּהַהוּא אֲתַר דְּיִשְׁתַּכְּחוּן אִינּוּן דְּלָעָאן בְּאוֹרַיְיתָא, וְאִשְׁתְּכַח בֵּינַיְיהוּ סֵפֶר תּוֹרָה דְּלָא מִשְׁתַּכַּר בֵּיהּ, כַּד מַפְקֵי הַאי, בְּגִינֵיהּ מִתְעָרֵי עִלָּאֵי וְתַתָּאֵי. וְכָל שֶׁכֵּן אִי אִכְתִּיב בֵּיהּ שְׁמָא קַדִּישָׁא כַּדְקָא חֲזֵי, וְהָא אוֹלִיפְנָא מִלָּה.

317. The people in the world will cry out, but there will be no one to protect them. They will look to all the directions of the world TO FIND RELIEF, but shall not return with a remedy TO THEIR TROUBLES. I have found but one remedy in the world and no more, wherever there will be people who are occupied in the Torah, and a scroll of the Torah with them, without any error. When it will be taken out, the upper and lower beings will be roused, especially if the Holy Name therein is properly written, as we have already learned.

318. וַוי לְדָרָא דְּאִתְגַּלְיָיא בֵּינַיְיהוּ סֵפֶר תּוֹרָה, וְלָא מִתְעָרֵי עֲלֵיהּ לְעֵילָּא וְתַתָּא. מַאן אִתְעַר עֲלֵיהּ בְּשַׁעְתָּא דְּעַלְמָא בְּצַעֲרָא טְפֵי, וְאִצְטְרִיךְ עַלְמָא לְמִטְרָא, וְאִצְטְרִיךְ לְאַגְלָאָה סֵפֶר תּוֹרָה יַתִּיר בְּדוֹחֲקָא דְּעַלְמָא.

318. Woe to the generation, where the scroll of the Torah is banished BY BEING TAKEN OUT TO THE STREETS IN ORDER TO PRAY. But no one was awakened above or below, FOR THEIR PRAYER WAS NOT ACCEPTED, FOR IT WAS NOT JOINED BY FASTING OR ATONEMENT BELOW. HE ASKS: Who shall be roused to pray when the world is in great sorrow and in need of rain as the scroll of the Torah is further banished because of the hardship in the world.

319. דְּכַד עַלְמָא בְּצַעֲרָא, וּבְעָאן בְּנֵי נָשָׁא רַחֲמִין עֲלֵי קִבְרֵי, כֻּלְּהוּ מֵתִין מִתְעָרִין עֲלֵיהּ, דְּהָא נַפְשָׁא אַקְדִּימַת וּמוֹדָעָא לְרוּחָא, דְּהָא ס״ת

אִשְׁתְּכַח בְּגָלוּתָא, דְּאִגְלֵי בְּדוּחֲקָא דְעָלְמָא, וְחַיָּיא אָתָאן וּבָעָאן רַחֲמֵי.

319. HE ANSWERS: When the world is in sorrow and people ask for mercy by the graves, all the dead are aroused to ask on behalf of the world, for the Nefesh hastens to tell the Ruach that the scroll of the Torah is in exile, and has been exiled due to hardship in the world, and the living have come TO THE GRAVES to ask for mercy.

320. כְּדֵין רוּחָא מוֹדְעָא לְנִשְׁמָה, וְנִשְׁמָה לְקוּדְשָׁא בְּרִיךְ הוּא, וּכְדֵין קוּדְשָׁא בְּרִיךְ הוּא אִתְעַר, וְחָס עַל עַלְמָא, וְדָא עַל גָּלוּתָא דְּס״ת מֵאַתְרֵיה, וְחַיָּיא אָתִין לְמִבְעֵי רַחֲמֵי עַל קִבְרֵי מֵתַיָי. וַוי לְדָרָא, אִי אִצְטְרִיךְ ס״ת לְאַגְלָאָה לֵיה מֵאֲתַר לַאֲתַר, אֲפִילוּ מִבֵּי כְּנִישְׁתָּא לְבֵי כְּנִישְׁתָּא, דְּהָא לָא אִשְׁתְּכַח בֵּינַיְיהוּ עַל מַה יַשְׁגְּחוּן עֲלַיְיהוּ.

320. Then the Ruach informs the Neshamah, and the Neshamah the Holy One, blessed be He. Then is the Holy One, blessed be He, aroused in pity on the world. All this is caused by the exile of the scroll of the Torah from its place, WHEN the living came to ask for mercy upon the graves of the dead. Woe to the generation which must exile the scroll of the Torah from place to place, or even from one synagogue to another IN ORDER TO PRAY, for there will be no one among them to take care of them AND PRAY FOR THEM, SINCE THERE ARE NO RIGHTEOUS AMONG THEM.

321. וְדָא לָא יַדְעִין כֻּלְּהוּ בְּנֵי נָשָׁא, דְּהָא שְׁכִינְתָּא כַּד אִתְגַּלְיָיא, גָּלוּתָא בַּתְרָאָה, עַד לָא תִסְתַּלַּק לְעֵילָא, מַה כְּתִיב מִי יִתְּנֵנִי בַּמִּדְבָּר מְלוֹן אוֹרְחִים. לְבָתַר בְּזִמְנָא דְּדַחֲקָא דְּאִשְׁתְּכַח טְפֵי בְּעָלְמָא, תַּמָּן אִשְׁתְּכַחַת, וּבְגָלוּתָא דְּס״ת, תַּמָּן הִיא, וְכֹלָּא מִתְעָרִין עֲלֵיה, עִלָּאֵי וְתַתָּאֵי.

321. Yet no man knows THE REASON FOR this. For when the Shechinah was exiled the last time, in order not to go up above, it is written THAT SHE SAID: "Oh, that I were in the wilderness, in a lodging place of wayfaring men" (Yirmeyah 9:1), AND NOT GONE ABOVE. FOR SHE WISHED TO

EXILE WITH YISRAEL. Later, WHEN SHE ALREADY WAS IN EXILE WITH YISRAEL, in a time of great distress for the world, She was IN THE DESERT, THE ABODE OF THE KLIPOT. Also in the exile of the scroll of the Torah She is there IN THE DESERT, and everyone is stirred AND SUFFERS for Her, the upper and lower beings.

322. אָמַר רִבִּי שִׁמְעוֹן, אִי הַנֵּי בַּבְלָאֵי טִפְּשָׁאֵי, יִנְדְּעוּן מִלִּין דְּרָזֵי דְּחָכְמְתָא, עַל מַה קָאֵים עָלְמָא, וְסָמְכוֹי עַל מַה קָא מִתְרַגְּשָׁן, כַּד יִשְׁתַּכַּח בְּדוֹחֲקָא, יִנְדְּעוּן שְׁבָחָא דְּרַב יֵיבָא סָבָא. כַּד אִשְׁתַּכַּח בֵּינַיְיהוּ, וְלָא הֲווֹ יָדְעֵי שְׁבָחֵיה. וְהָא אַשְׁכַּחְנָא מִלּוֹי מִתְקַשְׁרָן בְּמִלּוֹי דִשְׁלֹמֹה מַלְכָּא, בְּרָזָא עִלָּאָה דְּחָכְמְתָא, וְאִינוּן לָא הֲווֹ יָדְעֵי שְׁבָחֵיה.

322. Rabbi Shimon said: Had those stupid Babylonians known the secret verses of Wisdom, such as why the world exists, or why its supporting pillars quake when it is in distress, they would know the worth of Rav Hamnuna Saba, who dwelt among them without their knowing his worth. I find that his words are connected to those of King Solomon in the high secret of Wisdom, but they did not guess his worth.

323. וְהַשְׁתָּא אָזְלִין בָּתַר מִלֵּי דְּחָכְמְתָא, וְלֵית מַאן דְּקָאֵים עֲלָה, וְלֵית מַאן דְּקָרֵי. וְעִם כָּל דָּא, אִית בֵּינַיְיהוּ פִּקְחִין בְּעִבּוּרָא דְּשַׁתָּא, וּבִקְבִיעוּתָא דְּיַרְחֵי, אע״ג דְּלָא אִתְיְיהִיב לְהוֹ, וְלָא אִתְמְסַר בִּידַיְיהוּ.

323. Now they strive after words of wisdom but there is no one to uncover THEIR SECRET, and no one to teach it. With all that, there are sages among them in the field of establishing the beginning of months and the intercalation of years, though it is not their duty TO INTERCALATE THE YEARS AND SANCTIFY THE MONTHS, WHICH ARE FIXED ONLY IN THE LAND OF YISRAEL.

324. תָּנֵינָן, תְּרֵיסַר יַרְחֵי, הַאי נֶפֶשׁ אִיהִי מִתְקַשְׁרָא בְּגוּפָא בְּקִבְרָא, וְאִתְדָּנוּ בְּדִינָא כַּחֲדָא, בַּר הַהִיא נֶפֶשׁ דְּצַדִּיקַיָּיא, כְּמָה דְּאוֹקְמוּהָ, וּזְמִינָא בְּקִבְרָא, וְיָדַע בְּצַעֲרָא דִּילֵיה, וּבְצַעֲרָא דְּחַיֵּי יָדַע, וְלָא אִשְׁתַּדְּלַת עֲלַיְיהוּ.

324. We have learned that the Nefesh is attached to the body inside the grave for twelve months, and they are judged together, except the Nefesh of the righteous, as we explained. It dwells inside the grave and feels pain OF PUNISHMENT, and the pain of the living, yet it does not strive TO PRAY for them.

325. וּלְבָתַר תְּרֵיסַר יַרְחֵי, אִתְלַבַּשׁ בִּלְבוּשָׁא חַד, וְאָזֵיל וְשָׁאט בְּעַלְמָא, וְיָדַע מִן רוּחָא מַה דְּיָדַע, וְאִשְׁתַּדַּל צַעֲרָא לְעַלְמָא, וּלְמִבְעֵי רַחֲמֵי. וּלְמִנְדַּע צַעֲרָא דְּחַיֵּי.

325. After twelve months, the Nefesh dons a garment and goes to roam about the world, and learns certain things from the Ruach. It strives to ask for mercy for the world's pain, and to feel the sorrow of the living.

326. וּמַאן אִתְעַר לְכָל הַאי, בְּזִמְנָא דְּאִית זַכָּאָה, דְּאוֹדַע לְהוּ כִּדְקָא יָאוֹת, וְהַהוּא זַכָּאָה אִשְׁתְּמוֹדַע בֵּינַיְיהוּ. דְּתַנְיָא, זַכָּאָה כַּד אִשְׁתְּאַר בְּעַלְמָא, בֵּין חַיָּיא, וּבֵין מֵיתַיָּא אִשְׁתְּמוֹדַע, דְּהָא כָּל יוֹמָא מַכְרְזֵי עֲלֵיהּ בֵּינַיְיהוּ, וְכַד צַעֲרָא טָפֵי בְּעַלְמָא, וְהוּא לָא יָכִיל לְאַגָּנָא עַל דָּרָא, הוּא אוֹדַע לְהוּ צַעֲרָא דְּעַלְמָא.

326. HE ASKS: Who arouses all that, THE NEFASHOT OF THE DEAD TO PRAY FOR THE LIVING? HE REPLIES: When there is a righteous man in the world, he duly informs them. The righteous is well known among them. For we have learned that when there remains a righteous man in the world, known among the living and the dead, he is proclaimed every day. When the world is in great distress and he cannot protect the people, he informs them of the pain in the world AND THEY ASK FOR MERCY UPON THE LIVING.

327. וְכַד לָא אִשְׁתַּכַּח זַכָּאָה דְּמַכְרְזֵי עֲלֵיהּ בֵּינַיְיהוּ, וְלָא אִשְׁתַּכַּח מַאן דְּאִתְעַר לְהוּ בְּצַעֲרָא דְּעַלְמָא, אֶלָּא ס״ת. כְּדֵין עִלָּאֵי וְתַתָּאֵי מִתְעָרִין עֲלֵיהּ, וְצְרִיכִין כֹּלָּא דְּיִשְׁתַּכְּחוּן בְּהַהִיא זִמְנָא בִּתְשׁוּבָה, וְאִי לָא מִשְׁתַּכְּחֵי, הָא מָארֵי דְּדִינָא אִתְעָרוּן עֲלַיְיהוּ, וַאֲפִילוּ רוּחַ דְּגִנְתָא דְּעֵדֶן, מִתְעָרִין עֲלַיְיהוּ, בְּגִינֵיהּ דְּסֵפֶר תּוֹרָה, כִּדְאִתְּמַר.

327. When there is no proclaimed righteous among them and no one to stir THE NEFASHOT about the sorrow of the world but a scroll of the Torah, then the upper and lower are stirred for its sake TO PRAY FOR THE WORLD. Yet at that time, everyone should do penance, for if they do not, the accusers are aroused upon them TO PUNISH THEM FOR MOVING ABOUT THE SCROLL OF THE TORAH. THIS APPLIES NOT ONLY FOR THE NEFESH, as the Ruach in the Garden of Eden is also stirred for the sake of the scroll of the Torah TO ASK FOR MERCY, as we have learned.

328. תָּאנָא, וְשָׁכַבְתִּי עִם אֲבוֹתַי: בְּגוּפָא, בְּנַפְשָׁא, בְּרוּחָא, בְּנִשְׁמָתָא, בִּרְתִיכָא חֲדָא, בְּדַרְגָּא עִלָּאָה. א"ר יְהוּדָה, כַּמָּה אֲטִימִין מִכֹּלָּא בְּנֵי עָלְמָא, דְּלָא יָדְעֵי, וְלָא מַשְׁגִּיחֵי, וְלָא שָׁמְעֵי, וְלָא מִסְתַּכְּלֵי בְּמִלֵּי דְעָלְמָא. וְהֵיךְ קוּדְשָׁא בְּרִיךְ הוּא מִשְׁתַּכַּח עֲלַיְיהוּ בְּרַחֲמִין, בְּכָל זְמַן וְעִידָן, וְלֵית מַאן דְּיַשְׁגַּח.

328. We learned: "And I will lie with my fathers"; namely in body, Nefesh, Ruach, and Neshamah, all included within one Chariot of a high grade. TO WIT, THE VERSE ALLUDES TO THE BODY AND ALL THE ASPECTS OF THE SOUL, WHICH WILL BE TOGETHER WITH HIS FATHERS. Rabbi Yehuda said: How senseless are the children in the world who do not know, nor care, hear or see what happens in the world, that the Holy One, blessed be He, is filled with Mercy for the world at any time and season. But no one pays attention.

329. תְּלַת זִמְנִין בְּיוֹמָא, עָאל רוּחָא חֲדָא בִּמְעַרְתָּא דְכָפֶלְתָּא, וְנָשִׁיב בְּקִבְרֵי אֲבָהָתָא, וְאִתְסְיָין כָּל גַּרְמִין, וְקַיְימֵי בְּקִיּוּמָא, וְהַהוּא רוּחָא נָגִיד טַלָּא מִלְעֵילָא, מֵרֵישָׁא דְמַלְכָּא, אֲתָר דְּמִשְׁתַּכְּחֵי אֲבָהָן עִלָּאֵי. וְכַד מָטֵי הַהוּא טַלָּא מִנַּיְיהוּ, מִתְעָרִין אֲבָהָן דִּלְתַתָּא.

329. Three times a day, a certain spirit comes into the cave of the Machpelah and breathes over the tombs of the fathers so that their bones are healed and they endure. The spirit draws dew from over the King's head, CHOCHMAH, BINAH, AND DA'AT OF ZEIR ANPIN, where the supernal patriarchs are. When the dew flows in, the lower patriarchs are awakened IN THE CAVE OF THE MACHPELAH.

330. וְתָאנָא, נָחִית הַהוּא טַלָּא בְּדַרְגִּין יְדִיעָן, דַּרְגָּא בָּתַר דַּרְגָּא, וּמָטֵי לְגַן עֵדֶן דִּלְתַתָּא. וּמֵהַהוּא טַלָּא, אִתְסְחֵי בְּבוּסְמִין דְּגִנְתָּא דְעֵדֶן, וְאִתְעַר רוּחָא חָדָא, דְּכָלִיל בִּתְרֵין אָחֳרָנִין וְסָלֵיק וְשָׁאט בֵּינֵי בּוּסְמִין, וְעָיֵיל בְּפִתְחָא דִּמְעַרְתָּא, כְּדֵין מִתְעָרִין אֲבָהָן, אִינוּן וְזִיווּגָן, וּבַעָאן רַחֲמֵי עַל בְּנוֹי.

330. We have learned that the dew flows down certain grades, one grade after another, and reaches the lower Garden of Eden, where the perfumes are bathed in it. Then a certain spirit awakens, which comprises two others; NAMELY A SPIRIT OF THE CENTRAL COLUMN, JACOB, WHICH INCLUDES THE TWO COLUMNS, ABRAHAM AND ISAAC. It ascends and hovers above the perfumes and comes in through the opening of the cave. Then the patriarchs are awakened with their wives and ask for Mercy for their children.

331. וְכַד אִשְׁתְּכַח עַלְמָא בְּצַעֲרָא, בְּגִין דְּאִינוּן דְּמִיכִין עַל חוֹבֵי עַלְמָא, וְהַהוּא טַלָּא לָא אִתְנְגֵיד, וְלָא אִשְׁתְּכַח, עַד דְּאִתְעַר ס״ת, כְּדִקָא חֲזֵי בְּעַלְמָא, וְנַפְשָׁא אוֹדְעָא לְרוּחָא, וְרוּחָא לִנְשַׁמְתָא, וְנִשְׁמְתָא לְקוּדְשָׁא בְּרִיךְ הוּא, כְּדֵין, יָתֵיב מַלְכָּא בְּכָרְסַיָּיא דְּרַחֲמֵי, וְנָגֵיד מֵעַתִּיקָא קַדִּישָׁא עִלָּאָה, נְגִידוּ דְּטַלָּא דִּבְדוֹלְחָא, וּמָטֵי לְרֵישָׁא דְּמַלְכָּא, וּמִתְבָּרְכִין אֲבָהָן, וְנָגֵיד הַהוּא טַלָּא, לְאִינוּן דְּמִיכִין, וּכְדֵין מִתְחַבְּרָן כֻּלְּהוּ, וְחָיֵיס קוּדְשָׁא בְּרִיךְ הוּא עַל עַלְמָא. וְתָאנָא, לָא חָיֵיס קוּדְשָׁא ב״ה עַל עַלְמָא, עַד דְּאוֹדַע לַאֲבָהָן וּבְגִינַיְיהוּ עַלְמָא אִתְבָּרְכָא. א״ר יוֹסֵי, וַדַּאי הָכִי הוּא, וְהָא אַשְׁכַּחֲנָא מִלֵּי בְּסִפְרָא דִּשְׁלֹמֹה מַלְכָּא, הַהוּא עִלָּאָה, דְּקָרָא לֵיהּ עֵיטָא דְּחָכְמְתָא דְכֹלָּא.

331. When the world is in distress AND NOT ANSWERED, and due to its sins THE PATRIARCHS sleep and the dew does not arouse them, for it cannot be found or drawn, THEN, when the scroll of the Torah is stirred in the world, the Nefesh informs the Ruach, the Ruach the Neshamah, which tells the Holy One, blessed be He. The King then sits on the throne of mercy and draws from the supernal Atika Kadisha, ARICH ANPIN, the crystal dew, which flows upon the King's head, CHOCHMAH, BINAH AND DA'AT OF

ZEIR ANPIN, and the patriarchs, CHESED, GVURAH AND TIFERET OF ZEIR ANPIN, are blessed. The dew then flows upon the sleeping FATHERS IN THE CAVE OF THE MACHPELAH, who then join IN PRAYING FOR THE WORLD. The Holy One, blessed be He, then has Mercy upon the world. We have learned the Holy One, blessed be He, does not have mercy on the world until He notifies the Patriarchs, and for their merit the world is blessed. Rabbi Yosi said: Surely this is so. I also found it in the book of King Solomon, the high one who is called every MAN'S wise counsel, AS IT SAYS, "FOR HE WAS WISER THAN ALL MEN" (I MELACHIM 5:11).

332. וְרַב הַמְנוּנָא, הָכֵי גַּלֵי וַאֲמַר, דְּהָא אַחְזִיוּ לֵיהּ, דְּיַתִּיר עָבְדַת רָחֵל, דְּקַיְימָא בְּפָרָשַׁת אוֹרְחִין, בְּכָל זִמְנָא דְּאִצְטְרִיךְ עַלְמָא, מִכֻּלְּהוּ, וְרָזָא דְמִלָּה, אָרוֹן וְכַפּוֹרֶת וּכְרוּבִים, בְּחוּלְקָא דְּבִנְיָמָן, דְּאִתְיְלֵיד בְּאוֹרְחָא, וּשְׁכִינְתָּא עַל כֹּלָּא.

332. Rav Hamnuna also said the same and that it was revealed to him in a dream, that Rachel achieved more THAN ALL THE PATRIARCHS by standing at the highway whenever the world is in need OF MERCY. The secret of this matter is that the ark, its covering and the Cherubs are in the portion of Benjamin, RACHEL'S SON, who was born on the highway, and the Shechinah is above ALL HIS PORTION, AS IT SAYS, "HE SHALL COVER HIM ALL THE DAY LONG" (DEVARIM 33:12).

32. "And Israel bowed himself upon the bed's head"

A Synopsis

Rabbi Shimon begins the discussion by explaining that the bed in the title verse signifies the foundation of the world, and the bed's head signifies the Shechinah. We learn that by his action, Israel bowed to the Supernal Throne. Rabbi Yehuda then explains that although Jacob's soul departed while he was still in Egypt, it was united with the Shechinah and his body was buried alongside the patriarchs, as he had wished.

The text then addresses the verse, "And Joseph shall put his hand on your eyes." Rabbi Yesa reveals that this verse indicates both Jacob's importance and that his son would be alive at the time of Jacob's death. Rabbi Chizkiyah then speaks about the custom of a man's son putting dust on his father's eyes as a sign of respect when he dies. This leads to a discourse on the symbolic significance of each color of the eye. After offering further explanations for the custom of closing a man's eyes after his death, the conversation turns to the subject of the Nefesh of the departed soul. Finally, the rabbis return to the spiritual significance of Jacob's actions described in the title verse.

The Relevance of this Passage

The Light of the Shechinah is summoned into our world, helping The reader climb out of darkness and negativity [Egypt], and in doing so, merit closeness to the great patriarchs in the World to Come. These verses also help elevate the souls of our fathers if they have passed on.

333. וַיִּשְׁתַּחוּ יִשְׂרָאֵל עַל רֹאשׁ הַמִּטָּה, מַאן רֹאשׁ הַמִּטָּה. דָּא שְׁכִינְתָּא. אר"ש, ח"ו. אֶלָּא לְדִידֵיהּ כָּרַע וְסָגֵיד. תָּא חֲזֵי, מִטָּה: דָּא שְׁכִינְתָּא. דִּכְתִיב הִנֵּה מִטָּתוֹ שֶׁלִּשְׁלֹמֹה. רֹאשׁ הַמִּטָּה מַאן הוּא. דָּא יְסוֹדָא דְּעַלְמָא, דְּהוּא רֵישָׁא דְּעַרְסָא קַדִּישָׁא. עַל רֹאשׁ: דָּא יִשְׂרָאֵל, דְּקָאֵים עַל רֹאשׁ הַמִּטָּה, בְּגִינֵי כָּךְ, יִשְׂרָאֵל לְדִידֵיהּ קָא סָגֵיד.

333. "And Israel bowed himself upon the bed's head" (Beresheet 47:31). HE ASKS: What is the bed's head? HE ANSWERS: It is the Shechinah, WHICH IS ALWAYS PRESENT AT THE HEAD OF A SICK MAN. Rabbi Shimon said: Heaven forbid THAT HE WAS BOWING DOWN BEFORE THE SHECHINAH, SINCE HE WAS A CHARIOT OF TIFERET, WHICH IS ABOVE THE SHECHINAH. He bowed to his own attribute, TIFERET. HE EXPLAINS HIS WORDS: Come and behold: the bed is the Shechinah, of which it says,

"Behold it his litter, that of Solomon" (Shir Hashirim 3:7). The bed's head is the foundation (Yesod) of the world, the head of the sacred bed, THE SHECHINAH; the head refers to Israel, TIFERET, standing at the bed's head, WHICH IS YESOD, FOR TIFERET IS ABOVE YESOD, and therefore Israel bowed to himself, NAMELY TO TIFERET.

334. וְאִי תֵימָא, הָא בְּהַהוּא זִמְנָא, לָא הֲוָה מָרַע, דְּהָא לְבָתַר כְּתִיב, וַיְהִי אַחַר הַדְּבָרִים הָאֵלֶּה וַיֹּאמֶר לְיוֹסֵף הִנֵּה אָבִיךְ חוֹלֶה, וּבְשַׁעְתָּא דְּסָגֵיד, לָא הֲוָה חוֹלֶה, וְעַל דְּיָדַע, דְּהָא בְּהַהוּא זִמְנָא, סָלֵיק בְּדַרְגָּא עִלָּאָה קַדִּישָׁא כָּרְסְיָיא שְׁלֵימָתָא, בְּגִינֵי כָּךְ סָגֵיד לְהַהוּא רְתִיכָא, כָּרְסְיָיא עִלָּאָה, שְׁלִימוּ דְּאִילָנָא רַבְרְבָא וְתַקִּיף, דְּאִקְרֵי עַל שְׁמֵיהּ. וְעַל דָּא, וַיִּשְׁתַּחוּ יִשְׂרָאֵל עַל רֹאשׁ הַמִּטָּה, עַל רֹאשׁ הַמִּטָּה וַדַּאי, דְּהָא אִסְתַּלָּק לְאַתְרֵיהּ וְאִתְעַטַּר בְּעַטְרוֹי דְּמַלְכָּא קַדִּישָׁא.

334. You might say THAT HE BOWED DOWN TO THE SHECHINAH, WHICH IS ABOVE THE HEAD OF A SICK MAN. At that time, he was not yet ill, only later. It is written: "And it came to pass after these things, that one told Joseph, 'Behold, your father is sick'" (Beresheet 48:1). But when he bowed down, he was not sick. Of necessity, he bowed down because he knew that he then ascended to the holy supernal grade of the whole throne TIFERET. He therefore bowed down to that Chariot, the supernal throne. FOR CHESED, GVURAH AND TIFERET ARE THE SUPERNAL THRONE OF BINAH, AND TIFERET IS INCLUDED OF THEM ALL. It is the perfection of the great and strong tree which is named after him, NAMELY TIFERET CALLED ISRAEL AFTER HIS NAME. Therefore, "Israel bowed himself upon the bed's head," for surely he was elevated into his own grade and adorned with crowns, MOCHIN, of the Holy King TIFERET.

335. וַיֹּאמֶר הִשָּׁבְעָה לִי וַיִּשָּׁבַע לוֹ וַיִּשְׁתַּחוּ יִשְׂרָאֵל עַל רֹאשׁ הַמִּטָּה, רִבִּי חִיָּיא פָּתַח וְאָמַר, כָּל זֶה נִסִּיתִי בַחָכְמָה אָמַרְתִּי אֶחְכָּמָה וְהִיא רְחוֹקָה מִמֶּנִּי. הָא תָּנֵינָן, שְׁלֹמֹה מַלְכָּא, יָרֵית סִיהֲרָא מִכָּל סִטְרוֹי, וּבְיוֹמוֹי קַיְימָא בִּשְׁלֵמוּתָא, הַהִיא סִיהֲרָא דְּאִתְבָּרְכָא מִכֹּלָּא, וְכַד בָּעָא לְמֵיקַם עַל נִימוּסֵי אוֹרַיְיתָא, אָמַר אָמַרְתִּי אֶחְכָּמָה וְגוֹ'.

335. "And he said: 'Swear to me.' And he swore to him. And Israel bowed himself upon the bed's head." Rabbi Chiya opened the discussion saying:

"All this have I proved by Wisdom: I said, 'I will be wise'; but it was far from me" (Kohelet 7:23). We have learned that King Solomon inherited the moon, THE NUKVA, together with all her aspects. In his days the moon was in fullness, being blessed by all THE GRADES. When he wanted to understand the statutes of the Torah he said: "I said, 'I will be wise'; but it was far from me."

336. אָמַר רִבִּי יְהוּדָה, יַעֲקֹב אָמַר, וְשָׁכַבְתִּי עִם אֲבוֹתַי וּנְשָׂאתַנִי מִמִּצְרַיִם וּקְבַרְתַּנִי בִּקְבוּרָתָם, תַּמָּן תָּנִינָן, מַאן דְּנָפַק נִשְׁמָתֵיהּ, בִּרְשׁוּתָא אַחֲרָא, וְגוּפָא דִּילֵיהּ אִתְקְבַּר בְּאַרְעָא קַדִּישָׁא, עֲלֵיהּ כְּתִיב וַתָּבֹאוּ וַתְּטַמְּאוּ אֶת אַרְצִי וְנַחֲלָתִי שַׂמְתֶּם לְתוֹעֵבָה, וְיַעֲקֹב אָמַר וּקְבַרְתַּנִי בִּקְבוּרָתָם, וְנִשְׁמָתֵיהּ נָפְקָא בִּרְשׁוּתָא אַחֲרָא.

336. Rabbi Yehuda said: Jacob said, "but I will lie with my fathers and you shall carry me out of Egypt and bury me in their place of burial" (Beresheet 47:30). In connection with this, we learned that a man whose soul departed in another domain, NAMELY OUTSIDE THE LAND OF YISRAEL, and whose body was buried in the Holy Land, scripture says of him: "But when you entered, you defiled my land, and made my heritage an abomination" (Yirmeyah 2:7). Yet Jacob said: "And bury me in their place of burial," though his soul departed in another domain, IN EGYPT.

337. א"ר יְהוּדָה, שָׁאנֵי יַעֲקֹב, דִּשְׁכִינְתָּא הֲוַת אֲחִידַת בֵּיהּ, וְאִתְדַּבְּקַת בֵּיהּ, הַהִ"ד אָנֹכִי אֵרֵד עִמְּךָ מִצְרַיְמָה, לְדַיְירָא עִמָּךְ בְּגָלוּתָא. וְאָנֹכִי אַעַלְךָ גַם עָלֹה, לְאִזְדַּוּוּגָא בִּי נִשְׁמָתָךְ, וּלְאִתְקַבְּרָא גוּפָךְ בְּקִבְרֵי אֲבָהָתָךְ, מַאי קָא מַיְירֵי, אע"ג דְּקָא נָפְקַת נִשְׁמָתֵיהּ בִּרְשׁוּתָא אַחֲרָא.

337. Rabbi Yehuda said: Jacob is different THAN OTHER MEN, since the Shechinah held him and cleaved to him. This is the meaning of the words, "I will go down with you into Egypt" (Beresheet 46:4) to dwell with you in exile "and I will also surely bring you up again" (Ibid.), for your soul shall be united with Me, and your body shall be buried in the graves of your fathers. This comes to teach us that his soul left in another domain, YET "I WILL ALSO SURELY BRING YOU UP AGAIN" TO BE BURIED IN THE GRAVES OF HIS FATHERS.

338. וְיוֹסֵף יָשִׁית יָדוֹ עַל עֵינֶיךָ, יוֹסֵף וַדַּאי, דְּהָא הוּא בּוּכְרָא דְּהִרְהוּרָא דְּלַבָּא, בּוּכְרָא דְּטִפָּה קַדְמָאָה הֲוַת, כִּדְאִתְּמָר. וּבְגִין דְּיָדַע קוּדְשָׁא בְּרִיךְ הוּא טְמִירָא דָּא, אִתְבַּשַּׂר לֵיהּ בְּיוֹסֵף, דְּהָא כָּל רְחִימוּתָא בֵּיהּ תַּלְיָא.

338. "And Joseph shall put his hand on your eyes" (Ibid.). Surely because he was the firstborn, AND IT IS FOR THE FIRSTBORN TO PUT HIS HAND ON HIS FATHER'S EYES. For according to thought, he was the firstborn of the first seed, as we learned. Since the Holy One, blessed be He, knew this secret THAT HE THOUGHT OF RACHEL, He let him know that it would be Joseph, WHO WILL PUT HIS HANDS ON HIS EYES, whom he greatly loved.

339. יָשִׁית יָדוֹ עַל עֵינֶיךָ, מַאי קָא מַיְירֵי. א"ר יֵיסָא, בְּגִין יְקָרָא דְּיַעֲקֹב, וּלְאִתְבַּשְּׂרָא דְּהָא יוֹסֵף קַיָּים, וְיִשְׁתַּכַּח עֲלֵיהּ בְּמִיתָתֵיהּ. רַבִּי חִזְקִיָּה אָמַר, מִלָּה אוֹלִיפְנָא, וְדָחֵילְנָא לְגַלָּאָה, וּבְעוֹבָדֵי עַלְמָא חָכְמְתָא אִשְׁתַּכַּח. אָתָא רַבִּי אַבָּא, בָּטַשׁ בֵּיהּ, אֲמַר אֵימָא מִילָךְ, וְחֵיֵי זַיְינָךְ, בְּיוֹמוֹי דְּרַבִּי שִׁמְעוֹן מִלִּין אִתְגַּלְיָין.

339. "Shall put his hand on your eyes": HE ASKS: What does this come to teach us? Rabbi Yisa said: This teaches us of Jacob's importance, THAT HIS SON, A KING, WILL PUT HIS HAND ON HIS EYES, and also informs him that Joseph is alive and will be present at his death. Rabbi Chizkiyah said: I have learned something, yet I fear of revealing it, since Wisdom abides with the common customs. Rabbi Aba tapped him and said: Speak up and pluck up your courage, for everything is disclosed in the days of Rabbi Shimon AND THERE IS NO NEED TO BE AFRAID.

340. אֲמַר, אוֹלִיפְנָא מִפִּרְקִין דְּרַב יֵיסָא סָבָא, בְּנִמּוּסֵי עַלְמָא, בַּר נָשׁ דְּזָכֵי לְבַר בְּהַאי עַלְמָא, לִיבָּעֵי לֵיהּ לְנַגְדָּא עַפְרָא עַל עֵינוֹי כַּד אִתְקַבַּר, וְדָא הוּא יְקָרָא דִּילֵיהּ, לְאַחֲזָאָה דְּעַלְמָא אַסְתִּים מִנֵּיהּ, וְהוּא יָרֵית לֵיהּ לְעַלְמָא תְּחוֹתוֹי.

340. RABBI CHIZKIYAH said: We learned from the book of Rabbi Yesa Saba (the elder), in the chapter about customs, that when a man merits a son in this world, THE SON should put dust on his eyes when his father is buried as a sign of respect, an indication that the world is now concealed from him, and that he, THE SON, inherits it in his stead.

בְּגִין דְּעֵינוֹי דְּבַר נָשׁ, חֵיזוּ דְּעָלְמָא בֵּיהּ אִתְחֲזֵי, וְכָל גְּווֹנִין הָכֵי .341 אִינוּן דְּאִסְתַּחֲרוּ, חִוָּורָא דְּבֵיהּ, הוּא יַמָּא רַבָּא אוֹקְיָנוֹס, דְּאִסְתַּחַר כָּל עָלְמָא בְּכָל סִטְרֵי, גּוֹוָנָא אַחֲרָא הוּא יַבֶּשְׁתָּא, דַּאֲפִיקוּ מַיָּא, וְיַבֶּשְׁתָּא קָאִים בֵּין מַיָּא, הָכֵי הוּא גּוֹוָנָא בֵּין מַיָּא.

341. This is because a man's eyes reflect the world and contain all the colors. The white color in them is like a great sea which surrounds the world on all sides. Another is like the ground dug out from the water. The ground stands in the midst of the water and so does the color in the midst of the water, NAMELY IN THE MIDST OF THE WHITE COLOR WHICH INDICATES THE WATER OF THE OCEAN.

גּוֹוָנָא אַחֲרָא תְּלִיתָאָה, הִיא בִּמְצִיעוּתָא דְּבֵיהּ, דָּא יְרוּשָׁלֵַם, 342 דְּהִיא אֶמְצָעוּתָא דְּעָלְמָא. גּוֹוָנָא רְבִיעָאָה, הִיא חֵיזוּ דְּכָל עֵינָא, וְאִקְרֵי בַּת עַיִן, דְּבַהֲהוּא בַּת עַיִן, אִתְחֲזֵי פַּרְצוּפָא, וְחֵיזוּ יְקָרָא מִכֹּלָּא דָּא צִיּוֹן, דְּאִיהִי נְקוּדָה אֶמְצָעוּתָא מִכֹּלָּא, דְּחֵיזוּ דְּכָל עָלְמָא תַּמָּן אִתְחֲזֵי, וְתַמָּן שַׁרְיָא שְׁכִינְתָּא, דְּהִיא שַׁפִּירוּ דְּכֹלָּא, וְחֵיזוּ דְּכֹלָּא, וְעֵינָא דָּא הוּא יְרוּתַת עָלְמָא. וּבְגִינֵי כָּךְ, הַאי שָׁבִיק לֵיהּ, וְהַאי נָטִיל לֵיהּ, וְיָרֵית לֵיהּ.

342. The third color in the middle of the eye is Jerusalem, the center of the world. The fourth color in the eye is where the power of sight dwells; NAMELY THE BLACKNESS IN THE EYE. It is called "the apple of the eye" (Tehilim 17:8), where the face is seen and the most dear sight of all, Zion, the innermost point of all, where the whole world is seen, where the Shechinah dwells, which is the beauty and sight of all. The eye is the worldly inheritance, and therefore he WHO DIES leaves this and HIS SON takes it and inherits it.

א"ל שַׁפִּיר קָאֲמָרְתְּ, אֲבָל מִלָּה סְתִימָא אִיהוּ יַתִּיר, וּבְנֵי עָלְמָא 343 לָא יָדְעִין, וְלָא מִסְתַּכְּלָן, דְּהָא בְּשַׁעְתָּא דְּבַר נָשׁ נָפִיק מֵעָלְמָא. נַפְשָׁא דִּילֵיהּ טְמִירָא עִמֵּיהּ, וְעַד לָא נָפְקַת, עֵינוֹי דְּב"נ חָמוּ מַה דְּחָמוּ, כְּמָה

-174-

דְּאוֹקִימְנָא דִּכְתִיב כִּי לֹא יִרְאַנִי הָאָדָם וָחָי. בְּחַיֵּיהוֹן לָא חָמָאן, אֲבָל בְּמִיתַתְהוֹן חָמָאן.

343. He said to him: This was well said, but this matter has an even deeper meaning, though the children of the world do not know or look for it. For when a man departs from the world, his Nefesh is hidden with him, and before it leaves the body his eyes see certain things, as we have explained in relation to the verse: "For no man shall see Me, and live" (Shemot 33:20), that men do not see in their lives what they see in their death.

344. וְעֵינוֹי פְּקִיחָן מֵהַהוּא חֵיזוּ דְּחָמָא, וְאִינוּן דְּקַיְימִין עֲלֵיה, בָּעָא לְשַׁוָּאָה יָדָא עַל עֵינוֹי, וּלְאַסְתְּמָא עֵינוֹי, בְּגִין הַהוּא דְּאוֹלִיפְנָא בְּרָזָא דִּנְמוֹסֵי עַלְמָא, דִּבְשַׁעְתָּא דְּאִשְׁתְּאָרוּ עֵינוֹי פְּקִיחָן, מֵהַהוּא חֵיזוּ יַקִּירָא דְּחָמָא, אִי זָכֵי לְבַר, בְּרָא קָדֵים לְשַׁוָּאָה יְדֵיה עַל עֵינוֹי וּלְאַסְתְּמָא לוֹן, כְּמָה דִכְתִיב וְיוֹסֵף יָשִׁית יָדוֹ עַל עֵינֶיךָ. בְּגִין, דְּהָא חֵיזוּ אָחֳרָא דְּלָא קַדִּישָׁא אִזְדַּמְּנַת לְקַבְלֵיה, וְעֵינָא דְּחָמָא הַשְׁתָּא חֵיזוּ קַדִּישָׁא עִלָּאָה, לָא יִסְתַּכַּל בְּחֵיזוּ אָחֳרָא.

344. His eyes are opened to the sight they have just seen, and those standing by should put a hand on his eyes and close them, because of what we learned about common customs. When the eyes remain open to the dear vision, if he has a son, the son should be the first to put his hand over his eyes and close them. It says, "And Joseph shall put his hand on your eyes," for another unholy sight is come before him and the eye that beheld the supernal holy sight must not look at the other sight.

345. וְעוֹד, דְּהַהוּא נֶפֶשׁ סְמִיכַת לְקַבְלֵיה בְּבֵיתָא, וְאִי אִשְׁתְּאַר עֵינָא פְּקִיחָא, וְהַהוּא חֵיזוּ אָחֳרָא יִשְׁרֵי עַל עֵינוֹי, בְּכָל מַה דְּאִסְתַּכַּל אִתְלַטְיָא, וְלָאו יְקָרָא דְּעֵינָא הוּא, וְכָל שֶׁכֵּן מִקְרִיבוֹי, וְכָל שֶׁכֵּן מִן מִיתָא, דְּלָאו יְקָרָא דִּילֵיה לְאִסְתַּכְּלָא בַּמֶּה דְּלָא אִצְטְרִיךְ, וּלְאַשְׁרָיָא עַל עֵינוֹי מִלָּה אָחֳרָא, לְבָתַר אִתְכַּסְיָא בְּעַפְרָא, וְהָא אִתְעָרוּ חַבְרַיָיא עַל דִּינָא דְּקִבְרָא מַהוּ. וִיקָרָא הוּא, דְּיִסְתְּיֵם עֵינָא מִן כֹּלָא, עַל יְדָא דִּבְרֵיה דְּשָׁבֵק בְּעַלְמָא.

345. Another reason is that the Nefesh is close by in the house, and if the eye is open, and the other sight OF THE OTHER SIDE will be upon his eyes, whatever he beholds shall be cursed. AND SINCE HIS NEFESH IS STANDING IN FRONT OF HIM, HE MIGHT LOOK AT IT AND IT WILL BE ACCURSED. This is not respectful to the eye, or to any of the dead man's relatives, especially to the dead man himself. It is degrading for him to behold what he should not BEHOLD, and lay his eyes on another thing; NAMELY THE OTHER SIDE. Therefore he is covered by dust. The friends have already spoken about the judgment which THE DEAD MAN undergoes in the grave, AND THIS IS NOT THE PLACE TO SPEAK ABOUT IT. It is a sign of respect that the eye be closed by his son he left in the world.

346. תָּא חֲזֵי, כָּל שִׁבְעָה יוֹמִין, נַפְשָׁא אָזְלָא מִבֵּיתָא לְקִבְרָא, וּמִקִּבְרָא לְבֵיתָא, וְאִתְאַבָּלַת עֲלֵיהּ, וּתְלַת זִמְנִין בְּיוֹמָא, אִתְדָּנוּ כַּחֲדָא נַפְשָׁא וְגוּפָא, וְלֵית מַאן דְּיָדַע בְּעַלְמָא, וְיַשְׁגַּח לְאִתְעָרָא לִבָּא.

346. Come and see, for seven days AFTER THE DEMISE, the Nefesh goes from the grave to the house and back and mourns him. Three times a day, the Nefesh and the body are judged together, though nobody in the world knows it, or observes it so as to awaken his heart.

347. לְבָתַר, גּוּפָא אִתְטְרִיד, וְנַפְשָׁא אָזְלָא וְאִסְתַּחְיָא בַּגֵּיהִנֹּם, וְנָפְקָא וְשָׁטָא בְּעַלְמָא, וּמְבַקְּרָא לְקִבְרֵיהּ, עַד דְּמִתְלַבְּשָׁא בַּמֶּה דְּאִתְלַבְּשָׁא.

347. Afterwards, the body is sealed IN THE GRAVE and the Nefesh goes to bathe in Gehenom, then goes out to roam about the world and visit THE BODY IN the grave, until it wears that which it wears.

348. לְבָתַר תְּרֵיסַר יַרְחֵי, נָיְיחִין כֹּלָּא, גּוּפָא שָׁבֵיק בְּעַפְרָא. נַפְשָׁא אִתְצְרִיר וְאִתְנְהִיר בְּרוּחָא, בְּמָאנָא דְּאִתְלַבֵּשׁ. רוּחָא אִתְעַנַּג בְּגִנְתָא דְּעֵדֶן. נִשְׁמָתָא סָלְקָא לִצְרוֹרָא דְּעֵנוּגָא דְּכָל עִנּוּגִין. וְכֹלָּא אִתְקְשַׁר דָּא בְּדָא לְזִמְנִין יְדִיעָן.

348. After twelve months everybody rests. The body reposes in the dust and the Nefesh is bound and enlightened by the Ruach, which in its garment is satisfied in the Garden of Eden. The Neshamah ascends to the bundle of life,

THE NUKVA, the greatest pleasure of all. All of them are attached to each other, THE NEFESH TO THE RUACH AND THE RUACH TO THE NESHAMAH, at certain times, ON SHABBAT, HOLIDAYS AND THE FIRST DAY OF THE MONTH.

349. תָּא חֲזֵי, וַוי לוֹן לִבְנֵי נָשָׁא, דְּלָא מִסְתַּכְּלִין, וְלָא יָדְעִין, וְלָא אִשְׁתְּמוֹדְעָן, עַל מַה קַיְימֵי, וְיִתְנְשֵׁי מִנַּיְיהוּ, לְמֶעְבַּד פְּקוּדֵי אוֹרַיְיתָא. דְּאִית פְּקוּדֵי אוֹרַיְיתָא, דְּעָבְדֵי לְבוּשׁ יְקָר לְעֵילָּא, וְאִית פְּקוּדֵי אוֹרַיְיתָא, דְּעָבְדֵי לְבוּשׁ יְקָר לְתַתָּא, וְאִית פְּקוּדֵי אוֹרַיְיתָא, דְּעָבְדֵי לְבוּשֵׁי יְקָר לְהַאי עָלְמָא, וְכֹלָּא אִצְטְרִיכָן לֵיהּ לְב"נ, וּמִן יוֹמוֹי מַמָּשׁ, כֻּלְּהוּ מִתְתַּקְּנָן, כְּמָה דְּאוֹקִימְנָא.

349. Come and see: Woe to the people who do not regard, who do not know nor understand why they exist, and neglect to observe the precepts of the Torah. Some of the precepts of the Torah are made into a holy garment above IN THE UPPER GARDEN OF EDEN, and some are made into a holy garment below IN THE LOWER GARDEN OF EDEN. Some precepts are made into a holy garment in this world. Man needs them all. They are made of man's days as we explained.

350. רִבִּי יְהוּדָה סָבָא, אִתְרְגִישׁ בְּדַעְתֵּיהּ יוֹמָא חַד, וְאַחֲזוּ לֵיהּ בְּחֶלְמֵיהּ, חַד דְּיוֹקְנָא מִנְּהוֹרָא דִילֵיהּ, תַּקִּיף, דְּאַזְדְּהַר לְאַרְבַּע סִטְרִין, אֲמַר לֵיהּ מַאי הַאי. אֲמַר לֵיהּ, לְבוּשָׁא דִילָךְ הוּא, לְדִיּוּרָא דְהָכָא, וּמֵהַהוּא יוֹמָא הֲוָה חָדֵי.

350. Rabbi Yehuda Saba (the elder) was very anxious one day TO KNOW WHAT HE WOULD HAVE IN THE WORLD OF TRUTH. He was shown in a dream a certain image made of bright light which shines to the four directions. He asked what it was, and they said to him: This is your garment, which you shall wear here. From that day ONWARD, he was happy.

351. אֲמַר רִבִּי יְהוּדָה, כָּל יוֹמָא וְיוֹמָא, רוּחִין דְּצַדִּיקַיָּיא יַתְבִין בִּלְבוּשֵׁיהוֹן, שׁוּרִין שׁוּרִין בְּגִנְתָא דְעֵדֶן, וּמְשַׁבְּחָן לְקוּדְשָׁא בְּרִיךְ הוּא, בִּיקָרָא עִלָּאָה, הֲדָא הוּא דִכְתִיב אַךְ צַדִּיקִים יוֹדוּ לִשְׁמֶךָ יֵשְׁבוּ יְשָׁרִים אֶת פָּנֶיךָ. אֲמַר רִבִּי

אַבָּא, בְּקַדְמֵיתָא מַה כְּתִיב וַיִּשְׁתַּחוּ יִשְׂרָאֵל וגו', כְּמָה דְאוֹקִימְנָא, מַאן מַטָה, דָּא כ"י. רֹאשׁ הַמִּטָה: דָּא צַדִּיק. עַל רֹאשׁ הַמִּטָה: דָּא מַלְכָּא קַדִּישָׁא, דִּשְׁלָמָא כֹּלָּה דִּילֵיהּ, כְּמָה דִכְתִיב הִנֵּה מִטָתוֹ שֶׁלִּשְׁלֹמֹה. דְּיַעֲקֹב לְדִידֵיהּ קָא סָגִיד, לְהַהוּא דְּקָאִים עַל רֹאשׁ הַמִּטָה, יִשְׂרָאֵל שְׁמֵיהּ, בְּגִינֵי כָּךְ, וַיִּשְׁתַּחוּ יִשְׂרָאֵל עַל רֹאשׁ הַמִּטָה.

351. Rabbi Yehuda said: On each day the spirits of the righteous sit, clothed in their garments in rows in the Garden of Eden and praise the Holy One, blessed be He, with the highest glory, as it is written: "Surely the righteous shall give thanks to Your name: the upright shall dwell in Your presence" (Tehilim 140:14). Rabbi Aba said: It is first written, "And Israel bowed himself..." As we explained, the bed is the Congregation of Yisrael, THE NUKVA; the bed's head is the Righteous; "upon the bed's head" refers to the Holy King, that the peace is His, NAMELY TIFERET, as it is written: "Behold his litter, that of Solomon" (Shir Hashirim 3:7). For he bowed to himself, BEING THE CHARIOT OF TIFERET, to him who stands upon the bed's head whose name is Yisrael, AS TIFERET IS CALLED YISRAEL. Therefore, "And Israel bowed himself upon the bed's head."

352. לְבָתַר, כֵּיוָן דְּיָדַע יַעֲקֹב, דְּהָא בְּדַרְגָּא עִלָּאָה אִשְׁתְּלֵים, וְדַרְגָּא דִּילֵיהּ הוּא לְעֵילָּא עִם אֲבָהָתָא, וְהוּא בִּלְחוֹדוֹי תִּקּוּנָא שְׁלֵימָתָא, אַחֲסִין לְבֵיהּ, וְחָדֵי וְאִתְתַּקַּף בִּרְעוּתָא עִלָּאָה דְּקוּדְשָׁא בְּרִיךְ הוּא בֵּיהּ, מַה כְּתִיב בֵּיהּ וַיִּתְחַזֵּק יִשְׂרָאֵל וַיֵּשֶׁב עַל הַמִּטָה, עַל הַמִּטָה מַמָּשׁ, דְּהָא בְּדַרְגָּא עִלָּאָה יַתִּיר אִשְׁתַּלֵּם, זַכָּאָה חוּלְקֵיהּ.

352. Afterwards, when Jacob saw that he was perfected in the highest grade, and that his grade, TIFERET, was high, together with the patriarchs, CHESED AND GVURAH, and that he alone was wholly mended, FOR TIFERET IS THE CENTRAL COLUMN WHICH INCLUDES CHESED AND GVURAH AND MEASURED AGAINST ALL CHESED, GVURAH AND TIFERET, his heart rejoiced and he was strengthened by the supernal will of the Holy One, blessed be He, WHO WAS PLEASED with him. Then it was said of him, "And Yisrael strengthened himself, and sat upon the bed," on the bed itself, THE SECRET OF MALCHUT, since he was perfected in a higher grade, TO WIT, HE WAS MADE WHOLE BY THE ATTRIBUTE OF TIFERET WHICH IS ABOVE MALCHUT. Happy is his portion.

33. The world is judged four times a year

A Synopsis
Rabbi Yehuda discusses the four times of the year that the world is judged. During these four times of the year, Chesed, Gvurah, Tiferet and Malchut are present to judge the world. We learn of the significance of corn to the judgment on Passover, the significance of the fruits of the tree to the judgment on the Feast of Weeks, and the significance of water to the judgment on Sukkot. We are also told that the New Year is the head of God's year, and it is the time when all the inhabitants of the world pass before God. Finally, Rabbi Yosi reminds us that man's deeds are recorded every day. Each morning his soul entreats him to repent and to follow the righteous path. Those who ignore this warning will have their deeds recorded. Only the righteous have nothing to fear in this world and in the World to Come.

The Relevance of this Passage
The awesome power of the major holidays and their particular rituals is released into our world, helping us atone for our sins, lessen judgments decreed against us, and transform our inner character. Relative to the degree of atonement in our heart, this passage helps us alter our destiny in positive ways by controlling the seed and "head of God's year." Awareness of the importance of penitence and spiritual growth is deepened in our consciousness, inspiring us to pursue self-transformation for the purpose of achieving closeness to the Light of The Creator

353. תָּאנָא, אֲמַר ר' יְהוּדָה, בְּמַתְנִיתָא דִּילָן אוּקִימְנָא, הָא דִּתְנִינָן בְּאַרְבְּעָה פְּרָקִים בַּשָּׁנָה הָעוֹלָם נִדּוֹן, בְּפֶסַח עַל הַתְּבוּאָה, בַּעֲצֶרֶת עַל פֵּירוֹת הָאִילָן, בְּרֹאשׁ הַשָּׁנָה כָּל בָּאֵי הָעוֹלָם עוֹבְרִים לְפָנָיו כִּבְנֵי מָרוֹן, וּבֶחַג נִדּוֹנִין עַל הַמַּיִם, הָא אוּקִימְנָא מִלֵּי, וְרָזָא דְמַתְנִיתָא אוּקִימְנָא, בְּפֶסַח עַל הַתְּבוּאָה וכו', לָקֳבֵיל רְתִיכָא עִלָּאָה, רָזָא דַּאֲבָהָן, וְדָוִד מַלְכָּא. בְּפֶסַח עַל הַתְּבוּאָה, דְּהָכֵי הוּא מַמָּשׁ, וְהָא אוּקִימְנָא מִלָּה דָא, עַל מָה אַתְיָיא מַצָּה בְּפֶסַח, וְהָא דִינָא הוּא, דִּינָא דְמַלְכוּתָא דִינָא, וְדָא שֵׁירוּתָא, דְּשָׁרִיאוּ יִשְׂרָאֵל לְמֵיעַל בְּחוּלָקָא קַדִּישָׁא דְּקוּדְשָׁא בְּרִיךְ הוּא, וּלְבַעֲרָא מִנַּיְיהוּ חָמֵץ, דְּאִיהוּ טַעֲוָון אָחֳרָנִין, דִּי מְמַנָּן עַל עַמִּין עכו"ם, דְּאִקְרוּן אֱלֹהִים אֲחֵרִים, אֱלֹהֵי נֵכָר, וְאִקְרוּן חָמֵץ, יֵצֶר הָרָע, וּלְמֵיעַל בְּמַצָּה, חוּלָקָא קַדִּישָׁא דְּקוּדְשָׁא בְּרִיךְ הוּא. בְּגִין כָּךְ, בְּפֶסַח

נְדוֹנִין עַל הַתְּבוּאָה, וְאוֹקִימְנָא דְּעָלְמָא אִתְדָּן עַל דִּינָא דְה"א.

353. We learned that Rabbi Yehuda said: We have explained in the Baraita that the world is judged four times a year: in Pesach (Passover) in respect to corn; in Shavuot (Holiday of the Weeks) in respect to the fruits of the tree; on Rosh Hashanah, when all the inhabitants of the world pass before Him like a flock of sheep; and on Sukkot when water is apportioned to them. We have explained the secret of the Baraita: that corn on Pesach, corresponded to the supernal Chariot, the secret of the patriarchs, CHESED, GVURAH AND TIFERET, and King David, MALCHUT. TO WIT, THE FOUR TIMES BROUGHT UP IN THE BARAITA ARE THE SECRET OF THE FATHERS AND KING DAVID. HE EXPLAINS, judgment is pronounced on Pesach in respect to corn literally. And we have already explained, in relation to it why Matzah is connected to Pesach: because it is a law, and the law of the kingdom is the prevailing law. THUS, THE MATZAH IS A LAW. This is the starting point for Yisrael to enter the holy portion of the Holy One, blessed be He, and remove the leavened bread, which is a strange deity appointed over the idolatrous nations called other Elohim, foreign Elohim, and also called leavened bread and the Evil Inclination. To enter the Matzah, MALCHUT, is to enter the holy portion of the Holy One, blessed be He. This is the reason judgment is pronounced on Pesach concerning corn, as we explained that the world is sentenced in respect to *Hei*, MALCHUT. TVUAH (ENG. 'CORN') IS COMPOSED OF THE SYLLABLES *TAVO - HEI* (LIT. 'HEI SHALL COME').

354. בַּעֲצֶרֶת עַל פֵּירוֹת הָאִילָן. פֵּירוֹת הָאִילָן, פֵּירוֹת הָאִילָנוֹת מִבָּעֵי לֵיהּ, מַאן פֵּירוֹת הָאִילָן. אֶלָּא, דָּא הוּא אִילָנָא רַבְרְבָא וְתַקִּיף לְעֵילָא. פֵּירוֹת הָאִילָן, כְּמָה דִכְתִיב, אֲנִי כִּבְרוֹשׁ רַעֲנָן מִמֶּנִּי פֶּרְיְךָ נִמְצָא.

354. On Shavuot, the fruits of the tree are pronounced. HE ASKS: Why "the fruits of the tree"; shouldn't it have said 'the fruits of the trees'? HE ANSWERS: This is the great and strong tree above, ZEIR ANPIN. The fruits of the tree are mentioned in the verse, "I am like a leafy cypress tree; from Me is your fruit found" (Hoshea 14:9), WHICH ALLUDES TO THE SOULS OF THE RIGHTEOUS, THE FRUITS OF ZEIR ANPIN, CALLED TREE. THEY ARE SENTENCED AT ATZERET, AN ALLUSION TO TIFERET.

355. בְּרֹאשׁ הַשָּׁנָה עוֹבְרִין לְפָנָיו כִּבְנֵי מָרוֹן, תָּנָא רֹאשׁ הַשָּׁנָה, דָּא

הוּא רֵישָׁא דְשַׁתָּא דְמַלְכָּא, וּמַאן הוּא רֹאשׁ הַשָּׁנָה, דָּא יִצְחָק, דְּאִקְרֵי
רֹאשׁ, דְּאִיהוּ חַד רֵישָׁא דְמַלְכָּא, אֲתַר דְּאִקְרֵי שָׁנָה, בְּגִינֵי כָּךְ כָּל בָּאֵי
עוֹלָם עוֹבְרִין לְפָנָיו כִּבְנֵי מָרוֹן, וְעַל דָּא תָּנֵינָן, בְּרֹאשׁ הַשָּׁנָה, דְּהָא
בְּרֵישָׁא דְשַׁתָּא שָׁארֵי יִצְחָק.

355. On Rosh Hashanah, they pass before Him like a flock of sheep. We
learned that Rosh Hashanah (lit. 'head of the year') is the King's head of the
year, which is Isaac called head, the head of the King, ZEIR ANPIN, THE
HEAD HIS GVURAH. This place is called year, and therefore all the
inhabitants of the world pass before Him like a flock of sheep. We therefore
learned that on Rosh Hashanah, all the inhabitants of the world pass before
Him like a flock of sheep, for then Isaac abides there, WHO IS THE HEAD OF
THE LEFT WHERE JUDGMENTS DWELL. HENCE, IT IS SAID THAT ON
ROSH HASHANAH "HIS LEFT HAND IS UNDER MY HEAD" (SHIR
HASHIRIM 2:6).

356. וּבֶחַג נְדוֹנִין עַל הַמַּיִם, דָּא הוּא שֵׁירוּתָא דִּימִינָא דְמַלְכָּא, וְעַל
דָּא חֶדְוָותָא דְמַיָא אִשְׁתְּכַח בְּכֹלָּא, בְּשַׁעְתָּא דְּנָסְכֵי מַיָא, וְשָׁאֲבֵי לוֹן,
בְּגִין דְּמַיִם דָּא יְדִיעָא. וְעַל דָּא בְּאַרְבָּעָה פְּרָקִים אִלֵּין, כֹּלָּא מִשְׁתַּכְּחִין.

356. On Sukkot, Judgment is pronounced in respect to water. This is the
beginning OF THE ILLUMINATION of the King's right side, WHICH IS
CHASSADIM CALLED WATER. IT IS SAID OF SUKKOT "AND HIS RIGHT
HAND EMBRACES ME" (IBID.). The rejoicing in water is everywhere when
water is sprinkled or drawn, for water is known TO BE CHASSADIM.
Therefore, everything exists in these four times, ON PESACH THE
JUDGMENT IS IN THE SECRET OF MALCHUT CALLED CORN, ON
SHAVUOT IT IS IN THE SECRET OF TIFERET CALLED TREE, ON ROSH
HASHANAH IN THE SECRET OF GVURAH AND ON SUKKOT ON THE
SECRET OF CHESED.

357. אֲמַר רִבִּי יוֹסֵי, כַּד יִסְתַּכְּלוּן מִלֵּי, כֹּלָּא אִשְׁתְּכַח בְּהָנֵי פְּרָקִין,
אַבְרָהָם יִצְחָק וְיַעֲקֹב, דָּוִד מַלְכָּא, וּבְהָנֵי עַלְמָא אִתְדָּן, וּבְאַרְבַּע פְּרָקִין
בְּנֵי נָשָׁא אִתְדָנוּ, בְּיוֹמִין דְּאִשְׁתַּכְּחוּ בְּעַלְמָא, וּבְכָל יוֹמָא וְיוֹמָא, סִפְרִין
פְּתִיחָן, וְעוֹבָדִין כְּתִיבִין, וְלֵית מַאן דְּיַשְׁגַּח, וְלֵית מַאן דְּיַרְכִּין אוּדְנֵיהּ,

וְאוֹרַיְיתָא אַסְהִידַת בֵּיהּ בְּכָל יוֹמָא, וְקָלָא קָרֵי בְחֵילָא, מִי פֶּתִי יָסוּר הֵנָּה חֲסַר לֵב אָמְרָה לוֹ, וְלֵית מַאן דְּיָצֵית לְקַלֵיהּ.

357. Rabbi Yosi said: When you examine this, there is everything in these four times, Abraham, Isaac and Jacob, CHESED, GVURAH AND TIFERET, and King David, MALCHUT, ACCORDING TO THE EXPLANATION OF THE LAST PARAGRAPH. The world is judged by CHESED, GVURAH, TIFERET, AND MALCHUT and people are judged on these four times, THE DAYS WHEN CHESED, GVURAH, TIFERET AND MALCHUT ARE IN THE WORLD. Every day, the books are open and MEN'S deeds are recorded, yet no one heeds or lends an ear. The Torah gives testimony every day and says, "Whoever is simple, let him turn in here: for him that lacks understanding, she says to him" (Mishlei 9:4), but no one listens to its voice.

358. תָּאנָא בְּשַׁעְתָּא דְּבַר נָשׁ קָאִים בְּצַפְרָא, סָהֲדִין קַיְימִין לְקִבְלֵיהּ, וְסָהֲדִין בֵּיהּ, וְהוּא לָא אַשְׁגַּח. נִשְׁמְתָא אַסְהִידַת עֲלֵיהּ, בְּכָל עִדָן, וּבְכָל שַׁעְתָּא, אִי אָצֵית יָאוֹת, וְאִי לָאו, הָא סִפְרִין פְּתִיחִין, וְעוֹבָדִין כְּתִיבִין. אָמַר ר' חִיָּיא, זַכָּאִין אִינוּן צַדִּיקַיָּיא, דְּלָא מִסְתָּפוֹ מִן דִּינָא, לָא בְּעַלְמָא דֵין, וְלָא בְּעַלְמָא דְּאָתֵי, הה"ד וְצַדִּיקִים כִּכְפִיר יִבְטָח. וּכְתִיב צַדִּיקִים יִירְשׁוּ אָרֶץ.

358. We learned that when a man wakes up in the morning, witnesses stand before him and adjure him, but he does not heed that the soul adjures him every hour. If he hears, well, but if he does not, the books are open and his deeds recorded. Rabbi Chiya said: Happy are the righteous, who are not afraid of judgment neither in this world nor in the World to Come. Hence it says, "But the righteous are secure as a young lion" (Mishlei 28:1) and "the righteous shall inherit the earth" (Tehilim 37:29).

34. "And when the sun was going down"

A Synopsis
Rabbi Chizkiyah begins by explaining that the title verse refers to the day of strict judgment, when a man's soul departs from his body. We learn that thirty days before his death, man's Neshamah departs. As a consequence, his shadow disappears and all desire leaves him. When man is judged above, the Neshamah ascends to the Upper court of justice where it gives testimony to the thoughts and deeds of that man. If that man is sick and his judgment is favorable, he may recover. However, if his judgment condemns him, he may yet survive if God sees that he will later have merit or that he will give birth to a righteous son.

The Relevance of this Passage
Here we help cleanse our souls of sin and wrongdoing in order to sweeten judgments set forth against us. The desire to pursue spiritual development and growth is increased within us so that we may merit long life in this physical world and draw closer to the Light of The Creator through positive deeds. In addition, blessing and righteousness are bestowed upon our children, helping them to recognize and embrace the benefits of spirituality and Torah, which further increases our quality and length of life.

359. רִבִּי חִזְקִיָּה פָּתַח וְאָמַר וַיְהִי הַשֶּׁמֶשׁ לָבֹא וְתַרְדֵּמָה נָפְלָה עַל אַבְרָם וְגוֹ', הַאי קְרָא אוֹקְמוּהָ, אֲבָל דָּא יוֹמָא דְּדִינָא קַשְׁיָא, דְּאַפְקֵי לֵיהּ לְבַ"נ מֵהַאי עַלְמָא. דְּתַנְיָא, זִמְנָא דְּמָטָא, דְּבַר נָשׁ נָפֵיק מֵהַאי עַלְמָא, הַהוּא זִמְנָא יוֹמָא דְּדִינָא רַבָּא, דְּאִתְחֲשַׁךְ שִׁמְשָׁא מִן סִיהֲרָא, כְּמָה דִּכְתִיב, עַד אֲשֶׁר לֹא תֶחְשַׁךְ הַשֶּׁמֶשׁ, דָּא נִשְׁמָתָא קַדִּישָׁא, דְּאִתְמְנָעַת מִבַּר נָשׁ, תְּלָתִין יוֹמִין, עַד לָא יִפּוֹק מֵעַלְמָא, וְחָמָא דְּצוּלְמָא דְּאִתְמְנָעַת מִנֵּיהּ וְלָא אִתְחֲזֵי.

359. Rabbi Chizkiyah opened the discussion with the verse, "And when the sun was going down, a deep sleep fell upon Abram" (Beresheet 15:12). This verse has been explained, yet here is the secret of the day of strict Judgment, which removes man from this world. We have learned that when the time is come for man to depart from this world, it is the time of great Judgment, when the sun is darkened and does not shine unto the moon, as is written: "before the sun is darkened" (Kohelet 12:2). It refers to the holy Neshamah,

which is withheld from man thirty days before he departs from the world, and he sees that his shadow is withheld and not to be seen.

360. מַאי טַעְמָא אִתְמְנָעַת מִנֵּיהּ. בְּגִין דְּנִשְׁמָתָא קַדִּישָׁא סָלְקַת, וְאִתְעֲבָרַת מִנֵּיהּ, וְלָא אִתְחֲזֵי. דְּלָא תֵימָא, דְּכַד מִית בַּר נָשׁ וְאִתְחַלָּשׁ, הַאי נִשְׁמָתָא אִתְעֲבָרַת מִנֵּיהּ, אֶלָּא כַּד אִיהוּ בְּחַיָּיו, בְּתוֹקְפֵּיהּ, אִתְעֲבָרַת מִנֵּיהּ הַאי נִשְׁמָתָא, וְלָא נָהֲרָא לְרוּחָא, וְרוּחָא לָא נָהֵיר לְנַפְשָׁא, כְּדֵין צוּלְמָא אִתְעֲבָרַת מִנֵּיהּ, וְלָא נָהֵיר לֵיהּ. מֵהַהוּא יוֹמָא, כֹּלָּא מַכְרְזֵי עֲלֵיהּ, וַאֲפִילוּ צִפֳּרֵי שְׁמַיָּא. מַאי טַעְמָא. בְּגִין דְּנִשְׁמָתָא הָא סָלְקָא מִנֵּיהּ, וְרוּחָא לָא נָהֵיר לְנַפְשָׁא, כְּדֵין נַפְשָׁא אִתְחַלָּשַׁת, וּמֵיכְלָא וְכָל תֵּיאוֹבְתָּא דְגוּפָא, סָלְקָא מִנֵּיהּ וְאִתְעֲבַר.

360. HE ASKS: What is the reason his shadow is gone from him? HE ANSWERS: Because the holy Neshamah is gone and departed from him. It is not that when a man weakens and dies that the soul is removed from him, but in his life, when he is in vigor that his Neshamah departs from him, and does not shine upon the Ruach. The Ruach does not shine upon the Nefesh, and then the shadow is gone and does not illuminate upon him. From that day onward, every one proclaims that he will die, even the birds in the sky. Why? Because his Neshamah is gone from him, the Ruach no longer shines upon the Nefesh, and it is weakened and eating and every desire of the body is gone from him.

361. וְאָמַר רִבִּי יְהוּדָה, וַאֲפִילוּ כָּל זִמְנָא דְּנָפֵיל אִינִישׁ בְּבֵי מַרְעֵיהּ, וְלָא יָכֵיל לְצַלָּאָה, נִשְׁמָתָא אִתְעֲבָרַת וְסָלְקָא מִנֵּיהּ, וּכְדֵין לָא נָהֵיר רוּחָא לְנַפְשָׁא, עַד דִּדְיְיְנִין דִּינֵיהּ דְּבַר נָשׁ. וְאִי דְיְיְנִין לֵיהּ לְבַר נָשׁ לְטַב, כְּדֵין נִשְׁמָתָא אִתְהַדְּרַת לְאַתְרָהּ, וּנְהִירָא לְכֹלָּא. הָא בְּזִמְנָא דְּקַיְימָא מִלָּה בְּדִינָא. וּבְזִמְנָא דְּלָא קַיְימָא מִלָּה בְּדִינָא, תְּלָתִין יוֹמִין אַקְדִּימַת נִשְׁמָתָא לְכֹלָּא, וְצוּלְמָא אִתְעֲבַר מִנֵּיהּ.

361. Rabbi Yehuda said: Even when a man falls ill and cannot pray, the Neshamah is gone and removed from him. The Ruach does not then shine upon the Nefesh until verdict is given. If the sentence is good, the Neshamah returns to its place and shines upon everyone; NAMELY THE

RUACH AND THE NEFESH. This is true as long as Judgment is not yet pronounced. When it is, AND IT IS ALREADY DECIDED THAT HE WILL DIE, thirty days before the others, the Neshamah is gone and his shadow passes away.

362. תָּאנָא, בְּזִמְנָא דְּדַיְינִין לֵיהּ לְבַר נָשׁ לְעֵילָא, סָלְקִין לְנִשְׁמָתֵיהּ לְבֵי דִינָא, וְדַיְינִין עַל מֵימְרָהָא, וְהִיא אַסְהִידַת בְּכֹלָּא, וְאַסְהִידַת בְּכָל רַעֲיוֹנֵי דְּבַר נָשׁ, וּבְעוֹבָדִין לָא אַסְהִידַת, דְּהָא כֻּלְּהוּ בְּסִפְרָא כְּתִיבִין. וְכֻלְּהוּ דַיְינִין לֵיהּ לב״נ, בְּהַהִיא שַׁעְתָּא דְּדַיְינִין לֵיהּ לב״נ לְעֵילָא, כְּדֵין דְּחֲקָא דְגוּפָא אִשְׁתַּכַּח, יַתִּיר מִשְׁאָר זִמְנַיָּיא.

362. We learned that when a man is sentenced above, his Neshamah is brought up to the court of justice, where the trial proceeds according to its testimony. It testifies to everything and to evil thoughts he harbored, but not to evil deeds, since they are all recorded in a book. A man is judged for everything at the time of sentence above, BOTH FOR THOUGHTS AND DEEDS. The body is then in trouble more than in any other time.

363. אִי דַיְינִין לֵיהּ לְטַב, כְּדֵין אַרְפִּין מִנֵּיהּ. וְזֵיעָא אִתְבְּקַע עַל גּוּפָא, וְנִשְׁמָתָא אֲהַדְרַת לְבָתַר, וְנָהֲרָא לְכֹלָּא. וְלָא סָלֵיק בַּר נָשׁ מִבֵּי מַרְעֵיהּ לְעָלְמִין, עַד דְּדַיְינִין דִּינֵיהּ לְעֵילָא. וְאִי תֵימָא, הָא כַּמָּה חַיָּיבֵי עָלְמָא, כַּמָּה רַשִׁיעֵי עָלְמָא, קַיְימִין בְּקִיּוּמַיְיהוּ. אֶלָּא, קוּדְשָׁא בְּרִיךְ הוּא אַשְׁגַּח בְּדִינֵיהּ דב״נ, אע״ג דְּהַשְׁתָּא לָא זָכֵי, וְהוּא חָמֵי דְּהָא לְבָתַר זָכֵי, דְּאִין לֵיהּ לְטַב. אוֹ לְזִמְנִין דְּאוֹלִיד בַּר, דְּיֶהֱוֵי זַכָּאָה בְּעָלְמָא, וע״ד קוּדְשָׁא בְּרִיךְ הוּא דָּאִין לֵיהּ לְטַב.

363. If he is favorably judged, he is released. Sweat breaks out over the body and the Neshamah returns later to shine upon all, THE RUACH AND THE NEFESH. A man is never cured from his disease until he is sentenced above. You may say that there are yet many evil people who remain alive; NAMELY RECOVER FROM THEIR ILLNESS. HE ANSWERS: The Holy One, blessed be He, watches over his sentence. Even if he has no merit yet THE HOLY ONE, BLESSED BE HE, sees that he will later, He acquits him. Or sometimes He sees he will beget a righteous son and therefore the Holy One, blessed be He, judges him favorably.

364. וְכָל עוֹבָדוֹי וְדִינוֹי דְּקוּדְשָׁא בְּרִיךְ הוּא לְטַב, וּבְכֹלָּא אַשְׁגַּח, כְּמָה דִּכְתִיב חַי אָנִי נְאֻם ה' וגו' אִם אֶחְפּוֹץ בְּמוֹת הָרָשָׁע כִּי אִם בְּשׁוּב רָשָׁע מִדַּרְכּוֹ. וּבְגִין דָּא, כָּל אִינוּן חַיָּיבֵי עַלְמָא, דְּקַיְימִין בְּקִיּוּמַיְיהוּ, קוּדְשָׁא בְּרִיךְ הוּא דָּאִין לוֹן לְטַב.

364. All the works and judgments of the Holy One, blessed be He, are for the good, and He watches over everything, as it is written: "'Have I any pleasure at all that the wicked should die?' says Hashem Elohim: and not that he should return from his ways, and live?" (Yechezkel 18:23). Therefore the Holy One, blessed be He , judges favorably all the evil in the world who recover.

365. וּלְזִמְנִין, דְּאִינוּן מַרְעִין אִשְׁתַּלִּימוּ זְמַנַיְיהוּ, מִלְמִשְׁרֵי תַּמָּן, כְּד"א וָחֳלָאִים רָעִים וְנֶאֱמָנִים, דַּעֲבָדוּ מְהֵימְנוּתָא, דְּכַד שָׁרְיָאן עֲלֵיהּ דְּבַר נָשׁ מִסְתַּלְּקֵי מִנֵּיהּ לְבָתַר דְּאַשְׁלִימוּ זְמַנַיְיהוּ, בֵּין לְצַדִּיקַיָּיא, בֵּין לְחַיָּיבַיָּא, וְכֹלָּא אִתְעֲבַד בְּדִינָא כִּדְקָאֲמָרָן.

365. Sometimes, when the illness has run its course that was allotted it to afflict man, as it says, "And severe sicknesses, and of long continuance (also: 'faithful')" (Devarim 28:59), they act faithfully in dwelling upon man and leave after the set period, either the righteous or the evil. All is done according to justice, like we said.

35. "And Israel saw Joseph's sons"

A Synopsis

Rabbi Yitzchak begins this discussion by explaining the title verse. We learn that through the Holy Spirit, the righteous Israel was able to see that Joseph's sons would one day worship idols. We also learn that all the generations of the world stand in the presence of God before they are born into the world.

The Relevance of this Passage

The strength and wisdom to free oneself from idol - worshipping is bestowed upon the reader through the righteousness of Israel. Idol worshipping refers to any form of egocentric behavior where pleasure is derived from external sources as opposed to true contentment that is generated internally in our souls. Before a soul enters this world, all the secrets of the Torah are revealed to it. The soul promises The Creator that during physical existence, it will pursue the path of Torah and spiritual growth. Prior to the moment of birth, the wisdom of the Torah is then forgotten, along with our promise, and thus begins the true work of "remembering" our commitment and "reacquiring" our spiritual knowledge. This passage helps us to remain true to our promise to walk the path of the Light, and it regenerates the seeds of mystical wisdom implanted within our soul prior to our birth.

366. וַיַּרְא יִשְׂרָאֵל אֶת בְּנֵי יוֹסֵף וַיֹּאמֶר מִי אֵלֶּה, אָמַר ר׳ יִצְחָק, הַאי קְרָא קַשְׁיָא, דִּכְתִיב וַיַּרְא יִשְׂרָאֵל, וּכְתִיב וְעֵינֵי יִשְׂרָאֵל כָּבְדוּ מִזּוֹקֶן לֹא יוּכַל לִרְאוֹת, אִי לֹא יוּכַל לִרְאוֹת, מַהוּ וַיַּרְא יִשְׂרָאֵל. אֶלָּא דְּחָמָא בְּרוּחַ קוּדְשָׁא, אִינּוּן בְּנֵי יוֹסֵף, דְּאִינּוּן יָרָבְעָם וַחֲבֵירָיו, דְּיָרָבְעָם עָבַד תְּרֵין עֶגְלֵי זָהָב, וַאֲמַר אֵלֶּה אֱלֹהֶיךָ יִשְׂרָאֵל. וּבְגִין כָּךְ, מִי אֵלֶּה, מַאן הוּא דְּזַמִּין לְמֵימַר אֵלֶּה אֱלֹהֶיךָ לְטַעֲוָון אָחֳרָן, וּבְגִין כָּךְ וַיַּרְא יִשְׂרָאֵל אֶת בְּנֵי יוֹסֵף.

366. "And Israel saw Joseph's sons, and said: 'Who are these?'" (Beresheet 48:8). Rabbi Yitzchak said: This verse is difficult to understand. It is written, "And Israel saw" (Ibid. 10), yet also "And the eyes of Israel were dim from age, so that he could not see." If he cannot see, how come then: "And Israel saw"? HE ANSWERS: "AND ISRAEL SAW" MEANS that he saw through the Holy Spirit Joseph's descendants, Jeroboam and his fraternity, the same Jeroboam who made the two golden calves, and said: "These are

your Elohim, Yisrael" (I Melachim 12:28). Hence he said: "Who are these?" Who is he that will say, "These are your Elohim," about idol? It is therefore written: "And Israel saw Joseph's sons."

367. מִכָּאן, דְּצַדִּיקַיָּיא חָמָאן עוֹבָדָא לְמֵרָחוֹק, וְקוּדְשָׁא בְּרִיךְ הוּא מְעַטֵּר לוֹן בְּעִטְרָא דִּילֵיהּ, מַה קוּדְשָׁא בְּרִיךְ הוּא חָמֵי לְמֵרָחוֹק, כְּמָה דִּכְתִיב וַיַּרְא אֱלֹקִים אֶת כָּל אֲשֶׁר עָשָׂה וְהִנֵּה טוֹב מְאֹד, דְּקוּדְשָׁא בְּרִיךְ הוּא חָמָא כָּל עוֹבָדִין, עַד לָא יַעֲבֵד לוֹן, וְכֻלְּהוּ אַעֲבָרוּ קַמֵּיהּ.

367. From this, WE UNDERSTAND that the righteous see things afar, BEFORE THEY ARE MANIFEST IN THE WORLD, since the Holy One, blessed be He, adorns them with His crown. For the Holy One, blessed be He, sees into the distance, as said: "And Elohim saw everything that He had made, and, behold, it was very good" (Beresheet 1:31); the Holy One, blessed be He, sees all deeds before they are done, and they all pass before Him.

368. כְּגַוְונָא דָא, כָּל דָּרִין דְּעָלְמָא, מִסְּיָיפֵי עָלְמָא, עַד סְיָיפֵי עָלְמָא, כֻּלְּהוּ אִתְעַתְּדוּ וְקַיְימוּ קַמֵּיהּ עַד לָא יֵיתוּן לְעָלְמָא, קוֹרֵא הַדּוֹרוֹת מֵרֹאשׁ, עַד לָא אִתְבְּרֵי עָלְמָא. בְּגִין דְּכָל נִשְׁמָתִין דְּנַחְתִּין לְעָלְמָא, עַד לָא יֵיחֲתוּן, כֻּלְּהוּ קַיְימֵי קַמֵּיהּ דְּקוּדְשָׁא בְּרִיךְ הוּא, בְּדִיוּקְנָא דְּקַיְימֵי בְּהַאי עָלְמָא, וְאִקְרוּן בִּשְׁמָהָן, דִּכְתִיב לְכֻלָּם בְּשֵׁם יִקְרָא.

368. In the same manner, all the generations of the world from one world's end to the other stand before Him before coming into the world. This is written in the verse, "He who calls the generations from the beginning" (Yeshayah 41:4), NAMELY before the universe was created, for all the souls that descend into the world stand before the Holy One, blessed be He, before going into it, assuming their worldly shape and names. It is written: "He calls them all by names" (Yirmeyah 40:26).

369. אוֹף הָכֵי צַדִּיקַיָּיא, קוּדְשָׁא ב"ה אַחֲמֵי לוֹן כָּל דָּרִין דְּעָלְמָא, עַד לָא יֵיתוּן וְיִשְׁתַּכְּחוּן בְּעָלְמָא. מ"ל מֵאָדָם דַּהֲוָה קַדְמָאָה. דְּקוּדְשָׁא בְּרִיךְ הוּא אַחֲמֵי לֵיהּ כָּל אִינוּן דָּרִין עַד לָא יֵיתוּן, כִּדְכְתִיב זֶה סֵפֶר תּוֹלְדוֹת, דְּתָנֵינָן, אַחֲמֵי לֵיהּ, כָּל אִינוּן דָּרִין דְּזַמִּינִין לְמֵיתֵי לְעָלְמָא.

וְכֵן לְמֹשֶׁה, דִּכְתִיב וַיַּרְאֵהוּ ה' אֶת כָּל הָאָרֶץ, דְּקוּדְשָׁא בְּרִיךְ הוּא
אַחְמֵי לֵיהּ, כָּל דָּרִין דְּעָלְמָא, וְכָל אִינוּן מַנְהִיגֵי עָלְמָא, וְכָל שְׁאָר
נְבִיאֵי, עַד לָא יֵיתוּן לְעָלְמָא.

369. The righteous too are shown by the Holy One, blessed be He, all the
generations of the world, before they come into it. Whence do we know
that? From Adam, who was the first to be shown by the Holy One, blessed
be He, the generations before they came, as it is written: "This is the book
of the generations of Adam" (Beresheet 5:1). We learned that He showed
him all the generations destined to come into the world. Moses too was
shown, as it is written: "And Hashem showed him all the land" (Devarim
34:1), WHICH MEANS THAT the Holy One, blessed be He, showed him all
the generations of the world and all its leaders and prophets before they
were born.

370. אוֹף הָכָא, וַיַּרְא יִשְׂרָאֵל אֶת בְּנֵי יוֹסֵף, חָמָא לְמֵרָחוֹק, וְאִזְדַּעְזַע,
וַאֲמַר מִי אֵלֶּה, וְהַאי קְרָא אַשְׁלֵים לִתְרֵין סִטְרִין, לְהַאי סִטְרָא, וּלְהַאי
סִטְרָא. וְעַ"ד אָתֵיב יוֹסֵף וַאֲמַר, בָּנַי הֵם אֲשֶׁר נָתַן לִי אֱלֹהִים בָּזֶה.
וּמְנָ"ל דְּקוּדְשָׁא בְּרִיךְ הוּא אַחְמֵי לֵיהּ בְּרוּחָא דְקוּדְשָׁא. דִּכְתִיב וְהִנֵּה
הֶרְאָה אֹתִי אֱלֹקִים גַּם אֶת זַרְעֶךָ. גַּם, לְאַסְגָּאָה אִינוּן דְּנָפְקִין מִנֵּיהּ
כִּדְקָאֲמָרָן.

370. Here too, "And Israel saw Joseph's sons" means that he saw far off,
THAT THEY WILL WORSHIP IDOLS, and he trembled and said: "Who are
these?" The verse refers both to this, JEROBOAM WHO SAID: "THESE ARE
YOUR ELOHIM, YISRAEL" and to ITS SIMPLE MEANING ABOUT EPHRAIM
AND MENASHE THEMSELVES. Joseph answered it by saying: 'They are my
sons, whom Elohim had given me in this place.' TO WIT, THEY ARE GOOD,
YET HE DID NOT ANSWER HIM IN RELATION TO JEROBOAM AND HIS
FRIENDS. How do we know that the Holy One, blessed be He, showed him
through the Holy Spirit ABOUT JEROBOAM AND HIS FRIENDS? From the
verse: "And, lo, Elohim has shown me also your children" (Beresheet
48:11), "also" alludes to THE GENERATIONS that will issue from him, as we
said.

36. "And he blessed Joseph"

A Synopsis

From the explanations provided by Rabbi Yosi and Rabbi Elazar, we learn that the title verse indicates that a blessing was conferred on both Joseph and his sons, since a man's children are his own blessing. We also learn that the particle *Et* placed before Joseph is an allusion to Malchut. This means that he blessed the sign of the Holy Covenant, Malchut. According to the rabbis, all blessings originate in Binah, the source of life. They are then received by Jacob and passed to Malchut. Therefore, when a blessing is given, God must be blessed first if it is to be fulfilled. During morning prayer, we should first bless God and then bless the people of the world. We learn that when Jacob's father blessed him, he first blessed God in the statement, "the smell of my son is like the smell of a field"

The discussion then turns to the meaning of the verse, "These are your gods, Yisrael," The word "these," we are told, is a reference to the Serpent and its rider, the male and female of the Other Side who are not joined in unity like the Male and Female of Holiness. Following this, the verse, "For these I weep" is explained as a reference to the sin of the golden calf and the destruction of the temple. The word "these" is also written in relation to Holiness. However, through the Holy Spirit, Jacob saw that Jeroboam worshipped idols and correctly interpreted the verse, "These are your gods, Yisrael." He therefore blessed God and his sons, and ensured that his blessing would not be bestowed upon Jeroboam.

The Relevance of this Passage

By connecting us to the supernal blessings bestowed upon Joseph, we draw countless blessings upon our world, the dimension referred to as Malchut. This connection also ensures that all of our blessings take place after the blessings of our Creator. The Light aroused herein helps protect us from the Other Side and remove the negativity and darkness in our world resulting from the building of the Golden Calf and the destruction of the second temple.

371. וַיְבָרֶךְ אֶת יוֹסֵף וַיֹּאמַר הָאֱלֹקִים אֲשֶׁר וגו', בְּהַאי קְרָא אִית לְאִסְתַּכְּלָא בֵּיהּ, וַיְבָרֶךְ אֶת יוֹסֵף, דְּלָא אַשְׁכְּחָן הָכָא בְּרָכָה דִּבְרִיךְ לֵיהּ לְיוֹסֵף אֶלָּא לִבְנוֹי, אִי לִבְנוֹי, וַיְבָרְכֵם מִבָּעֵי לֵיהּ, מַהוּ וַיְבָרֶךְ אֶת יוֹסֵף, וְלָא אַשְׁכְּחָן הָכָא דְּאִתְבְּרִיךְ יוֹסֵף.

371. "And he blessed Joseph" (Beresheet 48:15). We have to examine this verse, since it is written, "And he blessed Joseph," yet no blessing was

conferred upon Joseph, but upon his sons. It should have been written: 'And he blessed them.' Why is it said that he blessed Joseph if Joseph was not blessed?

372. א״ר יוֹסֵי, אֶת דַּיְיקָא, כְּתִיב אֶת יוֹסֵף, בִּרְכְתָא דִּבְנוֹי הֲוָה, וְכַד אִתְבָּרְכָאן בְּנוֹי, אִיהוּ מִתְבָּרֵךְ, דְּבִרְכְתָא דִּבְנוֹי דְּבַר נָשׁ בִּרְכָתֵיהּ אִיהִי.

372. Rabbi Yosi said: The particle 'Et' before 'Joseph' ALLUDES TO MALCHUT. It is written "Et Joseph," which is the blessing for his sons SINCE HIS SONS, MENASHE AND EPHRAIM, ARE CONSIDERED TO BE MALCHUT CALLED ET. When his sons are blessed, he is blessed before them, therefore it is written also "Joseph," for man's children are his own blessing.

373. א״ר אֶלְעָזָר, וַיְבָרֶךְ אֶת יוֹסֵף, אֶת דַּיְיקָא, דִּבְרִיךְ לְאָת קַיָּימָא, רָזָא דִּבְרִית דְּנָטַר יוֹסֵף, וּבְג״כ אִקְרֵי צַדִּיק, אֶת דְּיוֹסֵף, רָזָא דִּבְרִית דְּקָיְימָא בַּהֲדֵיהּ דְּיוֹסֵף.

373. Rabbi Elazar said: "And he blessed (et) Joseph" Et is precise ALLUDING TO MALCHUT. For he blessed the sign of the covenant, NAMELY THE SECRET OF THE COVENANT that Joseph kept, WHICH IS MALCHUT. For this reason, the righteous, Joseph, is called Et, as it is written "Et Joseph" since Joseph includes the secret of the covenant, MALCHUT, that is present with him.

374. הָאֱלֹקִים אֲשֶׁר הִתְהַלְּכוּ אֲבוֹתַי לְפָנָיו. הָאֱלֹקִים: דָּא רָזָא דִּבְרִית קַדִּישָׁא, קָיְימָא קַדִּישָׁא. אֲבוֹתַי לְפָנָיו, דַּיְיקָא לְפָנָיו, דְּאִינּוּן קַדְמָאֵי עִלָּאֵי, מִקַּמֵּי רָזָא דְּנָא, אַבְרָהָם וְיִצְחָק, דְּהָא מִנְּהוֹן אִתְּזָן וְיָנְקָא הַהוּא אֲתַר.

374. "The Elohim, before whom my fathers Abraham and Isaac walked" (Ibid.): "Elohim" is the secret of the holy covenant, NAMELY MALCHUT CALLED HOLY COVENANT. My fathers indeed walked before him, WHICH MEANS THAT MY FATHERS ARE before and above this secret, NAMELY BEFORE MALCHUT. FOR MY FATHERS ARE Abraham and Isaac, CHESED

AND GVURAH OF ZEIR ANPIN, WHICH PRECEDE MALCHUT AND ARE HIGHER THAN HER, as that place, MALCHUT, is sustained and nourished by them.

375. הָאֱלֹקִים הָרוֹעֶה אוֹתִי, מַאי טַעֲמָא זִמְנָא אַחֲרָא הָאֱלֹקִים. אֶלָּא רָזָא עִלָּאָה אִיהוּ, וְהָכָא בָּרֵיךְ לְהַהוּא אֲתַר, בְּרָזָא דְּאֱלֹקִים חַיִּים, מְקוֹרָא דְּחַיֵּי, דְּמִנֵּיהּ נָפְקִין בִּרְכָאן, וּבְגִין דָּא אַדְכַּר גַּרְמֵיהּ בְּהַאי אֲתַר, וַאֲמַר הָאֱלֹקִים הָרוֹעֶה אוֹתִי, בְּגִין דְּכָל בִּרְכָאן דְּנָגְדֵי מִמְּקוֹרָא דְּחַיֵּי, יַעֲקֹב נָטִיל לוֹן, וְכֵיוָן דְּנָטִיל לוֹן אִיהוּ, הַאי אֲתַר נָטַל בִּרְכָאן, וְכֹלָּא אִיהוּ תַּלְיָיא בִּדְבוּרָא, וְעַל דָּא וַיְבָרֶךְ אֶת יוֹסֵף כְּתִיב.

375. "The Elohim who has been my shepherd": HE ASKS: What is the reason he repeats the word "The Elohim"? HE ANSWERS: This is a high secret. He blessed the place, MALCHUT, in the secret of living Elohim, BINAH, the source of life, whence blessings are drawn. He therefore mentioned himself in this place by saying: "The Elohim who has been my shepherd." For all blessings originate in the source of life, BINAH, and are received by Jacob, THE SECRET OF THE CENTRAL COLUMN. When he receives them, that place, MALCHUT, receives them from him, as all comes from the male, JACOB. Hence it says, "And he blessed *et* Joseph," ET BEING MALCHUT WHICH RECEIVED HER BLESSINGS FROM JACOB, ZEIR ANPIN.

376. בְּגִין כָּךְ, בְּכָל אֲתַר דְּבִרְכָאן אִצְטְרִיכוּ לְבָרְכָא, בָּעֵי קוּדְשָׁא בְּרִיךְ הוּא לְאִתְבָּרְכָא בְּקַדְמֵיתָא, וּלְבָתַר אִתְבָּרְכוּ אַחֲרָנִין, וְאִי קוּדְשָׁא בְּרִיךְ הוּא לָא אִתְבָּרֵיךְ בְּקַדְמֵיתָא, אִינוּן בִּרְכָאן לָא מִתְקַיְּימִין.

376. For this reason, wherever blessings are to be given, the Holy One, blessed be He, WHO IS MALCHUT, should be blessed first; for if He is not, the blessings are not fulfilled.

377. וְאִי תֵימָא, הָא יַעֲקֹב, דְּבִרְכֵיהּ אֲבוּהָ, וְלָא בָּרְכֵיהּ לְקוּדְשָׁא בְּרִיךְ הוּא בְּקַדְמֵיתָא. תָּא חֲזֵי , בְּשַׁעְתָּא דְּבָרֵיךְ יִצְחָק לְיַעֲקֹב, לָא בָּרְכֵיהּ, עַד דְּבָרֵיךְ לְקוּדְשָׁא בְּרִיךְ הוּא בְּקַדְמֵיתָא, כֵּיוָן דְּבָרֵיךְ לְקוּדְשָׁא בְּרִיךְ

-192-

הוּא בְּקַדְמֵיתָא, בָּרְכֵיהּ לְיַעֲקֹב. מנ״ל, דִּכְתִיב וַיֹּאמֶר רְאֵה רֵיחַ בְּנִי
כְּרֵיחַ שָׂדֶה אֲשֶׁר בֵּרְכוֹ ה׳, הָכָא קַיָּים בְּרָכָה לְקוּדְשָׁא בְּרִיךְ הוּא,
דִּכְתִיב אֲשֶׁר בֵּרְכוֹ ה׳, אִתְבָּרֵךְ בְּקִיּוּמָא דְּבִרְכָאן, וּלְבָתַר כְּתִיב בַּתְרֵיהּ,
וְיִתֶּן לְךָ וגו׳. כֵּיוָן דְּהַהוּא שָׂדֶה אִתְקַיַּים בְּקַיְימָא דְּבִרְכָאן, דְּנָפְקֵי
מִינֵיהּ בִּרְכָאן, לְבָתַר דְּאִיהוּ אִתְקַיַּים בְּבִרְכוֹי. כְּגַוְונָא דָא בָּרִיךְ יַעֲקֹב
בְּקַדְמֵיתָא לְקוּדְשָׁא בְּרִיךְ הוּא, וּלְבָתַר בָּרִיךְ לִבְנוֹי. תָּא חֲזֵי, בְּצַפְרָא
בָּעֵי ב״נ לְאַקְדָּמָא בִּרְכָאן לְקוּדְשָׁא בְּרִיךְ הוּא, וּלְבָתַר לִשְׁאָר בְּנֵי
עָלְמָא, וְהָא אוֹקִימְנָא דִּכְתִיב בַּבֹּקֶר יֹאכַל עַד וגו׳.

377. But you may say that when Jacob's father blessed him, he did not first bless the Holy One, blessed be He. HE ANSWERS: Come and see that when Isaac blessed Jacob, he did not do so before blessing the Holy One, blessed be He. After he did that, he blessed Jacob. Whence do we know that? From the verse: "...and said, 'See, the smell of my son is like the smell of a field which Hashem has blessed'" (Beresheet 27:27). There is a blessing here for the Holy One, blessed be He, in the words "which Hashem has blessed," and He was blessed with the establishment of the blessings. Then it says: "Therefore the Elohim give you" (Ibid. 28) since the field, MALCHUT, was established by the blessings, for they issue only from it after it is already established by the blessings. In the same manner, first Jacob blessed the Holy One, blessed be He, and then did he bless his sons. Come and see; in the morning, a man should first bless the Holy One, blessed be He, and then the other inhabitants of the world. We have explained it in relation to the verse: "In the morning shall he devour the prey..." (Beresheet 49:27).

378. וְתָּא חֲזֵי, כַּד בָּעָא יַעֲקֹב לְבָרְכָא לְאִינוּן בְּנֵי יוֹסֵף, חָמָא בְּרוּחַ
קוּדְשָׁא, דְּזַמִּין לְנָפְקָא מֵאֶפְרַיִם יָרָבְעָם בֶּן נְבָט, פְּתַח וַאֲמַר מִי אֵלֶּה.
מַאי שְׁנָא דַּאֲמַר בַּעֲבוֹדָה דָא דְּסִטְרָא דַּע״ז אֵלֶּה אֱלֹהֶיךָ יִשְׂרָאֵל. אֶלָּא
רָזָא אִיהוּ, כָּל אִינוּן סִטְרִין דְּהַהוּא חִוְיָא בִּישָׁא, וּמִסִּטְרָא דְּהַהוּא רוּחַ
מְסָאֲבָא הַהוּא חִוְיָא וְאִית מַאן דִּרְכֵיב עֲלֵיהּ, וְכַד מִזְדַּוְּוגָן, אִקְרוּן
אֵלֶּה. וְאִינוּן מִזְדַּמְּנִין בְּעָלְמָא, בְּכָל אִינוּן סִטְרִין דִּלְהוֹן.

378. Come and see: When Jacob wanted to bless the sons of Joseph, he saw through the Holy Spirit that Jeroboam, son of Nevat would issue from

Ephraim. He opened the discussion with the words, "Who are these" WHO SAID: "THESE ARE YOUR ELOHIM, YISRAEL"? (SHEMOT 32:4). HE ASKS: What is the reason he said, in relation to idol worshipping: "...these are your Elohim, Yisrael"? HE REPLIES: This is a secret. Of all the sides of the evil serpent, there is the side of the spirit of defilement considered to be the aspect of the serpent, and there is its rider, SAMAEL – IN OTHER WORDS, THEY ARE MALE AND FEMALE. When they mate, they are called 'these' IN THE PLURAL, TO SHOW THAT THEY ARE NOT JOINED IN UNITY LIKE THE MALE AND FEMALE OF HOLINESS BUT ARE SEPARATED, BECAUSE THE OTHER SIDE BEGINS UNITED BUT ENDS IN SEPARATION. They appear in the world in their several aspects; ALL THAT ARE DRAWN FROM THE SERPENT ISSUE FROM THE MATING OF THE MALE AND THE FEMALE CALLED 'THESE'.

379. וְרוּחַ דְּקוּדְשָׁא אִקְרֵי זֹאת, דְּאִיהוּ רָזָא דִּבְרִית, רְשִׁימָא קַדִּישָׁא דְּאִשְׁתַּכַּח תָּדִיר בְּב״נ, וְכֵן זֶה אֵלִי וְאַנְוֵהוּ, זֶה ה׳. אֲבָל אִלֵּין, אִקְרוּן אֵלֶּה, וְעַל דָּא כְּתִיב אֵלֶּה אֱלֹהֶיךָ יִשְׂרָאֵל.

379. The spirit of holiness, THE NUKVA OF ZEIR ANPIN, called *zot* (Eng. 'this', fem.) which is the secret of the covenant, is an imprint that is always upon man, THE IMPRINT OF CIRCUMCISION. Also "this is my El, and I will praise Him" (Shemot 15:2) and "this is Hashem," ZEIR ANPIN, WHICH ARE IN THE SINGULAR. But THE MALE AND FEMALE OF THE OTHER SIDE, SAMAEL AND THE SERPENT, are called these IN THE PLURAL. Hence it is written, "These are your Elohim, Yisrael."

380. וּבְג״כ כְּתִיב גַּם אֵלֶּה תִּשְׁכַּחְנָה, וְאָנֹכִי רָזָא דְזֹאת, לֹא אֶשְׁכָּחֵךְ, וּכְתִיב עַל אֵלֶּה אֲנִי בוֹכִיָּה, דְּהַהוּא חוֹבָא גָּרְמָא לוֹן לְמִבְכֵּי כַּמָּה בְכִיִּין. ד״א עַל אֵלֶּה אֲנִי, מ״ט. בְּגִין דְּאִתְיְהֵיב רְשׁוּ לַאֲתַר דָּא לְשַׁלְטָאָה עַל יִשְׂרָאֵל, וּלְחָרְבָא בֵּי מַקְדְּשָׁא, וּבְגִין דְּאִתְיְיהֵיב לוֹן רְשׁוּ לְשַׁלְטָאָה, אֲנִי בוֹכִיָּה, דָּא רוּחַ קוּדְשָׁא דְּאִקְרֵי אֲנִי.

380. Therefore it is written, "Even these may forget" (Yeshayah 49:15), REFERRING TO THE MALE AND FEMALE OF THE OTHER SIDE, "and I" – the secret of this, THE NUKVA OF ZEIR ANPIN - "will not forget." It is also written: "For these I weep" (Eichah 1:16), for the sin OF THE GOLDEN CALF

CALLED THESE brought them much weeping, BEING THE CAUSE FOR THE DESTRUCTION OF THE TEMPLE. Another explanation for, "For these I weep": The reason for this is that permission was given to this place, NAMELY TO THE SERPENT AND SAMAEL, to rule over Yisrael and destroy the Temple. Since they were given permission I weep, I being the Holy Spirit, NAMELY THE NUKVA called I.

381. וְאִי תֵימָא, הָא כְּתִיב אֵלֶּה דִּבְרֵי הַבְּרִית. הָכֵי הוּא וַדַּאי, דְּכָל אִלֵּין לָא מִתְקַיְימֵי, אֶלָּא מִגּוֹ אֵלֶּה, דְּתַמָּן כָּל לְוָוטִין שַׁרְיָין, כְּמָה דְּאוֹקִימְנָא דְּאִיהוּ אָרוּר, וּבְגִין דָּא אַקְדֵּים וַאֲמַר אֵלֶּה, דְּקַיְימָא לְמַאן דַּעֲבַר דִּבְרֵי הַבְּרִית.

381. It may be said that it is written, "These are the words of the covenant" (Devarim 28:69). CAN YOU SAY THAT 'THESE' IS THE NAME OF THE MALE AND FEMALE OF THE OTHER SIDE? HE ANSWERS: Assuredly those curses are not fulfilled save through these, WHICH ARE OF THE OTHER SIDE, where all the curses abide, like we explained about THE SERPENT that it is cursed, "CURSED ABOVE...EVERY BEAST OF THE FIELD" (BERESHEET 2:14). The Torah therefore preceded, saying "these" for those who transgress the words of the covenant.

382. אֵלֶּה הַמִּצְוֹת אֲשֶׁר צִוָּה ה', בְּגִין דְּכָל פִּקּוּדָא דְאוֹרַיְיתָא לְאִתְדַּכָּאָה ב"נ, וְלָא יִסְטֵי מֵאוֹרְחָא דָא, וְיִסְתַּמַּר מִתַּמָּן, וְיִתְפְּרֵשׁ מִנַּיְיהוּ. וְאִי תֵימָא אֵלֶּה תּוֹלְדוֹת נֹחַ. הָכֵי הוּא וַדַּאי, דְּהָא נָפַק חָם, דְּאִיהוּ אֲבִי כְנַעַן, וּכְתִיב אָרוּר כְּנַעַן וְאִיהוּ רָזָא דָא דְּאֵלֶּה.

382. HE ASKS: "These are the commandments, which Hashem commanded" (Vayikra 27:34), WHY IS IT WRITTEN "THESE" EVEN IN RELATION TO HOLINESS? HE ANSWERS: This is because all the precepts of the Torah purify man so he shall not deviate from the path and keep away FROM THE OTHER SIDE. THEREFORE, IT SAYS IN RELATION TO THE COMMANDMENTS "THESE." What then about, "And these are the generations of the sons of Noah" (Beresheet 10:1)? WHY DOES IT SAYS 'THESE'? HE REPLIES: Surely here too IT IS A NAME OF THE OTHER SIDE, for Ham, the father of Canaan, of whom it is written "Cursed be Canaan" (Beresheet 9:25). This is the secret of 'these'.

383. וְעַ״ד כְּתִיב וַיֹּאמְרוּ אֵלֶּה אֱלֹהֶיךָ יִשְׂרָאֵל, וְכָל הַנֵּי הַתּוֹכָא סוֹסְפִיתָא דְּדַהֲבָא. אַהֲרֹן קָרִיב דַּהֲבָא, דְּאִיהוּ סִטְרָא דִילֵיהּ, דְּכָלִיל אִיהוּ בְּתוּקְפָא דְּאֶשָּׁא, וְכֹלָּא חַד, וְסִטְרָא דָּא דַּהֲבָא וְאֶשָּׁא. רוּחַ מְסָאֲבָא, דְּאִשְׁתַּכַּח תָּדִיר בְּמַדְבְּרָא, אַשְׁכַּח אֲתַר בְּהַהוּא זִמְנָא, לְאִתְקַפָא בֵּיהּ.

383. Therefore it is written, "And they said: 'These are your Elohim, Yisrael'". It is the molten dross of gold. Aaron offered gold, which is of his side - THE LEFT SIDE - and is comprised of the power of fire. All is one because this side is considered to be gold and fire, AND THE DROSS OF GOLD IS THE KLIPOT AND DEFILEMENT. And the spirit of defilement, which is always in the desert, found then a place to gain power AND CLING TO YISRAEL.

384. וּמַה דַּהֲווֹ יִשְׂרָאֵל דַּכְיָין מֵהַהוּא זוּהֲמָא קַדְמָאָה דְּאָטִיל בְּעָלְמָא, דְּגָרֵים מוֹתָא לְעָלְמָא, כַּד קָמוּ עַל טוּרָא דְסִינַי, לְבָתַר אַהֲדְרוּ, וְגָרֵים לוֹ כְּמִלְקַדְמִין, לְסָאֲבָא לוֹן, וּלְאִתְתַּקְפָא עֲלַיְיהוּ, וְגָרֵים לוֹן מוֹתָא, וּלְכָל עָלְמָא, לְדָרֵיהוֹן בַּתְרַיְיהוּ, הה״ד אֲנִי אָמַרְתִּי אֱלֹקִים אַתֶּם וגו׳ אָכֵן כְּאָדָם וגו׳.

384. Before, Yisrael were purified from the primordial filth OF THE SERPENT, which he injected into the world and brought death unto it THROUGH THE SIN OF THE TREE OF KNOWLEDGE OF GOOD AND EVIL. FROM THIS, THEY WERE PURIFIED when they stood by Mount Sinai, but it returned again and the serpent defiled them as before and overpowered them and brought death unto them and unto the whole world for generations after. This is the meaning of the words, "I had said: 'You are angels... Nevertheless, you shall die like a man'" (Tehilim 6:7), FOR DUE TO THE SIN OF THE GOLDEN CALF, DEATH HAD POWER OVER THEM LIKE OVER ADAM.

385. וְעַ״ד כַּד חָמָא יַעֲקֹב לְיָרָבְעָם בֶּן נְבָט דְּעָבַד כּו״ם, וַאֲמַר אֵלֶּה אֱלֹהֶיךָ, אִזְדַעֲזַע, וַאֲמַר מִי אֵלֶּה, כַּד בָּעָא לְבָתַר לְבָרְכָא לוֹן, בָּרֵיךְ לֵיהּ לִשְׁכִינְתָּא בְּקַדְמֵיתָא, וּלְבָתַר בָּרֵיךְ לִבְנוֹי, כֵּיוָן דְּבָרֵיךְ לְקוּדְשָׁא

בְּרִיךְ הוּא בְּקַדְמֵיתָא, לְבָתַר מֵהַהוּא אֲתַר דְּבָרֵיךְ בְּקַדְמֵיתָא, בָּרֵיךְ לוֹן,
הה"ד הַמַּלְאָךְ הַגּוֹאֵל אוֹתִי מִכָּל רָע וגו'.

385. Therefore, when Jacob saw, through the Holy Spirit, Jeroboam, son of Nevat - who worshipped idols - who said, "These are your Elohim, Yisrael," he was shaken and asked, "Who are these?" When he later wished to bless them, he first blessed the Shechinah and then his sons. After blessing the Holy One, blessed be He, he then blessed them from that place, which he blessed first. Hence it says, "The angel who redeemed me from all evil..." (Beresheet 48:16); TO WIT, THE SHECHINAH CALLED ANGEL SHALL BLESS THEM. THIS WAY HE WAS SURE HIS BLESSING WOULD NOT BE CONFERRED UPON JEROBOAM, SON OF NEVAT.

37. "Then Hezekiah turned his face toward the wall"

A Synopsis

Rabbi Yehuda explains that he who does not beget children in this world has no life or existence in the World to Come. Therefore, because Hezekiah had no wife or children, he prayed with his face to the wall, an allusion to the Shechinah, so that the Shechinah would be with him. Hezekiah then chose a wife and prayed to The Creator. We learn that he kept and guarded the Covenant, and that he wept before God for redemption.

The Relevance of this Passage

The miraculous power of childbirth is transferred to all those experiencing difficulty bearing children. This divine force also strengthens spiritual bonds between parent and child for those who are blessed with children.

386. רִבִּי יְהוּדָה פָּתַח וְאָמַר, וַיַּסֵּב חִזְקִיָּהוּ פָּנָיו אֶל הַקִּיר וַיִּתְפַּלֵל אֶל ה'. הָא אוּקְמוּהָ, דְּלָא לִצְלֵי ב"נ אֶלָּא סָמוּךְ לְכוֹתְלָא, וְלָא יְהֵא מִלָּה חָצִיץ בֵּינֵיהּ לְבֵין כּוֹתְלָא, דִּכְתִיב וַיַּסֵּב חִזְקִיָּהוּ פָּנָיו אֶל הַקִּיר. מַאי שְׁנָא בְּכֻלְּהוּ דְּצַלֵי צְלוֹתָא, דְּלָא כְּתִיב בְּהוּ וַיַּסֵּב פָּנָיו אֶל הַקִּיר, דְּהָא דַי לֵיה דְּיֵימָא וְיִתְפַּלֵל אֶל ה', דְּהָא מַאן דְּמַצְלֵי צְלוֹתָא, אִיהוּ כַּוֵּון דַּעְתֵּיה כִּדְקָא יָאוּת, דְּהָא כְּתִיב בְּמֹשֶׁה, וַיִּתְפַּלֵל מֹשֶׁה אֶל ה', וַיִּצְעַק מֹשֶׁה אֶל ה' וְלָא כְּתִיב וַיַּסֵּב פָּנָיו, הָכָא בְּחִזְקִיָּהוּ, מ"ט וַיַּסֵּב חִזְקִיָּהוּ פָּנָיו אֶל הַקִּיר, וּלְבָתַר וַיִּתְפַּלֵל.

386. Rabbi Yehuda opened the discussion with the verse "Then Hezekiah turned his face toward the wall, and prayed to Hashem" (Yeshayah 38:2). It has been derived from the verse that a man should pray near the wall, and nothing should intervene between him and the wall, in accordance with the verse: "Then Hezekiah turned his face toward the wall." HE ASKS: Why is he different than others who prayed, of whom it does not say that they turned their faces to the wall, but it sufficed to say that they "prayed to Hashem"? For whoever prays does so with proper intention, EVEN IF HE DOES NOT TURN HIS FACE TO THE WALL, as it says of Moses, "And Moses prayed to Hashem" (Bemidbar 11:2). "And Moses cried to Hashem" (Shemot, 17:4), but not that he "turned his face toward the wall." Why does it say of Hezekiah that he "turned his face toward the wall," then prayed?

387. אֶלָּא רָזָא דְמִלָּה אִיהוּ, דְּתָנֵינָן, חִזְקִיָּה בְּהַהוּא זִמְנָא לָא הֲוָה
נָסִיב, וְלָא הֲוָה לֵיהּ אִנְתּוּ, וְלָא אוֹלִיד בְּנִין, מַה כְּתִיב וַיָּבֹא אֵלָיו וְגוֹ׳
כִּי מֵת אַתָּה וְלֹא תִחְיֶה, וְתָנֵינָן כִּי מֵת אַתָּה בָּעה״ז, וְלָא תִחְיֶה בְּעוֹלָם
הַבָּא, מ״ט. בְּגִין דְּלָא אוֹלִיד בְּנִין.

387. HE ANSWERS: The secret of the matter is what we learned of Hezekiah that he was not married at the time. He had no wife, nor did he beget any children. It is therefore written, "And Isaiah...came to him, and said to him...'For you shall die, and not live'" (Yeshayah 38:1). We derived from it that "you shall die" in this world "and not live" in the World to Come. Why? Because he did not beget children.

388. דְּכָל מַאן דְּלָא אִשְׁתַּדַּל לְאוֹלָדָא בְּנִין בְּהַאי עַלְמָא, לָא מִתְקַיֵּים
בְּעַלְמָא דְאָתֵי, וְלָא יְהֵא לֵיהּ חוּלָקָא בְּהַהוּא עַלְמָא, וְאִתְתָּרְכַת
נִשְׁמָתֵיהּ בְּעַלְמָא, וְלָא אַשְׁכְּחַת נַיְיחָא בַּאֲתַר דְּעַלְמָא, וְדָא הוּא
עוֹנָשָׁא דִּכְתִיב בְּאוֹרַיְיתָא, עֲרִירִים יָמוּתוּ, וּמְתַרְגְּמִינָן בְּלָא וְלָד, בְּגִין
דְּמַאן דְּאִיהוּ בְּלָא וְלָד, כַּד אָזִיל בְּהַהוּא עַלְמָא. מִית הוּא תַּמָּן, מִית
בְּעַלְמָא דֵין, וּבְעַלְמָא דְאָתֵי, וְע״ד כְּתִיב כִּי מֵת אַתָּה וְלֹא תִחְיֶה.

388. Whoever does not strive to beget children in this world has no existence in the World to Come, nor any portion thereof. His soul is driven from the world, and cannot find rest in any place in the world. This is the punishment indicted in the Torah by the words: "They shall die childless" (Vayikra 20:20). For when he goes to the World to Come, he who has no children dies there AND IS CONSIDERED DEAD in this world and in the World to Come. It is therefore written, "For you shall die, and not live."

389. וְלֹא עוֹד, אֶלָּא דִּשְׁכִינְתָּא לָא שַׁרְיָא עֲלוֹי כְּלָל, בְּדֵין כְּתִיב וַיַּסֵּב
חִזְקִיָּהוּ פָּנָיו אֶל הַקִּיר, אוֹלִיפְנָא דְּשַׁוֵּי רַעְיוֹנוֹי, וְכַוֵּין אַנְפּוֹהִי לְמֵיסַב
אִתְּתָא, בְּגִין דְּתִשְׁרֵי עֲלוֹי שְׁכִינְתָּא, רָזָא דְקִיר.

389. Moreover, the Shechinah did not rest upon him at all. From the words: "Then Hezekiah turned his face toward the wall," we learned that he made up his mind and decided to take a wife, so that the Shechinah, the secret of wall, would rest upon him, AS THE SHECHINAH IS CALLED WALL.

390. וּבְג"כ כְּתִיב לְבָתַר, וַיִּתְפַּלֵּל אֶל ה', מִכָּאן אוֹלִיפְנָא, דְּמַאן דְּאִית בֵּיהּ חוֹבָא, וּבָעֵי לְמִבְעֵי רַחֲמֵי עֲלוֹי, יְכַוֵּין אַנְפּוֹי וְרַעְיוֹנוֹי, לְאַתְקָנָא גַּרְמֵיהּ מֵהַהוּא חוֹבָא, וּלְבָתַר יִבְעֵי צְלוֹתָא, כְּד"א נַחְפְּשָׂה דְרָכֵינוּ וְנַחְקוֹרָה בְּקַדְמֵיתָא, וּלְבָתַר וְנָשׁוּבָה. אוֹף הָכָא, כֵּיוָן דְּיָדַע חִזְקִיָּהוּ חוֹבֵיהּ, מַה כְּתִיב וַיַּסֵּב חִזְקִיָּהוּ פָנָיו אֶל הַקִּיר, שַׁוֵּי אַנְפּוֹי לְאַתְקָנָא לְגַבֵּי שְׁכִינְתָּא, דְּהָא לְגַבֵּי אֲתַר דָּא חָב.

390. Hence it continues: "And prayed to Hashem." From this, we learned that whoever has sinned, and wishes to ask for forgiveness, should first fix his heart and thought upon purifying himself of that sin, and only then to pray, as it says, "Let us search and try our ways" (Eichah 3:40) first, then "turn back to Hashem" (Ibid.). Here too, since Hezekiah was conscious of his sin, it is written, "Then Hezekiah turned his face toward the wall," in resolution to be purified before the Shechinah CALLED WALL, for he sinned to that place.

391. בְּגִין דִּשְׁכִינְתָּא כָּל נוּקְבֵי דְעָלְמָא קַיְימִין בְּסִתְרָהָא, מַאן דְּאִית לֵיהּ נוּקְבָא, שַׁרְיָא אִיהִי לְגַבֵּיהּ, וּמַאן דְּלֵית לֵיהּ, לָא שַׁרְיָא לְגַבֵּיהּ, וְעַל דָּא אַתְקָן גַּרְמֵיהּ לְגַבָּהּ לְאַתְקָנָא, וְשַׁוֵּי עֲלֵיהּ לְאִתְנַסָּבָא, וּלְבָתַר וַיִּתְפַּלֵּל אֶל יְיָ'.

391. Since all the females in the world are in the secret of the Shechinah, the Shechinah rests upon whomever has a wife, but not upon him who does not. Therefore, Hezekiah resolved to be purified before Her, and took upon himself to marry a wife. Then he "prayed to Hashem."

392. קִיר: דָּא הוּא אֲדוֹן כָּל הָאָרֶץ, וְדָא שְׁכִינְתָּא, כְּד"א הִנֵּה אֲרוֹן הַבְּרִית אֲדוֹן כָּל הָאָרֶץ. קִיר: כְּד"א מְקַרְקֵר קִיר וְשׁוֹעַ. קַרְקוּרָא וּנְהִימָא דְקִיר, דְּאִיהוּ אֲדוֹן, כַּד אִתְחֲרִיב בֵּי מַקְדְּשָׁא, כְּד"א רָחֵל מְבַכָּה עַל בָּנֶיהָ, וְהָא אוֹקִימְנָא, וּבְגִין כָּךְ וַיַּסֵּב חִזְקִיָּהוּ פָנָיו אֶל הַקִּיר.

392. The wall is Master of all the earth, the Shechinah, as it says, "Behold, the Ark of the Covenant (of) the Master of all the earth" (Yehoshua 3:11). HENCE, THE ARK OF THE COVENANT IS THE SHECHINAH CALLED

MASTER OF ALL THE EARTH, and also called wall, as in "a breaking down of walls" (Yeshayah 22:5), WHICH MEANS the crying of the wall. For it is Master OF ALL THE EARTH, while the Temple was destroyed, as it says, "Rachel weeping for her children" (Yirmeyah 31:14), which we have already explained. Therefore, "Hezekiah turned his face toward the wall."

393. תָּא חֲזֵי, בִּצְלוֹתָא מַה כְּתִיב, אָנָא יי' זְכָר נָא אֶת אֲשֶׁר הִתְהַלַּכְתִּי לְפָנֶיךָ, רָמַז הָכָא, דְּנָטַר בְּרִית קַדִּישָׁא, וְלָא סָאִיב לֵיהּ, וְנָטַר לֵיהּ כְּדְקָא יָאוֹת, כְּתִיב הָכָא הִתְהַלַּכְתִּי לְפָנֶיךָ, וּכְתִיב הִתָם הִתְהַלֵּךְ לְפָנַי וֶהְיֵה תָמִים וְאֶתְּנָה בְרִיתִי בֵּינִי וּבֵינֶיךָ, דְּנָטַר בְּרִית קַדִּישָׁא כְּדְקָא יָאוֹת. בֶּאֱמֶת וּבְלֵב שָׁלֵם, דְּאִתְכַּוֵּון בְּכָל אִינוּן רָזֵי מְהֵימְנוּתָא דִּכְלִילָן בֶּאֱמֶת.

393. Come and see: It is said in his prayer, "Remember now, O Hashem, I beseech You, how I have walked before You" (Yeshayah 38:3). Here, he hints that he kept the holy covenant not to defile it but to guard it well, as it says here, "I have walked before You" and elsewhere "walk before Me, and be perfect. And I will make My covenant between Me and you" (Beresheet 17:1-2). AS "WALK" REFERS TO THE HOLY COVENANT, HERE TOO "I HAVE WALKED" MEANS that he kept well the holy covenant. "In truth and with a perfect heart" means that he was intent upon the secrets of faith comprised in Truth.

394. וְהַטּוֹב בְּעֵינֶיךָ עָשִׂיתִי, דְּסָמַךְ גְּאוּלָה לִתְפִלָּה, וְהָא אוֹקִימְנָא. וְהָא אוֹקְמוּהָ חַבְרַיָּיא, דְּאִתְכַּוֵּון לְיַחֲדָא יְחוּדָא כְּדְקָא יָאוֹת, וּבְגִין כָּךְ, וַיֵּבְךְּ חִזְקִיָּהוּ בְּכִי גָדוֹל, דְּלֵית תַּרְעָא דְּקַיְימָא קַמֵּי דִּמְעִין. גְּאוּלָה: דָּא הוּא מַלְאָךְ הַגּוֹאֵל, דְּדָא אִיהוּ דְּאִשְׁתַּכַּח בְּכָל פֵּרוּקָא דְּעָלְמָא, וְהָא אוֹקִימְנָא.

394. "And have done that which is good in Your sight" (Yeshayah 38:3) means that he did not interrupt his prayer between 'redemption (Ga'al Yisrael)' and the Amidah prayer, YESOD BEING CALLED REDEMPTION AND THE NUKVA, PRAYER. We have already explained, and the friends too, that he meant to declare the unison in a proper manner. He "wept sore" for no gate resists tears AND REMAINS CLOSED. Redemption COMBINED WITH

PRAYER is CALLED THE NUKVA, the redeeming angel, which may be found at every redemption in the world, as we have already explained.

38. "The angel who redeemed"

A Synopsis

Rabbi Elazar explains that the title verse indicates Jacob wished to join the high and the low, so that the blessings he bestowed on Malchut, our physical existence, would also be received by the lower spiritual bodies. We learn that the title verse alludes to Tiferet, who receives blessings from the higher grades and confers them on the upper Cherubs, Sandalfon and Metatron. The upper Cherubs spread out their wings over the place of the Ark three times daily and bestow blessings on the lower Cherubs.

The discourse then turns to address the verse, "House and riches are the inheritance of fathers" but a prudent wife is from The Creator." If man turns to the Other Side, he will receive from the Other Side. However, if God appreciates this man for his good deeds, He redeems him from the Other Side and provides him with a prudent wife. We learn that God matches couples according to the deeds of the righteous before they enter the world. A man may be matched with a "prudent wife", when he is born, but if he strays from the path of righteousness, his intended wife will be given to another. If he rectifies his ways by the time he is supposed to marry her, the other man will be rejected and he will have his rightful spouse.

Finally, the discussion reverts back to the subject of the hierarchical conferring of blessings. Rabbi Yehuda explains why the word *hayoshvi* is spelled with an extra *Yud* י *in* the verse, "To You I lift up my eyes" We also learn that the circle of the world is sustained by the central point, called "the house of the Holy of Holies."

The Relevance of this Passage

The celestial spirits that serve as conduits between mortals and the Light of The Creator, are accessible to readers of these mystical verses. Thus, sacred spiritual energy shines brighter in this world, infusing our lives with untold blessings. The good fortune to attract our true soulmate is kindled, as we become more cognizant of the illusionary material trappings that seduce us in this physical existence. This energy also enriches and deepens our marital relationships, enlightening us to the importance of building a marriage on a foundation of spiritual purpose and principles.

395. הַמַּלְאָךְ הַגּוֹאֵל אוֹתִי מִכָּל רָע. ר' אֶלְעָזָר אֲמַר, כֵּיוָן דִּבְרֵיךְ יַעֲקֹב וְאִתְכַּוֵּון מִתַּתָּא לְעֵילָא, כְּדֵין אַמְשִׁיךְ מֵעֵילָא לְתַתָּא, דִּכְתִיב הָאֱלֹקִים

הָרוֹעֶה אוֹתִי, כֵּיוָן דְּאִיהוּ נָטִיל, יָהֵיב בִּרְכָאן לְהַאי אֲתַר, כֵּיוָן דְּאַמְטֵי
בִּרְכָאן לְהַאי אֲתַר, כְּדֵין פָּתַח וַאֲמַר הַמַּלְאָךְ הַגּוֹאֵל וגו'.

395. "The angel who redeemed me from all evil" (Beresheet 48:16). Rabbi Elazar said: After Jacob gave the blessing he meant to bring unity from below upwards BY SAYING "THE ELOHIM," MALCHUT, "BEFORE WHOM MY FATHERS...DID WALK," CHESED AND GVURAH, continuing from above downwards in "The Elohim who has been my shepherd" THAT IS BINAH. HE DREW FROM BINAH UNTO HIS GRADE, TIFERET. Now that he has received, he gave to that place, THE NUKVA, and when the blessings reached it he opened the discussion saying: "The angel who redeemed..." SO THAT FROM HER BLESSINGS WILL BE DRAWN UNTO THE LOWER BEINGS.

396. פָּתַח וַאֲמַר כִּי הַכְּרוּבִים פּוֹרְשֵׂי כְנָפַיִם אֶל מְקוֹם הָאָרוֹן וגו'. תָּא
חֲזֵי, כְּרוּבִים בְּאָת וּבְנִיסָא הֲווֹ קַיְימֵי, תְּלַת זִמְנִין בְּיוֹמָא הֲווֹ פַּרְשֵׂי
גַדְפַּיְיהוּ, וְסָכְכֵי עַל אֲרוֹנָא לְתַתָּא, דִּכְתִיב פּוֹרְשֵׂי כְנָפַיִם, פְּרוּשֵׂי לָא
כְתִיב, אֶלָּא פּוֹרְשֵׂי.

396. He opened the discussion saying: "For the Cherubs spread out their two wings over the place of the ark" (I Melachim 8:7). The Cherubs stood there by miracle and three times a day spread their wings over the ark below, as it is written that they "spread their wings" and not that their wings were spread, WHICH WOULD MEAN THAT THEIR WINGS WERE ALWAYS SPREAD, BUT "SPREAD THEIR WINGS" MEANS THAT THEY DID SO THREE TIMES A DAY.

397. וְתָּא חֲזֵי קוּדְשָׁא בְּרִיךְ הוּא עָבֵיד לְתַתָּא כְּגַוְונָא דִּלְעֵילָא,
כְּרוּבִים: דְּיוֹקְנָא דִּלְהוֹן כְּחֵיזוּ רַבְיָין, וְקַיְימִין תְּחוֹת הַאי אֲתַר, מִימִינָא
וּמִשְּׂמָאלָא, וְאִלֵּין אִתְבָּרְכָן בְּקַדְמֵיתָא, מֵהַנְהוּ בִּרְכָאן דְּנָגְדָן מֵעֵילָא,
וּמֵהָכָא נַגְדֵי בִּרְכָאן לְתַתָּא.

397. Come and see: The Holy One, blessed be He, did below as He did above; TO WIT, THE CHERUBS AT THE TABERNACLE ARE LIKE THE CHERUBS ABOVE. The Cherubs above resemble boys and stand underneath that place, THE NUKVA OF ATZILUT, to its right and left. THEY, METATRON

AND SANDALFON, ABIDE AT THE HOLY OF HOLIES AT BRIYAH. They are first blessed from the blessings drawn from above, and from there blessings are drawn downward.

398. וְעַ"ד כְּתִיב הַמַּלְאָךְ הַגּוֹאֵל אוֹתִי מִכָּל רָע. אוֹתִי: דְּנָטֵיל בִּרְכָאן מִגְּוָונִין דִּלְעֵילָא, וְכֵיוָן דְּאִיהוּ נָטֵיל, יְבָרֵךְ אֶת הַנְּעָרִים, דָּא רָזָא דִּכְרוּבִים, דְּמִנַּיְיהוּ נָגְדֵי בִּרְכָאן מֵעִילָאֵי לְתַתָּאֵי.

398. It is therefore written "the angel who redeemed me from all evil," "me" BEING TIFERET, who receives blessings from the higher grades. Once it has received them, it will "bless the lads." This is the secret of the Cherubs, METATRON AND SANDALFON, from whom blessings are conferred by the higher to the lower.

399. הַמַּלְאָךְ הַגּוֹאֵל אוֹתִי מִכָּל רָע יְבָרֵךְ אֶת הַנְּעָרִים וְגו'. ר' חִיָּיא פְּתַח וַאֲמַר, בַּיִת וָהוֹן נַחֲלַת אָבוֹת, וְכִי נַחֲלַת אָבוֹת אִינְהוּ, וְהָא קוּדְשָׁא בְּרִיךְ הוּא יָהֵיב כֹּלָּא לְבַ"נ. אֶלָּא, דְּכֵיוָן דְּאַחְסֵין בֵּיתָא לְבַר נָשׁ וּמָמוֹנָא, לְזִמְנִין דְּיַחֲסֵין כֹּלָּא לִבְרֵיה, וִיהֵא אַחְסָנָא דְּאָבוֹת. אֲבָל וּמֵיְיָ' אִשָּׁה מַשְׂכָּלֶת, בְּגִין דְּאִתְּתָא, כַּד אַחְסֵין לָהּ בַּ"נ, מֵעִם קוּדְשָׁא בְּרִיךְ הוּא אַחְסֵין לָהּ, דְּהָא לָא יַחְסֵין לָהּ קוּדְשָׁא בְּרִיךְ הוּא לְבַ"נ, אֶלָּא כַּד מַכְרִיזִין עֲלֵיה בִּרְקִיעָא.

399. "The angel who redeemed me from all evil, bless the lads." Rabbi Chiya opened the discussion saying: "House and riches are the inheritance of fathers" (Mishlei 19:14). HE ASKS: How can they be the inheritance of fathers, as it is the Holy One, blessed be He, who gives a man all he has? HE ANSWERS: The Holy One, blessed be He, gives a man a house and riches, which he sometimes bequeaths to his son, for whom it is the inheritance of fathers. "But a prudent wife is from Hashem" (Ibid.), for when a man merits a wife, he receives her only from the Holy One, blessed be He, who gives her to him only after he is proclaimed throughout the firmament.

400. דְּקוּדְשָׁא בְּרִיךְ הוּא מְזַוֵּוג זִוּוּגִין, עַד לָא יֵיתוּן לְעַלְמָא. וְכַד זָכוּ

בְּנֵי נָשָׁא לְפוּם עוֹבָדֵיהוֹן, הָכֵי יַהֲבֵי לוֹן אִתְּתָא, וְכֹלָּא אִתְגַּלְיָין קַמֵיה דְקוּדְשָׁא בְּרִיךְ הוּא, וּלְפוּם עוֹבָדִין דְזַכָּאִין, הָכֵי מְזַוֵּוג זֻווּגִין.

400. For the Holy One, blessed be He, matches couples before they come into the world. Men are given a wife they deserve according to their deeds, and all men's actions are revealed to the Holy One, blessed be He. According to the deeds of the righteous, He matches couples BEFORE ENTERING THE WORLD.

401. וּלְזִמְנִין דְּקָא סְלִיקוּ בְּקְלִיטִין, וְאַסְטֵי הַהוּא ב"נ אָרְחֵיה, סָלֵיק זֻווּגֵיה לְאָחֳרָא, עַד דְּיַכְשַׁר עוֹבָדוֹי, וְכַד יַכְשַׁר עוֹבָדוֹי, אוֹ דְּמָטֵי זִמְנֵיה, אִתְדָּחֵי גְּבַר מִקַּמֵי גְּבַר, וְאָתֵי הַאי וְנָטֵיל דִילֵיה. וְדָא קַשֵׁי קַמֵי קוּדְשָׁא בְּרִיךְ הוּא מִכֹּלָּא לְדַחְיָא בַּר נָשׁ מִקַּמֵי גַּבְרָא אָחֳרָא, וּבְגִין כָּךְ קוּדְשָׁא בְּרִיךְ הוּא אִיהוּ יָהֵיב אִתְּתָא לב"נ, וּמִנֵּיה אַתְיָין זֻווּגִין. וְע"ד וּמֵיי' אִשָּׁה מַשְׂכָּלֶת.

401. Sometimes they are joined; TO WIT, IT HAS BEEN PROCLAIMED, BEFORE THEY CAME INTO THE WORLD, THAT THE DAUGHTER OF SO-AND-SO IS DESTINED FOR SO-AND-SO, BUT WHEN HE WAS BORN, man perverted his ways. His spouse was then given to another, until he rectifies his ways. If he does so by the time he is supposed to marry her, the other man is rejected and he comes to takes what is his, WHICH MEANS THAT THE OTHER ONE WHO MARRIED HIS SPOUSE BEFORE HE MADE RIGHT HIS DEEDS IS NOW REJECTED, NAMELY DIES, AND HE RECEIVES HIS SPOUSE FROM HIM. This is the most difficult task for the Holy One, blessed be He, to banish one man because of another. Therefore, it is the Holy One, blessed be He, who gives a wife to man, and by Him couples are formed. Hence, it says "but a prudent wife is from Hashem."

402. בְּגִין כָּךְ, קוּדְשָׁא בְּרִיךְ הוּא יָהֵיב כֹּלָּא לְבַר נָשׁ. וְאִי תֵימָא אִשָּׁה מַשְׂכָּלֶת וְלָא אָחֳרָא. תָּא חֲזֵי, אע"ג דְּקוּדְשָׁא בְּרִיךְ הוּא אַזְמִין טָבָאן לב"נ לְמֵיהַב לֵיה, וְהוּא אַסְטֵי אָרְחוֹי מֵעִם קוּדְשָׁא בְּרִיךְ הוּא לְגַבֵּי סִטְרָא אָחֳרָא, מֵהַהוּא סִטְרָא אָחֳרָא דְּאִתְדַּבַּק בֵּיה, יֵיתֵי לֵיה מַאן דְּיֵיתֵי, בְּכָל קָטְרוּגִין, וְכָל בִּישִׁין, וְלָא אַתְיָין לֵיה מֵעִם קוּדְשָׁא בְּרִיךְ

הוּא, אֶלָּא מֵהַהוּא סִטְרָא בִּישָׁא דְּאִתְדַּבַּק בֵּיה, בְּאִינוּן עוֹבָדִין דְּעָבַד.

402. Hence, THE TRUTH IS THAT the Holy One, blessed be He, gives a man everything. If you say that HE GIVES ONLY a prudent wife and nothing else, come and see, though the Holy One, blessed be He, prepares but goodness for men, if the man turns from the ways of the Holy One, blessed be He, to the Other Side, he will receive his due from the Other Side to which he cleft, together with accusations and evils. He does not receive them from the Holy One, blessed be He, but from the evil side to which he clung because of his deeds.

403. וְעַל דָּא, אִתְּתָא דְּלָאו אִיהִי מַשְׁכֶּלֶת, קָרָא ע״ד שְׁלֹמֹה, וּמוֹצֵא אֲנִי מַר מִמָּוֶת אֶת הָאִשָּׁה. בְּגִין דְּחוֹבוֹי דְּב״נ, הוּא מָשִׁיךְ עֲלֵיה, בְּאִינוּן עוֹבָדִין דְּעָבַד. וְעַל דָּא כַּד קוּדְשָׁא בְּרִיךְ הוּא אִתְרְעֵי בֵּיה בְּבַר נָשׁ, בְּגִין עוֹבָדוֹי דְּכָשְׁרָן, אִיהוּ אַזְמִין לֵיה אִנְתּוּ דְּאִיהִי מַשְׁכֶּלֶת, וּפָרֵיק לֵיה בְּפוּרְקָן, מִגּוֹ סִטְרָא אָחֳרָא.

403. Therefore Solomon says of a wife who is not prudent, "And I find more bitter than death the woman" (Kohelet 7:26), for one draws her to himself by the sins and deeds he commits INSTEAD OF FROM THE HOLY ONE, BLESSED BE HE. Therefore, when the Holy One, blessed be He, takes pleasure in man because of his good deeds, He provides for him a prudent wife, and redeems him from the Other Side.

404. וְעַל דָּא אֲמַר יַעֲקֹב, הַמַּלְאָךְ הַגּוֹאֵל אוֹתִי מִכָּל רָע. מַאי מִכָּל רָע, דְּלָא אִזְדַּמְנַת לִי אִתְּתָא, דְּאִיהִי מִגּוֹ סִטְרָא אָחֳרָא, וְלָא אִעְרַע פְּסוּל בְּזַרְעִי, דְּכֻלְּהוּ צַדִּיקֵי וּשְׁלֵימֵי בִּשְׁלֵימוּ, בְּגִין דְּאִתְפְּרַק מִכָּל רָע, וְיַעֲקֹב לָא אִתְדַּבַּק בְּהַהוּא סִטְרָא אָחֳרָא כְּלָל.

404. Jacob therefore said: "The angel who redeemed me from all evil." "From all evil" means that I was not provided with a wife from the Other Side, and that my children were not defective, but they were all righteous and complete to perfection, since Jacob was redeemed from all evil, THE OTHER SIDE, and did not cleave at all to the Other Side.

405. וְעַל דָּא, הַמַּלְאָךְ הַגּוֹאֵל אוֹתִי מִכָּל רָע יְבָרֵךְ אֶת הַנְּעָרִים. מ״ט אִתְחֲזוּ לְאִתְבָּרְכָא, בְּגִין דְּנָטֵיר יוֹסֵף, אֶת קַיָּימָא קַדִּישָׁא, וְעַל דָּא אָמַר יוֹסֵף בָּנַי הֵם אֲשֶׁר נָתַן לִי אֱלֹקִים בָּזֶה, אַחְמֵי לֵיהּ רָזָא דִּבְרִית דְּנָטַר לֵיהּ, וּבְגִין דְּנָטַר לֵיהּ אִתְחֲזוּ לְאִתְבָּרְכָא וְאִתְחֲזֵי אִיהוּ לְבִרְכָאן סַגִּיאִין, בְּגִין דָּא לְכֻלְּהוּ יְהַב בִּרְכָא חַד, וּלְיוֹסֵף בִּרְכָאן סַגִּיאִין, מַשְׁמַע דִּכְתִיב בִּרְכוֹת אָבִיךָ גָּבְרוּ עַל בִּרְכוֹת הוֹרַי וגו׳, בִּרְכוֹת שָׁדַיִם וָרָחַם תִּהְיֶיןָ לְרֹאשׁ יוֹסֵף.

405. Therefore "the angel who redeemed me from all evil, bless the lads." Wherefore are they worthy of being blessed? Because Joseph kept the holy covenant. Concerning this, Joseph said: "They are my sons, whom the Elohim has given me in this." To wit, he showed him the secret of the covenant CALLED "THIS," which he kept. Since he observed this, his sons are worthy of being blessed, and he deserves many blessings. Thus Jacob gave EACH one blessing, and to Joseph he gave many. This we derive from the verse, "The blessings of your father are potent above the blessings of my progenitors..." "blessings of the breasts, and of the womb...shall be on the head of Joseph" (Beresheet 49:25-26).

406. ר׳ יְהוּדָה פְּתַח וַאֲמַר, אֵלֶיךָ נָשָׂאתִי אֶת עֵינַי הַיּוֹשְׁבִי בַּשָּׁמָיִם, הַאי קְרָא אוֹקְמוּהָ, אֲבָל תָּא חֲזֵי, צְלוֹתָא דִב״נ דְּאִתְכַּוֵּון בָּהּ, אִיהוּ לְעֵילָא לְעוֹמְקָא עִלָּאָה, דְּמִתַּמָּן נָגְדֵי כָּל בִּרְכָאן וְכָל חֵירוּ, וּמִתַּמָּן נָפְקֵי לְקָיְימָא כֹּלָּא.

406. Rabbi Yehuda opened the discussion saying: "To You I lift up my eyes, O You who dwells (Heb. hayoshvi) in the heavens" (Tehilim 123:1). This verse has already been explained, yet come and see, a man's prayer offered with devotion is to be found above in the sublime deep, BINAH, whence all blessings are drawn FROM THE RIGHT COLUMN and freedom FROM THE LEFT. They all issue FROM ITS CENTRAL COLUMN to support all.

407. וְעַל דָּא יַתִּיר יוּ״ד, בְּגִין דְּלָא פָּסִיק יוּ״ד, מֵאֲתַר דָּא לְעָלְמִין, וּבְגִין דָּא כְּתִיב, הַיּוֹשְׁבִי בַּשָּׁמָיִם, אָחִיד לְעֵילָא, בְּרָזָא דְּחָכְמְתָא עִלָּאָה, וְאָחִיד לְתַתָּא דְּיָתֵיב עַל כֻּרְסְיָא דַּאֲבָהָן, יָתֵיב עַל כֻּרְסְיָא

דְּאִקְרֵי שָׁמָיִם, וּבְגִין כָּךְ הַיּוֹשְׁבִי בַּשָּׁמָיִם כְּתִיב.

407. Therefore, there is an extra *Yud* IN "HAYOSHVI" INSTEAD OF 'HAYOSHEV' IN HEAVEN. Thus *Yud*, WHICH IS CHOCHMAH, is never lacking from this place, AS CHOCHMAH AND BINAH ARE JOINED IN A NEVER-ENDING UNION. Therefore 'hayoshvi' is spelled WITH AN EXTRA *YUD*, for BINAH is attached above to supernal Chochmah CALLED *YUD*, and attached below by sitting on the throne of the Patriarchs, CHESED, GVURAH, AND TIFERET, the throne called heaven, ZEIR ANPIN WHICH INCLUDES CHESED, GVURAH AND TIFERET, WHICH ARE THE THREE LEGS OF THE HIGH THRONE BINAH. This is why it is written "hayoshvi" in heaven.

408. וּמֵהָכָא, כַּד בִּרְכָאן נָגְדֵי מֵעֵילָא מֵעוֹמְקָא דָא, כֻּלְּהוּ נָטִיל לוֹן הַאי אֲתָר דְּאִקְרֵי שָׁמָיִם, וּמֵהַאי נָגְדֵי לְתַתָּא, עַד דְּמָטוֹ לְצַדִּיקַיָּיא קַיָּימָא דְעָלְמָא, וּמֵהָכָא מִתְבָּרְכִין כָּל אִינוּן חַיָּילִין, וְכָל אִינוּן מַשְׁרְיָין לִזְנַיְיהוּ, וְהָא אוֹקְמוּהָ.

408. From this, we understand that when blessings are drawn from above, from the deep, BINAH, they are all received by the place called heaven, ZEIR ANPIN, from which they flow downward until they reach the righteous men, THE SECRET OF RIGHTEOUS AND RIGHTEOUSNESS, that are the covenant of the world, WHICH IS THE NUKVA, from which all the hosts and legions, THE LOWER BEINGS IN BRIYAH, YETZIRAH AND ASIYAH, are blessed as we already explained.

409. תָּא חֲזֵי, בְּשַׁבְעִין וּתְרֵין נְהוֹרִין, אִסְתַּלַּק עֲטָרָא דְּכָל מַשְׁרְיָין, עֲגוּלָא דְעָלְמָא, בְּשַׁבְעִין דּוּכְתֵּי, חַד עֲגוּלָא לְכֻלְּהוּ, בְּגוֹ הַהוּא עֲגוּלָא נְקוּדָה חֲדָא דְקַיְימָא בְּאֶמְצָעִיתָא, מֵהַאי נְקוּדָה, אִתְזָנַת כָּל הַהוּא עֲגוּלָא, בֵּית קֹדֶשׁ הַקֳּדָשִׁים, אִיהוּ אֲתָר לְהַהוּא רוּחָא דְּכָל רוּחִין, אִתְטַמַּר בְּגַוֵּיהּ, הַאי טְמִירוּ אִיהוּ בְּגוֹ חֵילָהָא, טְמִירָא אִיהוּ בְּגוֹ לְגוֹ, כַּד סָלְקָא דָא, כֹּלָּא סָלְקִין אֲבַתְרָהּ, הֵהֵ"ד מָשְׁכֵנִי אַחֲרֶיךָ נָּרוּצָה.

409. Come and behold: the crown of all armies is elevated through the 72 lights. It becomes the circle of the world in seventy places, all of them forming one circle. In it, there is a point in the middle, from which the circle is sustained. It is called the House of the Holy of Holies, a place for the spirit of all Spirits. Here is treasured the innermost secret, hidden among the legions. It is concealed in its innermost place. When it ascends, all THE WORLDS follow, as it is written: "Draw me, we will run after you" (Shir Hashirim 1:3).

39. "O remember not against us former iniquities"

A Synopsis

While travelling with Rabbi Chizkiyah and Rabbi Yosi, Rabbi Yehuda explains the title verse. We learn that because of Yisrael's sins, the Other Side and the heathen nations came to rule over the land of Yisrael. Knowing that they could not exist in the world without the mercy and compassion of God, they pray to Him so that He will remove their sins and protect them from the judgment of the Other Side.

The Relevance of this Passage

The knowledge and certitude that only God can protect us from the harsh accusations of the Other Side are awakened within us. The spiritual truth that we are never victims of other people's wickedness is made clearer in our own mind. Moreover, accountability for our own negative actions is kindled, inspiring us to seek out the Light of The Creator to help redeem us from our internal demons and selfish aspirations. This Light of redemption shines for all those who devoutly meditate upon the mystical letters of Hebrew with a contrite heart.

410. ר' חִזְקִיָּה וְר' יוֹסֵי וְר' יְהוּדָה הֲווֹ אָזְלֵי בְּאוֹרְחָא, א"ר יוֹסֵי, כָּל חַד וְחַד מִינָן, לֵימָא מִלֵּי דְאוֹרַיְיתָא. פָּתַח ר' יְהוּדָה וַאֲמַר, אַל תִּזְכָּר לָנוּ עֲוֹנוֹת רִאשׁוֹנִים מַהֵר יְקַדְּמוּנוּ וגו'. תָּא חֲזֵי, קוּדְשָׁא בְּרִיךְ הוּא, בְּרַחֲמוּתָא דְיִשְׂרָאֵל, רָחֵים לוֹן, דְאִינוּן עַדְבֵיהּ וְאַחֲסַנְתֵּיהּ, לָא מִסְתַּכַּל אָחֳרָא בְּדִינַיְיהוּ, בַּר אִיהוּ בִּלְחוֹדֵיהּ, וְכֵיוָן דְאִיהוּ מִסְתַּכַּל בְּדִינַיְיהוּ, אִתְמְלֵי עֲלַיְיהוּ רַחֲמִין, בְּגִין דְאִיהוּ כְּאָב דְרָחֵים עַל בָּנִים, כְּד"א כְּרַחֵם אָב עַל בָּנִים רַחֵם ה' וגו'. וְכֵיוָן דְאִשְׁתַּכַּח לוֹן חוֹבִין, מֵעֲבַר לוֹן רִאשׁוֹן רִאשׁוֹן, עַד דְאַעֲבַר לוֹן לְכֻלְּהוּ מִקַּמֵּיהּ, וְכֵיוָן דְאַעֲבַר לוֹן מִקַּמֵּיהּ, לָא אִשְׁתָּאַר עֲלַיְיהוּ חוֹבִין לְמֵיהַב שָׁלְטָנוּ לְסִטְרָא אָחֳרָא דְדִינָא עֲלַיְיהוּ.

410. Rabbi Chizkiyah, Rabbi Yosi and Rabbi Yehuda were journeying along the road. Rabbi Yosi said: Let each of us discourse upon the Torah. Rabbi Yehuda opened the discussion with the verse, "O remember not against us former iniquities: let Your tender mercies speedily come to meet us" (Tehilim 79:8). Come and see: The Holy One, blessed be He, in His

love for Yisrael, as they are His lot and portion, lets no one judge them but Himself. When He does, He is filled with compassion for them, like a father for his children, as it says, "As a father pities his children, so Hashem..." (Tehilim 103:13). If it is found that they have sinned, He removes the sins one by one, until all are removed from before Him, so that now they remain sinless so is no power for the Other Side to judge them ON THEIR ACCOUNT.

411. אָתֵי לְמֵיחַב קַמֵּיה כְּדִבְקַדְמֵיתָא, אִינּוּן חוֹבִין קַדְמָאֵי דְּאַעֲבַר מִקַּמֵּיה חָשִׁיב עֲלַיְיהוּ, וְע״ד כְּתִיב אַל תִּזְכָּר לָנוּ עֲוֹנוֹת רִאשׁוֹנִים מַהֵר יְקַדְּמוּנוּ רַחֲמֶיךָ וגו׳. דְּאִי רַחֲמֶיךָ לָא יַקְדִּימוּ עֲלַיְיהוּ דְּיִשְׂרָאֵל, לָא יָכְלִין לְקַיְּימָא בְּעָלְמָא. בְּגִין, דְּכַמָּה אִינּוּן מָארֵי דְּדִינָא קַשְׁיָא, מָארֵי תְרֵיסִין, וְכַמָּה דְּלָטוֹרִין דְּקַיְימֵי עֲלַיְיהוּ, דְּיִשְׂרָאֵל לְעֵילָא, וְאִלְמָלֵא דְּאַקְדִּים קוּדְשָׁא ב״ה רַחֲמִים עֲלַיְיהוּ דְּיִשְׂרָאֵל, עַד לָא יַשְׁגַּח בְּדִינֵיהוֹן, לָא יָכְלִין לְקַיְּימָא בְּעָלְמָא. וְעַל דָּא מַהֵר יְקַדְּמוּנוּ רַחֲמֶיךָ כִּי דַלּוֹנוּ מְאֹד, דַּלּוּתָא דְּעוֹבָדִין טָבִין, דַּלּוּתָא דְּעוֹבָדִין דִּכְשָׁרָן.

411. When they sin before Him as before, He is AGAIN reminded of the first sins, which were already removed. Therefore it is written, "O remember not against us former iniquities: let Your tender mercies speedily come to meet us." Unless Your tender mercies come upon Yisrael, they would not be able to exist in the world, for numerous adversaries and accusers await Yisrael from above. For unless the Holy One, blessed be He, would speedily send His mercies upon Yisrael before judging them, they would not be able to exist in the world. Therefore "let Your tender mercies speedily come to meet us: for we are very poor," poor in good deeds and in honest deeds.

412. תָּא חֲזֵי אִלְמָלֵי יְסַגְלוּן יִשְׂרָאֵל עוֹבָדִין דִּכְשָׁרָן קַמֵּי קוּדְשָׁא בְּרִיךְ הוּא, לָא הֲווֹ קָאִימוּ עֲלֵיה עַמִּין עכו״ם בְּעָלְמָא, אֲבָל יִשְׂרָאֵל אִינּוּן גַּרְמִין לִשְׁאָר עַמִּין עכו״ם לְזַקְפָא רֵישַׁיְיהוּ בְּעָלְמָא, דְּאִלְמָלֵי יִשְׂרָאֵל לָא יְהוֹן חָטָאן קַמֵּי קוּדְשָׁא בְּרִיךְ הוּא שְׁאָר עַמִּין עכו״ם אִתְכַּפְיָין קַמַּיְיהוּ.

412. Come and see: If Yisrael would have accumulated good deeds before

the Holy One, blessed be He, the idolatrous nations would not be standing against them. But Yisrael caused the other nations to raise their heads in the world, and if Yisrael would not have sinned before the Holy One, blessed be He, the other nations would be subdued before them.

413. וְתָא חֲזֵי, אִלְמָלֵא דְּאַמְשִׁיכוּ יִשְׂרָאֵל בְּעוֹבָדִין בִּישִׁין, לִסְטַר אָחֳרָא בְּאַרְעָא קַדִּישָׁא, הָא אִתְּמַר, דְּלָא שָׁלְטוּ שְׁאָר עַמִּין עעכו"ם בְּאַרְעָא קַדִּישָׁא, וְלָא אִתְגְּלוּ מֵעַל אַרְעָא, וְעַל דָּא כְּתִיב, כִּי דַלּוֹנוּ מְאֹד, דְּלֵית לָן עוֹבָדִין דִּכְשְׁרָן כְּדְקָא חֲזֵי, וּבְגִין כָּךְ כִּי דַלּוֹנוּ מְאֹד מַהֵר יְקַדְּמוּנוּ רַחֲמֶיךָ.

413. Come and see that were it not for Yisrael, who drew by evil deeds the Other Side to the land of Yisrael, the other heathen nations would not be ruling over it. And they would not be exiled from it. Hence it is written, "For we are very poor" in worthy good deeds: "since we are very poor" "let Your tender mercies speedily come to meet us."

40. "Serve Hashem with fear"

A Synopsis
Rabbi Yosi discourses on the title verse, explaining that the righteous should worship God in the morning and in the evening. The prayer should be performed with gladness and singing in order to bring union to Zeir Anpin. In the morning, our realm of Malchut is blessed by the two sides, Chesed and Gvurah, and in the evening she distributes the blessings to those who deserve it.

The Relevance of this Passage
The mystical Light that glows during the morning and evening hours through the prayer-connections made by the righteous radiates throughout this section. Harmony and union between the body and soul, and connection between the Lower and Upper Worlds, are achieved by meditating upon these verses with gladness and song in our hearts.

414. רְבִּי יוֹסֵי פָּתַח וַאֲמַר, עִבְדוּ אֶת ה' בְּיִרְאָה וְגִילוּ בִּרְעָדָה, וּכְתִיב עִבְדוּ אֶת ה' בְּשִׂמְחָה בֹּאוּ לְפָנָיו בִּרְנָנָה. תָּא חֲזֵי, כָּל ב"נ דְּאָתֵי לְמִפְלַח לֵיהּ לְקוּדְשָׁא בְּרִיךְ הוּא, בְּצַפְרָא וּבְפַנְיָא בָּעֵי לְמִפְלַח לֵיהּ לְקוּדְשָׁא בְּרִיךְ הוּא.

414. Rabbi Yosi opened the discussion saying: "Serve Hashem with fear, and rejoice with trembling" (Tehilim 2:10). It is also written: "Serve Hashem with gladness: come before His presence with singing" (Tehilim 100:2). Come and see, only a man who serves the Holy One, blessed be He, should worship Him morning and evening.

415. בְּצַפְרָא, כַּד סָלֵיק נְהוֹרָא, וְאִתְעֲרוּתָא דְּסְטַר יְמִינָא אִתְעַר בְּעָלְמָא, כְּדֵין בָּעֵי בַּר נָשׁ, לְאִתְקַשְׁרָא בִּימִינָא דְּקוּדְשָׁא בְּרִיךְ הוּא, וּלְמִפְלַח קַמֵּיהּ בְּפוּלְחָנָא דִּצְלוֹתָא. בְּגִין דִּצְלוֹתָא אַחְסִין תּוּקְפָּא לְעֵילָא, וְאַמְשִׁיךְ בִּרְכָאן מֵעוֹמְקָא עִלָּאָה, לְכֻלְּהוּ עָלְמִין, וּמִתַּמָּן אַמְשִׁיךְ בִּרְכָאן לְתַתַּאי, וְאִשְׁתַּכְּחוּ עִלָּאִין וְתַתָּאִין מִתְבָּרְכָאן, בְּהַהוּא פּוּלְחָנָא דִּצְלוֹתָא.

415. When light appears in the morning, there is an awakening of the right side, CHESED, in the world. It behooves man then to cling to the right of

the Holy One, blessed be He, and worship Him through prayer, for prayer brings power and strength from above, and draws blessings from the supernal deep, BINAH, to all the SUPERNAL worlds, whence blessings flow upon the lower beings. Thus, upper and lower are blessed through the service of prayer.

416. פּוּלְחָנָא דִצְלוֹתָא, דְקָא בָּעֵי בַּר נָשׁ לְמִפְלַח קַמֵּי קוּדְשָׁא בְּרִיךְ הוּא, בְּשִׂמְחָה וּבִרְנָנָה, לְאַכְלְלָא לִכְנֶסֶת יִשְׂרָאֵל בֵּינַיְיהוּ, וּלְבָתַר לְיַיחֲדָא יְחוּדָא כִּדְקָא חָזֵי, דִּכְתִיב דְּעוּ כִּי ה' הוּא אֱלֹקים, דָּא רָזָא דְיִחוּדָא בְּרָזָא דְפוּלְחָנָא.

416. The service prayer should be performed before the Holy One, blessed be He, with gladness and singing, CHESED AND GVURAH, in order to include the Congregation of Yisrael, THE NUKVA, between them, and to properly bring about unison TO ZEIR ANPIN, as it is written: "Know that Hashem He is Elohim" (Tehilim 100:3). This is the secret of unison in the secret of the service.

417. וְעִם כָּל דָּא, בָּעֵי בַּר נָשׁ לְמִפְלַח קַמֵּיה דְּקוּדְשָׁא בְּרִיךְ הוּא בְּחֶדְוָה, וּלְאַחֲזָאָה חֶדְוָה בְּפוּלְחָנֵיה, וְאִלֵּין תְּרֵין שִׂמְחָה וּרְנָנָה, לָקֳבֵל תְּרֵין אִלֵּין, תְּרֵין צְלוֹתִין, תְּרֵין קוּרְבָּנִין לְיוֹמָא לָקֳבֵל תְּרֵין אִלֵּין, דְּאִינוּן שִׂמְחָה וּרְנָנָה, שִׂמְחָה בְּצַפְרָא, וּרְנָנָה בְּרַמְשָׁא, וְעַל דָּא אֶת הַכֶּבֶשׂ אֶחָד תַּעֲשֶׂה בַבֹּקֶר וְאֵת הַכֶּבֶשׂ הַשֵּׁנִי תַּעֲשֶׂה בֵּין הָעַרְבָּיִם.

417. Nevertheless, man should worship the Holy One, blessed be He, with gladness and show joy in his service. Corresponding to the two, gladness and singing, are the two prayers and two daily offerings; of the two, gladness is in the morning and singing in the evening. Therefore, "The one lamb shall you offer in the morning, and the other lamb shall you offer at evening" (Bemidbar 28:4).

418. וְעַל דָּא, צְלוֹתָא דְעַרְבִית רְשׁוּת אִיהִי, בְּגִין דְּהַהִיא שַׁעְתָּא מְחַלֵּק טַרְפָּא לְכָל חֵילָהָא, וְלָאו שַׁעְתָּא לְאַדְכְּרָא אֶלָּא לְמֵיהַב מְזוֹנָא. בִּימָמָא הִיא מִתְבָּרְכַת מִתְּרֵין סִטְרִין אִלֵּין, בְּצַפְרָא וּבְרַמְשָׁא מִגּוֹ

שִׂמְחָה וּרְנָנָה, וּבְלֵילְיָא פָּלֵיג בִּרְכָאן לְכֹלָּא כִּדְקָא חָזֵי, הה"ד וַתָּקָם
בְּעוֹד לַיְלָה וַתִּתֵּן טֶרֶף לְבֵיתָהּ וגו'.

418. The evening service is therefore optional, since at that time She distributes prey among the legions. It is no time to be blessed but to deal sustenance. In the daytime, She is blessed by the two sides, CHESED AND GVURAH, in morning and evening with gladness and singing. At night, She gives the blessings to those who deserve it. Hence it says, "She rises also while it is yet night, and gives food to her household..." (Mishlei 31:15).

41. "Let my prayer be set forth before You like incense"

A Synopsis
Rabbi Chizkiyah discusses the title verse, explaining why incense is burned during the morning and evening services. We learn that incense is a token of gladness and creates bonds between the Sfirot, removing death, accusations, and anger, so they will have no power over the world. Rabbi Chizkiyah then explains to us the significance of the "evening oblation", mentioned in the title verse.

The Relevance of this Passage
The mystical power associated with the burning of incense is ignited in these verses, helping to remove from our midst the dark influences of the prosecuting Angel of Death.

419. פָּתַח רְבִּי חִזְקִיָּה וַאֲמַר, תִּכּוֹן תְּפִלָּתִי קְטֹרֶת לְפָנֶיךָ מַשְׂאַת כַּפַּי מִנְחַת עָרֶב. אַמַּאי מִנְחַת עָרֶב וְלָא צְלוֹתָא דְצַפְרָא, דְּלָא כְּתִיב תִּכּוֹן תְּפִלָּתִי בַּבֹּקֶר. אֶלָּא הָכֵי אִתְּמָר, תִּכּוֹן תְּפִלָּתִי קְטֹרֶת לְפָנֶיךָ, קְטֹרֶת לָא אַתְיָא אֶלָּא עַל חֶדְוָה, הה"ד שֶׁמֶן וּקְטֹרֶת יְשַׂמַּח לֵב. וְעַ"ד כַּהֲנָא כַּד אַדְלֵיק בּוֹצִינִין, הֲוָה מַקְרִיב קְטֹרֶת, כְּד"א בְּהֵטִיבוֹ אֶת הַנֵּרוֹת יַקְטִירֶנָּה וּבְהַעֲלוֹת אַהֲרֹן אֶת הַנֵּרוֹת בֵּין הָעַרְבַּיִם יַקְטִירֶנָּה. בְּצַפְרָא: עַל חֶדְוָה, דְּשַׁעְתָּא גָרֵים. בְּרַמְשָׁא: לְמֶחֱדֵי סְטַר שְׂמָאלָא, וְהָכֵי אִתְחֲזֵי. וּלְעָלַם לָא אָתֵי אֶלָּא עַל חֶדְוָה.

419. Rabbi Chizkiyah opened the discussion with the verse, "Let my prayer be set forth before You like incense; and the lifting up of my hands like the evening sacrifice" (Tehilim 141:2). HE ASKS: Why does it mention the "evening sacrifice" and not the morning service, for it does not say, 'Let my prayer be set in the morning'? HE ANSWERS: We have learned from the words, "Let my prayer be set forth before You like incense" that incense is a token of gladness, as it is written: "Oil and incense rejoice the heart" (Mishlei 27:9). Therefore, when he lit the candles, the priest used to offer incense, as it says, "When he dresses the lamps, he shall burn incense on it. And when Aaron lights the lamps at evening, he shall burn incense upon it" (Shemot 30:7-8). In the morning, HE BURNS INCENSE because of the joy brought by the season, AS MORNING IS A TIME OF JOY, and in the evening HE BURNS INCENSE to bring joy to the left side, as befits. Incense is ever a sign of joy.

420. וְתָא חֲזֵי קְטֹרֶת מְקַשֵּׁר קִשְׁרִין, וְאָחֵיד לְעֵילָא וְתַתָּא, וְדָא אַעֲבַר מוֹתָא וְקַטְרוּגָא וְרוּגְזָא, דְּלָא יָכֵיל לְשַׁלְטָאָה בְּעַלְמָא, כְּמָה דִכְתִיב וַיֹּאמֶר מֹשֶׁה אֶל אַהֲרֹן קַח אֶת הַמַּחְתָּה וְתֶן עָלֶיהָ אֵשׁ מֵעַל הַמִּזְבֵּחַ וְשִׂים קְטֹרֶת וְהוֹלֵךְ מְהֵרָה וגו'. לְבָתַר דָּא כְּתִיב וַיָּרָץ וגו', וַיְכַפֵּר עַל הָעָם, וּכְתִיב וַיַּעֲמֹד בֵּין הַמֵּתִים וּבֵין הַחַיִּים וַתֵּעָצַר הַמַּגֵּפָה. בְּגִין דְּלָא יָכְלִין כָּל סִטְרִין בִּישִׁין וְכָל מְקַטְרְגִין לְמֵיקַם קַמֵּי קְטֹרֶת, וְעַל דָּא אִיהוּ חֶדְוָה דְכֹלָּא וְקִשּׁוּרָא דְכֹלָּא.

420. Come and see how incense ties bonds BETWEEN THE SFIROT. It is attached above and below and removes death, accusations, and anger so they will have no power over the world, as it says, "And Moses said to Aaron. Take a censer, and put fire in it from off the altar, and put on incense, and take it quickly...and ran...and made atonement for the people. And he stood between the dead and the living; and the plague was stayed" (Bemidbar 17:11-13). For no evil aspect or accuser can exist before incense. Therefore, it brings gladness and connection among everything.

421. וּבְשַׁעֲתָּא דְמִנְחָה, דְּדִינָא שַׁרְיָא בְּעַלְמָא, אִתְכַּוֵּון דָּוִד בְּהַהוּא צְלוֹתָא, דִּכְתִיב תִּכּוֹן תְּפִלָּתִי קְטֹרֶת לְפָנֶיךָ וגו'. וְהַאי צְלוֹתָא דְסַלֵּיק, יַעֲבַר רוּגְזָא דְּדִינָא קַשְׁיָא, דְּשַׁלְּיט הַשְׁתָּא בְּהַאי זִמְנָא, בְּהַהוּא קְטֹרֶת, דְּדָחֵי וְאַעֲבַר קַמֵּיה כָּל רוּגְזָא, וְכָל קַטְרוּגָא דְעַלְמָא, הַיְינוּ דִכְתִיב מִנְחַת עָרֶב, דְּדִינָא תַּלְיָא בְּעַלְמָא.

421. At the time of Minchah, when Judgment rests upon the world, David was intent upon that prayer OF THE INCENSE, as it is written: "Let my prayer be set forth before You like incense." This prayer which he offered removed the wrath of strict Judgment which now ruled IN THE EVENING through the power of incense which rejects and removes wrath and any accusation in the world. Hence it says "evening sacrifice," for IT IS IN THE TIME OF MINCHAH THAT Judgment has sway upon the world.

422. תָּא חֲזֵי, כַּד אִתְחָרַב בֵּי מַקְדְּשָׁא, בְּשַׁעֲתָּא דְּאִתּוֹקַד, זְמַן מִנְחָה הֲוָה, וְעַל דָּא כְּתִיב, אוֹי לָנוּ כִּי פָנָה הַיּוֹם כִּי יִנָּטוּ צִלְלֵי עָרֶב. מַאן

צְלְלֵי עָרֶב. אִינּוּן מְקַטְרְגִין דְּעַלְמָא, וְרוֹגְזֵי דְּדִינִין, דִּזְמִינִין בְּהַהִיא
שַׁעֲתָא. וְע״ד תָּנִינָן, דְּבָעֵי בַּר נָשׁ לְכַוְּונָא דַעְתֵּיהּ, בִּצְלוֹתָא דְמִנְחָה.
בְּכֻלְּהוּ צְלוֹתָא בָּעֵי בַּר נָשׁ לְכַוְּונָא דַעְתֵּיהּ, וּבְהַאי צְלוֹתָא יַתִּיר
מִכֻּלְּהוּ, בְּגִין דְּדִינָא שַׁרְיָא בְּעַלְמָא. וְע״ד זְמַן צְלוֹתָא דְמִנְחָה, יִצְחָק
תַּקֵּין לֵיהּ, וְהָא אוּקְמוּהָ.

422. Come and see: When the Temple was destroyed, it was burned at the time of Minchah. Therefore it is written, "Woe to us! for the day declines, for the shadows of the evening are stretched out" (Yirmeyah 6:4). The evening shadows are the accusers in the world and the wrath of Judgment that are in wait at the time. We have therefore learned that it behooves man to pray with great intention at all prayers, but at Minchah more than the rest, since Judgment then rests upon the world. This is why it was Isaac who instituted the prayer of Minchah, WHICH IS OF JUDGMENT AND THE LEFT, as we have already explained.

42. A formidable mountain

A Synopsis

While walking, Rabbi Yosi, Rabbi Yehuda, and Rabbi Chizkiyah encounter a formidable mountain. Although Rabbi Yosi is initially afraid of the danger they may encounter, knowing that where danger is obvious, one should be afraid, the three continue on. Since all three are worthy of the Shechinah's protection, and knowing that demons and evil spirits will not attack a threesome, the companions are assured that no harm will come to them. They then discuss the verse, "The angel who redeemed me" Through their discourse, we learn that the "angel" is an allusion to the Shechinah. As long as man prays to God before he begins a journey, the Shechinah accompanies him and delivers him from harm.

The Relevance of this Passage

The protective Light from the righteous threesome of Rabbis Yosi, Yehuda, and Hezekiah filters into our lives, safeguarding us from unseen negative forces and evil entities that can wreak havoc in our lives. The blessings of The Creator emanate from these words, giving us further protection in our journeys, both physical and spiritual.

423. עַד דַּהֲווֹ אַזְלֵי, אָעֲלוּ בְּחַד טוּרָא, א"ר יוֹסִי, הַאי טוּרָא דַחֲלָא, נֶהַךְ וְלָא נִתְעַכֵּב הָכָא, בְּגִין דְּטוּרָא דְּחִילָא הוּא. אָמַר רַבִּי יְהוּדָה, אִי הֲוָה חַד, הֲוָה אֲמֵינָא הָכִי, דְּהָא תָּנִינָן דְּמַאן דְּאָזֵיל יְחִידָאי בְּאוֹרְחָא אִתְחַיֵּיב בְּנַפְשֵׁיהּ, אֲבָל תְּלָתָא לָא, וְכָל חַד וְחַד מִינָן, אִתְחֲזֵי דְּלָא תַעֲדֵי מִינָן שְׁכִינְתָּא.

423. While they were walking, they reached a mountain. Rabbi Yosi said: This mountain is formidable, let us not remain here but walk on. Rabbi Yehuda said: If you were solitary, I would advise it, for we have learned that he who walks alone on the road endangers his life, but this does not apply to three. Also, each of us is worthy OF PROTECTION, that the Shechinah will not depart from him.

424. א"ר יוֹסִי, הָא תָּנִינָן דְּלָא יִסְמוֹךְ בַּר נָשׁ עַל נִסָּא. מְנָלָן. מִשְׁמוּאֵל, דִּכְתִיב אֵיךְ אֵלֵךְ וְשָׁמַע שָׁאוּל וַהֲרָגָנִי, וְהָא אִתְחֲזֵי שְׁמוּאֵל יַתִּיר מִינָן. אָמַר לֵיהּ, אֲפִילוּ הָכִי, אִיהוּ הֲוָה חַד, וְהֶזֵּיקָא אִשְׁתַּכַּח

לְעֵינָא. אֲבָל אֲנַן תְּלָתָא, וְהֶזֵּיקָא לָא אִשְׁתַּכַּח לְעֵינָא. דְּאִי מִשּׁוּם מַזִּיקִין. הָא תָּנֵינָן, דְּלִתְלָתָא לָא מִתְחֲזֵי, וְלָא מַזְקֵי, וְאִי מִשּׁוּם לִסְטִים, לָא מִשְׁתַּכְּחֵי הָכָא, דְּהָא רָחִיק מֵיִשּׁוּבָא הַאי טוּרָא, וּבְנֵי נָשָׁא לָא מִשְׁתַּכְּחֵי הָכָא, בְּרַם דְּחִילוּ הוּא, דְּחֵיוָון בָּרָא דְּמִשְׁתַּכְּחִין הָכָא.

424. Rabbi Yosi said: We have learned that a man should not rely on a miracle. We know this from Samuel, as it is written: "How can I go? If Saul hears it, he will kill me" (I Shmuel 16:2), and Samuel was more worthy OF A MIRACLE than us. He said to him: Even so THAT HE WAS WORTHIER OF A MIRACLE THAN US, he was alone, and the danger was obvious, FOR IT WAS CERTAIN THAT SAUL WOULD HEAR OF IT AND KILL HIM. But we are three, and there is no danger in sight, TO WIT, IT IS NOT CERTAIN. If it be evil spirits, DEMONS, we have learned that they do not appear before or hurt a threesome; if it is a robber, there are none here, since the mountain is far from inhabited places, and there are no people here, but there is fear of wild beasts here.

425. פְּתַח וְאָמַר הַמַּלְאָךְ הַגּוֹאֵל אוֹתִי מִכָּל רַע, הַאי קְרָא אִית לְאִסְתַּכְּלָא בֵּיהּ, הַגּוֹאֵל, אֲשֶׁר גָּאַל מִבְּעֵי לֵיהּ, מַאי הַגּוֹאֵל. בְּגִין דְּהוּא מִשְׁתַּכַּח תָּדִיר לְגַבֵּי בְּנֵי נָשָׁא, וְלָא אַעֲדֵי מִבַּ"נ זַכָּאָה לְעָלְמִין. תָּא חֲזֵי, הַמַּלְאָךְ הַגּוֹאֵל אוֹתִי דָּא שְׁכִינְתָּא, דְּאָזִיל עִמֵּיהּ דְּבַ"נ תָּדִיר, וְלָא אַעֲדֵי מִנֵּיהּ, כַּד בַּ"נ נָטִיר פִּקּוּדֵי אוֹרַיְיתָא. וְעַ"ד יִזְדַּהַר בַּר נָשׁ, דְּלָא יִפּוֹק יְחִידָאי בְּאוֹרְחָא, מַאי יְחִידָאי. דְּיִזְדַּהַר בַּ"נ לְמִטַּר פִּקּוּדֵי דְּאוֹרַיְיתָא, בְּגִין דְּלָא תַעֲדֵי מִנֵּיהּ שְׁכִינְתָּא, וְיִצְטָרֵךְ לְמֵיזַל יְחִידָאי, בְּלָא זוּוּגָא דִּשְׁכִינְתָּא.

425. He opened the discussion saying: "The angel who redeemed (lit. 'redeems') me…" (Beresheet 48:16). HE ASKS: It says "redeems," while it should have been 'who redeemed.' Why the present tense? HE REPLIES: This is because he abides always with people, and never abandons a righteous man. Come and see: The angel who redeems me is the Shechinah, who continually accompanies man, never turns from him as long as he observes the precepts of the Torah. A man should therefore be careful not to go out alone on the road. HE ASKS: What is 'alone'? HE ANSWERS: A man should be careful to keep the precepts of the Torah, so that the Shechinah shall not depart from him, and he will have to go alone, unaccompanied by the Shechinah.

426. תָּא חֲזֵי, כַּד נָפֵיק בַּר נָשׁ לְאוֹרְחָא, יְסַדֵּר צְלוֹתָא קַמֵּי מָארֵיהּ, בְּגִין לְאַמְשָׁכָא עֲלֵיהּ שְׁכִינְתָּא, וּלְבָתַר יִפּוֹק לְאוֹרְחָא, וְיִשְׁכַּח זוּוּגָא דִשְׁכִינְתָּא, לְמִפְרַק לֵיהּ בְּאוֹרְחָא, וּלְשֵׁזָבָא לֵיהּ, בְּכָל מַה דְּאִצְטְרִיךְ.

426. Come and see: When a man sets out on his way, he should pray before his Master in order to draw the Shechinah upon him, and then go out on his way, joined by the Shechinah, who would redeem him on the way and save him in time of need.

427. מַה כְּתִיב בְּיַעֲקֹב, אִם יִהְיֶה אֱלֹקִים עִמָּדִי, דָּא זִוּוּגָא דִשְׁכִינְתָּא. וּשְׁמָרַנִי בַּדֶּרֶךְ הַזֶּה, לְמִפְרַק לִי מִכֹּלָּא, וְיַעֲקֹב יְחִידָאִי הֲוָה בְּהַהוּא זִמְנָא, וּשְׁכִינְתָּא אָזְלַת קַמֵּיהּ, כָּל שֶׁכֵּן חַבְרַיָּיא דְאִית בֵּינַיְיהוּ מִלִּין דְּאוֹרַיְיתָא, עַל אַחַת כַּמָּה וְכַמָּה.

427. It is written that Jacob said: "If Elohim will be with me," referring to the union with the Shechinah "and will keep me in this way" (Beresheet 28:20) to deliver him from any HARM. Jacob was solitary at the time, and the Shechinah walked before him. So much more for friends with the words of the Torah among them.

428. א"ר יוֹסֵי, מַאי נַעֲבֵיד, אִי נִתְעַכֵּב הָכָא, הָא יוֹמָא מָאִיךְ לְמֵיעַל, אִי נֵהַךְ לְעֵילָא, טוּרָא רַב אִיהוּ, וּדְחִילוּ דְחֵיוָון חַקְלָא דְּחֵילְנָא. א"ר יְהוּדָה, תְּוָוהְנָא עֲלָךְ ר' יוֹסֵי. א"ל הָא הָא תָּנִינָן דְּלָא יִסְמוֹךְ בַּר נָשׁ עַל נִיסָא, דְּקוּדְשָׁא בְּרִיךְ הוּא לָא יַרְחִישׁ נִיסָא בְּכָל שַׁעֲתָא. א"ל ה"מ יְחִידָאִי, אֲבָל אֲנַחְנָא תְּלָתָא, וּמַלֵּי אוֹרַיְיתָא בֵּינָנָא, וּשְׁכִינְתָּא עִמָּנָא, לָא דָחֵילְנָא.

428. Rabbi Yosi said: What shall we do? If we stay here, the day declines and if we climb, it is a great and formidable mountain and I fear the wild beasts. Rabbi Yehuda said: I am amazed at you THAT YOU ARE SO AFRAID.

Rabbi Yosi said to him: We have learned that a man should not rely on a miracle, since the Holy One, blessed be He, does not perform miracles at all times. He said to him: This is true for a lone man, but we are three. With words of the Torah between us, and the Shechinah with us, I have no fear.

429. עַד דַּהֲווֹ אַזְלֵי, חָמוּ לְעֵילָא בְּטוּרָא, טִנָּרָא חַד, וְחַד מְעַרְתָּא בְּגַוֵּוהּ. א״ר יְהוּדָה, נֵיהַךְ וְנֵיסַק לְהַהוּא טִינָרָא, דַּאֲנָא חָמֵי חֲדָא מְעַרְתָּא תַּמָּן. סְלִיקוּ לְתַמָּן, וְחָמוּ הַהִיא מְעַרְתָּא. א״ר יוֹסֵי, דָּחֵילְנָא, דִּילְמָא הַהִיא מְעַרְתָּא אֲתַר דִּלְחֵיוָון אִיהוּ, וְלָא יִפְגְּעוּ לוֹן הָכָא.

429. While they were walking they saw a rock with a cave in it. Rabbi Yehuda said: Let us climb to that rock, for I see a cave in it. They went there and saw the cave. Rabbi Yosi said: I am afraid, lest this cave is a lair of beasts, which might harm us.

430. א״ר יְהוּדָה לר׳ חִזְקִיָּה, הָא חָמֵינָא דְּר׳ יוֹסֵי דָּחֵיל אִיהוּ, אִי תֵּימָא בְּגִין דְּאִיהוּ חַטָּאָה, דְּכָל מַאן דְּדָחֵיל, חַטָּאָה אִיהוּ, דִּכְתִיב פָּחֲדוּ בְצִיּוֹן חַטָּאִים, הָא לָאו אִיהוּ חַטָּאָה, וּכְתִיב וְצַדִּיקִים כִּכְפִיר יִבְטָח. א״ר יוֹסֵי, בְּגִין דְּנִזְקָא שְׁכִיחַ.

430. Rabbi Yehuda said to Rabbi Chizkiyah, I see that Rabbi Yosi is afraid. You might say that this is since he is a sinner, for whoever fears is a sinner, as it is written: "The sinners in Zion are afraid" (Yeshayah 33:14). Yet is no sinner BUT A RIGHTEOUS MAN, and it is written, "But the righteous are bold as a lion" (Mishlei 28:1). Rabbi Yosi said: It is because danger is obvious AND WHEREVER DAMAGE IS OBVIOUS ONE SHOULD BE AFRAID.

43. Three watches

A Synopsis

Rabbi Yehuda, Rabbi Chizkiyah, and Rabbi Yosi enter a cave to rest for the night. They divide the night into three watches and begin discussing the verse, "I will sing the mercies of The Creator forever." We learn that Abraham is aligned completely with the attribute of Chesed. Therefore, God tested him so that he would be included in judgment, thus perfecting him. Another explanation reveals that this verse indicates God's kindness and truth to all creatures. We then learn that God revealed the secret of Faith to Abraham. Abraham in turn recognized that the world, the secret of Malchut, was created by judgment, but could not have endured without Chesed, mercy.

The discussion next turns to the verse, "In the beginning." We learn that this phrase includes the Female Principle and Chochmah as one. The first building of the world, the Female Principle, derived its existence from Chesed. On the second day it was included in Gvurah, thereby perfecting Zeir Anpin. After discussing the verse, "I have made a Covenant with My chosen," the rabbis speak of the verse, "I have sworn to David My servant." We're told that this oath is the secret of Faith and indicates that the Female Principle and Yesod will be separated only during the time of exile. During this joyless time, God finds pleasure only when Yisrael below study the Torah and sanctify the Holy Name.

Rabbi Yosi then opens a discussion of the verse, "Whereupon are its foundations fastened?" This question concerns the foundation upon which the seven pillars of the world rest. That is, if the universe rests on the seven pillars of the world, upon what do the seven pillars rest? There follows a discourse on "the foundation stone", the central point of the world found in Jerusalem, and we learn about the three watches of the night, during which the angels sing and chant praises to God.

The Relevance of this Passage

A delicate balance of judgement and mercy is attained within our souls, giving us the ability to share and love others in a pure and spiritual manner. Judgement, sweetened with the appropriate measure of mercy, is akin to a devoted parent reprimanding their child out of love and concern for the child's welfare. Because the universe reflects all of our behavioral actions towards others back at us, it is vital that we extend mercy and judgement in proper measure so that life treats us kindly in return.

431. א״ל אִי נִזְקָא שְׁכִיחַ, הָכִי הוּא, אֲבָל הָכָא לָא אִשְׁתַּכַּח נִזְקָא,

וּלְבָתַר דַּאֲנַן נֵיעוֹל לִמְעַרְתָּא, לָא לֵיעוֹל נִזְקָא, לְצַעֲרָא לָן. עָאלוּ
לִמְעַרְתָּא, א"ר יְהוּדָה, נִפְלוֹג לֵילְיָא לִתְלַת מִשְׁמָרוֹת דַּהֲוֵי לֵילְיָא, כָּל
חַד וְחַד מִנָּן, לֵיקוּם עַל קִיּוּמֵיהּ, בְּהָנֵי תְּלַת סִטְרֵי לֵילְיָא, וְלָא נִדְמוּךְ.

431. RABBI YEHUDA said TO RABBI CHIZKIYAH, If harm is probable, it is
SO AND WE SHOULD BE AFRAID, but it is not probable FOR WE SEE HERE
NO BEASTS WHICH COULD HARM US. And after we enter the cave, WE ARE
SAFE for no evil will follow to harm us. THEREFORE IT IS SAID: "BUT THE
RIGHTEOUS ARE BOLD AS A LION" (MISHLEI 28:1). They entered the
cave. Rabbi Yehuda said: We shall divide the night into three watches. Each
of us will stand guard at one watch of the night and we shall keep awake.

432. פָּתַח ר' יְהוּדָה וַאֲמַר, מַשְׂכִּיל לְאֵיתָן הָאֶזְרָחִי, הַאי תּוּשְׁבַּחְתָּא
אַבְרָהָם אָבִינוּ אַמְרָהּ בְּשַׁעְתָּא דְּאִשְׁתַּדַּל בְּפוּלְחָנָא דְקוּדְשָׁא בְּרִיךְ
הוּא, וְעָבֵיד חֶסֶד עִם בְּנֵי עַלְמָא, דְּיִשְׁתְּמוֹדְעוּן כֹּלָּא לְקוּדְשָׁא בְּרִיךְ
הוּא, דְּקוּדְשָׁא בְּרִיךְ הוּא שַׁלִּיט עַל אַרְעָא. וְאִקְרֵי אֵיתָן. בְּגִין, דְּאִתְקַּף
בְּתִקְפוּ בֵּיהּ בְּקוּדְשָׁא בְּרִיךְ הוּא.

432. Rabbi Yehuda opened the discussion saying: "A Maskil of Eitan the
Ezrachite" (Tehilim 89:1). This hymn was sung by the Patriarch Abraham
when he strove to serve the Holy One, blessed be He, by doing kindness
with the people of the world, in making them all acknowledge that the Holy
One, blessed be He, reigns over the land. He is called Eitan (lit. 'strong')
since he was strongly attached to the Holy One, blessed be He.

433. חַסְדֵּי ה' עוֹלָם אָשִׁירָה, וְכִי מִסִּטְרָא דַּחֲסִידִים אַתְיָין לְזַמְּרָא,
אֶלָּא הָכָא אִתְכְּלִיל סִטְרָא דִשְׂמָאלָא בִּימִינָא, וְעַ"ד קוּדְשָׁא בְּרִיךְ הוּא
נַסֵּי לְאַבְרָהָם, וּבָחֵין לֵיהּ, וְהָא אִתְּמַר דְּיִצְחָק בַּר תְּלָתִין וְשֶׁבַע שְׁנִין
הֲוָה בְּהַהוּא זִמְנָא, מַאי נִסָּה אֶת אַבְרָהָם, נִסָּה אֶת יִצְחָק מִבָּעֵי לֵיהּ.
אֶלָּא נִסָּה אֶת אַבְרָהָם, דְּיִשְׁתַּכַּח בְּדִינָא, וּלְאִתְכְּלָלָא בְּדִינָא, דְּיִשְׁתַּכַּח
שְׁלִים כִּדְקָא יָאוֹת, וְעַ"ד חַסְדֵּי ה' עוֹלָם אָשִׁירָה.

433. "I will sing the mercies (Heb. *chassadim*) of Hashem forever" (Tehilim
89:2): HE ASKS: Why does singing come from the side of the pious (Heb.

chassidim) WHO ARE OF THE RIGHT COLUMN, SEEING THAT SINGING COMES FROM THE LEFT COLUMN? HE ANSWERS: Here the left is included within the right. Therefore the Holy One, blessed be He, tried Abraham and tested him. We learned that Isaac was 37 at the time OF THE BINDING. Why does it say that He tried Abraham? It should have said that He tried Isaac. The reason it says that He tried Abraham is to make him be of Judgment, properly included in Judgment, SINCE HE WAS WHOLLY OF THE ATTRIBUTE OF CHESED. In this way will he be perfected. Therefore, "I will sing the Mercies of Hashem forever," SINCE HE WAS ALREADY INCLUDED OF THE LEFT COLUMN, WHENCE SINGING COMES FROM.

434. דְּאָ חַסְדֵּי ה' עוֹלָם אָשִׁירָה, אִינּוּן חֲסָדִים, דְּקוּדְשָׁא בְּרִיךְ הוּא עָבֵיד עִם עָלְמָא. לְדוֹר וָדוֹר אוֹדִיעַ אֱמוּנָתְךָ בְּפִי, טִיבוּ וּקְשׁוֹט, דְּעָבֵיד עִם כֹּלָּא. לְדוֹר וָדוֹר אוֹדִיעַ אֱמוּנָתְךָ, דָּא מְהֵימְנוּתָא דְּקוּדְשָׁא בְּרִיךְ הוּא דְּאוֹדַע אַבְרָהָם בְּעָלְמָא, וְאַדְכַּר לֵיהּ בְּפוּמָא דְּכָל בִּרְיָין, וְעַל דָּא אוֹדִיעַ אֱמוּנָתְךָ בְּפִי.

434. Another explanation for: "I will sing the Mercies of Hashem forever." These are the mercies that the Holy One, blessed be He, does by the world. "With my mouth I will make known Your faithfulness to all generations" (Ibid.) refers to the kindness and truth He confers upon all. It is the faith in the Holy One, blessed be He, that Abraham spread in the world, and caused Him to be mentioned on the tongue of all creatures. Therefore "with my mouth I will make known Your faithfulness."

435. וְקוּדְשָׁא בְּרִיךְ הוּא אוֹדַע לֵיהּ לְאַבְרָהָם רָזָא דִּמְהֵימְנוּתָא, וְכַד יָדַע רָזָא דִּמְהֵימְנוּתָא, יָדַע דְּאִיהוּ עִיקָּרָא וְקִיּוּמָא דְּעָלְמָא, דִּבְגִינֵיהּ אִתְבְּרֵי עָלְמָא, וְאִתְקַיַּים, הַהַ"ד כִּי אָמַרְתִּי עוֹלָם חֶסֶד יִבָּנֶה וְגו'. דְּכַד בָּרָא קוּדְשָׁא בְּרִיךְ הוּא עָלְמָא, חָמָא דְּלָא יָכִיל לְמֵיקַם, עַד דְּאוֹשִׁיט יְמִינָא עֲלֵיהּ וְאִתְקַיַּים, וְאִי לָאו דְּאוֹשִׁיט יְמִינָא עֲלֵיהּ, לָא אִתְקַיַּים, בְּגִין דְּעָלְמָא דָּא בְּדִינָא אִתְבְּרֵי, וְהָא אוֹקִימְנָא.

435. The Holy One, blessed be He, revealed to Abraham the secret of faith, WHICH IS THE NUKVA. When he knew it, ABRAHAM knew that the world was created and existed for his sake, FOR HE IS THE SECRET OF CHESED.

Hence, "For I have said: 'The world is built by love (lit. 'Chesed')'" (Tehilim 89:3). For when the Holy One, blessed be He, created the universe, THE NUKVA, He saw the world could not endure, so He extended His right hand, WHICH IS CHESED, and it endured. If He had not extended His right upon it, it would not have existed since this world, THE SECRET OF THE NUKVA, was created by Judgment AND THEREFORE CANNOT EXIST WITHOUT CHESED, as we have already explained.

436. וְאִתְּמָר בְּרֵאשִׁית, וְרָזָא כְּלָלָא חָדָא, תְּרֵין גְּווֹנִין הָכָא, בְּרֵאשִׁית, אע"ג דַּאֲמָרָן שֵׁירוּתָא מִתַּתָּא לְעֵילָּא, רֵאשִׁית הָכֵי נָמֵי מֵעֵילָּא לְתַתָּא, וְקָאַמְרִינָן ב' רֵאשִׁית, כִּדְקָאַמְרִינָן בֵּית קֹדֶשׁ הַקֳּדָשִׁים, דְּהַאי אִתְיְיהִיבַת לְהַהוּא רֵאשִׁית, וּמִלָּה כְּלִילָא אִיהִי כַּחֲדָא.

436. We have learned that the secret of: "In the beginning" (Beresheet 1:1) is that there are two principals in one. Though we said of it that it is the beginning from below upward, WHICH IS MALCHUT, "the beginning" also MEANS BEGINNING from above downward, WHICH IS CHOCHMAH; TO WIT, BINAH RETURNED TO BE CHOCHMAH. We have explained the word "In (the letter *Bet*) the beginning" as in the house (Heb. *bet*) of the Holy of Holies, WHICH IS THE NUKVA, THE HOUSE of the beginning, WHICH IS CHOCHMAH. The word "IN THE BEGINNING" includes THE NUKVA AND CHOCHMAH as one.

437. וּבְהַאי בֵּי"ת אִתְבְּרֵי עַלְמָא דָא, וְלָא אִתְקַיַּים אֶלָּא בִּימִינָא, וְהָא אוֹקִמוּהָ בְּהִבָּרְאָם: בְּאַבְרָהָם כְּתִיב, וּבְגִין כָּךְ, אָמַרְתִּי עוֹלָם חֶסֶד יִבָּנֶה. וּבְנִיָּינָא קַדְמָאָה דְּעַלְמָא, הַהוּא נְהוֹרָא דְּיוֹמָא קַדְמָאָה, הֲוָה בֵּיהּ לְקַיְּימָא. וּלְבָתַר בְּיוֹמָא תִּנְיָינָא, בִּשְׂמָאלָא. וּבְהוֹנְהוּ אַתְקַן שָׁמַיִם, וּכְתִיב שָׁמַיִם תָּכִין אֱמוּנָתְךָ בָּהֶם.

437. By this house, the world, THE NUKVA, was created, TO WIT, SHE IS BUILT AS A HOUSE FOR CHOCHMAH, BY RECEIVING FROM THE LEFT COLUMN AND THEREFORE LACKING IN CHASSADIM. Yet it exists only through the right, CHESED, FOR CHOCHMAH CANNOT EXIST WITHOUT CHESED. We have already explained that the word "*Behibar'am* (Eng. 'when they were created')" (Beresheet 2:4) has the same letters as '*BeAbraham*' (Eng. 'in Abraham'), THE SECRET OF CHESED. Therefore it

is written: "For I have said: 'The world is built by Chesed.'" The first building of the world, THE NUKVA, derived its existence from the light of the first day; NAMELY CHESED. Then on the second day, it was included within the left, WHICH IS GVURAH, and heaven, ZEIR ANPIN, was perfected by them, as it is written: "You do establish Your faithfulness in the heavens" (Tehilim 89:3). BY HEAVEN BEING ESTABLISHED BY THE TWO COLUMNS, CHESED AND GVURAH, FAITH, NAMELY THE NUKVA, IS MADE READY TO BE PERFECTED BY THE TWO COLUMNS, CHESED AND GVURAH.

438. ד"א שָׁמַיִם תָּכִין אֱמוּנָתְךָ בָּהֶם, שָׁמַיִם בְּאִינּוּן חֲסָדִים אִתַּקְנוּ, וְרָזָא דֶּאֱמוּנָה אִתְקָנַת בְּהוּ, דְּלֵית תִּקּוּנָהָא אֶלָּא מִגּוֹ שָׁמַיִם.

438. Another explanation for: "You do establish Your faithfulness in the heavens" is that the heaven, ZEIR ANPIN, was established by Chassadim, and the secret of faith, THE NUKVA, was established by them, AS IT SAYS "THE WORLD IS BUILT BY CHESED." THUS, THE HEAVEN INSPIRED CHESED UPON THE NUKVA CALLED 'WORLD', AND HENCE IT IS SAID: "YOU DO ESTABLISH YOUR FAITHFULNESS IN THE HEAVENS." For THE NUKVA cannot be established save by heaven, ZEIR ANPIN.

439. כָּרַתִּי בְרִית לִבְחִירִי, דָּא הוּא רָזָא דִמְהֵימְנוּתָא. ד"א, דָּא אִיהוּ צַדִּיק דְּמִינֵיהּ נָפְקִין בִּרְכָאן לְכֻלְּהוּ תַּתָּאֵי, וְכָל חֵיוָון קַדִּישָׁן, כֻּלְּהוּ אִתְבָּרְכָאן, מִן הַהוּא נְגִידוּ דְּנָגֵיד לְתַתָּאֵי, וּבְגִין כָּךְ כְּתִיב, כָּרַתִּי בְרִית לִבְחִירִי.

439. "I have made a covenant with My chosen" (Ibid. 4). THE COVENANT is the secret of faith CONFERRED UPON DAVID. Another explanation is that THE COVENANT is the Righteous, YESOD, from whom blessings flow upon the lower beings. The holy living creatures, WHICH ARE ANGELS, are all blessed by the abundance poured upon the lower beings. Therefore it is written, "I have made a covenant with My chosen," FOR HE WILL BE WORTHY OF THE COVENANT.

440. נִשְׁבַּעְתִּי לְדָוִד עַבְדִּי, דָּא רָזָא דִמְהֵימְנוּתָא, דְּאִיהוּ קַיָּימָא תָּדִיר בְּצַדִּיק דָּא, קִיּוּמָא דְעָלְמָא, דְּלָא יִתְבַּדְּרוּן לְעָלְמִין, בַּר בְּזִמְנָא

דְּגָלוּתָא, דִּנְגִידוּ דְבִרְכָאן אִתְמְנָעוּ, וְרָזָא דִמְהֵימְנוּתָא לָא אִשְׁתַּלֵּים, וְכָל חֶדְוָון אִתְמְנָעוּ. וְכַד עָיֵיל לֵילְיָא, מֵהַהוּא זִמְנָא, חֶדְוָון לָא עָאלוּ קַמֵּי מַלְכָּא.

440. "I have sworn to David My servant" (Tehilim 89:3). This oath is the secret of faith, WHICH IS THE NUKVA, which is always supported by the Righteous, YESOD. This oath is forever, so they will never be separated, save at the time of exile WHEN THEY WILL BE SEPARATED, when the abundance of blessings is withheld, the secret of faith cannot be perfected and there is no joy. At night, also, no joys come before the King.

441. וְאע"ג דְּחֶדְוָון לָא אִתְעָרוּ, אֲבָל לְבַר קָיְימֵי וּמְזַמְּרֵי שִׁירָתָא, וְכַד אִתְפְּלֵיג לֵילְיָא, וְאִתְעָרוּתָא סָלְקָא מִתַּתָּא לְעֵילָא, כְּדֵין קוּדְשָׁא בְּרִיךְ הוּא אַתְעַר כָּל חֵילֵי שְׁמַיָא לְבִכְיָה, וּבָעַט בִּרְקִיעָא, וְאִזְדַּעְזְעָן עִלָּאֵי וְתַתָּאֵי.

441. Though joys do not waken up AT NIGHT, ANGELS stand and chant hymns outside the King's temple. At midnight, the awakening rises from below upward. The Holy One, blessed be He, then awakens all the celestial armies to weep, and strikes the firmament. There is trembling high and low.

442. וְלֵית נַיְיחָא קַמֵּיה, בַּר בְּזִמְנָא דְּמִתְעָרֵי לְתַתָּא בְּאוֹרַיְיתָא, כְּדֵין, קוּדְשָׁא בְּרִיךְ הוּא, וְכָל אִינוּן נִשְׁמָתִין דְּצַדִּיקַיָּא, כֻּלְּהוּ צַיְיתִין וְחָדְיָין לְהַהוּא קָלָא וּכְדֵין נַיְיחָא. קַמֵּיה אִשְׁתַּכַּח. בְּגִין דְּמִיּוֹמָא דְּאִתְחָרֵיב מַקְדְּשָׁא לְתַתָּא, אוֹמֵי קוּדְשָׁא בְּרִיךְ הוּא, דְּלָא יֵיעוֹל בְּגוֹ יְרוּשְׁלֵם דִּלְעֵילָא, עַד דְּיֵיעֲלוּן יִשְׂרָאֵל לִירוּשְׁלֵם דִּלְתַתָּא, דִּכְתִיב בְּקִרְבְּךָ קָדוֹשׁ וְלֹא אָבוֹא בְּעִיר, וְהָא אוּקְמוּהָ חַבְרַיָיא.

442. He finds no pleasure save when there is awakening below to the Torah. Then the Holy One, blessed be He, and all the souls of the righteous listen joyfully to the sound, and He is pleased. Since the day the Temple was destroyed below, the Holy One, blessed be He, swore that He would not enter the celestial Jerusalem until Yisrael would enter the terrestrial Jerusalem, as it is written: "The Holy One in the midst of you: and I will not come into the city" (Hoshea 11:9), WHICH MEANS THAT "THE HOLY ONE IN THE MIDST OF YOU," NEVERTHELESS "I WILL NOT COME INTO THE CITY," WHICH IS THE CELESTIAL JERUSALEM, UNTIL YISRAEL SHALL ENTER THE TERRESTRIAL JERUSALEM .

443. וְכָל אִינוּן מְזַמְּרֵי, קַיְּימֵי לְבַר, וְאָמְרֵי שִׁירָתָא, בִּתְלַת פַּלְגֵי לֵילְיָא, וְכֻלְהוּ מְשַׁבְּחָן בְּתוּשְׁבַּחְתָּן יְדִיעָאן, וְכֻלְהוּ חֵילֵי שְׁמַיָּא, כֻּלְהוּ מִתְעָרֵי בְּלֵילְיָא, וְיִשְׂרָאֵל בִּימָמָא, וּקְדוּשָׁה לָא מְקַדְּשֵׁי לְעֵילָא, עַד דִּמְקַדְּשֵׁי יִשְׂרָאֵל לְתַתָּא, וּכְדֵין כָּל חֵילֵי שְׁמַיָּא מְקַדְּשֵׁי שְׁמָא קַדִּישָׁא כַּחֲדָא. וְעַ"ד יִשְׂרָאֵל קַדִּישִׁין, מִתְקַדְּשִׁין מֵעֵלָּאֵי וְתַתָּאֵי כַּחֲדָא, הה"ד קְדוֹשִׁים תִּהְיוּ כִּי קָדוֹשׁ אֲנִי ה' אֱלֹהֵיכֶם.

443. All the singers stand outside THE TEMPLE and chant during the three watches of the night, WHICH CORRESPOND TO THE THREE COLUMNS, all singing certain praises. The hosts of heaven are all awakened by night and Yisrael by day. Sanctification is not recited above until the children of Yisrael recite it below, then all the heavenly hosts sanctify together the Holy Name. Hence, holy Yisrael are sanctified high and low. This is the secret of the verse, "You shall be holy: for I Hashem your Elohim am holy" (Vayikra 19:2).

444. פְּתַח ר' יוֹסֵי וַאֲמַר, עַל מָה אֲדָנֶיהָ הָטְבָּעוּ, הַאי קְרָא קוּדְשָׁא בְּרִיךְ הוּא א"ל, בְּגִין דְּכַד בָּרָא עַלְמָא, לָא בָּרָא לֵיהּ אֶלָּא עַל סָמְכִין, דְּאִינוּן ז' סָמְכִין דְּעַלְמָא, כְּד"א חָצְבָה עַמּוּדֶיהָ שִׁבְעָה, וְאִינוּן סָמְכִין לָא אִתְיְידַע עַל מָה קַיְימִין.

444. Rabbi Yosi opened the discussion saying: "Whereupon are its foundations fastened?" (Iyov 38:6). The Holy One, blessed be He, said this TO JOB. For when He created the universe, THE NUKVA, He put it on pillars, the seven pillars of the world CHESED, GVURAH, TIFERET, NETZACH, HOD, YESOD AND MALCHUT, as it says "she has hewn out her seven pillars" (Mishlei 9:1). Upon what the pillars rest is unknown.

445. בְּגִין דְּאִיהוּ רָזָא עֲמִיקָא סְתִימָא דְּכָל סְתִימָן, וְעַלְמָא לָא אִתְבְּרֵי, עַד דְּנָטַל אַבְנָא חֲדָא, וְאִיהוּ אַבְנָא דְּאִתְקְרֵי אֶבֶן שְׁתִיָּה, וְנָטַל לָהּ

קוּדְשָׁא בְּרִיךְ הוּא, וְזָרַק לָהּ לְגוֹ תְהוֹמָא, וְאִתְנְעִיץ מֵעֵילָא לְתַתָּא, וּמִנֵּיהּ אִשְׁתִּיל עַלְמָא, וְאִיהִי נְקוּדָה אֶמְצָעִיתָא דְעַלְמָא, וּבְהַאי נְקוּדָה קַיְימָא קֹדֶשׁ הַקֳּדָשִׁים, הה״ד אוֹ מִי יָרָה אֶבֶן פִּנָּתָהּ, כְּד״א אֶבֶן בֹּחַן פִּנַּת יִקְרַת, וּכְתִיב אֶבֶן מָאֲסוּ הַבּוֹנִים הָיְתָה לְרֹאשׁ פִּנָה.

445. HE ANSWERS: It is a very deep and inscrutable secret that the world, THE NUKVA, was not created until He took a stone called "the foundation stone." The Holy One, blessed be He, took it and threw it into the abyss, where it was stuck upside down. From it the world, THE NUKVA, was planted. It is the central point of the world, where the Holy of Holies stands. It is alluded to by the verse, "who laid its corner stone" (Iyov 38:6), "a tried stone, a precious corner stone" (Yeshayah 28:16) as in "The stone which the builders rejected has become the head stone of the corner" (Tehilim 118:22). ALL THESE REFER TO THE SECRET OF THE FOUNDATION STONE.

446. תָּא חֲזֵי, הַאי אֶבֶן, אִתְבְּרֵי מֵאֶשָּׁא וּמֵרוּחָא וּמִמַּיָּא, וְאִתְגְּלִיד מִכֻּלְּהוּ, וְאִתְעֲבֵיד אַבְנָא חֲדָא, וְקַיְימָא עַל תְּהוֹמֵי, וְלִזְמְנִין נָבְעִין מִנֵּיהּ מַיָּא, וְאִתְמַלְּיָין תְּהוֹמֵי, וְהַאי אַבְנָא קַיְימָא לְאָת בְּאֶמְצָעִיתָא דְעַלְמָא, וְהַאי אִיהוּ אֶבֶן דְּקַיָּים וְאַשְׁתִּיל יַעֲקֹב, שְׁתִילוּ וְקִיּוּמָא דְעַלְמָא, הה״ד וַיִּקַּח יַעֲקֹב אֶבֶן וַיְרִימֶהָ מַצֵּבָה.

446. Come and see: This stone was created from fire, wind and water. TO WIT, IT RECEIVES FROM THE THREE COLUMNS OF ZEIR ANPIN, and was hardened into one stone, standing upon the abyss. Sometimes, water flows from it and the deeps are filled. This stone stands as a sign in the middle of the universe. It is the stone which Jacob set and implanted for the world to expand and be established by. Hence the words: "And Jacob took a stone, and set it up for a pillar" (Beresheet 31:45).

447. וְהָאֶבֶן הַזֹּאת אֲשֶׁר שַׂמְתִּי מַצֵּבָה וְגוֹ', וְכִי הַאי אֶבֶן שַׁוֵּי לֵיהּ יַעֲקֹב, וְהָא הַאי אֶבֶן אִתְבְּרֵי בְּקַדְמֵיתָא, כַּד בָּרָא קוּדְשָׁא בְּרִיךְ הוּא עַלְמָא. אֶלָּא דְשַׁוֵּי לָהּ קִיּוּמָא דִלְעֵילָא וְתַתָּא, וְעַל דָּא אֲשֶׁר שַׂמְתִּי מַצֵּבָה כְּתִיב, מַאי אֲשֶׁר שַׂמְתִּי. דִּכְתִיב יִהְיֶה בֵּית אֱלֹקִים, דְּשַׁוֵּי מְדוֹרָא דִלְעֵילָא הָכָא.

447. "And this stone, which I have set for a pillar" (Beresheet 28:22). HE ASKS: How could this stone be put there by Jacob, if it was created in the beginning, when the Holy One, blessed be He, created the world? HE ANSWERS: He only put it there as a support for the high and low. Therefore it says, "Which I have set for a pillar," "I put" so it "shall be Elohim's house" (Ibid.), by putting here the upper storey; NAMELY, THAT HE DREW INTO IT THE SUPERNAL MOCHIN.

448. תָּא חֲזֵי הַאי אֶבֶן אִית עֲלָהּ שִׁבְעָה עֵינַיִם, כְּד"א עַל אֶבֶן אַחַת שִׁבְעָה עֵינַיִם, עַל מָה אִתְקְרִיאַת שְׁתִיָּיה. חַד דְּמִנָּהּ אִשְׁתִּיל עָלְמָא. וְחַד, שְׁתִיָּיה. שָׁת יָהּ, דְּשַׁוֵּי קוּדְשָׁא בְּרִיךְ הוּא לָהּ, לְאִתְבָּרְכָא מִנָּהּ עָלְמָא, בְּגִין דְּעָלְמָא מִנָּהּ מִתְבָּרְכָא.

448. Come and see: This stone has seven eyes, as said: "Upon one stone are seven eyes" (Zecharyah 3:9). THE EYES ARE THE SECRET OF CHOCHMAH, AND WHEN CHOCHMAH IS REVEALED BY CHESED, GVURAH, TIFERET, NETZACH, HOD, YESOD AND MALCHUT OF THE NUKVA IT IS CALLED 'SEVEN EYES'. Why is it called a foundation (Heb. shetiyah) stone? Since the world was planted from it. The word 'shetiyah' contains the letters shat Yah (lit. 'Yah put'), for the Holy One, blessed be He, WHO IS BINAH CALLED YAH, has put it so that the world will be blessed by it, and indeed it is blessed by it.

449. וְתָא חֲזֵי בְּשַׁעְתָּא דְּעָאל שִׁמְשָׁא, הַנֵּי כְּרוּבִים דְּקַיְימִין בְּהַאי דוּכְתָּא, וַהֲווֹ יָתְבֵי בָּאת, הֲווֹ אַקְשָׁן גַּדְפַּיְיהוּ לְעֵיל, וּפָרְשֵׂי לוֹן, וְאִשְׁתְּמַע קוֹל נְגוּנָא דְּגַדְפַּיְיהוּ לְעֵילָא, וּכְדֵין שָׁרָאן לְנַגְּנָא אִינוּן מַלְאָכִין, דְּאָמְרֵי שִׁירָתָא בְּשֵׁירוּתָא דְּלֵילְיָא, בְּגִין דְּיִסַּלַּק יְקָרֵיה דְּקוּדְשָׁא בְּרִיךְ הוּא, מִתַּתָּא לְעֵילָא. וּמַאי שִׁירָתָא הֲווֹ אָמְרוּ, הַהוּא נְגוּנָא דְּגַדְפַּיְיהוּ דִּכְרוּבִים, הִנֵּה בָּרְכוּ אֶת ה' כָּל עַבְדֵי ה' וְגו', שְׂאוּ יְדֵיכֶם קֹדֶשׁ וְגו', וּכְדֵין אִיהוּ שִׁירָתָא לְאִינוּן מַלְאֲכֵי עִלָּאֵי לְזַמְּרָא.

449. Come and see when the sun sets, IN THE FIRST WATCH AT NIGHT, the Cherubs stand in this place, THE HOLY OF HOLIES, WHICH STANDS ON THE CENTRAL POINT, THE FOUNDATION STONE. They stand there by a miracle THROUGH THE LIGHTS OF BINAH, WHICH DO NOT BELONG TO IT, AND

ARE THEREFORE CONSIDERED A MIRACLE. They beat their wings and spread them, and the sound of their wings' song is heard above. Then the angels, who chant at the beginning of the night, start to sing so that the Holy One, blessed be He, will be glorified above and below. What do the wings of the Cherubs chant? "Behold, bless Hashem, all you servants of Hashem... Lift up your hands in the sanctuary" (Tehilim 134:1-2). It is then time for the supernal angels to sing.

450. בְּמִשְׁמַרְתָּא תִּנְיָינָא, הַנֵּי כְּרוּבִים אַקְשֵׁי גַדְפַּיְיהוּ לְעֵילָא, וְאִשְׁתְּמַע קוֹל נִגּוּנָא דִּלְהוֹן, וּכְדֵין שָׁרָאן לְנַגְּנָא אִינוּן מַלְאָכִין דְּקַיְימִין בְּמִשְׁמַרְתָּא תִּנְיָינָא, וּמַאי שִׁירָתָא הֲווֹ אָמְרֵי בְּהַאי שַׁעֲתָא, נִגּוּנָא דְּגַדְפַּיְיהוּ דִּכְרוּבִים, הַבּוֹטְחִים בַּה׳ כְּהַר צִיּוֹן לֹא יִמּוֹט וְגו׳. וּכְדֵין אִיהוּ שֵׁירוּתָא לְאִינּוּן דְּקַיְימֵי בְּהַאי מִשְׁמָרָה תִּנְיָינָא לְנַגְּנָא.

450. On the second watch, the Cherubs beat their wings above and the sound of their singing is heard. Then the angels of the second watch start to chant. What do the Cherubs' wings sing at that hour? "They who trust in Hashem shall be like Mount Zion..." (Tehilim 125:1). It is then time for the angels of the second watch to sing.

451. בְּמִשְׁמָרָה תְּלִיתָאָה, הַנֵּי כְּרוּבִים אַקְשׁוּ גַדְפַּיְיהוּ, וְאָמְרֵי שִׁירָתָא, וּמַאי הִיא. הַלְלוּיָהּ הַלְלוּ עַבְדֵי ה׳ וְגו׳, יְהִי שֵׁם ה׳ מְבוֹרָךְ וְגו׳, מִמִּזְרַח שֶׁמֶשׁ וְגו׳. כְּדֵין אִינּוּן מַלְאָכִין דְּקַיְימֵי בְּמִשְׁמָרָה תְּלִיתָאָה, כֻּלְּהוּ אָמְרֵי שִׁירָתָא.

451. On the third watch, the Cherubs beat their wings and chant hymns. They sing, "Haleluyah! Give praise, O servants of Hashem... Blessed be the name of Hashem...From the rising of the sun..." (Tehilim 113:1-3). Then all the angels of the third watch sing.

452. וְכֻלְּהוּ כּוֹכְבֵי וּמַזָּלֵי דִּבְרְקִיעָא, פָּתְחֵי שִׁירָתָא, כְּמָה דִכְתִיב, בְּרָן יַחַד כּוֹכְבֵי בֹקֶר וַיָּרִיעוּ כָּל בְּנֵי אֱלֹקִים. וּכְתִיב הַלְלוּהוּ כָּל כּוֹכְבֵי אוֹר, דְּהָא אִינּוּן כֹּכְבֵי דִנְהוֹרָא, מְנַגְּנָן עַל נְהוֹרָא.

452. All the stars and constellations in the firmament start to sing ON THE THIRD WATCH, as it is written: "when the morning stars sang together, and all the sons of Elohim shouted for joy" (Iyov 38:7), and "praise Him, all you stars of light" (Tehilim 148:3), as all these stars of light play music upon the light; TO WIT, THROUGH SINGING LIGHT IS DRAWN.

453. כַּד אָתֵי צַפְרָא, וּכְדֵין נָטְלֵי שִׁירָתָא אֲבַתְרַיְיהוּ דְיִשְׂרָאֵל לְתַתָּא, וְסָלְקָא יְקָרֵיהּ דְקוּדְשָׁא בְּרִיךְ הוּא, מִתַּתָּא וּמִלְעֵילָא, יִשְׂרָאֵל לְתַתָּא בִּימָמָא, וּמַלְאֲכֵי עִלָּאֵי לְעֵילָא, בְּלֵילְיָא, וּכְדֵין אִשְׁתְּלֵים שְׁמָא קַדִּישָׁא בְּכָל סִטְרִין.

453. When morning rises, Yisrael follow them with their singing and the Holy One, blessed be He, is glorified from below and from above. Yisrael sing below by day and the supernal angels at night. Then the Holy Name is perfected on all sides.

454. וְהַאי אֶבֶן דְקָאֲמַר, כֻּלְּהוּ מַלְאֲכֵי עִלָּאֵי, וְיִשְׂרָאֵל לְתַתָּא, כֻּלְּהוּ אִתְקְפוּ בְּהַאי אֶבֶן, וְאִיהִי סָלְקָא לְעֵילָא, לְאִתְעַטְּרָא גּוֹ אֲבָהָן בִּימָמָא. וּבְלֵילְיָא, קוּדְשָׁא בְּרִיךְ הוּא אָתֵי לְאִשְׁתַּעְשְׁעָא עִם צַדִּיקַיָּא בְּגִנְתָא דְעֵדֶן.

454. All the supernal angels and Yisrael below are strengthened by the stone we referred to. It rises above to be adorned by the fathers by day. By night, the Holy One, blessed be He, ZEIR ANPIN, comes to the Garden of Eden to be delighted by the righteous.

455. זַכָּאִין אִינוּן כָּל דְקַיְימֵי בְּקִיּוּמַיְיהוּ, וּמִשְׁתַּדְּלִין בְּאוֹרַיְיתָא בְּלֵילְיָא, בְּגִין דְקוּדְשָׁא בְּרִיךְ הוּא, וְכָל אִינוּן צַדִּיקַיָּיא דִּבְגִנְתָא דְעֵדֶן, שָׁמְעוּ קָלַיְיהוּ דִּבְנֵי נָשָׁא, אִינוּן דְמִשְׁתַּדְּלֵי בְּאוֹרַיְיתָא, כְּמָה דִכְתִיב הַיּוֹשֶׁבֶת בַּגַּנִּים וְגו'.

455. Happy are those who are established in their existence and study the Torah at night, since the Holy One, blessed be He, and all the righteous in the Garden of Eden listen to the voices of men who study the Torah, as it is written: "You that dwells in the gardens, the companions hearken for your voice: cause me to hear it" (Shir Hashirim 8:13).

456. תָּא חֲזֵי , הַאי אֶבֶן, אִיהוּ אֶבֶן טָבָא, וְדָא הוּא רָזָא דִכְתִיב וּמִלֵּאתָ בוֹ מִלוּאַת אֶבֶן אַרְבָּעָה טוּרֵי אָבֶן. וְאִלֵּין אִינוּן סִדְרִין דְּאֶבֶן טָבָא, אַשְׁלָמוּתָא דְּאֶבֶן יְקָרָה, בְּגִין דְּאִית אֶבֶן אָחֳרָא. דִּכְתִיב וַהֲסִירוֹתִי אֶת לֵב הָאֶבֶן וְגו', וּכְתִיב וְאֶת רוּחִי אֶתֵּן בְּקִרְבְּכֶם. וְהַאי אִיהוּ אֶבֶן בֹּחַן פִּנַּת יְקָרַת וְאוֹקִמוּהָ.

456. Come and see: This stone is a precious stone, FOR IT WAS SWEETENED BY BINAH AND IS GOODLY AND WORTHY OF RECEIVING MOCHIN. This is the secret of the verse, "And you shall set in it settings of stones, even four rows of stones" (Shemot 28:17). They are the arrangements of the precious stone, the setting of the goodly stone; TO WIT, THEY ARE THE SECRET OF THE MOCHIN OF THE ILLUMINATION OF CHOCHMAH RECEIVED IN MALCHUT ACCORDING TO THE SECRET OF THREE TIMES FOUR WHICH AMOUNT TO TWELVE. For there is another stone, NAMELY MALCHUT THAT WAS NOT SWEETENED IN BINAH, of which it is written, "And I shall remove the heart of stone." "And I will put my spirit within you" (Yechezkel 36:26), WHICH MEANS THAT AS LONG AS THE HEART OF STONE IS NOT REMOVED, THE SPIRIT OF HASHEM DOES NOT DWELL IN US, SINCE IT IS NOT SWEETENED BY BINAH. IT IS ALSO CALLED "a tried stone, a precious corner stone" (Yeshayah 28:16).

457. וְעַל רָזָא דָא כְּתִיב, לוּחוֹת הָאֶבֶן, דְּאִינוּן לוּחוֹת אִתְגְּזָרוּ מֵהָכָא, וְעַ"ד אִקְרוּן עַל שְׁמֵיהּ דְּהַאי אֶבֶן, וְהַאי הוּא רָזָא דִכְתִיב, מִשָּׁם רוֹעֶה אֶבֶן יִשְׂרָאֵל כְּמָה דְּאִתְּמָר.

457. In regard to this secret, it is written "tablets of stone" (Shemot 31:18), for this is where the stones were hewn, FROM THE PRECIOUS STONE. They are therefore named after this stone. This is the secret of the verse, "From thence the shepherd, the stone of Yisrael" (Beresheet 49:24), as we learned, THAT THIS TOO IS THE SECRET OF THE PRECIOUS STONE.

458. פָּתַח ר' חִזְקִיָּה וַאֲמַר, וְהָאֲבָנִים תִּהְיֶיןָ עַל שְׁמֹת בְּנֵי יִשְׂרָאֵל שְׁתֵּים עֶשְׂרֵה, אִלֵּין אַבְנֵי יְקָרִין עִלָּאִין, דְּאִתְקְרוּן אַבְנֵי הַמָּקוֹם, כְּד"א

וַיִּקַּח מֵאַבְנֵי הַמָּקוֹם. וְהָא אוּקְמוּהָ. וְהָאֲבָנִים עַל שְׁמוֹת בְּנֵי יִשְׂרָאֵל,
כְּמָה דְאִית י״ב שְׁבָטִים לְתַתָּא, הָכִי נָמֵי לְעֵילָא תְּרֵיסַר שְׁבָטִין, וְאִינּוּן
תְּרֵיסַר אֲבָנִין יַקִּירִין, וּכְתִיב שֶׁשָּׁם עָלוּ שְׁבָטִים וְגו׳, עֵדוּת לְיִשְׂרָאֵל דָּא
יִשְׂרָאֵל, רָזָא דִלְעֵילָא, וְכֻלְּהוּ לְהוֹדוֹת לְשֵׁם ה׳, וְע״ד וְהָאֲבָנִים תִּהְיֶיןָ
עַל שְׁמוֹת בְּנֵי יִשְׂרָאֵל.

458. Rabbi Chizkiyah opened the discussion saying: "And the stones shall be with the names of the children of Yisrael, twelve" (Shemot 28:21). These are the supernal precious stones called the stones of the place, as it is written: "And he took of the stones of that place" (Beresheet 28:11), as has been explained. THESE ARE THE SFIROT OF THE NUKVA, AND THE NUKVA IS CALLED PLACE. "And the stones shall be with the names of the children of Yisrael" as there are twelve tribes below, so there above, IN THE NUKVA, twelve tribes which are twelve precious stones. It is also written: "There the tribes go up, the tribes of Yah, for a testimony unto Yisrael" (Tehilim 122:4). This is the secret of the supernal Yisrael; NAMELY ZEIR ANPIN WHICH POURS THESE TWELVE UNTO THE NUKVA. They are all there "to give thanks to the name of Hashem" (Ibid.), WHICH IS THE NUKVA CALLED THE NAME OF HASHEM. Therefore it is written, "And the stones shall be with the names of the children of Yisrael."

459. וּכְמָה דְאִית י״ב שָׁעֵי בִּימָמָא, הָכִי אִית י״ב שָׁעֵי בְּלֵילְיָא, בְּיוֹמָא
לְעֵילָא, בְּלֵילְיָא לְתַתָּא, כֹּלָּא דָא לָקֳבֵל דָא, הַנֵּי י״ב שָׁעֵי דִּבְלֵילְיָא
מִתְפַּלְּגֵי לִתְלַת פְּלָגָאן, וְכַמָּה מְמַנֵּי תְּרֵיסִין קַיְימֵי תְּחוֹתַיְיהוּ, דַּרְגִּין עַל
דַּרְגִּין, כֻּלְּהוּ מְמַנָּן בְּלֵילְיָא, וְנָטְלֵי טַרְפָּא בְּקַדְמֵיתָא.

459. Just as there are twelve hours in the day, THE TWELVE OF ZEIR ANPIN, so there are twelve hours at night, THE TWELVE OF THE NUKVA. The daytime ones are above, and the nightly below, THE TWELVE OF ZEIR ANPIN BEING ABOVE AND THOSE OF THE NUKVA BELOW, TO WIT, THEY RECEIVE FROM THE TWELVE OF ZEIR ANPIN WHICH ARE ABOVE. The ones correspond to the others. The twelve nightly hours are divided into three parts, THE THREE WATCHES WE MENTIONED. Numerous legions are stationed beneath them over various grades, all of them in charge by night. They first receive their food, AND THEN CHANT HYMNS, AS IT IS WRITTEN:

"SHE RISES ALSO WHILE IT IS YET NIGHT, AND GIVES FOOD TO HER HOUSEHOLD..." (MISHLEI 31:15).

460. וּכְדֵין כַּד אִתְפְּלֵיג לֵילְיָא, קַיְימִין תְּרֵין סִדְרִין מִסִּטְרָא דָא, וּתְרֵין סִדְרִין מִסִּטְרָא אָחֳרָא, וְרוּחָא עִלָּאָה נָפַק בֵּינַיְיהוּ, וּכְדֵין כָּל אִינוּן אִלָנִין דִּבְגִנְתָּא דְעֵדֶן, כֻּלְּהוּ פָּתְחֵי שִׁירָתָא, וְקוּדְשָׁא בְּרִיךְ הוּא עָאל בְּגִנְתָּא דְעֵדֶן, הה"ד אָז יְרַנְּנוּ וגו' כִּי בָא לִשְׁפּוֹט אֶת הָאָרֶץ, כְּמָה דִכְתִיב, וְשָׁפַט בְּצֶדֶק דַּלִּים. בְּגִין דְּמִשְׁפָּט עָאל בֵּינַיְיהוּ וְאִתְמַלְיָא מִנֵּיה גַּן עֵדֶן.

460. At midnight, there are two settings on the one side and two settings on the other side. A Supernal Spirit comes out from between them. Then, all the trees in the Garden of Eden start to sing and the Holy One, blessed be He, enters the Garden of Eden. This is described in the verse: "Then shall the trees of the wood sing for joy at the presence of Hashem, because He comes to judge the earth" (I Divrei Hayamim 16:33), as it is written: "With righteousness shall He judge the poor" (Yeshayah 11:4). For justice, ZEIR ANPIN comes in between them and the Garden of Eden is filled with it.

461. וְרוּחָא דְצָפוֹן אִתְעַר בְּעָלְמָא, וְחֶדְוָה אִשְׁתַּכַּח וְנָשֵׁיב הַהוּא רוּחָא בְּאִינוּן בּוּסְמִין, וְסַלְקִין רֵיחִין לְעֵילָא, וּמִתְעַטְּרִין צַדִּיקַיָּא בְּעִטְרַיְיהוּ, וּמִתְהַנָּן מִגּוֹ זִיוָא דְאַסְפַּקְלַרְיָאה דְנָהֲרָא.

461. And a northern wind is stirred in the world and joy abounds, FOR AFTER THE BALANCING OF THE CENTRAL COLUMN, NORTH IS CLOTHED BY SOUTH, AND CHOCHMAH BY CHASSADIM. THEN THERE IS JOY IN THE ILLUMINATION OF THE NORTH, THE LEFT COLUMN. HE EXPLAINS, The wind, THE CENTRAL COLUMN, blows at the perfumes, THE SECRET OF THE ILLUMINATION OF CHOCHMAH, THROUGH WHICH THE ILLUMINATION OF CHOCHMAH IS CLOTHED BY PERFUMES OF CHASSADIM WITHIN THE SPIRIT, and THE PERFUMES raise scent from below upward, and the righteous are adorned with their crowns MEANING THAT THEY RECEIVE MOCHIN, and enjoy the splendor of the shining mirror, ZEIR ANPIN.

462. זַכָּאִין אִינוּן צַדִּיקַיָּא, דְּזָכָאן לְהַהוּא נְהוֹרָא עִלָּאָה, וְהַהוּא נְהוֹרָא

דְּאִסְפַּקְלַרְיָאה דְּנָהֲרָא, נָהִיר לְכָל סִטְרִין, וְכָל חַד וְחַד מֵאִלֵּין צַדִּיקַיָּא, נָטִיל לְחוּלָקֵיהּ כַּדְקָא חָזֵי לֵיהּ, וַהֲוָה נָטִיל כָּל חַד וְחַד כְּפוּם עוֹבָדוֹי דְּעָבַד בְּהַאי עַלְמָא, אִית מִנְּהוֹן דְּמִתְכַּסְּפֵי, מֵהַהוּא נְהִירוּ דְּנָטִיל חַבְרֵיהּ יַתִּיר וְנָהִיר, וְהָא אוֹקְמוּהָ.

462. Happy are the righteous who attain that supernal light and the light of the mirror which shines to all sides, RIGHT AND LEFT. Each of the righteous receives his appropriate share, according to his deeds in this world. Some of them are in shame before the light since their neighbor has received more to illuminate. This has already been explained.

463. חוּלָקֵיהּ דְּלֵילְיָא, מִכַּד שָׁאֲרֵי לֵילְיָא לְמֵיעַל. כַּמָּה גַּרְדִּינֵי נְמוּסִין מִתְעָרִין, וְשָׁטָאן בְּעַלְמָא, וּפָתְחִין סְתִימִין, וּלְבָתַר כַּמָּה זִינִין לְזַנַּיְיהוּ, כְּמָה דְּאוֹקִימְנָא. וּכְדֵין כַּד אִתְפְּלִיג לֵילְיָא, סִטְרָא דְּצָפוֹן נָחִית מֵעֵילָא לְתַתָּא, וְאָחִיד בֵּיהּ בְּלֵילְיָא, עַד תְּרֵין חוּלָקִין דְּלֵילְיָא.

463. The watches in the night ARE from the setting of night, several accusers are awakened to roam about the world and the ports OF LIGHTS are closed. THIS IS THE FIRST WATCH. Afterwards, DURING THE SECOND WATCH, all sorts OF EMISSARIES OF JUDGMENT ARE ROUSED as we explained, THAT THE SECOND WATCH PERTAINS TO THE LEFT COLUMN, THE NORTH WIND, FOR AS LONG AS IT IS NOT CONNECTED WITH THE SOUTH WIND, WHICH IS OF THE RIGHT, MANY JUDGMENTS WILL COME FROM IT. At midnight IN THE MIDDLE OF THE SECOND WATCH, the northern wind descends from above downward and holds on to night, WHICH IS THE NUKVA, until the end of the second watch.

464. וּלְבָתַר סִטְרָא דְּדָרוֹם אִתְּעַר, עַד דְּאָתֵי צַפְרָא, וְכַד אָתֵי צַפְרָא, כְּדֵין דָּרוֹם וְצָפוֹן אֲחִידוּ בֵּיהּ, וּכְדֵין אָתָאן יִשְׂרָאֵל לְתַתָּא, סַלְּקִין לָהּ בִּצְלוֹתְהוֹן וּבָעוּתְהוֹן לְעֵילָא, עַד דְּסַלְקָא וְאִתְגְּנִיזַת בֵּינַיְיהוּ, וְנָטְלָא בִּרְכָאן מֵרֵישָׁא דְּכָל רֵישִׁין.

464. Then, AT THE THIRD WATCH, the south side, CHESED, is aroused TO BE ATTACHED TO THE NORTH THROUGH THE CENTRAL COLUMN until morning. When morning comes, SOUTH AND NORTH ARE ALREADY ATTACHED TO THE NUKVA. Then Yisrael come below with their prayer and request and raise Her above TO ZEIR ANPIN until She ascends to be concealed among THE LIGHTS OF ZEIR ANPIN. TO WIT, SHE REDUCED HERSELF AND BECAME NULL TO THE GRADE OF ZEIR ANPIN, then receives blessings from the King's head.

465. וְאִתְבָּרְכָא מֵהַהוּא טַלָּא דְּאִתְמַשְׁכָא מִלְעֵילָא, וּמֵהַהוּא טַלָּא פָּרֵישׁ לְכַמָּה סִטְרִין, וְכַמָּה רִבְבָוָן אִתְּזָנוּ מִנֵּיה מֵהַהוּא טַלָּא, וּמִנֵּיה עֲתִידִין לְאַחֲיָיא מֵיתַיָּיא, הה"ד הָקִיצוּ וְרַנְּנוּ שׁוֹכְנֵי עָפָר כִּי טַל אוֹרֹת טַלֶּךָ, טַלָּא מֵאִינּוּן נְהוֹרִין עִלָּאִין דְּנָהֲרִין לְעֵילָא.

465. She is blessed from the dew that flows UNTO ZEIR ANPIN from above. The dew is divided TO ILLUMINATE on several sides, BOTH RIGHT AND LEFT. AND THOUGH THE DEW ITSELF IS BUT THE LIGHT OF CHESED, myriads of grades are sustained by it, which will raise the dead in the future. This is the meaning of the verse: "Awake and sing, you that dwell in dust: for your dew is as the dew on herbs (lit. 'of lights')" (Yeshayah 26:19); TO WIT, the dew from the supernal lights which shine above.

466. עַד דַּהֲווֹ יָתְבֵי אִתְפְּלֵיג לֵילְיָא, א"ל ר' יְהוּדָה לר' יוֹסֵי, הַשְׁתָּא רוּחָא דְּצָפוֹן אִתְעַר, וְלֵילְיָא אִתְפְּלַג, וְהַשְׁתָּא עִדָּנָא דְּקוּדְשָׁא ב"ה תָּאִיב לְקָלֵהוֹן דְּצַדִּיקַיָא בְּהַאי עַלְמָא, אִינּוּן דְּמִשְׁתַּדְּלֵי בְּאוֹרַיְיתָא, הַשְׁתָּא קוּדְשָׁא בְּרִיךְ הוּא צַיֵּית לָן, בְּהַאי אֲתַר, לָא נִפְסוֹק מִלֵּי דְּאוֹרַיְיתָא.

466. While they were sitting, midnight arrived. Rabbi Yehuda said to Rabbi Yosi, Now that the north wind is awakened at midnight, it is time when the Holy One, blessed be He, longs for the voices of the righteous in this world who are occupied in the Torah. The Holy One, blessed be He, now listens to them. Let us not stop from studying the Torah in this place.

44. "The angel who redeemed," part two

A Synopsis
The redeeming angel, Metatron, receives blessings and then bestows them upon the world. This angel is male when procuring blessings for the world, and is female when there is judgment in the world. The angel includes all the colors – red, white, and green – and has many shapes.

The Relevance of this Passage
The power of redemption, blessing, and balance between mercy and judgement and male and female energies, is made available to the readers of this ancient text. This effect is achieved through a mystical connection to the angel Metatron.

467. פְּתַח וַאֲמַר, הַמַּלְאָךְ הַגּוֹאֵל אוֹתִי מִכָּל רָע, הָא אִתְּמָר וְאוּקְמוּהָ. אֲבָל תָּא חֲזֵי, כְּתִיב הִנֵּה אָנֹכִי שׁוֹלֵחַ מַלְאָךְ וגו', דָּא הוּא מַלְאָךְ דְּאִיהוּ פָּרוֹקָא דְעָלְמָא, נְטִירוּ דִּבְנֵי נָשָׁא, וְהַאי דְּאִיהוּ דְּאַזְמִין בִּרְכָאן לְכָל עָלְמָא, בְּגִין דְּאִיהוּ נָטִיל לוֹן בְּקַדְמֵיתָא, וּלְבָתַר אִיהוּ אַזְמִין לוֹן בְּעָלְמָא, וּבְגִין דָּא כְּתִיב, הִנֵּה אָנֹכִי שׁוֹלֵחַ מַלְאָךְ לְפָנֶיךָ. וְשָׁלַחְתִּי לְפָנֶיךָ מַלְאָךְ.

467. He opened the discussion saying: "The angel who redeemed me from all evil" (Beresheet 48:16). We have studied it already, yet it is written, "Behold, I send an angel before you..." (Shemot 23:20). This is the angel who redeems the world, CALLED THE REDEEMING ANGEL, who protects people, AS IT SAYS "TO KEEP YOU IN THE WAY" (IBID.). It secures blessings for the whole world, first receiving them, and then providing them to the world; NAMELY THE ANGEL METATRON. It is therefore written, "Behold, I send an angel before you" and "and I will send an angel before you" (Shemot 33:2).

468. וְהַאי אִיהוּ מַלְאָךְ, דִּלְזִמְנִין דָּכָר, וּלְזִמְנִין נוּקְבָא, וְהָכֵי אִיהוּ, דְּבִזְמָנָא דְּאִיהוּ אַזְמִין בִּרְכָאן לְעָלְמָא, כְּדֵין אִיהוּ דָּכָר, וְאִקְרֵי דָּכָר. כְּדְכוּרָא דְּאַזְמִין בִּרְכָאן לְנוּקְבָא. הָכֵי אִיהוּ אַזְמִין בִּרְכָאן לְעָלְמָא. וּבִזְמָנָא דְּקַיְימָא בְּדִינָא עַל עָלְמָא, כְּדֵין אִקְרֵי נוּקְבָא, כְּנוּקְבָא דְּאִיהִי

-240-

עוֹבָדָא, הָכֵי אִיהוּ אִתְמְלֵי מִן דִּינָא, וּכְדֵין אִקְרֵי נוּקְבָא. וְעַל דָּא לִזְמְנִין אִקְרֵי דְכוּרָא, וּלְזִמְנִין אִקְרֵי נוּקְבָא, וְכֹלָּא רָזָא חֲדָא.

468. This angel is now male, now female. When procuring blessings for the world he is male and called male. As a male, he orders blessings for the female. And when there is judgment in the world, she is called female, and as a pregnant female, she is filled with judgments, and is then called a female. Therefore, now he is male, and now she is female. All this is one mystery.

469. כְּגַוְונָא דָּא כְּתִיב, וְאֶת לַהַט הַחֶרֶב הַמִּתְהַפֶּכֶת, מַלְאָכִין אִית שְׁלָחוּן בְּעַלְמָא, דְּמִתְהַפְּכִין לְכַמָּה גְוָונִין, לִזְמְנִין נוּקְבֵי, לִזְמְנִין דְּכוּרֵי, לִזְמְנִין דִּינָא, לִזְמְנִין רַחֲמֵי, וְכֹלָּא בְּחַד גַּוְונָא. כְּגַוְונָא דָּא הַאי מַלְאָךְ, בִּגְוָונִין סַגִּיאִין אִיהוּ, וְכָל גְּוָונִין דְּעַלְמָא, כֻּלְהוּ אִיתְנָהוּ בְּהַאי אֲתָר. וְרָזָא דָּא כְּמַרְאֵה הַקֶּשֶׁת אֲשֶׁר יִהְיֶה בֶעָנָן בְּיוֹם הַגֶּשֶׁם כֵּן מַרְאֵה הַנֹּגַהּ סָבִיב הוּא מַרְאֵה דְּמוּת כְּבוֹד ה'. וּכְמָה דְּאִית בֵּיה כָּל אִינּוּן גְּוָונִין, הָכֵי נָמֵי אַנְהֵיג לְכָל עָלְמָא.

469. It is likewise written: "And the bright blade of a revolving sword" (Beresheet 3:24); NAMELY there are angel messengers in the world which revolve and turn into several shapes, sometimes female and sometimes male, now Judgment and now Mercy, and all is the same matter. In the same manner, this angel has many shapes, and all the colors, WHITE, RED AND GREEN, of the world, THE NUKVA, are in this place. This is the mystery of: "As the appearance of the bow that is in the cloud in the day of rain, so was the appearance of the brightness round about. This was the appearance of the likeness of the glory of Hashem" (Yechezkel 1:28). THE APPEARANCE OF THE BOW, THE NUKVA, CONTAINS THE THREE COLORS. Since THE ANGEL has the three colors, he leads the world.

45. Three colors

A Synopsis

Here we first learn that the colors white, red and green correspond to the Right, Left and Central Columns respectively. These colors are connected, they encircle the realm of Malchut, and they are reflected in the Malchut. The illumination of Malchut, we learn, is concealed from those below. Whoever tries to behold her will be rejected if they lack the appropriate merit. And whoever understands how to unite and adjust the three colors properly will be preserved in this world and in the next.

The Relevance of this Passage

The ability to balance and manage the three primal spiritual energy forces known as Right, Left and Central Columns is bestowed up the reader. The colors white, red and green embody these three forces and they shine brightly in our souls so that our lives are more balanced, harmonious, and aligned with the spiritual structure of creation. This balance brings forth the wisdom to know when and how to receive for the purpose of sharing with others.

תּוֹסֶפְתָּא

470. רְחִימֵי עִלָּאֵי, מָארֵי דְסָכְלְתָנוּ אִסְתַּכָּלוּ, הוּרְמָנֵי יְדִיעָן בְּקוּלְפֵי דְסִיכְתָא, קְרִיבוּ לְמִנְדַע, מַאן מִנְכוֹן מָארֵי דְעַיְינִין בְּסָכְלְתָנוּ, וְיָדַע בְּשַׁעֲתָא דְסָלֵיק בִּרְעוּתָא דְרָזָא דְרָזִין, לְאַפָּקָא תְּלַת גְּוָונִין כַּחֲדָא כְּלִילָן, וְאִינוּן: חִוָּור וְסוּמָק וְיָרוֹק, תְּלַת גְּוָונִין כַּחֲדָא אִשְׁתְּלִיבָאן דָּא עִם דָּא, מִזְדַּוְּוגָן דָּא עִם דָּא, מַגְרוֹפַיָא תַּתָּאָה אִצְטַבַּע, וְנָפְקָא מִגוֹ גְּוָונִין אִלֵּין.

Tosefta (addendum)

470. Exalted, beloved men of intelligence, behold THE SOULS FROM THE RIGHT COLUMN. Litigants with a sailor stick, approach so you may know, THOSE OF THE LEFT COLUMN, WHENCE ARE JUDGMENTS. Those of you of intelligent eyes, OF THE CENTRAL COLUMN, WHO GAINED CHOCHMAH RECEIVED THROUGH TEVUNAH, know that when the wish came up of the mystery of mysteries to issue forth three colors bound together, the white, red and green, THE THREE COLUMNS: RIGHT IS WHITE, LEFT IS RED, AND THE CENTRAL GREEN, the three colors combined and mingled

together. Then the lower shovel, THE NUKVA, was dyed and came out of these colors.

471. וְכָל גּוֹוָנִין אָלֵין, אִתְחֲזוּן בְּהַאי, חֵיזוּ אִיהוּ לְאַסְתַּכְּלָא, כְּעֵינָא דִבְדוֹלְחָא אִתְחֲזֵי בְּשַׁעְתָּא, כְּגַוְונָא דְבָטַשׁ בְּגַוֵּוה, הָכִי אִתְחֲזֵי לְבַר, אָלֵין תְּלַת גּוֹוָנִין סַחֲרָן לְהַאי, וְגַוְונָא אָזְלָא סַלְקָא וְנָחֲתָא, קַסְטוֹרִין דִּקְטָרָא קְבִיעֵי בְּגַוֵּוה.

471. All these colors, WHITE, RED AND GREEN, are reflected IN THE NUKVA, a looking-glass mirror, SINCE ONLY IN IT ONE CAN SEE when it is crystal-like. When he struck it, THE NUKVA was seen outside. The three colors circle TO ITS RIGHT, LEFT AND MIDDLE; the color goes up and down. TO WIT, THE WHITE COLOR, RIGHT, GOES TO BE INCLUDED WITHIN THE LEFT; THE RED COLOR, LEFT, GOES UP, NAMELY SHINES FROM BELOW UPWARD; THE GREEN IN THE MIDDLE GOES DOWN, BY SHINING FROM ABOVE DOWNWARD. There are executioners in charge within Her, WHO PUNISH THOSE WHO DRAW THE ILLUMINATION OF THE LEFT FROM ABOVE DOWNWARD.

472. גּוֹוָנִין סָחֲרִין כְּלִילָן כַּחֲדָא, סָלְקִין לָהּ לְעֵילָא בִּימָמָא, וְנָחֲתָא בְּלֵילְיָא, שְׁרָגָא דְּדָלֵיק אִתְחֲזֵי בְּלֵילְיָא, בִּימָמָא אִסְתַּתְּרַת נְהוֹרָא, טְמִירָא בְּמָאתָן וְאַרְבְּעִין וּתְמַנְיָא עָלְמִין, כֻּלְּהוּ אָזְלִין לְגַוֵּוה מִלְעֵילָא לְתַתָּא, גּוֹ תְּלַת מְאָה וְשִׁתִּין וְחָמֵשׁ שַׁיְיפִין גְּנִיזָא וְאִתְכַּסְיָא לְתַתָּא.

472. The colors that are connected which encircle THE NUKVA, raise Her up by day, and She descends by night. SHE IS LIKE a burning candle, WHOSE ILLUMINATION is seen by night, and by day it is concealed AND CANNOT BE SEEN. The light is hidden in 248 worlds, which all shine within Her from above downward into 365 parts, which are concealed and covered from below.

473. מַאן דִּמְפַשְׁפֵּשׁ לְאַשְׁכְּחָא לָהּ, יִתְבַּר גַּדְפִין קְלִיפִין טְמִירִין, וְיִפְתַּח תַּרְעִין, מַאן דְּזָכֵי לְמֶיחֱמֵי, יֶחֱמֵי גּוֹ יְדִיעָה וְסֻכְלְתָנוּ, כְּמַאן דְּחָמֵי בָּתַר כּוֹתְלָא. בַּר מִן מֹשֶׁה, מְהֵימָנָא עִלָּאָה, דַּהֲוָה חָמֵי לֵיהּ עֵינָא בְּעֵינָא, לְעֵילָא בַּאֲתַר דְּלָא אִתְיְידַע.

473. Whoever solicits to attain Her will break the wings WHICH CONCEAL HER and the hidden Klipot, and then open the gates. Whoever may look will behold with knowledge and intelligence as if from behind a wall, save the exalted faithful prophet Moses, who saw it eye to eye above, where it is inconceivable.

474. מַאן דְּלָא זָכֵי, דָּחוּ לֵיהּ לְבַר, כַּמָּה חֲבִילֵי טְהִירִין אִזְדַּמְּנוּ לְגַבֵּיהּ, אִזְדַּמְּנָן נָפְקֵי עֲלֵיהּ, וְאַפָּקוּ לֵיהּ דְּלָא יִסְתַּכַּל בְּעִנּוּגָא דְּמַלְכָּא, וַוי לוֹן לְאִינּוּן חַיָּיבִין דְּעָלְמָא, דְּלָא זָכָאן לְאִסְתַּכְּלָא, כְּד"א וְלֹא יָבֹאוּ לִרְאוֹת כְּבַלַּע אֶת הַקֹּדֶשׁ וגו'.

474. Whoever did not merit it is rejected outside. Several battalions of angels are ready for him, to go out to him and escort him out so he will not behold the pleasure of the King. Woe to the wicked in the world, who have not the merit of beholding, as it says, "But they shall not go in to see when the holy things are covered..." (Bemidbar 4:20).

475. אֲמַר רִבִּי יְהוּדָה, מִסְתַּכֵּל הֲוֵינָא, וְהָא מִגּוֹ זְהִירִין אִלֵּין, מִסְתַּכְּלָן נִשְׁמָתְהוֹן דְּצַדִּיקַיָּא, כַּד אִתְדַּבְּקוּ בְּהַאי אֲתַר, מִגּוֹ זְהִירִין אִלֵּין מִסְתַּכְּלִין נִשְׁמָתְהוֹן דְּצַדִּיקַיָּא. אִינּוּן גּוָוֹנִין, סָלְקִין וְאִתְכְּלִילָן כַּחֲדָא. זַכָּאָה אִיהוּ מַאן דְּיָדַע לְאַכְלָלָא וּלְיַחֲדָא כֻּלְּהוּ כַּחֲדָא, לְאַתְקְנָא כֹּלָּא בְּלָא בַּאֲתַר דְּאִצְטְרִיךְ לְעֵילָא לְעֵילָא, וּכְדֵין אִתְנְטֵיר בַּר נָשׁ בְּהַאי עָלְמָא, וּבְעָלְמָא דְּאָתֵי.

ע"כ תוספתא

475. Rabbi Yehuda said: I was looking and, behold, through these lights, THE THREE COLORS, the souls of the righteous are looking. When they cleave to this place, THE NUKVA, the souls of the righteous look from among these lights. The colors, WHITE, RED AND GREEN, go up to be included together. Happy is he who knows how to comprise and unite them all as one, and correct all where it is needed to be, high above. Then man is preserved in this world and in the World to Come.

End of Tosefta

46. "The king's strength also loves judgment"

A Synopsis
Rabbi Yosi explains that the title verse refers to God and the power by which He strengthened the realm of Malchut. This power was derived through judgment. Malchut, and therefore the Congregation of Yisrael, was established through judgment - that is, the Mochin that includes Chochmah and Chassadim together.

The Relevance of this Passage
Spiritual balance between mercy and judgment is created within our souls and the world around us by virtue of the spiritual energy bottled up within the mystical words of this ancient text. Balance is critical if we are to live a life of fulfillment. For instance, if the scales are tipped towards the side of judgement, we'll find the world extra hard on us. The objective of this passage is to balance our ability to extend mercy and judgement to others so that we receive the same compassionate blend of judgment and mercy from the world.

476. פָּתַח רִבִּי יוֹסֵי וַאֲמַר, וְעֹז מֶלֶךְ מִשְׁפָּט אָהֵב אַתָּה כּוֹנַנְתָּ מֵישָׁרִים וְגו', וְעֹז מֶלֶךְ מִשְׁפָּט אָהֵב, דָּא קוּדְשָׁא בְּרִיךְ הוּא. וְעֹז מֶלֶךְ: תּוֹקְפָא דְּאַתְקַף קוּדְשָׁא בְּרִיךְ הוּא, לָאו אִיהוּ אֶלָּא בְּמִשְׁפָּט, דְּהָא בְּמִשְׁפָּט אִתְקַיַּים אַרְעָא, כְּד"א מֶלֶךְ בְּמִשְׁפָּט יַעֲמִיד אָרֶץ.

476. Rabbi Yosi opened the discussion saying: "The king's strength also loves judgment (or: 'justice'), You do establish equity" (Tehilim 99:4). "The king's strength also loves justice" refers to the Holy One, blessed be He, NAMELY THE NUKVA WHO LOVES JUSTICE, WHICH IS MOCHIN INCLUDED OF RIGHT AND LEFT TOGETHER. "The king's strength" is the power with which the Holy One, blessed be He, strengthened THE NUKVA, which comes only through justice, as it is written: "The king by justice establishes the land" (Mishlei 29:4) BY BEING INCLUDED OF CHOCHMAH AND CHASSADIM TOGETHER, CHASSADIM ON THE RIGHT AND CHOCHMAH ON THE LEFT.

477. וּבְגִין כָּךְ, וְעֹז מֶלֶךְ מִשְׁפָּט אָהֵב, וְלָא אִתְתַּקְנַת כְּנֶסֶת יִשְׂרָאֵל אֶלָּא בְּמִשְׁפָּט, בְּגִין דְּמִתַּמָּן אִתְזָנַת, וְכָל בִּרְכָאן דְּנַטְלָא, מִתַּמָּן נַטְלָא. וּבְגִין כָּךְ וְעֹז מֶלֶךְ מִשְׁפָּט אָהֵב, כָּל תִּאוּבוֹ, וְכָל רְחִימוּ דִילָהּ לָקֳבֵיל

מִשְׁפָּט. אַתָּה כּוֹנַנְתָּ מֵשָׁרִים, רָזָא דִּתְרֵין כְּרוּבִים לְתַתָּא, דְּאִינּוּן תִּקּוּנָא
וְיִישׁוּבָא דְעָלְמָא, וְהָא אִתְּמָר.

477. This is the reason SCRIPTURE SAYS, "The king's strength also loves justice," for the Congregation of Yisrael, THE NUKVA, is not established save through justice, WHICH IS MOCHIN INCLUDED OF CHOCHMAH AND CHASSADIM TOGETHER. Since it is fed thereof, THE SECRET OF CHASSADIM and all the blessings it receives are from there, THE SECRET OF CHOCHMAH. Therefore, "the king's strength also loves justice," for all it desires and craves is to receive justice. "You do establish equity (lit. 'equities')" is the secret of the two Cherubs below CALLED EQUITIES, who rectify and render the world inhabited.

47. "Haleluyah! Give praise, O servants of Hashem"

A Synopsis

The rabbis explain that when one person praises another, the praise should be in accordance with that person's merit. This is because praise given that is not deserved becomes a reproach. Through a discussion of the title verse, we learn that the name 'Haleluyah' is among the highest kinds of praise to God since it contains both the highest name as well the praise itself. The rest of the title portion reveals the name of the praised and those who address the praise. This means that they, the servants of The Creator, praised the place called "the Name of Yah," Malchut. We're then told of the significance of the *Yud* י in the Hebrew translation of the word *let,* and its relationship to "the drawing from the most hidden." The discourse then reveals the meaning of the words, "From the rising of the sun to its setting." This alludes to Zeir Anpin, whence the sun shines and Malchut, the place to which Faith is bound.

The Relevance of this Passage

The wisdom to offer praise to others with purity and in the appropriate measure is awakened in us. The Holy Name of "Haleluyah" and the letter *Yud* י connect us to lofty levels in the spiritual atmosphere, arousing Light, blessing, and praise throughout our physical world [Malchut]. We are inspired to become worthy of praise through spiritual growth and transformation.

478. רִבִּי חִזְקִיָּה פָּתַח וַאֲמַר, הַלְלוּ יָהּ הַלְלוּ עַבְדֵי ה' הַלְלוּ אֶת שֵׁם ה', הַאי קְרָא אִית לְאִסְתַּכְּלָא בֵּיהּ, כֵּיוָן דַּאֲמַר הַלְלוּיָה, אַמַּאי הַלְלוּ עַבְדֵי ה', וּלְבָתַר הַלְלוּ אֶת שֵׁם ה'. אֶלָּא הָכֵי תָּנֵינָן, מַאן דִּמְשַׁבַּח לְאַחֲרָא, אִצְטְרִיךְ לְשַׁבָּחָא לֵיהּ כְּפוּם יְקָרֵיהּ, וּכְפוּם יְקָרֵיהּ הָכֵי אִצְטְרִיךְ שְׁבָחֵיהּ, וְתָנֵינָן מַאן דִּמְשַׁבַּח לְאַחֲרָא, בִּשְׁבָחָא דְּלֵית בֵּיהּ, הוּא גָּלֵי גְּנוּתֵיהּ, וְצָבֵי לְגַלָּאָה לֵיהּ, וְעַל דָּא, מַאן דְּעָבֵיד הֶסְפֵּדָא עַל בַּר נָשׁ, אִצְטְרִיךְ כְּפוּם יְקָרֵיהּ, וְלָא יַתִּיר, דְּמִגּוֹ שְׁבָחֵיהּ אָתֵי לִגְנוּתֵיהּ, וּבְכֹלָּא שְׁבָחָא אִצְטְרִיךְ כְּפוּם יְקָרֵיהּ.

478. Rabbi Chizkiyah opened the discussion with the verse, "Haleluyah! Give praise, O servants of Hashem, praise the name of Hashem" (Tehilim 113:1). Let us examine this verse. After saying Haleluyah, why ADD "Give praise, O servants of Hashem" and then "praise the name of Hashem"? HE ANSWERS: We have so learned that whoever praises someone else should do so in accordance with his merits, and praise should be the extent of that person's merit. We have learned that he who gives him praise which he does not deserve, it is considered to be a reproach; TO WIT, his blame shall be revealed. Therefore, he who mourns another man should do so according to his merit and no more. For the praise might turn EVENTUALLY into blame. Praise should always agree with merits.

479. תָּא חֲזֵי, הַלְלוּיָהּ: הָכָא אִית שְׁבָחָא עִלָּאָה דְּמָארֵי דְכֹלָּא, אֲתָר דְּלָא שָׁלְטָא בֵּיהּ עֵינָא לְמִנְדַע וּלְאִסְתַּכְּלָא, דְּאִיהוּ טְמִירָא דְכָל טְמִירִין, וּמַאן אִיהוּ. י״ה, שְׁמָא עִלָּאָה עַל כֹּלָּא.

479. Come and see: "Haleluyah." There is here a supreme praise to the Master of everything, whom no eye can behold or know, who is most hidden. Who is He? THE NAME OF Yah, the highest name of all.

480. וּבְגִ״כ הַלְלוּיָהּ: שְׁבָחָא וּשְׁמָא כַּחֲדָא, כְּלִילָן כַּחֲדָא, וְהָכָא סְתִים מִלָּה דַּאֲמַר הַלְלוּיָהּ, וְלָא אֲמַר מַאן הַלְלוּיָהּ, לְמַאן אָמְרוּ הַלְלוּ, אֶלָּא כְּמָה דְּי״ה סָתִים, הָכֵי שְׁבָחָא דְּשַׁבּוּחֵי סָתִים אִינוּן, דִּמְשַׁבְּחֵי לָא יְדַעְנָא מַאן אִינוּן, וְהָכֵי אִצְטְרִיךְ לְמֶהֱוֵי כֹּלָּא סָתִים, בְּרָזָא עִלָּאָה, וּלְבָתַר דְּסָתִים בְּרָזָא עִלָּאָה, גַּלֵּי וַאֲמַר, הַלְלוּ עַבְדֵּי ה׳ הַלְלוּ אֶת שֵׁם ה׳, בְּגִין דְּדָא אִיהוּ אֲתָר, דְּלָא סָתִים, כְּהַהוּא עִלָּאָה טְמִירָא דְכָל טְמִירִין, דָּא הוּא אֲתָר דְּאִקְרֵי שֵׁם, כְּד״א אֲשֶׁר נִקְרָא שֵׁם שֵׁם ה׳.

480. Therefore "Haleluyah (lit. 'praise Yah')" contains a praise and a name in one. Here it is undisclosed since he says Haleluyah, yet does not mention the speaker, or to whom the word is addressed. As the name Yah is undisclosed, so is the praise, and I do not know who are those who address the praise. All should be thus covered in the supernal secret. After being concealed by the supernal secret, it is now revealed and said: "Give praise, O servants of Hashem, praise the name of Hashem," BY WHICH THE NAME OF THOSE WHO PRAISE AND THE PRAISED ARE MADE KNOWN. This is because the place is not as hidden as that supernal and most hidden of all, WHICH IS YAH, but is the place called name, NAMELY THE NUKVA, as it is

written: "Whose name is called by the name of Hashem" (II Shmuel 6:2), WHICH MEANS THE NUKVA CALLED NAME.

481. קַדְמָאָה סָתִים דְּלָא גַּלְיָא, תִּנְיָינָא סָתִים וְגַלְיָא, וּבְגִין דְּקַיְימָא בְּאִתְגַּלְיָיא, אֲמַר אִינוּן דְּקָא מְשַׁבְּחֵי לְהַהוּא אֲתַר מָאן אִינוּן, וְקָאֲמַר דְּאִינוּן עַבְדֵי ה', דְּאִתְחֲזוּן לְשַׁבְּחָא לַאֲתַר דָּא.

481. The first one, YAH, is covered and undisclosed, while the second, THE NAME OF YAH, is both undisclosed and disclosed. And since it may be revealed, SCRIPTURE says that they praise the place CALLED THE NAME OF YAH. Who are those who praise? The servants of Hashem, who are worthy of praising this place, THE NUKVA.

482. יְהִי שֵׁם ה' מְבוֹרָךְ, מַאי שְׁנָא דְּקָאֲמַר יְהִי. אֶלָּא יְהִי, רָזָא דְּאַמְשָׁכוּתָא מֵהַהוּא אֲתַר עִלָּאָה, דְּאִיהוּ סָתִים דְּקָאֲמָרָן, דְּאִיהוּ י"ה, עַד רָזָא דִּבְרִית, דְּאִיהוּ יוּ"ד תַּתָּאָה, כְּגַוְונָא דְיוּ"ד עִלָּאָה, שֵׁירוּתָא כְּסוֹפָא.

482. "Blessed be the name of Hashem" (Tehilim 113:2). HE ASKS: Why does it say here "be (Heb. *yehi* – or *Yud-Hei-Yud*)"? HE REPLIES: This word is the secret of drawing from that supernal, hidden place we mentioned, Yah, unto the secret of the covenant, the lower *Yud* which resembles the upper *Yud*; the beginning is like the end.

483. וּבְגִין כָּךְ יְהִי, רָזָא דְּאַמְשָׁכוּתָא מִטְּמִירָא דְּכָל טְמִירִין, עַד דַּרְגָּא תַּתָּאָה, וּבְמִלָּה דָּא אִתְקַיַּים כָּל עוֹבָדָא דִּבְרֵאשִׁית, כְּד"א יְהִ"י רָקִיעַ, יְהִ"י מְאוֹרֹת, יְהִ"י אוֹר.

483. Therefore '*Yud-Hei-Yud*' is the secret of drawing from the most hidden, THE FIRST *YUD* OF *YUD-ALEPH-HEI-DALET-VAV-NUN-HEI-YUD* unto the lower grade, THE LAST *YUD* OF *YUD-ALEPH-HEI-DALET-VAV- NUN -HEI-YUD*. THIS IS THE SECRET OF THE TWO *YUDS* OF *YUD-HEI-YUD*. With its support the Creation prevailed, as it says, "Let (Heb. *yehi*) there be firmament" (Beresheet 1:6), "let there be lights" (Ibid. 14), and "let there be light" (Ibid. 3).

484. בְּכָל אִינוּן עוֹבָדִין דִּלְעֵילָא כְּתִיב יְהִי, בְּכָל אִינוּן עוֹבָדִין דִּלְתַתָּא, לָא כְּתִיב יה"י, בְּגִין דְּרָזָא דָא דְּאִיהוּ אַמְשָׁכוּתָא מֵרָזָא עִלָּאָה, סְתִימִין דְּכָל סְתִימִין, לָא אִתְקַיָּים אֶלָּא בְּמִלִּין עִלָּאֵי דִּלְעֵילָא, וְלָא אִתְּמָר בְּאִינוּן מִלִּין תַּתָּאִין דִּלְתַתָּא.

484. In all the works above, THE FIRMAMENT, LIGHT AND THE LIGHTS, it is written *Yud-Hei-Yud*; in all the works below, THE EARTH, THE SEAS AND ALL THAT IS IN THEM, it does not say *Yud-Hei-Vav*, since the secret OF *YUD-HEI-VAV*, the drawing from the most hidden, THE FIRST *YUD* OF *YUD-ALEPH-HEI-DALET-VAV-NUN-HEI-YUD*, does not prevail save by the supernal works above and not those below.

485. וּבְדָא מִתְבָּרַךְ שְׁמָא קַדִּישָׁא בְּכֹלָּא, וְעַל דָּא כְּתִיב יְהִי שֵׁם יי' מְבוֹרָךְ וְגו', מִמִּזְרַח שֶׁמֶשׁ עַד מְבוֹאוֹ, דָּא אֲתַר עִלָּאָה, דְּקָא נָהִיר מִנֵּיהּ שִׁמְשָׁא, וְנָהִיר לְכֹלָּא, וְדָא הוּא אֲתַר רֵישָׁא עִלָּאָה סְתִימָאָה.

485. Through this, the most Holy Name is blessed by everything. It is therefore written: "Blessed be (*Yud-Hei-Yud*) the name of Hashem." "From the rising of the sun" (Tehilim 113:3) is the supernal place whence the sun, ZEIR ANPIN, shines from, the place of the supernal undisclosed head, THE HEAD OF ARICH ANPIN.

486. וְעַד מְבוֹאוֹ: דָּא הוּא אֲתַר קִשְׁרָא, דְּאִתְקַשַּׁר בֵּיהּ מְהֵימְנוּתָא כִּדְקָא חָזֵי, וּמִתַּמָּן נָפְקָן בִּרְכָאן לְכֹלָּא, וְעָלְמָא מֵהָכָא אִתְּזַן, כְּמָה דְּאִתְּמָר, וּבְגִין כָּךְ קַיְּימָא הַאי אֲתַר לְאִתְּזָנָא מֵעֵילָא, וּלְאִתְבָּרְכָא מִתַּמָּן, וְכֹלָּא קַיְּימָא בְּאִתְעֲרוּתָא דִּלְתַתָּא, דְּמִתְעָרֵי אִינוּן עַבְדֵי יי', כַּד מְבָרְכֵי שְׁמָא קַדִּישָׁא, כִּדְקָאֲמָרָן. וּבְגִין כָּךְ דְּאִיהוּ בְּאִתְגַּלְּיָיא, כְּתִיב הַלְלוּ עַבְדֵי יי' הַלְלוּ אֶת שֵׁם יי'.

486. "To its setting" (Ibid.): To this place to which faith, THE NUKVA, is well bound, BEING THE PLACE OF THE UNISON BETWEEN ZEIR ANPIN AND THE NUKVA, whence blessings issue forth to all, and the world, THE NUKVA, is fed thereof, as we learned. Hence this place, THE NUKVA, is fed and blessed from above. All depends upon awakening below, when the

servants of Hashem are aroused while blessing the Holy Name, THE NUKVA, like we said. And when She is revealed, it is written, "Give praise, O servants of Hashem, praise the name of Hashem."

487. אַדְהָכֵי הֲוָה נָהֵיר צַפְרָא, נָפְקוּ מִן מְעַרְתָּא, וּבְהַהוּא לֵילְיָא לָא דְמִיכוּ, אָזְלוּ בְּאָרְחָא, כַּד נָפְקוּ מֵאִינּוּן טוּרִין, יָתְבוּ וְצַלּוּ צְלוֹתָא, מָטוּ לְחַד כְּפַר, וְיָתְבוּ תַּמָּן כָּל הַהוּא יוֹמָא, בְּהַהוּא לֵילְיָא נָמוּ, עַד דַּהֲוָה פַּלְגוּת לֵילְיָא קָמוּ, לְאִתְעַסְּקָא בְּאוֹרַיְיתָא.

487. By this time, the morning broke and they came out of the cave, not having slept that night. They walked along the way and when they came out of the mountains, they sat down and prayed. They reached a village where they sat the whole day. At night, they slept until midnight when they rose to study the Torah.

48. "And he blessed them that day"

A Synopsis

The discussion begins with an interpretation of the title verse. We are told that the phrase "that day" signifies the unity between Zeir Anpin and Binah. "By you" alludes to the unity of the blessings from both high and low grades. "Yisrael," we learn, is an allusion to Yisrael-Saba, who receives blessings from above and confers them on Malchut. The rabbis then explain why the name Ephraim is mentioned first in the verse, "Elohim make you as Ephraim and Menashe." The first explanation of the title verse concludes with the teaching that love of one's grandchildren often surpasses the love of one's own children.

Rabbi Yosi provides an additional explanation for the title verse, revealing that men are blessed first, since women are blessed only through the blessings of men.

The Relevance of this Passage

In order for a lamp to illuminate a darkened room, it must be connected to a source of energy. Likewise, for spiritual Light to brighten our darkened world, we must connect ourselves to the source of energy that powers the entire cosmos. The word "that day" indicates a connection between Zeir Anpin and Binah, two Sfirot that occupy the Upper Worlds. The phrases "By you" and "Israel" correspond to the connection between our souls and the entire physical dimension to Zeir Anpin. Spiritual current is now free to flow and illuminate all of mankind once these cosmic "power stations" are connected to one another.

488. פָּתַח רִבִּי יְהוּדָה וְאָמַר וַיְבָרְכֵם בַּיּוֹם הַהוּא לֵאמוֹר בְּךָ יְבָרֵךְ יִשְׂרָאֵל וְגוֹ', וַיְבָרְכֵם בַּיּוֹם הַהוּא, מַאי בַּיּוֹם הַהוּא, דְּהָא סַגֵּי דְּקָאֲמַר וַיְבָרְכֵם. וְתוּ, כָּל לֵאמוֹר כְּתִיב חָסֵר, וְהָכָא לֵאמוֹר בְּוי"ו כְּתִיב, מַאי שְׁנָא.

488. "And he blessed them that day, saying (Heb. *lemor*), 'By you shall Israel bless'" (Beresheet 48:20). HE ASKS: What is the meaning of "that day"? It would have been enough to say just "And he blessed them." Also the word 'lemor' is normally spelled without *Vav*, but here there is an additional *Vav*. What is the reason for the difference?

489. אֶלָּא רָזָא אִיהוּ, וַיְבָרְכֵם בַּיּוֹם הַהוּא, מַאי בַּיּוֹם הַהוּא, רָזָא

דְּדַרְגָּא דְּאִתְמַנָּא עַל בִּרְכָאן לְעֵילָא. יוֹם הַהוּא. יוֹם מֵהַהוּא אֲתַר
עִלָּאָה, דְּאִקְרֵי הוּא, וְהַאי יוֹם הַהוּא, דְּלֵית פֵּרוּדָא בֵּין יוֹם וּבֵין הוּא,
וּבְכָל אֲתַר הַיּוֹם הַהוּא, דָּא תְּרֵין דַּרְגִּין, דַּרְגָּא עִלָּאָה וְתַתָּאָה דְּאִינּוּן
כַּחֲדָא.

489. HE ANSWERS: "And he blessed them that day" is a mystery. That day
is the secret of the grade in charge over the blessings above, BINAH; "That
day" is the day, ZEIR ANPIN, which is from the supernal place called "that
(lit. 'he')" WHICH IS BINAH. "That day" INDICATES THAT there is no
separation between "day" and "that." Wherever IT IS SAID "that day," there
are two grades: the supernal grade, BINAH, and the lower, ZEIR ANPIN,
when they are together; TO WIT, WHEN ZEIR ANPIN ASCENDED TO BINAH
AND BECAME LIKE IT.

490. וּבְגִין כָּךְ, כַּד בָּעָא יַעֲקֹב לְבָרְכָא לִבְנוֹי דְּיוֹסֵף, בָּרֵיךְ לוֹן בְּיִחוּדָא
דִּלְעֵילָא וְתַתָּא כֻּלְּהוּ כַּחֲדָא, בְּגִין דְּיִתְקַיֵּים בִּרְכַתְהוֹן, וּלְבָתַר כָּלֵיל
כֹּלָּא כַּחֲדָא, וַאֲמַר בְּךָ יְבָרֵךְ יִשְׂרָאֵל. מַאי בְּךָ. וַדַּאי דָּא רָזָא דְּיִחוּדָא,
בְּקַדְמֵיתָא מִתַּתָּא לְעֵילָא, וּלְבָתַר נָחִית לְאֶמְצָעִיתָא, וּלְתַתָּא. לֶאֱמוֹר
בְּוא"ו הָא אֶמְצָעִיתָא. וּלְבָתַר נָחִית לְתַתָּא בְּךָ. וְהָכֵי הוּא יָאוֹת כִּדְקָא
חֲזֵי, מִתַּתָּא לְעֵילָא, וּמֵעֵילָא לְתַתָּא.

490. This is why when Jacob wished to bless Joseph's children, he blessed
them all as one by the unison of high and low, so that their blessing would
prevail. He then included them all together, saying: "By you shall Israel
bless." What is "By you"? Assuredly this is the secret of unison. First he
blessed from below upward, TO WIT, IN "AND HE BLESSED THEM THAT
DAY," WHICH IS ZEIR ANPIN AND BINAH TOGETHER, and then he
descended into the middle TO ZEIR ANPIN and down TO THE NUKVA.
'Lemor' with *Vav* is the middle, SINCE *VAV* IS AN ALLUSION TO ZEIR
ANPIN. He then went down, SAYING "by you," WHICH REFERS TO THE
NUKVA. Thus THE BLESSING is well formed, being from below upward and
from above downward.

491. בְּךָ יְבָרֵךְ יִשְׂרָאֵל, מַאי יִשְׂרָאֵל, יִשְׂרָאֵל סָבָא, יְבוֹרְךָ יִשְׂרָאֵל לָא
כְּתִיב, אֶלָּא יְבָרֵךְ, דְּהָא יִשְׂרָאֵל נָטִיל בִּרְכָאן מִלְּעֵילָא, וּלְבָתַר אִיהוּ

מְבָרֵךְ לְכֹלָּא, בְּהַאי דַרְגָּא תַּתָּאָה דַיְיקָא, דְקָאָמַר, בְּךָ יְבָרֵךְ יִשְׂרָאֵל לֵאמֹר.

491. "By you shall Israel bless": HE ASKS: What is Israel? HE ANSWERS: It is Yisrael Saba, ZEIR ANPIN OF BINAH. It does not say, 'Shall Israel be blessed' but "Shall Israel bless," WHICH MEANS HE WILL BLESS OTHERS. This is because Yisrael-SABA receives blessings from above and then blesses all through the low grade, THE NUKVA, by saying "By you shall Israel bless, saying:" WHICH MEANS THAT THROUGH "BY YOU (HEB. BECHA)," BY THE NUKVA, YISRAEL-SABA SHALL BLESS ALL.

492. יְשִׂימְךָ אֱלֹהִים כְּאֶפְרַיִם וְכִמְנַשֶּׁה, אַקְדִּים לֵיהּ לְאֶפְרַיִם בְּקַדְמֵיתָא, בְּגִין דְּאֶפְרַיִם עַל שְׁמָא דְיִשְׂרָאֵל אִקְרֵי. מְנָ"ל. מֵהָא, דְּכַד שִׁבְטָא דְאֶפְרַיִם נָפַק, עַד לָא אִשְׁתְּלִים זִמְנָא דְשִׁעְבּוּדָא דְמִצְרַיִם, דָּחֲקוּ שַׁעְתָּא וְנָפְקוּ מִן גָּלוּתָא, קָמוּ עֲלֵיהוֹן שַׂנְאֵיהוֹן וְקַטְלוּ לוֹן, וּכְתִיב בֶּן אָדָם הָעֲצָמוֹת הָאֵלֶּה כָּל בֵּית יִשְׂרָאֵל הֵמָּה, מַשְׁמַע דִּכְתִיב כָּל בֵּית יִשְׂרָאֵל הֵמָּה, וְעַל דָּא אַקְדִּים לְאֶפְרַיִם קֳדָם מְנַשֶּׁה. בְּגִין כָּךְ אֶפְרַיִם מָטוֹלֵיהּ לִסְטַר מַעֲרָב, וּמַטְלָנוֹי הֲוָה.

492. "Elohim make you as Ephraim and Menashe" (Ibid.): He mentions Ephraim first, since Ephraim is called by the name of Yisrael. Whence do we know that? The tribe of Ephraim left before the time was over of the Egyptian enslavement, by trying to force time and come out of exile, and their foes rose against them and killed them. It is written, "Son of man, these bones are the whole house of Yisrael" (Yechezkel 37:11). From this, it is understood that EPHRAIM IS CONSIDERED AS YISRAEL, since it says "the whole house of Yisrael." Jacob therefore put Ephraim before Menashe. Thus Ephraim journeyed on the west side, which was his path, AS THE SHECHINAH IS ON THE WEST, WHO COMPRISES ALL YISRAEL. THEREFORE EPHRAIM, BEING CALLED YISRAEL, WAS ON THE SIDE OF THE SHECHINAH.

493. תָּא חֲזֵי , בִּרְכְתָא דְּבָרֵיךְ לִבְנֵי יוֹסֵף, אַמַּאי אַקְדִּים לוֹן בִּרְכָאן, עַד לָא יְבָרֵךְ לִבְנוֹי. אֶלָּא מִכָּאן, דַּחֲבִיבוּתָא דִּבְנֵי בְּנוֹי, חָבִיב עֲלֵיהּ

דב״נ יַתִּיר מִבְּנוֹי, וּבְגִין כָּךְ, אַקְדֵּים חֲבִיבוּתָא דִּבְנֵי בְּנוֹי קוֹדֶם לִבְנוֹי, לְבָרְכָא לוֹן בְּקַדְמֵיתָא.

493. Come and see: Why did the blessing he gave to Joseph's children precede that of his own children? HE ANSWERS: This teaches us that love of grandchildren surpasses the love of one's own children. Therefore, SINCE HIS LOVE FOR HIS GRANDCHILDREN IS STRONGER THAN THAT FOR HIS CHILDREN, he blessed them first.

494. וַיְבָרְכֵם בַּיּוֹם הַהוּא לֵאמֹר, ר' יוֹסֵי פְּתַח וַאֲמַר, יי' זְכָרָנוּ יְבָרֵךְ יְבָרֵךְ אֶת בֵּית יִשְׂרָאֵל וגו', יי' זְכָרָנוּ יְבָרֵךְ: אִלֵּין גּוּבְרִין. יְבָרֵךְ אֶת בֵּית יִשְׂרָאֵל: אִלֵּין נָשִׁין. בְּגִין דְּדְכוּרִין בָּעְיָין לְאִתְבָּרְכָא בְּקַדְמֵיתָא, וּלְבָתַר נָשִׁין, וְנָשִׁין לָא מִתְבָּרְכָן אֶלָּא מִבִּרְכָתְהוֹן דִּדְכוּרִין, דְּכַד דְּכוּרִין מִתְבָּרְכָן כְּדֵין נָשִׁין מִתְבָּרְכָן. וְאִי תֵימָא מֵהָא, דִּכְתִיב וְכִפֶּר בַּעֲדוֹ וּבְעַד בֵּיתוֹ, דְּבָעֵי לְכַפְּרָא עֲלֵיהּ בְּקַדְמֵיתָא, וּלְבָתַר עַל בֵּיתֵיהּ, בְּגִין דְּמִתְבָּרְכָא מִנֵּיהּ.

494. "And he blessed them that day, saying": Rabbi Yosi opened the discussion saying: "Hashem has remembered us: He will bless, He will bless the house of Yisrael" (Tehilim 115:12). WHY IS IT WRITTEN TWICE "BLESS"? HE SAYS, "Hashem has remembered us: He will bless" refers to the men. "He will bless the house of Yisrael" refers to the women. For the men should be blessed first and then the women, since women are blessed only through the blessing of men. When the men are blessed, the women are blessed. THIS MAY BE DERIVED from the verse, if you wish "And shall make atonement for himself and for his house" (Vayikra 16:6). One should first atone for himself and only then for his house, SINCE MEN COME BEFORE WOMEN, so that she will be blessed from him.

495. תָּא חֲזֵי, דְּנָשִׁין לָא מִתְבָּרְכָן אֶלָּא מִגּוּבְרִין, כַּד אִתְבָּרְכָן אִינּוּן בְּקַדְמֵיתָא, וּמֵהַאי בִּרְכָתָא מִתְבָּרְכָן. אֶלָּא בְּמַאי אוֹקִימְנָא יְבָרֵךְ אֶת בֵּית יִשְׂרָאֵל, אֶלָּא קוּדְשָׁא בְּרִיךְ הוּא יָהַב תּוֹסֶפֶת בִּרְכָאן לִדְכוּרָא דְּנָסִיב, בְּגִין דְּמִתְבָּרְכָא מִנֵּיהּ אִתְּתָא וְכֵן בְּכָל אֲתָר, יְהִיב קוּדְשָׁא

בְּרִיךְ הוּא תּוֹסֶפֶת בִּרְכָאן לִדְכוּרָא דְּנָסֵיב, בְּגִין דְּמִתְבָּרְכָא מֵהַהוּא
תּוֹסֶפֶת דְּבִרְכָאן. כֵּיוָן דְּאִנְסֵיב ב״נ יָהֵיב לֵיהּ תְּרֵין חוּלָקִין, חַד לֵיהּ
וְחַד לְנוּקְבֵיהּ, וְאִיהוּ, נָטֵיל כֹּלָּא, חוּלָקֵיהּ וְחוּלָק נוּקְבֵיהּ.

495. Come and see: Women are blessed only through men, who are blessed first, and by their blessings they are blessed, AND NEED NO SPECIAL BLESSING FOR THEMSELVES. HE ASKS: How can we account for the words: "He will bless the house of Yisrael," SEEING THAT WOMEN NEED NO SPECIAL BLESSING FOR THEMSELVES? HE ANSWERS: The Holy One, blessed be He, gives an additional blessing to a married man, so that his wife may be blessed from him. So always, the Holy One, blessed be He, gives an extra blessing to a married man, and gives him two portions, the one for him and another for his wife. And he receives everything, his own, and his wife's portion. HENCE THERE IS A SPECIAL BLESSING FOR THE WOMEN "HE WILL BLESS THE HOUSE OF YISRAEL," SINCE IT IS THEIR OWN PORTION. THOUGH MEN RECEIVE THEIR PORTION TOO, THEY LATER GIVE IT TO THEM, AS EXPLAINED.

496. תָּא חֲזֵי וַיְבָרֲכֵם בַּיּוֹם הַהוּא, לְבָתַר לֵאמוֹר בּוא״ו, הָכָא
אִתְרְמִיזָא בְּרָא בּוּכְרָא, בְּנִי בְכוֹרִי יִשְׂרָאֵל, וּכְתִיב וְאֶפְרַיִם בְּכוֹרִי הוּא,
וְעַל דָּא תּוֹסֶפֶת וא״ו.

496. "And he blessed them that day" is joined by the word 'lemor' (Eng. 'saying'), with Vav. Here is an allusion to a firstborn son, SINCE VAV ALLUDES TO BIRTHRIGHT, as it is written: "Israel is My son, My firstborn" (Shemot 4:22) and "Ephraim is My firstborn" (Yirmeyah 31:8). For this, there is an additional Vav, FOR EPHRAIM WHO WAS INCLUDED WITHIN THAT BLESSING.

49. "Your eyes did see my unshaped flesh"

A Synopsis

Rabbi Chizkiyah discourses on the title verse, revealing that before descending to earth, all souls stand before God in the same shape and form that they will possess in this world. The title verse alludes to this fact, since God sees all before they are seen in the world.

The Relevance of this Passage

Before a soul descends into the physical dimension, it stands before The Creator and promises to complete its correction process, seeking redemption for past life iniquities by way of spiritual transformation. The negative angel Satan and the trappings of our seductive material world cause forgetfulness. We succumb to temptations that glorify our own ego and thus, break our commitment to The Creator. Here we can awaken remembrance of our divine promise and receive inspiration and passion to pursue the path of spiritual transformation.

497. ר' חִזְקִיָּה פָּתַח, גָּלְמִי רָאוּ עֵינֶיךָ וְעַל סִפְרְךָ כֻּלָּם יִכָּתֵבוּ וגו', הַאי קְרָא אוֹקְמוּהָ בְּכַמָּה אֲתַר. אֲבָל תָּא חֲזֵי, כָּל אִינּוּן נִשְׁמָתִין דַּהֲווֹ מִיּוֹמָא דְּאִתְבְּרֵי עַלְמָא, כֻּלְּהוּ קַיְימֵי קַמֵּי קוּדְשָׁא בְּרִיךְ הוּא עַד לָא נָחֲתוּ לְעַלְמָא, בְּהַהוּא דִּיּוּקְנָא מַמָּשׁ דְּאִתְחֲזוּן לְבָתַר בְּעַלְמָא, וְהַהוּא חֵיזוּ דְּגוּפָא דְּבַר נָשׁ דְּקָאֵים בְּהַאי עַלְמָא, הָכִי קָאֵים לְעֵילָּא.

497. Rabbi Chizkiyah opened the discussion saying: "Your eyes did see my unshaped flesh; for in Your book all things are written" (Tehilim 139:16). This verse has been expounded in several places. Yet come and see: All the souls which have existed since the Creation of the world, all stand before the Holy One, blessed be He, before descending into the world, assuming the very shape in which they are seen in the world. In that same appearance of the person's body that lives in this world, so does it remain above.

498. וּבְשַׁעֲתָא דְּנִשְׁמָתָא דָּא זְמִינָא לְאַחֲתָא בְּעַלְמָא, הַהִיא נִשְׁמָתָא בְּהַהִיא דִּיּוּקְנָא מַמָּשׁ דְּקַיְימָא בְּהַאי עַלְמָא, הָכִי קָאֵים קַמֵּי קוּדְשָׁא בְּרִיךְ הוּא, וְאוֹמֵי לָהּ קוּדְשָׁא בְּרִיךְ הוּא דְּיִטּוֹר פִּקּוּדֵי אוֹרַיְיתָא, וְלָא יַעֲבָר עַל קְיָימִין.

498. When the soul is ready to descend into the world with the very shape it is about to have in this world, it stands before the Holy One, blessed be He, who adjures it to observe the precepts of the Torah and never transgress them.

499. וּמְנַ"ל דְּקָיְימִין קַמֵּיהּ, דִּכְתִיב חַי יי' אֲשֶׁר עָמַדְתִּי לְפָנָיו, עָמַדְתִּי וַדַּאי, וְהָא אוּקְמוּהָ. וּבג"כ גָּלְמִי רָאוּ עֵינֶיךָ, עַד לָא יִתְחֲזֵי בְּעַלְמָא. וְעַל סִפְרְךָ כֻּלָּם יִכָּתֵבוּ, דְּהָא כָּל נִשְׁמָתִין, בְּהַהוּא דְּיוֹקָנָא דִּלְהוֹן, כֻּלְּהוּ בְּסִפְרָא כְּתִיבִין. יָמִים יֻצָּרוּ, הָא אוּקְמוּהָ יֻצָּרוּ וַדַּאי, וְלֹא אֶחָד בָּהֶם, בְּהַאי עַלְמָא לְמֵיקַם בְּקִיּוּמָא דְּמָארֵיהוֹן, כִּדְקָא חָזֵי.

499. Whence do we know that THE SOULS stand before Him? From the verse: "As Hashem, the Elohim of Yisrael lives, before whom I stood" (I Melachim 17:1), stood assuredly BEFORE BEING CREATED, as has been explained. Therefore, "Your eyes did see my unshaped flesh" before it was seen in the world; "for in Your book all things are written" as all the souls in their very shapes are recorded in a book. "The days also in which they are to be fashioned" (Tehilim 139:16), indeed they are fashioned, as explained, TO WIT, THEY ARE MADE A GARMENT TO WEAR; "there was not one of them" (Ibid.), AS NOT ONE DAY in this world could stand properly before its Master.

50. "The measure of my days, what it is?"

A Synopsis

The discussion opens to reveal that the days of the righteous who gain merit through good deeds are blessed from Binah. We're also told that the phrase "my end" indirectly alludes to David. Rabbi Yehuda then states that the title verse relates to the seventy years that were taken from Adam and apportioned to David. We learn that David corresponds to Malchut, upon whom the seven Sfirot shine. David wished to know why the rest of the supernal lights had light of their own while he did not - he was, however, denied permission.

The Relevance of this Passage

The quality and length of one's days is directly affected by the deeds and degree of spiritual change a person seeks and attains in his lifetime. Upon the merit of the righteous, we draw blessings of long life from above [Binah] and shower them upon the entire world [David, the embodiment of Malchut]. We are inspired to use this Light and increased longevity to accomplish our spiritual purpose and correction.

500. תָּא חֲזֵי, יוֹמִין דְּב"ג, כַּד זָכֵי בְּהַאי עַלְמָא בְּעוֹבָדִין טָבָאן, יוֹמִין דִּילֵיהּ אִתְבָּרְכָאן לְעֵילָא, מֵהַהוּא אֲתַר דְּאִיהוּ מִדַּת יוֹמוֹי. פָּתַח וַאֲמַר הוֹדִיעֵנִי יי' קִצִּי וּמִדַּת יָמַי מַה הִיא וְגו', הַאי קְרָא אוּקְמוּהָ, אֲבָל תָּא חֲזֵי, קִצִּי: דָּא קֵץ הַיָּמִין, דְּאִיהוּ מִתְקַשַּׁר בֵּיהּ בְּדָוִד. וּמִדַּת יָמַי מַה הִיא, דָּא אִיהוּ דְּאִתְמַנֵּי מַמָּשׁ עַל יוֹמוֹי.

500. Come and see that when a man has merit in this world through good deeds, his days are blessed above from the place called "the measure of days," WHICH IS BINAH. He opened the discussion saying: "Hashem, make me to know my end, and the measure of my days, what it is" (Tehilim 39:5). This verse has already been explained, yet "my end" is the end of the right, which is connected to David. "The measure of my days" is in charge of his days, WHICH IS BINAH.

501. א"ר יְהוּדָה, הָא שָׁמַעְנָא מֵר' שִׁמְעוֹן, דְּהַאי קְרָא אִתְּמַר, עַל אִינוּן יוֹמִין דְּאִתְגְּזָרוּ עֲלוֹי מֵאָדָם קַדְמָאָה, דְּאִינוּן ע'. דְּהָא אִתְּמַר, דְּחַיִּין כְּלַל לָא הֲווֹ לֵיהּ, אֶלָּא דְּיָהֵיב לֵיהּ אָדָם מֵאִינוּן יוֹמִין דִּילֵיהּ, שַׁבְעִין שְׁנִין.

501. Rabbi Yehuda said: I have heard from Rabbi Shimon that this verse talks about the days that were portioned from Adam, seventy years. For we have learned that David had no life whatsoever, but the seventy years given him by Adam.

502. וְרָזָא דָא, וִילוֹן לָא מְשַׁמֵּשׁ כְּלוּם, וְסִיהֲרָא לָא נָהֲרַת מִגַּרְמָהּ כְּלַל, וְשַׁבְעִין שְׁנִין נָהֲרִין לָהּ, בְּכָל סִטְרָהָא. וְאִינוּן חַיֵּי דָוִד סְתָם. וְעַל דָּא בָּעָא דָוִד לְקוּדְשָׁא בְּרִיךְ הוּא, לְמִנְדַע רָזָא דָא, עַל מָה לֵית לֵהּ חַיִּין לְסִיהֲרָא מִגַּרְמָהּ, וּלְמִנְדַּע עִקָּרָא דִילָהּ.

502. It is a mystery THAT THE FIRMAMENT IS a curtain WHICH CORRESPONDS TO MALCHUT, which serves no purpose, since the moon, MALCHUT, has no light of her own. THE SECRET IS THAT DAVID, WHO CORRESPONDS TO MALCHUT, HAS NO LIFE. Seventy years shine upon her, UPON MALCHUT, on all her sides, BEING THE SECRET OF CHESED, GVURAH, TIFERET, NETZACH, HOD, YESOD AND MALCHUT OF ZEIR ANPIN, EACH INCLUDES OF TEN, WHICH ALTOGETHER AMOUNT TO SEVENTY. This is the life of David. He therefore desired to learn from the Holy One, blessed be He, this secret of why the moon has no life of her own, and wanted to know of her root.

503. וּמִדַּת יָמַי מַה הִיא, דָּא הוּא דַרְגָּא עִלָּאָה סְתִימָא, דְּאִיהוּ קַיְימָא עַל כָּל אִינוּן יוֹמִין, דְּאִינוּן חַיִּין דִּילָהּ, אֲתַר דְּנָהֵיר לְכֹלָּא. אֵדְעָה מֶה חָדֵל אָנִי: אֲמַר דָּוִד: אִנְדַּע עַל מַה חָדֵל אֲנָא נְהוֹרָא מִגַּרְמִי, וְאִתְמְנַע מִנִּי, כִּשְׁאָר כָּל אִינוּן נְהוֹרָאִין עִלָּאִין דְּאִית לוֹן חַיִּין לְכֻלְּהוּ, וַאֲנָא עַל מָה אֲנָא חָדֵל, וְעַל מַה אִתְמְנַע מִנִּי. וְדָא הוּא דִּבְעָא דָוִד לְמִנְדַּע, וְלָא אִתְיְיהִיב לֵיהּ רְשׁוּתָא לְמִנְדַּע.

503. "And the measure of my days, what it is": This is a supernal, undisclosed grade, BINAH, CALLED THE MEASURE OF MY DAYS, since it is situated over all the days which form the life OF MALCHUT, AS CHESED, GVURAH, TIFERET, NETZACH, HOD, YESOD AND MALCHUT ARE DRAWN FROM BINAH, a place which shines upon everything. "I will know how frail I am" (Tehilim 39:5). David said: Let me know wherefore I have not MY OWN light, and cannot be like the rest of the supernal lights, which have

THEIR OWN lives, why MY LIGHT IS frail, and wherefore it is withheld from me. This is what David desired to know, but was not given permission to know.

51. All blessings were given to this grade

A Synopsis
Malchut is called "a cup of blessing," because although she has no light of her own, all the blessings, joy, and goodness are in it and issue from her. All the Sfirot are included in Malchut, and she possesses all the supernal blessings. We therefore recite the Halel prayer to praise Malchut. The three grades of the Halel are the pious, the righteous, and the Congregation of Yisrael, corresponding to the right, left, and central Columns.

The Relevance of this Passage
The supernal blessings embedded into the world of Malchut are unleashed in all their splendor. The balance and harmony of the Three Column System, and the energy aroused through the prayer, connection known as Halel, are instilled within us as our eyes make contact with the mystical verses composing this passage.

504. תָּא חֲזֵי, כָּל בִּרְכָאן עִלָּאִין, כֻּלְּהוּ אִתְמְסָרוּ לְהַאי דַרְגָּא, לְבָרְכָא לְכֹלָּא. וְאע״ג דְּלֵית לָהּ נְהוֹרָא מִגַּרְמָהּ, כָּל בִּרְכָאן, וְכָל חֵידוּ, וְכָל טִיבוּ, כֻּלְּהוּ קַיְימִין בָּהּ, וּמִנָּהּ נָפְקֵי, וְעַל דָּא אִתְקְרִיאַת כּוֹס שֶׁל בְּרָכָה. וְאִקְרֵי בְּרָכָה מַמָּשׁ, כְּמָה דִּכְתִיב בִּרְכַּת ה' הִיא תַעֲשִׁיר, וְעַל דָּא כְּתִיב וּמָלֵא בִּרְכַּת ה' יָם וְדָרוֹם יְרָשָׁה.

504. Come and see: All the supernal blessings were given to this grade, MALCHUT, so it would bless everything. And though it has not its own light, yet all the blessings, joy and goodness are in it, and issue from it. It is therefore called "a cup of blessing," an actual blessing, as it says, "The blessing of Hashem, it makes rich" (Mishlei 10:22), AS THE BLESSING OF HASHEM IS MALCHUT. It is therefore written: "And full with the blessing of Hashem: possess you the west and the south" (Devarim 33:23).

505. וּבְגִין כָּךְ אִית לָהּ בְּכֻלְּהוּ שִׁיּוּר, וּמִכֻּלְּהוּ אִתְמַלְיָא, וּמִכֻּלְּהוּ אִית בָּהּ, וְאִתְבָּרְכָא מִכָּל אִינוּן בִּרְכָאן עִלָּאִין, וְאִתְמְסָרוּ לָהּ בִּרְכָאן לְבָרְכָא, מְנָלָן, דַּאֲמַר רִבִּי יִצְחָק, יַעֲקֹב בָּרֵיךְ לִבְנוֹי דְיוֹסֵף, מֵאֲתַר דָּא דְּכָל בִּרְכָאן אִתְמְסָרוּ בִּידֵיהּ לְבָרְכָא, כְּד״א וְהָיָה בְּרָכָה, מִכָּאן וּלְהַלְאָה בִּרְכָאן אִתְמְסָרוּ בְּיָדֶךְ.

505. Hence MALCHUT has a residue of all THE SFIROT, SINCE THEY ARE ALL INCLUDED WITHIN HER, and she is filled by them all and has something from them all. She is blessed from supernal blessings, which were handed to her to confer. HE ASKS: Whence do we know that? HE REPLIES: Rabbi Yitzchak said: Jacob blessed Joseph's sons from this place, which was given all the blessings to confer, as it says, "And you shall be a blessing" (Beresheet 12:2), WHICH MEANS HE WILL MERIT MALCHUT, THE SECRET OF BLESSING, AND THEN from now on the blessings were delivered to you, SINCE ALL BLESSINGS ARE IN THE HANDS OF MALCHUT.

‏506. תָּא חֲזֵי, כְּגַוְונָא דָא אֲנַן מְבָרְכָן וּמְשַׁבְּחִין לִשְׁמָא דָא, וְעַ"ד הַלֵּילָא, דְּאִינוּן יוֹמִין דְּקָאַמְרֵי הַלֵּילָא. דַּאֲמַר רַבִּי חִיָּיא בְּהַלֵּילָא צְרִיכִין ג' דַּרְגִּין, חֲסִידִים, צַדִּיקִים, וְיִשְׂרָאֵלִים. חֲסִידִים, מִסִּטְרָא דִּימִינָא, צַדִּיקִים מִסִּטְרָא דִּשְׂמָאלָא, וְיִשְׂרָאֵל מִכָּל אִינוּן סִטְרִין, בְּגִין דְּיִשְׂרָאֵל כְּלִילָן מִכֻּלְּהוּ, וְעַל דָּא אִסְתַּלַּק תּוּשְׁבַּחְתָּא דְּקוּדְשָׁא בְּרִיךְ הוּא מִכֹּלָא, וְכֵן בְּכָל אֲתַר דְּיִשְׂרָאֵל מְשַׁבְּחָן לֵיהּ לְקוּדְשָׁא בְּרִיךְ הוּא מִתַּתָּא, אִסְתַּלַּק יְקָרֵיהּ בְּכֹלָּא.

506. Come and behold: in the same manner SHE IS ESTABLISHED BY THE SEVEN SFIROT OF ZEIR ANPIN, we bless and praise this name, MALCHUT, and hence the Halel (lit. 'praise') prayer we recite during certain days. Rabbi Chiya said: We need three grades to the Halel: the pious, the righteous and Yisrael. The pious are on the right, the righteous on the left and Yisrael on all sides, since Yisrael comprise all, BEING THE CENTRAL COLUMN, WHICH INCLUDES THE TWO COLUMNS RIGHT AND LEFT. THEY CORRESPOND TO THE THREE COLUMNS, WHICH MALCHUT RECEIVES FROM ZEIR ANPIN, THOUGH SHE HAS NOTHING OF HER OWN. Therefore the praise of the Holy One, blessed be He, MALCHUT, was raised above THE SFIROT. Also, wherever Yisrael praise the Holy One, blessed be He, from below, THAT IS, RAISE MAYIN NUKVIN (FEMALE WATERS), His glory is elevated throughout THE SFIROT.

52. The sound of a wheel rolling

A Synopsis

The powers appointed over punishment and reward turn the wheel continually. The sound of the chirping of the two birds, Chochmah and Binah, joins with the sound of the wheel, illuminating the lights described in the poem for Shabbat day. Blessings are drawn by a whisper from the Right Column to the Central Column through the sound of the Shofar or ram's horn. When the turning wheel, the Central Column, is filled with Chesed, Chochmah is clothed with Chassadim and ceases to whisper, shining fully. When someone has merit, the wheel brings the illuminations of the three columns under the power of the right, and that person enjoys the illumination of supernal blessings. However, the wheel draws judgment upon he whom does not deserve supernal blessings.

The Relevance of this Passage

Conversing in the lyrical language of metaphor, the Zohar describes the intimate connection between human behavior, the cosmos, the concepts of punishment and reward, and the spiritual tools of the Torah that can help one draw blessing into their life and remove judgments. By virtue of this discourse, the energy of blessing and the cleansing power of the Light fill our lives so that judgement and mercy shine upon us in perfect measure.

תּוֹסֶפְתָּא

507. קָל גַּלְגַּלָּא מִתְגַּלְגְּלָא מִתַּתָּא לְעֵילָּא, רְתִיכָהָא טוֹרְקָהָא אָזְלִין וּמִתְגַּלְגְּלֵי. קָל נְעִימוּתָא סָלְקָא, וְנָחֲתָא, אָזְלָא וְשַׁטְיָא בְּעָלְמָא. קָל שׁוֹפָרָא נָגֵיד בְּעוֹמְקֵי דְּדַרְגֵּי אַסְחַר גַּלְגַּלָּא סַחֲרָנָהָא.

Tosefta (addendum)

507. The sound of a wheel rolling from below upward, closed Chariots roll about, a pleasant voice rises and falls, roams about the world. The sound of a Shofar is heard through the depth of the grades and the wheel turns round.

508. יָתְבִין תְּרֵין מַגְרוֹפִין, מִימִינָא וּמִשְׂמָאלָא, בִּתְרֵין גּוֹוְנִין מִשְׁתַּאֲבִין דָּא בְּדָא, דָּא חִוָּור וְדָא סוּמָק, וְתַרְוַוייְהוּ סָחֲרִין גַּלְגַּלָּא

לְעֵילָא, אַסְחַר לִימִינָא חִוָּורָא סַלְקָא, וְאַסְחַר לִשְׂמָאלָא סוּמְקָא נָחֲתָא. וְגַלְגַּלָּא אַסְחַר תָּדִיר וְלָא שָׁכֵיךְ.

508. Two shovels are placed, THE POWERS APPOINTED OVER PUNISHMENT AND REWARD, DRAWN from the right and left, included within each other by two colors, the one white, and the other red. Both turn the wheel up. When it turns to the right, the white ascends and when it turns to the left, the red descends. The wheel keeps turning and never rests.

509. תְּרֵין צִפֳּרִין סָלְקִין, דְּקָא מְצַפְצְפָן, חַד לִסְטַר דָּרוֹם, וְחַד לִסְטַר צָפוֹן. פָּרְחִין בַּאֲוִירָא צִפְצוּפָא, וְקָל נְעִימוּ דְגַלְגַּלָּא מִתְחַבְּרָן כַּחֲדָא, כְּדֵין מִזְמוֹר שִׁיר לְיוֹם הַשַּׁבָּת. וְכָל בִּרְכָאן נָגְדִין בִּלְחִישׁוּ בְּדָא נְעִימוּ, מִגּוֹ רְחִימוּ דְּקוֹל שׁוֹפָרָא.

509. Two birds, CHOCHMAH AND BINAH OF THE NUKVA, go up and chirp, the one, CHOCHMAH, to the south and the other, BINAH, to the north, and soar in the air. TO WIT, THEY SHINE ONLY UPON THE SIX EXTREMITIES OF CHOCHMAH AND BINAH CALLED AIR. The chirping OF THE BIRDS, WHICH IS THE SECRET OF THE NUKVA, and the pleasant sound of the wheel, THE SECRET OF ZEIR ANPIN, join together and then: "A Psalm, a poem for the Shabbat day" (Tehilim 92:1). TO WIT, WHEN THEY JOIN THE LIGHTS ILLUMINATE WHICH ARE DESCRIBED IN THE POEM FOR THE SHABBAT DAY. All the blessings, WHICH ARE THE SECRET OF CHOCHMAH, are drawn by a whisper, clothed by the pleasantness OF THE WHEEL, WHICH IS THE RIGHT COLUMN OF ZEIR ANPIN, WHICH IS CHASSADIM through the love of the sound of the Shofar, WHICH IS THE CENTRAL COLUMN OF ZEIR ANPIN.

510. לְקַבְּלָא אִינוּן בִּרְכָאן, נָחֲתִין מִלְעֵילָא לְתַתָּא, וְאִתְגְּנִיזוּ כַּחֲדָא בְּגוֹ עוֹמְקָא דְבֵירָא, נְבִיעוּ דְבֵירָא דְּלָא פָסְקָא בִּלְחִישׁוּ, עַד דְּאִתְמַלְּיָא הַהוּא גַּלְגַּלָּא סַחֲרָא.

510. In order to receive the blessings, SO THAT CHOCHMAH WILL BE CLOTHED BY CHASSADIM, the blessings go down from above, WHICH ARE THE SECRET OF CHOCHMAH, to be treasured deep inside the well, THE NUKVA; TO WIT, IT CANNOT SHINE WITHOUT CHASSADIM. The spring from the well does not cease to whisper, WHICH MEANS IT DOES NOT ILLUMINATE, until the turning wheel is filled, WHICH IS THE CENTRAL COLUMN, THE PRINCIPAL THAT TURNS THE WHEELS.

511. אִינּוּן תְּרֵין מַגְרוֹפִין סָחֲרָן, חַד דִּימִינָא, קָרֵא בְחֵיל וַאֲמַר, זְהִירוּ דִּזְהֲרִין דְּסַלְקָא וְנָחֲתָא, תְּרֵי אַלְפֵי עָלְמִי"ן אִזְדָּהֲרוּ. עָלְמָא דְאֶמְצָעִיתָא בְּגַוַוְיְיהוּ, אִזְדָּהַר בְּזוֹהֲרָא דְמָארָךְ. כָּל אִינּוּן מָארֵי דְעַיְינִין, אִסְתַּכָּלוּ וּפְקָחוּ עֵינַיְכוֹן, וְתִזְכּוּן לְהַאי נְהִירוּ, לְהַאי עֲדוּנָא, אִלֵּין אִינּוּן בִּרְכָאן דְּנַגְדֵי מִלְעֵילָּא, מַאן דְזָכֵי, גַּלְגַּלָּא סַלְקָא אַסְחַר לִימִינָא, וְאַנְגִּיד וְאַמְשִׁיךְ לְהַהוּא דְזָכֵי, וְאִתְעַדַּן מֵאלֵּין בִּרְכָאן עִלָּאִין דִּזְהֲרָן, זַכָּאִין אִינּוּן דְּזָכָאן בְּהוּ.

511. Of the two turning shovels, the one to the right, WHICH ROLLS THE THREE COLUMNS UNDER THE POWER OF THE RIGHT, cries loudly, saying, the illumination of the lights which ascend and descend, SINCE BEING RIGHT, ITS ILLUMINATION GOES FROM ABOVE DOWNWARD, the two thousand worlds, CHOCHMAH AND BINAH CALLED THOUSANDS AND DRAWN FROM THE TWO COLUMNS RIGHT AND LEFT, shine! The middle world inside them, DA'AT, DRAWN FROM THE CENTRAL COLUMN, shine by the light of your Master! All those who have eyes; TO WIT, THOSE WORTHY OF ATTAINING CHOCHMAH CALLED EYES, look and open your eyes, to attain this light, this delight. These are the blessings which are drawn from above. When someone has merit, the wheel goes up and turns to the right. TO WIT, IT BRINGS THE ILLUMINATIONS OF THE THREE COLUMNS UNDER THE POWER OF THE RIGHT, and brings and draws them upon he who achieved it, and he takes pleasure in the supernal luminous blessings. Happy are those who attained them.

512. וְכַד לָא זָכֵי, גַּלְגַּלָּא אַסְחַר, וְהַהוּא מַגְרוֹפָא דִּלְסְטַר שְׂמָאלָא, אַסְחַר וְנָחַת לְתַתָּא, וְאַמְשִׁיךְ דִּינָא עַל הַאי דְלָא זָכֵי, וְקָלָא נָפְקַת, וַוי לְאִינּוּן חַיָּיבִין דְּלָא זָכוּ. מֵהַהוּא סִטְרָא, נָפִיק אֶשָׁא דְּשַׁלְהוֹבָא דְּדָלֵיק, דְּשַׁרֵי עַל רֵישֵׁיהוֹן דְּחַיָּיבַיָּא. זַכָּאִין אִינּוּן, כָּל אִינּוּן דְּאֲזָלוּ בְּאוֹרַח קְשׁוֹט בְּהַאי עַלְמָא, לְמִזְכֵּי לְהַהוּא נְהוֹרָא עִלָּאָה, בִּרְכָאן דְּצַחְצְחָן, כְּמָה דְאַתְּ אָמֵר וְהִשְׂבִּיעַ בְּצַחְצָחוֹת נַפְשֶׁךָ.

עד כאן תוספתא

512. For he who does not achieve it, the wheel turns and the shovel on the left side turns it. TO WIT, IT BRINGS ABOUT THE ILLUMINATION OF THE COLUMNS UNDER THE POWER OF THE LEFT, and brings LIGHT down BY DRAWING THE ILLUMINATION OF THE LEFT FROM ABOVE DOWNWARD, thus drawing Judgment upon he who did not attain it. A voice resounds, saying: Woe to the wicked who have no merit. From the LEFT side, a flame comes out to burn and abides on the head of the wicked. Happy are those who walk the true path in this world and attain the supernal light, the blessings of brightness, as it says, "And satisfy your soul in drought (also: 'brightness')" (Yeshayah 58:11).

End of Tosefta

53. "Gather yourselves together, that I may tell you"

A Synopsis

Rabbi Aba first discourses on the verse, "He turned to the prayer of the lonely" He explains that God accepts all public prayers, whether they are from righteous or sinful people. However, when a solitary man offers a prayer to God, he becomes subject to scrutiny. God examines that man's sins and virtues. Therefore, we're told, a man should say his prayers in public. Another explanation for this verse interprets it as a reference to Jacob, who is included within the many. Therefore, his prayer is like a public prayer.

The discourse then reveals the meaning and significance of the word "called" (Heb. *vayikra*) in a number of contexts. We learn that when Jacob called for his sons, they appeared, accompanied by the spirit of the Shechinah. The title verse, we're further told, indicates that Jacob commanded his sons to bond themselves to their supernal roots in Malchut, so that he could draw the secret of wisdom upon them. Jacob then quoted the title verse and told them of the exile that would occur when the Yisrael entered the Holy Land.

The Relevance of this Passage

The power of unity and harmony between people underscores this passage of Zohar. When people congregate in love and unity to make connections with the Light of The Creator, the most sinful soul among the group will see his prayer ascend to the same lofty heights as the most righteous soul among the group, such is the power of unity. By connecting us to Jacob, who embodies the collective souls of humankind, this passage ensures that all our prayers will be considered to have been made in public and thus, will reach the same majestic heights as the prayers of Jacob.

513. וַיִּקְרָא יַעֲקֹב אֶל בָּנָיו וַיֹּאמֶר הֵאָסְפוּ וגו', רְבִּי אַבָּא פָּתַח וְאָמַר, פְּנָה אֶל תְּפִלַּת הָעַרְעָר וְלֹא בָזָה אֶת תְּפִלָּתָם, הַאי קְרָא אוֹקְמוּהָ, וְאַקְשׁוּ בֵּיהּ חַבְרַיָּיא, פְּנָה, הַקְשִׁיב מִבָּעֵי לֵיהּ, אוֹ שָׁמַע, מַאי פְּנָה.

513. "And Jacob called to his sons, and said: 'Gather yourselves together...'" (Beresheet 49:1). Rabbi Aba opened the discussion saying: "He turned to the prayer of the lonely and did not despise their prayer" (Tehilim 102:18). This verse has already been explained, yet the friends found it difficult as to why it says "turned" when it should have been 'listened' or 'hearkened.'

514. אֶלָּא כָּל צְלוֹתִין דְּעָלְמָא צְלוֹתִין. וּצְלוֹתָא דְּיָחִיד, לָא עָאל קַמֵּי מַלְכָּא קַדִּישָׁא, אֶלָּא בְּחֵילָא תַּקִּיפָא. דְּעַד לָא עָאלַת הַהִיא צְלוֹתָא לְאִתְעַטְּרָא בְּדוּכְתָּהּ, אַשְׁגַּח בָּהּ קוּדְשָׁא בְּרִיךְ הוּא, וְאִסְתְּכֵי בָּהּ, וְאִסְתְּכֵי בְּחוֹבוֹי וּבִזְכוּתֵיהּ דְּהַהוּא ב״נ, מַה דְּלָא עָבֵיד כֵּן בִּצְלוֹתָא דְּסַגִּיאִין, דִּצְלוֹתָא דְּסַגִּיאִין כַּמָּה אִינּוּן צְלוֹתִין דְּלָא מִן זַכָּאִין אִינּוּן, וְעָאלִין כֻּלְּהוּ קַמֵּי קוּדְשָׁא בְּרִיךְ הוּא, וְלָא אַשְׁגַּח בְּחוֹבַיְיהוּ.

514. HE ANSWERS: All the prayers in the world, THAT IS, THE PUBLIC PRAYERS, are considered prayers, but the prayer of a solitary man does not enter before the Holy King, save through great effort. For before the prayer enters to be adorned in its place, the Holy One, blessed be He, examines it and searches that man's sins and virtues. He does not do this to the prayers of the many, and though some of the prayers come not of the righteous, yet they all come before the Holy One, blessed be He, and He does not regard their sins.

515. בְּג״כ, פָּנָה אֶל תְּפִלַּת הָעַרְעָר, מְהַפֵּךְ וְאִסְתְּכֵי בָּהּ, וְאִסְתְּכֵי בָּהּ בַּמֶּה רְעוּתָא אִתְעֲבֵיד, וּמַאן הַהוּא ב״נ דְּצַלֵּי צְלוֹתָא דָא, וּמַאן אִינּוּן עוֹבָדוֹי. בְּג״כ, לִיבָּעֵי לֵיהּ לְב״נ, דִּלְצַלֵּי צְלוֹתָא בְּצִבּוּרָא. מַאי טַעְמָא, בְּגִין דְּלָא בָזָה אֶת תְּפִלָּתָם, אע״ג דְּלָאו כֻּלְּהוּ בְּכַוָּונָה וּרְעוּתָא דְּלִבָּא.

515. Therefore, "He turned to the prayer of the lonely." It means that He turned the prayer and examined every side to find out with what mind it was offered, who is the man who prayed and what his deeds were like. A man therefore should say his prayers in public. Why? Since He "did not despise their prayer," though not all are offered with devotion and a willing heart.

516. ד״א פָּנָה אֶל תְּפִלַּת הָעַרְעָר, דָּא יְחִידָאֵי דְּאִתְכְּלִיל בְּסַגִּיאִין. וּמַאן הוּא יְחִידָאֵי דְּאִתְכְּלֵיל בְּסַגִּיאִין, הֲוֵי אֵימָא דָּא יַעֲקֹב, דְּאִיהוּ כָּלִיל בִּתְרֵין סִטְרִין, וְקָרָא לִבְנוֹי, וְצַלֵּי צְלוֹתֵיהּ עֲלַיְיהוּ. מַאן צְלוֹתָא דְּיִתְקַבְּלוּן בִּשְׁלִימוּ לְעֵילָא, צְלוֹתָא דְּלָא יִשְׁתְּצוּן בְּגָלוּתָא.

516. Another explanation for: "He turned to the prayer of the lonely": IT SIMPLY MEANS THAT HE ACCEPTS HIS PRAYER, ONLY THAT this is the

individual who becomes part of the many, AND THEREFORE HIS PRAYER IS AS A PUBLIC PRAYER. Who is the individual, who is included within the many? He is said to be Jacob, who is included within the two sides, RIGHT AND LEFT, ABRAHAM AND ISAAC. He called to his sons and prayed for them. What is the prayer which is wholly accepted above? That Yisrael shall not perish in exile.

517. בְּהַאי שַׁעְתָּא דְּיַעֲקֹב קָרָא לוֹן, אִסְתַּלַּק מִנֵּיהּ שְׁכִינְתָּא, וְהָא אוּקְמוּהָ. וְתָא חֲזֵי, בְּשַׁעְתָּא דְּיַעֲקֹב הֲוָה קָאֲרֵי לִבְנוֹי, אִזְדַּמְּנוּ אַבְרָהָם וְיִצְחָק תַּמָּן, וּשְׁכִינְתָּא עַל גַּבַּיְיהוּ. וּשְׁכִינְתָּא הֲוָה בֵּיהּ חָדֵי בְּיַעֲקֹב, לְאִתְחַבְּרָא בַּאֲבָהָן, לְאִתְקַשְּׁרָא עִם נַפְשַׁיְיהוּ כְּחַד, לְמֶהֱוֵי רְתִיכָא.

517. When Jacob sent for them, the Shechinah departed from him, as was already explained. Come and see: When Jacob called for his sons, Abraham and Isaac appeared there with the Shechinah upon them. The Shechinah rejoiced in Jacob, that he would be united with the fathers, to become a Chariot together with their souls.

518. בְּשַׁעְתָּא דְּפָתַח יַעֲקֹב, וַאֲמַר הֵאָסְפוּ וְאַגִּידָה לָכֶם אֵת אֲשֶׁר יִקְרָא אֶתְכֶם בְּאַחֲרִית הַיָּמִים, בְּאַחֲרִית: דָּא שְׁכִינְתָּא, כִּבְיָכוֹל יְהַב עֲצִיבוּ בֵּיהּ, וְאִסְתַּלַּק. וּלְבָתַר אַהֲדְרוּ לָהּ בְּנוֹי, בְּיִחוּדֵי דְּמִלַּיְיהוּ, וּפָתְחוּ וְאָמְרוּ שְׁמַע יִשְׂרָאֵל וְגו'. בְּהַהִיא שַׁעְתָּא קָאֵים לָהּ יַעֲקֹב, וַאֲמַר בשכמל"ו, וְאִתְיַישְּׁבַת שְׁכִינְתָּא בְּדוּכְתָּהּ.

518. When Jacob opened the discussion saying: "Gather yourselves together, that I may tell you that which shall befall you in the latter end of days," the latter end being the Shechinah, THE LAST OF THE SFIROT, BY MENTIONING "THAT WHICH SHALL BEFALL YOU IN THE LATTER END OF DAYS," HE MENTIONED THE EXILE. The Shechinah was saddened and departed. Later, his sons brought Her back by the unison created by the words they uttered, "Hear, O Yisrael..." (Devarim 6:4). Then Jacob stayed Her and said: 'Blessed be the name of the glory of His sovereignty for evermore.' The Shechinah then settled in Her place.

519. וַיִּקְרָא יַעֲקֹב, מַאי קְרִיאָה הָכָא. אֶלָּא קְרִיאָה, לְקַיְּימָא דּוּכְתַּיְיהוּ,

לְקַיְּימָא לוֹן לְעֵילָא וְתַתָּא. תָּא חֲזֵי, בְּכָל אֲתַר קְרִיאָה בְּהַאי גַוְונָא,
דִּכְתִיב וַיִּקְרָא מֹשֶׁה לְהוֹשֵׁעַ בֶּן נוּן יְהוֹשֻׁעַ, לְקַיְּימָא דוּכְתֵּיה, בַּאֲתַר
דְּאִצְטְרִיךְ, וּלְקַשְׁרָא לֵיה. וְכֵן וַיִּקְרָא שְׁמוֹ יַעֲקֹב. וּכְתִיב וַיִּקְרָא לוֹ אֵל
אֱלֹהֵי יִשְׂרָאֵל, קוּדְשָׁא בְּרִיךְ הוּא קַיָּים לֵיה לַאֲתַר דָּא בִּשְׁמָא דָא.
קְרִיאָה לְקִיּוּמָא קָא אַתְיָא.

519. "And Jacob called": HE ASKS: What call is this? HE REPLIES: This
call establishes their place, MALCHUT CALLED PLACE, FOR WHEN HE
CALLED THEM HE CONNECTED THEM TO THEIR ROOT; to establish them
above IN THEIR ROOT, and below IN THIS WORLD. Come and see, wherever
"calling" is mentioned, it is always in the same way, as it is written: "And
Moses called Hosea son of Nun, Joshua" (Bemidbar 13:6), IN ORDER to
secure his place, WHICH IS MALCHUT, where it should be and connect him
to it. It also says, "And he called his name Jacob" (Beresheet 25:26), and
"and called it El, the Elohim of Yisrael" (Beresheet 33:20), thus establishing
this place through the name he gave it, as naming brings securing AND
STRENGTHENING.

520. אִי תֵימָא וַיִּקְרְאוּ אֶל אֱלֹקִים, קָרָאתִי מִצָּרָה לִי אֶל ה', הָכֵי הוּא
וַדַּאי, לְקַשְׁרָא וּלְקַיְּימָא קִיּוּמָא לְעֵילָא, וּמַאן אִיהוּ, סִדּוּרָא דְשִׁבְחָא
דְמָארֵיה, וְכָל אִינוּן מִלִּין דִּבְעָאן קַמֵּי מָארֵיה, קִיּוּמָא יָהֵיב לֵיה
לְמָארֵיה, דְּאַחֲזֵי דְּבֵיה תַּלְיָא כֹּלָּא, וְלָא בַּאֲתַר אָחֳרָא, הָא כֹּלָּא קַיָּים
קִיּוּמָא. כה"ג וַיִּקְרָא יַעֲקֹב אֶל בָּנָיו, קַיָּים לוֹן בְּקִיּוּמָא שְׁלִים. כְּגַוְונָא
דָא וַיִּקְרָא אֶל מֹשֶׁה, אִתְקַיַּים בְּקִיּוּמֵיה.

520. You may ask about the verse: "And called mightily to Elohim" (Yonah
3:7), and "I called from my sorrow unto Hashem" (Yonah 2:3), WHAT
ESTABLISHING IS HERE? HE ANSWERS: Assuredly THE CALLING HERE
connects and establishes it above. How so? The arranging of the praises of
his Master and all the words of prayer give strength and might to his Master,
thus showing that all depends upon Him and not on any other place. Hence,
THE CALLING HERE brings endurance. In the same manner "Jacob called to
his sons," thus wholly establishing them, and also "Hashem called (Heb.
vayikra) to Moses" (Vayikra 1:1), THUS establishing him in his place.

521. אָמַר רִבִּי יִצְחָק, א׳ דְּוַיִּקְרָא, אַמַּאי הִיא זְעֵירָא. א״ל, אִתְקַיַּים מֹשֶׁה בִּשְׁלִימוּ, וְלָא בְּכֹלָּא, דְּהָא אִסְתַּלַּק מֵאִתְּתֵיהּ. בְּסִפְרֵי קַדְמָאֵי אַמְרֵי לְשַׁבְחָא, וַאֲנַן הָכֵי תְּנִינָן, מַאי דְּאִסְתַּלַּק לְעֵילָּא, יִתְקַשַּׁר לְעֵילָּא וּלְתַתָּא, וּכְדֵין, אִיהוּ שָׁלִים. תּוּ, אָל״ף זְעֵירָא מֵאֲתַר זְעֵירָא הֲוָה, זְעֵירָא דְּאִיהוּ רַב בְּאִתְחַבְּרוּתֵיהּ לְעֵילָּא.

521. Rabbi Yitzchak said: Why is the *Aleph* in the word 'vayikra' small, IF IT IS SUPPOSED TO INDICATE EXISTENCE AND STRENGTH? He said to him: Moses was wholly established THROUGH THE CALLING, but not in every respect, since he abstained BECAUSE OF THIS from his wife. THEREFORE THE *ALEPH* IS SMALL. In ancient books, it is said that THE SEPARATION FROM HIS WIFE is a praise to him AND DOES NOT DIMINISH HIM. But we have learned that he separated FROM HIS WIFE AND CLOVE above, when he had to connect both above and below, TO WIT, TO HIS WIFE TOO. Then he would be perfect. THE SEPARATION FROM HIS WIFE IS THEN CONSIDERED AS DIMINISHING, TO WHICH THE SMALL *ALEPH* ALLUDES. Also, the small *Aleph* indicates the small place it came from; TO WIT, THE CALLING IS FROM THE SMALL PLACE, MALCHUT, which is great when united above WITH ZEIR ANPIN, THE SECRET OF MOSES. THEREFORE "HASHEM CALLED TO MOSES" TO MAKE IT GREAT.

522. וַיֹּאמֶר, מַאי וַיֹּאמֶר. הָא אוֹקְמוּהָ, וְאָמַרְתָּ בִּלְבָבְךָ, אֲמִירָה בַּחֲשַׁאי. הֵאָסְפוּ, אִסְפוּ מִבָּעֵי לֵיהּ, כְּד״א אִסְפוּ לִי חֲסִידָי. אֶלָּא קִים לָן הֵאָסְפוּ מֵאֲתַר דִּלְעֵילָּא הוּא. הֵאָסְפוּ בְּקִשּׁוּרָא שְׁלִים בְּיִחוּדָא חַד. וְאַגִּידָה לָכֶם, מַאי וְאַגִּידָה, רָזָא דְחָכְמְתָא אִיהוּ.

522. "And said": HE ASKS: THE WORDS "AND SAID: GATHER YOURSELVES" MEAN THAT THEY WERE NOT WITH HIM THEN. What does "and said" means? TO WHOM DID HE THEN ADDRESS THE WORDS? HE ANSWERS: as in the verse "If you shall say in your heart" (Devarim 7:17), he whispered them; TO WIT, HE ADDRESSED UPWARDS THE WORDS "GATHER YOURSELVES," AND NOT TO HIS SONS. "GATHER YOURSELVES": HE ASKS: IF HE TOLD THE MESSENGERS TO GATHER HIS SONS, he should have said 'Gather' instead of "Gather yourselves," as in "Gather my pious ones together" (Tehilim 50:5). HE ANSWERS: It is clear to us that "Gather" is from a high place; TO WIT, HE TOLD THEM TO GATHER

THEMSELVES TO THEIR SUPERNAL ROOTS WITHIN MALCHUT, SO THAT THEY WOULD BE GATHERED into a complete bond, and union. "That I may tell you": HE ASKS: What does it mean? HE REPLIES: It is the secret of Wisdom; TO WIT, "I MAY TELL YOU" MEANS THAT HE WILL DRAW UPON THEM THE SECRET OF WISDOM.

523. רִבִּי יוֹסֵי שָׁאֵיל לְר"ש, א"ל, וְאַגִּידָה, אוֹ וַיַּגֵּד, אוֹ וַיַּגִּידוּ, וְכֵן כֻּלְּהוּ, דְּתָנִינָן דְּרָזָא דְחָכְמְתָא אִיהִי, אַמַּאי בְּמִלָּה דָא אִיהוּ רָזָא דְחָכְמְתָא. א"ל, בְּגִין דְּאִיהוּ מִלָּה דְּאַתְיָא בְּגִימ"ל דָּל"ת בְּלָא פֵרוּדָא, וְהַאי אִיהוּ רָזָא דְחָכְמְתָא. מִלָּה דְּאַתְיָא בִּשְׁלִימוּ בְּרָזָא דְאַתְוָון, הָכֵי הוּא, כַּד אִינוּן בְּחָכְמְתָא, אֲבָל דָּל"ת בְּלָא גִימ"ל, לָאו הוּא שְׁלִימוּ, וְכֵן גִימ"ל בְּלָא דָל"ת. דְּהָא דָא בְּדָא אִתְקַשְׁרוּ בְּלָא פֵרוּדָא, וּמַאן דְּאַפְרֵישׁ לוֹן, גָּרֵים לְגַרְמֵיהּ מוֹתָא, וְרָזָא דָא חוֹבָא דְאָדָם.

523. Rabbi Yosi asked Rabbi Shimon, "I may tell you," "he may tell" or "they may tell" are all DERIVED FROM "TELL" (HEB. *HAGADAH*), which we learned to be of the secret of Wisdom. Why does this word contain the secret of Wisdom? He said to him: It is because the word is spelled with *Gimel* and *Dalet* without division between them, WHICH HINTS AT THE WHOLE UNISON, FOR *GIMEL* IS THE SECRET OF YESOD AND *DALET* THE SECRET OF MALCHUT. It is the secret of wisdom that a word is perfected by the secret of the letters *GIMEL* AND *DALET*, because they are in THE SECRET OF Wisdom. But *Dalet* without *Gimel* brings no perfection, and also *Gimel* without *Dalet*, since they are connected to each other with nothing dividing them, and whoever separates them, brings death unto himself. This is the secret of Adam's sin, THE DRAWING OF LIGHT OF MALCHUT FROM ABOVE DOWNWARD AND SEPARATING HER FROM YESOD OF ZEIR ANPIN, AND *DALET* FROM *GIMEL*.

524. בְּג"כ, הוּא מִלָּה דְּרָזָא דְחָכְמְתָא, וְאע"ג דְּאִית יו"ד לְזִמְנִין בֵּין גִימ"ל לְדָל"ת, לָאו הֲוֵי פֵרוּדָא, וְכֹלָּא קְשׁוּרָא חָדָא, וְע"ד מִלָּה דָא הָכֵי הוּא וַדַּאי, וְאַגִּידָה לָכֶם, רָזָא דְחָכְמְתָא, בָּעָא לְגַלָּאָה סוֹפָא דְכָל עוֹבָדֵיהוֹן דְּיִשְׂרָאֵל.

524. Therefore, hagadah (Eng. 'telling') is a word which pertains to the secret of Wisdom, and though there may be *Yud* between *Gimel* and *Dalet*,

LIKE IN "*VE'AGIDAH* (ENG. 'THAT I MAY TELL')," there is no separation and all is connected into one knot, SINCE *YUD* ALSO ALLUDES TO YESOD. Therefore, this is surely the meaning of this word. HERE TOO: "That I may tell you" is the secret of Wisdom. He wished to reveal the outcome of Yisrael's deeds, NAMELY THE SECRET OF THE END.

525. וְאִי תֵּימָא, דְּלָא גְּלֵי מַאי דְּבָעָא לְגַלָּאָה, א״ה אַמַּאי כְּתִיב בְּאוֹרַיְיתָא מִלָּה דְּיַעֲקֹב שְׁלֵימָא, וְאִתְפְּגֵים לְבָתַר, וְלָא אִשְׁתְּלִים מִלָּה. אֶלָּא וַדַּאי אִשְׁתְּלִים, כָּל מַה דְּאִצְטְרִיךְ לְגַלָּאָה גַּלֵי וְסָתִים, אָמַר מִלָּה וְגַלֵּי לְבַר וְסָתִים לְגוֹ. וּמִלָּה דְּאוֹרַיְיתָא לָא אִתְפְּגֵים לְעָלְמִין.

525. You may say that he did not reveal what he wanted to reveal. Why then are the words of perfect Jacob written in the Torah, SEEING THAT they were belied later and were not perfected? Assuredly they were perfected, he revealed whatever was needful for him to reveal, and he concealed, revealing outwardly and withholding internally. A word of the Torah can never be defective.

526. וְכֹלָּא הוּא סָתִים בֵּיהּ בְּאוֹרַיְיתָא, בְּגִין דְּאוֹרַיְיתָא הוּא שְׁלִימוּ דְּכֹלָּא, שְׁלִימוּ דִּלְעֵילָּא וְתַתָּא, וְלָא אִית מִלָּה אוֹ אָת בְּאוֹרַיְיתָא פְּגִימוּ, וְיַעֲקֹב כָּל מַה דְּאִצְטְרִיךְ לֵיהּ לְמֵימַר אָמַר, אֲבָל גַּלֵּי וְסָתִים, וְלָא פָּגֵים מִכָּל מַה דְּבָעָא אֲפִילוּ אוֹת אֶחָת.

526. Everything in the Torah is undisclosed, since the Torah is the perfection of all, perfection above and below, not a word or a letter in the Torah is defective. Jacob said whatever he had to say, but he revealed and concealed. From what he wanted to reveal, he did not render defective even one letter.

527. רִבִּי יְהוּדָה וְרִ' יוֹסֵי, הֲווֹ יַתְבֵי יוֹמָא חַד אֲפִתְחָא דְּלוֹד. אָמַר רִבִּי יוֹסֵי לְרִבִּי יְהוּדָה, הָא דְּחָמֵינָן דְּיַעֲקֹב בָּרֵיךְ לִבְנוֹי, חָמֵינָן מִמַּה דִּכְתִיב, וַיְבָרֶךְ אוֹתָם, אֲבָל אָן בִּרְכָתָא דִּלְהוֹן. א״ל כֹּלָּא בִּרְכָאן אִינוּן דְּבָרֵיךְ לְהוֹ, כְּגוֹן, יְהוּדָה אַתָּה יוֹדוּךְ אַחֶיךָ. דָּן יָדִין עַמּוֹ. מֵאָשֵׁר שְׁמֵנָה לַחְמוֹ. וְכֵן כֻּלְּהוּ.

527. Rabbi Yehuda and Rabbi Yosi sat one day at the gate of Lod. Rabbi Yosi said to Rabbi Yehuda, We know that Jacob blessed his sons from the verse: "And blessed them" (Beresheet 49:28), but what are their blessings? He said to him: these are the blessings he blessed them, such as "Yehuda you are he whom your brethren shall praise," "Dan shall judge his people" and "Out of Asher his bread shall be fat" (Beresheet 49).

528. אֲבָל מַה דִּבְעֵי לְגַלֵּי לוֹן לָא גַּלֵּי, דִּבְעָא לְגַלָּאָה לְהוּ אֶת הַקֵּץ. וְהָא אוּקְמוּהָ, דְּאִית קֵץ לִימִינָא, וְאִית קֵץ לִשְׂמָאלָא, וּבְעָא לְגַלָּאָה לוֹן אֶת הַקֵּץ, בְּגִין לְאִסְתַּמְּרָא וּלְאִתְדַּכָּאָה מֵעָרְלָה. וּמַאן דְּגַלֵּי לוֹן אִתְיְדַע וְאִתְגַּלֵּי, עַד דְּעָאלוּ לְאַרְעָא קַדִּישָׁא, אֲבָל מִלִּין אָחֳרָנִין לָאו אִינוּן בְּאִתְגַּלְיָיא, וּסְתִימִין אִינוּן בְּאוֹרַיְיתָא, בְּהַאי פָּרְשָׁתָא דְּיַעֲקֹב, וּבְאִינוּן בִּרְכָאן.

528. But he did not reveal that which he wanted to reveal, for he wanted to reveal the end to them. It has been explained that there is an end of the right and an end of the left. He wanted to tell them of the end OF THE RIGHT, so that they will be kept and be purified from the foreskin OF THE END OF THE LEFT. What he revealed to them pertained to when they came to the Holy Land. But he did not disclose other things openly; they are hidden within the Torah in this portion of Jacob and in these blessings.

54. "Reuben, you are my firstborn"

A Synopsis

The discussion first reveals that the title verse indicates that Jacob placed Reuben's blessings in the hands of God to hold until Reuben was worthy of them.

Rabbi Elazar then comments on the verse, "Prophesy to the wind," revealing that it alludes to the lower and upper awakening of wisdom.

Rabbi Shimon then explains why God brings souls into the world knowing that they will one day die. We also learn that when the soul ascends to be attached to Malchut, it becomes perfected and Malchut and Zeir Anpin are united.

Finally, we are told that when Jacob departed from the world, the Shechinah was in front of his bed. Seeing this, he gathered his sons around her and he blessed his sons.

The Relevance of this Passage

Sometimes a person performs a positive action, but their previous sins create a black hole of negativity that consumes their rewards. However, the Light that we arouse in life can be entrusted into the hands of The Creator until such time that we cleanse ourselves of our negativity. Then we can receive our recompense. It's interesting to note that the Hebrew word for sin also means "to give over." This passage ensures that our Light is *given over* to The Creator for safekeeping, as opposed to the dark forces that seek to nourish from it. The power of Jacob's blessings, plus the energy of the Shechinah and the uniting of our Lower World with the Upper, takes place when our eyes allow the Light of these mystical verses to shine upon our souls. Other benefits associated with this Light include protection and the removal of darkness from the world and our personal lives.

529. פְּתַח וַאֲמַר, רְאוּבֵן בְּכֹרִי אַתָּה כֹּחִי וְרֵאשִׁית אוֹנִי, מַאי קָא חָמָא יַעֲקֹב לְמִפְתַּח בִּרְאוּבֵן, לִיפְתַּח בִּיהוּדָה, דְּאִיהוּ קַדְמָאָה לְכָל מַשְׁרְיָין, וְאִיהוּ מַלְכָּא, וְחָמֵינָן דְּלָא בָּרְכֵיהּ וְסָלֵיק בִּרְכָאן מִנֵּיהּ, עַד דְּאָתָא מֹשֶׁה וְצַלֵּי צְלוֹתָא עֲלֵיהּ, כְּמָה דְאַתְּ אָמֵר יְחִי רְאוּבֵן וְאַל יָמֹת.

529. He opened the discussion saying: "Reuben, you are my firstborn, my might and the beginning of my strength" (Beresheet 49:3). HE ASKS: Why did Jacob begin by blessing Reuben? Why not start with Judah, who, WHEN THE STANDARDS TRAVEL, is a king and is the first to journey among the

camps, AS IT SAYS, "THESE SHALL FIRST SET FORTH" (BEMIDBAR 2:9). Moreover, we saw that he did not bless REUBEN and the blessings were removed from him until Moses prayed for him, as it says, "Let Reuben live, and not die" (Devarim 33:6). ACCORDING TO THIS, IT WOULD HAVE BEEN BETTER TO BEGIN WITH JUDAH AND START WITH A BLESSING.

530. אֲבָל וַדַּאי בָּרְכֵיהּ, וְסָלְקָא הַהוּא בִּרְכְתָא לְאַתְרֵיהּ. לְבַר נָשׁ דַּהֲוָה לֵיהּ בַּר, כַּד מָטָא זִמְנֵיהּ לְאִסְתַּלְּקָא מֵעַלְמָא, אָתָא מַלְכָּא עֲלֵיהּ, אֲמַר, הָא כָּל מָמוֹנָא דִּילִי, לֶיהֱוֵי בִּידָא דְּמַלְכָּא נָטִיר לִבְרָאי. כַּד חָמֵי מַלְכָּא דִּבְרִי אִתְחֲזֵי, יָהֵיב לֵיהּ. כָּךְ יַעֲקֹב אֲמַר, רְאוּבֵן בְּכֹרִי אַתָּה, רְחִימָא דִּמֵעַיי אֲנַתְּ, אֲבָל בִּרְכָאן דִּילָךְ יִסְתַּלְּקוּן בִּידָא דְּמַלְכָּא קַדִּישָׁא, עַד דְּיֶחֱמֵי בָךְ, בְּגִין דַּאֲזַלְתְּ לְקֳבֵל אַפָּךְ וְגוֹ', כְּתַרְגּוּמוֹ.

530. HE ANSWERS: Assuredly he blessed REUBEN, and the blessing arose to its place. This is like the story of a man who had a son. When the time came for him to pass away from the world, the king came to him. He said: Let all my money be in the hands of the king, who will keep it for my son. When the king sees that my son is worthy of it, he will give it to him. Jacob also said: "Reuben, you are my firstborn," you are beloved of my heart and bowels, yet your blessings shall be in the hands of the Holy King until He shall see you ARE WORTHY OF THEM. THIS IS BECAUSE you followed your anger LIKE WATER, according to the Aramaic translation TO "UNSTABLE AS WATER."

531. רְאוּבֵן בְּכוֹרִי אַתָּה וְגוֹ'. רִבִּי אֶלְעָזָר פָּתַח וַאֲמַר, וַיֹּאמֶר אֵלַי הִנָּבֵא אֶל הָרוּחַ וְגוֹ'. כַּמָּה אֲטִימִין אִינוּן בְּנֵי נָשָׁא, דְּלָא יָדְעִין וְלָא מַשְׁגִּיחִין בִּיקָרָא דְּמַלְכָּא, דְּהָא אוֹרַיְיתָא אַכְרֵיז עֲלַיְיהוּ בְּכָל יוֹמָא, וְלֵית מַאן דְּצַיֵּית אוּדְנֵיהּ לְקַבְּלֵיהּ. הַאי קְרָא קַשְׁיָא, כֵּיוָן דִּכְתִיב הִנָּבֵא אֶל הָרוּחַ, אַמַּאי זִמְנָא אָחֳרָא הִנָּבֵא בֶן אָדָם וְאָמַרְתָּ אֶל הָרוּחַ.

531. "Reuben, you are my firstborn": Rabbi Elazar opened the discussion saying: "Then he said to me, 'Prophesy to the wind (also: 'breath')...'" (Yechezkel 37:9). How obtuse are people, who neither know nor care for the glory of the King. Though the Torah announces it to them daily, no one lends an ear. This verse is difficult to understand. After saying "Prophesy to the wind," why add: "Prophesy, son of man, and say to the wind."

532. אֶלָּא מִכָּאן אוֹלִיפְנָא רָזָא דְחָכְמְתָא, תְּרֵין קַיְימִין הָכָא, חַד לְאִתְעָרָא מִתַּתָּא לְעֵילָא, דְּאִי לָא מִתְעָרִין לְתַתָּא, לָא מִתְעָרִין לְעֵילָא, וּבְאִתְעָרוּתָא דִלְתַתָּא אִתְעַר לְעֵילָא. הִנָּבֵא אֶל הָרוּחַ מִתַּתָּא לְעֵילָא. הִנָּבֵא בֶן אָדָם וְאָמַרְתָּ אֶל הָרוּחַ, מֵעֵילָא לְתַתָּא.

532. From this, we learned the secret of Wisdom. There are two commands here, the first is to arouse from below upward, for if they are not wakened FIRST from below, there is no awakening above. Through the lower awakening, there is an upper awakening. THE SECOND COMMAND IS TO AROUSE FROM ABOVE DOWNWARD. "Prophesy to the wind" is from below upward, and "prophecy, son of man, and say to the wind" is from above downward.

533. דְּהָא אֲפִילוּ לְעֵילָא, בְּאִתְעָרוּתָא דִלְתַתָּא, נָקִיט הַהוּא עִלָּאָה מֵעִלָּאָה מִנֵּיהּ. כְּגוֹן הַאי קְרָא, כֹּה אָמַר ה' מֵאַרְבַּע רוּחוֹת בֹּאִי הָרוּחַ, מֵאַרְבַּע רוּחוֹת, דָּא דָרוֹם וּמִזְרָח וְצָפוֹן וּמַעֲרָב, וְרוּחַ אַתְיָא מִמַּעֲרָב, בְּאִתְחַבְּרוּתָא דְּאִלֵּין אַחֲרָנִין, כְּד"א כָּרוּהָ נְדִיבֵי הָעָם וגו'.

533. For even above, when there is stirring below, the supernal receives from that which is even superior to it, like it is said in the next words, "Come from the four winds, O wind" (Yechezkel 37:9). The four winds are south, east, north, west – CHESED, TIFERET, GVURAH AND MALCHUT. The wind coming from the west, MALCHUT, joins the others, SOUTH, NORTH, EAST, WHICH ARE CHESED, GVURAH AND TIFERET, as it says "that the nobles of the people delved" (Bemidbar 21:18).

534. וּמֵהָכָא נָפְקִין רוּחִין וְנִשְׁמָתִין לִבְנֵי עָלְמָא לְאִצְטַיְירָא בְּהוּ. וּפָחֵי: כְּד"א וַיִּפַּח בְּאַפָּיו נִשְׁמַת חַיִּים, תָּא חֲזֵי, נָקִיט מֵהַאי גִיסָא, וְיָהִיב בְּגִיסָא אָחֳרָא, וְעַל דָּא כָּל הַנְּחָלִים הוֹלְכִים אֶל הַיָּם וְהַיָּם אֵינֶנּוּ מָלֵא. אַמַּאי אֵינֶנּוּ מָלֵא, בְּגִין דְּנָקִיט וְיָהִיב, אָעֵיל וְאַפֵּיק.

534. Spirits and souls issue forth from MALCHUT to receive the impression from the inhabitants of the world; NAMELY TO RECEIVE THEIR SHAPES, THE SHAPE OF THE FIRST THREE SFIROT. "And breathe UPON THESE

SLAIN" as in the verse: "And breathed into his nostrils the breath of life" (Beresheet 2:7). Come and see: MALCHUT receives on one side and gives on another. This is the reason why "all the rivers run into the sea; yet the sea is not full" (Kohelet 1:7). It is not full since it receives and gives, takes in and out.

535. רְבִּי אֶלְעָזָר שָׁאִיל שְׁאֶלְתָּא לְר"ש, אָמַר, הוֹאִיל וְקוּדְשָׁא בְּרִיךְ הוּא גְּלֵי קַמֵּיה, דִּבְנֵי נָשָׁא יְמוּתוּן, אַמַּאי נָחִית נִשְׁמָתִין לְעָלְמָא, וְאַמַּאי אִצְטְרִיךְ לֵיה. א"ל שְׁאֶילְתָּא דָא קַמַּיְיהוּ דְרַבָּנָן שָׁאִילוּ כַּמָה וְכַמָה, וְאוֹקְמוּהָ. אֲבָל קוּדְשָׁא בְּרִיךְ הוּא יָהֵיב נִשְׁמָתִין דְּנָחֲתִין לְהַאי עָלְמָא, לְאִשְׁתְּמוֹדְעָא יְקָרֵיה, וְנָקִיט לוֹן לְבָתַר, אִי הָכֵי אַמַּאי נָחֲתוּ.

535. Rabbi Elazar asked Rabbi Shimon a question. He said: Since it is known to the Holy One, blessed be He, that people die, why then did He bring souls down into the world? What purpose do they serve? He said to him: Many sages were asked this question by their students. They explained it THOUGH IT IS DIFFICULT. The Holy One, blessed be He, sends souls into the world to declare His glory. Yet He takes them away. Wherefore did they descend?

536. אֶלָּא, רָזָא דָא, הָכֵי הוּא. פָּתַח וַאֲמַר, שְׁתֵה מַיִם מִבּוֹרֶךָ וְנוֹזְלִים מִתּוֹךְ בְּאֵרֶךָ, הָא אוֹקִימְנָא, בּוֹר: אֲתַר דְּלָא נְבִיעַ מִגַּרְמֵיה, וְאֵימָתַי נָבְעִין הַנֵּי מַיָּא, בְּשַׁעֲתָא דְּאִשְׁתְּלֵים נִשְׁמָתָא בְּהַאי עָלְמָא, כַּד סַלְקָא לְהַהוּא אֲתַר דְּאִתְקַשַּׁר בֵּיה, כְּדֵין הוּא שְׁלֵים, מִכָּל סִטְרִין מִתַּתָּא וּמֵעֵילָא.

536. HE ANSWERS: The explanation is as follows: He opened the discussion saying: "Drink waters out of your own cistern, and flowing streams out of your own well" (Mishlei 5:15). We have explained that a cistern is a place out of which no water flows, WHILE A WELL FLOWS BY ITSELF. When does water flow BY ITSELF? When the soul is perfected in this world, and ascends to where it is attached, MALCHUT. Then it is completed on all sides, above and below.

537. וְכַד נִשְׁמָתָא סַלְקָא, כְּדֵין אִתְעַר תֵּיאוּבְתָּא דְּנוּקְבָא לְגַבֵּי דְּכוּרָא,

וּכְדֵין נָבְעִין מַיָא מִתַּתָּא לְעֵילָא, וּבוֹר, אִתְעֲבֵיד בְּאֵר, מַיִין נְבִיעָאן, וּכְדֵין אִתְחַבְּרוּתָא וְיִחוּדָא וְתֵיאוּבְתָּא וְרַעֲוָא אִשְׁתַּכַּח, דְּהָא בְּנִשְׁמָתָא דְּצַדִּיקַיָא אִשְׁתְּלֵים הַהוּא אֲתָר, וְאִתְּעַר חֲבִיבוּתָא וּרְעוּתָא לְעֵילָא, וְאִתְחַבַּר כְּחַד.

537. When the soul ascends, the desire of the female is stirred toward the male, and then the water flows IN MALCHUT from below upward, AND THAT WHICH WAS a cistern becomes a well of flowing water. Then there is a joining in union and desire, for that place, MALCHUT, is perfected by the souls of the righteous, friendship and goodwill are aroused above, AND ZEIR ANPIN AND MALCHUT are joined as one.

538. רְאוּבֵן בְּכֹרִי אַתָּה, הָכֵי הוּא וַדַּאי, טִפָּה קַדְמָאָה דְּיַעֲקֹב הֲוָה, וּרְעוּתֵיה בַּאֲתָר אָחֳרָא הֲוָה כְּמָה דְאִתְּמָר. תָּא חֲזֵי, רְאוּבֵן וְכֻלְּהוּ שִׁבְטִין תְּרֵיסַר, כֻּלְּהוּ אִתְאַחֲדָן בִּשְׁכִינְתָּא, וְכַד חָמָא יַעֲקֹב לִשְׁכִינְתָּא עַל גַּבֵּיה, קָרָא לִבְנוֹי תְּרֵיסַר לְאִתְחַבְּרָא בָּה.

538. "Reuben, you are my firstborn." Assuredly so, for he was of the first seed of Jacob, WHO HAD NO POLLUTION IN HIS DAYS, whose thoughts were directed to another place, NAMELY RACHEL as we learned. Come and see Reuben and all the twelve tribes were joined with the Shechinah. When Jacob saw the Shechinah upon him, he called his sons to be united with Her.

539. וְתָא חֲזֵי, עַרְסָא שְׁלֵימָתָא לָא אִשְׁתַּכַּח, מִן יוֹמָא דְּאִתְבְּרֵי עַלְמָא, כְּהַהִיא שַׁעְתָּא דְּבָעָא יַעֲקֹב לְאִסְתַּלְּקָא מֵעַלְמָא, אַבְרָהָם מִימִינֵיה, יִצְחָק מִשְׂמָאלֵיה, יַעֲקֹב הֲוָה שָׁכֵיב בֵּינַיְיהוּ, שְׁכִינְתָּא קַמֵּיה. כֵּיוָן דְּחָמָא יַעֲקֹב כָּךְ, קָרָא לִבְנוֹי, וְאָחֵיד לוֹן סַחֲרָנֵיה דִּשְׁכִינְתָּא, וְסַדַּר לוֹן בְּסִדּוּרָא שְׁלִים.

539. Come and see: There was never a more complete bed since the universe was created. At the time when Jacob wanted to depart from the world, Abraham was on his right, Isaac on his left and Jacob was lying between them with the Shechinah in front of him. When Jacob saw this, he called his sons and placed them around the Shechinah with perfect order.

540. מנ"ל דְּסַדֵּר לוֹן סַחֲרָנֵיה דִּשְׁכִינְתָּא, דִּכְתִיב הֵאָסְפוּ, וּכְדֵין אִשְׁתַּכַּח תַּמָּן שְׁלִימוּ דְּכֹלָּא, וְכַמָּה רְתִיכִין עִלָּאִין סַחֲרָנַיְיהוּ. פְּתָחֵי וְאָמְרֵי, לְךָ ה' הַגְּדוּלָה וְהַגְּבוּרָה וְגוֹ', כְּדֵין אִתְכְּנֵישׁ שִׁמְשָׁא לְגַבֵּיהּ דְּסִיהֲרָא, וְאִתְקְרֵיב מִזְרָח בְּמַעֲרָב, הַה"ד וַיֶּאֱסֹף רַגְלָיו אֶל הַמִּטָּה, וְאִתְנְהֵיר סִיהֲרָא, וְאִשְׁתַּכַּח בִּשְׁלִימוּ, וּכְדֵין וַדַּאי תָּנִינָן, יַעֲקֹב אָבִינוּ לָא מִית. כֵּיוָן דְּחָמָא יַעֲקֹב סִטְרָא שְׁלִים, מַה דְּלָא אִשְׁתַּכַּח הָכִי לְבַר נָשׁ אָחֳרָא, חָדֵי, וְשַׁבַּח לֵיהּ לְקוּדְשָׁא בְּרִיךְ הוּא, וּפְתַח וּבָרֵיךְ לִבְנוֹי, כָּל חַד וְחַד כִּדְקָא יָאוֹת לֵיהּ.

540. Whence do we know that he arranged them around the Shechinah? From the words "Gather yourselves," THAT IS, GATHER ABOVE AROUND THE SHECHINAH. Then was everything brought to perfection with several supernal Chariots around them. They opened by saying: "Yours, O Hashem, is the greatness, and the power..." (I Divrei Hayamim 29:11). Then the sun, NAMELY JACOB WHO IS ZEIR ANPIN, was gathered to the moon, THE NUKVA, and east, ZEIR ANPIN, drew near to the west, THE NUKVA. This is what is meant by the verse: "He gathered up his feet into the bed" (Beresheet 49:33), WHICH IS AN INDICATION OF MATING, and the moon shone by him and attained perfection. We therefore learned that surely Jacob did not die, BUT UNITED WITH THE SHECHINAH. When Jacob saw the perfect order, which had never been vouchsafed to any man, he rejoiced and praised the Holy One, blessed be He, and started blessing each of his sons according to what he deserved.

55. "Out of Asher his bread shall be fat"

A Synopsis
Rabbi Yosi and Rabbi Yisa go to visit Rabbi Shimon to discover the meaning of the title verse. We learn that Asher is one of the pillars that support the world. It is the supernal gate of the righteous that, when blessed, gives blessings to the world. The meaning of the title verse, we're told, is that when the two Columns are joined, the bread of poverty is rectified by Asher.

The Relevance of this Passage
The Light that shines from the supernal gate of the righteous radiates into our lives, helping to remove poverty from the landscape of human civilization, while bringing readers of this passage the blessing of sustenance.

541. ר' יוֹסֵי וְרַבִּי יֵיסָא הֲווֹ אַזְלֵי בְּאָרְחָא, אָמַר ר' יֵיסָא הָא וַדַּאי תָּנֵינָן, כָּל בְּנוֹי דְּיַעֲקֹב אִתַּקְנוּ בְּסִדּוּרָא שְׁלִים, וְאִתְבָּרְכוּ כָּל חַד וְחַד כִּדְקָא יָאוֹת לֵיהּ, מַאי קָא נֵימָא בְּהַאי קְרָא, דִּכְתִיב מֵאָשֵׁר שְׁמֵנָה לַחְמוֹ וְגוֹ'. א"ל לָא יְדַעְנָא, בְּגִין דְּלָא שָׁמַעְנָא בֵּיהּ מִבּוּצִינָא קַדִּישָׁא, אֶלָּא אַנְתְּ וַאֲנָא נֵיזֵיל לְגַבֵּי בּוּצִינָא קַדִּישָׁא. אַזְלֵי כַּד מָטוּ לְגַבֵּי דְּרַבִּי שִׁמְעוֹן, אָמְרוּ מִלָּה, וְשָׁאִילוּ שְׁאִילְתָּא, אָמַר לוֹן, וַדַּאי רָזָא דְחָכְמְתָא הוּא.

541. Rabbi Yosi and Rabbi Yisa were walking along the road. Rabbi Yisa said: We have surely learned that all of Jacob's sons were put in a perfect order, BY BECOMING A CHARIOT TO THE ARRANGEMENT OF THE SUPERNAL SFIROT. They were blessed each according to his worth. What then is the meaning of this verse, "Out of Asher his bread shall be fat..." (Beresheet 49:20)? He said to him: I do not know, for I have not learned it from the Holy Luminary, WHICH IS RABBI SHIMON. Let us go, you and I, to the Holy Luminary. When they came before him, they spoke and raised that question. He said to them, Surely this is the secret of Wisdom.

542. פְּתַח וַאֲמַר, אָשֵׁר יָשַׁב לְחוֹף יַמִּים וְעַל מִפְרָצָיו יִשְׁכּוֹן, אַמַּאי יָתֵיב תַּמָּן. אֶלָּא מַאן דְּיָתֵיב בְּשִׂפְתָּא דְּיַמָּא, אִשְׁתַּמֵּשׁ בְּתַפְנוּקֵי עָלְמָא, וְהָכָא אָשֵׁר דָּא פְּתָחָא עִלָּאָה דְּצַדִּיק כַּד אִתְבָּרְכָא לְאַרְקָא בִּרְכָאן

בְּעָלְמָא. וְהַאי פִּתְחָא אִשְׁתְּמוֹדַע תָּדִיר בִּרְכָאן דְּעָלְמָא, וְאִקְרֵי אָשֵׁר,
וְדָא הוּא עַמּוּדָא מֵאִינוּן דְּקָאֵים עָלְמָא עֲלַיְיהוּ.

542. He opened the discussion saying: "Asher continued on the sea shore, and abode by his bays" (Shoftim 5:17). HE ASKS: Why did he dwell there? HE ANSWERS: For whoever dwells by the sea shore, YESOD OF MALCHUT CALLED SEA, has access to luxuries of the world, NAMELY MOCHIN FROM EDEN. Here, Asher is the supernal gate of the Righteous, YESOD, which, when blessed, pours blessings upon the world. This is the gate which sends blessings to the world, and is called Asher. It is one of the pillars upon which the world is supported.

543. וְהַהוּא אֲתַר דְּאִקְרֵי לֶחֶם עוֹנִי, מֵהַהוּא אֲתַר אַתְקַין, הה"ד
מֵאָשֵׁר שְׁמֵנָה לַחְמוֹ, מַה דַּהֲוָה לַחְמָא דְמִסְכֵּנָא, אִתְהַדַּר לֶחֶם פַּנַּג.
בְּגִין דְּאָרֵיק וְאַרְמֵי בֵּיהּ בִּרְכָאן וְתַפְנוּקִין, וְסוֹפָא דִקְרָא אוֹכַח, וְהוּא
יִתֵּן מַעֲדַנֵּי מֶלֶךְ. מַאן מֶלֶךְ, דָּא כְּנֶסֶת יִשְׂרָאֵל, דְּמִנָּהּ אִתְּזָן בְּתַפְנוּקֵי
עָלְמָא, וְדָא יָהִיב לְהַאי מֶלֶךְ כָּל בִּרְכָאן, כָּל חֵידוּ, וְכָל טִיבוּ, הוּא
יָהִיב, וּמִנָּהּ נַפְקֵי. אָמְרוּ, אִי לָא אֲתֵינָא לְעָלְמָא, אֶלָּא לְמִנְדַע דָּא טַב
לָן.

543. The place called bread of poverty, THE NUKVA WHILE RECEIVING FROM THE LEFT COLUMN ALONE, is rectified by the place ASHER, WHICH BECOMES A CURTAIN TO THE CENTRAL COLUMN, WHICH JOINS THE RIGHT AND THE LEFT COLUMNS. The meaning of, "Out of Asher his bread shall be fat," is that what was previously bread of poverty became once more, AFTER THE TWO COLUMNS WERE JOINED TOGETHER, millet bread, since he poured and gave it blessings and delicacies, as shown by the end of the verse, "and he shall yield royal delicacies (lit. 'dainties of the king')." Who is the king? It is the Congregation of Yisrael, NAMELY MALCHUT, from which THE WORLD is nourished by royal delicacies. It is he ASHER who gives the king, MALCHUT, all blessings, joy and goodness. He gives MALCHUT, and from her it pours down upon THE LOWER BEINGS. They said, were we to come into the world only to hear this, it would have sufficed.

56. "Unstable as water, you shall not excel"

A Synopsis
Rabbi Chiya interprets the title verse, explaining that it signifies Reuben was blessed. However, the kingship, priesthood, and birthright to which he was entitled were taken from him. This verse also reveals, we learn, that Reuben would dwell outside of the land of Yisrael. We are then told that Reuben is aligned with both Chesed and Gvurah. Rabbi Shimon next tells the rabbis that Reuben's sons are in exile, dispersed among the four corners of the world. One day, we hear, they will wage two wars in the land of Yisrael, and they will try to seize the kingship from the Messiah when he rises up to conquer the nations.

The Relevance of this Passage
Here we ignite a particular frequency of spiritual energy that helps to hasten the arrival of the Messiah in a merciful manner, for us personally, and for our neighbors who inhabit our global village.

544. רְאוּבֵן בּוּכְרָא דְיַעֲקֹב הֲוָה, אָמַר רִבִּי חִיָּיא, לֵיהּ הֲוָה אִתְחֲזֵי כֹּלָּא, וְאִתְעֲבַר מִינָהּ כֹּלָּא, וְאִתְיְהֵיב מַלְכוּ לִיהוּדָה, בְּכֵירוּתָא לְיוֹסֵף, כְּהוּנָתָא לְלֵוִי, הה"ד פַּחַז כַּמַּיִם אַל תּוֹתַר: לָא תִשְׁתָּאַר בְּהוֹ. וּמַה דַּאֲמַר כֹּחִי וְרֵאשִׁית אוֹנִי, הָכָא בָּרְכֵיהּ וּפַקְדֵיהּ לְקוּדְשָׁא בְּרִיךְ הוּא.

544. Reuben was Jacob's firstborn. Rabbi Chiya said: He was entitled to everything, KINGSHIP, BIRTHRIGHT AND PRIESTHOOD, but it was all taken from him. Kingship was given to Judah, the birthright to Joseph and the priesthood to Levi. This is the meaning of the words: "Unstable as water, you shall not excel (lit. 'leave')" (Beresheet 49:4); NAMELY you shall not be left with them. In saying "my might and the beginning of my strength" (Ibid. 3), he blessed him and remembered him to the Holy One, blessed be He.

545. לִרְחִימָא דְמַלְכָּא, יוֹמָא חַד אַעֲבַר בְּרֵיהּ בְּשׁוּקָא, אָמַר לְמַלְכָּא, דָּא הוּא בְּרִי, וַדַּאי רְחִימָא דְנַפְשָׁאי, שָׁמַע מַלְכָּא, וְיָדַע דְּהָא שָׁאִיל עַל בְּרֵיהּ. כָּךְ יַעֲקֹב, אָמַר רְאוּבֵן בְּכוֹרִי אַתָּה כֹּחִי וְגוֹ', הָכָא פַקְדֵיהּ לְמַלְכָּא.

545. This is like the favorite of the king. One day when his son went in the city, he said to the king, This is my son, beloved of my soul. The king heard and understood that he was asking of him TO FAVOR his son. Jacob said: "Reuben, you are my firstborn..." (Ibid.) to ask the King TO BE KINDLY TOWARD HIM.

546. פַּחַז כַּמַּיִם אַל תּוֹתַר, הָכָא אֲמַר מַה דְּאָעֲרַע לֵיהּ, דְּלָא אִשְׁתְּאַר בְּאַרְעָא, וְשָׁדֵי לֵיהּ לְבַר מֵאַרְעָא. לָקֳבֵל דָּא, חַד מְמַנָּא מִסִּטְרָא דְּמַשְׁכְּנָא לְעֵילָא, דִּי מְמַנָּא תְּחוֹת יָדָא דְּמִיכָאֵל, וְאָמְרֵי לָהּ תְּחוֹת יְדָא דְּגַבְרִי"אֵל. וּמִיכָאֵל הוּא רֵישָׁא בְּכָל אֲתַר מִסִּטְרָא דְּחֶסֶ"ד, וְגַבְרִיאֵל מִסִּטְרָא דִשְׂמָאלָא דִּגְבוּר"ה. וִיהוּדָה עֹד רָד עִם אֵל, סְטַר גְּבוּרָה, בֵּי דִּינָא אִקְרֵי, וְסָמִיךְ לֵיהּ רְאוּבֵן, אע"ג דְּמַלְכוּ הֲוָה דִיהוּדָה, רְאוּבֵן סָמוּךְ לְקַבְלֵיהּ הֲוָה.

546. "Unstable as water, you shall not excel." Here he stated his fate, that he would not remain in the land of Yisrael but dwell outside it, NAMELY EAST OF THE JORDAN. Correspondingly, the officer in charge, on the side of the tabernacle above, THE NUKVA, in charge under Michael, IS ALSO REJECTED OUTSIDE THE TABERNACLE. Some say THAT THE TRUSTEE THAT WAS REJECTED FROM THE TABERNACLE ABOVE WAS under Gabriel. AND THOUGH REUBEN IS CHESED, Michael is the first OF THE ANGELS on the side of Chesed, and Gabriel is THE FIRST on the left side, Gvurah, REUBEN IS NEVERTHELESS ALSO OF THE SIDE OF GVURAH, WHICH WE LEARN FROM THE VERSE, "But Judah still rules (also: 'descends') with El" (Hoshea 12:1), THE DESCENT WHICH INDICATES THAT HE IS OF the side of Gvurah and called court of justice. Reuben's inheritance was adjacent to his. JUDAH'S PORTION WAS WEST OF THE JORDAN AND REUBEN'S WAS EAST OF THE JORDAN. THIS SHOWS THAT REUBEN, TOO, IS OF THE SIDE OF GVURAH. And though kingship (Malchut), THE SECRET OF LOWER GVURAH, WAS TAKEN FROM REUBEN AND belongs to Judah, HE IS NEVERTHELESS NOT WHOLLY CLEANSED OF GVURAH, SINCE THE INHERITANCE OF Reuben is adjacent to his, WHICH IS AN INDICATION OF GVURAH.

547. אר"ש, זְמִינִין אִינוּן בְּנֵי רְאוּבֵן, לַאֲגָחָא תְּרֵין קְרָבִין בְּגוֹ אַרְעָא. תָּא חֲזֵי, כְּתִיב כֹּחִי, בְּגָלוּתָא דְּמִצְרַיִם. וְרֵאשִׁית אוֹנִי, דְּאִינוּן הֲווֹ

קַדְמָאִין לְגַבֵּי אֲחוּהוֹן לְקַרְבָא. יֶתֶר שְׂאֵת, לְגָלוּתָא דְאַשּׁוּר, דְמִתַּמָן גְלוּ בְּנֵי גָד וּבְנֵי רְאוּבֵן קַדְמָאי מִכֻּלְהוּ, וְסָבְלֵי כַּמָה בִּישִׁין, וְכַמָה עִנּוּיִין סָבְלוּ, וְלָא תָבוּ עַד כְּעַן.

547. Rabbi Shimon said: Reuben's sons will in the future wage two wars in the land of Yisrael. Come and behold: it is written "my might," namely, the exile in Egypt; "and the beginning of my strength," NAMELY they were the first among the brothers to fight. "The excellency of dignity" is the exile of Assyria (Ashur), where the sons of Gad and Reuben were the first to go down and suffered much torture, and did not return FROM THERE until now.

548. וְיֶתֶר עָז לְזִמְנָא דְמַלְכָּא מְשִׁיחָא יִתְעַר בְּעָלְמָא, אִינוּן יִפְקוּן וְיִגָחוּן קְרָבִין בְּעָלְמָא, וִינַצְחוּן, וְיִתְקְפוּן עַל עַמְמַיָא, וּבְנֵי עָלְמָא יִדְחֲלוּן מִנַּיְיהוּ וְיִרְתְּתוּן קַמַיְיהוּ, וְיַחְשִׁיבוּ לְאִתְגַּבְּרָא בְּמַלְכוּתָא, וְלָא יִשְׁתָּאֲרוּן בֵּיהּ, הֲהַ״ד פַּחַז כַּמַּיִם אַל תּוֹתַר, מַ״ט לָא יִשְׁתָּאֲרוּן בֵּיהּ, וַאֲפִילוּ בְּסִטְרָא חַד דְעָלְמָא, בְּגִין כִּי עָלִיתָ מִשְׁכְּבֵי אָבִיךָ, דִזְמִינִין לְאֵעָלָא וּלְאַגָחָא קְרָבִין בְּגוֹ אַרְעָא קַדִּישָׁא, מִשְׁכְּבֵי אָבִיךָ דַּיְיקָא, זוֹ יְרוּשָׁלֵם.

548. "And the excellency of power" refers to the time when Messiah will rise in the world and they will go forth and make war in the world and win, and conquer the nations. The inhabitants of the world will fear them and tremble before them. THE SONS OF REUBEN will plan to seize the kingship yet shall not retain it, hence the words: "Unstable as water, you shall not excel." Why will they not retain mastery even in one place in the world? Because "you went up to your father's bed" (Beresheet 49:4), for they are going to wage war within the Holy Land. "Your father's bed" is Jerusalem. THEY WILL STRIVE TO TAKE IT FROM MESSIAH.

549. תָּא חֲזֵי, בְּאַרְבַּע סִטְרֵי עָלְמָא, אִתְבַּדְרוּ בְּנֵי רְאוּבֵן בְּגָלוּתָא, לְקָבְלֵיהוֹן דְכָל יִשְׂרָאֵל, דְאִתְגְּלוּ בְּגָלוּתָא אַרְבַּע זִמְנִין, בְּאַרְבַּע סִטְרֵי עָלְמָא, הַהַ״ד, כֹּחִי חַד, וְרֵאשִׁית אוֹנִי תְּרֵי, יֶתֶר שְׂאֵת תְּלַת, וְיֶתֶר עָז אַרְבָּעָה. כְּגַוְונָא דָא זְמִינִין אִינוּן לְאַגָחָא קְרָבָא בְּאַרְבַּע סִטְרֵי עָלְמָא,

וּלְמִשְׁלַט בְּקַרְבַּיְיהוּ עַל כֹּלָּא, וִינַצְחוּן עֲמָמִין סַגִּיאִין, וְיִשְׁלְטוּן עֲלַיְיהוּ.

549. Come and see, the sons of Reuben dispersed into exile in the four corners of the world, in correspondence with all of Yisrael, who were exiled four times into the four corners of the world. Hence it says, "My might," which is the first exile; "and the beginning of my strength," the second; "the excellency of dignity" the third and "the excellency of power" the fourth. Likewise, they will wage war in the four corners of the world, thus ruling over everything. They will conquer many peoples and rule over them.

550. פַּחַז כַּמַּיִם אַל תּוֹתַר כִּי עָלִיתָ מִשְׁכְּבֵי אָבִיךָ, הָכָא אִתְרְמִיז עַל הִרְהוּרָא קַדְמָאָה דַּהֲוָה לֵיהּ לְיַעֲקֹב. בְּהַאי טִפָּה קַדְמָאָה בְּרָחֵל, דְּאִלְמָלֵא הִרְהוּרָא דְּהַהִיא טִפָּה הֲוָה בְּאַתְרָהּ, אִשְׁתְּאַר רְאוּבֵן בְּכֹלָּא, אֲבָל פַּחַז כַּמַּיִם אַל תּוֹתַר כִּי עָלִיתָ מִשְׁכְּבֵי אָבִיךָ, עָלִיתָ, בְּהִרְהוּרָא אָחֳרָא, אָז חִלַּלְתָּ וְגוֹ'.

550. "Unstable as water, you shall not excel; because you went up to your father's bed." Here is an allusion to the first thought Jacob had when issuing the first seed, which was about Rachel. Were the thought attached to the first seed in its place, LEAH, Reuben would retain all, THE KINGSHIP, THE PRIESTHOOD AND THE BIRTHRIGHT, but "unstable as water, you shall not excel; because you went up to your father's bed" namely you came up through other thoughts, and "then you did defile it..." (Ibid.).

551. דָּבָר אַחֵר, פַּחַז כַּמַּיִם אַל תּוֹתַר, דְּהָא כַּד יִגְחוּן קְרָבָא בְּנֵי רְאוּבֵן בְּעָלְמָא, וִינַצְחוּן עֲמָמִין סַגִּיאִין, לָא יִשְׁתָּאֲרוּן בְּמַלְכוּתָא, מ"ט, כִּי עָלִיתָ מִשְׁכְּבֵי, דִּזְמִינִין לְאַגָּחָא קְרָבָא בְּאַרְעָא קַדִּישָׁא דַּיְיקָא, דִּכְתִיב כִּי עָלִיתָ מִשְׁכְּבֵי אָבִיךָ דָּא יְרוּשָׁלַיִם. מִשְׁכְּבֵי, מִשְׁכַּב מִבָּעֵי לֵיהּ. אֶלָּא, אָבִיךָ דָּא יִשְׂרָאֵל סָבָא, מִשְׁכְּבֵי אָבִיךָ וְלָא מִשְׁכַּב, בְּגִין דְּהָא בִּתְרֵי זִמְנֵי אִתְבְּנֵי יְרוּשָׁלֵם, וּתְלִיתָאָה לְזִמְנָא דְּמַלְכָּא מְשִׁיחָא. וְעַל דָּא מִשְׁכְּבֵי אָבִיךָ. וְהָכָא אִתְגַּלְיָיא בְּרָכָה, וּמַאי דַּהֲוָה בְּהַהוּא זִמְנָא, וּמַה דַּהֲוָה כַּד עָאלוּ יִשְׂרָאֵל לְאַרְעָא, וּמַה דְּיִהֵא בְּזִמְנָא דְּמַלְכָּא מְשִׁיחָא בְּעוֹבָדָא דִּרְאוּבֵן.

551. Another explanation for "unstable as water, you shall not excel": When the sons of Reuben will wage war in the world and conquer many nations, they will not remain rulers. HENCE IT IS WRITTEN, "YOU SHALL NOT EXCEL." What is the reason for this? "Because you went up to your father's bed (lit. 'beds')," as they are destined to wage war in the Holy Land, precisely mentioned in the words "your father's bed," which refer to Jerusalem. HE ASKS: WHY DOES SCRIPTURE SAY "beds," instead of 'bed'? HE ANSWERS: "Your father" is Yisrael Saba, NAMELY ZEIR ANPIN, AND THEREFORE IT SAYS "beds" instead of 'bed', since Jerusalem was twice destroyed, and WILL BE BUILT a third time at the time of King Messiah. Hence the plural. Here, the blessing is revealed IN THE VERSE: "YOU ARE MY FIRSTBORN, MY MIGHT AND THE BEGINNING OF MY STRENGTH." And also what happened at that time THAT THE BIRTHRIGHT, KINGSHIP AND PRIESTHOOD WERE TAKEN FROM HIM, AS SAID "UNSTABLE AS WATER, YOU SHALL NOT EXCEL," that which will be when Yisrael shall come to the land of Yisrael, THAT HE WILL HAVE NO PORTION IN IT BUT ACROSS THE JORDAN. And Reuben's deeds at the time of Messiah, NAMELY THAT HE WILL WAGE WARS AGAINST MANY PEOPLES AND IN JERUSALEM.

57. "Simeon and Levi are brothers"

A Synopsis
Rabbi Yitzchak explains to Rabbi Yosi that Simeon was not worthy of a blessing and that Levi came from the side of strict judgment. After explaining the meaning of the verse, "So is the great and wide sea", Rabbi Yehuda reveals that Simeon and Levi were not blessed by their father, but rather were delivered to Moses to receive blessings. Rabbi Shimon then explains the reason for this. We learn that Jacob wished to bless Simeon and Levi when he was about to depart from the world; however, he did not because of the Shechinah, who stood over him. Knowing that to bless them would render the Shechinah defective, he decided to deliver them to Moses, the master of the house. Jacob knew that he would be able to bless Simeon and Levi without damaging the Shechinah. Rabbi Chiya concludes the passage by explaining that because they were both of strict judgment, Simeon and Levi were divided and dispersed so that all of Yisrael received from their strict judgment.

The Relevance of this Passage
Strict judgement is removed from our midst through the power of Moses, even though we and the rest of world may not be worthy of such cleansing. In addition, the Light of the Shechinah showers us with protection upon the merit of Moses.

552. שִׁמְעוֹן וְלֵוִי אַחִים, אָמַר ר' יִצְחָק, הָכָא אָחֵיד לוֹן, בְּסִטְרָא שְׂמָאלָא דִּשְׁכִינְתָּא. דְּחָמָא עוֹבָדֵין דְּדִינָא קַשְׁיָא, דְּלָא יָכֵיל עַלְמָא לְמִסְבַּל. אָמַר ר' יוֹסֵי, בִּרְכְתָא דִּלְהוֹן אָן הִיא. אָמַר רִבִּי יִצְחָק, שִׁמְעוֹן לָא אִתְחֲזֵי לְהַאי, דְּחָמָא לֵיהּ כַּמָּה עוֹבָדֵין בִּישִׁין. וְלֵוִי דְּאָתֵי מִסִּטְרָא דְּדִינָא קַשְׁיָא, וּבִרְכְתָא לָא תַּלְיָא בֵּיהּ, וַאֲפִילוּ כַּד אָתָא מֹשֶׁה, לָא תָּלֵי בִּרְכָתֵיהּ בֵּיהּ, דִּכְתִיב בָּרֵךְ ה' חֵילוֹ וּפוֹעַל יָדָיו תִּרְצֶה, בְּקוּדְשָׁא בְּרִיךְ הוּא תַּלְיָיא.

552. "Simeon and Levi are brothers" (Beresheet 49:5). Rabbi Yitzchak said: Here he attached them to the left side of the Shechinah, for he saw they have acted with strict judgment, which the world cannot endure. Rabbi Yosi asked, Where is their blessing? Rabbi Yitzchak said: Simeon was not worthy of it, for he saw in him many evil deeds. Levi came from the side of strict judgment, from which blessing does not stem. Even Moses did not

attach his blessing to him, as said: "Bless, Hashem, his substance, and accept the work of his hands" (Devarim 33:11), so that his blessing came from the Holy One, blessed be He.

553. תָּא חֲזֵי כְּתִיב זֶה הַיָּם גָּדוֹל וּרְחַב יָדַיִם שָׁם רֶמֶשׂ וְאֵין מִסְפָּר חַיּוֹת קְטַנּוֹת עִם גְּדוֹלוֹת. זֶה הַיָּם גָּדוֹל, דָּא שְׁכִינְתָּא, דְּקַיְימָא עֲלֵיהּ דְּיַעֲקֹב, כַּד בָּעָא לְאִסְתַּלְּקָא מֵעַלְמָא. וּרְחַב יָדַיִם, דְּהָא כָּל עָלְמָא אִמְלֵי וְאִשְׁתְּלִים וְאִתְצַמְצַם תַּמָּן. שָׁם רֶמֶשׂ וְאֵין מִסְפָּר, דְּכַמָּה מַלְאֲכֵי עִלָּאֵי וְקַדִּישָׁאֵי אִשְׁתַּכְּחוּ תַּמָּן. חַיּוֹת קְטַנּוֹת עִם גְּדוֹלוֹת, אִלֵּין אִינּוּן י"ב שְׁבָטִין, בְּנוֹי דְּיַעֲקֹב, דְּאִשְׁתַּכְּחוּ בְּהוֹן בִּשְׁלִימוּ, חַד אַיָּלָה, וְחַד זְאֵב, וְחַד אֲרִי, וְחַד טָלֶה. אָמַר רִבִּי יִצְחָק, אַרְיֵה חַד, וְטָלֶה חַד, חַד זְאֵב, וְחַד גְּדִי, וְכֵן כֻּלְּהוּ, לְאִשְׁתַּכְּחָא חַיּוֹת קְטַנּוֹת עִם גְּדוֹלוֹת.

553. Come and see, it is written: "So is the great and wide sea, wherein are creeping things innumerable, both small and great beasts" (Tehilim 104:25). The great sea is the Shechinah, which stood over Jacob when he wished to depart from the world. It is wide, for all the world is filled and made whole, and contracted within THE SHECHINAH, SINCE SHE WAS FILLED AND MADE WHOLE BY THE SOUTH AND CONTRACTED BY THE NORTH. "Wherein are creeping things innumerable," since there are many supernal and holy angels there. The "small and great beasts" are the twelve tribes, Jacob's sons, who are found there in wholeness. There is a hind, NAFTALI; a wolf, BENJAMIN; a lion, JUDAH; and a lamb, JOSEPH, AS SAID "THAT LEADS JOSEPH LIKE A FLOCK" (TEHILIM 80:2). Rabbi Yitzchak said: A lion and a lamb, a wolf and a kid (Heb. *gedi*), NAMELY GAD, and so on, there are small beasts with great ones.

554. רִבִּי יְהוּדָה אֲמַר, כֻּלְּהוּ שַׁפִּיר, אֲבָל יְהוּדָה אַרְיֵה, שִׁמְעוֹן שׁוֹר, וְהָא אוֹקִמוּהּ חַבְרַיָּיא דַּהֲווֹ מַשְׁגִּיחִין דָּא לָקֳבֵל דָּא, דָּא מִימִינָא, וְדָא מִשְׂמָאלָא. לְתוֹרָא דְּעוֹבְדוֹי בִּישִׁין, אַמְרוּ נְצַיֵּיר אִקּוּנִין דְּאַרְיֵה בְּקוּפְטֵיהּ, וְיִסְתַּכַּל בְּדָא וְיִדְחַל מִנֵּיהּ, כָּךְ שִׁמְעוֹן שׁוֹר, יְהוּדָה אַרְיֵה.

554. Rabbi Yehuda said: It was well said about all THE TRIBES, THAT THERE ARE GREAT AND SMALL BEASTS, but Judah is a lion and Simeon an

OX, AS SIMEON IS OF GVURAH, WHICH IS THE FACE OF AN OX. The friends have explained that they were facing each other, JUDAH on the right and SIMEON on the left. THIS IS LIKE A MAN WHO HAD a vicious ox. He said: I shall paint the figure of a lion in his stall, and it will see it and fear it. Thus Simeon is an ox and Judah a lion, AS SIMEON THE OX, NAMELY GVURAH, IS SUBDUED THROUGH LOOKING AT JUDAH THE LION, WHICH IS CHESED.

555. שִׁמְעוֹן לָא זָכָה לְבִרְכָאן, אֶלָּא טָפַל לֵיהּ בִּיהוּדָה, כְּתִיב הָכָא שְׁמַע ה' קוֹל יְהוּדָה, וּכְתִיב הָתָם כִּי שָׁמַע ה' כִּי שְׂנוּאָה אָנֹכִי. א"ר יְהוּדָה, שִׁמְעוֹן וְלֵוִי, אֲבוּהוֹן סָלֵיק לוֹן לְמֹשֶׁה. א"ל ר' יוֹסֵי, מ"ט אֲבוּהוֹן סָלֵיק לוֹן לְמֹשֶׁה. א"ל, אַף אֲנַן נַסְלֵיק לֵיהּ לְבוּצִינָא קַדִּישָׁא עִלָּאָה.

555. Simeon did not receive any blessing FROM JACOB, but Moses attached him to Judah, as it is written: "Hear (Heb. sh'ma), Hashem, the voice of Judah" (Devarim 33:7) and elsewhere "because Hashem has heard (Heb. shama) that I was hated" (Beresheet 29:33). THEREFORE, SHE NAMED HIM SIMEON. THERE IS AN ANALOGY BETWEEN THE VERSES. AS THERE IS HEARING IN THE NAME OF SIMEON, SO THE HEARING IN RELATION TO JUDAH INCLUDES SIMEON. Rabbi Yehuda said: Simeon and Levi WERE NOT BLESSED BY their father SINCE HE brought them to Moses TO BLESS THEM. Rabbi Yosi said to him: Wherefore DID their father NOT BLESS THEM BUT delivered them to Moses? Rabbi Yehuda said to him: We too shall bring THE QUESTION before the Holy Luminary, RABBI SHIMON.

556. אָתוּ שָׁאֲלוּ לֵיהּ לר"ש, אָמַר כַּמָּה חֲבִיבִין מִלִּין אַטְפַּח בִּידוֹי וּבְכָה, אָמַר מַאן יְגַלֵּי לָךְ מְהֵימְנָא קַדִּישָׁא, אִסְתַּלָּקַת בְּחַיָּיךְ עַל בְּנֵי נָשָׁא, אִסְתַּלָּקַת בְּמוֹתָךְ, וְאַסְתֵּים דְּיוֹקְנָךְ. מַפְתְּחָן דְּמָארֶךְ אִתְמַסְרוּ בִּידָךְ תָּדִיר.

556. They came and asked Rabbi Shimon. He said: How sweet are the words. He clapped his hands and wept. He said: Who will uncover you, holy faithful, NAMELY MOSES. In your lifetime you were raised above men, and in your death you were elevated and your image covered. The keys of your Master were always delivered to your hands.

557. תָּא חֲזֵי, יַעֲקֹב הֲוָה לֵיהּ אַרְבַּע נָשִׁין, וְאוֹלִיד בְּנִין מִכֻּלְּהוּ, וְאִשְׁתְּלֵים בִּנְשׁוֹי. כַּד בָּעָא יַעֲקֹב לְאִסְתַּלְּקָא, שְׁכִינְתָּא קַיְימֵי עֲלוֹי, בָּעָא לְבָרוּכֵי לְאַלֵּין, וְלָא יָכֵיל, מִקַּמֵּי שְׁכִינְתָּא דְּדָחֵיל, אָמַר, הֵיךְ אַעֲבֵיד, דְּהָא תַּרְוַוייְהוּ מִסִּטְרָא דְּדִינָא קַשְׁיָא קָא אַתְיָין, אִי אַתְקֵיף בִּשְׁכִינְתָּא לָא יָכֵילְנָא, דְּהָא אַרְבַּע נָשִׁין הֲווֹ לִי, וְאִשְׁתְּלֵימְנָא בְּהוֹן, אֶלָּא אֲסַלֵּק לוֹן לְמָארֵי דְּבֵיתָא, דְּהָא בֵּיתָא בִּרְעוּתֵיהּ קַיְימָא, וּמַה דְּבָעֵי יַעֲבֵיד.

557. Come and see: Jacob had four wives. He begot children by them all, and was perfected through his wives. When Jacob wished to depart FROM THE WORLD, the Shechinah stood over him. He wanted to bless SIMEON AND LEVI but could not, since he feared the Shechinah. He said to himself, How can I do this, seeing that both of them come from the side of strict judgment, AND TO BLESS THEM WILL RENDER THE SHECHINAH DEFECTIVE. I cannot force the Shechinah, since I had four wives WHO WERE DRAWN FROM THE FOUR ASPECTS, CHESED, GVURAH, TIFERET AND MALCHUT OF THE SHECHINAH, AND I WAS PERFECTED THROUGH THEM, SINCE THEY BORE ME TWELVE TRIBES, THE SECRET OF ALL PERFECTION. SINCE I RECEIVED MY PERFECTION FROM THE SHECHINAH, HOW CAN I BLESS SIMEON AND LEVI AGAINST Her wish? I shall deliver them to the landlord of the house, MOSES, THE HUSBAND OF THE MATRON, who is the owner, and he shall do as he pleases.

558. כָּךְ יַעֲקֹב אָמַר, חוּלְקִין דִּנְשִׁין וּבְנִין הָא נָסֵבִית בְּהַאי עַלְמָא, וְאִשְׁתַּלְּמְנָא, הֵיךְ אַתְקֵיף בְּמַטְרוֹנִיתָא יַתִּיר, אֶלָּא אֲסַלֵּק מִלִּין לְמָארֵי מַטְרוֹנִיתָא, וְהוּא יַעֲבֵד מַה דְּבָעֵי, וְלָא יִדְחַל.

558. Jacob said: I have received my portion of wives and children in this world FROM THE SHECHINAH, and become perfected. How can I force the Matron, THE SHECHINAH? I shall deliver the matter to the master of the Matron, MOSES, who will do as he pleases without fear.

559. תָּא חֲזֵי מַה כְּתִיב, וְזֹאת הַבְּרָכָה אֲשֶׁר בֵּרַךְ מֹשֶׁה אִישׁ הָאֱלֹקִים, מָארֵיהּ דְּבֵיתָא, מָארֵיהּ דְּמַטְרוֹנִיתָא. כְּמָה דִּכְתִיב אִישָׁה יְקִימֶנּוּ

וְאִישָׁה יְפֵרֶנּוּ. דְּהָא כַּלַּת מֹשֶׁה כְּתִיב. וְעַל דָּא, מֹשֶׁה בָּרֵיךְ מַאן דְּבָעָא
וְלָא דָחִיל, כִּדְאוֹקִימְנָא. וּבְגִין כָּךְ אָמַר יַעֲקֹב, הָא חָמֵינָן דִּבְנֵי אִלֵּין
בְּסִטְרָא דְּדִינָא קַשְׁיָא, יֵיתֵי מָארֵיה דְּבֵיתָא וִיבָרֵךְ לוֹן.

559. Come and see, it is written, "And this is the blessing, with which Moses the man of the Elohim blessed" (Devarim 33:1), which means master of the house, master of the Matron, SINCE MAN MEANS MASTER, as it is written: "Her husband (man) may let it stand, or her husband may make it void" (Bemidbar 30:14) and "Moses had finished (Heb. *kalot*)" (Bemidbar 7:1), FOR THE SHECHINAH IS CALLED 'MOSES' BRIDE (HEB. *KALAT*)'. Therefore, Moses may bless whomever he pleases, without fear OF DAMAGING THE SHECHINAH, SINCE HE CAN FIX HER ACCORDING TO HIS WISHES, as has been explained. Therefore Jacob said: I see that these sons of mine are from the side of strict judgment, let the master of the house come and bless them.

560. מֹשֶׁה וַדַּאי אִישׁ הָאֱלֹקִים הָיָה, וּרְעוּתֵיהּ עָבֵיד בְּבֵיתֵיהּ, כְּד"א
אִישָׁה יְקִימֶנּוּ. הה"ד וַיֹּאמֶר מֹשֶׁה קוּמָה ה'. וְאִישָׁה יְפֵרֶנּוּ, הה"ד
וּבְנֻחֹה יֹאמַר שׁוּבָה ה'. וַדַּאי רְעוּתֵיהּ עָבַד מָארֵיהּ דְּבֵיתָא וְלֵית דִּימְחֵי
בִידֵיהּ. כְּבָר נָשׁ דְּגָזַר עַל אִנְתְּתֵיהּ, וְעָבְדָא רְעוּתֵיהּ. וְעַל דָּא יַעֲקֹב
אע"ג דַּהֲוָה אָחִיד בְּאִילָנָא דְּחַיֵּי, לָא הֲוָה מָארֵי דְּבֵיתָא, אֶלָּא לְתַתָּא,
מֹשֶׁה הוּא לְעֵילָא, בְּגִין כָּךְ סָלֵיק לוֹן לְמָארֵיהּ דְּבֵיתָא.

560. Assuredly Moses was a man of Elohim, and did as he pleased in his house, as it says, "Her husband may let it stand" BY GIVING HER MOCHIN OF CHOCHMAH CALLED RISING UP, in accordance with the verse, "Moses said: Rise up, Hashem, and let Your enemies be scattered" (Bemidbar 10:35). BECAUSE ON THE WAY, THERE IS FOOTHOLD TO THE KLIPOT AND THE MOCHIN OF CHOCHMAH SCATTER THE KLIPOT. "Or her husband may make it void," which agrees with the words "And when it rested, he said: 'Return, Hashem'" (Ibid. 35), FOR WHEN THE SHECHINAH IS AT REST, THE KLIPOT CANNOT HOLD HER AND THERE IS NO FEAR. THEREFORE, "HER HUSBAND MAY MAKE IT VOID." BY STRENGTH OF THE CENTRAL COLUMN, HE MAKES VOID THE FIRST THREE SFIROT OF CHOCHMAH IN ORDER TO CLOTHE HER WITH CHASSADIM, THE SECRET OF THE VERSE "AND WHEN IT RESTED, HE SAID: 'RETURN, HASHEM.'"

Assuredly the master of the house does as he pleases and no one may protest, as a man who has decided for his wife and she does his bidding. Therefore, Jacob, though he was attached to the Tree of Life, ZEIR ANPIN, was not the master of the house LIKE MOSES for he was attached below and Moses above. Jacob therefore delivered them to the landlord TO BE BLESSED BY HIM.

561. בְּסוֹדָם אַל תָּבֹא נַפְשִׁי וגו', ר' אַבָּא פְּתַח וַאֲמַר סוֹד יי' לִירֵאָיו וגו'. סוֹד יי' לִירֵאָיו, רָזָא עִלָּאָה דְאוֹרַיְיתָא, לָא יָהִיב קוּדְשָׁא בְּרִיךְ הוּא אֶלָּא לְאִינוּן דַּחֲלֵי חַטָּאָה. וּמַאן דְּאִינוּן דַּחֲלֵי חַטָּאָה אִתְגְּלֵי לוֹן רָזָא עִלָּאָה דְאוֹרַיְיתָא, וּמַאן אִיהוּ, רָזָא עִלָּאָה דְאוֹרַיְיתָא, הֲוֵי אֵימָא, דָּא אָת קַיָּימָא קַדִּישָׁא, דְּאִקְרֵי סוֹד ה' בְּרִית קֹדֶשׁ.

561. "Let my soul not come into their council" (Beresheet 49:6). Rabbi Aba opened the discussion saying: "The counsel of Hashem is for them that fear Him" (Tehilim 25:14). It is the supernal mystery of the Torah that the Holy One, blessed be He, gives only to those who fear sin. Whoever fears sin, the supernal secret of the Torah is revealed to him, the sign of the holy covenant called the secret of Hashem.

562. שִׁמְעוֹן וְלֵוִי, אַטְרַחוּ גַּרְמַיְיהוּ עַל הַאי סוֹד, בְּאַנְשֵׁי שְׁכֶם, דְּיִגְזְרוּן גַּרְמַיְיהוּ וִיקַבְּלוֹי עֲלוֹן הַאי סוֹד. תּוּ בְּעוֹבָדָא דְזִמְרִי בֶּן סָלוּא, דְּפָסַל הַאי סוֹד. וְיַעֲקֹב אֲמַר בְּסוֹדָם אַל תָּבֹא נַפְשִׁי. מַאי נַפְשִׁי. דָּא נַפְשָׁא דְעָאֲלַת וְאִתְאַחֲדַת בִּבְרִית עִלָּאָה לְעֵילָא, וְאִקְרֵי נֶפֶשׁ צְרוֹרָא דְחַיֵּי.

562. Simeon and Levi took pains on account of that secret OF THE HOLY COVENANT, that the people of Shchem will circumcise themselves and accept that secret upon them; TO WIT, TO PRESERVE THE SIGN OF THE HOLY COVENANT. But the scripture bears testimony that it was done with guile. Also Zimri, son of Salu, WHO WAS A CHIEF OF A FAMILY OF THE TRIBE OF SIMEON, defiled that secret WITH KOZBI, THE DAUGHTER OF TZUR. IN RELATION TO THIS, Jacob said: "Let my soul not come into their council (lit. 'secret')" (Beresheet 49:6). What soul is this? The soul which rises up to be united with the supernal covenant above, NAMELY MALCHUT

WHICH IS UNITED WITH THE SUPERNAL COVENANT, YESOD OF ZEIR ANPIN, called the soul of the bundle of life.

563. בְּקִהָלָם אַל תֵּחַד כְּבוֹדִי. הָא אוֹקִמוּהָ, כְּד"א וַיַּקְהֵל עֲלֵיהֶם קֹרַח. אַל תֵּחַד כְּבוֹדִי, דָּא כְּבוֹד יִשְׂרָאֵל סְתָם. וְע"ד לָא בָּרֵיךְ לוֹן אֲבוּהוֹן, בְּגִין דְּסָלִיק לוֹן לְמֹשֶׁה. ר' חִיָּיא אָמַר מֵהֲנֵי קְרָאֵי מַשְׁמַע דְּלָא אִתְאַחֵיד דָּא בְּדָא, וְאִצְטְרִיךְ הָכֵי. וְע"ד אִית בֵּיהּ כֹּלָּא, וְלֵית לָךְ דָּרָא בְּעָלְמָא, דְּלָא נָחֲתָא דִּינָא דִּלְהוֹן לְקַטְרְגָא בְּעָלְמָא וְאַסְגִּיאוּ מְהַדְּרֵי עַל פִּתְחַיְיהוּ דִּבְנֵי נָשָׁא, הָא לָךְ כֹּלָּא.

563. "To their assembly let my honor not be united" (Ibid.). This has been explained to refer to the words, "And Korah gathered all the congregation" (Bemidbar 16:19), FOR JACOB'S NAME IS NOT MENTIONED, ONLY "KORAH, THE SON OF IZHAR, THE SON OF KOHATH THE SON OF LEVI," AND NOT "THE SON OF JACOB." "Let my honor not be united," the honor of Yisrael in general. Therefore, DUE TO THESE DEEDS, their father did not bless them but delivered them to Moses. Rabbi Chiya said: From these verses, we understand that they were not joined together, BUT SCATTERED, AS IT SAYS "I WILL DIVIDE THEM IN JACOB, AND SCATTER THEM IN YISRAEL" (BERESHEET 49:7), as should be, FOR THEY NEED SCATTERING DUE TO THEIR BEING OF STRICT JUDGMENT. Therefore there is everything in it, SINCE THEIR STRICT JUDGMENT PERVADES THROUGHOUT YISRAEL, FOR BY SCATTERING THEM IN YISRAEL, YISRAEL RECEIVED FROM THEIR STRICT JUDGMENT. There is no generation in the world, upon which their Judgment has not descended to bring accusation on the world, which causes beggars to multiply. Thus, all OF YISRAEL WERE HURT BY THEIR JUDGMENT.

58. The nations by the sun and Yisrael by the moon

A Synopsis
Here we find a discourse on the moon. The Yisraelites use the cycles of the moon to calculate seasons, holidays, and years. In contrast, the nations of the world use the cycles of the sun, which, we're told, comprise an inferior system.

The Relevance of this Passage
Like the moon, mankind has no Light of its own. As the moon derives its light from the sun, mankind and this entire earthly realm draw spiritual Light from the Upper World domain known as Zeir Anpin. This passage helps us rise above any negative celestial influences that appear throughout the lunar/solar calendar year, connecting us only to the positive energy that the moon and sun release into the cosmos.

564. יְהוּדָה אַתָּה יוֹדוּךְ אַחֶיךָ יָדְךָ בְּעֹרֶף אוֹיְבֶיךָ וגו'. ר' יוֹסֵי פָּתַח עָשָׂה יָרֵחַ לְמוֹעֲדִים וגו'. עָשָׂה יָרֵחַ בְּגִין לְקַדְּשָׁא בֵּיהּ רֵישׁ יַרְחִין, וְרֵישׁ שַׁתִּין. וּלְעָלְמִין סִיהֲרָא לָא נָהִיר אֶלָּא מִשִּׁמְשָׁא, וְכַד שִׁמְשָׁא שַׁלִּיט, סִיהֲרָא לָא שַׁלְטָא, כַּד אִתְכְּנֵישׁ שִׁמְשָׁא, כְּדֵין סִיהֲרָא שַׁלְטָא, וְלֵית חוּשְׁבַּן לְסִיהֲרָא אֶלָּא כַּד אִתְכְּנֵישׁ שִׁמְשָׁא.

564. "Judah you are he whom your brethren shall praise: your hand shall be on the neck of your enemies" (Beresheet 49:8). Rabbi Yosi opened the discussion saying: "He made the moon for seasons" (Tehilim 104:19). "He made the moon" with which to sanctify the first day of months and new years. The moon never shines but from the sun. When the sun reigns, the moon does not; when the sun is gathered, the moon rules. The moon is of no account, save when the sun is gathered.

565. וְתַרְוַוייְהוּ עֲבַד קוּדְשָׁא בְּרִיךְ הוּא לְאַנְהָרָא, הה"ד וַיִּתֵּן אֹתָם אֱלֹקִים בִּרְקִיעַ הַשָּׁמַיִם לְהָאִיר עַל הָאָרֶץ וגו'. וְהָיוּ לְאוֹתוֹת, אִלֵּין שַׁבָּתוֹת, דִּכְתִיב כִּי אוֹת הִיא. וּלְמוֹעֲדִים, אִינוּן י"ט. וּלְיָמִים, אִלֵּין רֵישֵׁי יַרְחִין. וּלְשָׁנִים, אִלֵּין רֵישֵׁי שְׁנִין. דְּלֶהֱוּוֹן אוּמוֹת הָעוֹלָם עָבְדִין חֻשְׁבַּן לְשִׁמְשָׁא, וְיִשְׂרָאֵל לְסִיהֲרָא.

565. The Holy One, blessed be He, made both so that they will shine, as it is written in the verse, "And Elohim set them in the firmament of heaven to give light upon the earth" (Beresheet 1:17), to "let them be for signs" (Ibid. 15). Shabbat CALLED SIGN, as in "It is a sign" (Shemot 31:17). "And for seasons," the holidays; "and for days," the days of the beginning of the month; "and years" (Beresheet 1:14), are new year days. The nations in the world reckon by the sun and Yisrael by the moon.

566, וְאָזְלָא הָא, כִּי הָא דַּאֲמַר ר׳ אֶלְעָזָר, כְּתִיב הִרְבִּיתָ הַגּוֹי לוֹ הִגְדַּלְתָּ הַשִּׂמְחָה. הִרְבִּיתָ הַגּוֹי, אִלֵּין יִשְׂרָאֵל, דִּכְתִיב בְּהוֹ כִּי מִי גוֹי גָּדוֹל. וּכְתִיב גּוֹי אֶחָד בָּאָרֶץ. לוֹ: בְּגִינֵיהּ. הִגְדַּלְתָּ הַשִּׂמְחָה, דָּא סִיהֲרָא, דְּאִתְרְבִיאַת בִּנְהוֹרָא בְּגִינֵיהוֹן דְּיִשְׂרָאֵל. אוּמוֹת הָעוֹלָם לְשִׁמְשָׁא, וְיִשְׂרָאֵל לְסִיהֲרָא, הֵי מִנַּיְיהוּ עָדִיף. וַדַּאי סִיהֲרָא לְעֵילָּא, וְשִׁמְשָׁא דְּאוּמוֹת הָעוֹלָם, תְּחוֹת הַאי סִיהֲרָא הוּא, וְהַהוּא שִׁמְשָׁא מֵהַאי סִיהֲרָא נָהִיר. חָמֵי מַה בֵּין יִשְׂרָאֵל, לְהוֹ. יִשְׂרָאֵל אֲחִידוּ בְּסִיהֲרָא, וְאִשְׁתַּלְשְׁלוּ בְּשִׁמְשָׁא עִלָּאָה, וְאִתְאַחֲדוּ בַּאֲתַר דְּנָהִירָא מְשַׁמְּשָׁא עִלָּאָה, וּמִתְדַּבְּקָן בֵּיהּ, דִּכְתִיב וְאַתֶּם הַדְּבֵקִים בַּיְיָ׳ אֱלֹהֵיכֶם חַיִּים כֻּלְּכֶם הַיּוֹם.

566. This accords with Rabbi Elazar's discourse upon the verse: "You have multiplied the nation, and increased its joy" (Yeshayah 9:2). The "nation" is Yisrael, of whom it says, "For what nation is there so great" (Devarim 4:7) and "a single nation on the earth" (I Divrei Hayamim 17:21). "Its" means 'for it', "increased its joy" of the moon, which light grew for Yisrael's sake. The nations of the world RECKON TIMES BY THE CYCLE OF the sun and Yisrael BY THE CYCLE OF the moon. HE ASKS: Which one is superior, THE RECKONING BY THE SUN OR BY THE MOON? HE REPLIES: Surely the moon is above, and the sun of the peoples of the world is underneath this moon. That sun RECEIVES LIGHT from the moon and illuminates. See the difference between Yisrael and THE NATIONS OF THE WORLD: The children of Yisrael are attached to the moon and linked to the Supernal Sun. They are united with the place which shines by the Supernal Sun and cleave to it, as it is written: "But you that did cleave unto Hashem your Elohim are alive every one of you this day" (Devarim 4:4).

59. "Judah you are he whom your brethren shall praise"

A Synopsis

Rabbi Shimon explains that the kingship was given to Judah, since he is the fourth leg of the supernal Throne and the Chariot to the attribute of Malchut. Rabbi Shimon proceeds by discussing the meaning of the verse, "The King's daughter is all glorious within." This, we learn, signifies that the Female Principle within Atzilut is clothed by and joined with Gvurah. The discourse then turns to address the verse, "So He drove out the man" This refers to Adam, who by his sin, brought death upon himself and the entire world, and drove the Female Principle out of the Garden of Eden. We learn that fiery flames guard the way to the Tree of Life, the Female Principle, which rests on the angels Metatron and Sandalfon. We also learn that after she was driven out, the Female Principle was flawed until she was rectified – first by Noah, and then by Abraham. She stood in wholeness by Abraham and his sons, and Judah cleaved to her and became stronger in his kingship because of this. Indeed, the verse, "The sons of your father shall bow down before you," signifies that all the tribes shall bow down to Judah. We also learn that Judah, referred to as a "lion," escaped the Angel of Death. The mighty Shechinah is also compared to a lion and a lioness because of her strength and because she crouches to await her prey, the idolatrous nations. Finally, we are told that the verse, "The staff shall not depart from Judah," indicates that the Shechinah shall rise up in exile.

The Relevance of this Passage

An abundance of Light radiates throughout this complex passage of Zohar. This Light helps correct the original sin of Adam, which in turn, assists in weakening the grip of the Angel of Death over mankind. Our souls are strengthened by the Light of Noah, Abraham and Judah, which helps us correct our owns transgressions and cleanse us of negativity, which also helps correct the original sin of Adam.

567. יְהוּדָה אַתָּה וגו'. ר' שִׁמְעוֹן אָמַר, מַלְכוּ לִיהוּדָה אִתְקַיַּים, וְהַיְינוּ דְּאַמְרִינָן, מַאי דִּכְתִיב, הַפַּעַם אוֹדֶה אֶת ה', בְּגִין דְּאִיהוּ רְבִיעָאָה, אוֹדֶה אֶת ה', בְּגִין דְּאִיהוּ רַגְלָא רְבִיעָאָה לְכָרְסְיָא. יה"ו, דָּא רְשִׁימָא דִּשְׁמָא עִלָּאָה, וּבַמֶּה אִשְׁתְּלִים, בְּה"א, וְהַיְינוּ ה"א בַּתְרָאָה דִּשְׁמָא קַדִּישָׁא, שְׁמָא קַדִּישָׁא שְׁלִים בְּאַתְווֹי, וְקֶשֶׁר דְּאָחִיד לוֹן, עַל דָּא יוֹדוּךָ אַחֶיךָ, דְּמַלְכוּ לָךְ אִתְחֲזֵיָא לְאִתְקַיְּימָא וַדַּאי. וִיהוּדָה עַד רַד עִם אֵל

וְעִם קְדוֹשִׁים נֶאֱמָן, מַאן קְדוֹשִׁים, אִלֵּין קְדוֹשִׁים עֶלְיוֹנִין, דְּכֻלְּהוּ אוֹדָן לְגַבֵּיהּ, וְשַׁוְיוּהָ נֶאֱמָן, בְּגִין כָּךְ הוּא קַדְמָאָה בְּכוֹלָּא, הוּא מַלְכָּא עַל כֹּלָּא.

567. "Judah, you are..." (Beresheet 49:8): Rabbi Shimon said: The kingship was assigned to Judah, as we said in relation to the words, "Now will I praise Hashem" (Beresheet 29:35), because he was the fourth. "I will praise Hashem," since He is the fourth leg of the throne. *Yud-Hei-Vav* of Yud Hei Vav Hei, WHICH ARE CHESED, GVURAH AND TIFERET, are the impress of the Supernal Name ZEIR ANPIN, which is completed by *Hei*, MALCHUT, the last *Hei* of the Holy Name, THROUGH WHICH the Holy Name is made whole with its letters. AND IT IS the knot which binds THE LETTERS OF THE HOLY NAME. Therefore "your brethren shall praise" (Beresheet 49:8) you, for thanks to you the kingship, Malchut, is able to exist, YOU BEING THE CHARIOT TO THE ATTRIBUTE OF MALCHUT. It is written, "Judah still rules with El, and is faithful with Holy Ones" (Hoshea 12:1). HE ASKS: Who are these Holy Ones? AND ANSWERS, They are the supernal Holy Ones, THE HOLY SFIROT CHESED, GVURAH AND TIFERET, who all acknowledged him and made him faithful, TO WIT, BY GIVING HIM ALL THAT IS IN THEM. He is therefore first in everything and king over all.

568. ר"ש פְּתַח וַאֲמַר, כָּל כְּבוּדָּה בַת מֶלֶךְ פְּנִימָה. כָּל כְּבוּדָּה, דָּא כנ"י, כְּבוּדָּה: בְּגִין דְּאִיהוּ כָבוֹד, דָּא עַל דָּא, דָּא דָּכָר, וְדָא נוּקְבָא, וְאִתְקְרֵי כְּבוּדָּה. בַּת מֶלֶךְ, הַיְינוּ בַּת שֶׁבַע, בַּת קוֹל דְּאִיהוּ קוֹל גָּדוֹל, וְהַאי מֶלֶךְ עִלָּאָה הוּא. פְּנִימָה: בְּגִין דְּאִית מֶלֶךְ דְּלָאו אִיהוּ לְגוֹ כַּוָּותֵיהּ, וְהַאי כְּבוּדָּה בַּת מֶלֶךְ.

568. Rabbi Shimon opened the discussion saying: "The king's daughter is all glorious (Heb. *kevudah*) within" (Tehilim 45:14). "Kevudah" refers to the Congregation of Yisrael, NAMELY THE NUKVA, CALLED 'KEVUDAH', because He, ZEIR ANPIN, IS CALLED 'kavod' (Eng. 'glory'); the one upon the other, AS BOTH ARE ONE; the one, ZEIR ANPIN, a male, IS CALLED 'KAVOD,' and the other, MALCHUT, a female, is called 'kevudah,' WITH THE ADDITIONAL *HEI* OF THE FEMININE. The king's daughter is Bathsheba (lit. 'daughter of seven'), WHICH IS THE NUKVA, AND ALSO an echo (lit. 'a voice's daughter'), while he is called a great voice, being the supernal King,

ZEIR ANPIN, WHILE THE NUKVA IS CALLED THE DAUGHTER OF A VOICE. It is "within" as there is a king, NAMELY MALCHUT, which is not as far within as him, FOR SOMETIMES MALCHUT IS CLOTHED IN BRIYAH, while the king's daughter is all glorious within IN ATZILUT.

569. מִמִּשְׁבְּצוֹת זָהָב לְבוּשָׁה, בְּגִין דְּאִתְלַבְּשַׁת וְאִתְאַחֲדַת בִּגְבוּרְתָּא עִלָּאָה, וְהַאי, אוֹף נָמֵי מֶלֶךְ אִקְרֵי, וּבְגִינָהּ קַיְימָא אַרְעָא, אֵימָתַי, בְּשַׁעְתָּא דְּאִתְאַחֲדַת בְּמִשְׁפָּט, כְּד"א מֶלֶךְ בַּמִּשְׁפָּט יַעֲמִיד אָרֶץ. וְדָא קָרֵינָן מַלְכוּ דִּשְׁמַיָא, וִיהוּדָה אִתְאֲחִיד בָּהּ, וְיָרֵית מַלְכוּתָא דִּבְאַרְעָא.

569. "Her clothing is inwrought with gold" (Ibid.), since she is clothed and joined by the supernal Gvurah, NAMELY THE LEFT SIDE OF IMA, WHO IS CALLED GOLD, ACCORDING TO THE SECRET OF THE VERSE, "GOLD COMES OUT OF THE NORTH" (IYOV 37:22). IMA is also called a king, and on her account the land endures, WHICH IS MALCHUT. When is MALCHUT established? When coupled with justice, WHICH IS ZEIR ANPIN, as it says, "The king by justice establishes the land" (Mishlei 29:4), WHICH IS MALCHUT. We call it the kingdom of heaven. Judah was united with it, and he therefore inherited the kingdom on earth.

570. ר' יְהוּדָה וְר' יִצְחָק הֲווֹ קָאַזְלֵי בְּאָרְחָא. אָמַר ר' יִצְחָק, נִפְתַּח בְּמִלֵּי דְאוֹרַיְיתָא וְנֵיזִיל. פָּתַח ר' יִצְחָק וְאָמַר, וַיְגָרֶשׁ אֶת הָאָדָם וַיַּשְׁכֵּן מִקֶּדֶם לְג"ע וגו'. הַאי קְרָא אוֹקְמוּהָ חַבְרַיָיא. אֲבָל וַיְגָרֶשׁ, כְּב"נ דִּגְרֵישׁ לְאַנְתְּתֵיהּ, אֶת הָאָדָם דַּיְיקָא.

570. Rabbi Yehuda and Rabbi Yitzchak were walking along the way. Rabbi Yitzchak said: Let us discourse on the words of the Torah as we go. Rabbi Yitzchak opened the discussion saying: "So He drove out the man; and He placed at the east of the Garden of Eden..." (Beresheet 3:24). This verse has been expounded upon by the friends. Yet "He drove" has the same meaning of a man divorcing his wife, TO WIT, THE HOLY ONE, BLESSED BE HE, DIVORCING THE NUKVA. "The man" is correct, AS THE NUKVA IS CALLED *ET* (ENG. 'THE').

571. תָּא חֲזֵי, רָזָא דְמִלָּה, אָדָם בַּמֶּה דְּחָטָא אִתְפַּס, וְגָרֵים מוֹתָא לֵיהּ וּלְכָל עָלְמָא, וְגָרֵים לְהַהוּא אִילָנָא דְּחָטָא בֵּיהּ, תֵּירוּכִין, לְאִתָּרְכָא

בֵּיהּ, וּלְאִתְתָּרְכָא בִּבְנוֹי לְעָלְמִין. הה"ד וַיְגָרֶשׁ אֶת הָאָדָם, אֶת דַּיְיקָא,
כְּמָה דִּכְתִיב וָאֶרְאֶה אֶת ה', אוֹף הָכֵי אֶת הָאָדָם.

571. Come and see the secret meaning of this matter. Adam was caught for his sin and brought death upon himself and upon the world, and caused the tree, by which he sinned, NAMELY THE NUKVA, to be driven out on his account, and be driven because of his descendants' SINS forever. Hence it says, "So He drove out the man," Et (the) having a precise meaning, such as in, "I saw (Heb. *et*) Hashem" (Yeshayah 6:1), WHICH MEANS THE NUKVA. Here too, "the man" REFERS TO THE NUKVA.

572. וַיַּשְׁכֵּן מִקֶּדֶם לְג"ע וגו', הַאי לְתַתָּא. וּכְמָה דִּכְרוּבִים לְעֵילָא, אִית
כְּרוּבִים לְתַתָּא, וְהַאי אִילָנָא אַשְׁרֵי עֲלַיְיהוּ. וְאֶת לַהַט הַחֶרֶב
הַמִּתְהַפֶּכֶת, אִינוּן טָפְסֵי דְּשַׁלְהוֹבֵי דְּאֶשָׁא, מֵהַהוּא חַרְבָּא דְּמִתְלַהֲטָא.
הַמִּתְהַפֶּכֶת, דָּא הַאי חַרְבָּא, דְּיָנְקָא בִּתְרֵין סִטְרִין, וְאִתְהַפְּכָא מִסְּטְרָא
דָּא לְסִטְרָא אָחֳרָא. ד"א הַמִּתְהַפֶּכֶת, דָּא לַהַט אִינוּן טָפְסֵי דְּשַׁלְהוֹבָא
דְּקָאֲמָרָן, דְּמִתְהַפְּכָן, לְזִמְנִין גּוּבְרִין וּלְזִמְנִין נָשִׁין וּמִתְהַפְּכָן
מְדוּכְתַּיְיהוּ לְכֹלָּא, וְכָל דָּא, לִשְׁמוֹר אֶת דֶּרֶךְ עֵץ הַחַיִּים. מַאן דֶּרֶךְ.
כְּד"א הַנּוֹתֵן בַּיָם דָּרֶךְ.

572. "And He placed at the east of the Garden of Eden," This is below ATZILUT. As there are Cherubs above IN ATZILUT, A MALE AND A FEMALE, so there are Cherubs below ATZILUT, THE ANGELS METATRON AND SANDALFON. The tree, WHICH IS THE NUKVA CALLED THE TREE OF KNOWLEDGE OF GOOD AND EVIL, rests upon them, and "the bright blade of a revolving sword" (Beresheet 3:24) is the shapes of fiery flames come out from the brightness of the sword, WHICH GUARD THE WAY TO THE TREE OF LIFE, NOT THE BRIGHT BLADE OF THE SWORD ITSELF. "Revolving" refers to the sword, which sucks from the two sides, RIGHT AND LEFT, and revolves now to this side, now to the other. According to another explanation, "revolving" alludes to the shapes of the fiery flames which are revolving, like we said. They revolve and change forms, now to men, now to women. They revolve in their places and change forms, in order to guard the way to the Tree of Life. What is a way? As in "who makes a way in the sea" (Yeshayah 43:16), IT REFERS TO YESOD OF THE NUKVA.

573. אֲמַר ר' יְהוּדָה שַׁפִּיר, וְהָכֵי הוּא וַדַּאי, דְּגָרֵים אָדָם לְהַהוּא
אִילָנָא דְּחָטָא בֵּיה לְאִתְּרָכָא, וַאֲפִילוּ שְׁאָר בְּנֵי עָלְמָא נָמֵי, כְּד"א
וּבְפִשְׁעֵיכֶם שֻׁלְחָה אִמְּכֶם, אֲבָל שַׁפִּיר קָאֲמָרְתְּ, דְּהָא מְדוּכְתֵּיה מַשְׁמַע,
דִּכְתִיב וַיְגָרֶשׁ אֶת הָאָדָם, בְּגִין דְּדָא שְׁלִימוּ דְּאָדָם הוּא.

573. Rabbi Yehuda said: Well said, and assuredly correct. Adam caused that
tree, in regard to which he sinned, WHICH IS THE NUKVA, to be driven out.
So did other men, WHICH CAUSE IT TO BE DRIVEN OUT THROUGH THEIR
SINS, as said in the verse, "And for your transgressions was your mother put
away" (Yeshayah 50:1). And yet it is true to say that it refers to himself, as
it is written, "He drove out the man," ET (ENG. 'THE') BEING THE NUKVA,
man's perfection. BY DRIVING HER OUT, HE LOST HIS WHOLENESS.

574. וּמֵהַהוּא יוֹמָא אִתְפְּגֵים סִיהֲרָא, עַד דְּאָתָא נֹחַ וְעָאל בְּתֵיבוּתָא.
אָתוּ חַיָּיבַיָּא וְאִתְפְּגֵים. עַד דְּאָתָא אַבְרָהָם, וְקָיְימָא בִּשְׁלִימוּ דְּיַעֲקֹב
וּבְנוֹי. וְאָתָא יְהוּדָה וְאָחֵיד בֵּיה, וְאִתְּקַף בְּמַלְכוּתָא, וְאַחְסֵין לֵיה
אַחְסָנַת עָלְמִין, הוּא וְכָל בְּנוֹי בַּתְרוֹי, הה"ד יְהוּדָה אַתָּה יוֹדוּךְ אַחֶיךָ.
וַדַּאי בְּשַׁעְתָּא דְּקָיְימוּ יִשְׂרָאֵל עַל יַמָּא, דְּכֻלְּהוּ אוֹדוּ לֵיה, וְנָחֲתוּ
אֲבַתְרֵיה בְּיַמָּא.

574. From the day SHE WAS DRIVEN OUT, the moon, THE NUKVA, became
flawed, until Noah entered the ark. Then came evil men, and she was flawed
again, until Abraham came AND RECTIFIED HER. She stood in wholeness
by Jacob and his sons, and Judah came, held on to her and became stronger
through the kingship, and inherited it for ever, for him and his sons after
him. Hence the verse: "Judah you are whom your brethren shall praise"
(Beresheet 49:8). Indeed, when Yisrael stood by the sea AND THE TRIBE OF
JUDAH WERE THE FIRST TO ENTER IT they all praised him and went into
the sea after him.

575. יָדְךָ בְּעֹרֶף אוֹיְבֶיךָ, כְּד"א יְהוּדָה יַעֲלֶה. יִשְׁתַּחֲווּ לְךָ בְּנֵי אָבִיךָ,
כְּלָלָא דְּכָל אִינוּן שְׁאָר שִׁבְטִין, בְּגִין דָּא בְּנֵי אָבִיךָ, וְלָא בְּנֵי אִמְּךָ, בְּנֵי
אָבִיךָ, הָא כֻּלְּהוּ שְׁאָר שִׁבְטִין, דְּאַף עַל גַּב דְּאִתְפְּלֵיג לִתְרֵין מַלְכְּוָון,

כַּד הֲווֹ סָלְקִין לִירוּשָׁלַם, הֲווֹ סְגִידִין וְכָרְעָן לְמַלְכָּא דְּבִירוּשָׁלַם, בְּגִין
דְּמַלְכוּתָא דִּירוּשָׁלַם, מִמַּלְכוּתָא קַדִּישָׁא מִנֵּיהּ הֲוָה.

575. "Your hand shall be on the neck of your enemies" (Ibid.) as it says,
"Judah shall go up" (Shoftim 1:2) TO WAR. "The sons of your father shall
bow down before you" (Beresheet 49:8) includes all the tribes, and hence
the words: "The sons of your father" instead of 'your mother' as the sons of
your father are the other tribes. And though Yisrael were divided into two
kingdoms, yet when they went up to Jerusalem, they would kneel and bow
to the king in Jerusalem, since the kingdom of Jerusalem WHICH DREW
from the holy kingdom, THE NUKVA, was from JUDAH.

576. יִשְׁתַּחֲווּ לָךְ, וְלָא כְּתִיב וְיִשְׁתַּחֲווּ, דְּאִי כְּתִיב וְיִשְׁתַּחֲווּ, לְאוֹסְפָא
לִשְׁאָר עַמִּין, וְיִשְׁתַּחֲווּ לָא כְּתִיב, אֶלָּא בְּזִמְנָא דְּיֵיתֵי מַלְכָּא מְשִׁיחָא,
דִּכְתִיב שָׂרִים וְיִשְׁתַּחֲווּ, הַשְׁתָּא דְּאָמַר יִשְׁתַּחֲווּ, לְאַחֲזָאָה דְּיִשְׂרָאֵל
כֻּלְּהוּ בִּלְחוֹדַיְיהוּ, כֻּלְּהוּ יִפְלְחוּן לְרֵישָׁא דְּגוֹלָה, לְרֹאשׁ דְּבָבֶל, וְלָא
שְׁאָר עַמִּין.

576. "Shall bow down before you": It does not say, 'And shall bow', which
would include other nations, AND MEAN THAT ALL THE NATIONS OF THE
WORLD WILL BOW DOWN TO HIM. It does not say 'And shall bow' save at
the time of Messiah, WHEN it is written: "Princes also shall prostrate
themselves" (Yeshayah 49:7). For now, he ONLY said "shall bow" to show
that Yisrael alone shall bow down to the exilarch in Babylon, and no other
nation.

577. גּוּר אַרְיֵה יְהוּדָה, בְּקַדְמֵיתָא גּוּר, וּלְבָתַר אַרְיֵה, וְרָזָא דְמִלָּה
בְּקַדְמֵיתָא נַעַר, וּלְבָתַר אִישׁ, יְיָ' אִישׁ מִלְחָמָה. מִטֶּרֶף בְּנִי עָלִיתָ, מַאי
מִטֶּרֶף. לְאַכְלְלָא מַלְאַךְ הַמָּוֶת, דְּאִיהוּ קַיְימָא עַל טֶרֶף, לְשֵׁיצָאָה בְּנֵי
עָלְמָא, וְלָא מְשֵׁזִיב, כְּד"א וְטָרַף וְאֵין מַצִּיל. וּמֵהַהוּא טֶרֶף אִסְתַּלְּקַת
שְׁכִינְתָּא.

577. "Judah is a lion's whelp" (Beresheet 49:9). First he was a whelp and
then a lion. HENCE THE REPETITION: A WHELP AND A LION. The secret of
the matter is that first, WHEN ZEIR ANPIN IS IN MOCHIN OF SMALLNESS,

IT IS CALLED a youth, and later, WHEN IN MOCHIN OF GREATNESS, IT IS
CALLED a man, AS IT IS WRITTEN: "Hashem is a man of war" (Shemot
15:3). JUDAH TOO, WHEN IN MOCHIN OF SMALLNESS, IS CALLED A
WHELP, AND WHEN IN MOCHIN OF GREATNESS, HE IS CALLED A LION.
"From the prey, my son, you are gone up" (Beresheet 49:9). HE ASKS:
What prey is this? It includes the Angel of Death, who stands by its prey to
exterminate the world, and none can save from it, as in "and tears in pieces,
and none can deliver" (Michah 5:7). From that prey, the Shechinah was
gone up. THE WORDS: "FROM THE PREY, MY SON, YOU ARE GONE UP"
MEAN THAT JUDAH ESCAPED THE ANGEL OF DEATH, WHICH IS THE
SATAN, THE EVIL INCLINATION, INSTEAD OF STUMBLING BY IT.

578. כָּרַע: בְּגָלוּתָא דְּבָבֶל. רָבַץ: בְּגָלוּתָא דֶאֱדוֹם. כְּאַרְיֵה: דְּאִיהוּ
תַּקִּיפָא. וּכְלָבִיא: דְּאִיהוּ תַּקִּיפָא יַתִּיר, כָּךְ יִשְׂרָאֵל תַּקִּיפִין אִינוּן דִּבְנֵי
עָלְמָא עעכו"ם, מְפַתִּין וְדָחֲקִין לוֹן, וְאִינוּן קָיְימֵי בְּדָתֵיהוֹן
וּבְנִימוּסֵיהוֹן כְּאַרְיֵה וּכְלָבִיא.

578. "He stooped down" (Beresheet 49:9) in the exile in Babylon "and he
couched" (Ibid.) in the exile of Edom "as a lion" which is mighty "and as a
lioness" which is mightier than a lion. So are Yisrael mighty, for though the
idolatrous people of the world entice and oppress them, they adhere to their
laws and customs like a lion and a lioness.

579. כָּךְ שְׁכִינְתָּא, דְּאע"ג דִּכְתִיב, נָפְלָה לֹא תוֹסִיף קוּם בְּתוּלַת
יִשְׂרָאֵל, הִיא תַּקִּיפָא כְּאַרְיֵה וּכְלָבִיא בְּהַאי נְפִילָה. מַה אַרְיֵה וְלָבִיא
לָא נָפְלִין, אֶלָּא בְּגִין לְמִטְרַף טַרְפָּא, וּלְשַׁלְטָאָה, דְּהָא מֵרַחֵיק אָרַח
טַרְפֵּיה, וּמִשַׁעְתָּא דְּאָרַח נָפַל, וְלָא קָם עַד דְּדָלִיג עַל טַרְפֵּיה וְאָכֵיל
לָהּ, כָּךְ שְׁכִינְתָּא לָא נָפְלָה אֶלָּא כְּאַרְיֵה וּכְלָבִיא, בְּגִין לְנַקְמָא מֵעַמִּין
עעכו"ם, וּלְדַלְגָא עֲלַיְיהוּ, כְּמָא דְאַתְּ אָמֵר צוֹעֶה בְּרוֹב כֹּחוֹ.

579. The Shechinah also is as strong as a lion and a lioness when She thus
falls, though it is written, "The virgin of Yisrael is fallen; she shall no more
rise" (Amos 5:2). As a lion and a lioness only crouch to hunt their prey, and
when they smell it from afar they fall; TO WIT, THEY CROUCH ON THE
GROUND TO PREPARE TO JUMP ON THE PREY and do not rise until they

jump upon it and eat it. The Shechinah also does not fall but as a lion and a lioness, in order to revenge the idolatrous nations, leap upon them, as it says "striding in the greatness of his strength" (Yeshayah 63:1).

580. מִי יְקִימֶנּוּ, הוּא לָא יָקוּם לְנַקְמָא מִנַּיְיהוּ נוּקְמָא זְעֵירָא, אֶלָּא מִי יְקִימֶנּוּ. מִי כְּדְ"א, מִי יִרְפָּא לָךְ, וְהוּא אִיהוּ עַלְמָא עִלָּאָה, דְּבֵיהּ שָׁלְטָנוּתָא לְאִתְתַּקְפָא לְכֹלָּא. וּכְתִיב, מִבֶּטֶן מִי יָצָא הַקָּרַח וְאוֹקְמוּהָ.

580. "Who shall rouse him up?" (Beresheet 49:9). He shall not rise to take petty vengeance upon them, but who shall rouse him, 'who' being, as in the verse "who can heal you" (Eichah 2:13). It is the supernal world, NAMELY BINAH CALLED WHO, which has dominion over all. It is written "out of whose womb (lit. 'the womb of who') came the ice?" (Iyov 38:29), which has been explained THAT THROUGH THE JUDGMENT CALLED ICE, IT SUBDUES ALL THE KLIPOT.

581. לֹא יָסוּר שֵׁבֶט מִיהוּדָה וגו', אוֹקְמוּהָ חַבְרַיָּא, אֲבָל עַד כִּי יָבֹא שִׁיל"ה בְּה"א, בְּגִין דְּשְׁאַר בּוֹ', לְאַחֲזָאָה הָכָא רָזָא דִשְׁמָא קַדִּישָׁא י"ה, בְּאֲתַר אָחֳרָא שִׁילוּ בְּלָא ה', בְּאֲתַר אָחֳרָא שִׁלֹה בְּלָא י', וְהָכָא שִׁיל"ה בְּיוּ"ד ה"א, רָזָא דִשְׁמָא קַדִּישָׁא עִלָּאָה, דִּשְׁכִינְתָּא תָּקוּם בִּשְׁמָא דִּי"ה וְאִיהוּ רָזָא מִ"י, כִּדְקָאֲמָרִינָן.

581. "The staff shall not depart from Judah" (Beresheet 49:10) has been explained by the friends, but "until Shiloh come" (Ibid.) is spelled with *Hei*, while in other PLACES IT IS SPELLED SHILO with *Vav*. This is an indication of the secret of the Holy Name *Yud-Hei*, for in other places it is spelled Shilo without *Hei*, or without *Yud*. Here it is spelled Shiloh with both *Yud* and *Hei*, which is the secret of the supernal Holy Name, and means that the Shechinah shall rise FROM HER FALL IN THE EXILE through this name of *Yud-Hei*, which, as we said, is the mystery of 'who', FOR YAH IS THE NAME OF BINAH, ALSO NAMED 'WHO'.

60. "Binding his foal to the vine," part one

A Synopsis

Here we learn that God protects and preserves the deserving in this world and in the next. The soul of he who does not have merit, however, will be dragged to Gehenom by legions of demons. This soul is then delivered to the angel Dumah, who takes it to be locked behind the seven gates of fire. Every Shabbat, the souls in Gehenom are allowed to go to the outer gates, where they meet with other souls that convene there but do not enter Gehenom. It is said that the evil are sentenced to the heat of the burning fire and then the intense cold of snow. Though they first feel relief when they enter the snow, they soon moan again, realizing they are still in Gehenom. The rabbis then explain that the title verse signifies the children of Yisrael and the Messiah are destined to conquer the idolatrous nations. The Messiah is called "poor', we're told, because He is drawn from the moon, Malchut, who has no illumination of her own. Proceeding on from this, the discussion turns to the subject of dreams and prophecy. Dreams are of a much lower grade than prophecy and are accessible to all, even the wicked. We learn that Joseph was able to correctly interpret his dream about the Pharaoh's cup of poison. Indeed, we are told that through the power of the vine, the Female Principle, the heathen nations were subjugated and their force subdued. The discourse then remarks upon the double precepts practiced by the Yisraelites so that they may avoid being sent to Gehenom of snow. Following an explanation of the verse, "She is not afraid of the snow of her household", the section concludes when the rabbis meet a young boy who travels without his former companion.

The Relevance of this Passage

The cleansing power of this passage purifies our souls, helping us merit a place in the World to Come without having to pass through the gates of Gehenom. The arrival of the Messiah is also quickened, and readers who peruse these verses with a pure heart, help to ensure that the appearance of the Messiah happens in a manner that is merciful for all mankind. In addition, we gain the ability to utilize our sleep and dream states in a fashion that will facilitate our spiritual development.

582. אֹסְרִי לַגֶּפֶן עִירֹה וְלַשֹּׂרֵקָה בְּנִי אֲתֹנוֹ וְגוֹ'. רִבִּי חִיָּיא פָּתַח, ה' יִשְׁמָרְךָ מִכָּל רָע יִשְׁמוֹר אֶת נַפְשֶׁךָ, כֵּיוָן דַּאֲמַר ה' יִשְׁמָרְךָ מִכָּל רָע, אֲמַאי יִשְׁמוֹר אֶת נַפְשֶׁךָ. אֶלָּא ה' יִשְׁמָרְךָ מִכָּל רָע, בְּהַאי עָלְמָא. יִשְׁמוֹר אֶת נַפְשֶׁךָ בְּהַהוּא עָלְמָא.

582. "Binding his foal to the vine, and his ass's colt to the choice vine" (Beresheet 49:11): Rabbi Chiya opened the discussion saying: "Hashem shall preserve you from all evil: He shall preserve your soul" (Tehilim 121:7). HE ASKS: After saying: "Hashem shall preserve you from all evil," why add "He shall preserve your soul"? HE ANSWERS: "Hashem shall preserve you from all evil" in this world and "shall preserve your soul" in the world of Truth.

583. שְׁמִירָה דְּהַאי עַלְמָא הוּא, לְמֶהֱוֵי נָטִיר ב״נ, מִכַּמָּה זְנִין בִּישִׁין מְקַטְרְגִין, דְּאַזְלִין לְקַטְרְגָא בְּנֵי נָשָׁא בְּעַלְמָא, וּלְאִתְדַּבְּקָא בְּהוּ. בְּהַהוּא עַלְמָא מַאי הוּא, כְּמָה דַאֲמָרָן, כַּד נָפֵיק ב״נ מֵהַאי עַלְמָא, אִי אִיהוּ זָכֵי, נִשְׁמָתָא דִּילֵיהּ סָלְקָא וְאִתְעַטְּרַת בְּאַתְרֵיהּ. וְאִי לָא, כַּמָּה חֲבִילִין טְרִיקִין אִזְדַּמְּנָן, לְאַנְגְּדָא לֵיהּ לַגֵּיהִנָּם, וּלְאִמְסְרָא לֵיהּ בִּידָא דְּדוּמָה, דְּאִתְמַסְּרָא לִמְמַנָּא עַל גֵּיהִנָּם, וּתְלֵיסַר אֶלֶף רִבּוֹא מְמַנָּן עִמֵּיהּ, וְכֻלְּהוּ אִזְדַּמְּנָן עַל נַפְשַׁיְיהוּ דְחַיָּיבַיָּא.

583. By the keeping in this world is meant that a man is protected from evil accusing demons, which go in the world to bring charges against people and cling to them. By the keeping in the world of Truth is meant that when a man passes away from this world, if he be meritorious, his soul ascends to be adorned in its place. But if he is not MERITORIOUS, several legions of demons appear before him and drag him into Gehenom, where he is delivered to the hands of Dumah, who hands him to the chief in charge over Gehenom. There are 13,000 chieftains with him, who all await the souls of the wicked.

584. תָּא חֲזֵי, שִׁבְעָה מְדוֹרִין אִית בֵּיהּ בַּגֵּיהִנָּם, וְשִׁבְעָה פִּתְחִין. וְנִשְׁמָתָא דְּחַיָּיבַיָּא עָאלַת, וְכַמָּה טְרִיקִין, טְהִירִין, נְטוּרֵי תַּרְעֵי, וַעֲלַיְיהוּ חַד מְמַנָּא בְּכָל תַּרְעָא וְתַרְעָא, וְנִשְׁמַתְהוֹן דְּחַיָּיבַיָּא אִתְמַסְרוּן לְאִינּוּן מְמַנָּן, עַל יְדָא דְּדוּמָה, כֵּיוָן דְּאִתְמַסְּרָן בִּידַיְיהוּ, סָתְמִין תַּרְעִין דְּאֶשָׁא דְּמַלַהֲטָא.

584. Come and see: There are seven chambers in Gehenom, and seven gates. The soul of the wicked enters THERE. There are several fiends, spirits and gate keepers, and one chief in charge over each gate. The souls of the wicked are delivered to these chiefs by Dumah. Once they are delivered, THEY close the gates of burning fire.

585. דְּהָא תַּרְעִין בָּתַר תַּרְעִין הֲווֹ, תַּרְעִין כֻּלְּהוּ פְּתִיחִין וּסְתִימִין, אִינוּן דִּלְבַר פְּתִיחִין, דִּלְגוֹ סְתִימִין. וּבְכָל שַׁבָּת וְשַׁבָּת כֻּלְּהוּ פְּתִיחִין, וְנָפְקִין חַיָּיבַיָּא עַד אִינוּן פִּתְחִין דִּלְבַר, וּפָגְעִין נִשְׁמָתִין אַחֲרָנִין, דְּמִתְעַכְּבִין בְּפִתְחִין דִּלְבַר. כַּד נָפַק שַׁבַּתָּא, כְּרוֹזָא קָאי בְּכָל פִּתְחָא וּפִתְחָא, וְאָמַר יָשׁוּבוּ רְשָׁעִים לִשְׁאוֹלָה וגו'. תָּא חֲזֵי, נִשְׁמָתִין דְּצַדִּיקַיָּיא, קוּדְשָׁא בְּרִיךְ הוּא נָטִיר לוֹן, דְּלָא יִתְמַסְּרוּן בִּידָא דְּדוּמָה, דְּהוּא מְמַנָּא, הה"ד, יִשְׁמֹר צֵאתְךָ וּבוֹאֶךָ וּכְתִיב יִשְׁמֹר אֶת נַפְשֶׁךָ.

585. There are double gates, which are opened and closed, the outer ones are open and the inner closed. Every Shabbat all of them are open. The wicked go out as far as the outer gates, where they meet other souls, which tarry there, BUT DO NOT ENTER GEHENOM. When Shabbat goes out, the herald comes out to each gate and says "The wicked shall return to Sheol" (Tehilim 9:18). Come and behold: the souls of the righteous are protected by the Holy One, blessed be He, from being delivered into the hands of the chieftain Dumah, as it is written: "Hashem shall preserve your going out and your coming in" (Tehilim 121:8) and "He shall preserve your soul."

586. אֹסְרִי לַגֶּפֶן עִירֹה. מַאי גֶּפֶן, דָּא כְּנֶסֶת יִשְׂרָאֵל, כד"א גֶּפֶן מִמִּצְרַיִם תַּסִּיעַ. וּכְתִיב אֶשְׁתְּךָ כְּגֶפֶן פּוֹרִיָּה, אֶשְׁתְּךָ, כְּהַאי גֶפֶן קַדִּישָׁא. א"ר יוֹסֵי, הַאי גֶפֶן, דִּמְבָרְכִינָן בֵּיהּ בּוֹרֵא פְּרִי הַגָּפֶן. בּוֹרֵא, הַיְינוּ דִּכְתִיב, עֵץ עוֹשֶׂה פְּרִי. פְּרִי הַגָּפֶן, דָּא עֵץ פְּרִי. עוֹשֶׂה פְּרִי, דְּכַר, עֵץ פְּרִי דָּא נוּקְבָא. בְּגִינֵי כָּךְ, בּוֹרֵא פְּרִי הַגָּפֶן דָּא דְּכַר וְנוּקְבָא כַּחֲדָא.

586. "Binding his foal to the vine": HE ASKS: What is a vine? HE SAYS, It is the Congregation of Yisrael, THE NUKVA, as it says, "You have brought a vine out of Egypt" (Tehilim 80:9) and "Your wife shall be like a fruitful vine" (Ibid. 128:3). Your wife is as the holy vine, THE SUPERNAL NUKVA. Rabbi Yosi said about the vine over which we say the benediction – 'Who created the fruit of the vine (Heb. *bore peri hagefen*)' – 'created' means "a tree yielding fruit" (Beresheet 1:12). 'The fruit of the vine' is a fruit tree,

'yielding fruit' is the male, NAMELY ZEIR ANPIN, and the 'fruit tree' is a female, NAMELY THE NUKVA OF ZEIR ANPIN. Therefore, "who created the fruit of the vine" includes a male and a female together, MALE AND FEMALE.

587. אָסְרִי לַגֶּפֶן עִירֹה, דָּא מַלְכָּא מְשִׁיחָא, דְּזַמִּין לְשַׁלְטָאָה עַל כָּל חֵילֵי עֲמַמְיָא, חֵילִין דִּי מְמַנָּן עַל עַמִּין עעכו״ם, וְאִינּוּן תּוּקְפָּא דִלְהוֹן לְאִתְתַּקְפָא, וְזַמִּין מַלְכָּא מְשִׁיחָא לְאִתְגַּבְּרָא עֲלַיְיהוּ.

587. "Binding his foal to the vine": This is King Messiah, who will rule over the nations' armies, and over the hosts in charge of the idolatrous nations who derive their strength from them. King Messiah is destined to overpower them.

588. בְּגִין דְּהַאי גֶּפֶן, שַׁלִּיט עַל כָּל אִלֵּין כִּתְרִין תַּתָּאִין, דְּשַׁלְטֵי בְּהוֹ עֲמַמְיָא עעכו״ם, הַאי נָצַח לְעֵילָא. יִשְׂרָאֵל, דְּאִינּוּן שֹׂרֵקָה, יְשֵׁיצוּן וִינַצְחוּן חֵילִין אָחֳרָנִין לְתַתָּא, וְעַל כֻּלְּהוּ יִתְגַּבַּר מַלְכָּא מְשִׁיחָא. הה״ד עָנִי וְרוֹכֵב עַל חֲמוֹר וְעַל עַיִר. עַיִר וַחֲמוֹר תְּרֵין כִּתְרִין אִינּוּן, דְּשַׁלְטֵי בְּהוֹ עֲמַמְיָא עעכו״ם, וְאִינּוּן מִסְטַר שְׂמָאלָא סִטְרָא דְּחוֹל.

588. Because this vine, THE NUKVA, rules over the lower crowns, through which the idolatrous nations reign, and is victorious above, the children of Yisrael, who are called "the choice vine," will conquer and annihilate the other legions below, and King Messiah will overpower all of them. It is written "poor and riding upon an donkey, and upon a colt" (Zecharyah 9:9). The donkey and the colt are two crowns, through which the idolatrous nations rule. They are of the left side, the side of profanity. AND KING MESSIAH OVERCOMES THEM.

589. וּמַה דַּאֲמַר עָנִי, וְכִי מַלְכָּא מְשִׁיחָא עָנִי אִקְרֵי. אֶלָּא הָכֵי אֲמַר ר״ש, בְּגִין דְּלֵית לֵיהּ מִדִּילֵיהּ וְקָרִינָן לֵיהּ מֶלֶךְ הַמָּשִׁיחַ. דָּא הוּא סִיהֲרָא קַדִּישָׁא לְעֵילָא, דְּלֵית לָהּ נְהוֹרָא אֶלָּא מִשִׁמְשָׁא.

589. HE ASKS: Why DOES SCRIPTURE SAY ABOUT KING MESSIAH THAT he is poor? Can King Messiah be called poor? HE ANSWERS: Rabbi

Shimon said it is so, because he has nothing of his own, SINCE IT IS THE NUKVA OF ZEIR ANPIN which is called King Messiah. But it is the holy moon above, THE NUKVA OF ZEIR ANPIN, which has no light of her own, save what she receives from the sun, ZEIR ANPIN. SHE IS THEREFORE CALLED POOR.

590. מַלְכָּא מְשִׁיחָא דָא, יִשְׁלוֹט בְּשָׁלְטָנֵיה, יִתְיַיחֵד בְּדוּכְתֵּיה, וּכְדֵין הֲוָה מַלְכֵּךְ יָבֹא לָךְ סְתָם. אִי לְתַתָּא עָנִי הוּא, דְּהָא בְּסִטְרָא דְסִיהֲרָא הוּא. אִי לְעֵילָא עָנִי, אַסְפַּקְלַרְיָא דְּלָא נָהֲרָא. לֶחֶם עֹנִי. וְעִם כָּל דָּא, רוֹכֵב עַל חֲמוֹר וְעַל עַיִר, תּוּקְפָא דְּעַמִּין דְּעעכו״ם, לְאַכַּפְיָיא תְּחוֹתֵיה, וְיִתְתַּקַּף קוּדְשָׁא בְּרִיךְ הוּא בְּדוּכְתֵּיה.

590. King Messiah, THE NUKVA, will have dominion and will be united in his place above. Then "behold, your king comes to you" (Zecharyah 9:9). It does not say what king, SINCE HE INCLUDES THE NUKVA ABOVE AND KING MESSIAH BELOW. Below he is poor because he is of the aspect of the moon, WHICH IS THE SUPERNAL NUKVA. FOR MESSIAH BELOW IS DRAWN FROM THE NUKVA, AND IS THEREFORE CALLED POOR LIKE HER. Above She is poor, THE NUKVA HERSELF, because She is the mirror which does not shine OF HER OWN, BUT FROM ZEIR ANPIN, AND IS THEREFORE CALLED bread of poverty. With all that, MESSIAH IS "riding upon an donkey, and upon a colt," which are the stronghold of the idolatrous nation, to subdue them. The Holy One, blessed be He, THE NUKVA, will be strengthened in His place ABOVE, AS THE VERSE: "BEHOLD, YOUR KING COMES TO YOU" INCLUDES THEM BOTH.

591. כִּבֵּס בַּיַּיִן לְבוּשׁוֹ, כְּד״א מִי זֶה בָּא מֵאֱדוֹם חֲמוּץ בְּגָדִים מִבָּצְרָה, וּכְתִיב פּוּרָה דָרַכְתִּי לְבַדִּי וגו׳. כִּבֵּס בַּיַּיִן דָּא סְטַר גְּבוּרָה, דִּינָא קַשְׁיָא, לְמֶהֱוֵי עַל עֲמַמְיָא עעכו״ם, וּבְדַם עֲנָבִים סוּתֹה, דָּא אִילָנָא לְתַתָּא, בֵּי דִּינָא דְּאִקְרֵי עֲנָבִים, וְיֵינָא אִתְמְסַר בְּדַם עֲנָבִים, בְּגִין לְאִתְלַבְּשָׁא בְּתַרְוַוְיְיהוּ, לְתַבְּרָא תְּחוֹתֵיה כָּל שְׁאָר עַמִּין עעכו״ם וּמַלְכִין דְּעָלְמָא.

591. "He washes his garments in wine" (Beresheet 49:11) is like the verses: "Who is this that comes from Edom, with crimsoned garments from Botzra?" (Yeshayah 63:1) and "I have trodden the winepress alone" (Ibid.

3). The wine is the side of Gvurah OF ZEIR ANPIN, of strict Judgment upon the idolatrous nations. "And his clothes in the blood of grapes" (Beresheet 49:11) refers to the lower tree, THE NUKVA, the court of law called grapes. The wine is mingled with the blood of grapes in order to be clothed by both THE STRICT JUDGMENT OF ZEIR ANPIN AND THE JUDGMENT OF THE NUKVA, to crush beneath it all the other idolatrous nations and the kings of the world.

592. ר' יוֹסֵי פָּתַח וְאָמַר אֹסְרִי לַגֶּפֶן עִירה. וּכְתִיב וּבַגֶּפֶן שְׁלֹשָׁה שָׂרִיגִים וְהִיא כְפוֹרַחַת עָלְתָה נִצָּה. תָּא חֲזֵי, כַּמָּה אֲטִימִין אִינּוּן בְּנֵי נָשָׁא, דְּלָא יָדְעִין וְלָא מַשְׁגִּיחִין בִּיקָרָא דְמָארֵיהוֹן, וְלָא מִסְתַּכְּלֵי בְּמִלֵּי דְאוֹרַיְיתָא, וְלָא יָדְעֵי אָרְחַיְיהוּ בַּמֶּה יִתָּפְסוּן, דִּכְתִיב דֶּרֶךְ רְשָׁעִים כָּאֲפֵלָה לֹא יָדְעוּ בַּמֶּה יִכָּשֵׁלוּ.

592. Rabbi Yosi opened the discussion with the verses, "Binding his foal to the vine" and "And on the vine were three tendrils: and it was as though it budded, and its blossoms shot forth" (Beresheet 40:10). Come and see how stupid are people who neither know nor care for the glory of their Master, or regard the words of the Torah. They do not know their ways, or what they are caught in, as it is written: "The way of the wicked is like darkness: they know not at what they stumble" (Mishlei 4:19).

593. בְּזִמְנָא קַדְמָאָה הֲוַת נְבוּאָה שַׁרְיָא עֲלַיְיהוּ דִּבְנֵי נָשָׁא, וַהֲווֹ יָדְעִין וּמִסְתַּכְּלֵי לְמִנְדַע בִּיקָרָא עִלָּאָה. כֵּיוָן דְּפָסְקָא נְבוּאָה מִנַּיְיהוּ, הֲווֹ מִשְׁתַּמְּשֵׁי בְּבַת קוֹל. הַשְׁתָּא פָּסְקָא נְבוּאָה וּפָסְקָא בַּת קוֹל, וְלָא מִשְׁתַּמְּשֵׁי בְּנֵי נָשָׁא אֶלָּא בְּחֶלְמָא.

593. At the earliest time, prophecy rested upon people who would know and look to know the highest glory. When prophecy was stopped from them, they resorted to divine voices. Now both have ceased, and people resort only to dreams.

594. וְחֶלְמָא דַּרְגָּא תַּתָּאָה הוּא לְבַר, דְּהָא תָּנֵינָן חֶלְמָא אֶחָד מִשִּׁשִּׁים לִנְבוּאָה. מַאי טַעְמָא, בְּגִין דְּאַתְיָיא מִדַּרְגָּא שְׁתִיתָאָה לְתַתָּא, וְהָא אִתְּמַר. תָּא חֲזֵי, חֶלְמָא לְכֹלָּא אִתְחֲזֵי, בְּגִין דְּחֶלְמָא מִסְטַר שְׂמָאלָא

אַתְיָיא, וְנָחֵית בְּכַמָּה דַרְגִּין, וְאִתְחֲזֵי חֶלְמָא, אֲפִילוּ לְחַיָּיבַיָא. וַאֲפִילוּ לעכו״ם.

594. The dream is from the lower grade outside, for we learn that a dream is the sixtieth part of prophecy. Why? Because it comes from the sixth grade below, as was already explained, THAT IT IS FROM HOD OF THE NUKVA, WHICH IS THE SIXTH GRADE FROM NETZACH AND HOD OF ZEIR ANPIN WHERE PROPHECY IS. Come and behold: dream is accessible to all, since it is from the left side, HOD OF THE NUKVA, and descends many grades DOWN TO THE ANGEL GABRIEL, WHO DELIVERS THE DREAMS. A dream may be seen even by wicked men and even by gentiles.

595. בְּגִין דְּזִמְנִין, נָקְטִין חֶלְמָא וְשַׁמְעִין הַנֵּי זִינֵי בִישִׁין, וּמוֹדְעִין לִבְנֵי נָשָׁא, מִנַּיְיהוּ דְּחַיְיכָן בִּבְנֵי נָשָׁא, וּמוֹדִיעִין לוֹן מִלִּין כְּדִיבִין. וּלְזִמְנִין מִלִּין דִּקְשׁוֹט דְּשָׁמְעִין. וּלְזִמְנִין דְּאִינוּן שְׁלוּחִין לְחַיָּיבַיָא, וּמוֹדָעֵי לוֹן מִלִּין עִלָּאִין.

595. Sometimes evil angels receive and hear the dream, and inform men. Some of them mock at men and tell them false things, and sometimes true things which they heard. Sometimes, they are sent to the evil to tell them lofty matters.

596. הַאי רָשָׁע מַאי כְּתִיב בֵּיה, חָמָא חֶלְמָא דִּקְשׁוֹט, דִּכְתִיב וּבַגֶּפֶן שְׁלֹשָׁה שָׂרִיגִים. מַאי גֶּפֶן. דָּא כְּנֶסֶת יִשְׂרָאֵל, דִּכְתִיב הַבֵּט מִשָּׁמַיִם וּרְאֵה וּפְקוֹד גֶּפֶן זֹאת. מִשָּׁמַיִם, דְּהָא מֵאֲתַר דָּא אִתְרְמֵי, כְּד״א הִשְׁלִיךְ מִשָּׁמַיִם אֶרֶץ. וּפְקוֹד גֶּפֶן זֹאת, גֶּפֶן דְּהִיא זֹאת, וַדַּאי.

596. It is written of this wicked man that he saw a true dream, as it is written: "And on the vine were three tendrils." What is the vine? It is the Congregation of Yisrael, THE NUKVA, as it is written: "Look down from heaven, and behold, and be mindful of this vine" (Tehilim 80:15). It says "from heaven" IN "LOOK DOWN FROM HEAVEN," since it has been cast from there, according to the words: "And cast down from heaven to earth" (Eichah 2:1). "And be mindful of this vine," NAMELY the vine which is "this," THE NUKVA CALLED "THIS."

597. שְׁלֹשָׁה שָׂרִיגִם, כְּד"א שְׁלֹשָׁה עֶדְרֵי צֹאן רֹבְצִים עָלֶיהָ. וְהִיא כְּפוֹרַחַת, דִּכְתִיב, וַתֵּרֶב חָכְמַת שְׁלֹמֹה, דְּאִתְנְהֵיר סִיהֲרָא. עָלְתָה נִצָּה, דָּא יְרוּשָׁלַם דִּלְתַתָּא. ד"א עָלְתָה נִצָּה, לְעֵילָא, הַהוּא דַּרְגָּא דְּקַיְימָא עֲלָה וְיַנֵּיק לָהּ, כְּד"א אֲשֶׁר זַרְעוֹ בוֹ עַל הָאָרֶץ. הִבְשִׁילוּ אַשְׁכְּלוֹתֶיהָ עֲנָבִים, לְנַטְרָא בְּהוֹ יַיִן דְּמִנְטְרָא.

597. "Three tendrils" as in the verse: "There were three flocks of sheep lying by it" (Beresheet 29:2), ARE THE SECRET OF THE THREE COLUMNS. "And it was as though it budded," as it is written: "And Solomon's Wisdom excelled" (I Melachim 5:10) means that the moon shone, THE NUKVA CALLED SOLOMON'S WISDOM; "and its blossoms shot forth" refers to the lower Jerusalem, THE NUKVA. Another explanation for, "and its blossoms shot forth": It refers to the grade above THE NUKVA, which suckles Her, NAMELY YESOD, as it says, "whose seed is in itself, upon the earth" (Beresheet 1:11), WHICH ALLUDES TO YESOD, THAT POURS UPON THE NUKVA CALLED EARTH. "And its clusters brought forth ripe grapes" (Beresheet 40:10), in which to keep the preserved wine, SO THAT THE KLIPOT WILL NEVER HAVE A HOLD ON IT.

598. חָמֵי כַּמָּה חָמָא הַהוּא רָשָׁע, מַה כְּתִיב, וְכוֹס פַּרְעֹה בְּיָדִי וָאֶקַּח אֶת הָעֲנָבִים וָאֶשְׁחַט אוֹתָם. הָכָא חָמָא הַהוּא כּוֹס תַּרְעֵלָה, יַנִּיקָא דְּבֵי דִּינָא, דְּנָפֵיק מֵאִינּוּן עֲנָבִים דְּאִתְיְיהֵיב לְפַרְעֹה וְשָׁתֵי לֵיהּ, כְּמָה דַּהֲוָה בְּגִינֵיהוֹן דְּיִשְׂרָאֵל. כֵּיוָן דְּשָׁמַע יוֹסֵף דָּא, חָדֵי, וְיָדַע מִלָּה דִּקְשׁוֹט בְּהַאי חֶלְמָא. בְּגִינֵי כָּךְ פְּשַׁר לֵיהּ חֶלְמָא לְטַב, עַל דְּבִשַּׂר לְיוֹסֵף בְּהַאי.

598. See how much this wicked man saw. It is written: "And Pharaoh's cup was in my hand: and I took the grapes, and pressed them" (Beresheet 40:11). He saw here the cup of poison, the branch of the court of justice, which issues from these grapes. It was given to Pharaoh, who drank it, as it came to pass AT THE TIME OF THE EXODUS FROM EGYPT, on account of Yisrael. When Joseph heard this, he rejoiced and recognized the truth in that dream. Hence, he interpreted his dream for the good, for bringing him good tidings.

599. תָּא חֲזֵי, אֹסְרִי לַגֶּפֶן עִירֹה, דְּאִתְכַּפְיָין תְּחוֹת הַאי גֶּפֶן כָּל אִינּוּן

חֵילִין תַּקִּיפִין דְּעַמִּין עכו"ם, כִּדְאֲמָרָן, בְּגִין הַאי גֶּפֶן, אִתְקַשַּׁר
וְאִתְכַּפְיָיא הַהוּא חֵילָא דִּלְהוֹן. וְאִתְּמַר.

599. Come and see: "Binding his foal to the vine" since strong forces of the heathen nations were subjugated underneath this vine, as we said that through the power of the vine, THE NUKVA, their force was bound up and subdued, as has been explained.

600. ר' שִׁמְעוֹן אָמַר, אִית גֶּפֶן, וְאִית גֶּפֶן. אִית גֶּפֶן קַדִּישָׁא עִלָּאָה,
וְאִית גֶּפֶן דְּאִקְרֵי, גֶּפֶן סְדוֹם, וְאִית גֶּפֶן נָכְרִיָּה בַּת אֵל נֵכָר. בְּגִין כָּךְ
כְּתִיב גֶּפֶן זֹאת, הַהִיא דְּאִקְרֵי כֻּלֹּה זֶרַע אֱמֶת. שׂוֹרֵק אֵלּוּ יִשְׂרָאֵל,
דְּנָפְקֵי מֵהַאי גֶּפֶן. כַּד חָבוּ יִשְׂרָאֵל, וְשָׁבְקוּ לְהַאי גֶּפֶן, מַה כְּתִיב, כִּי
מִגֶּפֶן סְדוֹם גַּפְנָם וְגו'. וּבְגִין כָּךְ אִית גֶּפֶן וְאִית גֶּפֶן.

600. Rabbi Shimon said: There is a vine and there is a vine. There is a holy supernal vine, THE NUKVA, and there is a vine called "the vine of Sodom" (Devarim 32:32), WHICH IS AN EVIL KLIPAH. There is also "a strange vine" (Yirmeyah 2:21), the daughter of a strange El. Therefore, it is written "this vine," WHICH HINTS THAT SHE IS THE NUKVA CALLED "this," the same that is called "an entirely right seed" (Ibid.) "a noble vine," AS IT SAYS, "AND I HAD PLANTED YOU A NOBLE VINE" (IBID.), refers to Yisrael who issued from this vine. When Yisrael sinned and abandoned this vine, it says, "For their vine is of the vine of Sodom" (Devarim 32:32).

601. ר' יְהוּדָה וְר' יִצְחָק הֲווֹ אָזְלֵי בְּאָרְחָא. א"ר יְהוּדָה לְר' יִצְחָק,
נֵיזִיל בְּהַאי חֲקַל, דְּהוּא אֹרַח מֵישַׁר יַתִּיר. אֲזָלוּ. עַד דַּהֲווֹ אָזְלֵי, אָמַר
רַבִּי יְהוּדָה, כְּתִיב לֹא תִירָא לְבֵיתָהּ מִשָּׁלֶג כִּי כָל בֵּיתָהּ לָבֻשׁ שָׁנִים.
הַאי קְרָא, רַבִּי חִזְקִיָּה חַבְרָנָא אוֹקִים בֵּיהּ, דַּאֲמַר, דִּינָא דְּחַיָּיבֵי דְּגֵיהִנֹּם
תְּרֵיסַר יַרְחִין, פַּלְגָּא מִנַּיְיהוּ בְּחַמָּה וּפַלְגָּא מִנַּיְיהוּ בְּתַלְגָּא.

601. Rabbi Yehuda and Rabbi Yitzchak were walking along the road. Rabbi Yehuda said to Rabbi Yitzchak, Let us walk through this field, which is more level. While they were walking, Rabbi Yehuda said: It is written, "She is not afraid of the snow for her household: for all her household are clothed with scarlet" (Mishlei 31:21). This verse has been explained by our friend Rabbi Chizkiyah. He said that the evil are sentenced to twelve months in Gehenom, half of them in heat OF BURNING FIRE and half in snow.

602. בְּשַׁעְתָּא דְעָאלִין לְנוּרָא, אִינוּן אָמְרֵי דָא הוּא וַדַּאי גֵּיהִנֹּם, עָאלִין לְתַלְגָּא, אָמְרֵי דָא חֲרִיפָא דְסִיתְוָא דְקוּדְשָׁא בְּרִיךְ הוּא. שָׁרָאן וְאָמְרִין וַה, וּלְבָתַר אָמְרִין וַוי. וְדָוִד אָמַר וַיַּעֲלֵנִי מִבּוֹר שָׁאוֹן מִטִּיט הַיָּוֵן וַיָּקֶם וגו'. מֵאֲתַר דְּאָמְרֵי וַה, וּלְבָתַר וַוי.

602. When they enter the fire, they say, This must be Gehenom. When they go into the snow, they say, This is surely the intense cold of the Holy One's, blessed be He, winter. They start with, 'Hurrah', AND REJOICE FOR COMING OUT OF GEHENOM, but later, WHEN THEY UNDERSTAND IT IS A GEHENOM OF SNOW, they say, 'Woe'. David said: "He brought me up also out of the gruesome pit, out of the miry clay, and set my feet..." (Tehilim 40:3); NAMELY from where they first say 'Hurrah' and then 'Woe', AS THE WORD HAYAVEN (ENG. 'MIRE') CONTAINS BOTH VAV-HEI (ENG. 'HURRAH') AND VAV-YUD (ENG. 'WOE').

603. וְהֵיכָן מִשְׁתַּלְמֵי נַפְשַׁיְיהוּ, בַּשֶּׁלֶג, כְּד"א, בְּפָרֵשׂ שַׁדַּי מְלָכִים בָּה תַּשְׁלֵג בְּצַלְמוֹן. יָכוֹל אַף יִשְׂרָאֵל כֵּן, ת"ל לֹא תִירָא לְבֵיתָהּ מִשָּׁלֶג. מ"ט. בְּגִין דְּכָל בֵּיתָהּ לָבוּשׁ שָׁנִים. אַל תִּקְרֵי שָׁנִים אֶלָּא שְׁנַיִם: כְּגוֹן מִילָה וּפְרִיעָה, צִיצִית וּתְפִילִין, מְזוּזָה וְנֵר חֲנוּכָּה כו'.

603. Where are their souls perfected? In A GEHENOM OF snow, as said: "When the Almighty scatters kings in it, snow falls in Tzalmon" (Tehilim 68:15). One might think this also applies to Yisrael, THAT THEY ARE SENTENCED TO SNOW. Of this, the verse says, "She is not afraid of the snow for her household" Why? "For all her household are clothed with scarlet." The word shanim (Eng. 'scarlet') may also be pronounced 'two (Heb. shnayim)'; to wit, the circumcision and uncovering, the Tzitzit (fringes) and the Tefilin, the Mezuzah and the Chanukah candle, and so on. TO WIT, YISRAEL ARE QUICK IN OBSERVING THE PRECEPTS AND HAVE DOUBLE PRECEPTS, FOR IN CIRCUMCISION THERE IS BOTH CIRCUMCISION AND UNCOVERING, IN PRAYER-THE TZITZIT (FRINGES) AND THE TEFILIN, AND ON THEIR DOORS THEY HAVE THE MEZUZAH AND THE CHANUKAH

CANDLE. THEREFORE THEY ARE NOT AFRAID OF THE GEHENOM OF SNOW, WHICH COMES FOR LAZINESS AND SLACKNESS IN OBSERVING THE PRECEPTS.

604. תָּא חֲזֵי, לֹא תִירָא לְבֵיתָהּ מִשָּׁלֶג, דָּא כְּנֶסֶת יִשְׂרָאֵל, דְּאִיהִי כָּל בֵּיתָהּ לְבוּשׁ שָׁנִים, כְּמָה דַּאֲמָרָן, דִּכְתִיב חֲמוּץ בְּגָדִים וְגוֹ', לְבוּשָׁא דְּדִינָא קַשְׁיָא, לְאִתְפָּרְעָא מֵעַמִּין עכו"ם, וְזַמִּין קוּדְשָׁא בְּרִיךְ הוּא לְמִלְבַּשׁ לְבוּשָׁא סוּמָקָא, וְחַרְבָּא סוּמָקָא, וּלְאִתְפָּרְעָא מִן סוּמָקָא. לְבוּשָׁא סוּמָקָא, דִּכְתִיב, חֲמוּץ בְּגָדִים, וּכְתִיב מַדּוּעַ אָדוֹם לִלְבוּשֶׁךָ. סַיְיפָא סוּמָקָא, דִּכְתִיב חֶרֶב לַה' מָלְאָה דָם. וּלְאִתְפָּרְעָא מִן סוּמָקָא, דִּכְתִיב כִּי זֶבַח לַה' בְּבָצְרָה וְגוֹ'. תּוּ, כִּי כָל בֵּיתָהּ לְבוּשׁ שָׁנִים דְּהָא מִסִּטְרָא דְּדִינָא קַשְׁיָא קָא אַתְיָיא.

604. Come and behold: "She is not afraid of the snow for her household." This is the Congregation of Yisrael, whose "household are clothed with scarlet," like we said in relation to the words "crimsoned garments" (Yeshayah 63:1), which is a robe of strict Judgment, in which punishment is exacted from the idolatrous nations. The Holy One, blessed be He, will don a red garment and a red sword and punish the red, ESAU. The garment is red as in "crimsoned garment" and "Why is your apparel red" (Ibid. 2). Of the red sword, we learn from the verse "The sword of Hashem is filled with blood" (Yeshayah 34:6). He will punish the red, as it is written: "For Hashem has a sacrifice in Botzra" (Ibid.). Also "her household are clothed with scarlet," since THE NUKVA comes from strict Judgment, AND THEREFORE "SHE IS NOT AFRAID OF THE SNOW."

605. א"ר יִצְחָק, וַדַּאי הָכֵי הוּא, אֶלָּא כָּל בֵּיתָהּ לְבוּשׁ שָׁנִים, מַאי שָׁנִים, אִלֵּין שָׁנִים קַדְמוֹנִיּוֹת, בְּגִין דְּאִיהִי אִתְכְּלִילַת מִכֻּלְּהוּ, וְיָנְקָא מִכָּל סִטְרִין, כְּדִכְתִיב כָּל הַנְּחָלִים הוֹלְכִים אֶל הַיָּם.

605. Rabbi Yitzchak said: This is indeed so, but we should explain the words "her household are clothed with scarlet (Heb. shanim)." These are the primordial years (Heb. shanim), THE SECRET OF THE SEVEN SFIROT CHESED, GVURAH, TIFERET, NETZACH, HOD, YESOD AND MALCHUT, for she is included of them all and sucks from all sides, as it is written: "All

the rivers run into the sea" (Kohelet 1:7). SHE THEREFORE DOES NOT FEAR THE JUDGMENTS, WHICH ARE SNOW.

606. עַד דַּהֲווֹ אָזְלֵי, פָּגְעוּ בֵּיהּ בְּהַהוּא יְנוּקָא, דַּהֲוָה אָזִיל לְקַפּוֹטְקְיָא בְּקַסְטִירָא דַחֲמָרָא, וְחַד סָבָא רָכֵיב. אָמַר הַהוּא סָבָא לְהַהוּא יְנוּקָא, בְּרִי, אֵימָא לִי קְרָאֶיךָ. אָמַר לֵיהּ, קְרָאֵי לָאו חַד הוּא, אֶלָּא חַד חוֹת לְתַתָּא, אוֹ אַרְכֵּב לְקַמָּךְ, וְאֵימָא לָךְ. אָמַר לֵיהּ, לָא בָּעֵינָא, אֲנָא סָבָא וְאַנְתְּ רַבְיָא, דְּאִתְקַל גַּרְמִי בַּהֲדָךְ. אָמַר לֵיהּ, אִי הָכִי אַמַּאי שָׁאֵלְתְּ קְרָאֵי. אָמַר לֵיהּ, בְּגִין דְּנֵיזֵיל בְּאוֹרְחָא. אָמַר תִּיפַּח רוּחֵיהּ דְּהַהוּא סָבָא, דְּהוּא רָכֵיב וְלָא יָדַע מִלָּה, וַאֲמַר דְּלָא יִתְקַל בַּהֲדִי, אִתְפְּרַשׁ מֵהַהוּא סָבָא, וַאֲזֵיל לֵיהּ בְּאוֹרְחָא.

606. While they were walking, they met a child who was walking to Cappadocia behind a donkey, upon which rode an old man. The man said to the child, My son, read to me a passage of scripture. He said to him: I KNOW not one BUT MANY PASSAGES, but alight first, or let me ride before you, and I will recite it. THE OLD MAN said to him: I am old and you are a child and I do not want to be put on the same level WITH YOU. THE CHILD said to him: Why then did you ask me to recite verses to you? He said: so that we shall walk together. The child said: may this old man hang himself, who rides and knows nothing but says he does not wish to be on a level with me. He left the old man and walked on the road.

607. כַּד מָטוֹ ר' יְהוּדָה וְר' יִצְחָק, קָרֵיב לְגַבַּיְיהוּ שָׁאִילוּ לֵיהּ, וְסַח לוֹן עוֹבָדָא, אָמַר לֵיהּ ר' יְהוּדָה, שַׁפִּיר קָא עֲבַדְתְּ, זִיל בַּהֲדָן, וְנֵיתִיב הָכָא, וְנִשְׁמַע מִלָּה מִפּוּמָךְ. אָמַר לוֹן, לָאֵי אֲנָא, דְּלָא אָכֵילְנָא יוֹמָא דֵין. אַפִּיקוּ נַהֲמָא, וִיהִיבוּ לֵיהּ. אִתְרְחִישׁ לוֹן נִיסָּא, וְאַשְׁכָּחוּ חַד נְבִיעָא דְּמַיָּא דַּקִּיק תְּחוֹת אִילָנָא, שָׁתֵי מִנַּיְיהוּ, וְאִינוּן שָׁתוּ וִיתִיבוּ.

607. When Rabbi Yehuda and Rabbi Yitzchak arrived, the child approached them. They asked him and he told them what happened. Rabbi Yehuda said: You have acted rightly, come with us and let us sit here and hear your words. He said to them, I am weary since I have not eaten today. They took out bread and gave it to him. A miracle happened and they found a streamlet under a tree. He drank of it, and they drank and sat down.

61. "Fret not yourself because of evil doers"

A Synopsis

The child whom the rabbis encounter in the previous section opens a discussion about the title verse. We learn that this verse is not a prayer or a song, but rather, it was spoken by the Holy Spirit. The verse warns us not to challenge the wicked, since we do not know about the previous incarnations of our own souls, let alone anyone else's. Furthermore, this verse instructs us that we should not look on the deeds of others for fear of feeling envious. Envy of another, we're told, transgresses three negative precepts commanded by God.

The Relevance of this Passage

Casting a jealous eye towards our friends and foe's possessions and/or positions in life diverts our attention away from our own lot. We fail to appreciate our good fortune. Continued lack of appreciation inevitably leads to the loss of all that we should've held dear to our hearts. The mystical effect of these verses shifts our attention away from others and redirects it towards our own spiritual treasures. Additionally, passing judgement upon others causes us to neglect negative deeds and immoral traits ingrained in our own nature. A spiritual individual realizes that the trials and tribulations that challenge us are a direct result of prior incarnations and they cannot be measured against the deeds and fortunes of others, for all is relative in the overall scheme of spiritual evolution.

608. פָּתַח הַהוּא יְנוּקָא וַאֲמַר, לְדָוִד אַל תִּתְחַר בַּמְּרֵעִים אַל תְּקַנֵּא בְּעוֹשֵׂי עַוְלָה. לְדָוִד, אִי שִׁירָתָא לָא קָאֲמַר, אִי תְּפִלָּה לָא קָאֲמַר, אֶלָּא בְּכָל אֲתַר לְדָוִד סְתָם, רוּח הַקֹּדֶשׁ אֲמָרוֹ.

608. The child opened the discussion saying: "To David. Fret not yourself because of evil doers, nor be envious against the workers of iniquity" (Tehilim 37:1). HE ASKS: "To David" shows it is not a song, like in "A psalm of David" nor a prayer, AS IN "A PRAYER OF DAVID." HE ANSWERS: Wherever it says just "To David," it was spoken by the Holy Spirit.

609. אַל תִּתְחַר בַּמְּרֵעִים. מַאי אַל תִּתְחַר בַּמְּרֵעִים, אַל תִּתְחַבַּר מִבָּעֵי לֵיהּ. אֶלָּא אַל אַל תַּעֲבֵיד תַּחֲרוּת בַּמְּרֵעִים, בְּגִין דְּלָא יָדַעְתְּ יְסוֹדָא דְּגַרְמָךְ, וְלָא תֵיכוּל לֵיהּ, דִּילְמָא אִיהוּ אִילָנָא דְּלָא אִתְעֲקַר לְעָלְמִין,

וְתִתְדְּחֵי קַמֵּיהּ.

609. "Fret not yourself because of evil doers." HE ASKS: What is the meaning thereof? It should have been 'Join not EVIL DOERS.' HE REPLIES: Do not challenge the wicked, for you do not know your origins, TO WIT, THE INCARNATIONS OF YOUR SOUL. IT MIGHT BE that you will not prevail against him, if he is a tree which was never uprooted, A SOUL WHICH WAS NEVER INCARNATED BEFORE, WHICH IS VERY STRONG. Then you will be repulsed by him.

610. וְאַל תְּקַנֵּא בְּעוֹשֵׂי עַוְלָה, דְּלָא תַשְׁגַּח בְּעוֹבָדֵיהוֹן, וְלָא תֵיתֵי לְקַנְּאָה עֲלַיְיהוּ, דְּכָל מַאן דְּחָמֵי עוֹבָדֵיהוֹן, וְלָא קַנֵּי לְקוּדְשָׁא בְּרִיךְ הוּא, אַעֲבַר עַל תְּלַת לָאוִין, דִּכְתִיב לֹא יִהְיֶה לְךָ אֱלֹהִים אֲחֵרִים עַל פָּנָי. לֹא תַעֲשֶׂה לְךָ פֶסֶל וְכָל תְּמוּנָה. לֹא תִשְׁתַּחֲוֶה לָהֶם וְלֹא תָעָבְדֵם כִּי אָנֹכִי ה' אֱלֹהֶיךָ אֵל קַנָּא.

610. "Nor be envious against the workers of iniquity": Do not look at their deeds, for you might be envious of them. For whoever sees their works and is not zealous for the glory of the Holy One, blessed be He, transgresses three negative precepts: "You shall have no other Elohim beside Me: You shall not make for yourself any carved idol, or any likeness of any thing...you shall not bow down to them, nor serve them: for I Hashem your Elohim am a jealous El" (Shemot 20:5).

62. Small Aleph

A Synopsis

Here, the child, whom the rabbis encountered in section 59, first discourses on the verse, "And The Creator called to Moses." The small *Aleph* א in this verse, he explains, refers to Malchut alone. This is also the case in the verse, "and The Creator spoke to him out of the tent of meeting," since these words also came from Malchut alone. The Tent of Meeting is the Malchut, upon whom the calculation of time, all festivals, and Shabbat depends. The verse indicates that God spoke from above, from Binah. Zeir Anpin receives from Binah and gives to Malchut. In this way, Malchut was given permission from above to reveal supernal knowledge. We then learn about the verse, "And they brought the Tabernacle to Moses." The reason the Tabernacle was brought to Moses is that he corresponds to Zeir Anpin. Therefore, Moses is the master of the house and may do what no other man can. When Moses is addressed in the verse, "If any man of you bring an offering," it is Binah who is speaking. We are told that "an offering to The Creator" involves bringing the lower to join with that which is above, and "your offering" involves joining the upper with that which is below. All this is alluded to in the opening verses of Vayikra.

The Relevance of this Passage

Light radiates in the lives of all mankind when the realm of Zeir Anpin, the Upper World, enjoins with Malchut, our Lower World. Here, we connect to the Hebrew letter, the small *Aleph* א, which embodies our physical dimension of time, space and motion, known as Malchut. The Zohar's reference to the festivals, Shabbat, the Tabernacle, and Moses, is the mechanism by which Malchut [our world] makes contact with Zeir Anpin. Thus, each time our eyes fall upon these words, the two worlds are united and the Light of The Creator sparks our souls.

611. בְּג"כ, בָּעֵי לֵיה לְב"ן לְאִתְפָּרְשָׁא מִנַּיְיהוּ, וּלְמִסְטֵי אוֹרְחֵיה מִנַּיְיהוּ, עַל דָּא אִתְפָּרְשָׁנָא וְסָטִינָא אָרְחָאי. מִכָּאן וּלְהָלְאָה דְּאַשְׁכַּחְנָא לְכוּ, אֵימָא הַנֵּי קְרָאֵי קַמֵּיכוֹן. פָּתַח וַאֲמַר, וַיִּקְרָא אֶל מֹשֶׁה, הָכָא אָלֶ"ף זְעֵירָא אַמַּאי, בְּגִין דְּהַאי קְרִיאָה לָא הֲוָה בִּשְׁלִימוּ. מַאי טַעֲמָא דְּהָא לָא הֲוָה אֶלָּא בְּמִשְׁכְּנָא, וּבְאַרְעָא אָחֳרָא, בְּגִין דִּשְׁלִימוּ לָא אִשְׁתַּכַּח אֶלָּא בְּאַרְעָא קַדִּישָׁא.

611. A man should therefore keep away from them, and turn his way from them. I therefore left and turned away from him. Now that I have found you, I shall recite these verses before you. He opened the discussion saying: "And (Hashem) called (Heb. *vayikra*) to Moses" (Vayikra 1:1). Here IN VAYIKRA, the *Aleph* is small. HE ASKS why? HE ANSWERS: THIS SHOWS US that this calling was not perfect. Why? Because it was only in the tabernacle, WHICH IS TEMPORARY, and in a foreign land. For perfection is to be found only in the land of Yisrael.

612. תּוּ, הָכָא שְׁכִינְתָּא, הָתָם שְׁלִימוּ דִּדְכַר וְנוּקְבָא: אָדָם שֵׁת אֱנוֹשׁ. אָדָם: שְׁלִימוּ דְּכַר וְנוּקְבָא, הָכָא, נוּקְבָא. תּוּ סֵיפָא דִקְרָא, וַיְדַבֵּר ה' אֵלָיו מֵאֹהֶל מוֹעֵד לֵאמֹר, בְּגִין כָּךְ אָלֶ"ף זְעֵירָא.

612. WE HAVE TO EXPLAIN further ABOUT THE SMALL *ALEPH*, THAT IT IS SO BECAUSE here, IN THIS CALLING TO MOSES, is the Shechinah, while there is perfection of a male and a female TOGETHER, AS IT IS WRITTEN "Adam, Seth, Enosh" (I Divrei Hayamim 1:1), 'Adam' IS SPELLED WITH A BIG *ALEPH*, WHICH ALLUDES TO the perfection of male and female IN UNION. But here THE *ALEPH* IS SMALL, WHICH ALLUDES TO the Nukva ALONE; NAMELY THE SHECHINAH. ANOTHER EVIDENCE comes from the end of the verse "and Hashem spoke to him out of the Tent of Meeting" (Vayikra 1:1). THE TENT OF MEETING IS THE NUKVA, HENCE THE WORDS CAME FROM THE NUKVA ALONE. Therefore the *Aleph* is small, AS SMALL LETTERS ALLUDE TO THE NUKVA, REGULAR ONES TO ZEIR ANPIN AND THE BIG TO IMA, OR TO THE PERFECTION OF MALE AND FEMALE TOGETHER, WHICH COMES THROUGH IMA ALONE.

613. תּוּ אָלֶ"ף זְעֵירָא, מְתַל לְמַלְכָּא, דַּהֲוָה יָתֵיב בְּכָרְסְיֵהּ, וְכִתְרָא דְמַלְכוּתָא עֲלֵיהּ, אִקְרֵי מֶלֶךְ עִלָּאָה, כַּד נָחֵית וַאֲזַל לְבֵי עַבְדֵיהּ, מֶלֶךְ זוּטָא אִקְרֵי, כָּךְ קוּדְשָׁא בְּרִיךְ הוּא, כָּל זִמְנָא דְּאִיהוּ לְעֵילָא עַל כֹּלָּא, מֶלֶךְ עִלָּאָה אִקְרֵי, כֵּיוָן דְּנָחֵית מְדוֹרֵיהּ לְתַתָּא, מֶלֶךְ אִיהוּ, אֲבָל לָאו עִלָּאָה כְּקַדְמֵיתָא, בְּגִין כָּךְ אָלֶ"ף זְעֵירָא.

613. Further explanation CONCERNING the small *Aleph*: There is a story of a king who sat upon his throne, with a crown on his head. He is then called the supreme king. When he goes down to visit the house of his servant he is called little king. The Holy One, blessed be He, too, as long as He is above all, is called a supreme King. Once He comes to dwell below in the tabernacle, he is still a King, but not supreme as before. Therefore the *Aleph* is small.

614. וַיִּקְרָא: הָכֵי תְּנִינָן, זַמִּין לֵיהּ לְהֵיכָלֵיהּ. מֵאֹהֶל מוֹעֵד. מַאן אֹהֶל מוֹעֵד. אֹהֶל דְּבֵיהּ תַּלְיָין מוֹעֵד וְחַגָּא וְשַׁבַּתָּא לְמִמְנֵי, כְּד"א וְהָיוּ לְאֹתוֹת וּלְמוֹעֲדִים, בֵּיהּ שַׁרְיָא חוּשְׁבְּנָא לְמִמְנֵי. וּמַאן אִיהוּ, סִיהֲרָא, כְּמָא דְאַתְּ אָמֵר אֹהֶל בַּל יִצְעָן בַּל יִסַּע יְתֵדוֹתָיו לָנֶצַח.

614. "And he called" as we learned MEANS THAT he called and invited him to his palace. "From the Tent of Meeting (Heb. *moed*)": What is it? It is a tent, upon which depends the reckoning of times (Heb. *moed*), festivals and Shabbat, as it says, "And let them be for signs, and for seasons" (Beresheet 1:14). In her abides the reckoning. Who is she? The moon, NAMELY THE NUKVA, FROM WHICH COME ALL THE CHANGES FROM WEEK DAYS TO FESTIVALS AND SHABBAT, THROUGH CHANGES IN THE STATURE OF HER MOCHIN, as it says, "A tent that shall not be taken down: its pegs shall not be removed for ever" (Yeshayah 33:20), WHICH ALLUDES TO THE NUKVA CALLED TENT.

615. לֵאמֹר, מַאי לֵאמֹר. בְּגִין לְגַלָּאָה, מַה דַּהֲוָה סָתִים לְגוֹ. וּבְכָל אֲתַר לֵאמֹר, כְּד"א וַיְדַבֵּר ה' אֶל מֹשֶׁה לֵאמֹר, דְּאִתְיְיהֵיב רְשׁוּ לְגַלָּאָה. אֲבָל כֹּלָּא חַד הוּא, וְשַׁפִּיר הוּא, בְּגִין דְּהָא אִתְמַנֵּי לְסִיהֲרָא הַהִיא מִלָּה, מֵאֲתַר דְּמֹשֶׁה קַיְימָא.

615. "Saying": HE ASKS: What does this mean? HE ANSWERS: IT MEANS revealing what is hidden inside. Wherever it says "saying," like in: "And Hashem spoke to Moses, saying," it means that permission was given to reveal. Yet all is one, and it is well since the revelation was given to the moon, THE NUKVA, from where Moses stands, ZEIR ANPIN, ACCORDING TO ORDER.

616. וַיְדַבֵּר ה', לְעֵילָא. אֶל מֹשֶׁה, בְּאֶמְצָעִיתָא. לֵאמֹר, בַּתְרַיְיתָא, אֲתַר, דְּאִית רְשׁוּ לְגַלָּאָה. תּוּ, וַיִּקְרָא אֶל מֹשֶׁה מַה כְּתִיב לְעֵילָא,

וַיָּבִיאוּ אֶת הַמִּשְׁכָּן אֶל מֹשֶׁה וְגוֹ'. אַמַּאי אֶל מֹשֶׁה. הָכֵי אָמְרוּ, בְּגִין
דְּמֹשֶׁה חָמָא לֵיהּ בְּטוּרָא, וְקוּדְשָׁא בְּרִיךְ הוּא אַחֲמֵי לֵיהּ בְּחֵיזוּ דְּעַיְנָא,
כְּד"א כַּאֲשֶׁר הֶרְאָה אוֹתְךָ בָּהָר, וּכְתִיב כַּמַּרְאֶה אֲשֶׁר הֶרְאָה ה' אֶת
מֹשֶׁה וְגוֹ'. וּכְתִיב וּרְאֵה וַעֲשֵׂה בְּתַבְנִיתָם אֲשֶׁר אַתָּה מָרְאֶה בָּהָר,
הַשְׁתָּא אַיְיתִיאוּ לֵיהּ, בְּגִין דְּיֶחֱמֵי, אִי אִיהוּ כְּהַהוּא מִשְׁכְּנָא דְּחָמָא.

616. "And Hashem spoke," above, BINAH, "to Moses," who is in the
middle, ZEIR ANPIN, AS BINAH GIVES TO ZEIR ANPIN, "saying," which is
the last one, THE NUKVA, WHO RECEIVES FROM ZEIR ANPIN. She is the
place where permission to reveal is given. "And (Hashem) called to Moses":
It is written before, "And they brought the tabernacle to Moses" (Shemot
39:33). Why bring it to Moses? They said: "Moses saw it upon Mount Sinai,
for the Holy One, blessed be He, showed it to him before his eyes, as it says
"as it was shown you in the mountain" (Shemot 27:8) "according to the
pattern which Hashem had shown Moses" (Bemidbar 8:4) and "And look
that you make them after their pattern, which was shown to you in the
mountain" (Shemot 25:40). They THEREFORE brought him THE TABERNACLE
now, so he will see whether it resembles the tabernacle he has seen.

617. אֲבָל אַמַּאי וַיָּבִיאוּ אֶת הַמִּשְׁכָּן אֶל מֹשֶׁה. אֶלָּא, לְמַלְכָּא דְּבָעָא
לְמִבְנֵי פַּלְטְרִין לְמַטְרוֹנִיתָא, פַּקִּיד לְאוּמָנִין הֵיכָלָא דָּא בְּדוּךְ פְּלַן,
וְהֵיכָלָא דָּא בְּדוּךְ פְּלַן, הָכָא אֲתַר לְעַרְסָא, וְהָכָא אֲתַר לְנַיְיחָא. כֵּיוָן
דַּעֲבִידוּ לוֹן אוּמָנִין, אַחֲמִיוּ לְמַלְכָּא. כָּךְ וַיָּבִיאוּ אֶת הַמִּשְׁכָּן אֶל מֹשֶׁה,
מָארֵי דְּבֵיתָא, אִישׁ הָאֱלֹקִים, כֵּיוָן דְּאִשְׁתַּכְלַל הֵיכָלָא, מַטְרוֹנִיתָא
זְמִינַת לְמַלְכָּא לְהֵיכָלָא, זְמִינַת לְבַעֲלָהּ עִמָּהּ, בְּגִין כָּךְ וַיִּקְרָא אֶל
מֹשֶׁה.

617. But ACCORDING TO THIS, IT IS YET HARD TO UNDERSTAND why they
brought the tabernacle to Moses, INSTEAD OF MOSES COMING TO THE
TABERNACLE. This is like a king who wanted to build a palace for the
Matron. He ordered the craftsmen to build a room in one place, and a room
in another place. Here will be the bed and there a place to recline. When the
craftsmen finished it, they showed it to the king. So "they brought the
tabernacle to Moses," who is the master of the house and a man of Elohim.
MOSES DID NOT GO TO THE TABERNACLE BUT IT WAS BROUGHT TO HIM.

When the palace was built, the Matron invited the king to it, invited her husband THE KING to be with her. Therefore "called to Moses" IS SPELLED WITH A SMALL *ALEPH*. THE SMALL *ALEPH*, WHICH IS THE NUKVA, CALLED TO MOSES, ZEIR ANPIN, HER HUSBAND, TO BE WITH HER.

618. וּבְגִין דְּמֹשֶׁה מָאבֵי דְבֵיתָא אִיהוּ, מַה כְּתִיב, וּמֹשֶׁה יִקַח אֶת הָאֹהֶל וְנָטָה לוֹ מִחוּץ לַמַּחֲנֶה, מֹשֶׁה דְּאִיהוּ מָאבֵי דְבֵיתָא, עָבֵיד הָכֵי, מַה דְּלֵית רְשׁוּ לְבַר נָשׁ אָחֳרָא לְמֶעְבַּד הָכֵי.

618. And since Moses is the master of the house, NAMELY ZEIR ANPIN, THE HUSBAND OF THE MATRON, it says, "And Moses would take the Tent" – THE NUKVA CALLED TENT-"and pitch it outside the camp" (Shemot 33:6). Moses, who is the master of the house, may do what no other man may.

619. וַיְדַבֵּר ה' אֵלָיו, דַּרְגָּא אָחֳרָא עִלָּאָה, וּכְדֵין בְּשַׁעְתָּא דְּאִזְדַּמַּן מֹשֶׁה לְמֵיעַל, כְּדֵין פְּתַח וַאֲמַר, אָדָם כִּי יַקְרִיב מִכֶּם. מַאי אָדָם הָכָא. אֶלָּא כַּד אִתְחַבָּרוּ שִׁמְשָׁא וְסִיהֲרָא כַּחֲדָא, פְּתַח וַאֲמַר אָדָם. כְּדִכְתִיב, שֶׁמֶשׁ יָרֵחַ עָמַד זְבוּלָה, עָמַד, וְלֹא עָמְדוּ.

619. "And Hashem spoke to him." This is a different, supernal grade, BINAH. "AND HE CALLED," THE NUKVA CALLED "TO MOSES," TIFERET, "AND HASHEM SPOKE" IS BINAH. And so when Moses was entering THE NUKVA, BINAH opened the discussion saying: "If any man of you bring an offering" (Vayikra 1:2); BINAH IS THE SPEAKER HERE. HE ASKS: Why say "man" HERE WHEN IT WOULD HAVE SUFFICED TO SAY, 'IF ANY OF YOU BRING AN OFFERING'? HE ANSWERS: When the sun and moon were united, TIFERET AND MALCHUT TOGETHER, BINAH opened and said: "Man," IF "ANY MAN" BRING AN OFFEEFERING, HE SHOULD BE "OF YOU," THAT IS, AS MALE AND FEMALE LIKE YOU. AND THEY WERE BOTH NAMED "MAN" IN THE SINGULAR, as it is written: "The sun and moon stood still in their habitation" (Chavakuk 3:11), "stood still" in the singular instead of the plural, BECAUSE THE SCRIPTURE SPEAKS OF THEIR BEING IN UNION.

620. כִּי יַקְרִיב מִכֶּם, הָכָא אִתְרְמִיז, מַאן דְּיַעֲבֵיד פּוּלְחָנָא דְקָרְבְּנָא

שְׁלִים, דְּיִשְׁתְּכַּח דְּכַר וְנוּקְבָא. מַשְׁמַע דִּכְתִיב מִכֶּם, דְּיִשְׁתְּכַּח בְּחֵיזוּ דִּלְכוֹן. קָרְבָּן לַה' דְּאַקְרֵיב כֹּלָּא, לְאִתְאַחֲדָא כַּחֲדָא, לְעֵילָא וְתַתָּא.

620. "If any man of you bring an offering": It is hinted here that whoever makes a service of sacrifice flawlessly, should be there as male and female; NAMELY BE MARRIED. This is derived from the words "of you (plur.)," which indicates that he will have your images; TO WIT, BINAH SAID THIS TO TIFERET AND MALCHUT, WHICH ARE THE SECRET OF MOSES CALLED "MAN." "An offering to Hashem," by sacrificing all in order to be united both above and below. HENCE IT IS FIRST SAID "AN OFFERING TO HASHEM," WHICH IS THE JOINING FROM BELOW UPWARD, AND THEN "YOUR OFFERING," JOINING FROM ABOVE DOWNWARD, AS WAS SAID BEFORE.

621. מִן הַבְּהֵמָה, לְאַחֲזָאָה אָדָם וּבְהֵמָה, כֹּלָּא כַּחֲדָא. מִן הַבָּקָר וּמִן הַצֹּאן, אִלֵּין רְתִיכִין, דְּאִינוּן דַּכְיִין, דְּכֵיוָן דַּאֲמַר מִן הַבְּהֵמָה, יָכוֹל מִכֹּלָּא, בֵּין דַּכְיִין, בֵּין מְסָאֲבָן, הֲדַר וַאֲמַר מִן הַבָּקָר וּמִן הַצֹּאן.

621. "Of the cattle" (Vayikra 1:2) shows the unity of man and beast as one, AS WAS SAID BEFORE: "AN OFFERING TO HASHEM" IS MAN, WHO IS THE UNISON FROM BELOW UPWARD, WHENCE IT IS DRAWN DOWNWARD BY THE SECRET OF "YOUR OFFERING" OF THE CATTLE. THE TWO UNISONS ILLUMINATE TOGETHER. "Of the oxen and of the sheep" (Ibid.): These are pure Chariots. In saying "of the cattle (lit. 'animal')," one might think it refers to all animals, both clean and unclean. It therefore continues "of the oxen and of the sheep."

622. תַּקְרִיבוּ אֶת קָרְבַּנְכֶם. קָרְבָּנִי מִבָּעֵי לֵיהּ, מַאי קָרְבַּנְכֶם. אֶלָּא בְּקַדְמֵיתָא קָרְבָּן לַה', וְהַשְׁתָּא קָרְבַּנְכֶם. קָרְבָּן לַה' אָדָם. קָרְבַּנְכֶם מִן הַבְּהֵמָה מִן הַבָּקָר וּמִן הַצֹּאן: לְאַחֲזָאָה יְחוּדָא מִתַּתָּא לְעֵילָא, וּמֵעֵילָא לְתַתָּא. מִתַּתָּא לְעֵילָא, הַיְינוּ קָרְבָּן לַה'. מֵעֵילָא לְתַתָּא, הַיְינוּ קָרְבַּנְכֶם.

622. "Shall you bring your offering": HE ASKS: It should have been 'His offering', AS IT IS WRITTEN BEFORE "AN OFFERING TO HASHEM." Why say "your offering"? HE ANSWERS: First it should have been "an offering to Hashem" and now "your offering." HE EXPOUNDS UPON IT: "An offering to Hashem" is THE UNITY CALLED MAN, NAMELY THE RAISING OF THE NUKVA TO BE UNITED ABOVE THE CHEST OF ZEIR ANPIN, CALLED man. "Your offering...of the oxen, and of the flock" CONTINUES THE ILLUMINATION OF THE UNION OF THE CHEST UPWARD UNTO THE LOWER BEINGS WHO ARE FROM THE CHEST DOWNWARD in order to demonstrate the unison from below upward and from above downward. From below upward is "the offering to Hashem" and from above downward is "your offering."

623. לְמַלְכָּא, דְּאִיהוּ יָתֵיב בְּטוּרְסְקָא עִלָּאָה, לְעֵילָא לְעֵילָא, וְכֻרְסְיָא אִתְתַּקַּן עַל הַהוּא טוּרְסְקָא, וּמַלְכָּא עִלָּאָה עַל כֹּלָּא. בַּר נָשׁ דְּקָרֵיב דּוֹרוֹנָא לְמַלְכָּא, בָּעָא לְסַלְּקָא מִדַּרְגָּא לְדַרְגָּא, עַד דְּסָלֵיק מִתַּתָּא לְעֵילָא לַאֲתַר דְּמַלְכָּא יָתִיב, עִלָּאָה עַל כֹּלָּא, וּכְדֵין יָדְעִין דְּהָא סָלְקִין דּוֹרוֹנָא לְמַלְכָּא, וְהַהוּא דּוֹרוֹנָא דְּמַלְכָּא אִיהוּ. נָחֵית דּוֹרוֹנָא מֵעֵילָא לְתַתָּא, הָא יָדְעִין דְּהַהוּא דּוֹרוֹנָא דְּמַלְכָּא נָחֵית מֵעֵילָא, לִרְחִימָא דְּמַלְכָּא, דְּאִיהוּ לְתַתָּא.

623. This is like a king who sits high upon a great mountain, and his throne is fixed on it. The king WHO SITS ON THE THRONE is higher than anyone. A man who offers the king a present, should take it up step by step until he reaches the top where the king sits up high. Everyone knows then that a present is brought up to the king. And this is the present to the king. When a present is brought down, then surely it is a present from the king above to his friend below.

624. כָּךְ בְּקַדְמֵיתָא, אָדָם סָלֵיק בְּדַרְגּוֹי מִתַּתָּא לְעֵילָא, וּכְדֵין קָרְבָּן לַה'. מִן הַבְּהֵמָה מִן הַבָּקָר, נָחֵית בְּדַרְגּוֹי מֵעֵילָא לְתַתָּא, וּכְדֵין קָרְבַּנְכֶם. בְּגִינֵי כָּךְ כְּתִיב, אָכַלְתִּי יַעֲרִי עִם דִּבְשִׁי שָׁתִיתִי יֵינִי עִם חֲלָבִי, הַיְינוּ אָדָם וְקָרְבָּן לַה'. אִכְלוּ רֵעִים, הַיְינוּ מִן הַבְּהֵמָה מִן הַבָּקָר וּמִן הַצֹּאן, וּכְדֵין תַּקְרִיבוּ אֶת קָרְבַּנְכֶם.

624. So at first, man mounts the grades from below upward. This is "an offering to Hashem." "Of the cattle and of the oxen," he descends down the grades from above. This is "your offering." Hence it is written, "I have eaten my honeycomb with my honey; I have drunk my wine with my milk" (Shir Hashirim 5:1), which is a man and "an offering to Hashem," FOR IT IS THE HOLY ONE, BLESSED BE HE, WHO SAYS, "I HAVE EATEN…"; "Eat, O dear ones" "of the cattle, of the oxen and of the sheep." Then, "shall you bring your offering."

625. אֲתוֹ ר' יִצְחָק וְרַבִּי יְהוּדָה, וּנְשָׁקוּהָ עַל רֵישֵׁיהּ, אֲמָרוּ, בְּרִיךְ רַחֲמָנָא דְּזָכֵינָא לְמִשְׁמַע דָּא, וּבְרִיךְ רַחֲמָנָא, דְּלָא אִתְאֲבִידוּ מִלִּין אִלֵּין בְּהַהוּא סָבָא. קָמוּ וַאֲזָלוּ, עַד דַּהֲווֹ אָזְלֵי, חָמוּ חַד גֶּפֶן נְטִיעַ בְּחַד גִּנָּא.

625. Rabbi Yitzchak and Rabbi Yehuda came to him and kissed his forehead. They said: 'Blessed be the Merciful One that we merited to hear these words, and they were not wasted on that old man', WHO WOULD NOT HAVE UNDERSTOOD THEM, AND THE WORDS WOULD BE LOST. They rose and went. While they were walking, they saw a vine planted in a garden.

63. "Binding his foal to the vine," part two

A Synopsis

This second discussion of the title verse interprets it as containing a warning against the Klipah of the mule and the foal. Were it not for the aspect of the Holy Name included here, we are told, these Klipot would have destroyed the world. The vine signifies the congregation of Yisrael, which accepts none, but God, as a vine will receive no graft from another tree. The child and the rabbis then discuss the verse "He washed his garments in wine." This is interpreted as signifying the Messiah, the Female Principle, who will overpower the idolatrous nations. Another explanation is that the Yisraelites draw from Malchut in Holiness and she therefore brings them mercy and joy. The idolatrous nations, however, draw from Malchut excessively and are consequently subject to Judgment. We then learn the significance of the verse, "His eyes are red with wine, and his teeth white with milk." The Written Law of the Torah is called milk, and the Oral Law is called wine. The passage is an allusion to the illumination of Binah and the intoxicating Torah, Malchut, which transfers judgment to those who draw it downwards from above. Following this, through an interpretation of the verse, "And wine that makes glad the heart of man", we learn that wine begins in joy and ends in judgment. The "oil to brighten the face" signifies the drawing of Chassadim from Aba, through which all judgments are cancelled. The final verse of this discourse is "and bread which sustains the heart of man." It is a reference to the bread that sustains the world, signifying Zeir Anpin. The world depends on both bread and wine, the Female Principle and Zeir Anpin, since they sustain the world together. Therefore, when saying grace, there must be bread on the left side of the table and wine on the right, in order to pronounce a proper blessing on the Holy Name.

The Relevance of the Passage

All things must be in balance in order to generate and sustain fulfillment. Too much of a good thing eventually brings negativity. Common phrases, such as "killing him with kindness," help convey the lesson and Light being distilled in this passage. The wisdom and discipline to balance our desires to receive with our desire to share are infused into our being. We are inspired to direct and channel our desires for spiritual purposes as opposed to selfish, indulgent pursuits, the former generating fulfillment, the latter bringing judgement down upon this world.

626. פָּתַח הַהוּא יְנוּקָא וַאֲמַר, אֹסְרִי לַגֶּפֶן עִירֹה וְלַשּׂוֹרֵקָה בְּנִי אֲתֹונוֹ

הַאי קְרָא רָזָא עִלָּאָה הוּא. אֹסְרִי, אָסַר מִבָּעֵי לֵיהּ. עִירֹה, עַיִר מִבָּעֵי
לֵיהּ. אֶלָּא רָזָא הוּא, לְדַרְדְּקֵי דְּאִינּוּן בְּבֵי רַב, לְאִסְתַּמְּרָא מֵהַהוּא גִּירָא
דְּעַיִר, וּשְׁמָא קַדִּישָׁא אִתְכְּלִיל תַּמָּן י"ה.

626. The child opened the discussion saying: "Binding his foal to the vine, and his ass's colt to the choice vine" (Beresheet 49:11). This verse contains a high mystery. HE ASKS: Why does it say "*osri* (Eng. 'binding')" instead of the customary '*oser*' and "*iroh* (Eng. 'ass')" instead of '*ayir*'? HE ANSWERS: It is the secret that the schoolchildren should beware of the sharp edge OF THE KLIPAH of the donkey. The Holy Name *Yud-Hei* is included there in order to subdue it, TO WIT, THE *YUD* OF 'OSRI' TOGETHER WITH THE *HEI* OF 'IROH'.

627. וּכְמָה דְּהָכָא אִתְרְמִיז שְׁמָא קַדִּישָׁא, הָכֵי נָמֵי וְלַשֹּׂרֵקָה, שׂוֹרֵק
מִבָּעֵי לֵיהּ. בְּנִי בֶּן מִבָּעֵי לֵיהּ. שׂוֹרֵק, כִּדְכְתִיב וְאָנֹכִי נְטַעְתִּיךְ שֹׂרֵק.
בֶּן, כְּד"א בֶּן אֲתוֹנוֹת. אַמַּאי שׂוֹרֵקָה, וְאַמַּאי בְּנִי.

627. Just as the Holy Name is hinted here, IT IS HINTED ALSO IN THE WORDS "AND HIS ASS'S COLT TO THE CHOICE VINE." It says "*sorekah*" (Eng. 'choice vine') instead of '*sorek*' and *bni* (Eng. 'colt') instead of *ben*, as it is written: "And I have planted you a noble vine (Heb. *sorek*)" (Yirmeyah 2:21) WITHOUT *HEI* and "upon a colt (Heb. *ben*)" (Zecharyah 9:9) WITHOUT *YUD*. Why then is it written here sorekah and bni?

628. אֶלָּא, כְּמָה דְּאִית שְׁמָא קַדִּישָׁא לְאַכְפְּיָא לְעַיִר, הָכֵי נָמֵי, אִית
שְׁמָא קַדִּישָׁא, לְאַכְפְּיָא חֵילָא אָחֳרָא, דְּאִיהִי חֲמָרָא, דְּאִלְמָלֵא דִּשְׁמָא
קַדִּישָׁא אִתְרְמִיז הָכָא, הֲווֹ מְטַרְטְשֵׁי עָלְמָא, י"ה בְּחֵילָא דָּא, וְי"ה
בְּחֵילָא דָּא, לְאִסְתַּמְּרָא עָלְמָא מִנַּיְיהוּ, וּלְאִסְתַּמְּרָא בַּר נָשׁ, דְּלָא
יִשְׁלְטוּן בֵּיהּ בְּעָלְמָא.

628. As there is a Holy Name which subdues the KLIPAH foal, so there is a Holy Name to subdue the power of another KLIPAH, the donkey. IT IS THE *YUD* OF 'BNI' AND THE *HEI* OF 'SOREKAH'. Were it not for the Holy Name hinted here, THESE TWO KLIPOT would have destroyed the world.

Therefore, there is *Yud-Hei* against this force and *Yud-Hei* against the other force, which protect the world against them, and preserve man so they would have no mastery over him in the world.

629. אָסְרִי לַגֶּפֶן, מַאי גֶּפֶן. דָּא כְּנֶסֶת יִשְׂרָאֵל, אַמַּאי אִתְקְרִיאַת גֶּפֶן. אֶלָּא מַה גֶּפֶן, לָא מְקַבְּלָא עֲלָהּ נְטִיעָא אָחֳרָא, הָכִי נָמֵי כְּנֶסֶת יִשְׂרָאֵל, לָא מְקַבְּלָא עֲלָהּ אֶלָּא לְקוּדְשָׁא בְּרִיךְ הוּא, וּבְגִין כְּנֶסֶת יִשְׂרָאֵל, אִתְכַּפְיָין קַמָּהּ כָּל חֵילִין אָחֳרָנִין, וְלָא יָכְלִין לְאַבְאָשָׁא, וּלְשַׁלְטָאָה בְּעַלְמָא, וְעַ״ד אַטִּיל קְרָא שְׁמָא קַדִּישָׁא בֵּינַיְיהוּ, בְּהַאי גִיסָא וּבְהַאי גִיסָא. בְּנִי אֲתוֹנוֹ, דְּאִתְעֲקַר בְּגִין הַהוּא שׂוֹרֵק, כְּמָה דְאַתְּ אָמֵר, וְאָנֹכִי נְטַעְתִּיךְ שׂוֹרֵק וְגו׳.

629. "Binding his foal to the vine": What is the vine? It is the Congregation of Yisrael. Wherefore is it called vine? As a vine will receive no graft from another tree, so the Congregation of Yisrael accepts none but the Holy One, blessed be He. Therefore, in front of the Congregation of Yisrael all other forces are subdued, THE FOAL AND THE DONKEY, and they cannot harm nor rule the world. Therefore scripture inserts between them the Holy Name YUD-HEI on the side OF THE FOAL and the side OF THE DONKEY. The ass's colt is uprooted due to the choice vine, THE CONGREGATION OF YISRAEL, as said: "And I have planted you a noble vine."

630. כִּבֵּס בַּיַּיִן לְבוּשׁוֹ וְגו׳, כִּבֵּס, כּוֹבֵס מִבָּעֵי לֵיהּ. אֶלָּא כִּבֵּס, מִיּוֹמָא דְּאִתְבְּרֵי עַלְמָא, וּמַאן אִיהוּ דָּא מַלְכָּא מְשִׁיחָא. בַּיַּיִן: סְטַר שְׂמָאלָא. וּבְדַם עֲנָבִים: סְטַר שְׂמָאלָא. לְתַתָּא. וְזַמִּין מַלְכָּא מְשִׁיחָא לְשַׁלְטָאָה לְעֵילָא עַל כָּל חֵילִין אָחֳרָנִין דְּעַמִּין עכו״ם, וּלְתַבְרָא תּוּקְפֵּיהוֹן מֵעֵילָא וּמִתַּתָּא.

630. "He washed his garments in wine" (Beresheet 49:11). HE ASKS: Why does it say "washed" IN THE PAST TENSE instead of "washes"? HE ANSWERS: He has been washing since the world was created. Who has? King Messiah, THE NUKVA; THEREFORE "WASHED" IS IN THE PAST TENSE. "Wine" is the left side, NAMELY GVURAH OF ZEIR ANPIN; "the blood of grapes" is the left side below, NAMELY THE LEFT SIDE OF THE

NUKVA. WITH THE TWO GVUROT, OF ZEIR ANPIN AND OF THE NUKVA HERSELF, SHE WASHES HER GARMENTS. King Messiah, THE NUKVA, will rule above over all the other forces of the idolatrous nations, and crush their stronghold above and below.

631. ד״א כְּבֶס בַּיַּין לְבוּשׁוֹ, כְּגַוונָא דְּהַאי חַמְרָא, אַחֲזֵי חֵידוּ, וְכוּלֵּיהּ דִּינָא, הָכֵי נָמֵי מַלְכָּא מְשִׁיחָא, יֶחֱזֵי חֵדוּ לְיִשְׂרָאֵל, וְכוּלֵּיהּ דִּינָא לְעַמִּין עעכו״ם. כְּתִיב וְרוּחַ אֱלֹקִים מְרַחֶפֶת עַל פְּנֵי הַמַּיִם, דָּא רוּחָא דְּמַלְכָּא מְשִׁיחָא, וּמִן יוֹמָא דְּאִתְבְּרֵי עַלְמָא, אַסְחֵי לְבוּשֵׁיהּ בְּחַמְרָא עִלָּאָה.

631. Another explanation for "He washed his garments in wine": Wine is a sign of joy, AS IN THE VERSE, "MY WINE, WHICH CHEERS ELOHIM AND MAN" (SHOFTIM 9:13), and is all judgment, so King Messiah, WHO IS THE NUKVA, brings joy to the children of Yisrael, WHO DRAW FROM IT IN HOLINESS, but is all judgment to the idolatrous nations, WHO DRAW FROM IT EXCESSIVELY. It is written, "And the spirit of Elohim hovered over the surface of the waters" (Beresheet 1:2). This is the spirit of King Messiah, WHICH HOVERS TO AND FRO BETWEEN JUDGMENT AND MERCY. From the Creation of the world, He washes His garment in the holy wine, AS SAID ABOVE.

632. חָמֵי מַה כְּתִיב בַּתְרֵיהּ, חַכְלִילִי עֵינַיִם מִיַּיִן וּלְבֶן שְׁנַּיִם מֵחָלָב, דָּא חַמְרָא עִלָּאָה, דְּאוֹרַיְיתָא דְּמַרְוֵי, מִנֵּיהּ שָׁתֵי. וּלְבֶן שְׁנַּיִם מֵחָלָב, דְּהָא אוֹרַיְיתָא יַיִן וְחָלָב, תּוֹרָה שֶׁבִּכְתָב, וְתוֹרָה שֶׁבְּעַל פֶּה.

632. The following words are, "His eyes are red with wine, and his teeth white with milk" (Beresheet 49:12). "HIS EYES ARE RED WITH WINE" refers to the supernal wine, NAMELY THE ILLUMINATION OF THE LEFT OF BINAH. The Torah, THE NUKVA, when it intoxicates NAMELY TRANSFERS JUDGMENT TO THOSE WHO DRAW IT FROM ABOVE DOWNWARD, drinks it AND THEREFORE BINAH IS CONSIDERED, AS IF JUDGMENT COME FROM HER. "And his teeth white with milk" REFERS TO THE WRITTEN TORAH, ZEIR ANPIN, WHICH ACCEPTS CHASSADIM CALLED MILK, for the Torah is called wine and milk; the Written Torah, ZEIR ANPIN, IS CALLED MILK, and the Oral Law, THE NUKVA IS CALLED WINE. WINE COMES FROM BINAH AND MILK FROM ABA.

633. כְּתִיב וְיַיִן יְשַׂמַּח לְבַב אֱנוֹשׁ לְהַצְהִיל פָּנִים מִשָּׁמֶן, וַדַּאי מֵאֲתַר דְּאִתְקְרֵי שָׁמֶן. תָּא חֲזֵי, שֵׁירוּתָא דְּחַמְרָא חֶדְוָה, הוּא אֲתַר דְּכָל חֵידוּ מִנֵּיהּ נַפְקָא. וְסוֹפֵיהּ דִּינָא, מ"ט. בְּגִין דְּסוֹפָא דִּילֵיהּ, אֲתַר כְּנִישׁוּ דְּכֹלָּא, דִּינָא הוּא, וּבֵיהּ אִתְדָּן עַלְמָא, וְעַל דָּא שֵׁירוּתָא חֶדְוָה, וְסוֹפָא דִּינָא, בְּגִינֵי כָּךְ, לְהַצְהִיל פָּנִים מִשָּׁמֶן. מֵאֲתַר דְּכָל חֶדְוָה מִנֵּיהּ נַפְקָא.

633. It is written, "And wine that makes glad the heart of man; oil to brighten the face" (Tehilim 104:15). Indeed it is from the place called oil, WHICH IS ABA. HE EXPLAINS HIS WORDS, Come and behold: wine first makes glad, because it is a place whence all joys come from, NAMELY BINAH, and ends in Judgment WHEN IT EXPANDS TOWARDS THE NUKVA. Why? Because its ending is the place of gathering of all THE SFIROT, NAMELY THE NUKVA, WHICH IS THEREFORE CALLED THE CONGREGATION OF YISRAEL, NAMELY THE PLACE OF GATHERING OF ZEIR ANPIN. It is Judgment by which the world is sentenced. Therefore, since wine starts with joy and ends in Judgment, therefore there is "oil to brighten the face," whence all the joys issue.

634. וְלֶחֶם לְבַב אֱנוֹשׁ יִסְעָד, מַאן לֶחֶם. אֶלָּא לֶחֶם עַלְמָא סָעִיד, וְאִי תֵּימָא, דְּבֵיהּ תַּלְיָיא סְעִידוּ דְּעַלְמָא בִּלְחוֹדוֹי, לָאו הָכִי, דְּהָא לֵילְיָא בְּלָא יוֹמָא, לָא אִשְׁתַּכַּח, וְלָא בָּעֵי לְאַפְרְשָׁא לוֹן. וּמַאן דְּאַפְרִישׁ לוֹן, יִתְפְּרַשׁ מֵחַיִּין, וְהַיְינוּ דִּכְתִיב, לְמַעַן הוֹדִיעֲךָ כִּי לֹא עַל הַלֶּחֶם לְבַדּוֹ יִחְיֶה הָאָדָם. בְּגִין דְּלָא בָּעֵי לְאִתְפְּרָשָׁא.

634. "And bread which sustains the heart of man" (Tehilim 104:15): HE ASKS: What is the bread MENTIONED HERE? HE RESPONDS: It is the bread which sustains the world, THE SECRET OF CHASSADIM DRAWN FROM CHESED, GVURAH AND TIFERET OF ZEIR ANPIN. You might say that the world depends on it alone. This is not true. IT NEEDS ALSO WINE, THE SECRET OF THE ILLUMINATION OF CHOCHMAH, AS WAS SAID BEFORE, since night cannot exist without day. BUT THE DAY, WHICH IS ZEIR ANPIN, AND THE NIGHT, WHICH IS THE NUKVA, SHOULD BE JOINED TOGETHER. HENCE WE NEED BREAD FROM ZEIR ANPIN AND WINE FROM THE NUKVA, WHICH BOTH TOGETHER NOURISH THE WORLD. One must not separate them, AND DRAW BREAD ALONE FROM ZEIR ANPIN WITHOUT THE

NUKVA. Whoever separates them is separated from life, as it is written: "That He might make you know that man does not live by bread only" (Devarim 8:3). Thus one should not separate them.

635. וְאִי תֵימָא, דָּוִד הֵיךְ קָאֲמַר וְלֶחֶם לְבַב אֱנוֹשׁ יִסְעָד, הוֹאִיל וְלָא תַּלְיָיא בֵּיהּ בִּלְחוֹדוֹי סְעִידוּ דְּעָלְמָא. אֶלָּא דַּיְיקָא דְּמִלָּה, וְלֶחֶם, וא"ו אִיתּוֹסַף, כְּמוֹ וַה', וְעַל דָּא, כֹּלָּא אִשְׁתַּכַּח כַּחֲדָא.

635. It may be asked why David said: "And bread which sustains the heart of man," seeing that the world does not depend on it alone for nourishment. HE ANSWERS: The exact meaning of the words IS THAT in "and bread" there is an extra *Vav* (= and) like "and Hashem," WHICH INCLUDES THE NUKVA, FOR WHEREVER IT SAYS "AND HASHEM," IT INCLUDES HIM AND HIS COURT OF JUSTICE, WHICH IS THE NUKVA. HERE TOO "AND" INCLUDES THE NUKVA, and therefore all is together, NAMELY IN UNISON.

636. תָּא חֲזֵי , מַאן דִּמְבָרֵךְ עַל מְזוֹנָא, לָא יְבָרֵךְ עַל פָּתוֹרָא רֵיקַנְיָא, וּבָעֵי נַהֲמָא לְאִשְׁתַּכְּחָא עַל פָּתוֹרָא, וְכַסָּא דְחַמְרָא בִּימִינָא, מַאי טַעְמָא, בְּגִין לְקַשְּׁרָא שְׂמָאלָא בִּימִינָא, וְנַהֲמָא דְּיִתְבָּרַךְ מִנַּיְיהוּ, וּלְאִתְקַשְּׁרָא בְּהוֹ, וּלְמֶהֱוֵי כֹּלָּא חַד קְשׁוּרָא, לְבָרְכָא שְׁמָא קַדִּישָׁא כְּדְקָא יָאוֹת. דְּהָא לֶחֶם אִתְקַשַּׁר בְּיַיִן, וְיַיִן בִּימִינָא, וּכְדֵין בִּרְכָאן שַׁרְיָין בְּעַלְמָא, וּפָתוֹרָא אִשְׁתְּלֵים כְּדְקָא יָאוֹת.

636. HE FURTHER EXPLAINS: Come and see, when saying grace after meals, one should not bless over an empty table. There should be bread, THE ABUNDANCE OF ZEIR ANPIN, WHICH IS RIGHT, on the table, WHICH IS THE SECRET OF THE NUKVA, ON THE LEFT SIDE, and a glass of wine, WHICH IS THE ABUNDANCE OF THE NUKVA, on the right side, WHICH ALLUDES TO ZEIR ANPIN. What is the reason for this? It attaches the left to the right AND BINDS THEM. Thus the bread, WHICH IS RIGHT, will be blessed by them, THROUGH THE UNION WITH THE LEFT, and be attached to them, and they will all become one knot for the proper blessing of the Holy Name. For bread, WHICH IS THE RIGHT, FROM ZEIR ANPIN, is connected to wine, WHICH IS LEFT, FROM THE NUKVA, and wine, WHICH IS OF THE LEFT, will be attached to the right. Then blessings rest on the world, and the table, WHICH IS THE NUKVA, is properly perfected.

637. א"ר יִצְחָק, אִלְמָלֵא לָא אִזְדַּמָּן לָן אוֹרְחָא דָא אֶלָּא לְמִשְׁמַע מִלִּין אִלֵּין, דַּי לָן. א"ר יְהוּדָה. אָוֹת הוּא לְהַאי יְנוֹקָא, דְּלָא יִנְדַּע כָּל הַאי, וַאֲנָא מִסְתָּפֵינָא עֲלֵיהּ, אִי יִתְקַיִּים בְּעַלְמָא בְּגִין הַאי. א"ר יִצְחָק וְלָמָּה. א"ל, בְּגִין דְּהַאי רַבְיָא יָכֵיל לְאִסְתַּכְּלָא, בְּאַתְרָא דְּלֵית רְשׁוּ לְבַר נָשׁ לְאִסְתַּכְּלָא בֵּיהּ, וּמִסְתָּפֵינָא עֲלוֹי, דְּעַד לָא יִמְטֵי לְפָרְקוֹי, יַשְׁגַּח וְיִסְתַּכַּל וְיַעַנְשׁוּן לֵיהּ.

637. Rabbi Yitzchak said: Had we gone this way only to hear these words, it would have been worth our while. Rabbi Yehuda said: It would have been better for this child not to know so much, and I fear that for this, he might not survive in the world. Why, said Rabbi Yitzchak? He said: Since this boy can look upon a place where a man is not permitted to look, I am afraid for him that he will observe and look there before the time will come for him to marry, BEFORE HE WILL COME OF AGE, and be punished for it.

638. שָׁמַע הַהוּא יְנוֹקָא, אָמַר לָא מִסְתָּפֵינָא מֵעוֹנָשָׁא לְעָלְמִין, דְּהָא בְּשַׁעְתָּא דְּאִסְתָּלִיק אַבָּא מֵעַלְמָא, בָּרֵיךְ לִי וְצַלֵּי עָלַי. וְיִדַעְנָא דִזְכוּתָא דְאַבָּא יָגֵין עָלַי. אֲמָרוּ לֵיהּ וּמַאן הוּא אֲבוּךְ. אֲמַר בְּרֵיהּ דְּרַב הַמְנוּנָא סָבָא, נָטְלוּ לֵיהּ, וְאַרְכְּבוּהּ עַל כִּתְפַיְיהוּ, תְּלַת מִילִין.

638. The boy heard and said: I never fear punishment, because when my father passed away, he blessed me and prayed for me, and I know that my father's merit will protect me. They asked him, And who is your father? He said: I am the son of Rav Hamnuna Saba (the elder). They took him on their shoulders for three miles.

64. "Out of the eater came forth food"

A Synopsis

The rabbis explain the title verse to the young son of Rav Hamnuna Saba (the elder). Their interpretation reveals that Yesod consumes the abundance from the Sfirot of Zeir Anpin. Through the strength of the Strict Judgment of Zeir Anpin, the Upper Worlds, signifying the Written Law, Malchut, our physical world, receives an abundance of illumination from the left. The Oral Law, called "honey," is this illumination of the left within Malchut. The righteous, we're told, provide "food" for the world, without which Malchut would be unable to endure. After delivering the young boy to his mother, the companions relate their experiences to Rabbi Shimon. A discussion of the verse, "Gird your sword upon your thigh," ensues. One interpretation provided reveals that this alludes to the vengeance of the Holy Covenant that the avenging sword wreaks on he who impairs the imprinted sign of the Holy Covenant. He who desires to protect the Holy Covenant should prepare and arm himself against the Evil Inclination by drawing this sword upon his thigh before it. Another explanation instructs us that before setting out on a journey, one should prepare oneself through prayers and supplication, and gird oneself with righteousness.

The Relevance of this Passage

Here, judgments that are hanging over us are sweetened with supernal "honey". The Light and the blessings of the righteous blanket us with protection and help generate sustenance. We are inspired to seek the path of the Torah and, in turn, we gain the strength to triumph over our Evil Inclinations. Finally, this passage provides us with protection for all of our journeys by igniting sparks of righteousness within our soul.

639. קָרוֹ עֲלֵיהּ, מֵהָאוֹכֵל יָצָא מַאֲכָל וּמֵעַז יָצָא מָתוֹק וגו'. אֲמַר לוֹן הַהוּא יְנוֹקָא, מִלָּה אָתָא לִידַיְיהוּ, פָּרִישׁוּ לָהּ. אֲמָרוּ לֵיהּ, קוּדְשָׁא בְּרִיךְ הוּא זַמִּין לָן אָרְחָא דְחַיֵּי, אֵימָא אַנְתְּ.

639. They recited about him the verse, "Out of the eater came forth food, and out of the strong came forth sweetness" (Shoftim 14:14). The boy said to them: You have spoken THIS VERSE, now explain it. They said to him: The Holy One, blessed be He, appointed us a path of life, you speak!

640. פְּתַח וְאָמַר, מֵהָאוֹכֵל יָצָא מַאֲכָל וּמֵעַז יָצָא מָתוֹק. הַאי קְרָא,

אַסְמַכְתָּא אִית לָן בֵּיהּ, מֵהָאוֹכֵל, דָּא צַדִּיק, דִּכְתִיב צַדִּיק אוֹכֵל
לְשׂוֹבַע נַפְשׁוֹ, צַדִּיק אוֹכֵל וַדַּאי, וְנָטִיל כֹּלָּא, אַמַּאי, לְשׂוֹבַע נַפְשׁוֹ,
לְמֵיהַב שָׂבְעָא, לְהַהוּא אֲתָר דְּאִקְרֵי נַפְשׁוֹ דְּדָוִד. יָצָא מַאֲכָל, דְּאִלְמָלֵא
הַהוּא צַדִּיק, לָא יִפּוֹק מְזוֹנָא לְעָלְמִין, וְלָא יָכִיל עַלְמָא לְקַיְּימָא. וּמֵעַז
יָצָא מָתוֹק, דָּא יִצְחָק, דְּבָרֵיךְ לְיַעֲקֹב בְּטַל הַשָּׁמַיִם וּמִשְׁמַנֵּי הָאָרֶץ.

640. He opened the discussion saying: "Out of the eater came forth food, and out of the strong came forth sweetness." There is another verse which shows that the eater is the righteous, which says, "The righteous eats to satisfy his soul" (Mishlei 13:25). The Righteous, YESOD, indeed eats and takes all THE ABUNDANCE FROM THE SFIROT OF ZEIR ANPIN. Why? "To satisfy his soul" and to satisfy that place called David's soul, NAMELY THE NUKVA. "Came forth food": Were it not for the righteous, no food would be provided for the world, and the world, THE NUKVA, would not have been able to endure. "And out of the strong came forth sweetness." This is Isaac, who blessed Jacob "of the dew of heaven, and the fatness of the earth" (Beresheet 27:28).

641. תּוּ, אע״ג דְּכֹלָּא חַד, אִלְמָלֵא תּוּקְפָּא דְּדִינָא קַשְׁיָא, לָא נָפְקָא
דְּבַשׁ. מַאן דְּבַשׁ. דָּא תּוֹרָה שֶׁבְּעַל פֶּה, דִּכְתִיב וּמְתוּקִים מִדְּבַשׁ וְנֹפֶת
צוּפִים. מֵעַז: דָּא תּוֹרָה שֶׁבִּכְתָב, דִּכְתִיב ה׳ עֹז לְעַמּוֹ יִתֵּן. יָצָא מָתוֹק,
דָּא תּוֹרָה שֶׁבְּעַל פֶּה.

641. TO EXPLAIN further, though all THE SFIROT ARE one, YET were it not for the strength of the strict Judgment OF THE LEFT OF ZEIR ANPIN, no honey would have come forth, WHICH IS THE ABUNDANCE OF THE ILLUMINATION OF THE LEFT WITHIN THE NUKVA, RECEIVED FROM THE LEFT OF ZEIR ANPIN. What is this honey? It is the Oral Law, THE NUKVA, of which it says, "Sweeter also than honey and the honeycomb" (Tehilim 19:11). ACCORDING TO THIS, "the strong" is the Written Torah, WHICH IS THUS CALLED as it is written: "Hashem gives strength to His people" (Tehilim 29:11), ZEIR ANPIN WILL GIVE STRENGTH. "Came forth sweetness": The Oral Law, NAMELY THE NUKVA, IN WHICH IS THE SECRET OF HONEY.

642. אַזְלוּ כַּחֲדָא תְּלַת יוֹמִין, עַד דְּמָטוּ לְטוּרְסָא דְּקִירָא דְּאִמֵּיהּ, כֵּיוָן

דְּחָמַאת לוֹן אַתְקְנֵית בֵּיתָא, וְיַתְבוּ תַּמָּן תְּלַת יוֹמִין אָחֳרָנִין. בָּרְכוּהוּ,
וַאֲזָלוּ, וְסִדְּרוּ מִלִּין קַמֵּיהּ דְּרַבִּי שִׁמְעוֹן. אֲמַר, וַדַּאי יְרוּתַת אוֹרַיְיתָא
אַחְסִין, וְאִלְמָלֵא זְכוּתָא דַּאֲבָהָן יִתְעֲנַשׁ מִלְּעֵילָא, אֲבָל קוּדְשָׁא בְּרִיךְ
הוּא לְאִינּוּן דְּאַזְלִין בָּתַר אוֹרַיְיתָא, אַחְסִינוּ לָהּ אִינּוּן וּבְנַיְיהוּ לְעָלְמִין,
הה״ד וַאֲנִי זֹאת בְּרִיתִי אוֹתָם אָמַר ה׳ רוּחִי אֲשֶׁר עָלֶיךָ וְגו׳.

642. They went together for three days until they reached the village where the CHILD'S mother LIVED. When she saw them she prepared the house and they stayed there for three more days, blessed him and went. They related what happened to Rabbi Shimon. He said: Surely he inherited the Torah. Were it not for ancestral merits OF RABBI HAMNUNA SABA (THE ELDER), he would have been punished from above. But the Holy One, blessed be He, is with those who follow the Torah. They inherit it and their descendants after them forever, as it is written: "As for Me, this is My covenant with them, says Hashem; My spirit that is upon you" (Yeshayah 59:21).

643 זְבוּלוּן לְחוֹף יַמִּים יִשְׁכּוֹן וְהוּא לְחוֹף אֳנִיּוֹת אֶנְיוֹת וְיַרְכָתוֹ וְגו׳. ר׳ אַבָּא
פָּתַח, חֲגוֹר חַרְבְּךָ עַל יָרֵךְ גִּבּוֹר הוֹדְךָ וַהֲדָרֶךָ. וְכִי דָּא הוֹד וְהָדָר, לְמֵיזַן
זַיְינָא, וּלְאִזְדַּרְזָא בְּהַאי. מַאן דְּאִשְׁתַּדַּל בְּאוֹרַיְיתָא, וְאַגַּח קְרָבָא
בְּאוֹרַיְיתָא, וְזָרֵיז גַּרְמֵיהּ בָּהּ, דָּא הוּא שְׁבָחָא, דָּא הוּא הוֹד וְהָדָר, וְאַתְּ
אֲמַרְתְּ חֲגוֹר חַרְבְּךָ.

643. "Zebulun shall dwell at the shore of the sea; and he shall be a haven for ships, and his border (or: 'thigh')..." Rabbi Aba opened the discussion saying: "Gird your sword upon your thigh, O mighty warrior: Your glory and your majesty" (Tehilim 45:4). HE ASKS: Is there glory and majesty in girding and wearing a weapon? Whoever studies the Torah and is engaged in war for the Torah, and arms himself with it, he is praiseworthy. This is glory and majesty. Why does it say, "Gird your sword...YOUR GLORY AND YOUR MAJESTY"?

644. אֶלָּא, וַדַּאי עִקְּרָא דְּמִלָּה, אָת קַיְּימָא קַדִּישָׁא, יְהַב קוּדְשָׁא בְּרִיךְ
הוּא, וְרָשִׁים לֵיהּ בִּבְנֵי נָשָׁא. בְּגִין דְּיִנְטְרוּן לֵיהּ, וְלָא יִפְגְּמוּן לֵיהּ
בִּפְגִימוּ לְהַאי רְשִׁימָא דְּמַלְכָּא, וּמַאן דְּפָגֵים לֵיהּ, הָא קָאֵים לְקַבְּלֵיהּ

חֶרֶב נֹקֶמֶת נְקַם בְּרִית, לְנַקְמָא נוּקְמָא דִּבְרִית קַדִּישָׁא, דְּאִתְרְשִׁים בֵּיהּ, וְהוּא פָּגִים לֵיהּ.

644. HE ANSWERS: Assuredly the meaning of this is that the Holy One, blessed be He, imprinted the sign of the holy covenant upon men to preserve it and not blemish the impress of the King. Whoever impairs it, the avenging sword rises before him and takes the vengeance of the holy covenant, which was imprinted upon him, yet he who impaired.

645. וּמַאן דְּבָעֵי לְנַטְרָא הַאי אֲתַר, יִזְדְּרֵז וְיִתַּקַן גַּרְמֵיהּ, וִישַׁוֵּי לְקַבְלֵיהּ, בְּשַׁעֲתָא דְּיִצְרָא בִּישָׁא יִתְקַף עֲלוֹי, לְהַאי חֶרֶב דְּקָיְימָא עַל יָרֵךְ, לְאִתְפָּרְעָא מִמַּאן דְּפָגִים הַאי אֲתַר, וּכְדֵין חֲגוֹר חַרְבְּךָ עַל יָרֵךְ גִּבּוֹר, גִּבּוֹר אִיהוּ, גִּבּוֹר אִתְקְרֵי. וְעַל דָּא הוֹדְךָ וַהֲדָרֶךָ.

645. He who desires to keep this place, THE HOLY COVENANT, should prepare and arm himself, and when the Evil Inclination assails him, he should draw before it this sword which is upon the thigh, thus taking vengeance upon him who impairs that place CALLED THIGH. Hence, "Gird your sword upon your thigh, O mighty warrior." He is mighty, WHO VANQUISHES THE EVIL INCLINATION, and is called mighty. This is "your glory and majesty."

646. ד"א חֲגוֹר חַרְבְּךָ עַל יָרֵךְ גִּבּוֹר. מַאן דְּנָפֵיק בְּאָרְחָא, יְתַקַן גַּרְמֵיהּ בִּצְלוֹתָא דְּמָארֵיהּ, וְיִזְדְּרֵז בְּהַאי צֶדֶק, חֶרֶב עִלָּאָה, בִּצְלוֹתָא וּבָעוּתִין עַד לָא יִפּוֹק לְאָרְחָא, כְּדִכְתִיב צֶדֶק לְפָנָיו יְהַלֵּךְ וְיָשֵׂם לְדֶרֶךְ פְּעָמָיו.

646. Another explanation for, "Gird your sword upon your thigh, O mighty warrior": Before setting out on a journey, one should prepare himself with a prayer to his Master, and gird himself with righteousness, NAMELY MALCHUT, which is the supernal sword, through prayers and supplication, as it is written: "Righteousness shall go before him, and walk in the way of his steps" (Tehilim 85:14).

647. תָּא חֲזֵי, זְבוּלוּן נָפֵיק תְּדִירָא לִשְׁבִילִין, וְאָרְחִין, וְאַגַּח קְרָבִין, וְאִזְדְּרֵז בְּהַאי חֶרֶב עִלָּאָה, בִּצְלוֹתָא וּבָעוּתִין, עַד לָא נָפֵיק בְּאָרְחָא,

וּכְדֵין נָצַח עַמִּין, וְאִתְתַּקַּף עֲלַיְיהוּ. וְאִי תֵימָא יְהוּדָה, הָא אִתְתַּקַּן
בְּהַאי, לְאַגָּחָא קְרָבִין, וְתִקּוּנִין, בְּהַאי חֶרֶב, אַמַּאי זְבוּלוּן. אֶלָּא, תָּא
חֲזֵי, הַנֵּי תְּרֵיסַר שִׁבְטִין, כֻּלְּהוּ תִּקּוּנָא דְמַטְרוֹנִיתָא הֲווֹ.

647. Come and see: Zebulun always went out on ways and paths, and engaged in wars, and armed himself with this supernal sword, WHICH IS THE NUKVA ON THE SIDE OF JUDGMENTS OF THE ILLUMINATION OF THE LEFT, with prayers and supplication, before setting out on his way. He then overcame and conquered nations. You may say that this was assigned to Judah, who was ready with the sword to wage wars and prepare amendments, FOR HE IS OF THE ASPECT OF MALCHUT; why then Zebulun? HE ANSWERS, Come and behold: the twelve tribes were the adornments of the Matron, WHO IS MALCHUT. THUS ZEBULUN TOO IS OF THE ASPECT OF MALCHUT.

65. Two improvements of the Nukva

65. Two improvements of the Nukva

A Synopsis

In Shir Hashirim, King Solomon made two corrections of the Nukva [Malchut]. One relates to the Jubilee, signifying Binah, and the other to the adornment of the bride, the Sabbatical year, signifying the Nukva. We learn that the creation was manifest in two places, the Upper and the Lower Worlds resembling each other perfectly. The upper Female Principle was corrected by Binah. These corrections were then drawn to the lower Nukva, thereby perfecting Malchut. The supernal correction is both concealed and revealed, because prophecy does not dwell outside the land of Yisrael. The lower correction is more exposed.

The Relevance of this Passage

Here we draw down Divine Light from the realm known as Binah that helps correct our souls and the entire world from previous iniquities. We draw the force of perfection from King Solomon, which helps bring about the final correction of the world and the age of Messiah.

648. תְּרֵין תִּקּוּנִין דְּנוּקְבֵי אָמַר שְׁלֹמֹה בְּשִׁיר הַשִּׁירִים, חַד לְרַעְיָא עִלָּאָה יוֹבְלָא, וְחַד לְכַלָּה, שְׁנַת הַשְּׁמִיטָה. חַד תִּקּוּנָא לְעֵילָא, וְחַד תִּקּוּנָא לְתַתָּא. עוֹבָדָא דִּבְרֵאשִׁית, הָכִי הוּא נָמֵי, בְּהַנֵּי תְּרֵי אַתְרֵי, חַד עוֹבָדָא לְעֵילָא, וְחַד עוֹבָדָא לְתַתָּא, וְעַ״ד פְּתִיחָא דְאוֹרַיְיתָא בְּב׳, עוֹבָדָא דִּלְתַתָּא, כְּגַוְונָא דִּלְעֵילָא, דָּא עֲבַד עָלְמָא עִלָּאָה, וְדָא עֲבַד עָלְמָא תַּתָּאָה. כְּגַוְונָא דָא, תְּרֵין תִּקּוּנִין דְּנוּקְבֵי קָאֲמַר שְׁלֹמֹה, חַד לְעֵילָא, וְחַד לְתַתָּא, חַד לְעֵילָא, בְּתִקּוּנָא עִלָּאָה דִּשְׁמָא קַדִּישָׁא, חַד לְתַתָּא, בְּתִקּוּנָא תַּתָּאָה כְּגַוְונָא דִּלְעֵילָא.

648. Solomon mentioned two improvements of the Nukva in "Shir Hashirim," one for the supernal shepherdess, the Jubilee, NAMELY BINAH, and one for the bride, the Sabbatical year, NAMELY THE NUKVA, one correction above IN BINAH and one below IN THE NUKVA. The Creation too was manifest in two places, one work above IN BINAH, and one below IN THE NUKVA. This is why the Torah begins with *Bet* (= 2), WHICH ALLUDES TO THE TWO NUKVAS. The work below resembled IN ITS PERFECTION the work above. ABA made the upper world, BINAH and ZEIR ANPIN made the lower world, THE NUKVA. In the same manner, of the two improvements of

the Nukvas mentioned by Solomon, the one is above and the other below. The upper one is fixed by the upper establishment of the Holy Name, WHICH IS BINAH, and the lower by the establishment of the lower one, THE NUKVA, like the upper establishment IN BINAH. ALL THE IMPROVEMENTS HE MADE IN THE SUPERNAL NUKVA, HE DREW UNTO THE LOWER NUKVA, BY WHICH THE LOWER NUKVA, MALCHUT, WAS PERFECTED AS THE UPPER ONE, BINAH.

649. תָּא חֲזֵי, זַכָּאָה חוּלָקֵיה דְּיַעֲקֹב קַדִּישָׁא, דְּזָכָה לְהַאי. וְהָא אִתְּמָר מִיּוֹמָא דְּאִתְבְּרֵי עָלְמָא, לָא אִשְׁתַּכַּח עַרְסָא שְׁלֵימָתָא כְּעַרְסֵיה דְּיַעֲקֹב. וּבְשַׁעְתָּא דְּבָעָא לְאִסְתַּלָּקָא מֵעָלְמָא, כְּדֵין הֲוָה שָׁלִים, בְּכָל סִטְרוֹי, אַבְרָהָם מִימִינֵיה, יִצְחָק מִשְׂמָאלֵיה, הוּא בְּאֶמְצָעִיתָא, שְׁכִינְתָּא קַמֵּיה, כֵּיוָן דְּחָמָא יַעֲקֹב הַאי, קָרָא לִבְנוֹי, וַאֲמַר לוֹן הֵאָסְפוּ, בְּגִין דְּיִשְׁתַּכַּח תִּקּוּנָא דִּלְעֵילָא וְתַתָּא.

649. Come and see: Happy is the portion of holy Jacob, who merited this. We learned that since the world was created, there was not a more complete bed than Jacob's bed. When Jacob prepared to depart from the world, he was whole on all sides, Abraham, CHESED, on his right, Isaac, GVURAH, on his left, and he himself, TIFERET, in the middle. The Shechinah was before him. THIS IS THE SECRET OF THE PERFECTION OF THE FOUR LEGS OF THE SUPERNAL THRONE, EACH OF CHESED, GVURAH, TIFERET AND MALCHUT INCLUDES THREE, AMOUNTING TO TWELVE, AND BINAH ABOVE THEM. When Jacob saw this, he called his sons and said to them, "Gather yourselves" so there will be adornment above and below.

650. תָּא חֲזֵי רָזָא דְּמִלָּה, תְּרֵין תִּקּוּנִין אִשְׁתַּכָּחוּ תַּמָּן, חַד עִלָּאָה, וְחַד תַּתָּאָה, לְמֶהֱוֵי כֹּלָּא שְׁלִים כְּדְקָא יָאוֹת. תִּקּוּנָא עִלָּאָה, תִּקּוּנָא סְתִים וְגַלְיָא, דְּהָא תִּקּוּנָא דְּיוֹבֵלָא אִיהוּ, הַהוּא דַּאֲמַר שְׁלֹמֹה בְּשִׁיר הַשִּׁירִים כְּדְקָאָמְרָן, רֵישָׁא סְתִים הֲוָה דְּלָא אִתְגַּלְיָיא הָכָא, וְלָא יָאוֹת לְאִתְגַּלְיָיא. דְּרוֹעִין וְגוּפָא אִתְגַּלְיָין, וְהָא יְדִיעִין. שׁוֹקִין סְתִימוּ וְלָא אִתְגַּלְיָין. מ"ט, בְּגִין דִּנְבוּאָה לָא שַׁרְיָא אֶלָּא בְּאַרְעָא קַדִּישָׁא. וְתִקּוּנָא דָּא סְתִים וְגַלְיָיא.

650. Come and see: The secret of the matter is that two establishments were there, an upper and a lower one, so that all will be perfected; TO WIT, THE NUKVA PERFECTED LIKE BINAH. HE EXPLAINS, The supernal correction is concealed and revealed, since it is the adornment of the Jubilee, which Solomon mentioned in "Shir Hashirim," which we said TO BE BINAH. The head, THE FIRST THREE SFIROT OF ZEIR ANPIN, is concealed, since it is not revealed here, nor should it be, AS THE HEAD OF ZEIR ANPIN IS ESTABLISHED BY CHESED AND GVURAH; the arms and the body, CHESED, GVURAH AND TIFERET, are exposed and known; the legs, NETZACH AND HOD, are concealed and cannot be seen. Why? Because prophecy, THE SECRET OF ABUNDANCE OF NETZACH AND HOD, does not dwell outside the land of Yisrael, WHICH IS THE NUKVA, TO WIT, THEIR ABUNDANCE IS REVEALED IN THE NUKVA, THE ILLUMINATION OF CHOCHMAH WHICH BELONGS TO HER, AND NOT TO ZEIR ANPIN. And this establishment is concealed and revealed.

651. תִּקוּנָא אָחֳרָא תַּתָּאָה, תִּקוּנָא דְּכַלָּה דְּקָאֲמַר שְׁלֹמֹה בְּשִׁיר הַשִּׁירִים, הַאי תִּקוּנָא דְּאִתְגַּלְיָיא יַתִּיר, וְתִקוּנָא דָא בִּתְרֵיסַר שִׁבְטִין דְּאִינוּן תְּחוֹתָה, וְתִקוּנָא דְגוּפָא דִילָה.

651. Another lower establishment (also: 'adornment') is the adornment of the bride, which Solomon mentioned in "Shir Hashirim," THE NUKVA. This adornment is more visible SINCE THE ILLUMINATION OF CHOCHMAH IS SHINING HERE. This adornment is done through the twelve tribes under her, and the adornment of her body; THEY ARE THE FOUR SFIROT CHESED AND GVURAH, NETZACH AND HOD, THREE KNOTS IN EACH AND TWELVE IN ALL. THE NUKVA, TIFERET BETWEEN THEM, IS ABOVE THEM, AS SHALL BE WXPLAINED.

66. Corrected by twelve in two worlds

A Synopsis

Rabbi Aba begins the discussion by quoting the verse, "And he made a molten sea" It stood upon twelve oxen" We learn that when Jacob saw the adornment of the upper sea by the twelve chariots appointed from above, he wished to complete the adornment of the lower sea. He therefore called to his twelve sons to prepare to perfect the Faith. Thus, the Lower World, the Nukva, [Malchut] was perfected by the twelve tribes. Three tribes look to each of the four directions of the world, signifying Chesed, Gvurah, Netzach and Hod, the arms and legs of the body of the Shechinah. We also learn that "The seven eyes of The Creator" allude to the seventy members of the Sanhedrin. The hairs on his head are signified by the great numbers in the camp of Reuben and in the camp of Judah. The discourse then turns again to supernal correction of the Jubilee discussed in the previous section. Finally, the rabbis expand upon the significance of the twelve supports of Binah and the Nukva, the structure of the metaphorical body, the seven supernal eyes, and the hairs of the head.

The Relevance of this Passage

Readers of this passage rise above the negative celestial influences of the twelve constellations. Ascending over the signs allows us to become the captains of our own destiny. In addition, the protective Light of the Shechinah encircles our souls. The twelve tribes also signify the support and foundation of the spiritual worlds, and thus, we draw support for our own efforts towards spiritual evolvement.

652. פְּתַח ר' אַבָּא וְאָמַר, וַיַּעַשׂ אֶת הַיָּם מוּצָק וגו'. וּכְתִיב עוֹמֵד עַל שְׁנֵי עָשָׂר בָּקָר שְׁלֹשָׁה פוֹנִים צָפוֹנָה וּשְׁלֹשָׁה פוֹנִים יָמָּה וּשְׁלֹשָׁה פוֹנִים נֶגְבָּה וגו' וְהַיָּם עֲלֵיהֶם מִלְמַעְלָה וגו'. וּכְתִיב וְאֶת הַבָּקָר שְׁנֵים עָשָׂר תַּחַת הַיָּם. עוֹמֵד עַל שְׁנֵי עָשָׂר בָּקָר, הָכֵי הוּא וַדַּאי, דְּדָא יָם מִתַּקְּנָא בִּי"ב בִּתְרֵין עָלְמִין, בִּתְרֵיסַר לְעֵילָא רְתִיכִין מְמַנָּן, לְעֵילָא בִּתְרֵיסַר, לְתַתָּא תְּרֵיסַר שִׁבְטִין. כֵּיוָן דְּחָמָא יַעֲקֹב תִּקּוּנָא עִלָּאָה, וְחָמָא שְׁכִינְתָּא קָאֵים לְקַבְּלֵיהּ, בָּעָא לְאַשְׁלָמָא תִּקּוּנְהָא, קָרָא לִבְנוֹהִי תְּרֵיסַר, וַאֲמַר לוֹן הֵאָסְפוּ, אַתְקִינוּ גַּרְמַיְיכוּ לְאַשְׁלָמָא מְהֵימְנוּתָא.

652. Rabbi Aba opened the discussion with the verse, "And he made a molten sea... It stood upon twelve oxen, three looking towards the north,

and three looking towards the west, and three looking towards the south, and three looking towards the east: and the sea was set above upon them" (I Melachim 7:23-25) and "twelve oxen under the sea" (Ibid. 44). "It stood upon twelve oxen" surely, for the sea is adorned by twelve within both worlds, THE SUPERNAL WORLD BINAH AND THE LOWER WORLD THE NUKVA. The upper twelve are the Chariots appointed from above. THEY ARE CHESED, GVURAH, TIFERET AND MALCHUT ABOVE THE CHEST OF ZEIR ANPIN, EACH INCLUDING THREE. TOGETHER THEY AMOUNT TO TWELEVE AND BINAH RIDES OVER THEM. HENCE THE CHESED, GVURAH, TIFERET AND MALCHUT ARE CONSIDERED AS CHARIOTS. And the lower twelve are the twelve tribes, BEING CHESED, GVURAH, NETZACH AND HOD OF THE NUKVA EACH INCLUDING THREE AND TOGETHER AMOUNTING TO TWELVE. THE NUKVA, TIFERET BETWEEN THEM, RIDES OVER THEM. When Jacob saw the supernal adornment, CHESED, GVURAH AND TIFERET, and the Shechinah in front of him, WHICH IS MALCHUT, THE SECRET OF THE FOUR LEGS OF THE SUPERNAL THRONE, he wanted to complete the adornment, so he called for his twelve sons and said to them "Gather yourselves" and prepare yourselves to perfect the faith, THE NUKVA. THEY SHOULD RECTIFY THEMSELVES WITH THE SECRET OF THE ADORNMENT OF THE NUKVA'S TWELVE, SO THAT THE NUKVA WILL BE COMPLETED, LIKE THE NUKVA ABOVE, BINAH, AND THE ADORNMENT WILL BE COMPLETED.

653. תָּא חֲזֵי, תְּרֵיסַר שִׁבְטִין, בְּד׳ דְּגָלִין, בְּד׳ סִטְרִין, שְׁלֹשָׁה פּוֹנִים צָפוֹנָה וּשְׁלֹשָׁה פּוֹנִים יָמָּה וּשְׁלֹשָׁה פּוֹנִים נֶגְבָּה וּשְׁלֹשָׁה פּוֹנִים מִזְרָחָה וְהַיָּם עֲלֵיהֶם. וְהָכֵי הוּא וַדַּאי תְּלַת שִׁבְטִין לְכָל סְטַר, לְד׳ רוּחֵי עַלְמָא, וּתְלַת שִׁבְטִין לִדְרוֹעָא דִּימִינָא, וּתְלַת שִׁבְטִין לִדְרוֹעָא דִשְׂמָאלָא, וּתְלַת שִׁבְטִין, לְיַרְכָא יְמִינָא, וּתְלַת שִׁבְטִין לְיַרְכָא שְׂמָאלָא, וְגוּפָא דִשְׁכִינְתָּא עֲלַיְיהוּ, הה״ד וְהַיָּם עֲלֵיהֶם.

653. Come and see the twelve tribes with four standards to the four directions: "Three looking towards the north, and three looking towards the west, and three looking towards the south, and three looking towards the east: and the sea was set above upon them." So three tribes look to each of the four directions of the world, three tribes to the right arm, CHESED, and three tribes to the left arm, GVURAH, three tribes to the right leg, NETZACH, and three tribes to the left leg, HOD. And the body of the Shechinah,

TIFERET CALLED BODY, is above them, as it is written: "and the sea was set above upon them," AS THE SEA IS THE SHECHINAH.

654. מַאי טַעְמָא תְּלַת שִׁבְטִין לִדְרוֹעָא, וּתְלַת שִׁבְטִין לִיַרְכָא, וְכֵן לְכֹלָּא. אֶלָּא רָזָא דְמִלָּה, תְּלַת קִשְׁרִין אִינוּן בִּדְרוֹעָא יְמִינָא, וּתְלַת בִּשְׂמָאלָא, וּתְלַת בִּיַרְכָא יְמִינָא, וּתְלַת קִשְׁרִין בִּיַרְכָא שְׂמָאלָא, אִשְׁתַּכָּחוּ תְּרֵיסַר קִשְׁרִין לְאַרְבַּע סִטְרִין, וְגוּפָא עֲלַיְיהוּ. אִשְׁתַּכָּחוּ תְּרֵיסַר עִם גּוּפָא בְּגַוְונָא דִלְעֵילָא. מְנָ"ל, דִּכְתִיב כָּל אֵלֶּה שִׁבְטֵי יִשְׂרָאֵל שְׁנֵים עָשָׂר, וְזֹאת, בְּגִין דְּבָהּ אִשְׁתְּלֵים חוּשְׁבְּנָא, כְּמָה דְּאִתְּמַר וְהַיָּם עֲלֵיהֶם מִלְמָעְלָה.

654. Why are there three tribes per arm and three tribes per leg? The secret of this is that there are three joints in the right arm OF THE LOWER BODY, and so in the left arm, the right leg and the left leg. They are twelve altogether, attached to the body as above. Whence do we know that? From the verse, "All these are the twelve tribes of Yisrael: and this" (Beresheet 49:28). HE ATTACHED: "AND THIS IS THAT WHICH THEIR FATHER SPOKE TO THEM," THE NUKVA CALLED 'THIS', because the reckoning is complete with her, as it says, "And the sea was set above upon them," WHICH IS THE NUKVA CALLED SEA. THUS, THE TWELVE TRIBES ARE ATTACHED TO THE BODY OF THE NUKVA ABOVE THEM.

655. שִׁבְעָה עֵינֵי ה' אִינוּן שִׁבְעָה עֵינֵי הָעֵדָה. שִׁבְעִין סַנְהֶדְרִין. שַׂעֲרָהָא: כְּמָה דִכְתִיב, כָּל הַפְּקוּדִים לְמַחֲנֵה יְהוּדָה מְאַת אֶלֶף וְגו'. כָּל הַפְּקוּדִים לְמַחֲנֵה רְאוּבֵן, וְכֵן לְכֻלְּהוּ.

655. "The seven eyes of Hashem" (Zecharyah 4:10) are the seven eyes of the congregation, NAMELY, CHESED, GVURAH, TIFERET, NETZACH, HOD, YESOD AND MALCHUT OF THE HEAD OF THE NUKVA CALLED HEAD CONGREGATION. BEING THE MOCHIN OF CHOCHMAH, THEY ARE ONSIDEREED TO BE EYES. They are the seventy members of the Sanhedrin, AS EACH OF CHESED, GVURAH, TIFERET, NETZACH, HOD, YESOD AND MALCHUT IS INCLUDED OF TEN, SEVENTY IN ALL, IN THE SECRET OF THE VERSE "FOR THE JUDGMENT IS ELOHIM" (DEVARIM 1:17). The hairs THAT GROW FROM THIS HEAD ARE ALLUDED TO in the verse, "All

that were numbered in the camp of Judah were a hundred thousand" (Bemidbar 2:9). "All that were numbered in the camp of Reuben..." (Ibid. 16). ALL THOSE GREAT NUMBERS ARE CONSIDERED TO BE THE HAIRS OF THE NUKVA.

656. וְאִי תֵימָא, בְּמִצְרַיִם דְּיַעֲקֹב סַלְּקוּ מֵעַלְמָא, דְּאִשְׁתַּכַּח שְׁלִימוּ בְּהַהִיא שַׁעְתָּא, כּוּלֵי הַאי אָן הוּא. וַדַּאי שַׁבְעִין נַפְשִׁין הֲווֹ, וְכָל אִינּוּן דְּאוֹלִידוּ בְּשֶׁבַע עֶשְׂרֵה שְׁנִין, דְּלֵית לוֹן חוּשְׁבְּנָא, כְּמָה דִּכְתִיב וּבְנֵי יִשְׂרָאֵל פָּרוּ וַיִּשְׁרְצוּ וַיִּרְבּוּ וַיַּעַצְמוּ בִּמְאֹד מְאֹד, וּכְתִיב עָצְמוּ מִשַּׂעֲרוֹת רֹאשִׁי. זַכָּאָה חוּלָקֵיהּ דְּיַעֲקֹב שְׁלֵימָא, דְּהוּא אִשְׁתְּלִים לְעֵילָא וְתַתָּא.

656. You may ask: In Egypt, when Jacob departed from the world, where was perfection at that time, where were all those WHO WERE NUMBERED IN THE CAMPS, WHO ARE CONSIDERED THE HAIRS OF THE NUKVA? IF THEY WERE NOT THERE, THE NUKVA WOULD THEN BE IMPERFECT, FOR THEY ARE HER HAIRS. HE ANSWERS: Indeed they were seventy souls WHEN THEY ARRIVED IN EGYPT, CORRESPONDING TO THE MOCHIN OF THE SEVENTY MEMBERS OF THE SANHEDRIN, and they begot innumerable descendants during the seventeen years THAT JACOB LIVED IN EGYPT, as it is written: "And the children of Yisrael were fruitful, and increased abundantly, and multiplied, and grew exceedingly mighty (Heb. vaya'atzmu)" (Shemot 1:7). THEY WERE ALSO CONSIDERED AS THE HAIRS OF THE NUKVA, as it is written: "They are more (Heb. atzmu) than the hairs of my head" (Tehilim 40:13). THE WORD 'VAYA'ATZMU' ALSO REFERS TO HAIRS. THEY LIVED AT THE TIME OF JACOB'S DEPARTURE FROM THE WORLD, AND THEREFORE PERFECTION WAS NOT INCOMPLETE. Happy is the portion of perfect Jacob, who was perfected above and below.

657. אָמַר ר' אֶלְעָזָר, וַדַּאי הָכֵי הוּא, אֲבָל בְּתִקּוּנָא עִלָּאָה דְּיוֹבְלָא, הֵיךְ אִשְׁתַּכַּח כּוּלֵי הַאי. א"ל, אַרְיָא, כֵּיוָן דְּסַדַּר רַגְלוֹי לְמֵיעָאל בְּכַרְמָא, מַאן אִיהוּ דְּעָיֵיל בַּהֲדֵיהּ.

657. Rabbi Elazar said TO RABBI ABA, Surely this is AS YOU SAID. But concerning the supernal correction of the Jubilee, BINAH, how could there be so much there, NAMELY THE TWELVE ASPECTS? RABBI ABA said to him: After the lion was set to enter the vineyard, who should follow? WHICH MEANS, EXPLAIN IT YOURSELF.

658. פָּתַח רָבִּי אֶלְעָזָר וַאֲמַר, וְהוּא בְאֶחָד וּמִי יְשִׁיבֶנּוּ וְנַפְשׁוֹ אִוְּתָה
וַיַּעַשׂ. הַאי תִּקּוּנָא עִלָּאָה, הוּא כֹּלָּא חַד, לָא הֲוֵי בֵּיהּ פָּרוֹדָא, כְּהַאי
תַּתָּאָה, דְּהָא כְתִיב וּמִשָּׁם יִפָּרֵד וְהָיָה לְאַרְבָּעָה רָאשִׁים. וְאע"ג דְּאִית
בֵּיהּ פָּרוֹדָא, כַּד יִסְתַּכְּלוּן מִלֵּי, כֹּלָּא סַלְקָא לְחַד.

658. Rabbi Elazar opened the discussion with the verse, "But He is unchangeable (lit. 'in one'), and who can turn Him? and what His soul desires, even that He does" (Iyov 23:13). The supernal establishment IN BINAH is all one, and there is no division in it, like in the lower ESTABLISHMENT IN THE NUKVA, as it says "and from thence it was parted, and branched into four streams" (Beresheet 2:10), FOR THERE IS SEPARATION WITHIN THE NUKVA. Though it is divided, it all comes to one when you examine it, FOR EVEN THE SEPARATION IN HER IS FIXED BY THE CORRECTION OF THE TWELVE, AND THEN SHE IS ALL ONE. BUT BINAH WAS NEVER DIVIDED, AND NEEDS NO CORRECTION OF THE TWELVE TO FIX HER.

659. אֲבָל הַאי תִּקּוּנָא עִלָּאָה דְּיוֹבְלָא, קַיְימָא עַל תְּרֵיסַר, כְּהַאי
תַּתָּאָה, וְאע"ג דְּאִיהוּ חַד, הַאי חַד אַשְׁלִים לְכָל סְטַר, בְּהַאי סְטַר,
וּבְהַאי סְטַר. אִינּוּן שִׁית סְטְרִין עִלָּאִין תְּרֵיסַר הֲווֹ. דְּכָל חַד אוֹזִיף
לְחַבְרֵיהּ, וְאִתְכְּלִיל מִנֵּיהּ, וְאִשְׁתַּכְּחוּ תְּרֵיסַר, וְכֹלָּא קַיְימָא עַל
תְּרֵיסַר. מַאן גּוּפָא, דָּא יַעֲקֹב, וְהָא אִתְּמַר, אֶלָּא רֵישָׁא וְגוּפָא בְּחַד
קַיְימֵי.

659. But the establishment of the supernal Jubilee, BINAH, is also supported by twelve like the lower one, THE NUKVA. And though it is one, AND WAS NEVER PARTED, yet it perfects every side, this and that side – IN OTHER WORDS, THE ONENESS OF THE SFIROT TO THE RIGHT COMPLETES THE LEFT SIDE, AND VICE VERSA. Thus the six supernal extremities, CHESED, GVURAH, TIFERET, NETZACH, HOD AND YESOD OF BINAH, become twelve, since each of them lends ITS LIGHTS to its neighbor and is included of its neighbor's LIGHTS. Hence they are twelve, with the body OF BINAH ABOVE THEM. THEREFORE, everything is based on twelve. What is the body? It is Jacob, as we learned, NAMELY TIFERET, AND NOT BINAH WHICH IS THE HEAD AND NOT THE BODY. HOW CAN YOU SAY THAT

BINAH IS THE BODY OVER THE TWELVE? HE ANSWERS: the head and the body are together, TO WIT, THEY ARE INCLUDED WITHIN EACH OTHER, AND THEREFORE THE ASPECT OF TIFERET EXISTS ALSO IN THE HEAD OF BINAH.

660. תּוּ תְּרֵיסַר, תְּלַת קָשְׁרִין דִּדְרוֹעָא יְמִינָא חֶסֶ״ד חֲסָדִים. תְּלַת קָשְׁרִין דִּדְרוֹעָא שְׂמָאלָא גְּבוּר״ה גְּבוּרוֹת. תְּלַת קָשְׁרִין בְּיַרְכָא יְמִינָא, נֶצַ״ח נְצָחִים. תְּלַת קָשְׁרִין בְּיַרְכָא שְׂמָאלָא, הוֹ״ד וְהוֹדוֹת. הָא תְּרֵיסַר. וְגוּפָא קַיְימָא עֲלַיְיהוּ הָא תְּלֵיסַר. תּוּ, בִּתְלֵיסַר מְכִילָן אוֹרַיְיתָא אִתְפְּרַשׁ, וְכֹלָּא חַד, מֵעֵילָא לְתַתָּא בְּיִחוּדָא, עַד הַהוּא אֲתַר דְּקַיְימָא עַל פְּרוֹדָא.

660. WE SHOULD further EXPLAIN THE SECRET OF twelve. There are three joints in the right arm, Chesed - Chassadim, WHICH MEANS ALL THREE PERTAIN TO CHESED, and three joints in the left arm, Gvurah - Gvurot, THAT IS THREE TIMES GVUROT, three joints in the right leg, Netzach - Netzachim, THAT IS, THREE TIMES NETZACH, and three joints in the left leg, Hod and Hodot. Together, there are twelve, and with the body, TIFERET, which stands above them, there are thirteen. The Torah too is expounded by the thirteen attributes, THE THIRTEEN ATTRIBUTES OF MERCY DRAWN FROM THE THIRTEEN CHARACTERISTICS OF THE BEARD OF ARICH ANPIN, which are all one WITHOUT, HEAVEN FORBID, ANY SEPARATION. They are drawn from above downward as one, until they reach that place, which is in division, THE NUKVA.

661. שִׁבְעָה עַיְנִין עִלָּאִין, אִלֵּין דִּכְתִיב, עֵינֵי ה׳ הֵמָּה מְשׁוֹטְטִים דְּכוּרִין, דְּהָא אֲתַר דִּדְכוּרָא אִיהוּ. הָכָא עֵינֵי ה׳ מְשׁוֹטְטוֹת, בְּתִקּוּנֵי שְׁכִינְתָּא לְתַתָּא, אֲתַר דְּנוּקְבָּא. שִׁבְעָה עַיְנִין עִלָּאִין, לָקֳבֵיל הָא דִּכְתִיב, לְךָ ה׳ הַגְּדוּלָּה וְהַגְּבוּרָה וגו׳. הַאי אֲתַר, אַשְׁלִים לְכָל סְטַר.

661. There are seven supernal eyes, THE SEVEN SFIROT CHESED, GVURAH, TIFERET, NETZACH, HOD, YESOD AND MALCHUT OF THE MOCHIN OF CHOCHMAH CALLED EYES. There are "the eyes of Hashem, they rove (masc.) to and fro through the whole earth" (Zecharyah 4:10); they are male; NAMELY OF ZEIR ANPIN, since it is the place of the male. It

is written elsewhere, "For the eyes of Hashem run (fem.) to and fro" (II Divrei Hayamim 16:9), they are part of the adornments of the Shechinah below, the place of the female. The seven supernal eyes, EITHER OF THE MALE OR OF THE FEMALE, correspond to the verse, "Yours, O Hashem, is the greatness (Chesed), and the Gvurah, AND THE TIFERET, AND THE NETZACH AND THE HOD: FOR ALL THAT IS IN HEAVEN AND ON EARTH (YESOD) IS YOURS; YOURS IS THE KINGDOM (MALCHUT), O HASHEM" (I Divrei Hayamim 29:11). This place, MALCHUT, completes each end OF THE SIX EXTREMITIES CHESED, GVURAH, TIFERET, NETZACH, HOD AND YESOD.

662. תּוּ שַׁעֲרָא, כְּמָה דִכְתִיב, מִי יְמַלֵּל גְּבוּרוֹת ה'. הה"ד, עָצְמוּ מִשַּׁעֲרוֹת רֹאשִׁי. וּכְתִיב חַסְדֵי ה' כִּי לֹא תָמְנוּ וגו'. וְתִקּוּנִין אִלֵּין אִסְתַּלָּקוּ לַאֲתַר אָחֳרָא. וְאע"ג דְּהָכָא אִתְּמַר טְפֵי, וְאִסְתַּלֵּיק בְּמַתְקְלָא יַד עִלָּאָה וְתַתָּאָה, וּשְׁלֹמֹה מַלְכָּא אֲמָרָן, וְאִצְטְרִיכְנָא לְפָרְשָׁא לוֹן. זַכָּאָה חוּלְקֵהוֹן דְּצַדִּיקַיָּא יַתִּיר, דְּיָדְעִין אָרְחָא דְקוּדְשָׁא בְּרִיךְ הוּא, וְהָכָא כֹּלָּא אִתְגַּלְיְיא לְיָדְעֵי מִדִּין.

662. We have to look at the hairs OF THE MALE AND THE FEMALE, as it is written: "Who can utter the mighty acts (Heb. Gvurot) of Hashem?" (Tehilim 106:2). FOR THE HAIRS ARE CONSIDERED TO BE GVUROT. IT ALSO SAYS, "They are more than the hairs of my head" (Tehilim 40:13), and "Hashem's Chassadim have not ceased" (Eichah 3:22), SINCE THE HAIRS ARE GVUROT YET INNUMERABLE CHASSADIM ARE DRAWN THROUGH THEM, OF WHICH IT SAYS, THE "HASHEM'S CHASSADIM HAVE NOT CEASED." These adornments rise to another place, TO MOCHIN WITHOUT RECKONING, though this place, THE MOCHIN OF RECKONING, THE SECRET OF THE SEVEN EYES OF HASHEM, is spoken of more, and put on a scale, NAMELY UPON THE CENTRAL COLUMN, WHICH BALANCES THE TWO SIDES OF THE SCALES, THE RIGHT AND THE LEFT, the upper, BINAH and the lower, MALCHUT. King Solomon expounded THE TWO NUKVAS, IN "SHIR HASHIRIM," and they need explaining UNLIKE THE MOCHIN OF THE HAIRS WHICH NEEDS NO EXPLAINING. Happier is the portion of the righteous who know the ways of the Holy One, blessed be He. And in here, IN THE MOCHIN OF RECKONING, all is made known to the knowledgeable in judgment and law.

67. "Zebulun shall dwell at the shore of the seas"

A Synopsis

Rabbi Yehuda discourses on the title verse, explaining that the merchant Zebulun made an agreement with Issachar, promising to support him while Issachar studied the Torah. Zebulun was a merchant of the sea and he therefore dwelled among seamen for purposes of commerce. His border, we're told, reached Tzidion, a place of commerce. Although he did not occupy himself with the Torah, Zebulun is always placed before Issachar during the blessings, because he took bread from his own mouth and gave to Issachar. He who supports scholars of the Torah receives blessings from above and below, meriting wealth in this world and a portion in the World to Come. Rabbi Aba then quotes the verse, "Nor shall you suffer the salt of the Covenant." We learn that salt is important because it washes away and perfumes bitterness to give it taste. Without salt, the world would be unable to endure the bitterness of judgment, and it is through judgment that the world learns righteousness. Salt signifies Yesod, the Covenant that supports the world. Therefore, a meal lacking salt symbolically separates Yesod and the Female Principle, a division that brings death. Rabbi Aba and Rabbi Yosi conclude with a discussion of the verse, "And that you will save alive my father and my mother" Their interpretation reveals that Rachav asked for a token of life, which, she said, rests upon the letter of truth. She was given a cord of scarlet thread, a token of Joshua, because the time had come for the moon to rule. She thus received a token of the moon, signifying Malchut.

The Relevance of this Passage

A profound spiritual truth emerges from this text concerning the ultimate purpose of Torah and the dangers of blind religiosity. The purpose of Torah study is not in any way related to academic, religious, or scholarly pursuits. Rather, the Torah is a tool for spiritual development with the sole intention of leading one to the ultimate objective of "loving thy neighbor as thyself." Remarkably, many "devout" and religious men will behave with intolerance towards others in the name of God and for the sake of their own religious objectives. This is completely contrary to the underlying purpose of the Torah. The Zohar stresses this point by explaining that the biblical character of Zebulun, who was not a student of the Torah, is always placed before Issachar during the blessings because he took bread from his own mouth and gave to a man named Issachar. Additionally, this passage helps sweeten the judgments that must appear in our lives, demonstrating that the Torah and the Light of the Zohar offer mankind a path to spiritual perfection that is most merciful and meaningful.

663. א"ר יְהוּדָה, זְבוּלֵן וְיִשָׂשׁכָר תְּנַאי עֲבָדוּ, חַד יָתֵיב וְלָעֵי בְּאוֹרַיְיתָא, וְחַד נָפֵיק וְעָבֵיד פְּרַקְמַטְיָא, וְתָמִיךְ לְיִשָׂשׁכָר, דִּכְתִיב וְתוֹמְכֶיהָ מְאוּשָּׁר. וַהֲוָה פָּרֵישׁ בְּיַמֵּי לְמֶעְבַּד פְּרַקְמַטְיָא, וְחוּלָקֵיהּ הָכִי הֲוָה, דְּהָא יַמָּא הֲוָה אַחֲסַנְתֵּיהּ.

663. Rabbi Yehuda said: Zebulun and Issachar made an agreement between them that one will sit and study the Torah, ISSACHAR, and the other will be a merchant, ZEBULUN, and support Issachar, as it is written: "And happy are those who hold (also: 'support') her" (Mishlei 3:18). He used to traverse the seas with merchandise. It fell in his portion since his inheritance was by the sea.

664. וּבְגִינֵי כָּךְ קָרֵי לֵיהּ יָרֵךְ. דַּרְכֵּיהּ דִּיָרֵךְ לְנָפְקָא וּלְמֵיעַל, הה"ד, שָׂמַח זְבוּלוּן בְּצֵאתֶךָ וְיִשָׂשׁכָר בְּאֹהָלֶךָ. לְחוֹף יַמִּים יִשְׁכֹּן, בְּאִינוּן פְּרִישֵׁי יַמִּים, לְמֶעְבַּד פְּרַקְמַטְיָא. לְחוֹף יַמִּים, אע"ג דְּחַד יַמָּא הֲוָה לֵיהּ בְּאַחֲסַנְתֵּיהּ, בִּתְרֵין יַמִּין שָׁרְיָיא.

664. He is therefore called "leg (Heb. *yerech*)," AS IT SAYS, "AND HIS BORDER (HEB. *YARCHATO*) SHALL BE AT TZIDON" (Beresheet 49:13), for it is the function of the leg to go to and fro. Hence it is written, "Rejoice, Zebulun, in your going out; and Issachar in your tents" (Devarim 33:18). "Zebulun shall dwell at the shore of the seas" (Beresheet 49:13) among the seamen for the purposes of commerce. "The shore of the seas," though his inheritance was by one sea, THE GREAT SEA, YET "SEAS" IS IN THE PLURAL, since it dwelt between two seas, THE GREAT SEA AND THE SEA OF GALILEE, THOUGH ITS INHERITANCE DID NOT REACH THE SEA OF GALILEE.

665. ר' יוֹסֵי אָמַר, כָּל שְׁאָר יַמִּין, הֲווֹ מְהַדְּרָן קַרְפּוֹלִין בְּיַמָּא דִּילֵיהּ. וְהוּא לְחוֹף אֲנִיּוֹת, אֲתַר דְּכָל אַרְבִּין מִשְׁתַּכְּחִין לְמֶעְבַּד סְחוֹרְתָּא. וְיַרְכָתוֹ, אָמַר ר' חִזְקִיָּה, יַרְכָתֵיהּ דִּילֵיהּ מָטֵי עַל סְפַר צִידוֹן, וְתֵחוּמָא פָּרֵישׁ לְהַהוּא אֲתַר, וּפְרַקְמַטְיָא דְּכָל מָארֵי סְחוֹרְתָּא, סָחֲרִין וְתָיְיבִין

בִּסְחוֹרָתַיְהוּ לְהַהוּא אֲתַר.

665. Rabbi Yosi said: All the merchants of the other seas were interested in the merchandise of his own sea. HENCE IT SAYS "THE SHORE OF THE SEAS" IN THE PLURAL. "And he shall be a haven for ships," NAMELY, where all ships would assemble to trade. "And his border": THIS IS DIFFICULT TO EXPLAIN, FOR THE BORDER OF TZIDON IS FAR FROM ZEBULUN. Rabbi Chizkiyah said to him: His leg reaches the border of Tzidon, A THIN STRIP OF LAND, RESEMBLING A LEG, STRETCHED FROM ZEBULUN TO TZIDON. THROUGH THIS MEANS, Zebulun's border reached THE BORDER OF TZIDON, WHICH WAS a place of commerce, where all the tradesmen would come and go there with their merchandise.

666. רִבִּי אַחָא אֲמַר, כְּתִיב וְלֹא תַשְׁבִּית מֶלַח בְּרִית אֱלֹהֶיךָ מֵעַל מִנְחָתֶךָ עַל כָּל קָרְבָּנְךָ תַּקְרִיב מֶלַח, וְכִי אַמַּאי מֶלַח. אֶלָּא בְּגִין דְּאִיהוּ מְמָרֵק וּמְבַשֵּׂם מְרִירָא לְאַטְעָמָא, וְאִי לָאו מִלְחָא, לָא יָכִיל עַלְמָא לְמִסְבַּל מְרִירָא. הה"ד כִּי כַּאֲשֶׁר מִשְׁפָּטֶיךָ לָאָרֶץ לָמְדוּ יוֹשְׁבֵי תֵבֵל. וּכְתִיב צֶדֶק וּמִשְׁפָּט מְכוֹן כִּסְאֶךָ.

666. Rabbi Acha said: It is written, "Nor shall you suffer the salt of the covenant of your Elohim to be lacking from your meal offering: with all your offerings you shall offer salt" (Vayikra 2:13). Why is salt SO IMPORTANT? Because it washes away and perfumes the bitterness to give it taste. Without salt, the world would not endure the bitterness. Hence it says, "For when Your judgments are on the earth, the inhabitants of the world learn righteousness" (Yeshayah 26:9). It is also written, "Righteousness and justice are the foundation of Your throne" (Tehilim 89:15), FOR RIGHTEOUSNESS IS PERFECTED BY JUSTICE, THE SECRET OF SALT.

667. וּמֶלַח אִיהוּ בְּרִית, דְּעַלְמָא קַיְימָא בֵּיהּ, דִּכְתִיב אִם לֹא בְרִיתִי יוֹמָם וָלַיְלָה חֻקּוֹת שָׁמַיִם וָאָרֶץ לֹא שָׂמְתִּי. בְּגִין כָּךְ, אִקְרֵי בְּרִית אֱלֹהֶיךָ, וְאִקְרֵי יַם הַמֶּלַח, וְיַמָּא אִקְרֵי עַל שְׁמֵיהּ.

667. Salt is the covenant, YESOD, which supports the world, THE NUKVA, as it is written: "Thus says Hashem; If My covenant be not day and night, it were as if I had not appointed the ordinances of heaven and earth"

(Yirmeyah 33:25). Hence, THE CENTRAL COLUMN, YESOD, COMES ABOVE IT, SALT is called the covenant of your Elohim, YESOD BEING CALLED COVENANT, and the Salt Sea. The sea, WHICH IS THE NUKVA is called after THE SALT WHICH SWEETENS IT.

668. ר' חִיָּיא אֲמַר, כְּתִיב כִּי צַדִּיק ה' צְדָקוֹת אָהֵב, דָּא מִלְחָא בְּיַמָּא. וּמַאן דְּפָרֵישׁ לוֹן, גָּרֵים לְגַרְמֵיהּ מִיתָה, בְּג"כ כְּתִיב, לא תַשְׁבִּית מֶלַח, דְּהָא דָּא בְּלָא דָּא לָא אָזְלָא.

668. Rabbi Chiya said: It is written, "For Hashem is righteous, He loves righteousness" (Tehilim 11:7). This is the salt, YESOD, of the sea, MALCHUT, RIGHTEOUS BEING YESOD AND RIGHTEOUSNESS BEING MALCHUT. Whoever divides between them brings death upon himself. Therefore, it is written: "Nor shall you suffer the salt...TO BE LACKING FROM YOUR MEAL OFFERING" THUS SEPARATING YESOD, WHICH IS SALT, FROM THE MEAL OFFERING, WHICH IS THE NUKVA. They are inseparable.

669. אֲמַר ר' אֲחָא, יַם חַד הוּא, וְאִקְרֵי יַמִּים. אֶלָּא אֲתַר אִית בְּיַמָּא דְּאִיהוּ מַיִין צְלִילָן, וַאֲתַר דְּאִית בֵּיהּ מַיִּין מְתִיקָן, וַאֲתַר דְּאִית בֵּיהּ מַיִּין מְרִירָן, בְּג"כ יַמִּים קַרֵינָן, וְע"ד לְחוֹף יַמִּים. אֲמַר ר' אַבָּא, כָּל שִׁבְטָא וְשִׁבְטָא, וְכָל חַד וְחַד קִשְׁרָא חַד, מֵאִינּוּן קִשְׁרִין דְּמִתְחַבְּרָן בְּגוּפָא.

669. Rabbi Acha said: The sea is one, but is called 'seas', IN THE VERSE, "ZEBULUN SHALL DWELL AT THE SHORE OF THE SEAS," as the water is clear in some places, in ome place water is sweet, in another it is bitter. Hence, SINCE THERE ARE DIFFERENT PLACES, it is called seas. Thus it says, "At the shore of the seas." Rabbi Aba said: Each tribe corresponds to one of the joints connected to the body, THE NUKVA. SINCE THERE ARE DIFFERENT PLACES WITHIN THE NUKVA CALLED SEA, ACCORDING TO THE PARTICULAR TRIBE, SHE IS THEREFORE CALLED SEAS IN THE PLURAL.

670. ר' אַבָּא הֲוָה יָתִיב לֵילְיָא חַד, וְקָם לְמִלְעֵי בְּאוֹרַיְיתָא, עַד דַּהֲוָה יָתִיב, אָתָא רַבִּי יוֹסֵי, וּבָטַשׁ אֲפִתְחָא, אֲמַר סִיפְטָא בְּטוּפְסְרָא קַפְטְלָאי

שְׁכִיחֵי.

670. Rabbi Aba rose one night to study the Torah. While he was sitting, Rabbi Yosi knocked on the door. He said: In the prince's chest there are jewels, TO WIT, HE WANTED TO HEAR PEARLS OF WISDOM OF THE TORAH FROM HIM.

671. יָתְבוּ וְלָעוּ בְּאוֹרַיְיתָא. אַדְהָכֵי קָם בְּרֵיהּ דְּאוּשְׁפִּיזָא, וְיָתֵיב קַמַּיְיהוּ, אֲמַר לוֹן מַאי דִּכְתִּיב וְהַחֲיִיתֶם אֶת אָבִי וְאֶת אִמִּי וגו'. וּכְתִיב וּנְתַתֶּם לִי אוֹת אֱמֶת. מַאי קָא בָּעֵאת מִנַּיְיהוּ. א"ר אַבָּא יָאוֹת שָׁאֵלְתְּ, אֲבָל אִי שְׁמַעְתְּ מִידֵי אֵימָא בְּרִי. אֲמַר תּוּ שְׁאֶלְתָּא, דְּהָא אִינּוּן יַהֲבוּ לָהּ מַה דְּלָא בָּעֵאת מִנַּיְיהוּ, דִּכְתִּיב, אֶת תִּקְוַת חוּט הַשָּׁנִי הַזֶּה תִּקְשְׁרִי בַּחֲלוֹן וגו'.

671. They sat, occupied with the Torah. The son of the innkeeper rose and sat before them. He asked, What is the meaning of the verse, "And that you will save alive my father, and my mother" (Yehoshua 2:13) and before that "and give me a true token" (Ibid. 12). What did she ask of them? Rabbi Aba said: You have asked a good question, but tell me son, if you have heard something. He said: I HAVE another question: They did not give her what she asked for, but "you shall bind this cord of scarlet thread in the window" (Ibid. 18), WHICH ALLUDES TO MALCHUT, THE SECRET OF THE VERSE, "YOUR LIPS ARE LIKE A THREAD OF SCARLET" (SHIR HASHIRIM 4:3), WHEN SHE ASKED FOR A TOKEN OF TRUTH, WHICH ALLUDES TO TIFERET, AS WAS SAID BEFORE.

672. אֶלָּא הָכֵי אוֹלִיפְנָא, הִיא בָּעֵאת סִימָנָא דְּחַיֵּי, דִּכְתִּיב וְהַחֲיִיתֶם אֶת אָבִי וגו', וַאֲמָרָה, סִימָנָא דְּחַיֵּי לָא שַׁרְיָיא, אֶלָּא בְּאוֹת אֱמֶת, וּמַאי אִיהוּ אוֹת אֱמֶת, דָּא אָת ו', בְּגִין דְּבֵיהּ שַׁרְיָין חַיִּין. הָכֵי אוֹלִיפְנָא, סִימָנָא דְּמֹשֶׁה קָא בָּעֵאת, וְאִינּוּן אַמַּאי יַהֲבוּ לָהּ תִּקְוַת חוּט הַשָּׁנִי.

672. HE ANSWERS: I have learned that she asked for a token of life, as it is written: "And that you will save alive my father, and my mother." She also said that the token of life rests only upon the letter of Truth, which is *Vav*

OF THE NAME YUD HEI VAV HEI, TIFERET, where there is life, BEING THE TREE OF LIFE. I have learned that she asked for the token of Moses, THE SECRET OF TIFERET. Why did they give her the cord of scarlet thread, WHICH IS A TOKEN OF JOSHUA, THE SECRET OF MALCHUT?

673. אֶלָּא אִינוּן אָמְרֵי, מֹשֶׁה הָא אִסְתַּלַּק מֵעַלְמָא, דְּהָא אִתְכְּנֵישׁ שִׁמְשָׁא, וְהָא מָטָא זִמְנָא דְּסִיהֲרָא לְמִשְׁלַט, סִימָנָא דְּסִיהֲרָא אִית לָן לְמֵיהַב לָךְ, וּמַאי אִיהוּ. תְּקוּת חוּט הַשָּׁנִי הַזֶּה, כְּד"א כְּחוּט הַשָּׁנִי שִׂפְתוֹתַיִךְ, סִימָנָא דִּיהוֹשֻׁעַ יְהֵא גַבָּךְ, בְּגִין דְּשׁוּלְטָנוּתָא דְּסִיהֲרָא הַשְׁתָּא. קָמוּ ר' אַבָּא וְר' יוֹסֵי וּנְשָׁקוּהוּ. אָמְרוּ. וַדַּאי זַמִּין אַנְתְּ לְמֶהֱוֵי רֵישׁ מְתִיבְתָּא, אוֹ גַּבְרָא רַבָּא בְּיִשְׂרָאֵל, וּמַנּוּ. רִבִּי בּוֹן.

673. They told her that Moses passed away from the world, since the sun has set, WHICH IS TIFERET AND THE ASPECT OF MOSES. The time has come for the moon to rule. Therefore we give you the token of the moon, MALCHUT. What is it? The cord of scarlet thread, as it is written: "Your lips are like a thread of scarlet." You shall have the token of Joshua, THE SECRET OF MALCHUT, because now is the rule of the moon. Rabbi Aba and Rabbi Yosi rose and kissed him. They said: Surely you shall be a head of a Yeshivah, or a great man in Yisrael. Who is he? Rabbi Bon.

674. תּוּ שָׁאִיל וַאֲמַר, בְּנוֹי דְּיַעֲקֹב כֻּלְּהוּ תְּרֵיסַר שִׁבְטִין, אִתְסַדְּרוּ לְתַתָּא כְּגַוְונָא דִלְעֵילָא, אַמַּאי אַקְדֵּים בְּבִרְכָאן, זְבוּלוּן לְיִשָּׂשכָר תָּדִיר, וְהָא יִשָּׂשכָר אִשְׁתַּדְּלוּתֵיהּ בְּאוֹרַיְיתָא, וְאוֹרַיְיתָא אַקְדֵּים בְּכָל אֲתָר, אַמַּאי אַקְדֵּים לֵיהּ זְבוּלוּן בְּבִרְכָאן, אֲבוֹי אַקְדֵּים לֵיהּ, מֹשֶׁה אַקְדֵּים לֵיהּ.

674. He asked further: All of Jacob's sons, the twelve tribes, were arranged below according to the order above, THE TWELVE KNOTS OF CHESED AND GVURAH, NETZACH AND HOD OF THE NUKVA. Why is Zebulun always placed before Issachar during the blessings, although Issachar was occupied with the Torah, which is universally put first? In the blessings, why was Zebulun placed before both by his father and Moses?

675. אֶלָּא זְבוּלוּן זָכָה, עַל דְּאָפֵּיק פִּתָּא מִפּוּמֵיהּ, וְיָהַב לְפוּמֵיהּ

דְּיִשָּׂשכָר, בְּגִינֵי כָּךְ אַקְדֵּים לֵיהּ בְּבִרְכָאן. מֵהָכָא אוֹלִיפְנָא, מַאן דְּסָעֵיד לְמָרֵיהּ דְּאוֹרַיְיתָא, נָטֵיל בִּרְכָאן מֵעֵילָא וְתַתָּא. וְלָא עוֹד אֶלָּא דְּזָכֵי לִתְרֵי פָּתוֹרֵי, מַה דְּלָא זָכֵי ב"נ אַחֲרָא, זָכֵי לְעוֹתְרָא דְּיִתְבָּרֵךְ בְּהַאי עַלְמָא, וְזָכֵי לְמֶהֱוֵי לֵיהּ חוּלָקָא בְּעַלְמָא דְּאָתֵי. הה"ד זְבוּלוּן לְחוֹף יַמִּים יִשְׁכֹּן וְהוּא לְחוֹף אֳנִיּוֹת. כֵּיוָן דִּכְתִיב לְחוֹף יַמִּים, אַמַּאי וְהוּא לְחוֹף אֳנִיּוֹת. אֶלָּא, לְחוֹף יַמִּים, בְּעַלְמָא דֵּין. לְחוֹף אֳנִיּוֹת, בְּעַלְמָא דְּאָתֵי, כִּד"א שָׁם אֳנִיּוֹת יְהַלֵּכוּן וְגו'. דְּתַמָּן הוּא נְגִידוּ דְּעַלְמָא דְּאָתֵי.

675. HE ANSWERS: Zebulun was honored BY BEING PLACED BEFORE ISSACHAR, since he took bread out of his own mouth and gave to Issachar. He is therefore placed before ISSACHAR in the blessings. From this, we learn that whoever supports a student of the Torah, receives blessings from above and below. He also merits two tables, which no other man is granted. He deserves to be blessed with wealth in this world, and a portion in the World to Come. Hence it says "Zebulun shall dwell at the shore of the sea; and he shall be a haven for ships." Since it says "at the shore of the sea," why add "a haven for ships"? The "shore of the sea" is in this world and the "haven for ships" is in the World to Come, as it is written: "There go the ships" (Tehilim 104:26), WHICH WAS SAID OF "THIS GREAT AND WIDE SEA" (IBID. 25), WHICH IS BINAH, THE SECRET OF THE WORLD TO COME, for there abides the abundance of the World to Come.

68. "I charge you, O daughters of Jerusalem"

A Synopsis

One explanation of the title verse tells us that the daughters of Jerusalem are the souls of the righteous, whom are always close to the King, informing Him daily of the welfare of Malchut. When a soul descends into this world, Malchut makes it swear to tell God of her love for Him so that He will be pleased with her. Man does this by proclaiming the union of the Holy Name with his mouth, heart, and soul. Another explanation of this verse interprets the daughters of Jerusalem as signifying the twelve tribes. Malchut stands upon twelve mountains and includes seven sides. The daughters of Jerusalem testify before God, declaring Yisrael love for Him. In this way, Malchut's love for Zeir Anpin is affirmed.

The Relevance of this Passage

Drawing upon the spiritual power of the righteous souls who have walked this earth throughout history, and the devout who dwell in our midst today, we unite our body and soul and our physical world with the Upper World realm called Zeir Anpin. This union produces bountiful beams of Light that brighten the lives of all mankind. The reference to the twelve Tribes is an indication to the twelve signs and the Zohar's assistance in helping us transcend the influences the stars and planets. Thus, control over our fate and fortunes is awarded to us through the spiritual power associated with this passage.

676. פָּתַח וַאֲמַר, הִשְׁבַּעְתִּי אֶתְכֶם בְּנוֹת יְרוּשָׁלַיִם אִם תִּמְצְאוּ אֶת דּוֹדִי מַה תַּגִּידוּ לוֹ שֶׁחוֹלַת אַהֲבָה אָנִי. וְכִי מַאן קָרִיב לְמַלְכָּא כִּכְנֶסֶת יִשְׂרָאֵל, דְּאִיהִי אָמְרַת אִם תִּמְצְאוּ אֶת דּוֹדִי מַה תַּגִּידוּ לוֹ. אֶלָּא בְּנוֹת יְרוּשָׁלַיִם, אִלֵּין אִינּוּן נִשְׁמָתְהוֹן דְּצַדִּיקַיָּיא דְּאִינּוּן קְרֵיבִין לְמַלְכָּא תָּדִיר, וּמוֹדְעִין לְמַלְכָּא בְּכָל יוֹמָא עִסְקוֹי דְמַטְרוֹנִיתָא.

676. He opened the discussion saying: "I charge you, O daughters of Jerusalem, if you find my beloved, that you tell him, that I am sick with love" (Shir Hashirim 5:8). HE ASKS: Who is closer to the King than the Congregation of Yisrael, THE NUKVA? Why then does she charge them, "If you find my beloved, that you tell him." HE REPLIES: The daughters of Jerusalem are the souls of the righteous who are always near the King, and inform Him daily of the welfare of the Matron, THE NUKVA.

677. דְּהָכֵי אוֹלִיפְנָא, בְּשַׁעְתָּא דְּנִשְׁמָתָא נָחֲתַת לְעַלְמָא, כְּנֶסֶת יִשְׂרָאֵל, עָאלַת עֲלָה בְּקִיּוּמָא דְּאוּמָאָה, דִּיחֲוֵי לְמַלְכָּא, וְיוֹדַע לֵיהּ רְחִימוּתָא דִּילָהּ לְגַבֵּיהּ, בְּגִין לְאִתְפַּיְּיסָא בַּהֲדֵיהּ.

677. For so we have learnt that when a soul descends into the world, the Congregation of Yisrael, THE NUKVA, makes it swear to tell the King and inform Him of her love for Him, so He shall be pleased with her.

678. וּבַמֶּה, בְּגִין דְּחִיּוּבָא עַל ב"נ לְיַחֲדָא שְׁמָא קַדִּישָׁא בְּפוּמָא, בְּלִבָּא בְּנַפְשָׁא, וּלְאִקְשְׁרָא כֹּלָּא, כְּשַׁלְהוֹבָא דְּאִתְקְשָׁרָא בְּטִיפְסָא, וּבְהַהוּא יִחוּדָא דְּעָבֵיד, גָּרֵים לְאִתְפַּיְּיסָא מַלְכָּא בְּמַטְרוֹנִיתָא, וְאוֹדַע לֵיהּ לְמַלְכָּא רְחִימוּתָא דִּילָהּ לְגַבֵּיהּ.

678. By which means DO THE SOULS INFORM THE KING OF THE LOVE OF THE NUKVA FOR HIM? A man should proclaim the unison of the Holy Name, THE NUKVA OF ZEIR ANPIN, by mouth, heart and soul, and attach himself wholly TO ZEIR AND THE NUKVA, like a flame to a burning coal, by the union which causes the King to be well disposed towards the Queen, and to proclaim before the King her love for Him.

679. ד"א בְּנוֹת יְרוּשָׁלַם, אִלֵּין תְּרֵיסַר שִׁבְטִין. דְּתָנִינָן יְרוּשָׁלַם עַל תְּרֵיסַר טוּרִין קַיְימָא. וּמַאן דְּאָמַר עַל שִׁבְעָה, לָא קָאָמַר לְאַשְׁלָמָא שְׁלִימוּ, וְאע"ג דְּכֹלָּא חַד, דְּאִית שִׁבְעָה, וְאִית ד', וְאִית תְּרֵיסַר, וְכֹלָּא חַד.

679. Another explanation: The daughters of Jerusalem are the twelve tribes; NAMELY THE TWELVE KNOTS OF CHESED AND GVURAH, NETZACH AND HOD UPON WHICH STANDS THE BODY OF THE NUKVA. For we have learned that Jerusalem, THE NUKVA, is established upon twelve mountains. Those who say that she stands upon only seven are not wholly correct, though all is one, for she includes seven SIDES; NAMELY CHESED, GVURAH, TIFERET, NETZACH, HOD, YESOD AND MALCHUT, and has the four ASPECTS CHESED, GVURAH, TIFERET AND MALCHUT and twelve ASPECTS, WHICH ARE THE TWELVE KNOTS WE MENTIONED. All is one,

ONLY THAT THESE ARE GRADES WITHIN HER, BUT TWELVE IS PERFECTION.

680. וְדַאי עַל תְּרֵיסַר טוּרִין קַיְימָא, תְּלַת טוּרִין לְסִטְרָא דָא, וּתְלַת טוּרִין לְסִטְרָא דָא, וְכֵן לְאַרְבַּע זִוְיָין, וּכְדֵין אִתְקְרֵי חַיָּה. כְּד"א הִיא הַחַיָּה אֲשֶׁר רָאִיתִי תַּחַת אֱלֹהֵי יִשְׂרָאֵל. וְאִלֵּין אִקְרוּן בְּנוֹת יְרוּשָׁלַיִם, בְּגִין דְּקַיְימָא עֲלַיְיהוּ. וְאִינוּן סָהֲדֵי סַהֲדוּתָא לְמַלְכָּא עַל כְּנֶסֶת יִשְׂרָאֵל, הה"ד, שִׁבְטֵי יָה עֵדוּת לְיִשְׂרָאֵל לְהוֹדוֹת לְשֵׁם יי'. אָמַר רַבִּי יְהוּדָה, זַכָּאָה חוּלְקֵהוֹן דְּיִשְׂרָאֵל, דְּיָדְעֵי אוֹרְחוֹי דְקוּדְשָׁא בְּרִיךְ הוּא, עֲלַיְיהוּ כְּתִיב, כִּי עַם קָדוֹשׁ אַתָּה לַיי' אֱלֹהֶיךָ וּבְךָ בָּחַר יי' וְגו'.

680. Surely she is established upon twelve mountains, three to each side, THREE KNOTS TO THE SIDE OF CHESED, THREE TO GVURAH, THREE TO NETZACH AND THREE TO HOD, AND THE BODY OF THE NUKVA ABOVE THEM. They are then called living creature, as it is written: "This is the living creature that I saw under the Elohim of Yisrael" (Yechezkel 10:20). They are called the daughters of Jerusalem, since JERUSALEM, THE NUKVA, stands above them. They testify before the King OF THE LOVE of the Congregation of Yisrael, WHO CHARGES THEM, "IF YOU FIND MY BELOVED, THAT YOU TELL HIM, THAT I AM SICK WITH LOVE." Hence it says, "There the tribes used to go up, the tribes of Yah as a testimony unto Yisrael, to give thanks unto the name of Hashem" (Tehilim 122:4), TO TESTIFY BEFORE YISRAEL, ZEIR ANPIN, OF THE LOVE OF THE NUKVA. Rabbi Yehuda said: Happy is the portion of Yisrael, who know the ways of the Holy One, blessed be He. Of them it is written, "For you are a holy people to Hashem your Elohim, and Hashem has chosen you..." (Devarim 14:2).

69. "Issachar is a strong donkey"

A Synopsis

Issachar is compared to a donkey because just as a donkey will lie anywhere and accepts its burden without kicking its master, so Issachar accepted the burden of the Torah and cared nothing for his own honor, only that of his Master. Another explanation of the title verse tells us that when night falls, dogs and donkey roam, and fiends have permission to wreak havoc in the world. He who rises at night to study the Torah relegates the evil demons to the holes of the great abyss and subdues the Klipah of the donkey, bringing it down into the holes underneath the ground. Through his study of the Torah, Issachar subdued the Klipah of the mule, forcing it to descend and thereby preventing it from harming the world. Indeed, Issachar studied the Torah constantly and cleaved so strongly to God that he weakened himself through his devotion. While walking, Rabbi Shimon, Rabbi Yosi, and Rabbi Chiya continue this discussion. Rabbi Shimon comments that he who studies the Torah receives a supernal reward that no other attains. This reward is alluded to in the name Issachar. Indeed, we are told that when the truly righteous study the Torah, the power of the other nations will be subdued and the nations of the world will ask Yisrael to be their leaders. However, if the righteous do not study the Torah, the Klipah of the donkey will cause Yisrael to go into exile, and they will be ruled by other nations. Rabbi Shimon next begins a discourse on the verse, "As I looked, thrones were placed" This means that when the Temple was destroyed, two thrones fell. The two thrones above are of Jacob and David, and the lower thrones signify Jerusalem and the students of the Torah.

The discussion then addresses the meaning of the verse, "The mandrakes give a fragrance." This alludes to Issachar, who caused new and old studies of the Torah to be in the synagogues and colleges. We learn that all new expositions of the Torah ascend to the Garden of Eden where God sees them and rejoices. These words are then recorded in the supernal book. The section concludes by explaining that Judah, Issachar, and Zebulun are all included in the same portion, each illuminating one of the three Columns.

The Relevance of this Passage

Each negative action that we've committed, large and small, knowingly or unknowingly, creates a negative blockage [Klipah] that dims the Light of our soul and diminishes the Light of The Creator in our lives. Torah study after midnight with a contrite heart summons forth awesome streams of Light that removes these blockages from our lives and the world, as evidenced by the Zohar's story of Issachar.

This mystical Light of the night shines forth in this passage when the eyes of man touch the letters that bespeak this ancient wisdom. Hence, we can remove the blockages [Klipot] that currently darken our daily lives through our connection to Issachar. Moreover, we are inspired to pursue the secrets of the Torah through continued learning of Zohar, helping to hasten the final redemption. Issachar embraced his burdens with great dedication, and so when our study of Torah and its spiritual treasures becomes difficult, that is when we draw upon the strength and character of Issachar to struggle onward. These difficult times of study are when the greatest amount of Light is ready to be revealed.

681. יִשָּׂשכָר חֲמוֹר גָּרֶם רוֹבֵץ בֵּין הַמִּשְׁפְּתָיִם. אָמַר רבּי אֶלְעָזָר, וְכִי יִשָּׂשכָר חֲמוֹר אִקְרֵי. אִי בְּגִין דְּאִשְׁתַּדַּל בְּאוֹרַיְיתָא, נִקְרְיֵיה לֵיהּ סוּס אוֹ אַרְיֵה, אוֹ נָמֵר, אַמַּאי חֲמוֹר. אֶלָּא אָמְרוּ, בְּגִין דַּחֲמוֹר נָטִיל מָטוֹלָא, וְלָא בָּעֵיט בְּמָארֵיהּ כִּשְׁאָר בְּעִירֵי, וְלָא אִית בֵּיהּ גַּסּוּת הָרוּחַ, וְלָא חָיֵישׁ לְמִשְׁכַּב בְּאֲתַר מִתְתַּקָּן. אוּף הָכֵי יִשָּׂשכָר, דְּאִשְׁתַּדְלוּתֵיהּ בְּאוֹרַיְיתָא, נָטִיל מָטוֹלָא דְּאוֹרַיְיתָא, וְלָא בָּעֵיט בֵּיהּ בְּקוּדְשָׁא בְּרִיךְ הוּא, וְלָא אִית בֵּיהּ גַּסּוּת הָרוּחַ, כַּחֲמוֹר, דְּלָא חָיֵישׁ לִיקָרָא דִילֵיהּ, אֶלָּא לִיקָרָא דְּמָרֵיהּ. רוֹבֵץ בֵּין הַמִּשְׁפְּתָיִם, כִּדְאַמְרִינָן וְעַל הָאָרֶץ תִּישַׁן, וְחַיֵּי צַעַר תִּחְיֶה, וּבַתּוֹרָה אַתָּה עָמֵל.

681. "Issachar is a strong donkey couching down between the shipfolds" (Beresheet 49:14) Rabbi Elazar said: Why is Issachar called an donkey? If it is because he studied the Torah, he should be called a horse, a lion or a leopard. Why an donkey? Because it is known that an donkey would bear any burden without kicking his master like other animals. It is not fastidious and would lie anywhere. Issachar too is occupied with the Torah, accepts the burden of the Torah and does not kick the Holy One, blessed be He. He is not haughty and, like the donkey, does not care for his honor, but for the honor of his Master. He is "couching down between the sheepfolds" as we said, that one should lie on the ground, live a life of privation and labor for the Torah.

682. ד"א יִשָּׂשכָר חֲמוֹר גָּרֶם רוֹבֵץ וְגוֹ'. פָּתַח וְאָמַר, לְדָוִד ה' אוֹרִי וְיִשְׁעִי מִמִּי אִירָא יי' מָעוֹז חַיַּי מִמִּי אֶפְחָד, כַּמָּה חֲבִיבִין אִינוּן מִלִּין דְּאוֹרַיְיתָא, כַּמָּה חֲבִיבִין אִינוּן דְּמִשְׁתַּדְּלֵי בְּאוֹרַיְיתָא, קַמֵּי קוּדְשָׁא

בְּרִיךְ הוּא, דְּכָל מַאן דְּאִשְׁתַּדַּל בְּאוֹרַיְיתָא, לָא דָּחִיל מִפְּגְעֵי עַלְמָא, נָטִיר הוּא לְעֵילָא, נָטִיר הוּא לְתַתָּא. וְלָא עוֹד, אֶלָּא דְּכָפִית לְכָל פְּגִיעֵי דְּעָלְמָא, וְאָחֵית לוֹן לְעוֹמְקֵי דִּתְהוֹמָא רַבָּא.

682. Another explanation for "Issachar is a strong donkey": He opened the discussion saying: "To David. Hashem is my light and my salvation; whom shall I fear? Hashem is the stronghold of my life: of whom shall I be afraid?" (Tehilim 27:1). How dear are the words of the Torah, how beloved those who study the Torah before the Holy One, blessed be He. He who studies the Torah need not be afraid of the fiends in the world, for he is protected above and protected below. Moreover, he subdues the demons in the world and pushes them down into the great abyss.

683. תָּא חֲזֵי, בְּשַׁעֲתָא דְּעָאל לֵילְיָא, פְּתָחִין סְתִימִין, וְכַלְבֵּי וַחֲמָרֵי שַׁרְיָין וְשָׁטָאן בְּעָלְמָא, וְאִתְיְיהִיבַת רְשׁוּ לְחַבָּלָא, וְכָל בְּנֵי עַלְמָא נַיְימֵי בְּעַרְסַיְיהוּ, וְנִשְׁמָתְהוֹן דְּצַדִּיקַיָּיא סָלְקִין לְאִתְעַנְּגָא לְעֵילָא. כַּד אִתְעַר רוּחַ צָפוֹן, וְאִתְפְּלִיג לֵילְיָא, אִתְעָרוּתָא קַדִּישָׁא אִתְעַר בְּעָלְמָא, וְאִתְּמַר בְּכַמָּה דּוּכְתֵּי.

683. Come and see: when night falls, the UPPER gates are closed, and dogs and donkeys dwell and roam about the world. Permission is given to the fiends to destroy, and the inhabitants of the world sleep in their beds. The souls of the righteous ascend to take pleasure above. When the north wind stirs at midnight, there is holy awakening in the world, as has been explained in several places.

684. זַכָּאָה חוּלְקֵיה דְּהַהוּא ב"נ, דְּאִיהוּ קָאִים בְּהַהִיא שַׁעֲתָא, וְאִשְׁתַּדַּל בְּאוֹרַיְיתָא, כֵּיוָן דְּאִיהוּ פָּתַח בְּאוֹרַיְיתָא, כָּל אִינוּן זִינִין בִּישִׁין אָעִיל לוֹן בְּנוּקְבֵי דִּתְהוֹמָא רַבָּה, וְכָפִית לֵיה לַחֲמוֹר, וְנָחֵית לֵיה בְּטַפְסְרֵי דִּתְחוֹת עַפְרָא, דְּזוּהֲמֵי קַסְרָא.

684. Happy is the portion of the man who rises from his bed at that time, to study the Torah. When he studies the Torah, he puts all the evil demons into the holes of the great abyss and subdues THE KLIPAH OF the donkey and

-362-

brings it down into the holes underneath the ground, into the filth of the refuse and the dung.

685. בְּגִינֵי כָּךְ, יִשָּׂשכָר, דְּאִשְׁתַּדְּלוּתֵיה בְּאוֹרַיְיתָא, כָּפֵית לֵיה לַחֲמוֹר, וְנָחֵית לֵיה. מֵהַהוּא גֶּרֶם הַמַּעֲלוֹת, דְּאִיהוּ סָלִיק לְנִזְקָא עַלְמָא, וְשַׁוֵּי מָדוֹרֵיה בֵּין הַמִּשְׁפְּתָיִם, בֵּין זוּהֲמֵי דְּטַפְסְרֵי דְּעַפְרָא.

685. Hence Issachar, who studied the Torah, subdued THE KLIPAH OF the donkey, and brought it down. THE DONKEY, who climbed the stairs (Heb. *gerem*) in order to harm the world, AS IT IS WRITTEN: "A STRONG (HEB. *GAREM*) DONKEY," was NOW brought into its place between the shipfolds, NAMELY AMONG THE REFUSE, the filth of the holes in the ground. THE VERSE TEACHES US THAT ISSACHAR, BY STUDYING THE TORAH, BROUGHT DOWN THE KLIPAH OF THE STRONG DONKEY AND CAUSED HIM TO COUCH DOWN BETWEEN THE SHIPFOLDS, BY CASTING HIM DOWN INTO THE HOLES IN THE GROUND, AMONG THE REFUSE.

686. תָּא חֲזֵי, מַה כְּתִיב, וַיַּרְא מְנוּחָה כִּי טוֹב וְאֶת הָאָרֶץ כִּי נָעֵמָה וַיֵּט שִׁכְמוֹ לִסְבּוֹל וַיְהִי לְמַס עוֹבֵד. וַיַּרְא מְנוּחָה כִּי טוֹב, דָּא תּוֹרָה שֶׁבִּכְתָב. וְאֶת הָאָרֶץ כִּי נָעֵמָה, דָּא תּוֹרָה שֶׁבְּעַ"פ. וַיֵּט שִׁכְמוֹ לִסְבּוֹל, לְמִסְבַּל עוֹלָא דְּאוֹרַיְיתָא, וּלְדַבְּקָא בָּה יוֹמֵי וְלֵילֵי. וַיְהִי לְמַס עוֹבֵד, לְמֶהֱוֵי פָּלַח לְקוּדְשָׁא בְּרִיךְ הוּא, וּלְאִתְדַּבְּקָא בֵּיה, וּלְאַתָּשָׁא גַּרְמֵיה בָּה.

686. Come and behold: It is written: "And he saw that rest was good and the land that it was pleasant and became a servant to tribute" (Beresheet 49:15). "And he saw that rest was good" is the Written Law; while "and the land that it was pleasant" is the Oral Law. "And he bowed his shoulder to bear" the yoke of the Torah, and cleave to it days and nights, "and became a servant to tribute" to serve the Holy One, blessed be He, and cling to Him, thus weakening himself for it, BY STUDYING THE TORAH CONSTANTLY.

687. ר"ש וְר' יוֹסֵי וְר' חִיָּיא, הֲווֹ קָא אָזְלֵי מִגָּלִילָא עַלָּאָה לִטְבֶרְיָה, אֲר"ש, נֵיהַךְ וְנִשְׁתַּדֵּל בְּאוֹרַיְיתָא, דְּכָל מַאן דְּיָדַע לְאִשְׁתַּדְּלָא בְּאוֹרַיְיתָא, וְלָא אִשְׁתַּדֵּל, אִתְחַיַּיב בְּנַפְשֵׁיה. וְלָא עוֹד אֶלָּא דְּיַהֲבִין לֵיה עוֹלָא דְּאַרְעָא, וְשִׁעְבּוּדָא בִּישָׁא, דִּכְתִיב בְּיִשָּׂשכָר, וַיֵּט שִׁכְמוֹ לִסְבּוֹל,

מַהוּ וַיֵּט, סָטָא. כְּד"א וַיִּטּוּ אַחֲרֵי הַבָּצַע. מַאן דְּסָטָא אָרְחֵיהּ וְגַרְמֵיהּ, דְּלָא לְמִסְבַּל עוּלָא דְּאוֹרַיְיתָא, מִיָּד וַיְהִי לְמַס עוֹבֵד.

687. Rabbi Shimon, Rabbi Yosi and Rabbi Chiya were walking from the upper Galilee to Tiberias. Rabbi Shimon said: Let us discourse upon the Torah as we walk, for whoever can study the Torah but does not do so, risks his life and suffers besides from worldly cares, and evil oppression OF THE GOVERNMENT, like it is said of Issachar, "And he bowed his shoulder to bear." What is the meaning of "bowed (also: 'turned aside')"? It means he turned aside, as it says, "But turned aside after unjust gain" (I Shmuel 8:3); NAMELY TURNED ASIDE FROM THE PATH OF RIGHTEOUSNESS. For whoever turns aside and prefers not to suffer the yoke of the Torah, he forthwith "became a servant to tribute," WHICH MEANS HE SANK UNDER THE BURDEN OF THE LAW AND THE OPPRESSION OF THE GOVERNMENT.

688. פָּתַח ר"ש וַאֲמַר, לְהַנְחִיל אוֹהֲבַי יֵשׁ וְאוֹצְרוֹתֵיהֶם אֲמַלֵּא. זַכָּאִין אִינוּן בְּנֵי עָלְמָא, אִינוּן דְּמִשְׁתַּדְּלֵי בְּאוֹרַיְיתָא, דְּכָל מַאן דְּאִשְׁתַּדֵּל בְּאוֹרַיְיתָא, אִתְרְחִים לְעֵילָא, וְאִתְרְחִים לְתַתָּא, וְאָחֲסִין בְּכָל יוֹמָא, יְרוּתָא דְּעָלְמָא דְּאָתֵי, הה"ד, לְהַנְחִיל אוֹהֲבַי יֵשׁ. מַאי יֵשׁ. דָּא עָלְמָא דְּאָתֵי דְּלָא פָּסַק מֵימוֹי לְעָלְמִין, וְנָטַל אֲגַר טַב עִלָּאָה, דְּלָא זָכֵי בֵּיהּ ב"נ אָחֳרָא, וּמַאי אִיהוּ. יֵ"שׁ. וּבְגִינֵי כָּךְ, רָמֵיז לָן שְׁמָא דְּיִשָּׂשכָר דְּאִשְׁתַּדֵּל בְּאוֹרַיְיתָא, יֵשׁ שָׂכָר. דָּא הוּא אַגְרָא דְּאִינוּן דְּמִשְׁתַּדְּלֵי בְּאוֹרַיְיתָא, יֵ"שׁ.

688. Rabbi Shimon opened the discussion saying: "That I may cause those who love Me to inherit substance; and I will fill their treasures" (Mishlei 8:21). Happy are the children of the world who study the Torah, for whoever is occupied with the Torah is beloved above and beloved below. He inherits the World to Come, as it is written: "That I may cause those who love Me to inherit substance." The substance is the World to Come, BINAH, whose water, ITS ABUNDANCE, never stops flowing. FOR HE WHO STUDIES THE TORAH receives supernal reward, which no other man attains. What is it? It is substance (Heb. *yesh*), BINAH. This is alluded to by the name Issachar, who studied the Torah, SINCE HIS NAME CONTAINS THE SYLABLES *Yesh sachar* (lit. 'there is a reward'), the reward for those who study the Torah; NAMELY THE MENTIONED *Yesh*.

689. כְּתִיב חָזֵה הֲוֵית עַד דִּי כָרְסָוָון רְמִיו וְעַתִּיק יוֹמִין יְתִיב וְגו' חָזֵה הֲוֵית עַד דִּי כָרְסָוָון רְמִיו, כַּד אִתְחָרַב בֵּי מַקְדְּשָׁא, תְּרֵי כָּרְסָוָון נָפְלוּ, תְּרֵי לְעֵילָא, תְּרֵי לְתַתָּא. תְּרֵי לְעֵילָא, בְּגִין דְּאִתְרְחִיקַת תַּתָּאָה מֵעִלָּאָה, כָּרְסַיָּיא דְיַעֲקֹב אִתְרְחִיקַת מִכָּרְסַיָּיא דְּדָוִד. וְכָרְסַיָּיא דְּדָוִד נָפְלַת, הה"ד הִשְׁלִיךְ מִשָּׁמַיִם אֶרֶץ. תְּרֵי כָּרְסָוָון לְתַתָּא: יְרוּשָׁלַם, וְאִינוּן מָארֵי דְאוֹרַיְיתָא. וְכָרְסָוָון דִּלְתַתָּא בְּגַוְונָא דְכָרְסָוָון דִּלְעֵילָא, מָרֵיהוֹן דְּאוֹרַיְיתָא הַיְינוּ כָּרְסַיָּיא דְיַעֲקֹב. יְרוּשָׁלַם הַיְינוּ כָּרְסַיָּיא דְּדָוִד, וְעַל דָּא כְּתִיב, עַד דִּי כָרְסָוָון, וְלָא כָּרְסְיָא. כָּרְסָוָון סַגִּיאִין נָפְלוּ, וְכֻלְּהוּ לָא נָפְלוּ, אֶלָּא מֵעֶלְבּוֹנָה דְּאוֹרַיְיתָא.

689. It is written, "As I looked, thrones were placed, and an ancient of days did sit" (Daniel 7:9), WHICH MEANS THAT when the Temple was ruined, two thrones fell, for there are two thrones above and two below. HE EXPLAINS, There are two thrones above, THE THRONE OF JACOB, ZEIR ANPIN, AND THE THRONE OF DAVID, MALCHUT. When the lower throne was removed from the upper throne, the throne of Jacob from that of David, the latter fell. Hence it says, "And cast down from heaven (to) earth" (Eichah 2:1). The two thrones below, Jerusalem and the students of the Torah, resemble the thrones above, for the students of the Torah are the throne of Jacob, ZEIR ANPIN, and Jerusalem is the throne of David, MALCHUT. HENCE TWO THRONES FELL, THE UPPER THRONE OF DAVID, THE NUKVA, AND THE THRONE OF THE TERRESTRIAL JERUSALEM. It is therefore written: "Thrones were placed" IN THE PLURAL instead of 'throne' IN THE SINGULAR, for more than one throne fell, for the sole reason of the insult to the Torah.

690. תָּא חֲזֵי, כַּד אִינוּן זַכָּאֵי קְשׁוֹט מִשְׁתַּדְּלֵי בְּאוֹרַיְיתָא, כָּל אִינוּן תּוּקְפִין דִּשְׁאָר עַמִּין, דִּשְׁאָר חֵילִין, וְכָל חֵילִין דִּלְהוֹן, אִתְכַּפְיָין, וְלָא שָׁלְטֵי בְּעָלְמָא, וְיִשְׂרָאֵל אִזְדַּמַּן עֲלַיְיהוּ לְסַלְקָא לוֹן עַל כֹּלָּא, וְאִי לָא, חֲמוֹר גָּרְמָא לוֹן לְיִשְׂרָאֵל לְמֵיהַךְ בְּגָלוּתָא, וּלְמִנְפַּל בֵּינֵי עַמְמַיָא, וּלְמִשְׁלַט עֲלַיְיהוּ. וְכָל דָּא אֲמַאי, בְּגִין וַיַּרְא מְנוּחָה כִּי טוֹב, וּמְתַקְּנָא קַמֵּיהּ, וְיָכִיל לְמִרְוַוח בְּגִינָהּ כַּמָּה טָבִין וְכַמָּה כְּסוּפִין, וְסָטָא אוֹרְחֵיהּ דְּלָא לְמִסְבַּל עוּלָא דְּאוֹרַיְיתָא, בְּגַ"כ וַיְהִי לְמַס עוֹבֵד.

690. Come and see: when the truly righteous study the Torah, all the forces of the other nations and the armies, with all their power and legions, are subdued and no longer rule the world. Yisrael are appointed BY THE NATIONS OF THE WORLD, TO WIT, THEY ARE ASKED BY THEM to be their leaders. THIS IS THE SECRET OF THE NAME ISSACHAR, YESH-SACHAR AS EXPLAINED. But if not, THE KLIPAH OF the donkey causes Yisrael to go into exile and fall into the hands of the peoples and be ruled by them. And all this is because, "he saw rest that it was good," HE SAW THAT THE TORAH IS GOOD AND ready before him, and he could receive as his reward her benefits and comforts, yet he turned his way so as not to bear the burden of the Torah, and therefore "became a servant to tribute" IN EXILE.

691. כְּתִיב הַדּוּדָאִים נָתְנוּ רֵיחַ וְעַל פְּתָחֵינוּ כָּל מְגָדִים חֲדָשִׁים גַּם יְשָׁנִים וְגוֹ'. הַדּוּדָאִים נָתְנוּ רֵיחַ, אִלֵּין אִינוּן דְּאַשְׁכַּח רְאוּבֵן. כְּד"א, וַיִּמְצָא דוּדָאִים בַּשָּׂדֶה, וְלָא אִתְחַדְּשָׁן מִלֵּי דְאוֹרַיְיתָא, אֶלָּא עַל יְדוֹי בְּיִשְׂרָאֵל, כְּד"א וּמִבְּנֵי יִשָּׂשכָר יוֹדְעֵי בִינָה לְעִתִּים וְגוֹ'.

691. It is written, "The mandrakes give a fragrance, and at our gates are all manner of choice fruits, new and old" (Shir Hashirim 7:14). Reuben found those mandrakes in the field, as it is written: "And found mandrakes in the field" (Beresheet 30:14). New expositions of the Torah among Yisrael are discoursed only by him, as it is written: "And of the sons of Issachar were those who had knowledge of the times" (I Divrei Hayamim 12:32).

692. וְעַל פְּתָחֵינוּ כָּל מְגָדִים, אִינוּן גָּרְמוּ לְמֶהֱוֵי עַל פְּתָחֵינוּ, עַל פִּתְחֵי בָּתֵּי כְנֵסִיּוֹת וּבָתֵּי מִדְרָשׁוֹת, כָּל מְגָדִים. חֲדָשִׁים גַּם יְשָׁנִים, כַּמָּה מִלֵּי חַדְתָּאן וְעַתִּיקִין דְּאוֹרַיְיתָא, דְּאִתְגַּלְיָין עַל יְדַיְיהוּ, לְקָרְבָא לְיִשְׂרָאֵל לַאֲבוּהוֹן דִּלְעֵילָא, הֲדָא הוּא דִכְתִיב לָדַעַת מַה יַּעֲשֶׂה יִשְׂרָאֵל.

692. "And at our gates are all manner of choice fruits": It is THE CHILDREN OF ISSACHAR, who caused them to be at our gates; NAMELY the doors to the synagogues and Torah academies. "All manner of choice fruits, new and old" are studies of the Torah, new and old, which are revealed through them in order to bring near Yisrael to their Father above. Hence it says, "to know what Yisrael ought to do" (Ibid.).

693. דּוֹדִי צָפַנְתִּי לָךְ, מֵהָכָא אוֹלִיפְנָא כָּל מַאן דְּאִשְׁתַּדַּל בְּאוֹרַיְיתָא כִּדְקָא יָאוֹת, וְיָדַע לְמֶחֱדֵי מִלִּין, וּלְחַדְתּוּתֵי מִלִּין כִּדְקָא יָאוֹת, אִינוּן מִלִּין סַלְקִין עַד כָּרְסְיָיא דְּמַלְכָּא, וּכְנֶסֶת יִשְׂרָאֵל פְּתַח לוֹן תַּרְעִין, וְגָנֵיז לוֹן. וּבְשַׁעֲתָּא דְּעָאל קוּדְשָׁא בְּרִיךְ הוּא לְאִשְׁתַּעְשְׁעָא עִם צַדִּיקַיָּיא בְּגִנְתָּא דְּעֵדֶן, אֲפִיקַת לוֹן קַמֵּיהּ, וְקוּדְשָׁא בְּרִיךְ הוּא מִסְתַּכֵּל בְּהוֹ וְחָדֵי, כְּדֵין קוּדְשָׁא בְּרִיךְ הוּא מִתְעַטַּר בְּעִטְרִין עִלָּאִין, וְחָדֵי בְּמַטְרוֹנִיתָא, הה"ד, חֲדָשִׁים גַּם יְשָׁנִים דּוֹדִי צָפַנְתִּי לָךְ. וּמֵהַהִיא שַׁעֲתָּא, מִלּוֹי כְּתִיבִין בְּסִפְרָא, הֲדָא הוּא דִכְתִיב, וַיִּכָּתֵב סֵפֶר זִכָּרוֹן לְפָנָיו.

693. "Which I have laid up for you, O my beloved" (Shir Hashirim 7:14): From this we learned that whoever studies the Torah appropriately and knows new, joyous words, these words rise up to the King's throne, WHICH IS THE NUKVA, THE THRONE OF ZEIR ANPIN. And the Congregation of Yisrael, THE NUKVA, opens the gates before them and conceals them. And when the Holy One, blessed be He, enters the Garden of Eden to take delight in the righteous AT MIDNIGHT, she brings THE NEW EXPOSITIONS ON THE TORAH before Him, and the Holy One, blessed be He, sees them and rejoices. He then crowns Himself with supernal crowns and rejoices with the Matron, THE NUKVA. This is the meaning of the words "new and old, which I have laid up for you O my beloved," WHICH SHE UTTERS AT MIDNIGHT, WHEN BRINGING OUT THE NEW EXPOSITIONS ON THE TORAH BEFORE THE HOLY ONE, BLESSED BE HE. From that time on, the words OF THE STUDENT, WHO GLADDENS BY HIS WORDS, are written in the SUPERNAL book, as it says "and a book of remembrance was written before Him" (Malachi 3:16).

694. זַכָּאָה חוּלְקֵיהּ, מַאן דְּאִשְׁתַּדַּל בְּאוֹרַיְיתָא כִּדְקָא יָאוֹת, זַכָּאָה הוּא בְּהַאי עַלְמָא, וְזַכָּאָה הוּא בְּעַלְמָא דְּאָתֵי. עַד הָכָא שׁוּלְטָנוּתָא דִּיהוּדָה, דְּרוֹעָא דְּאִתְכְּלֵיל בְּכֹלָּא, בְּחֵילָא דְּכָל סִטְרִין, תְּלַת קִשְׁרִין דִּדְרוֹעָא, לְאִתְגַּבְּרָא עַל כֹּלָּא.

694. Happy is the portion of him who studies the Torah appropriately, for he is happy in this world and will be happy in the World to Come. So far extends the sway of Judah, the arm which includes all THE THREE

COLUMNS, through the strength of the sides, SOUTH, NORTH AND EAST, the three joints of the arm. TO WIT, JUDAH, ISSACHAR AND ZEBULUN ARE PLACED TOGETHER IN THIS PORTION, AS IN RELATION TO THE STANDARDS, FOR JUDAH IS THE ILLUMINATION OF THE RIGHT COLUMN, ISSACHAR THE LEFT AND ZEBULUN THE CENTRAL COLUMN, so that Judah will overcome all THE OTHER SIDE.

70. "Dan shall judge his people"

A Synopsis
The Zohar expounds upon the tribe of Dan. When the Jews were trekking through the desert, the tribe of Dan was placed in the rear to watch over the other tribes. The Zohar then speaks of the spiritual routes taken by each of the tribes, and in doing so, reveals that each route was already inscribed a cosmic blueprint designed to arouse spiritual Light in this world. Jacob specifically blessed the tribe of Dan with the words "Dan should be snake on the road." The Zohar then asks what this blessing means. The lower most dimension, in this case the end of the procession, represents the lowest level of Light and therefore represents the beginning and opening for negativity to enter. Dan is the watch guard protecting all the tribes from any intrusions from the negative snake known as the Satan.

The Relevance of this Passage
The cosmic sentinel that is the tribe of Dan, blankets us with a protective armor of Light that keeps negative entities, evil thoughts, and destructive emotions incited by the angel Satan, at bay.

695. דָּן יָדִין עַמּוֹ כְּאַחַד שִׁבְטֵי יִשְׂרָאֵל. רִבִּי חִיָּיא אָמַר, הַאי קְרָא הָכֵי אִית לֵיהּ לְמֵימַר, דָּן יָדִין לְשִׁבְטֵי יִשְׂרָאֵל, אוֹ דָּן יָדִין לְשִׁבְטֵי יִשְׂרָאֵל כְּאֶחָד, מַהוּ דָּן יָדִין עַמּוֹ. וּלְבָתַר כְּאַחַד שִׁבְטֵי יִשְׂרָאֵל.

695. "Dan shall judge his people, as one of the tribes of Yisrael" (Beresheet 49:16). Rabbi Chiya said: This verse should have been, 'Dan shall judge the tribes of Yisrael' or 'Dan shall judge the tribes of Yisrael as one.' What is the meaning of "Dan shall judge his people" followed by "as one of the tribes of Yisrael"?

696. אֶלָּא דָּן, הוּא דִּכְתִיב בֵּיהּ, מְאַסֵּף לְכָל הַמַּחֲנוֹת, דְּהוּא יַרְכָא שְׂמָאלָא, וְאָזֵיל לְבַתְרַיְיתָא. תָּא חֲזֵי כֵּיוָן דִּיהוּדָה וּרְאוּבֵן נַטְלִין, לֵיוָאֵי וַאֲרוֹנָא פָּרְשִׁין דְּגָלִין, וְנָטֵיל דִּגְלָא דְּאֶפְרַיִם דְּאִיהוּ לְמַעֲרָב, יַרְכָא יְמִינָא נָטֵיל, בְּקַפְסִירֵי קַסְטָא. וְאִי תֵּימָא, זְבוּלֻן דְּאִיהוּ עָאל, וְנָפֵיק, דִּכְתִיב בֵּיהּ, שְׂמַח זְבוּלֻן בְּצֵאתֶךָ, וּכְתִיב וְיַרְכָתוֹ וְגוֹ'. אֶלָּא וַדַּאי, יְהוּדָה אִתְכְּלֵיל מִכֹּלָא.

696. HE ANSWERS: Dan, whom it says was "rearward of all the camps" (Bemidbar 10:25), is the left thigh, NAMELY HOD, and went last. HE EXPLAINS, Come and see: when Judah and Reuben march, the Levites and the ark unfurl their standard and then the standard of Ephraim marches to the west. The right thigh marches according to order, BY WHICH THE RIGHT THIGH GOES BEFORE THE LEFT THIGH, DAN. THEREFORE DAN IS THE LAST TO MOVE. You may say that Zebulun is the one who goes in and out, as it says of him, "Rejoice, Zebulun, in your going out" (Devarim 33:18), FOR HE PERTAINS TO THE THIGH, AS EXPRESSLY STATED, "And his border (also: 'thigh') shall be at Tzidon" (Beresheet 49:13). ZEBULUN THEN SHOULD BE THE THIGH AND NOT EPHRAIM. HE ANSWERS: Judah comprises all of them.

697. תָּא חֲזֵי, מַלְכוּ דִּלְעֵילָא אִתְכְּלִיל מִכֹּלָּא, וִיהוּדָה אִיהוּ מַלְכוּ תַּתָּאָה. כְּמָה דְמַלְכוּ עִלָּאָה אִתְכְּלִיל מִכֹּלָּא, הָכֵי נָמֵי מַלְכוּ תַּתָּאָה, אִתְכְּלִיל מִכֹּלָּא, מִגּוּפָא מִיַּרְכָּא, בְּגִין לְאִתְגַּבְּרָא בְּתוּקְפֵיה.

697. HE EXPLAINS THE ARRANGEMENT OF THE FOUR STANDARDS, SAYING: come and behold: the upper Malchut, THE NUKVA OF ZEIR ANPIN, comprised everything, ALL THE TWELVE BODY SEGMENTS, and Judah is the lower Malchut. As the upper Malchut comprises everything, so does the lower Malchut (kingdom), Judah, comprise the whole body and the thigh; NAMELY TIFERET AND THE TWELVE JOINTS IN THE ARMS AND LEGS, in order to grow in strength.

698. כְּתִיב מִימִינ"וֹ אֵ"שׁ דָּ"ת לָמוֹ, אוֹרַיְיתָא מִסְּטְרָא דִגְבוּרָה אִתְיְיהִיב, וּגְבוּרָה אִתְכְּלִיל בִּימִינָא, וּבְגוּפָא, וְיַרְכָא, וּבְכֹלָּא. הָכֵי נָמֵי סִדְרָא קַדְמָאָה, יְהוּדָה אִיהוּ, מַלְכוּ דְאָתֵי מִסְּטַר גְּבוּרָה, וְאִתְכְּלִיל בִּימִינָא, בְּגוּפָא, וּבְיַרְכָא, בְּכֹלָּא אִתְכְּלִיל. כְּמָה דְמַלְכוּ דִלְעֵילָא, אִתְכְּלִיל מִכֹּלָּא.

698. It is written, "From His right hand went a fiery law for them" (Devarim 33:2), which means that the Torah was given from the side of Gvurah, WHICH IS FIRE. BUT Gvurah was included within the right, CHESED, in the body, TIFERET, and the thigh, NETZACH AND HOD, and all THE SFIROT. The first corps OF THE STANDARDS is Judah's, which is Malchut from the side of Gvurah, BUT included within the right in the body and in the thigh, and all THE SFIROT, like Malchut above, THE NUKVA OF ZEIR ANPIN, comprises all THE SFIROT.

699. סִדְרָא תִּנְיָינָא רְאוּבֵן, דְּאִיהוּ לִסְטַר דָּרוֹם, וְדָרוֹם אִיהוּ יְמִינָא, וְכָל חֵילָא דְּיָמִינָא, יְהוּדָה נָטִיל לֵיהּ, בְּגִין דִּרְאוּבֵן אִתְעֲבִיר מִנֵּיהּ מַלְכוּ, כְּד"א פַּחַז כַּמַּיִם אַל תּוֹתַר, וְנָטִיל לֵיהּ יְהוּדָה, וְאִתְגַּבַּר בְּתוּקְפָּא דְּיָמִינָא, דַּהֲוָה מֵרְאוּבֵן, וְכֵן כְּתִיב בְּדָוִד, נְאֻם יי' לַאדֹנִי שֵׁב לִימִינִי. בְּגִין דִּשְׂמָאלָא אִתְכְּלִיל בְּיָמִינָא, וְאִתְתַּקַּף בְּחֵילֵיהּ, הה"ד, יְמִין יי' עוֹשָׂה חָיִל וְגו'. יְהוּדָה וּרְאוּבֵן תְּרֵין דְּרוֹעִין הֲווֹ.

699. The second corps of the standards is Reuben's, who was on the south side, which is right, CHESED. But the strength of the right, OF REUBEN, was taken by Judah, since the kingship was removed from Reuben, for "unstable as water, you shall not excel" (Beresheet 49:4). So Judah took it and was reinforced with the power of the right, which was Reuben's. It is also said of David, WHO IS COME FROM JUDAH, "Hashem says to my master, 'Sit at My right hand'" (Tehilim 110:1), because left is included in the right and has become strengthened. And so is written, "The right hand of Hashem does valiantly" (Tehilim 118:16). SINCE JUDAH TOOK ALL REUBEN'S POWER OF THE RIGHT, HE WAS THE FIRST TO MARCH. Judah and Reuben were the two arms, REUBEN THE RIGHT AND JUDAH THE LEFT ARM.

700. סִדְרָא תְּלִיתָאָה, אֶפְרַיִם, דְּאִיהוּ יַרְכָא יְמִינָא, וְנָטְלָא קַמֵּי שְׂמָאלָא תָּדִיר, וְדָן דְּאִיהוּ יַרְכָא שְׂמָאלָא, נָטִיל לְבַתְרַיְיתָא, וְעַל דָּא הוּא הַמְאַסֵּף לְכָל הַמַּחֲנוֹת לְצִבְאוֹתָם, וְאָזֵיל לְבַתְרַיְיתָא.

700. The third corps OF THE STANDARDS is that of Ephraim, who is the right thigh, NETZACH, which always goes before the left. Dan, who is the left thigh, HOD, goes last and is therefore "the rearward of all the camps" and marches last.

701. יְהוּדָה נָטִיל חֵילָא בִּתְרֵין דְּרוֹעִין, בְּגִין דִּרְאוּבֵן דְּאִיהוּ יְמִינָא, אִתְאֲבִיד מִנֵּיהּ בְּכֵירוּתָא כְּהוּנָתָא וּמַלְכוּתָא, וְעַל דָּא כְּתִיב בִּיהוּדָה,

יָדָיו רָב לוֹ וְעֵזֶר מִצָּרָיו תִּהְיֶה.

701. Judah had a portion in the two arms, CHESED AND GVURAH, since Reuben, who is the right arm, lost his birthright, priesthood and the kingship. It therefore says of Judah, "Let his hands be sufficient for him; and be you a help to him from his enemies" (Devarim 33:7), WHICH REFERS TO THE TWO HANDS, CHESED AND GVURAH.

702. תָּא חֲזֵי, כְּתִיב וַיַּעַשׂ הַמֶּלֶךְ שְׁלֹמֹה כִּסֵּא שֵׁן גָּדוֹל. כָּרְסַיָּיא דִּשְׁלֹמֹה, עֲבַד לֵיהּ כְּגַוְונָא דִּלְעֵילָּא, וְכָל דְּיוֹקְנִין דִּלְעֵילָּא עֲבַד הָכָא. וְעַל דָּא כְּתִיב, וַיֵּשֶׁב שְׁלֹמֹה עַל כִּסֵּא ה' לְמֶלֶךְ, מֶלֶךְ מִלָּה סְתִימָא הוּא. וְכֵן וּשְׁלֹמֹה יָשַׁב עַל כִּסֵּא דָוִד אָבִיו וַתִּכּוֹן מַלְכוּתוֹ מְאֹד, דְּקַיְימָא סִיהֲרָא בְּאַשְׁלָמוּתָא.

702. Come and behold: It is written: "The king made a great throne of ivory" (I Melachim 10:18). The throne of Solomon was constructed after the supernal pattern, and all the supernal forms, NAMELY THE LION, THE OX, AND SO ON, were upon it. THUS THE LOWER MALCHUT, SOLOMON, WHO IS A DESCENDANT OF JUDAH, INCLUDES ALL THE SFIROT LIKE THE UPPER MALCHUT. Of this says the verse, "Then Solomon sat on the throne of Hashem as king" (I Divrei Hayamim 29:23). The word king without attributes POSSIBLY DOES NOT REFER TO SOLOMON, BUT ALLUDES TO THE SUPERNAL MALCHUT. THE LESSON OF THE VERSE IS THAT "SOLOMON SAT ON THE THRONE OF HASHEM" LIKE A KING, THE SUPERNAL MALCHUT, AND LIKE IT COMPRISED ALL THE SFIROT. "Then Solomon sat upon the throne of David his father; and his kingdom was firmly established" (I Melachim 2:12). "HIS KINGDOM" REFERS TO THE SUPERNAL MALCHUT, WHICH MEANS THAT the moon, THE SUPERNAL KINGDOM, was full. HERE TOO, "AS KING" ALLUDES TO THE SUPERNAL MALCHUT.

703. דָּן יָדִין עַמּוֹ בְּקַדְמֵיתָא, וּלְבָתַר שִׁבְטֵי יִשְׂרָאֵל כְּאֶחָד: כִּיחִידוֹ שֶׁל עוֹלָם כְּמָה דַּהֲוָה בְּשִׁמְשׁוֹן, דְּאִיהוּ יְחִידָאי עָבֵיד דִּינָא בְּעַלְמָא, וְדָאִין וְקָטִיל כַּחֲדָא, וְלָא אִצְטְרִיךְ סְמָךְ.

703. "Dan shall judge his people" first, and then "the tribes of Yisrael." THE WORD "as one" MEANS like the lone one in the world, TO WIT, HE JUDGED

ON HIS OWN LIKE THE ONLY ONE OF THE WORLD. This applies to Samson, who singlehandedly executed justice in the world, sentenced and killed by himself and needed no help.

704. דָּן יָדִין עַמּוֹ. ר' יִצְחָק אֲמַר, דָּן, הַיְינוּ חִוְיָא, כְּמִין עַל אוֹרְחִין וּשְׁבִילִין. וְאִי תֵימָא דְּעַל שִׁמְשׁוֹן בִּלְחוֹדוֹי הוּא. אוֹף הָכֵי נָמֵי לְעֵילָא, דָּא הוּא נָחָשׁ זוּטָא מְאַסֵּף לְכָל הַמַּחֲנוֹת, וְכָמִין לְאוֹרְחִין וּשְׁבִילִין. לְבָתַר, חֵילִין וּמַשִׁירְיָין מֵהָכָא נָפְקֵי, אִינוּן דְּכָמְאַן לִבְנֵי נָשָׁא, עַל חוֹבִין, דְּרָאמִין לְהוֹ לַאֲחוֹרָא, בָּתַר כִּתְפַּיְיהוּ. אֲמַר רָבִּי חִיָּיא, נָחָשׁ הַקַּדְמוֹנִי לְעֵילָא, עַד דְּלָא יִתְבַּסֵּם בְּחַמְרָא דְּחֵידוּ.

704. "Dan shall judge his people" (Beresheet 49:16). Rabbi Yitzchak said: Dan is a serpent which lurks in ways and paths. It may be said that this is true for Samson alone. NOT SO, but this is also true above. It is the little serpent in "the rearward of all the camps" AT THE END OF THE GRADES OF HOLINESS. It lurks in the ways and paths, and from it issue armies and hosts OF FIENDS, which lurk in wait for people, TO PUNISH THEM for the sins they cast behind their backs, TO WIT, WHICH THEY DID NOT NOTICE, AND THEN SAY THEY DO NOT COMMIT. Rabbi Chiya said: This was the primordial serpent above before it was tempered by the gladdening wine.

705. נָחָשׁ עֲלֵי דֶרֶךְ. תָּא חֲזֵי, כְּמָה דְאִית דֶּרֶךְ לְעֵילָא, הָכֵי נָמֵי אִית דֶּרֶךְ לְתַתָּא, וּמִתְפַּרְשָׁא יַמָּא, לְכַמָּה אוֹרְחִין בְּכָל סְטַר. וְאִית אוֹרְחָא חַד, דְּאָתֵי וְאַסְגֵּי יַמָּא, וְרַבֵּי נוּנִין בִּישִׁין לְזַנְיְיהוּ, כְּמָה דַּאֲפִיקוּ מַיִין לְתַתָּא, נוּנִין טָבִין, נוּנִין בִּישִׁין, נוּנֵי עוּרְדְּעָנַיָּא, כְּגַוְונָא דָא, נוּנִין בִּישִׁין לְזַנְיְיהוּ.

705. "A serpent by the way" (Ibid. 17): Come and see: as there is a way above IN BINAH, so there is a way below IN MALCHUT. The sea is divided THROUGH THESE TWO WAYS into several paths on each side, EACH INCLUDED OF BOTH. There is one path, which adds MOCHIN OF THE FIRST THREE SFIROT to the sea, MALCHUT. It breeds all kinds of bad fish, FOR THE KLIPOT APPROACH TO SUCK ABUNDANCE FROM THERE AND THUS GROW. As the water below breed good fish, bad fish and frogs, so bad fish issue FROM THE SUPERNAL SEA.

706. וְכַד מִשְׁתַּמְּשֵׁי מֵאָרְחָא דְיַמָּא, אִתְחֲזוּן רָכְבִין עַל סוּסַיְיהוּ. וְאִלְמָלֵא דְּהַאי חִוְיָא, דְּאִיהוּ כָּנֵישׁ לְכָל מַשִּׁירְיָין, כְּמִין לְסוֹף אָרְחִין, וּבַדַּר לוֹן לַאֲחוֹרָא, הֲווֹ מְטַשְׁטְשֵׁי עַלְמָא. מִסִּטְרָא דְּהַנֵּי נַפְקִין חֲרָשִׁין לְעָלְמָא. תָּא חֲזֵי, בְּבִלְעָם כְּתִיב, וְלֹא הָלַךְ כְּפַעַם בְּפַעַם לִקְרַאת נְחָשִׁים, בְּגִין דְּאִינוּן קַיְימִין לְלַחֲשָׁא בַּחֲרָשֵׁי עַלְמָא.

706. When THE KLIPOT go by way of the sea, SUCKING ABUNDANCE FROM IT, they are seen riding on horses, and were it not for the serpent in the rearward of the camps, NAMELY DAN, THE LITTLE SERPENT which lies in the end of the paths and wards them off, they would destroy the world. OF THEM SAYS THE VERSE, "THAT BITES THE HORSE'S HEELS, SO THAT HIS RIDER SHALL FALL BACKWARD" (IBID.). THESE ARE THE DEMONS WHO RIDE HORSES. From the side OF THE KLIPOT, sorcerers come into the world. Come and behold: it is written of Bilaam: "He went not, as at other times, to seek for enchantments (lit. 'serpents')" (Bemidbar 24:1), which are made to cast spells with their charms.

707. חָמֵי מַה כְּתִיב, יְהִי דָן נָחָשׁ עֲלֵי דֶרֶךְ. מַאי עֲלֵי דֶרֶךְ. אֶלָּא נָחָשׁ, מַאן דְּאִשְׁתַּדַּל אֲבַתְרֵיה, אַבְחִישׁ פַּמַּלְיָא דִלְעֵילָא, וּמַאי אִיהוּ, הַהוּא דֶרֶךְ עִלָּאָה דְּנָפַק מִלְעֵילָא, כְּדְ"א הַנּוֹתֵן בַּיָּם דֶּרֶךְ וְגו'. נָחָשׁ, מַאן דְּאִשְׁתַּדַּל אֲבַתְרֵיה, כְּאִילוּ אָזִיל עַל הַהוּא דֶרֶךְ עִלָּאָה לְאַבְחָשָׁא לֵיה, בְּגִין דְּמֵהַהוּא דֶרֶךְ, אִתְּזָנוּ עָלְמִין עִלָּאֵי.

707. See the words: "Dan shall be a serpent by the way." HE ASKS: What way is this? HE ANSWERS: Whoever follows the serpent, rejects the household of heaven, CAUSES DIMINUTION IN THE HOLY HOSTS IN THE SUPERNAL WORLD. How so? Because this is a way which begins above, as it is written: "Who makes a way in the sea" (Yeshayah 43:16). Whoever follows the serpent, it is as if he treads this way and lessens it, BY DIMINISHING ITS ABUNDANCE, since from this way the upper worlds are sustained. HE SPOILS THEIR NOURISHMENT AND CAUSES THEM TO BECOME THIN.

708. וְאִי תֵימָא, דָן, אַמַּאי אִיהוּ בְּדַרְגָּא דָא, אֶלָּא כְּדִכְתִיב, וְאֶת לַהַט

-374-

הַחֶרֶב הַמִּתְהַפֶּכֶת לִשְׁמוֹר אֶת דֶּרֶךְ עֵץ הַחַיִּים, הָכִי נָמֵי הַנּוֹשֵׁךְ עִקְּבֵי
סוּס וְגוֹ', בְּגִין לְנַטְרָא לֵיהּ לְכָל מַשִּׁירְיָין. אָמַר רִבִּי אֶלְעָזָר, תִּקוּנָא
דְכוּרְסַיָּיא אִיהוּ, תָּא חֲזֵי, כָּרְסַיָּיא דִשְׁלֹמֹה מַלְכָּא, חַד חִוְיָא מְרַפְרֵף,
בְּקִטּוּרֵי שַׁרְבִּיטָא לְעֵילָא מֵאַרְיְוָתָא.

708. You may ask why Dan is in this grade, WHICH IS OF THE ASPECT OF THE EVIL KLIPAH. HE ANSWERS: Like "the bright blade of a revolving sword to guard the way to the Tree of Life" (Beresheet 3:24), IT SAYS here "that bites the horse's heels..." for the protection of all the camps. Rabbi Elazar said: This is the fixing of the throne. TO WIT, DAN HOLDING TO THE GRADE OF THE KLIPAH IS THE UPHOLDING OF THE NUKVA, TO KEEP HER FROM THE SUCKING OF THE FIENDS WHICH RIDE HORSES. Come and see: Upon Solomon's throne, there is a serpent dangling from the scepter above the lions THAT ARE ON THE THRONE, WHICH TEACHES US THAT THERE IS A SERPENT IN THE MAKING OF THE THRONE.

709. כְּתִיב וַתָּחֶל רוּחַ ה' לְפַעֲמוֹ בְּמַחֲנֵה דָן וְגוֹ'. תָּא חֲזֵי, שִׁמְשׁוֹן נְזִיר
עוֹלָם הֲוָה, וּפָרִישׁ עָלְמָא אִיהוּ, וְאִתְגַּבַּר בֵּיהּ חֵילָא תַּקִּיפָא, וְהוּא הֲוָה
חִוְיָא בְּהַאי עַלְמָא, לָקֳבֵל עַמִּין עכו"ם, דְּהָא אַחְסָנַת חוּלָקָא דְבִרְכָתָא
דְדָן אֲבוּהִי יָרֵית, דִּכְתִיב וִיהִי דָן נָחָשׁ עֲלֵי דֶרֶךְ וְגוֹ'.

709. It is written: "And the spirit of Hashem began to move him in the camp of Dan" (Shoftim 13:25). Come and see: Samson was a permanent Nazirite and a recluse of great strength. He was a serpent in this world against the heathen nations, for he inherited the portion of blessings of his ancestor Dan, as it is written: "Dan shall be a serpent by the way."

710. אָמַר ר' חִיָּיא, נָחָשׁ יְדִיעָא, שְׁפִיפוֹן מַאי נִיהוּ. א"ל, רָזָא דְתִקוּנָא
דַּחֲרָשִׁין, דְּנָחָשׁ אִיהוּ שְׁפִיפוֹן, הָכִי נָמֵי הַהוּא רָשָׁע דְּבִלְעָם, בְּכֹלָּא
הֲוָה יָדַע. תָּא חֲזֵי, כְּתִיב וַיֵּלֶךְ שֶׁפִי, לְזִמְנִין בְּהַאי, וּלְזִמְנִין בְּהַאי.

710. Rabbi Chiya said: We understand about the serpent, but what of the adder? He said to him: The secret of making spells is that the serpent is an adder, THOUGH THEY ARE TWO DIFFERENT SPECIES, THEY CAST THE SAME SPELLS AS IF THEY WERE OF THE SAME KIND. It is written also of the evil Bilaam, who was omniscient, that he "went to a steep place (Heb. *shefi*)" (Bemidbar 23:3), WHICH ALLUDES TO THE ADDER (HEB. *SHEFIFON*), THOUGH BEFORE IT IS WRITTEN: "HE WENT NOT, AS AT OTHER TIMES, TO SEEK FOR ENCHANTMENTS (OR: SERPENTS)" (BEMIDBAR 24:1). He used now the one now the other, NOW THE SERPENT AND NOW THE ADDER, SINCE HE HAD KNOWLEDGE OF BOTH.

711. וְאִי תֵימָא דָן, לָאו דַּרְגֵּיהּ בְּהַאי. הָכֵי הוּא וַדַּאי, אֶלָּא אִתְמַנָּא עַל דַּרְגָּא דָא, לְמֶהֱוֵי סִטְרָא בַּתְרַיְיתָא, וְשַׁבְחָא אִיהוּ דִילֵיהּ, מִמַּנָּן דְּמַלְכָּא בְּהַאי, וּמְמַנָּא עַל הַאי, וִיקָרָא אִיהוּ לְכָל אִינוּן מְמֻנִּין. וְכַרְסְיָיא דְּמַלְכָּא, בְּכָל אִינוּן מְמַנָּן אִתְתַּקַּן, בְּכָל הַנֵּי מְמַנָּן תְּחוֹתַיְיהוּ מִתְפָּרְשָׁן אוֹרְחִין וְדַרְגִּין, הֵן לְטַב, הֵן לְבִישׁ, וְכֻלְּהוּ אִתְאַחֲדָן בְּהַנֵּי תִּקּוּנֵי דְּכַרְסְיָיא, וּבְגִינֵי כָּךְ דָּן לְסְטַר צָפוֹן, בְּנוּקְבָּא דִּתְהוֹמָא רַבָּא, דִּסְטַר צָפוֹן כַּמָּה חֲבִילֵי טְרִיקִין אִזְדַּמְּנָן תַּמָּן, וְכֻלְּהוּ טַפְסִירָא דְקַסְטְרָא לְאַבְאָשָׁא עַלְמָא.

711. You may say that it does not pertain to Dan's grade to use THE SERPENT AND THE ADDER. HE REPLIES: Indeed it does not, but he was appointed over this grade TO USE IT FOR THE NEEDS OF HOLINESS, being of the last grade. This is to his honor, for there are chieftains charged by the King over this or that, and it is considered to be an honor to all the appointes TO BE APPOINTED BY THE KING, REGARDLESS OF WHAT THEY ARE APPOINTED OVER, for the King's throne is fixed through all the chiefs together, and under them there are paths and grades for the good and for evil, all of them united in the making of the throne, THE NUKVA. Hence Dan is to the north, NAMELY THE LEFT THIGH OF THE NUKVA WHICH IS HOD. In a hole of the great abyss, IN THE END OF THE LEFT THIGH, WHICH IS BINAH OF THE KLIPAH, there are many battalions of evil demons, all in charge of harming the world.

712. בְּגִינֵי כָּךְ צַלֵּי יַעֲקֹב וַאֲמַר, לִישׁוּעָתְךָ קִוִּיתִי ה'. בְּכָל שְׁבָטִים לָא קָאֲמַר לִישׁוּעָתְךָ אֶלָּא בְּהַאי. בְּגִין דְּחָמָא לֵיהּ תּוֹקְפָא תַּקִּיפָא דְּחִוְיָא, מְרַחֲשָׁא דִינָא לְאִתְגַּבְּרָא.

712. For this reason, Jacob prayed, saying, "I wait for Your salvation, O Hashem" (Beresheet 49:18). HE ASKS: Why does he not ask for salvation in

regard to the other tribes, only to this one. HE REPLIES: This is because he has seen the force and strength of the serpent, when judgment is aroused to overpower HOLINESS. HE THEREFORE PRAYED FOR SALVATION.

713. ר' יוֹסֵי וְר' חִזְקִיָּה, הֲווֹ אָזְלֵי לְמֶחֱמֵי לְר"ש בְּקַפּוֹטְקִיָּא, אֲמַר רַבִּי חִזְקִיָּה, הַאי דְּאַמְרִינָן לְעוֹלָם יְסַדֵּר בַּר נָשׁ שְׁבָחָא דְּמָרֵיהּ, וּלְבָתַר יְצַלֵּי צְלוֹתֵיהּ, הַאי מַאן דְּלַבֵּיהּ טָרֵיד, וּבָעֵי לְצַלָּאָה צְלוֹתֵיהּ, וְאִיהוּ בְּעָקוּ, וְלָא יָכִיל לְסַדְּרָא שְׁבָחָא דְּמָרֵיהּ כִּדְקָא יָאוֹת, מַאי הוּא.

713. Rabbi Yosi and Rabbi Chizkiyah were going to visit Rabbi Shimon in Cappadocia. Rabbi Chizkiyah said: It is known that a man should first pronounce the praises of his Master and only then to say his prayer. A QUESTION ARISES: What of a man who is in distress or in trouble and wishes to pray, yet cannot pronounce his Master's praises?

714. א"ל, אע"ג דְּלָא יָכִיל לְכַוְּונָא לִבָּא וּרְעוּתָא, סְדוּרָא וְשִׁבְחָא דְּמָרֵיהּ אַמַּאי גָּרַע, אֶלָּא יְסַדֵּר שְׁבָחֵיהּ דְּמָארֵיהּ, אע"ג דְּלָא יָכִיל לְכַוְּונָא, וִיצַלֵּי צְלוֹתֵיהּ. הה"ד תְּפִלָּה לְדָוִד שִׁמְעָה ה' צֶדֶק הַקְשִׁיבָה רִנָּתִי, שִׁמְעָה ה' צֶדֶק בְּקַדְמֵיתָא, בְּגִין דְּאִיהוּ סְדוּרָא דִּשְׁבָחָא דְּמָרֵיהּ. וּלְבָתַר הַקְשִׁיבָה רִנָּתִי הַאֲזִינָה תְפִלָּתִי. מַאן דְּיָכִיל לְסַדְּרָא שְׁבָחָא דְּמָרֵיהּ, וְלָא עָבֵיד, עֲלֵיהּ כְּתִיב, גַּם כִּי תַרְבּוּ תְפִלָּה אֵינֶנִּי שׁוֹמֵעַ יְדֵיכֶם וְגוֹ'.

714. Rabbi Yosi said to him: He is not fully devoted in heart and will, yet why should he fail to praise his Master? He should first pronounce his Master's praises, though not with perfect devotion, and then say his prayer. This is the meaning of "A prayer of David. Hear the right, O Hashem, attend to my cry" (Tehilim 17:1). First, "Hear the right, O Hashem," which is the praises for the Master, and only then "attend to my cry give ear to my prayer." Whoever can praise his Master, yet does not do so, of him it is written: "Even when you make many prayers, I will not hear..." (Yeshayah 1:15).

715. כְּתִיב אֶת הַכֶּבֶשׂ הָאֶחָד תַּעֲשֶׂה בַּבֹּקֶר וְאֵת הַכֶּבֶשׂ הַשֵּׁנִי תַּעֲשֶׂה בֵּין הָעַרְבָּיִם. תְּפִלּוֹת כְּנֶגֶד תְּמִידִין תִּקְנוּם. תָּא חֲזֵי, בְּאִתְעֲרוּתָא

דִּלְתַתָּא, אִתְעַר הָכֵי נָמֵי לְעֵילָא, וּבְאִתְעֲרוּתָא דִּלְעֵילָא, הָכֵי נָמֵי
לְעֵילָא מִנֵּיהּ, עַד דְּמָטֵי אִתְעֲרוּתָא לַאֲתַר דְּבָעֵיָא בּוּצִינָא לְאַדְלָקָא
וְאַדְלֵיק, וּבְאִתְעֲרוּתָא דִתְנָנָא דִּלְתַתָּא, אַדְלֵיק בּוּצִינָא לְעֵילָא, וְכַד
הַאי אַדְלֵיק, כֻּלְּהוּ בּוּצִינִין אָחֳרָנִין דָּלְקִין, וּמִתְבָּרְכָאן מִנֵּיהּ כֻּלְּהוּ
עָלְמִין. אִשְׁתַּכַּח, דְּאִתְעֲרוּתָא דְּקָרְבָּנָא תִּקּוּנָא דְעָלְמָא, וּבִרְכָאן
דְעָלְמִין כֻּלְּהוּ.

715. It is written, "The one lamb shall you offer in the morning, and the other lamb shall you offer at evening" (Bemidbar 28:4). The prayers were ordained in the place of the daily offerings, THE MORNING PRAYER CORRESPONDS TO THE MORNING OFFERING, MINCHAH TO THE EVENING OFFERING. Come and see: by the awakening below CAUSED BY THE SACRIFICE OF THE OFFERING, there is also awakening above. Through the awakening above towards that which is higher still, IT IS AROUSED too, until the awakening reaches the place where the candle is to be lit, and it is lit. Thus IT IS FOUND THAT through the ascent of the smoke WHICH RISES FROM THE OFFERING below, the candle is lit above, WHICH IS THE NUKVA. When this candle is lit, all other candles are lit and all the worlds are blessed through it. Thus the awakening of the offering is the support of the world, and the blessings of all worlds.

716. הָא כֵיצַד, שָׁאֲרֵי תְּנָנָא לְסַלְּקָא, אִינּוּן דְּיוֹקְנִין קַדִּישִׁין דִּמְמַנָּן עַל
עָלְמָא אִתְתַּקְּנָן לְאִתְעָרָא, וּמִתְעָרִין לְדַרְגִּין בְּכִסּוּפָא דִּלְעֵילָא, כְּד"א
הַכְּפִירִים שׁוֹאֲגִים לַטָּרֶף וגו'. אָלֵין אִתְעָרִין לְדַרְגִּין עִלָּאִין דַּעֲלַיְיהוּ,
עַד דְּמָטֵי אִתְעֲרוּתָא, עַד דְּבָעֵי מַלְכָּא לְאִתְחַבְּרָא בְּמַטְרוֹנִיתָא.

716. HE EXPLAINS HIS WORDS: How is this performed? When the smoke from the offering commences to rise, the holy forms appointed over the world OF ASIYAH are prepared to rouse AND RAISE MAYIM NUKVIN (FEMALE WATERS.) They are aroused towards the grades above them IN THE WORLD OF YETZIRAH, with great desire, as it says, "The young lions roar after their prey..." (Tehilim 104:21). Those OF THE WORLD OF YETZIRAH are aroused toward the grades above them IN THE WORLD OF BRIYAH, UNTIL THE AWAKENING REACHES THE PLACE WHERE THE CANDLE IS TO BE LIT; NAMELY until the King, ZEIR ANPIN, wishes to join the Matron, THE NUKVA.

717. וּבְכְסוּפָא דִּלְתַתָּא, נָבְעִין מַיִּין תַּתָּאִין, לְקַבְּלָא מַיִּין עִלָּאִין, דְּהָא
לָא נָבְעִין מַיִּין עִלָּאִין, אֶלָּא בְּאִתְעָרוּתָא דִּכְסוּפָא דִּלְתַתָּא, וּכְדֵין
תֵּיאוֹבְתָּא אִתְדַּבַּק, וְנָבְעִין מַיִּין תַּתָּאִין לָקֳבֵל מַיִּין עִלָּאִין, וְעַלְמִין
מִתְבָּרְכָאן, וּבוּצִינִין כֻּלְּהוּ דְּלִיקָן, וְעִלָּאִין וְתַתָּאִין מִשְׁתַּכְּחֵי בְּבִרְכָאן.

717. HE EXPLAINS THE MEANING OF MAYIN NUKVIN, saying that through the desire below, the lower waters, NAMELY MAYIN NUKVIN, rise to receive the upper waters FROM THE GRADE ABOVE IT. The lower waters do not flow save through the arousal of the desire of the lower one. Then the desire OF THE LOWER AND THE UPPER cleave together, the lower waters flow to meet the DESCENDING upper waters, AND THE MATING IS CONSUMMATED. The worlds are blessed, all the candles lit, and the upper and lower beings are endowed with blessings.

718. תָּא חֲזֵי , כַּהֲנֵי וְלֵיוָאֵי, מִתְעָרֵי לְאִתְחַבְּרָא שְׂמָאלָא בִּימִינָא. אֲמַר
ר' חִזְקִיָּה, כֹּלָּא הָכֵי הוּא וַדַּאי, אֲבָל הָכֵי שְׁמַעְנָא, כַּהֲנֵי וְלֵיוָאֵי, דָּא
אִתְעַר שְׂמָאלָא, וְדָא אִתְעַר יְמִינָא, בְּגִין דְּאִתְחַבְּרוּתָא דִּדְכוּרָא לְגַבֵּי
נוּקְבָּא, לָאו אִיהוּ אֶלָּא בִּשְׂמָאלָא וְימִינָא, כְּד"א שְׂמֹאלוֹ תַּחַת לְרֹאשִׁי
וִימִינוֹ תְּחַבְּקֵנִי. וּכְדֵין אִתְחַבַּר דְּכַר בְּנוּקְבָּא, וְתֵיאוּבְתָּא אִשְׁתַּכַּח,
וְעַלְמִין מִתְבָּרְכִין, וְעִלָּאֵי וְתַתָּאֵי בְּחֵידוּ.

718. Come and see: the priests FROM THE RIGHT COLUMN and the Levites FROM THE LEFT COLUMN are aroused WHEN THEY SACRIFICE THE OFFERING, so as to join the right with the left. Rabbi Chizkiyah said: This is true, yet I have heard AN EXPLANATION TO THIS. AT THE TIME OF OFFERING, the one stirs the left, NAMELY THE LEVITES, and the other, THE PRIESTS, the right. For the union of the male and the female occurs only through left and right, as it says, "His left hand is under my head, and his right hand embraces me" (Shir Hashirim 2:6). AFTER THE EMBRACE OF RIGHT AND LEFT, the male is united to the female with desire, all the worlds are blessed and there is joy high and low.

719. וְעַל דָּא, כַּהֲנֵי וְלֵיוָאֵי, מִתְעָרֵי מִלָּה לְתַתָּא, לְאִתְעָרָא בְּסוּפָא
וַחֲבִיבוּתָא לְעֵילָא, דְּכֹלָּא תַּלְיָא בִּימִינָא וּשְׂמָאלָא, אִשְׁתַּכַּח דְּקָרְבְּנָא

יְסוֹדָא דְעָלְמָא, תִּקּוּנָא דְעָלְמָא, חֵידוּ דְעֶלְאִין וְתַתָּאִין. אָמַר ר' יוֹסֵי
וַדַּאי שַׁפִּיר קָא אֲמַרְתְּ, וְהָכֵי הוּא, וְהָכֵי שְׁמַעְנָא מִלָּה, וְאַנְשֵׁינָא לָהּ,
וַאֲנָא שְׁמַעְנָא הָא, וְכֹלָּא בְּחַד סַלְקָא.

719. The priests and Levites then stir below THE OFFERING in order to arouse desire and love above, DESIRE BEING THE SECRET OF THE LEFT AND LOVE THE SECRET OF THE RIGHT, since all depends upon right and left. FOR THE CENTRAL COLUMN ONLY BRINGS THEM TOGETHER. It is found that the sacrifice is the foundation of the world, the making of the world, the joy of the upper and lower. Rabbi Yosi said: You have spoken well, and this is so. I, TOO, have heard the same, yet I forgot it. NOW that I hear it from you, it all comes up to one, NAMELY THROUGH THE CENTRAL COLUMN, WHICH BRINGS TOGETHER RIGHT AND LEFT AND COMPLETES THEM.

720. הַשְׁתָּא צְלוֹתָא בַּאֲתַר דְּקָרְבָּנָא, וּבְעֵי ב"ן לְסַדְרָא שְׁבָחָא דְמָרֵיהּ
כִּדְקָא יָאוֹת, וְאִי לָא יְסַדֵּר, לָאו צְלוֹתֵיהּ צְלוֹתָא. תָּא חֲזֵי סִדּוּרָא
שְׁלִים דְּשְׁבָחָא דְקוּדְשָׁא בְּרִיךְ הוּא, מַאן דְּיָדַע לְיַחֲדָא שְׁמָא קַדִּישָׁא
כִּדְקָא יָאוֹת, דִּבְהַאי מִתְעָרִין עֶלְאִין וְתַתָּאִין, וְנַגְדֵּי בִּרְכָאן לְכֻלְּהוּ
עָלְמִין.

720. Now that prayer has taken the place of sacrifice, man should first pronounce the praise of the Holy One, blessed be He, fittingly, for if he does not, his prayer is no prayer. Come and see: The perfect praise for the Holy One, blessed be He, is made by him who knows how to properly unite the Holy Name, WHO CAN RAISE MAYIN NUKVIN TO UNITE MALE AND FEMALE, for through this the upper and lower are awakened and draw blessings upon all the worlds.

721. א"ר חִזְקִיָּה, לָא אַשְׁרֵי קוּדְשָׁא בְּרִיךְ הוּא לְיִשְׂרָאֵל בְּגָלוּתָא בֵּינֵי
עַמְמַיָא, אֶלָּא בְּגִין דְּיִתְבָּרְכוּן שְׁאָר עַמִּין בְּגִינֵיהוֹן, דְּהָא אִינּוּן נַגְדִּין
בִּרְכָאן מִלְּעֵילָא לְתַתָּא כָּל יוֹמָא.

721. Rabbi Chizkiyah said: The Holy One, blessed be He, put the children of Yisrael in exile among the nations for the sole purpose that the other nations be blessed through Yisrael, who daily draw blessings from above downward.

722. אַזְלוּ, עַד דַּהֲווֹ אָזְלֵי, חָמוּ חַד חִוְיָא דַּהֲוָה קָמַסְחַר בְּאָרְחָא. סָטוּ מֵאָרְחָא. אָתָא ב״נ אָחֲרָא לְגַבַּיְיהוּ, קָטֵיל לֵיהּ חִוְיָא. אַהֲדָרוּ רֵישַׁיְיהוּ, וְחָמוּ לֵיהּ, לְהַהוּא ב״נ דְּמִית. אָמְרוּ, וַדַּאי הַהוּא נָחָשׁ, שְׁלִיחוּתָא דְּמָרֵיהּ קָא עָבֵיד. בְּרִיךְ רַחֲמָנָא דְּשֵׁזְבִינָנָא.

722. They went. As they were walking, they saw a snake on the road and turned aside. Another man came and the snake killed him. They turned their heads and saw the man dead. They said: Surely the snake acted by his Master's bidding; TO WIT, THE HOLY ONE, BLESSED BE HE, ORDERED HIM TO KILL THAT MAN. Blessed be the Merciful One who saved us.

723. פָּתַח רִבִּי יוֹסֵי וַאֲמַר, יְהִי דָן נָחָשׁ עֲלֵי דֶרֶךְ. אֵימָתַי הֲוָה דָן נָחָשׁ, בְּיוֹמוֹי דִּירָבְעָם, דִּכְתִיב וְאֶת הָאֶחָד נָתַן בְּדָן אַמַּאי אִתְּיְיהֵיב תַּמָּן עֲלֵי דֶרֶךְ. עַל הַהוּא אֹרַח, דְּיִתְמְנַע דְּלָא יִסְלְקוּן לִירוּשָׁלַם. וְדָא דָן, הֲוָה לוֹן נָחָשׁ לְיִשְׂרָאֵל עֲלֵי דֶרֶךְ, עֲלֵי דֶרֶךְ וַדַּאי, כְּד״א וַיִּוָּעַץ הַמֶּלֶךְ וגו'. שְׁפִיפֹן עֲלֵי אֹרַח. דְּעָקִיץ לוֹן לְיִשְׂרָאֵל. וְכֹלָּא לָא הֲוָה אֶלָּא עֲלֵי דֶרֶךְ, וַעֲלֵי אוֹרְחָא, לְאִתְמַנְּעָא מִיִּשְׂרָאֵל דְּלָא יִסְלְקוּן לִירוּשָׁלַם, לְמֵיחַג חַגַּיְיהוּ, וּלְקָרְבָא קָרְבָּנִין וְעִלָּוָון, לְמִפְלַח תַּמָּן.

723. Rabbi Yosi opened the discussion with the verse: "Dan shall be a serpent by the way." When was Dan a serpent? In the days of Jeroboam, as it is written: "And the other put he in Dan" (I Melachim 12:29). BECAUSE "A SNAKE" REFERS TO IDOL WORSHIPPING. And why was he put there "by the road"? "By the way," so as to prevent the pilgrimage to Jerusalem. Dan was then a snake "by the way" of Yisrael. "By the way" indeed, as it says, "the king took counsel, AND MADE TWO CALVES OF GOLD, AND SAID TO THEM, IT IS TOO MUCH FOR YOU TO GO UP TO JERUSALEM" (IBID. 28). HE THUS MADE THIS SNAKE BY THE WAY TO JERUSALEM TO PREVENT THEIR GOING THERE ON PILGRIMAGE. "An adder in the path" bit Yisrael. They were put "by the way" and in the path to prevent the children of Yisrael from going up to Jerusalem to celebrate their festivals, offer sacrifices and offering and worship there.

724. תָּא חֲזֵי בְּשַׁעְתָּא דְּמָטוּ בִּרְכָאן לִידָא דְּמֹשֶׁה, לְבָרְכָא לְכֻלְּהוּ שִׁבְטִים, חָמָא לְדָן דַּהֲוָה קָטִיר בְּחִוְיָא, אַהֲדַר קָטַר לֵיהּ בְּאַרְיָא, הֲדָא הוּא דִּכְתִיב וּלְדָן אָמַר דָּן גּוּר אַרְיֵה יְזַנֵּק מִן הַבָּשָׁן. מ"ט, בְּגִין דִּיהֵא שֵׁירוּתָא וְסוֹפָא דְּד' דְּגָלִין קָטִיר בִּיהוּדָה דְּאִיהוּ מַלְכָּא, כְּד"א, גּוּר אַרְיֵה יְהוּדָה, וְהוּא שֵׁירוּתָא דְּדִגְלִין, וְסוֹפָא דְּדִגְלִין דָּן, דִּכְתִיב דָּן גּוּר אַרְיֵה וְגו', לְמֶהֱוֵי שֵׁירוּתָא וְסוֹפָא קָטִיר בְּחַד אֲתַר.

724. Come and see: when it was time for Moses to bless the tribes, he saw that Dan was attached to the serpent, and linked him again to the lion, WHICH IS CHESED. This is the meaning of the verse, "And of Dan he said: 'Dan is a lion's whelp, that leaps from Bashan'" (Devarim 33:22). Wherefore did he do this? So as to connect the first and the last of the four standards: Judah's who is king, as it is written: "Judah is a lion's whelp," the first of the standards, and Dan's in the rear, as is written, "Dan is a lion's whelp..." so as to link the beginning and the end to one place, THE LION WHICH IS CHESED.

725. לִישׁוּעָתְךָ קִוִּיתִי ה', רִבִּי חִיָּיא אָמַר, כְּד"א וְהוּא יָחֵל לְהוֹשִׁיעַ אֶת יִשְׂרָאֵל מִיַּד פְּלִשְׁתִּים. אָמַר ר' אַחָא, וְכִי אַמַּאי קִוִּיתִי וְהָא סָלִיק הֲוָה יַעֲקֹב מֵעַלְמָא בְּהַהוּא זִמְנָא מִכַּמָּה שְׁנִין, אַמַּאי אָמַר דְּאִיהוּ מְחַכֶּה לְהַהוּא יְשׁוּעָה. אֶלָּא וַדַּאי רָזָא דְּמִלָּה, כְּדִכְתִיב, וְהָיָה כַּאֲשֶׁר יָרִים מֹשֶׁה יָדוֹ וְגָבַר יִשְׂרָאֵל, יִשְׂרָאֵל סְתָם. אוּף הָכָא וְהוּא יָחֵל לְהוֹשִׁיעַ אֶת יִשְׂרָאֵל, יִשְׂרָאֵל סְתָם. בְּגִינֵי כָּךְ אָמַר, לִישׁוּעָתְךָ קִוִּיתִי ה'. אָמַר ר' חִיָּיא. וַדַּאי הָכִי הוּא, וְשַׁפִּיר. זַכָּאָה חוּלָקְהוֹן דְּצַדִּיקַיָּיא, דְּיָדְעֵי לְאִשְׁתַּדְּלָא בְּאוֹרַיְתָא, לְמִזְכֵּי בָּהּ לְחַיִּין דִּלְעֵילָא. כְּד"א כִּי הִיא חַיֶּיךָ וְאֹרֶךְ יָמֶיךָ לָשֶׁבֶת עַל הָאֲדָמָה וְגו'.

725. "I wait (lit. 'waited') for your salvation, O Hashem" (Beresheet 49:18): Rabbi Chiya said: It is written, "And he shall begin to deliver Yisrael out of the hand of the Philistines" (Shoftim 13:5). THIS IS THE SALVATION JACOB WAITED FOR. Rabbi Acha said: Why DOES IT SAY, "I waited"? Jacob would have been dead these many years by then. Why did he say he was waiting for salvation? The secret of this matter is the verse, "And it came to pass, when Moses held up his hand, that Yisrael prevailed" (Shemot 17:11).

The word Yisrael without attributes IS ZEIR ANPIN; NAMELY THE ASPECT OF JACOB. THUS THE SALVATION THROUGH SAMSON CONCERNS JACOB, THOUGH HE HAD ALREADY PASSED AWAY. Hence he said: "I wait (lit. 'waited') for your salvation, O Hashem." Rabbi Chiya said: Surely this is correct and well. Happy is the portion of the righteous who know how to study the Torah and merit through her life eternal, as it says "for He is your life, and the length of your days: that you may dwell in the land..." (Devarim 30:20).

71. "Gad, raiders shall maraud him"

A Synopsis

Rabbi Yisa explains the name Gad indicates that many hosts and legions are dependent on him, and that armies will issue from him and engage in war. The name Gad also signifies the sustenance that the water of the river flowing from the Garden of Eden provides to the poor and the needy. Indeed, if not for his lineage, Gad would have risen higher than all the tribes because of his name. We learn that, similar to Reuben, he was born at a propitious time. However, perfection later departed from him, and also like Reuben, he thus did not receive a portion in the Holy Land, but instead dwelt on the other side of the river Jordan.

The Relevance of this Passage

The spiritual strength and fortitude to wage war on our own Evil Inclination is instilled within us. Additionally, we awaken the spiritual Light that brings forth sustenance into our lives, helping to remove both spiritual and physical poverty from the landscape of human civilization.

726. גָּד גְּדוּד יְגוּדֶנּוּ וְהוּא יָגֻד עָקֵב. רִבִּי יֵיסָא אָמַר, מִגָּד אִשְׁתְּמַע, דְּהָא חֵילִין יִפְּקוּן לְאַגָּחָא קְרָבָא, מַשְׁמַע דִּכְתִיב גָּד, בְּכָל אֲתָר גִימֶ"ל דַּלֶ"ת, חֵילִין וּמַשְׁרְיָין נָפְקֵי מִנַּיְיהוּ. דְּהָא גִימֶ"ל יָהִיב, וְדַלֶ"ת לָקִיט. וּמֵהָכָא כַּמָּה חֵילִין, וְכַמָּה מַשִׁרְיָין, תַּלְיָין בְּהוּ.

726. "Gad, raiders shall maraud him, but he shall overcome at the last" (Beresheet 49:19). Rabbi Yisa said: From THE NAME Gad, we understand that armies will issue from him and engage in war. This is derived from the spelling of Gad, which is always spelled *Gimel* and *Dalet*, YESOD AND MALCHUT, from which UNION armies come forth, as Gimel gives, BEING YESOD, and Dalet receives, BEING MALCHUT. From this we understand how many hosts and legions come from them. HENCE IT SAYS, "GAD, RAIDERS SHALL MARAUD HIM..."

727. תָּא חֲזֵי, הַהוּא נָהָר דְּנָגִיד וְנָפִיק מֵעֵדֶן, לָא פָּסְקִין מֵימוֹי לְעָלְמִין, וְהוּא אַשְׁלִים לְמִסְכְּנֵי, וְעַל דָּא, קַיְימֵי כַּמָּה חֵילִין, וְכַמָּה מַשִׁרְיָין, וְאִתְחֲזוּן מֵהָכָא. וְעַל דָּא גָד, דָּא אַפִּיק וְיָהִיב, וְדָא לָקִיט

-384-

וְנָקֵיט, וְאִתְּזָן בֵּיתָא, וְכָל אַנְשֵׁי בֵּיתָא.

727. Come and see: the water of that river which comes out and flows from the Garden of Eden, BINAH, never stops flowing. It supports the poor BY GIVING THE LIGHT OF CHASSADIM THROUGH GIMEL WHICH IS YESOD TO MALCHUT, WHICH IS DALET, THAT IS POOR (HEB. *DALA*) AND NEEDY. Hence, hosts and legions wait here for sustenance FROM BINAH, THE SECRET OF THE SAID RIVER. THIS UNION is therefore CALLED BY THE NAME OF Gad, THE GIMEL taking out FROM BINAH to give and DALET accepting and receiving from it. The house, THE NUKVA, is sustained together with the household men, THE HOSTS AND LEGIONS OF ANGELS THAT EXTEND FROM HER.

728. א"ר יִצְחָק, אִלְמָלֵא דַּהֲוֵי גָד מִבְּנֵי שְׁפָחוֹת, שַׁעְתָּא קַיְימָא לֵיה לְאַשְׁלָמָא יַתִּיר מִכֹּלָּא, הֲה"ד בָּא גָד קְרִי, וּכְתִיב בָּגָד חָסֵר אָלֶ"ף, דְּהָא שַׁעְתָּא קַיְימָא בִּשְׁלִימוּ, וְאִסְתַּלַּק מִנֵּיה, הֲה"ד, אַחַי בָּגְדוּ כְמוֹ נָחַל, בְּגִין דְּהַהוּא נָהָר דְּנָגֵיד, אִסְתַּלַּק בְּהַהִיא שַׁעְתָּא, וּכְתִיב בָּגַד חָסֵר אָלֶ"ף, וְעַל דָּא, לָא זָכָה בְּאַרְעָא קַדִּישָׁא וְאִסְתַּלַּק מִינָה.

728. Rabbi Yitzchak said: Were Gad not of the sons of a handmaids, WHO ARE CONSIDERED HINDER PARTS, he would have succeeded in rising higher than all the tribes, BECAUSE OF THE HIGH AND PERFECT ORIGIN OF THE NAME GAD. It is written "*Ba Gad* (Eng. 'Fortune comes')" (Beresheet 30:10), but spelled "*Bagad* (Eng. 'betrayed')" without *Aleph*, since the hour of his birth was propitious, but later PERFECTION departed from him. This is the meaning of the words: "My brethren have dealt deceitfully (Heb. *bagdu*) like a river" (Iyov 6:15), since the flowing river, WHICH IS BINAH CALLED RIVER, turned away at that time, SINCE GAD WAS OF THE HINDER PARTS, UPON WHICH THE RIVER BINAH DOES NOT FLOW, AND GIMEL HAD NOTHING TO POUR UPON DALET. HENCE, it says "bagad" without *Aleph*, WHICH ALLUDES TO THE LACK OF BINAH'S ABUNDANCE. He therefore did not receive a portion in the Holy Land, BUT DWELT ACROSS THE JORDAN.

729. ר' יְהוּדָה אָמַר, מִנַּיִן לִרְאוּבֵן דַּהֲוָה כְּהַאי גַוְונָא, כְּדִכְתִיב פַּחַז כַּמַּיִם אַל תּוֹתַר דְּאִסְתַּלְּקוּ מַיִין, וְלָא נְגִידוּ, וְהָא אִתְּמָר בַּמֶּה אִפְגֵּים.

וְתַרְוַוְיְיהוּ לָא זָכוּ בְּאַרְעָא קַדִּישָׁא, וְחֵילִין וּמַשִׁירְיָין אֲפִיקוּ לְאַחְסָנָא
לְהוּ לְיִשְׂרָאֵל אַרְעָא. תָּא חֲזֵי, מַה דְּאִתְפַּגִּים בְּגָד, אִשְׁתְּלֵים בְּאָשֵׁר,
הה"ד מֵאָשֵׁר שְׁמֵנָה לַחְמוֹ וְהוּא יִתֵּן מַעֲדַנֵּי מֶלֶךְ. הַשְׁתָּא אַשְׁלֵים
גִימ"ל לְדל"ת.

729. Rabbi Yehuda said: Whence do we know that the same happened to Reuben, WHO WAS AT FIRST OF A GREATER GRADE, WHICH LATER DEPARTED FROM HIM? From the verse: "Unstable as water, you shall not excel" (Beresheet 49:4), WHICH MEANS that the water, THE LIGHTS OF BINAH, departed and did not flow. His deficiency was already explained THAT JACOB THOUGHT OF RACHEL, AND THEREFORE HIS BIRTHRIGHT WAS TAKEN FROM HIM AND GIVEN TO JOSEPH. Both REUBEN AND GAD did not receive a portion in the Holy Land, BUT ACROSS THE JORDAN, but they sent armies and troops AS THE VANGUARD BEFORE THE CHILDREN OF YISRAEL, to deliver the land to them. Come and behold: the flaw in Gad was made good in Asher, as it is written, "Out of Asher his bread shall be fat, and he shall yield royal delicacies" (Ibid. 20). Now Gimel perfects Dalet.

72. "Set me as a seal upon your heart"

A Synopsis
While sheltering themselves from the bright sun in a cave, Rabbi Aba and Rabbi Elazar discuss the title verse. Rabbi Elazar tells of Rabbi Shimon's interpretation of this verse, explaining that only the souls of the righteous can raise the Female Waters of the Female Principle. After the male and female were joined, the Female Principle quoted the title verse, desiring to retain a likeness even in separation. Similarly, Yisrael desired to remain with the Shechinah in some way, even in exile. Yisrael' love for God is so strong that any separation from Him is as difficult to bear as the day when the spirit leaves the body.

The discussion then turns to the verse, "Jealousy is cruel as Sheol." We learn that jealousy is a sign of true love. Therefore, a man should be jealous of his wife so that he will be attached to her in complete love and will not look at other women. Another explanation is that when the wicked are brought down to Sheol, their sins are announced and the jealous demand reckoning for these sins. We then learn that the "flame of Yah" is the burning flame that comes out of the Shofar, the burning the flame of Yisrael love for God. This love burns so strongly that rather than extinguishing it, the "many waters" of Chesed add to it. Rabbi Shimon, Rabbi Yehuda, and Rabbi Yitzchak then join Rabbi Elazar and Rabbi Aba to conclude the discussion.

The Relevance of this Passage
Deep love for The Creator burns within us as Light and love emanate from these poetic words. This energy also helps to remove envy and jealousy of others from our hearts, while stirring a positive form of jealousy, passion, and appreciation for our spouses.

730. ר' אֶלְעָזָר וְרִבִּי אַבָּא, אִשְׁתְּמִיטוּ בִּמְעַרְתָּא דְלוּד, דְּעָאלוּ קַמֵּי תּוֹקְפָּא דְשִׁמְשָׁא, דַּהֲווֹ אָזְלֵי בְּאָרְחָא. אָמַר רַבִּי אַבָּא נַסְחַר הַאי מְעַרְתָּא בְּמִלֵּי דְאוֹרַיְיתָא. פָּתַח ר' אֶלְעָזָר וַאֲמַר, שִׂימֵנִי כַחוֹתָם עַל לִבֶּךָ כַּחוֹתָם עַל זְרוֹעֶךָ וְגו', רְשָׁפֶיהָ רִשְׁפֵּי אֵשׁ שַׁלְהֶבֶת יָהּ, הַאי קְרָא אִתְעַרְנָא בֵּיהּ, אֲבָל לֵילְיָא חַד הֲוָה, כַּד הֲוֵינָא קָאִים קַמֵּי אַבָּא, וְשָׁמַעְנָא מִנֵּיהּ מִלָּה, דְּלֵית שְׁלִימוּ וּרְעוּתָא וְכִסּוּפָא דִכְנֶסֶת יִשְׂרָאֵל בְּקוּדְשָׁא בְּרִיךְ הוּא, אֶלָּא בְּנִשְׁמַתְהוֹן דְּצַדִּיקַיָּיא, דְּאִינוּן מִתְעָרֵי נְבִיעוּ דְמַיָא תַּתָּאֵי, לְקַבְּלֵי עִלָּאֵי, וּבְהַהִיא שַׁעְתָּא שְׁלִימוּ דִּרְעוּתָא וְכִסּוּפָא

בִּדְבִיקוּ חָדָא, לְמֶעְבַּד פֵּירִין.

730. Rabbi Elazar and Rabbi Aba entered a cave in Lod to escape the bright sun upon the road WHICH THEY COULD NOT BEAR. Rabbi Aba said: Let us encompass this cave with words of the Torah. Rabbi Elazar opened the discussion saying: "Set me as a seal upon your heart, as a seal upon your arm...its coals are coals of fire, the very flame of Yah" (Shir Hashirim 8:6). We have already roused this verse; NAMELY EXPLAINED IT. Yet one night, when I was attending to my father, RABBI SHIMON, I heard from him that the Congregation of Yisrael, THE NUKVA, had no perfection, desire or passion towards the Holy One, blessed be He, but from the souls of the righteous, who excite the flow of the lower waters OF THE NUKVA toward the supernal waters OF ZEIR ANPIN; TO WIT, THEY RAISE THE MAYIN NUKVIN (FEMALE WATERS) OF THE NUKVA. Then is a time of perfect will and passion to become one and produce fruit.

731. תָּא חֲזֵי , בָּתַר דְּאִתְדַּבְּקוּ דָּא בְּדָא, וְהִיא קַבֵּילַת רְעוּתָא, הִיא אָמְרַת שִׂימֵנִי כַחוֹתָם עַל לִבֶּךָ, אַמַּאי כַחוֹתָם. אֶלָּא אָרְחֵיהּ דְּחוֹתָם, כֵּיוָן דְּאִתְדַּבַּק בְּאֲתַר חַד, אע"ג דְּאִתְעֲדֵי מִינֵּיהּ, הָא אִשְׁתְּאַר רְשִׁימוּ בְּהַהוּא אֲתַר, וְלָא אַעֲדֵי מִנֵּיהּ, דְּכָל רְשִׁימוּ, וְכָל דְּיוֹקְנָא דִילֵיהּ, בֵּיהּ אִשְׁתְּאַר. כָּךְ אָמְרָה כְּנֶסֶת יִשְׂרָאֵל, הָא אִתְדַּבַּקְנָא בָּךְ, אע"ג דְּאִתְעֲדֵי מִינָךְ וְאֵזֵיל בְּגָלוּתָא, שִׂימֵנִי כַחוֹתָם עַל לִבֶּךָ, בְּגִין דְּיִשְׁתָּאַר כָּל דְּיוֹקְנִי בָּךְ, כְּהַאי חוֹתָם דְּיִשְׁתָּאַר כָּל דְּיוֹקְנֵיהּ, בְּהַהוּא אֲתַר דְּאִתְדַּבַּק בֵּיהּ.

731. Come and see: After THE MALE AND THE FEMALE cleaved to each other, and she was desirous OF ZEIR ANPIN, she said: "Set me as a seal upon your heart." Why a seal? Because a seal, when it is imprinted, even after it is removed, its impress remains there, and is never erased, but its shape and likeness stay. Thus said the Congregation of Yisrael, THE NUKVA: Now that I have cleaved to you, even though I shall leave and go into exile, "set me as a seal upon your heart" so that my likeness will remain with you, like the seal which leaves its imprint wherever it is pressed.

732. כִּי עַזָּה כַמָּוֶת אַהֲבָה, תַּקִּיפָא הִיא, כִּפְרִישׁוּ דְּרוּחָא מִן גּוּפָא. דְּתָנִינָן, בְּשַׁעֲתָא דְּב"נ מָטֵי לְאִסְתַּלָּקָא מִן עַלְמָא וְחָמֵי מַה דְּחָמֵי,

רוּחָא אָזְלָא בְּכָל שַׁיְיפֵי דְגוּפָא וְסָלֵיק גַּלְגֵּלוֹי, כְּמַאן דְּאָזֵיל בְּיַמָּא בְּלָא
שַׁיְיטִין, סָלֵיק וְנָחֵית וְלָא מֵהַנְיָיא לֵיהּ, אָתָא וְאִשְׁתָּאֵיל מִכָּל שַׁיְיפֵי
גוּפָא, וְלֵית תַּקִּיפוּ כְּיוֹמָא דְּפָרֵישׁ רוּחָא מִן גוּפָא. כָּךְ תַּקִּיפוּ דִּרְחִימוּ
דִּכְנֵ"י לְגַבֵּי קוּדְשָׁא בְּרִיךְ הוּא, כְּתַקִּיפוּ דְמוֹתָא, בְּשַׁעְתָּא דְבָעֵי רוּחָא
לְאִתְפָּרְשָׁא מִן גוּפָא.

732. "For love is strong as death" (Ibid.). It is as strong as the spirit taking leave of the body. For we have learned that when the time comes for a man to depart from the world and he sees certain sights, the spirit goes to every limb in the body and courses on waves like a passenger UPON A BOAT at sea, without oars, helplessly going up and down. Nothing is more difficult than the day when the spirit takes leave of the body. So the love of the Congregation of Yisrael for the Holy One, blessed be He, is as strong as death is, when the spirit departs from the body.

733. קָשָׁה כִּשְׁאוֹל קִנְאָה, כָּל מַאן דְּרָחֵים, וְלָא קָשֵׁיר עִמֵּיהּ קִנְאָה,
לָאו רְחִימוּתֵיהּ רְחִימוּתָא, כֵּיוָן דְּקַנֵּי, הָא רְחִימוּתָא אִשְׁתְּלֵים. מִכָּאן
אוֹלִיפְנָא דְּבָעֵי בַּ"נ לְקַנָּאָה לְאִנְתְּתֵיהּ, בְּגִין דְּיִתְקַשַּׁר עִמָּהּ רְחִימוּתָא
שְׁלֵים, דְּהָא מִגּוֹ כָּךְ לָא יָהֵיב עֵינוֹי בְּאִינְתּוּ אָחֳרָא. מַהוּ קָשָׁה כִּשְׁאוֹל.
אֶלָּא, מַה שְׁאוֹל קַשְׁיָא בְּעֵינַיְיהוּ דְּחַיָּיבִין לְמֵיחַת בֵּיהּ, כָּךְ קִנְאָה קַשְׁיָא
בְּעֵינַיְיהוּ דְּמַאן דְּרָחֵים וְקַנֵּי, לְאִתְפָּרְשָׁא מֵרְחִימוּתָא.

733. "Jealousy is cruel as Sheol..." (Ibid.). Whoever loves and is not jealous, his love is not true love. When he is jealous, love is perfected. From this we have learned that a man should be jealous of his wife, so as to be attached to her in complete love. For this way he does not look at other women. What is "cruel (lit. 'hard') as Sheol"? As it is hard for the wicked to descend to Sheol, so it is hard for the jealous lover to part from his love.

734. ד"א קָשָׁה כִּשְׁאוֹל קִנְאָה, מַה שְׁאוֹל, בְּשַׁעְתָּא דְנָחֲתִין לוֹן
לְחַיָּיבַיָּא בֵּיהּ, מוֹדִיעִין לוֹן חוֹבַיְיהוּ עַל מָה נָחֲתִין לֵיהּ, וְקַשְׁיָא לְהוּ.
כָּךְ, מַאן דְּקַנֵּי, הוּא תָּבַע עַל חוֹבֵיהּ, וְחָשֵׁיב כַּמָּה עוֹבָדִין, וּכְדֵין
קְשׁוּרָא דִּרְחִימוּתָא אִתְקַשַּׁר בֵּיהּ.

734. Another explanation for "jealousy is cruel as Sheol" is that when the wicked are brought down to Sheol, their sins are announced to them, for which they are brought down. They find it hard, so he who is jealous demands reckoning for sins, and enumerates all the SUSPICIOUS things SHE DID, and his love grows strong.

735. רְשָׁפֶיהָ רִשְׁפֵּי אֵשׁ שַׁלְהֶבֶת יָהּ, מַאן שַׁלְהֶבֶת יָהּ, דָּא שַׁלְהוֹבָא דְּאִתּוֹקְדָא וְנַפְקָא מִגּוֹ שׁוֹפָר, דְּאִיהוּ אִתְּעַר וְאוֹקִיד, וּמַאן אִיהוּ, שְׂמָאלָא. הה"ד שְׂמָאלוֹ תַּחַת לְרֹאשִׁי. דָּא אוֹקִיד שַׁלְהוֹבָא דִּרְחִימוּ דִּכְנֶסֶת יִשְׂרָאֵל, לְגַבֵּי קוּדְשָׁא בְּרִיךְ הוּא.

735. "Its coals are coals of fire, the very flame of Yah." What is the very flame of Yah? It is the burning flame which comes out of the Shofar, YESOD OF IMA CALLED YAH. Once it is aroused, it burns. What is it? The Left COLUMN OF IMA, as it is written: "His left hand is under my head" (Shir Hashirim 8:3). It burns the flame of the Congregation of Yisrael's love, THE SHECHINAH, for the Holy One, blessed be He.

736. וּבְגִינֵי כָךְ, מַיִם רַבִּים לֹא יוּכְלוּ לְכַבּוֹת אֶת הָאַהֲבָה. דְּהָא כַּד אָתֵי יְמִינָא דְּאִיהוּ מַיִם, אוֹסִיף יְקִידוּ דִּרְחִימוּתָא, וְלָא כָּבֵי שַׁלְהוֹבָא דִּשְׂמָאלָא, כְּד"א וִימִינוֹ תְּחַבְּקֵנִי, הַאי אִיהוּ מַיִם רַבִּים לֹא יוּכְלוּ לְכַבּוֹת אֶת הָאַהֲבָה, וְכֵן כֹּלָּא כְּהַאי גַוְונָא.

736. Therefore, "many waters cannot quench love" (Shir Hashirim 8:7), for when the right comes, which is water, CHESED, it adds to the burning of love, instead of extinguishing the flame of the left, as it says "and his right hand embraces me" (Ibid. 3). Hence "many waters cannot quench love." All THE FOLLOWING VERSES are EXPOUNDED UPON in this manner.

737. עַד דַּהֲוָה יַתְבֵי, שָׁמְעוּ קָלֵיהּ דְּרַבִּי שִׁמְעוֹן, דַּהֲוָה אָתֵי בְּאוֹרְחָא, הוּא וְרַבִּי יְהוּדָה וְרַבִּי יִצְחָק. קָרִיב לְמְעַרְתָּא, נָפְקוּ רַבִּי אֶלְעָזָר וְרַבִּי אַבָּא. אָמַר רַבִּי שִׁמְעוֹן, מִכּוֹתְלֵי דִמְעַרְתָּא חָמֵינָא, דִּשְׁכִינְתָּא הָכָא. יָתְבוּ. אָמַר ר' שִׁמְעוֹן בְּמַאי עַסְקִיתוּ. אָמַר ר' אַבָּא, בִּרְחִימוּתָא דִּכְנֶסֶת יִשְׂרָאֵל לְגַבֵּי קוּדְשָׁא בְּרִיךְ הוּא, וְר"א פָּרֵישׁ הַאי קְרָא בִּכְנֶסֶת יִשְׂרָאֵל,

שִׂימֵנִי כַחוֹתָם עַל לִבֶּךָ וגו'. אָמַר לֵיהּ, אֶלְעָזָר בִּרְחִימוּ עִלָּאָה וּקְשִׁירוּ דַּחֲבִיבוּתָא אִסְתַּכַּלְתְּ.

737. As they were sitting, they heard Rabbi Shimon, who was coming this way together with Rabbi Yehuda and Rabbi Yitzchak. RABBI SHIMON approached the cave, and Rabbi Elazar and Rabbi Aba came out. Rabbi Shimon said: From the walls of the cave I see that the Shechinah is here. They sat. Rabbi Shimon asked, What are you studying? Rabbi Aba said: The Congregation of Yisrael's love for the Holy One, blessed be He. Rabbi Elazar explained the verse, "Set me as a seal upon your heart" as referring to the Congregation of Yisrael. Rabbi Shimon said: Elazar, you have looked upon sublime love and the bond of amity.

738. אִשְׁתִּיק רִבִּי שִׁמְעוֹן שַׁעְתָּא, אֲמַר בְּכָל אֲתַר בָּעְיָיא שְׁתִיקוּ, בַּר שְׁתִיקוּ דְּאוֹרַיְיתָא. גִּנְזָא חֲדָא אִית לִי גְּנִיזָא, וְלָא בָּעֵינָא דְּיִתְאֲבֵיד מִנַּיְיכוּ, וְהִיא מִלָּה עִלָּאָה, וְאַשְׁכַּחְנָא לָהּ בְּסִפְרָא דְּרַב הַמְנוּנָא סָבָא.

738. Rabbi Shimon was silent for a while, then said: Silence is always good everywhere, except in relation to the Torah. I have a hidden secret, which I do not wish to be lost from you. It is a supernal matter, which I found in the book of Rav Hamnuna Saba (the elder).

739. תָּא חֲזֵי, בְּכָל אֲתַר דְּכוּרָא רָדֵיף בָּתַר נוּקְבָא, וְאִתְּעַר לְגַבָּהּ רְחִימוּתָא, וְהָכָא אַשְׁכַּחְנָא, דְּהִיא אִתְּעָרַת רְחִימוּתָא וְרָדְפָה אֲבַתְרֵיהּ, וְאוֹרְחֵיהּ דְּעָלְמָא, דְּלֵית שְׁבָחָא דְּנוּקְבָא, לְמִרְדַּף בַּתְרֵיהּ דִּדְכוּרָא. אֶלָּא, מִלָּה סְתִימָא הִיא, וּמִלָּה עִלָּאָה דְּבֵי גְּנָזַיָיא דְּמַלְכָּא.

739. Come and see: the male always chases after the female and arouses her love. Yet here I found that she arouses his love and courts him, AS SAID IN THE VERSE: "SET ME AS A SEAL UPON YOUR HEART…" According to custom, it is not proper that the female runs after the male. But OF NECESSITY this is a deep matter, a supernal matter HIDDEN among the King's treasures.

73. Three souls

A Synopsis

A discussion of the three souls reveals that there are actually four. The first is the supernal soul of all souls, which is hidden and never revealed. The second is the Nukva. The third and forth are the souls of the righteous below, which come from the soul of the female and the male, Zeir Anpin. Through the analogy of a king who sends his son away to be raised in a village until he is ready to learn the ways of the palace, we learn why the soul descends to this world only to leave at a later time. The soul never leaves this world until the Matron comes for it and delivers it to the King's palace, where it remains. The discourse then returns to the subject of the previous section, Yisrael love for God. We are told that the souls of the righteous, who are male, incite the female love and desire for Zeir Anpin. The rabbis conclude by explaining that the verse, "The righteous is the foundation of the world," alludes to both Yesod of Zeir Anpin and the souls of the righteous.

The Relevance of this Passage

The wisdom woven throughout this passage awakens a deep desire within us to know our true purpose in this world. A love for the Light of The Creator and for spiritual truths is kindled in our hearts and soul, which, in turn, help unite the Lower and Upper Worlds.

Spiritual work requires both an intellectual and emotional understanding in order to provide us with the impetus to continue onward. Here, an emotional awakening concerning our source and origin is born within us as we realize that spiritual growth brings us nearer to our supernal Father.

740. תָּא חֲזֵי, תְּלַת נִשְׁמָתִין אִינוּן, וְאִינוּן סָלְקִין בְּדַרְגִּין עִלָּאִין יְדִיעָן, וְעַל דְּאִינוּן תְּלָתָא אַרְבַּע אִינוּן. חַד נִשְׁמָתָא עִלָּאָה דְּלָא אִתְפַּס, וְלָא אִתְּעַר בֵּיהּ גִּזְבְּרָא דְּקַרְטִיטָאָה עִלָּאָה, כָּל שֶׁכֵּן תַּתָּאָה. וְהַאי נִשְׁמָתָא לְכָל נִשְׁמָתִין, וְהוּא סָתִים, וְלָא אִתְגַּלְיָא לְעָלְמִין, וְלָא אִתְיְידַע, וְכֻלְּהוּ בֵּיהּ תַּלְיָין.

740. Come and see: There are three souls which pertain to certain supernal grades. The three are really four. The first is a supernal soul, which cannot be perceived by the higher treasurer, much less by the lower one. It is the soul of all the souls, hidden and never revealed to be known. All stem from it.

741. וְהַאי אִתְעַטַּף בְּעִטוּפָא דְזָהֲרָא דְּכַרְמְלָא, בְּגוֹ זְהִירוּתָא וְנָטֵיף טִפִין מַרְגְּלָאן. וְאִתְקַשָּׁרוּ כֻּלְּהוּ כְּחַד, כְּקִשְׁרִין דְּשַׁיְיפֵי דְגוּפָא חַד. וְהוּא אָעִיל בְּגַוַוְייהוּ, וְאַחֲזֵי בְּהוּ עֲבִידְתֵּיה. הוּא וְאִינוּן חַד הוּא, וְלֵית בְּהוּ פְּרִישׁוּ. הַאי נִשְׁמָתָא עִלָּאָה טְמִירוּ דְכֹלָּא.

741. It is wrapped in a garment made of the splendor of the Carmel, which drips pearls, all linked as one like the limbs of the body. The supernal soul enters them, and displays through them its works, AS THE BODY REVEALS THE WORKS OF THE SOUL. It and they are one with nothing to divide them. This is the supernal soul, the most hidden.

742. נִשְׁמָתָא אָחֳרָא, נוּקְבָא דְמִטַּמְּרָא בְּגוֹ חֵילָהָא, וְהִיא נִשְׁמָתָא לְהוּ, וּמִנַּיְיהוּ אֲחִידָא גוּפָא, לְאַחֲזָאָה בְּהוּ עֲבִידְתָּא לְכָל עַלְמָא, כְּגוּפָא דְּאִיהוּ מָאנָא לְנִשְׁמָתָא, לְמֶעְבַּד בֵּיה עֲבִידְתָּא, וְאַלֵּין כְּגַוְונָא דְאִינוּן קְשִׁירִין טְמִירִין דִּלְעֵילָא.

742. Another soul is the Nukva, which hides among Her armies, it She is their soul and receives a body from them. SHE IS CLOTHED IN THEM AS A SOUL WITHIN A BODY, so as to display through them Her handiwork to all the world, just as the body is a vessel which executes Her works through it. They are ATTACHED AND UNITED TO EACH OTHER, like the hidden ones above are attached.

743 נִשְׁמָתָא אָחֳרָא, הִיא, נִשְׁמַתְהוֹן דְּצַדִּיקַיָּיא לְתַתָּא. נִשְׁמַתְהוֹן דְּצַדִּיקַיָּיא אַתְיָין מֵאִינוּן נִשְׁמָתִין עִלָּאִין, מִנִּשְׁמָתָא דְנוּקְבָא, וּמִנִּשְׁמָתָא דִדְכוּרָא. וּבְגִין כָּךְ, נִשְׁמָתִין דְּצַדִּיקַיָּיא עִלָּאִין, עַל כָּל אִינוּן חֵילִין וּמַשְׁרְיָין דִּלְעֵילָא.

743. Another soul is the souls of the righteous below. The souls of the righteous come from the supernal souls, the soul of the female and the soul of the male, ZEIR ANPIN. For this reason, the souls of the righteous are higher than all the armies and legions of angels above, SINCE ANGELS COME FROM THE OUTER PART OF THE NUKVA, BUT THE SOULS COME FROM THE INNER PART OF THE NUKVA AND ZEIR ANPIN, NAMELY FROM THEIR SOULS.

744. וְאִי תֵימָא, הָא עִלָּאִין אִינוּן מִתְּרֵין סִטְרִין, אַמַּאי נַחְתִּין לְהַאי עָלְמָא, וְאַמַּאי אִסְתַּלְּקוּ מִנֵּיה. לְמַלְכָּא דְּאִתְיְלִיד לֵיה בַּר, שַׁדַּר לֵיה לְחַד כְּפַר, לְמַרְבֵּה לֵיה, וּלְגַדְּלָא לֵיה, עַד דְּיִתְרַבֵּי, וְיוֹלְפוּן לֵיה אָרְחֵי דְהֵיכְלָא דְמַלְכָּא. שָׁמַע מַלְכָּא, דְּהָא בְּרֵיה רַב וְאִתְרַבֵּי. מַה עָבַד בִּרְחִימוּ דִבְרֵיה, מְשַׁדַּר לָה לְמַטְרוֹנִיתָא אִמֵּיה בְּגִינֵיה, וְאָעֵיל לְהֵיכְלֵיה, וְחָדֵי עִמֵּיה כָּל יוֹמָא.

744. HE ASKS: You may say that if the souls are elevated on two sides, OF ZEIR ANPIN AND THE NUKVA, AND COME FROM THEIR INWARDNESS, why then do they descend into this world, and why leave it? HE ANSWERS: THIS IS LIKE a king who begot a son. He sent him to be raised in a village until it was time for him to be taught the ways of the palace. When the king heard his son is grown up, out of love for him, he sent the Matron his mother to fetch him. She brought him to the palace, where he rejoiced with HIS SON every day.

745. כַּךְ קוּדְשָׁא בְּרִיךְ הוּא, אוֹלִיד בַּר בְּמַטְרוֹנִיתָא, וּמַאי אִיהוּ נִשְׁמָתָא עִלָּאָה קַדִּישָׁא, שַׁדַּר לֵיה לִכְפַר, לְהַאי עָלְמָא, דְּיִתְרַבֵּי בֵּיה, וְיוֹלְפוּן לֵיה אוֹרְחֵי דְהֵיכְלָא דְמַלְכָּא, כֵּיוָן דְּיָדַע מַלְכָּא דְּהָא בְּרֵיה אִתְרַבֵּי בְּהַאי כְּפַר, וְעִידָן הוּא לְמַיְיתֵי לֵיה לְהֵיכְלֵיה. עָבַד בִּרְחִימוּ דִבְרֵיה, מְשַׁדַּר לְמַטְרוֹנִיתָא בְּגִינֵיה וְאָעֵיל לֵיה לְהֵיכְלֵיה. נִשְׁמָתָא לָא סַלְקָא מֵהַאי עָלְמָא, עַד דְּאָתַת מַטְרוֹנִיתָא בְּגִינָה, וְאָעֵילַת לָה בְּהֵיכְלָא דְמַלְכָּא, וִיתֵיבַת תַּמָּן לְעָלְמִין.

745. The Holy One, blessed be He, also begot a son by the Matron. Who is he? The supernal Holy Soul, THE DESCENDANTS OF ZEIR ANPIN AND NUKVA. He sent him to the village, NAMELY to this world, to be raised and be brought up in the ways of the King's palace. When the King saw that His son was grown up in this village, and that it was time to bring him to the palace, what did he do? Out of love for his son, he sent the Matron, who fetched him to His palace. The soul never leaves this world until the Matron comes for it, and brings it to the King's palace where it remains forever.

746. וְעִם כָּל דָּא, אוֹרְחָא דְעָלְמָא, דְּאִינוּן בְּנֵי כְּפַר, בָּכָאן עַל פְּרִישׁוּ

דִּבְרֵיהּ דְּמַלְכָּא מִנַּיְיהוּ. חַד פִּקֵּחַ הֲוָה תַּמָּן, אֲמַר לוֹן עַל מָה אַתּוּן
בָּכָאן, וְכִי לָאו בְּרֵיהּ דְּמַלְכָּא אִיהוּ, וְלָא אִתְחֲזֵי לְמֵידַר יַתִּיר בֵּינַיְיכוּ,
אֶלָּא בְּהֵיכָלָא דַּאֲבוֹי. כָּךְ מֹשֶׁה, דַּהֲוָה פִּקֵּחַ, חָמָא בְּנֵי כְפַר דַּהֲוָה
בָּכָאן. עַל דָּא אֲמַר, בָּנִים אַתֶּם לַיְיָ׳ אֱלֹהֵיכֶם לֹא תִתְגּוֹדְדוּ.

746. Yet it is the way of the world that the inhabitants of the village weep when the King's son parts from them. There was a wise man there, who said: Wherefore are you crying, is he not a king's son? It is not meet that he shall dwell among you any longer, but in his father's palace. Moses too, who was wise, saw the inhabitants of the village crying, and said to them, "You are the children of Hashem your Elohim: you shall not gash yourselves" (Devarim 14:1).

747. תָּא חֲזֵי , אִילוּ הֲווֹ יָדְעִין כֻּלְּהוּ צַדִּיקַיָּיא הַאי, הֲווֹ חָדָאן הַהוּא
יוֹמָא דְּמָטֵי לוֹן לְאִסְתַּלְּקָא מֵהַאי עַלְמָא, וְכִי לָאו יְקָרָא עִלָּאָה הוּא,
דְּמַטְרוֹנִיתָא אָתַת בְּגִינַיְיהוּ, וּלְאוֹבָלָא לוֹן לְהֵיכָלָא לְמַלְכָּא, לְמֶחְדֵּי
בְּהוֹ מַלְכָּא כָּל יוֹמָא, דְּהָא קוּדְשָׁא בְּרִיךְ הוּא לָא אִשְׁתַּעְשַׁע אֶלָּא
בְּנִשְׁמַתְהוֹן דְּצַדִּיקַיָּא.

747. Come and see: if all the righteous knew that, they would be glad when the day comes for them to depart from this world. For is it not a high honor that the Matron comes for them to escort them into the King's palace, and that the King will daily rejoice in them? For the Holy One, blessed be He, amuses Himself only with the souls of the righteous.

748. תָּא חֲזֵי, אִתְעֲרוּתָא דִּרְחִימוּ דכנ״י, לְגַבֵּי קוּדְשָׁא בְּרִיךְ הוּא,
נִשְׁמָתְהוֹן דְּצַדִּיקַיָּא לְתַתָּא, מִתְעָרִין לָהּ, בְּגִין דְּאִינוּן אַתְיָין מִסִּטְרָא
דְּמַלְכָּא, מִסִּטְרָא דִּדְכוּרָא, וְאִתְעֲרוּתָא דָא מָטֵי לְנוּקְבָא מִסִּטְרָא
דִּדְכוּרָא, וְאִתְעַר רְחִימוּתָא. אִשְׁתַּכַּח, דִּדְכוּרָא אִתְעַר חֲבִיבוּ
וּרְחִימוּתָא לְנוּקְבָא, וּכְדֵין נוּקְבָא אִתְקַשְּׁרַת בִּרְחִימוּתָא, לְגַבֵּי דְכוּרָא.

748. Come and see: the love of the Congregation of Yisrael, THE NUKVA, for the Holy One, blessed be He, ZEIR ANPIN, is stirred by the souls of the righteous below. Since they come from the side of the King, ZEIR ANPIN, the side of the male, the female is aroused from the side of the male, and love is stirred. Thus the male incites affection and love within the female and she is united in love with the male. THIS SETTLES THE QUESTION, THAT IT IS NOT PROPER FOR THE FEMALE TO COURT THE MALE. NOW IT IS EXPLAINED, THAT THE SOULS OF THE RIGHTEOUS, WHO ARE MALE, INCITE IN HER THIS LOVE TO ZEIR ANPIN.

749. כְּהַאי גַוְונָא, תֵּיאוּבְתָּא דְנוּקְבָא, לְמִשְׁדֵי מַיִין תַּתָּאִין לְקַבֵּל מַיִין עִלָּאִין, לָאו אִיהוּ, אֶלָּא בְּנִשְׁמַתְהוֹן דְּצַדִּיקַיָּא. זַכָּאִין אִינוּן צַדִּיקַיָּא בְּהַאי עָלְמָא, וּבְעַלְמָא דְאָתֵי, דַּעֲלַיְיהוּ קַיְימִין עִלָּאִין וְתַתָּאִין. וְעַל דָּא וְצַדִּיק יְסוֹד עוֹלָם כְּתִיב סְתָם.

749. In the same manner, the desire of the female to pour forth lower waters towards the upper waters is aroused solely by the souls of the righteous. Happy are the righteous in this world and in the World to Come, for they support the upper and lower. Therefore it just says, "The righteous is the foundation of the world" (Mishlei 10:25), WHICH MAY MEAN EITHER THE SUPERNAL RIGHTEOUS, YESOD OF ZEIR ANPIN, OR THE SOULS OF THE RIGHTEOUS. BOTH MEANINGS ARE TRUE.

750. וְרָזָא דְכֹלָּא, צַדִּיק, אִיהוּ יְסוֹדָא דִלְעֵילָּא, וְאִיהוּ יְסוֹדָא לְתַתָּא, וּכְנֶסֶת יִשְׂרָאֵל אִתְכְּלִילַת מִצַּדִּיק, מִלְעֵילָּא וּמִתַּתָּא, צַדִּיק מֵהַאי סִטְרָא, וְצַדִּיק מֵהַאי סִטְרָא, יַרְתִין לָהּ, הה"ד צַדִּיקִים יִרְשׁוּ אָרֶץ. יִרְשׁוּ אָרֶץ וַדַּאי. תָּא חֲזֵי, צַדִּיק אַחְסִין לָהּ לְהַאי אֶרֶץ, וְאָרֵיק עֲלָהּ בִּרְכָאן בְּכָל יוֹמָא, וְיָהֵיב לָהּ תַּפְנוּקִין וְעִדּוּנִין, בִּנְגִידוּ עִלָּאָה דְּנָגֵיד עֲלָהּ, וְהָא אוֹקִימְנָא מִלָּה.

750. The secret thereof is that the Righteous is Yesod above, YESOD OF ZEIR ANPIN, and Yesod below OF THE NUKVA AND THE SOULS OF THE RIGHTEOUS. The Congregation of Yisrael, THE NUKVA, comprises the upper and lower Righteous. The Righteous on this side, YESOD OF ZEIR ANPIN, and the righteous on that side, THE SOUL OF THE RIGHTEOUS BELOW, inherit THE NUKVA. Hence it says, "The righteous shall inherit the earth" (Tehilim 38:29), and assuredly they will inherit THE NUKVA CALLED

earth. Come and see: The Righteous, Yesod of Zeir Anpin, inherits the earth, the Nukva, pours blessings upon it every day and furnishes it with delights and delicacies which he draws from Binah upon it. We have already explained this.

74. "Out of Asher his bread shall be fat," part two

A Synopsis

A discussion of the title verse interprets it as signifying Binah, which gives "royal delicacies" to Yesod, which in turn then gives to Malchut, our dimension of physical matter. There are two types of bread: the bread of poverty, which is the bread of Malchut, and millet bread, the bread of Zeir Anpin. The bread mentioned in the title verse is that of Zeir Anpin. Zeir Anpin nourishes Malchut through the righteous, and Malchut distributes the "royal delicacies" among the grades beneath her.

Following a description of the double bread of Shabbat, there ensues a discussion of the verse, "For the bread is spent." We are told that the upper bread of Zeir Anpin is referred to as masculine and includes all types of food, while the lower bread of the Nukva is feminine and refers only to bread. Finally, the discourse informs us Moses revealed that Asher is mentioned above in Binah. We also learn that Asher is mentioned below, in relation to Malchut and is included in the support of Malchut, below the twelve tribes.

The Relevance of this Passage

Here, the righteous sages of antiquity, and the pious who walk among us in the present, assist us in connecting our souls and the entire world [Malchut] to the level of Zeir Anpin, the fountainhead of spiritual energy, including financial sustenance for our physical reality.

751. וְרָזָא דִּכְתִיב מֵאָשֵׁר שְׁמֵנָה לַחְמוֹ וְהוּא יִתֵּן מַעֲדַנֵּי מֶלֶךְ. וְעִם כָּל דָּא, מִלָּה אָחֳרָא, כְּמָה דִכְתִיב, רָאוּהָ בָנוֹת וַיְאַשְּׁרוּהָ, וְעַל דָּא אָמְרָה לֵאָה, בְּאָשְׁרִי כִּי אִשְּׁרוּנִי בָנוֹת וְכֹלָּא שַׁפִּיר. וְתָא חֲזֵי מֵעַלְמָא דְּאָתֵי, אִתְמְשִׁיךְ וְנָגִיד לְהַאי צַדִּיק, לְמֵיהַב תַּפְנוּקִין וְעִדּוּנִין לְהַאי אֶרֶץ, דְּאִיהוּ לֶחֶם עוֹנִי, וְאִתְעֲבִיד לֶחֶם פַּנָּג, הֲדָא הוּא דִכְתִיב, מֵאָשֵׁר שְׁמֵנָה לַחְמוֹ וְהוּא יִתֵּן מַעֲדַנֵּי מֶלֶךְ וַדַּאי, וְהָא אוֹקִימְנָא.

751. This is the secret of the verse, "Out of Asher his bread shall be fat, and he shall yield royal delicacies" (Beresheet 49:20), WHICH MEANS THAT ASHER IS THE SAID RIGHTEOUS, YESOD OF ZEIR ANPIN, THAT POURS DELICACIES UPON THE NUKVA. Yet he is not YESOD OF ZEIR ANPIN, as it is written: "The daughters saw her, and called her happy" (Shir Hashirim 6:9), WHICH IS AN ASPECT OF THE NUKVA AND NOT YESOD OF ZEIR

ANPIN. Leah therefore said "for the daughters will call me happy (Heb. *oshri*)" (Beresheet 30:13). This is correct. Come and see: From the World to Come, BINAH, issues a flow upon the Righteous, YESOD OF ZEIR ANPIN, to pour delicacies and delicacies upon the earth, which has been bread of poverty turned millet bread. This is the meaning of, "Out of Asher his bread shall be fat, and he shall yield royal delicacies." We have already explained this. ASHER IS BINAH, WHICH GIVES ROYAL DELICACIES TO YESOD AND YESOD TO THE NUKVA.

752. תָּא חֲזֵי, מֵאָשֵׁר שְׁמֵנָה לַחְמוֹ. דָּא הוּא אֲתַר דְּכֹלָּא מְאַשְׁרִין לֵיהּ, וּמַאי אִיהוּ. עָלְמָא דְּאָתֵי, דְּעִלָּאֵי וְתַתָּאֵי מְאַשְׁרִין לֵיהּ, וּמְכַסְּפִין לֵיהּ. שְׁמֵנָה לַחְמוֹ, מַאן. עַד כָּאן לָא פָּרֵישׁ מַאן הוּא אֲתַר. אֶלָּא, אִית לֶחֶם, וְאִית לֶחֶם, כְּמָה דְּאִית אִילָנָא, וְאִית אִילָנָא, אִית אִילָנָא דְּחַיֵּי, וְאִית אִילָנָא דְּתַלְיָיא בֵּיהּ מוֹתָא. אִית לֶחֶם דְּאִקְרֵי לֶחֶם עוֹנִי, וְאִית לֶחֶם דְּאִקְרֵי לֶחֶם פַּנַג. וּמַאן אִיהוּ. דָּא ו', וְדָא הוּא לַחְמ"וֹ: לֶחֶ"ם ו', וְעַל דָּא כְּתִיב הִנְנִי מַמְטִיר לָכֶם לֶחֶם מִן הַשָּׁמַיִם, מִן הַשָּׁמַיִם וַדַּאי.

752. Come and see: "Out of Asher his bread shall be fat." This is the place which everyone calls happy. What is it? It is the World to Come, BINAH, which the upper and lower call happy and yearn for. "His bread shall be fat": HE ASKS: Whose BREAD? It does not specify the place OF BREAD. HE REPLIES: There is bread and bread, and in the same way there is a tree and a tree. There is the Tree of Life, ZEIR ANPIN, and the tree upon which death depends, THE NUKVA. So there is bread which is called bread of poverty, THE NUKVA, and there is bread called millet bread. What is THE MILLET BREAD? It is Vav OF THE NAME YUD HEI VAV HEI, WHICH IS ZEIR ANPIN. This is "his bread (Heb. *lachmo*)": the bread (Heb. *lechem*) of *Vav*, NAMELY THE BREAD OF ZEIR ANPIN. Hence it says "Behold, I will rain bread from heaven" (Shemot 16:4), from heaven indeed, WHICH IS ZEIR ANPIN CALLED HEAVEN.

753. וְעַל דָּא, מֵאָשֵׁר שְׁמֵנָה לַחְמוֹ, לֶחֶם ו', דְּהָא מִינֵּיהּ אִתְּזָן הַאי אִילָנָא, וְהוּא מְעַטְּרָא לֵיהּ, כְּדִכְתִיב בָּעֲטָרָה שֶׁעִטְּרָה לּוֹ אִמּוֹ. וְכַד אִיהוּ נָקִיט, וַדַּאי הוּא יִתֵּן מַעֲדַנֵּי מֶלֶךְ. וּמַאן מֶלֶךְ. דָּא כְּנֶסֶת יִשְׂרָאֵל, דְּהָא מִנֵּיהּ אִתְּזָנַת, וְהוּא יָהִיב לָהּ עַל יְדָא דְּצַדִּיק, דַּרְגָּא קַדִּישָׁא אֶת

קַיְּימָא. וּמֵהָכָא לִשְׁאָר דַּרְגִּין דִּלְתַתָּא, וְכֻלְּהוּ כְּגַוְונָא דִּלְעֵילָּא.

753. Hence, "out of Asher his bread shall be fat." "His bread" includes the syllables *lechem* and the letter *Vav*, TO WIT, THE BREAD OF ZEIR ANPIN CALLED 'VAV', since from him - FROM BINAH CALLED 'ASHER'-the tree is nourished, and he, BINAH, adorns it WITH THE FIRST THREE SFIROT, as it says "the crown with which his mother crowned him" (Shir Hashirim 3:11), TO WIT, BINAH CALLED 'MOTHER'. When ZEIR ANPIN receives, he shall surely "yield royal delicacies (lit. 'of the king')." Who is the king? The Congregation of Yisrael, NAMELY THE NUKVA, which is nourished BY ZEIR ANPIN, who gives to her via the Righteous, the holy grade of the sign of the covenant, NAMELY YESOD OF ZEIR ANPIN, and from THE NUKVA unto the other grades below IN BRIYAH, YETZIRAH AND ASIYAH, which resemble the ones above; TO WIT, THE IMPLEMENTS IN BRIYAH, YETZIRAH AND ASIYAH RESEMBLE THOSE IN ATZILUT.

754. בְּסִפְרָא דְּרַב הַמְנוּנָא סָבָא, אָמַר הָכִי, מֵאָשֵׁר שְׁמֵנָה לַחְמוֹ, דָּא לֶחֶם שַׁבָּת, דְּאִיהוּ פָּנַג, עַל חַד תְּרֵין, כִּדְכְתִיב לָקְטוּ לֶחֶם מִשְׁנֶה. מַאי לֶחֶם מִשְׁנֶה. אֶלָּא, תְּרֵי לֶחֶם: לֶחֶם מִן הַשָּׁמַיִם, וְלֶחֶם מִן הָאָרֶץ, דָּא הוּא לֶחֶם פָּנַג, וְדָא הוּא לֶחֶם דְּמִסְכֵּנָא, וּבְשַׁבָּת אִתְכְּלִיל לֶחֶם תַּתָּאָה, בְּלֶחֶם עִלָּאָה, וְאִתְבָּרֵךְ הַאי, בְּגִינֵי הַאי, וְאִיהוּ לֶחֶם מִשְׁנֶה.

754. In the book of Rav Hamnuna Saba (the elder), he said the following, "Out of Asher his bread shall be fat" refers to the Shabbat bread, which is doubly delightful, as it is written: "They gathered double bread" (Shemot 16:22). There are two kinds of breads, bread from heaven, FROM ZEIR ANPIN, and bread from the earth, FROM THE NUKVA. This is millet bread, BUT THE BREAD FROM THE EARTH DETACHED FROM THE BREAD FROM HEAVEN is the bread of poverty. On Shabbat, the lower bread OF THE NUKVA is included within the upper bread OF ZEIR ANPIN, and the lower is blessed by the upper. This is double bread.

755. וְתוּ הֲוָה אָמַר, לֶחֶם מִשְׁנֶה דְּשַׁבָּת, נָקִיט מִשַּׁבָּת עִלָּאָה, דְּאִיהוּ נָגִיד וְאַנְהֵיר לְכֹלָּא, וְאִתְחַבַּר לֶחֶם בְּלֶחֶם, וְאִיהוּ מִשְׁנֶה. וּבְכָל אֲתַר, רָזָא דְּלֶחֶם, נוּקְבָּא הִיא, בְּגִין כָּךְ שְׁמֵנָה כְּתִיב וְלֹא שָׁמֵן. וּכְתִיב כִּי אִם הַלֶּחֶם אֲשֶׁר הוּא אוֹכֵל, דָּא אַנְתְּתֵיהּ.

755. RAV HAMNUNA SABA (THE ELDER) also said that the double bread of Shabbat, WHICH IS THE BREAD OF THE NUKVA, receives from the supernal Shabbat, BINAH, which flows and shines upon everything. The bread OF THE NUKVA is united with the bread OF BINAH and becomes double. HE EXPLAINS WHY HE DOES NOT TALK OF THE BREAD OF THE NUKVA AND THE BREAD OF ZEIR ANPIN, BUT THE BREAD OF BINAH. IT IS that uniformly the secret of bread is the female, EITHER THE NUKVA OF ZEIR ANPIN, OR BINAH, WHICH IS ALSO A FEMALE. BUT THE ABUNDANCE OF ZEIR ANPIN IS NOT CALLED BREAD, SINCE IT IS MALE. Hence it is written: "Shall be fat" with a feminine suffix INSTEAD OF A MASCULINE. It also says "save the bread which he did eat" (Beresheet 39:6), WHICH ALLUDES TO the wife CALLED BREAD. HENCE BREAD IS AN ASPECT OF THE FEMALE.

756. וְאִי תֵּימָא וְהַלֶּחֶם אָזַל מִכֵּלֵינוּ, וְלָא כְּתִיב אָזְלַת. שְׁאָר מְזוֹנָא לֶחֶם קָרֵינָן לֵיהּ, וְאַשְׁתְּמוֹדְעָן מִלִּין, מַאן הוּא שְׁאָר מְזוֹנָא, וּמַאן הוּא לֶחֶם מַמָּשׁ. לֶחֶם דִּלְעֵילָּא, בְּכָל אֲתַר דְּכַר, לֶחֶם תַּתָּאָה, בְּכָל אֲתַר נוּקְבָא. וַאֲנַן אַשְׁכְּחִינָא דְּזִמְנִין כְּתִיב דְּכַר, וּלְזִמְנִין נוּקְבָא, וְכֹלָּא חַד מִלָּה, הַאי כְּהַאי, וְשַׁפִּיר כֹּלָּא.

756. One may ask about the verse: "For the bread is spent in our vessels" (I Shmuel 9:7), THAT THE WORD "SPENT" IS MASCULINE AND not feminine. THE REASON THEREOF IS THAT other victuals BESIDES BREAD are also called bread. It can be noticed what would be other victuals and what would be bread, for upper bread OF ZEIR ANPIN is uniformly male, AND REFERS TO ALL KINDS OF FOOD. The lower bread OF THE NUKVA is uniformly female, AND REFERS TO BREAD ALONE. We find that it is sometimes written as masculine and sometimes as feminine. All is the same, and the one is like the other, ONLY ONE IS IN ZEIR ANPIN AND THE OTHER IN THE NUKVA, and all is correct.

757. תָּא חֲזֵי, אָשֶׁר, רָשִׁים לְעֵילָּא, וְרָשִׁים לְתַתָּא, בְּתִקּוּנֵי כַּלָּה, וְכֻלְּהוּ תְּרֵיסַר שִׁבְטִין יַמָּא קָאִים עֲלַיְיהוּ, וְאִתְתַּקַּן בְּהוֹ, הה"ד וְהַיָּם עֲלֵיהֶם מִלְמָעְלָה. וְרָזָא דְמִלָּה, אִתְתַּקַּן לְעֵילָּא, וְאִתְתַּקַּן לְתַתָּא בְּאַרְעָא. אִתְתַּקַּן לְעֵילָּא בְּתִקּוּנִין יְדִיעָן, כְּגַוְונָא דְעָלְמָא עִלָּאָה. וְאִתְתַּקַּן לְתַתָּא בְּהָנֵי תְּרֵיסַר שִׁבְטִין כְּגַוְונָא דִלְעֵילָּא וְעַ"ד שְׁכִינְתָּא לְעֵילָּא וּשְׁכִינְתָּא

לְתַתָּא בְּגִינַיְיהוּ דְיִשְׂרָאֵל, וּבִתְרֵיסַר שְׁבָטִין אִתְכְּלִילַת וְאִתְתַּקְנַת. אָשֵׁר בְּתִקּוּנָהָא קַיְימָא, כִּשְׁאָר שְׁבָטִין.

757. Come and see: Asher is mentioned above IN BINAH and mentioned below in relation to the adornments of the bride, WHO IS THE NUKVA, since the sea, THE NUKVA, rests upon and is supported by all the twelve tribes, THE SECRET OF THE TWELVE OXEN. This is the meaning of: "And the sea was set above upon them" (I Melachim 7:25). ASHER THEN IS PART OF THE SUPPORT OF THE NUKVA. The secret of the matter is that it is established above IN BINAH and below on earth, THE NUKVA, through certain amendments after the pattern of the supernal world BINAH. It is established below through the twelve tribes WHO SUPPORT THE NUKVA, after the supernal pattern OF BINAH WHICH IS ESTABLISHED UPON THE TWELVE SUPPORTS OF ZEIR ANPIN. Hence there is the Shechinah above, BINAH, WHICH RESTS UPON THE TWELVE SUPPORTS OF ZEIR ANPIN, THE THREE COLUMNS, EACH OF THEM FOUR FACED and there is the Shechinah below, the NUKVA, through which Yisrael is included and established by the twelve tribes, and Asher is part of her support like the other tribes.

758. וְאִי לָאו דְּגָלֵי מֹשֶׁה, לָא אִתְיְידַע, דִּכְתִיב וְטוֹבֵל בַּשֶּׁמֶן רַגְלוֹ. לְאַחֲזָאָה אָן הוּא קִשְׁרָא דִּילֵיהּ בְּאַתְרֵיהּ, דְּאִיהוּ נָגִיד הַהוּא מְשַׁח רְבוּת מִלְעֵילָא, בְּגִינֵי כָּךְ כְּתִיב, בָּרוּךְ מִבָּנִים אָשֵׁר וְגוֹ'.

758. If it were not for Moses who revealed THAT ASHER IS IN BINAH, it would not be made known. Thus it says, "And let him dip his foot in oil" (Devarim 33:24) to indicate his attachment to his place, which pours the anointing oil from ITS PLACE above IN BINAH. Therefore it says, "Be Asher blessed above sons" (Ibid.).

75. "Naftali is a hind let loose"

A Synopsis
An interpretation of this difficult section reveals that while Malchut is considered female, anything that rises above her to Binah is considered male. We learn that a male is considered perfect when he is circumcised, because he possesses the sign of the Covenant. Therefore, the verse, "a male without blemish", alludes to the virile member which must not be castrated. Although Binah is often referred to as female, since she has many feminine aspects, when the "final part," the aspect of maleness, is revealed, all turns into male. The discussion next moves to the question of why God omitted Joseph and put Ephraim in his place when He ordered the four standards for the twelve tribes in order to adorn the Shechinah. We learn that although Joseph was righteous, he had the imprint of the male. Because the Shechinah's adornments are all female, Joseph was removed and Ephraim, who is of the feminine aspect, was put in his place. Finally, the rabbis provide further insight into the title verse through an explanation of the words, "and your mouth (speech) is comely." The voice, which signifies Zeir Anpin, guides the speech, which signifies Malchut. Just as there is no voice without speech and vice versa, Malchut and Zeir Anpin cannot illuminate without each other. Thus, the whole depends on the part, and the part depends on the whole.

The Relevance of this Passage
The realization of the interconnectedness and perfect harmony of all reality begins to take hold within our consciousness. We receive purification of our negative sexual deeds and thoughts through the Light that is set aflame during circumcision. Our efforts of meditating upon these verses help to couple Malchut and Zeir Anpin bringing Light to the planet and balance to the male and female energies that permeate all worlds.

759. ר"ש פְּתַח וַאֲמַר, נַפְתָּלִי אַיָּלָה שְׁלוּחָה הַנּוֹתֵן אִמְרֵי שָׁפֶר. הָא אִתְּמַר, דְּעָלְמָא עִלָּאָה עָלְמָא דִּדְכוּרָא אִיהוּ, כֵּיוָן דְּסַלְקָא מִלָּה מִכְּנֶסֶת יִשְׂרָאֵל וּלְעֵילָא, כֹּלָּא הוּא דְּכַר. מְנָלָן, מֵעוֹלָה, אַמַּאי אִתְקְרֵי עוֹלָה, בְּגִין דְּסַלְקָא לְעֵילָא מִן נוּקְבָא. וּבְגִינֵי כָּךְ, עוֹלָה זָכָר תָּמִים יַקְרִיבֶנּוּ וְגוֹ'.

759. Rabbi Shimon opened the discussion with: "Naftali is a hind let loose: he gives goodly words" (Beresheet 49:21). THIS VERSE IS CONSIDERED

DIFFICULT, FOR SINCE IT SAYS "A HIND LET LOOSE," IT SHOULD END WITH 'SHE GIVES GOODLY WORDS', INSTEAD OF "HE." We have learned that the supernal world, BINAH, is the world of the male. Once something rises from the Congregation of Yisrael, WHICH IS FEMALE, it becomes male. Whence do we know that? From the burnt offering (Heb. *olah*). Why is it called olah (lit. 'goes up', fem.)? Because it rises up from the Nukva. Therefore, "let him offer a male without blemish" (Vayikra 1:3), AS ABOVE THE NUKVA IT IS MALE. FOR THIS REASON THE SUPERNAL WORLD, BINAH, IS CONSIDERED THE WORLD OF THE MALE.

760. אַמַּאי תָּמִים, וְכִי פִּיסְקֵי פִּיסְקֵי בְּעִינָן לֵיהּ, דַּאֲמַר תָּמִים, מַהוּ תָּמִים. אֶלָּא, כִּדְכְתִיב הִתְהַלֵּךְ לְפָנַי וֶהְיֵה תָמִים. אֵימָתַי תָּמִים, בְּשַׁעְתָּא דְּאִתְגְּזַר, דְּהָא דְכוּרָא לָא הֲוֵי, וְלָא אִשְׁתְּמוֹדַע, אֶלָּא בְּהַהוּא אֲתַר דְּאִקְרֵי תָּמִים, וּמַאן אִיהוּ, דָּא אָת קַיָּימָא, דְּבֵיהּ אִשְׁתְּמוֹדַע דְּכוּרָא מִן נוּקְבָא, כִּדְכְתִיב אִישׁ צַדִּיק תָּמִים הָיָה. בְּגִינֵי כָּךְ זָכָר תָּמִים, דְּאִשְׁתְּמוֹדַע בֵּיהּ הַאי שַׁיְיפָא, וְלָא יְסָרְסוּן לֵיהּ.

760. HE ASKS: Why DOES SCRIPTURE say "A MALE without blemish"? Was there any intention of bringing it in pieces, that it admonishes "without blemish (lit. 'perfect')"? HE ANSWERS: What is perfect? It is expressed by the words: "Walk before me, and be perfect" (Beresheet 17:1). When was he perfect? At the time he was circumcised, since a male exists and is recognized only by the place called perfect, the sign of the covenant, which indicates the difference between male and female. Hence it says, "Noah was a righteous perfect man" (Beresheet 6:9), RIGHTEOUS BEING YESOD WHICH IS CALLED PERFECT. Therefore, the words "a male without blemish" allude to the virile member which must not be castrated.

761. וְאִי תֵימָא, הָא כְּתִיב, נְקֵבָה תְּמִימָה. הָכֵי הוּא וַדַּאי, כְּמָה דְּאִקְרֵי צַדִּיק תָּמִים, כָּךְ אִקְרֵי צֶדֶק תְּמִימָה. בְּגִין דְּכֹלָּא, נָטְלָא מִנֵּיהּ, בְּגִינֵי כָּךְ, עוֹלָה דְּסַלְקָא מִן נוּקְבָא לִדְכוּרָא, וּמֵהַאי אֲתַר וּלְעֵילָא, כֹּלָּא הוּא דְכוּרָא. וּמִן נוּקְבָא וּלְתַתָּא, כֹּלָּא הוּא נוּקְבָא, וְהָא אוֹקִימְנָא.

761. HE ASKS: Yet it also says "a female without blemish." HE ANSWERS: Assuredly, as YESOD is called "righteous perfect," so does the Nukva, since she receives everything from him AND IS THEREFORE CALLED PERFECT

LIKE HIM. BUT THE ATTRIBUTE "PERFECT" MAINLY REFERS TO THE MALE. Hence, the burnt offering which rises from the female unto the male IS MALE, since from that place, THE NUKVA, upwards, all is male. From the Nukva downward all is female, as has already been explained.

762. וְאִי תֵימָא, הָכֵי נָמֵי נוּקְבָא דִּלְעֵילָא. אֶלָּא, סִיּוּמָא דְגוּפָא אַחְזֵי עַל כָּל גּוּפָא דְּאִיהוּ דְכַר, רֵישָׁא דְגוּפָא נוּקְבָא, עַד דְּנָחֵית לְסִיּוּמָא, וְכַד סִיּוּמָא אִתְחֲזֵי, הָא עָבֵיד כֹּלָּא דְכַר. אֲבָל הָכָא, רֵישָׁא וְסוֹפָא נוּקְבָא, דְּהָא כָּל תִּקּוּן גּוּפָא נוּקְבָא.

762. HE ASKS: But there is also a female above, BINAH. HE REPLIES: The final part of the body shows that the whole body is male. The head and body OF BINAH – BEING CHOCHMAH, BINAH, DA'AT, CHESED, GVURAH AND TIFERET, are feminine until the final part, TO NETZACH, HOD AND YESOD, CLOTHED IN THE HEAD OF ZEIR ANPIN TO ASSUME THE ASPECT OF THE MALE LIKE HIM, and when the final part shows THE ASPECT OF MALENESS all turns into male, EVEN ITS CHOCHMAH, BINAH, DA'AT, CHESED, GVURAH AND TIFERET, WHICH ARE NOT CLOTHED WITH ZEIR ANPIN, ARE ALSO CONSIDERED TO BE MALE. But here IN THE NUKVA OF ZEIR ANPIN, the head and end are considered feminine, for her whole body is female, WITHOUT A TRACE OF MALE IN HER NETZACH HOD YESOD.

763. תָּא חֲזֵי, חַד רָזָא עִלָּאָה אִית בְּמִלָּה דָא, דְּהָא חָמֵינָן דְּיַעֲקֹב בָּרֵיךְ לְיוֹסֵף בְּגוֹ אֲחוֹהִי, כֵּיוָן דְּמַנֵּי קוּדְשָׁא בְּרִיךְ הוּא אַרְבַּע דְּגָלִים בִּשְׁכִינְתָּא, בִּתְרֵיסַר שִׁבְטִין לְאִתְתַּקְּנָא בְּהוּ, גָּרַע מִנַּיְיהוּ לְיוֹסֵף, וְשַׁוֵּי לְאֶפְרַיִם בְּאַתְרֵיה. מַ"ט אִסְתַּלַק יוֹסֵף מִנַּיְיהוּ, אִי תֵימָא בְּגִין חוֹבוֹי, לָאו הָכֵי, דְּהָא זַכָּאָה אִיהוּ.

763. Come and see: There is a supernal secret in this, for we notice that Jacob blessed Joseph together with his brothers. But when the Holy One, blessed be He, ordered the four standards of the Shechinah for the twelve tribes, through which to adorn the Shechinah, he omitted Joseph and put Ephraim in his place. Why did he omit Joseph? If you say that it was for his sins, this is not so, for he was righteous.

764. אֶלָּא, רָזָא דְמִלָּה, יוֹסֵף רְשִׁימָא דִּדְכוּרָא הֲוָה, דִּכְתִיב בֵּן פּוֹרָת

יוֹסֵף בֵּן פּוֹרָת עֲלֵי עָיִן. וּכְתִיב מִשָּׁם רוֹעֶה אֶבֶן יִשְׂרָאֵל, מִתַּמָּן אִתְּזָן, הַאי אֶבֶן יִשְׂרָאֵל. אֶבֶן: דָּא כְּנֶסֶת יִשְׂרָאֵל, וַעֲלָהּ אָמַר דָּוִד אֶבֶן מָאֲסוּ הַבּוֹנִים הָיְתָה לְרֹאשׁ פִּנָּה. וּבְגִין דְּיוֹסֵף אִיהוּ רְשִׁימוּ דִּדְכוּרָא, אִקְרֵי יוֹסֵף הַצַּדִּיק, דְּהָא אִיהוּ צַדִּיק וַדַּאי, מִשָּׁם רוֹעֶה אֶבֶן יִשְׂרָאֵל.

764. HE ANSWERS: The secret meaning of this is that Joseph was the imprint of the male, as it is written: "Joseph is a fruitful bough, a fruitful bough by a well" (Beresheet 49:22), WHICH IS THE ASPECT OF YESOD CALLED A FRUITFUL BOUGH, and "from thence he fed the stone of Yisrael" (Ibid. 24). The stone is the Congregation of Yisrael, NAMELY THE NUKVA, of which David said: "The stone which the builders rejected has become the head stone of the corner" (Tehilim 118:21). Since Joseph was the imprint of the male, he is called Joseph the righteous, for indeed he was righteous, YESOD. "From thence he fed the stone of Yisrael" WHICH GIVES TO THE NUKVA.

765. וּבְגִין דְּכָל תִּקּוּנֵי שְׁכִינְתָּא אִינוּן נוּקְבָן, אִסְתַּלַּק יוֹסֵף מִתַּמָּן, וְאִתְמַנֵּי תְּחוֹתֵיהּ אֶפְרַיִם, וְאִיהוּ נוּקְבָא לְתִקּוּנָהָא. וּבְגִין דְּאִיהוּ הָכִי, אִתְמַנֵּי לִסְטַר מַעֲרָב, אֲתַר דְּנוּקְבָא שַׁרְיָא, וְהַהוּא רְשִׁימוּ דְּאִיהוּ דִּדְכוּרָא, אִסְתַּלַּק מִתִּקּוּנָהָא, בְּגִין דְּאִיהוּ עָלְמָא דְנוּקְבָא, וְלָא עָלְמָא דִּדְכוּרָא, וְכָל תִּקּוּנָהָא בָּעְיָין נוּקְבֵי.

765. Since all the implements of the Shechinah are female, FOR FROM THE NUKVA DOWNWARD ALL IS FEMALE, Joseph was removed from them and Ephraim was assigned in his place to the TWELVE implements, for he is of the aspect of the female. He was then stationed on the west side, the dwelling of the Nukva, THE SHECHINAH BEING ON THE WEST, and the impress of the male, NAMELY JOSEPH, was removed from the implements, which are all of the world of the female and not of the world of the male. All implements need to bear the aspect of the female.

766. וּבְגִין כָּךְ, יוֹסֵף דְּאִיהוּ צַדִּיק, אִסְתַּלַּק מִתִּקּוּנָהָא, וְאִתְמַנֵּי אֶפְרַיִם תְּחוֹתֵיהּ. וְע"ד, כֻּלְּהוּ תְּרֵיסַר שְׁבָטִין, תִּקּוּנֵי שְׁכִינְתָּא אִינוּן, וְכֻלְּהוּ בָּעְיָין בְּגַוְונָא דִלְעֵילָא, בַּר דַּרְגָּא דְצַדִּיק, דְּאִיהוּ עָבִיד כָּל שַׁיְיפִין דְּכַר, וְלָא בָּעֵי לְאַכְחְשָׁא לֵיהּ.

766. Hence Joseph the righteous, YESOD WHICH IS MALE, was removed from the adornments and Ephraim was put in his stead. Therefore all the twelve tribes WHO ARE CONSIDERED FEMALE, are the adornments of the Shechinah, and must bear the likeness of above; TO WIT, TO BE FEMALES LIKE THE SHECHINAH, except the grade of righteous OF THE TRIBES, WHICH IS YESOD, which turn all the members of the body into male and should not be counted among the twelve implements so that there will be no need to deduct him.

767. נַפְתָּלִי אַיָּלָה שְׁלוּחָה הַנּוֹתֵן אִמְרֵי שָׁפֶר, הַיְינוּ דִכְתִיב וּמִדְבָּרֵךְ נָאוֶה, בְּגִין דְקוֹל מַדְבַּר לֵיהּ לְדִבּוּר, וְלֵית קוֹל בְּלָא דִבּוּר, וְהַהוּא קוֹל אִשְׁתַּלַּח מֵאֲתַר עֲמִיקָא דִלְעֵילָא, וְשָׁלִיחַ מִקַּמֵּיהּ, לְאַנְהָגָא לְדִבּוּר, דְּהָא לֵית קוֹל בְּלָא דִבּוּר, וְלָא דִבּוּר בְּלָא קוֹל, וְדָא כְּלָל דְּצָרִיךְ לִפְרָט, וּפְרָט דְּצָרִיךְ לִכְלָל, וְדָא קוֹל נָפְקָא מִדָּרוֹם, וּמַדְבַּר לְמַעֲרָב, יָרֵית לִתְרֵין סִטְרִין, וְדָא הוּא דִכְתִיב, וּלְנַפְתָּלִי אָמַר וגו', יָם וְדָרוֹם יְרָשָׁה, לְעֵילָא דְּכַר, לְתַתָּא נוּקְבָא, בְּגִין כָּךְ נַפְתָּלִי שְׁלוּחָה אַיָּלָה נוּקְבָא לְתַתָּא. כְּגַוְונָא דָּא דְּכַר לְעֵילָא, דִכְתִיב הַנּוֹתֵן אִמְרֵי שָׁפֶר, הַנּוֹתֵן כְּתִיב, וְלֹא הַנּוֹתֶנֶת.

767. "Naftali is a hind let loose: he gives goodly words" as it says "and your mouth (speech) is comely" (Shir Hashirim 4:3), for the voice, ZEIR ANPIN, guides the speech, THE NUKVA. There is no voice without speech. The voice is sent from a deep place above, BINAH, to guide the speech, since there is no voice without speech nor speech without voice. This is the whole needing the part, and the part in need of the whole. The voice comes forth from the south, WHICH IS THE RIGHT COLUMN, THE LIGHT OF CHASSADIM and leads the west, THE NUKVA, which inherits the two sides, THE LIGHT OF CHASSADIM FROM THE SOUTH AND THE LIGHT OF CHOCHMAH FROM THE WEST. Hence it is written, "And of Naftali he said...possess you the west and the south" (Devarim 33:23). Therefore it is said that "Naftali is a hind let loose," NAMELY the Nukva below. In the same manner, the male above SHINES TOGETHER WITH HER, FOR THEY DO NOT SHINE THE ONE WITHOUT THE OTHER. Hence, "he gives goodly words" is written in the masculine, WHICH IS ZEIR ANPIN, instead of the feminine.

76. Thought, voice, speech

A Synopsis

Thought, we are told, is the beginning of all. In the beginning, there was no separation between thought, voice, and speech, as signified by the verse, "The Creator shall be one, and His Name One." Thought then expanded and was named Binah (Understanding) when it came to the place where the spirit dwelt. The spirit expands and utters a voice, which includes all forces and guides the speech.

The Relevance of this Passage

The energy flowing from this passage transports our souls back to the moment before creation where all was one. This all-embracing unity radiates Light that returns our entire being back to an embryonic state when we were free of any negativity and defilement. This process has a refining and purifying effect on us, removing blockages and darkness from the recesses of our souls. The Light of rejuvenation ignites within us, giving us renewed strength and power to continue our spiritual transformation.

768. תָּא חֲזֵי, מַחֲשָׁבָה רֵאשִׁיתָא דְּכֹלָּא, וּבְגִין דְּאִיהִי מַחֲשָׁבָה, אִיהִי לְגוֹ סְתִימָא וְלָא אִתְיְידַע. כָּךְ אִתְפַּשַּׁט הַאי מַחֲשָׁבָה יַתִּיר, אַתְיָא לְאֲתַר דְּרוּחָא שַׁרְיָא, וְכַד מָטֵי לְהַהוּא אֲתַר אִקְרֵי בִּינָ"ה, וְהָא לָאו סְתִים כְּדְקַדְמֵיתָא, וְאע"ג דְּאִיהוּ סָתִים, הַאי רוּחָא אִתְפַּשַּׁט, וְאַפִּיק קָלָא, כָּלִיל מֵאֶשָׁא וּמַיָּא וְרוּחָא, דְּאִינוּן צָפוֹן וְדָרוֹם וּמִזְרָח. וְהַאי קָלָא, כְּלָלָא דְּכָל שְׁאָר חֵילִין, וְקָלָא דָּא מַדְבַּר לְדִבּוּר, וְדָא יָהֵיב מִלָּה בְּתִקּוּנָא, בְּגִין דְּקוֹל אִשְׁתַּלַּח מֵאֲתַר דְּרוּחָא, וְאָתֵי לְדַבְּרָא מִלָּה, לְאֲפָקָא מִלִּין תְּרִיצִין.

768. Come and see: Thought is the beginning of all. Thought is hidden inside and inscrutable. When thought further expanded, it came to where the spirit dwelt, and was there named Binah (understanding). Now it is not concealed as before, and though it is somewhat hidden, the spirit expands and utters a voice, which is composed of fire, water and wind, THE THREE COLUMNS north, south and east. This voice includes all forces, and guides the speech. It gives word its fixing, since it was sent from the place of the spirit and came to guide the word and utter correct words.

769. וְכַד תִּסְתַּכֵּל בְּדַרְגִּין, הוּא מַחֲשָׁבָה, הוּא בִּינָה, הוּא קוֹל, הוּא
דִבּוּר, וְכֹלָּא חַד, וְהִיא הִיא מַחֲשָׁבָה, רֵאשִׁיתָא דְּכֹלָּא, וְלָא הֲוֵי פֵּרוּד,
אֶלָּא כֹּלָּא חַד, וְקִשּׁוּרָא חַד, דְּאִיהוּ מַחֲשָׁבָה מַמָּשׁ אִתְקַשַּׁר בְּאַיִן, וְלָא
אִתְפָּרַשׁ לְעָלְמִין, וְדָא הוּא ה' אֶחָד וּשְׁמוֹ אֶחָד. וְעַל דָּא, הַנּוֹתֵן אִמְרֵי
שֶׁפֶר כְּתִיב, דָּא גוּפָא.

769. When you look at these grades, you shall find that thought, Binah, voice and speech are all one. This is the thought in the beginning of all. There was no separation but all was one and united. That very thought was attached to naught, KETER, never to separate. This is meant by: "Hashem shall be one, and His name One" (Zecharyah 14:9). Therefore "he gives goodly words" refers to the body.

77. "Joseph is a fruitful bough"

A Synopsis
The Zohar offers a complex discourse concerning the exact makeup of the great spiritual channel Joseph.

The Relevance of this Passage
Joseph is considered to be the foundation of our physical world. Within the structure of the Ten Sfirot, Joseph corresponds to the dimension of Yesod, the doorway through which all the energy of the Upper Worlds enters our material realm. Joseph also corresponds to sustenance. Hence, in this passage, we draw the power of good fortune and we strengthen our soul's connection to the true foundation of all spirituality.

770. סִיּוּמָא דְגוּפָא, דָּא דִּכְתִיב בֵּן פּוֹרָת יוֹסֵף בֵּן פּוֹרָת עֲלֵי עָיִן, אַמַּאי תְּרֵי זִמְנֵי. אֶלָּא בֵּן פּוֹרָת לְעֵילָא. בֵּן פּוֹרָת לְתַתָּא. וְאַמַּאי לָאו אִיהוּ בֵּן פּוֹרָת לְתַתָּא, בְּתִקּוּנֵי מַטְרוֹנִיתָא. בְּגִין דִּבְנָת צָעֲדָה, לְמֶהֱוֵי עֲלֵי שׁוּר, דְּבָעְיָין בָּנוֹת לְתִקּוּנְהָא וְלָא בָנִים. כְּד״א רַבּוֹת בָּנוֹת עָשׂוּ חָיִל וְגו'. רַבּוֹת בָּנוֹת עָשׂוּ חָיִל, אִלֵּין תְּרֵיסַר שִׁבְטִין.

770. The ending of the body, YESOD, is referred to in the verse: "Joseph is a fruitful bough, a fruitful bough by a well" (Beresheet 49:22). HE ASKS: Why does it say twice "A FRUITFUL BOUGH"? HE ANSWERS: There is a fruitful bough above and a fruitful bough below. Why is there no fruitful bough below among the implements of the Matron, NAMELY AMONG THE TWELVE TRIBES, THE SECRET OF THE TWELVE OXEN, WHICH SUPPORT THE MATRON ABOVE? HE REPLIES: "The daughters advanced upon the wall" (Idib.), WHICH MEANS THAT females are used as her implements, FEMALE ASPECTS, WHICH ARE THE SECRET OF THE TWELVE TRIBES, and not sons. AND JOSEPH IS YESOD, WHICH IS A SON, NAMELY MALE. Hence it says, "Many daughters have done virtuously" (Mishlei 31:29). "Many daughters have done virtuously" are the twelve tribes, WHO ARE MADE A THRONE FOR THE NUKVA. THUS, THE VERSE ENDS WITH "BUT YOU EXCEL (LIT. 'RISES ABOVE') THEM ALL" (IBID.).

771. תָּא חֲזֵי, מַלְכוּתָא קַדִּישָׁא, לָא קַבֵּיל מַלְכוּתָא קַדִּישָׁא שְׁלֵימָתָא, עַד דְּאִתְחַבַּר בַּאֲבָהָן, וְכַד אִתְחַבַּר בַּאֲבָהָן, אִתְבְּנֵי בִּנְיָינָא שְׁלֵימָא

מֵעַלְמָא עִלָּאָה, דְּאִיהוּ עַלְמָא דִּדְכוּרָא, וְעַלְמָא עִלָּאָה אִקְרֵי ז' שְׁנִין, בְּגִין דְּכֻלְּהוּ ז' שְׁנִין בֵּיהּ.

771. Come and see: the holy Malchut does not attain perfection as holy Malchut, until it is united with the Patriarchs, WHO ARE CHESED, GVURAH AND TIFERET FROM THE CHEST AND ABOVE OF ZEIR ANPIN. When it joins them, the kingdom was turned into a complete building by the upper world, which is the world of the male, NAMELY BINAH, SINCE THEN CHESED, GVURAH AND TIFERET OF ZEIR ANPIN RECEIVE FROM ITS RIGHT SIDE AND MALCHUT FROM BINAH'S LEFT SIDE. The supernal world is called seven years since it includes all seven years, AS BINAH INCLUDES WITHIN HER ALL THE SEVEN SFIROT CHESED, GVURAH, TIFERET, NETZACH, HOD, YESOD AND MALCHUT CALLED SEVEN YEARS.

772. וְסִימָנֶיךָ וַיִּבְנֵהוּ שֶׁבַע שָׁנִים, דָּא עַלְמָא עִלָּאָה, וְלָא כְּתִיב בְּשֶׁבַע שָׁנִים, כְּד"א כִּי שֵׁשֶׁת יָמִים עָשָׂה ה' אֶת הַשָּׁמַיִם וְאֶת הָאָרֶץ, וְלָא כְּתִיב בְּשֵׁשֶׁת וּכְתִיב אֵלֶּה תּוֹלְדוֹת הַשָּׁמַיִם וְהָאָרֶץ בְּהִבָּרְאָם: בְּאַבְרָהָם. וְאַבְרָהָם, ז' יָמִים אִקְרֵי, וּבֵיהּ אִתְבְּנֵי עַלְמָא עִלָּאָה, וְאִלֵּין אִקְרוּן עַלְמָא דִּדְכוּרָא.

772. This is indicated by: "And he built it seven years" (I Melachim 6:38). This is the upper world BINAH, WHICH INCLUDES SEVEN YEARS. It therefore does not say 'in seven years', BUT SEVEN, as in: "For six days Hashem made heaven and earth" (Shemot 31:17), instead of 'in six days.' THIS MEANS THAT THE SIX DAYS CHESED, GVURAH, TIFERET, NETZACH, HOD AND YESOD MADE HEAVEN AND EARTH; HERE ALSO IT MEANS THAT THE SEVEN YEARS, BINAH, BUILT IT. It is written: "These are the generations of the heaven and of the earth when they were created (Heb. be'hibar'am)" (Beresheet 2:4), the letters of "be'abraham (Eng. 'in Abraham')," for Abraham, WHO IS CHESED, is called seven days, and by him the upper world, BINAH, was built. They are called the 'world of the male'.

773. כְּגַוְונָא דָא לְתַתָּא, אִית ז' שְׁנִין, רָזָא דְּעַלְמָא תַּתָּאָה, וְרָזָא דָא, דִּכְתִיב ז' יָמִים וְז' יָמִים י"ד יוֹם. דְּכֵיוָן דַּאֲמַר שִׁבְעַת יָמִים וְשִׁבְעַת יָמִים, לָא יְדַעְנָא דְּאַרְבֵּיסַר אִינוּן. אֶלָּא, לְאַחֲזָאָה עַלְמָא עִלָּאָה,

וְעַלְמָא תַּתָּאָה. וְאִינּוּן שִׁבְעַת יָמִים וְשִׁבְעַת יָמִים. אִלֵּין דְּכוּרִין, וְאִלֵּין
נוּקְבִין. אִלֵּין נוּקְבֵי הַאי עָלְמָא עָלַיְיהוּ, דִּכְתִיב רַבּוֹת בָּנוֹת עָשׂוּ חָיִל,
אִלֵּין תְּרֵיסַר שְׁבָטִין, דְּאִינּוּן עָשׂוּ חָיִל, כְּדִכְתִיב כָּל הַפְּקוּדִים לְמַחֲנֵה
יְהוּדָה וְגו', וְכֵן כֻּלְּהוּ.

773. Likewise there are seven years below, CHESED, GVURAH, TIFERET, NETZACH, HOD, YESOD AND MALCHUT DIVIDED AMONG THE TWELVE TRIBES, the secret of the lower world, THE NUKVA. This is the secret meaning of the words:, "Seven days and seven days, fourteen days" (I Melachim 8:66). HE ASKS: From "seven days and seven days," do I not know they amount to fourteen, WHY ADD "FOURTEEN DAYS"? HE ANSWERS: THEIR PURPOSE IS to indicate the upper and lower worlds, which are seven days and seven days, ALLUDED TO BY THE FOURTEEN DAYS. Those OF THE UPPER WORLD are males and those OF THE LOWER WORLD are females. This world, THE NUKVA, is above the females, CHESED, GVURAH, TIFERET, NETZACH, HOD AND YESOD DIVIDED AMONG THE SAID TWELVE, as it is written: "Many daughters have done virtuously." This refers to the twelve tribes, that "have done virtuously," as "all that were numbered in the camp of Judah..." (Bemidbar 2:9) and the others MULTIPLIED EXCEEDINGLY. THUS THE VERSE ENDS WITH "BUT YOU RISE ABOVE THEM ALL," SINCE THE NUKVA IS OVER THEM.

774. וְאִי תֵימָא רַבּוֹת, וְהָא תְּרֵיסַר אִינּוּן, וְלָא יַתִּיר, בַּר הַהוּא חָיִל
דְּעָבְדוּ, מַאי רַבּוֹת. אֶלָּא כְּמָה דִּכְתִיב, זַעֲקַת סְדוֹם וַעֲמוֹרָה כִּי רַבָּה,
כְּמוֹ גָּדְלָה. וְכֵן רַבּוֹת גְּדוֹלוֹת, עֶלְאִין, וְרַבְרְבִין עַל כֹּלָּא. וְאִלֵּין אִקְרוּן
חַיּוֹת גְּדוֹלוֹת. עָשׂוּ חָיִל, הַהוּא חָיִל דְּעָבְדוּ דְּסָמְכִין עָלַיְיהוּ, אִקְרוּן
חַיּוֹת קְטַנּוֹת, עִם גְּדוֹלוֹת, לְאִתְחַבְּרָא כַּחֲדָא, לְאִתַּתְקְנָא בְּהוֹ
מַטְרוֹנִיתָא, לְמֶחֱדֵי בְּהוֹ עֶלְאִין וְתַתָּאִין, כְּד"א לִוְיָתָן זֶה יָצַרְתָּ לְשַׂחֶק
בּוֹ, בְּגִינֵי כָּךְ רַבּוֹת בָּנוֹת עָשׂוּ חָיִל.

774. HE ASKS: You may say that the verse says "many" yet they are but twelve, excepting their virtuous deeds, FOR EACH MULTIPLIED, AS HINTED BY THE WORDS "HAVE DONE VIRTUOUSLY." Why does it say "many (Heb. rabot) daughters"? HE REPLIES: Like in the verse: "Because the cry of Sodom and Amorah is great (Heb. rabah)" (Beresheet 18:20), "many" means that they are great, above all and greater than all. These are the great living creatures. They "have done virtuously" AS EACH TRIBE MULTIPLIED EXCEEDINGLY. "AND THOSE THAT ENCAMP BY HIM" (BEMIDBAR 2:5), ISSACHAR AND ZEBULUN BY THE STANDARD OF JUDAH, AND SO ON, are called 'small living creatures', which join as one the great living creatures, JUDAH, REUBEN, EPHRAIM AND DAN, so that the Matron, THE NUKVA, will be established by them. The upper and lower will rejoice in them. Hence it says, "There is the Leviathan, whom You have made to play therein" (Tehilim 104:26). THE LEVIATHAN IS THE CONNECTION BETWEEN THE SMALL AND GREAT LIVING CREATURES. Therefore "many daughters have done virtuously..."

775. וְעַל דָּא בָּנוֹת צָעֲדָה עֲלֵי שׁוּר. בָּנוֹת צָעֲדָה, צָעֲדוֹת מִבָּעֵי לֵיהּ, אֶלָּא הַהוּא עַיִן דִּכְתִיב לְעֵילָא, וּמַאן אִיהוּ, עַיִן מִשְׁפָּט, וְאִיהוּ קָאִים עֲלֵי עַיִן, וְאִיהוּ עַיִן, צָעֲדָה, וּפָסְעַת לְמֵיטַל בָּנוֹת לְתִקּוּנָהָא, וְהַיְינוּ בָּנוֹת צָעֲדָה, וְלָא בָנִים, בָּנוֹת צָעֲדָה, אִסְתַּכְּלַת לְתִקּוּנָהָא, וְלָא בָנִים. וַיְמָרְרוּהוּ וָרֹבּוּ, בְּאִסְתַּכְּלוּתָא דִּרְחִימוּ לְגַבֵּיהּ, כִּדְכְתִיב הָסֵבִּי עֵינַיִךְ מִנֶּגְדִּי שֶׁהֵם הִרְהִיבֻנִי. וְעַל דָּא וַיִּשְׂטְמֻהוּ בַּעֲלֵי חִצִּים.

775. Hence "the daughters advanced upon the wall" (Beresheet 49:22). HE ASKS: IT SAYS "daughters advanced (sing.)" INSTEAD OF IN THE PLURAL. HE ANSWERS: This is the reflection of that which is written above "A FRUITFUL BOUGH BY A WELL." What is this WELL? It is the well of justice, THE NUKVA, WHICH RECEIVES JUSTICE, TIFERET. JOSEPH gives to the well, THE NUKVA, which advances to take daughters for its adornment. "The daughters advanced": THE NUKVA ADVANCED WITH DAUGHTERS but not with sons, for daughters are worthy to establish Her, but sons are not. "They fiercely attacked him" (Beresheet 49:23) by looking lovingly at him, as it is written: "Turn away your eyes from me, for they have overcome me" (Shir Hashirim 6:5), FOR THEY BURN ME WITH YOUR LOVE'S FLAME. HERE TOO HE COULD NOT SUFFER THE NUKVA'S ARROWS OF LOVE. THIS IS THE MEANING OF "THEY FIERCELY ATTACKED HIM" and "the archers hated him" (Beresheet 49:23), THAT HE COULD NOT TOLERATE IT.

776. וַתֵּשֶׁב בְּאֵיתָן קַשְׁתּוֹ דָּא קֶשֶׁת. מַה קֶשֶׁת. דָּא בַּת זוּגוֹ. בְּאֵיתָן: תּוּקְפָּא אַלְבִּישַׁת עֲלוֹי, דְּלָא אַחְלְשַׁת חֵילָא, דְּהָא יְדַעַת דְּיוֹסֵף לָא

יִסְטֵי בְּהַהוּא דַרְגָּא, דְּאַת קַיְימָא דִילֵיהּ, לִימִינָא וְלִשְׂמָאלָא.

776. "But his bow abode in strength" (Beresheet 49:24). The bow IS THE NUKVA. HE ASKS: Why say "his bow" WHEN IT SHOULD HAVE BEEN 'BUT BOW ABODE…'? HE ANSWERS: It is JOSEPH'S spouse, AND THEREFORE IT SAYS "HIS BOW." "In strength" means that she clothed him in strength and might, and so his strength will not be enfeebled FOR HIS UNION WITH HER. For she knew that Joseph would not turn aside within his grade; TO WIT, HE WOULD NOT TURN, DUE TO MATING, TO THE LEFT GRADE, THE PLACE OF JUDGMENTS, since his sign of the covenant turns both right and left IN ONE.

777. וַיָּפֹזּוּ, מַאי וַיָּפֹזּוּ. אֶלָּא כִּדְכְתִיב הַנֶּחֱמָדִים מִזָּהָב וּמִפַּז רָב. וּכְתִיב וּתְמוּרָתָהּ כְּלִי פָז. אִתְיַיקְרוּ דְּרוֹעוֹי בְּמַרְגְּלִיתָא עִלָּאָה. מִידֵי אֲבִיר יַעֲקֹב, מֵאִינּוּן תְּרֵין סִטְרִין, דְּאַתְקִיף בְּהוֹ יַעֲקֹב. מִשָּׁם רוֹעֶה אֶבֶן יִשְׂרָאֵל, מִתַּמָּן אִתְּזָן הַהוּא אֶבֶן יְקָרָא, כִּדְקָאַמְרָן. תּוּ, מֵאִינּוּן תְּרֵיסַר סִטְרִין, אִתְּזָן הַהוּא אֶבֶן יְקָרָא, דְּאִינּוּן צָפוֹן וְדָרוֹם, וְהִיא אִתְיַיהֲבַת בֵּינַיְיהוּ, וְאִתְבָּרְכָא מִנַּיְיהוּ, וְאִתְּזָנָא מִנְהוֹן עַל יְדָא דְצַדִּיק.

777. What do the words "were made supple (Heb. *vayafozu*)" (Ibid.) mean? HE ANSWERS: As it says, "More to be desired are they than gold, even much fine gold (Heb. *paz*)" (Tehilim 19:11) and "nor shall it be valued with pure gold (Heb. *paz*)" (Iyov 28: 18). HERE TOO, VAYAFOZU IS DERIVED FROM PAZ, FINE GOLD AND PRECIOUSNESS, as his hands were precious with the sublime pearl, THE SUPERNAL NUKVA ABOVE THE CHEST, THAT RECEIVED ABUNDANCE FROM BEING UNITED. SHE RECEIVED "by the hand of the mighty One of Jacob" (Beresheet 49:24) from the two sides, RIGHT AND LEFT, by which Jacob was strengthened. "From thence he fed the stone of Yisrael" (Ibid.), from thence that precious stone, THE NUKVA, was fed, like we said. We should further explain that the precious stone was fed by the twelve sides, north and south, WHICH ARE THE HANDS OF JACOB, FOR THERE ARE CHESED, GVURAH, TIFERET, NETZACH, HOD AND YESOD TO THE NORTH AND CHESED, GVURAH, TIFERET, NETZACH, HOD AND YESOD TO THE SOUTH, ALTOGETHER TWELVE. THE NUKVA is put in their midst to be blessed by them, fed by them via JOSEPH the Righteous.

778. תָּא חֲזֵי, לְיוֹסֵף אִתּוֹסַף לֵיהּ בִּרְכָה אָחֳרָא, כְּד"א מֵאֵל אָבִיךָ
וְיַעְזְרֶךָ וְגו', הַאי קְרָא קַשְׁיָא, מֵאֵל אָבִיךָ, אֵל אָבִיךָ יַעְזְרֶךָ מִבְּעֵי לֵיהּ.
מַאי מֵאֵל אָבִיךָ וּלְבָתַר יַעְזְרֶךָ. וְאֵת שַׁדַּי, וְאֵל שַׁדַּי מִבָּעֵי לֵיהּ, כְּמָה
דִּכְתִּיב וְאֵל שַׁדַּי יִתֵּן לָכֶם רַחֲמִים לִפְנֵי הָאִישׁ. וִיבָרְכֶךָ, יְבָרֶכְךָ מִבָּעֵי
לֵיהּ.

778. Come and see: Joseph was bestowed yet another blessing "by the El of
your father, and He shall help you; AND BY (ET) SHADAI, AND HE SHALL
BLESS YOU" (Beresheet 49:25). This verse is hard to understand, since it
says "by the El of your father," when it should have been 'the El of your
father help you.' It says "Et Shadai" instead of 'El' as in "and El Shadai
give you Mercy before the man" (Beresheet 43:14). "And He shall bless
you" should have been 'He shall bless you.'

779. אֶלָּא אַחְסִין לֵיהּ לְעֵילָא וְתַתָּא. אַחְסִין לֵיהּ לְעֵילָא, מֵאֵל אָבִיךָ,
דְּאִיהוּ אַחְסָנָא עִלָּאָה, אֲתַר דְּאִקְרֵי שָׁמַיִם. וְיַעְזְרֶךָ, בְּגִין דְּלָא יַחֲלִיף
הַאי אֲתַר, לַאֲתַר אָחֳרָא, וְסִיּוּעָא דִּילֵיהּ לֶיהֱוֵי מֵאֲתַר דָּא, וְלָא
מֵאָחֳרָא.

779. HE REPLIES: He inherited both above IN ZEIR ANPIN and below IN
THE NUKVA. He inherited above, as it says "by the El of your father," which
is the supernal inheritance, a place called heaven, NAMELY ZEIR ANPIN,
WHICH CHARIOT JACOB WAS. "And He shall help you": He shall not
exchange it for another place, and His help shall be from this place and no
other.

780. וְאֵת שַׁדַּי, מַהוּ וְאֵת שַׁדַּי, אֶלָּא, אִיהוּ דַרְגָּא אָחֳרָא תַּתָּאָה, דְּהָא
תָּנֵינָן, בְּכָל אֲתַר אֶת ה', דָּא שְׁכִינְתָּא, כְּמוֹ וָאֵרָא אֶת ה', אֶת לְרַבּוֹת.
וְאֵת לְאַכְלָלָא יוֹם בְּלַיְלָה, וְלַיְלָה בְּיוֹם, כִּדְכְתִּיב וְאֵת שַׁדַּ"י, דְּהָא
מִתַּמָּן נָפְקִין בִּרְכָאן לְבָרְכָא עָלְמִין.

780. "And (Heb. et) Shadai": What is the meaning of this phrase, SHOULD
IT NOT HAVE BEEN 'EL SHADAI', AS ASKED ABOVE? But this is another
lower grade, as we have learned that uniformly "Et (Eng. 'the') Hashem" is

the Shechinah, as in "I saw (et) Hashem" (Yechezkel 6:1); Et includes THE SHECHINAH. "And the (Heb. *et*)" ALLUDES TO ZEIR ANPIN, thus comprising day, ZEIR ANPIN in night, and night in day, as it is written: "and (et) Shadai" WITH *VAV* (= AND), since from thence blessings issue into the world.

781. תּוּ, אַמַּאי לָא קָאַמַר וְאֵל שַׁדַּי, דְּהָא ה״ן מַשְׁמַע כִּדְקָאַמְרִינָן, דִּכְתִיב וְאֵל שַׁדַּי יִתֵּן לָכֶם רַחֲמִים, כֹּלָּא אֲתָר חַד הוּא, אַמַּאי שָׁבַק ל׳ וְכָתַב ת׳. אֶלָּא רָזָא אִיהוּ, דְּכַד אִינוּן שְׁבִילִין נָפְקִין מֵעֵילָא, כְּלָלָא דְּאוֹרַיְיתָא, אַחְסִין שָׁמַיִם, כְּד״א אֵת הַשָּׁמַיִם, כְּלָלָא דְּכ״ב אַתְוָון. וּמֵהָכָא נָפְקֵי לַתּוֹרָה שֶׁבְּע״פ דְּאִקְרֵי אֶרֶץ, כִּדְקָאַמְרִינָן וְאֵת הָאָרֶץ, כְּלָלָא דְּכ״ב אַתְוָון. וְשָׁמַיִם כָּלִיל כֹּלָּא כַּחֲדָא, וּכְדֵין מִתְעַטְּרָא סִיהֲרָא בְּכֹלָּא, וְיַתְבָא בְּאַשְׁלָמוּתָא, וּבִרְכָאן נָגְדִין כְּדֵין מִתַּמָּן, וְעַל דָּא וְאֶת שַׁדַּי.

781. We should explain further, Why it does not say 'And El Shadai', seeing that it has the same meaning as we said THAT IT TOO ALLUDES TO THE NUKVA, ALSO CALLED "EL SHADAI," as it is written: "and El Shadai give you mercy." All is the same SINCE "AND EL SHADAI" REFERS TO THE NUKVA LIKE "AND (ET) SHADAI." Why then omit the *Lamed* and replace IT with *Tav*? It is a mystery, that when these paths come from above, TO WIT, THE 22 LETTERS, FROM WHICH EVERY PERFECTION IS SUPPLIED, the whole of the Torah, THE ABUNDANCE OF ZEIR ANPIN, is inherited by heaven, ZEIR ANPIN, as it is written: "the (et) heaven" (Beresheet 1:1), ET (ALEPH TAV) including all the 22 letters FROM ALEPH TO TAV. From here, they depart to the Oral Law, called earth, NAMELY THE NUKVA, as it says "and the (et) earth" (Ibid.), ALEPH TAV including the 22 letters RECEIVED BY THE NUKVA. AT FIRST, heaven, ZEIR ANPIN, includes them all as one, and then the moon, THE NUKVA, is adorned by them all; TO WIT, SHE RECEIVES THEM FROM ZEIR ANPIN and dwells in perfection. Blessings are then drawn from there, and thus it says "and (et) Shadai," WHICH INDICATES THE GREAT PERFECTION OF THE INCLUSION OF THE 22 LETTERS OF THE NUKVA, WHENCE THERE ARE BLESSINGS.

782. וִיבָרְכֶךָ, בְּגִין דִּיהֵא לֵיהּ קִיּוּם תָּדִיר וְיַתִּיר, דְּהָא בְּכָל אֲתָר דְּאִית בֵּיהּ וא״ו, תּוֹסֶפֶת אִית לֵיהּ, וְקִיּוּמָא. עַד כָּאן כְּלָל, וּלְבָתַר עָבֵיד פְּרָט,

דִּכְתִיב בִּרְכוֹת שָׁמַיִם וְגו'.

782. "And (*Vav*) He shall bless you" IS SPELLED WITH *VAV*, for further lasting prevalence TO THE BLESSINGS. For wherever there is *Vav*, it is an indication of an increase and maintenance. Up to this point, it was said in general. Now he gives details, as is written: "blessings of heaven..."

783. בִּרְכוֹת אָבִיךָ גָּבְרוּ עַל בִּרְכוֹת הוֹרַי. בִּרְכוֹת אָבִיךָ גָּבְרוּ וַדַּאי, דְּהָא יַעֲקֹב אַחְסִין שְׁבְחָא דְּכֹלָּא, יַתִּיר מֵאֲבָהָן, דְּהָא הוּא שְׁלִים הֲוָה בְּכֹלָּא. וְכֹלָּא יָהַב לֵיהּ לְיוֹסֵף, מַ"ט. בְּגִין דְּהָכֵי אִתְחֲזֵי, דְּהָא צַדִּיק כֹּלָּא נָטֵיל, וְאַחְסִין כֹּלָּא כַּחֲדָא, וְכָל בִּרְכָאן בֵּיהּ שַׁרְיָין. הוּא אָרֵיק בִּרְכָאן מֵרֵישָׁא לְעֵילָּא, וְכָל שַׁיְיפֵי גוּפָא כֻּלְּהוּ אִתְתַּקָּנָן, לְאַרְקָא בֵּיהּ בִּרְכָאן, וּכְדֵין אִתְעֲבֵיד נָהָר דְּנָפֵיק מֵעֵדֶן.

783. "The blessings of your father are potent above the blessings of my progenitors" (Beresheet 49:26). The blessings of your father JACOB, THE CENTRAL COLUMN, are surely more potent THAN THE BLESSINGS OF ABRAHAM AND ISAAC, since Jacob inherited more praises than the Patriarchs, he being perfect in all. He gave it all to Joseph. Why? Because this is fit, for the Righteous, YESOD, NAMELY JOSEPH, takes and inherits all together; TO WIT, HE RECEIVES FROM ALL THE SFIROT OF ZEIR ANPIN TOGETHER; and all blessings dwell in him. He draws them from the head above, THE FIRST THREE SFIROT OF ZEIR ANPIN, and all the members of the body, CHESED, GVURAH, TIFERET, NETZACH, HOD AND YESOD OF ZEIR ANPIN, prepare to pass the blessings TO YESOD, and then YESOD turns into a river which flows from Eden.

784. מַאי מֵעֵדֶן, אֶלָּא, בְּכָל שַׁעְתָּא דְּכָל שַׁיְיפִין יָתְבִין בְּקִשּׁוּרָא חֲדָא, וְאִינוּן בְּעִדּוּנָא דְּתֵיאוּבְתָּא מֵרֵישָׁא לְעֵילָּא וּלְתַתָּא, וְכֻלְּהוּ מֵעִדּוּנָא וְתֵיאוּבְתָּא דִּלְהוֹן, מְרִיקִין בֵּיהּ, וְאִתְעֲבֵיד נָהָר דְּנָגֵיד וְנָפֵיק מֵעֵדֶן וַדַּאי. תּוּ מֵעֵדֶן מֵחָכְמָה עִלָּאָה, נָגֵיד כֹּלָּא לְאִתְמַשְּׁכָא, וְעָבֵיד נַהֲרָא, וְאִתְמַשְּׁכָא עַד דְּמָטֵי לְהַאי דַּרְגָּא, וּכְדֵין כֹּלָּא בְּבִרְכָאן, וְכֹלָּא חַד.

784. HE ASKS OF THE MEANING OF "from Eden (lit. 'delight')." HE SAYS, When all the limbs are linked together in delight and desire from the abundance in the head above and from below, they all pour UPON YESOD their delight and desire, and it becomes a river which flows and comes out from Eden. WE SHOULD further EXPLAIN THAT the word "from Eden" MEANS that from supernal Chochmah called Eden, all flows and turns into a river, which pours down until it reaches the grade OF YESOD, and then all THE SFIROT OF ZEIR ANPIN are blessed, and all is one.

785. עַד תַּאֲוַת גִּבְעוֹת עוֹלָם, תֵּיאוּבְתָּא דְּאִינּוּן גִּבְעוֹת עוֹלָם. וּמַאי נִינְהוּ. תְּרֵי נוּקְבֵי, חַד לְעֵילָא, וְחַד לְתַתָּא, דְּכָל חַד אִקְרֵי עוֹלָם. וְתֵיאוּבְתָּא דְּכָל שַׁיְיפֵי גוּפָא, בְּאִינּוּן תְּרֵין אִמָּהָן. תֵּיאוּבְתָּא לְיָנְקָא מֵאִמָּא עִלָּאָה. תֵּיאוּבְתָּא לְאִתְקַשְּׁרָא בְּאִמָּא תַּתָּאָה. וְתֵיאוּבְתָּא דְּכֹלָּא חַד, בְּגִין כָּךְ כֻּלְּהוּ, תִּהְיֶינָה לְרֹאשׁ יוֹסֵף וְגוֹ', לְאִתְבָּרְכָא הַהוּא דַרְגָּא דְּצַדִּיק, וּלְנַטְלָא כֹּלָּא, כִּדְקָא חָזֵי.

785. "To the utmost bound (also: 'desires') of the everlasting (lit. 'world') hills" (Beresheet 49:26) is the passion for the two everlasting hills. What are they? The two females, one above, BINAH, and one below, THE NUKVA OF ZEIR ANPIN, each called 'world'. The desire of all the members of the body, ALL THE SFIROT OF ZEIR ANPIN, is for these two mothers. They desire to suck from the upper mother, BINAH, and desire to be attached to the lower mother, THE NUKVA. These desires of them all is the same, and therefore "they shall be on the head of Joseph" (Ibid.), WHO IS YESOD, who will receive them all as befits.

786. זַכָּאִין אִינּוּן דְּאִקְרוּן צַדִּיקִים, דְּהָא צַדִּיק לָא אִקְרֵי, אֶלָּא מַאן דְּנָטִיר הַאי דַּרְגָּא, הַאי אָת קַיָּימָא קַדִּישָׁא. זַכָּאִין אִינּוּן בְּעָלְמָא דֵין, וּבְעָלְמָא דְּאָתֵי. נָפְקוּ מִן מְעַרְתָּא, אֲמַר ר' שִׁמְעוֹן, כָּל חַד וְחַד לֵימָא מִלָּה, וְנֵיהַךְ בְּאָרְחָא.

786. Happy are those who are called righteous, for only those who keep the grade of the sign of the holy covenant are so called. They are happy in this world and in the World to Come. They came out of the cave. Rabbi Shimon said: Let each of us discourse as we walk.

78. "Benjamin is a ravenous wolf"

A Synopsis
The first explanation for why Benjamin is called a wolf tells us that this was engraved upon the throne. The second explanation interprets it as a reference to the altar upon which he offered the flesh of sacrifice daily. The third explanation indicates that through sacrifices, Benjamin appeased the accusers, called "wolf," in order that they would accuse Yisrael. The discussion then reveals the meaning of the verse, "In the morning he shall devour the prey." We are told that in the morning, the offering causes pleasure. At this time only, Ad, of the supernal throne of Binah, consumes the sacrifice. We next learn that the smoke of the sacrifice rises and unites Zeir Anpin and the Female Principle. Wine is also poured below, thereby bringing joy to the wine above. The awakening below should be performed with fine flour in oil in order to effect the union. The first sacrifices of the day are offered entirely to God, Whom then confers blessings on the supernal armies. This unites Zeir Anpin and Malchut and connects the Upper and the Lower Worlds. Indeed, we're told, it is forbidden for a man to greet anyone in the morning before blessing God.

The Relevance of this Passage
The underlying meaning behind any sacrifice to The Creator concerns the sacrifice of our own immoral qualities that dwell deep within our nature. By meditating to uproot our negative traits, and acknowledging our jealousies, ego, and selfishness, the Light issuing through the words of these verses burns away our Evil Inclination, thus facilitating our spiritual evolution.

787. פָּתַח ר' אֶלְעָזָר קָרָא אֲבַתְרֵיהּ, בִּנְיָמִין זְאֵב יִטְרָף וגו'. בִּנְיָמִין זְאֵב יִטְרָף, זְאֵב אֲמַאי. אֶלָּא בְּגִין דְּהָכֵי אִתְרְשִׁים בְּכָרְסְיָיא, דְּהָא כָּל חֵיוָון רַבְרְבִין זְעִירִין רְשִׁימִין תַּמָּן, כְּמָה דִכְתִיב חַיּוֹת קְטַנּוֹת עִם גְּדוֹלוֹת. וְכָרְסְיָיא דַּעֲבַד שְׁלֹמֹה, הָכֵי אִתְרְשֵׁים, כְּגַוְונָא דִלְעֵילָא.

787. Rabbi Elazar opened the discussion with the following verse, "Benjamin is a ravenous wolf" (Beresheet 49:27). HE ASKS: Why is Benjamin called a wolf? HE ANSWERS: Because he was so engraved upon the throne, THE NUKVA, IN THE SHAPE OF A WOLF. For all the great and small living creatures are imprinted UPON THE THRONE, as it is written "both small and great beasts" (Tehilim 104:25). The throne made by

Solomon was also engraved in the same manner, after the pattern of the THRONE above.

788. תּוּ זְאֵב יִטְרָף, דְּהָא מִזְבֵּחַ בְּחוּלְקֵיהּ הֲוָה. וּמִזְבֵּחַ אִיהוּ זְאֵב. דְּאִי תֵימָא בִּנְיָמִין אִיהוּ זְאֵב, לָאו הָכֵי, אֶלָּא מִזְבֵּחַ דַּהֲוָה בְּחוּלְקֵיהּ, הוּא זְאֵב, דַּהֲוָה אָכֵיל בִּשְׂרָא כָּל יוֹמָא וּבִנְיָמִין הֲוָה זָן לֵיהּ, בְּגִין דְּהָא בְּחוּלְקֵיהּ הֲוָה, כִּבְיָכוֹל אִיהוּ מְפַרְנֵס וְזָן לְהַאי זְאֵב. תּוּ זְאֵב יִטְרָף, זְאֵב יְזוּן. וּמַאן אִיהוּ, אִלֵּין מָארֵי דְּבָבוּ, דְּאִינּוּן קַיְימֵי לְעֵילָא לְקַטְרְגָא, וְכֻלְּהוּ אִתְהֲנוּ וְאִתְתַּקָּנָן מִקׇרְבָּנָא, וּמִתְעָרֵי אִתְעָרוּתָא לְעֵילָא.

788. Another explanation for "a ravenous wolf" is that the altar was in Benjamin's portion, and the altar is a wolf. If you say that Benjamin is a wolf, it is not so, the altar on his territory was the wolf, since it consumed flesh every day; NAMELY THE SACRIFICES OFFERED UPON IT. Benjamin used to feed it WITH SACRIFICES, because it was in his territory. It was as if he nourished and fed that wolf. "RAVENOUS" MEANS FEEDING, THE VERSE MAY READ 'BENJAMIN SHALL FEED THE WOLF,' THE ALTAR. Another explanation for "a ravenous wolf" is that 'he shall feed the wolf'. Who is the wolf? ANGELS sworn to enmity who are ready to accuse Yisrael from above. They are all appeased by the sacrifices, aroused the awakening above. THUS BENJAMIN, IN WHOSE TERRITORY THE ALTAR LIES, FEEDS THE ACCUSERS CALLED WOLF, SO THAT THEY WILL NOT BRING ACCUSATION UPON YISRAEL.

789. בַּבֹּקֶר יֹאכַל עַד וְלָעֶרֶב יְחַלֵּק שָׁלָל. מַאי בַּבֹּקֶר יֹאכַל עַד. אֶלָּא בְּצַפְרָא, דְּאַבְרָהָם אִתְּעַר בְּעָלְמָא, וְשַׁעֲתָא דִּרְעוּתָא אִשְׁתְּכַּח, קׇרְבָּנָא עָבֵיד אִתְעָרוּתָא וְנַיְיחָא וְסַלְקָא עַד ע״ד, הַהוּא אֲתַר, דִּכְתִיב וְשַׁבְתָּ עַד ה׳ אֱלֹהֶיךָ.

789. "In the morning he shall devour the prey (Heb. *ad*), and at night he shall divide the spoil" (Beresheet 49:27). HE ASKS: What is the meaning of: "In the morning he shall devour the prey"? HE REPLIES: In the morning, when Abraham, CHESED, stirs in the world, and it is time of goodwill, the offering causes stirring and pleasure. It rises to 'ad', the place of which it says "and you shall return to (Heb. *ad*) Hashem your Elohim" (Devarim 30:2), WHICH IS ZEIR ANPIN, FROM THE CHEST UPWARD.

790. תּוּ בַּבֹּקֶר, מַאי בַּבֹּקֶר, דָּא אַבְרָהָם כִּדְקָאֲמָרָן, דִּכְתִיב וַיַּשְׁכֵּם אַבְרָהָם בַּבֹּקֶר, בְּזִמְנָא דִּרְעֲוָא אִשְׁתַּכַּח, בְּהַהִיא שַׁעֲתָא לָא הֲוָה אָכֵיל קָרְבָּנָא אָחֳרָא, וּמַאן הֲוָה אָכֵיל, הַהוּא אֲתַר דְּאִקְרֵי ע״ד, וְאִיהוּ כָּרְסְיָיא עִלָּאָה, דְּאִיהוּ עֲדֵי עַד, כִּדְכְתִיב עֲדֵי עַד וְגו'.

790. "In the morning" refers to Abraham like we said - WHO IS CHESED, as it is written: "And Abraham rose up early in the morning" (Beresheet 22:3) when it is the time of grace and no one else eats the sacrifice. Who would eat it? The place called Ad would. It is the supernal throne, CHESED, GVURAH AND TIFERET FROM THE CHEST OF ZEIR ANPIN UPWARD, THE THRONE OF BINAH, '*adey ad* (Eng. 'forever')', FOR EATING IS UNITING SHALL BE EXPLAINED.

791. וְזִמַן אֲכִילָה, בְּצַפְרָא דְּע״ד הוּא, וְהַאי עַד, לְעֵילָא, דִּכְתִיב בְּטָחוּ בַּיי' עֲדֵי עַד. וּבַבֹּקֶר, הַיְינוּ קָרְבַּן לַה', וַדַּאי. יֹאכַל עַד, וְלָא אָחֳרָא.

791. Ad eats in the morning, NAMELY WHEN CHESED OF ZEIR ANPIN HAS THE ASCENDANCY. Ad is above THE CHEST OF ZEIR ANPIN, A PLACE WHICH IS ALL CHASSADIM, as it is written: "Trust in Hashem for ever (Heb. *adey-ad*)" (Yeshayah 26:4). FROM THIS, WE UNDERSTAND THAT AD IS A VERY HIGH PLACE. In the morning, WHEN CHESED OF ZEIR ANPIN REIGNS, there is a sacrifice unto Hashem, WHEN THE NUKVA CALLED SACRIFICE IS UNITED WITH HASHEM; THEREFORE "he shall devour ad (or: 'ad shall devour')," THAT IS ZEIR ANPIN AND RIGHT, WHICH IS CHESED, SHALL, and no other GRADE.

792. תְּנָנָא סָלֵיק, וְאִתְּעָרוּתָא דִּרְחִימוּ קָשִׁיר, וְאִתְּעַר לְעֵילָא וְקָיְימָא דָּא לָקֳבֵל דָּא, וְנוּרָא דָּלֵיק, וְאַנְהֵיר בְּהַאי אִתְּעָרוּתָא דִּלְתַתָּא. וְכַהֲנָא אִתְּעַר, וְלֵיוָאֵי מְשַׁבְּחָן, וְאַחְזְיָין חֵידוּ, וּכְדֵין חַמְרָא אִתְנְסַךְ, לְאִתְקַשְּׁרָא בְּמַיָא, וְחַמְרָא נָהֵיר וְאַחֲזֵי חֵידוּ, בְּגִינֵי כָּךְ, חַמְרָא טַב לְתַתָּא, לְאַחֲזָאָה חֵידוּ, לְחַמְרָא אָחֳרָא דִּלְעֵילָא, וְכֹלָּא אִתְּעַר, לְאִתְקַשְּׁרָא שְׂמָאלָא בִּימִינָא.

792. HE EXPLAINS THE UNION WHICH IS BROUGHT ABOUT THROUGH THE SACRIFICE, SAYING the smoke OF THE SACRIFICE rises, THE AWAKENING

FROM BELOW, love is aroused above and connects BETWEEN ZEIR ANPIN AND THE NUKVA, and they stand facing each other. The candle, THE NUKVA, is kindled and shines from the awakening below, TO WIT, IT RECEIVES ABUNDANCE FROM ZEIR ANPIN. The priest is stirred and the Levites praise with joy. The wine, OF THE LEFT SIDE AND GVURAH, is mingled with water, WHICH IS RIGHT AND CHESED. The wine illuminates and brings joy, FOR WHEN GVUROT ARE CLOTHED IN CHASSADIM, THEY ARE CALLED 'GLADDENING WINE'. Therefore good wine should be poured from below, so as to gladden the other wine above. All then are aroused to connect the left with the right.

793. וְלֶחֶם דְּאִיהוּ סֹלֶת, מַלְכוּתָא דְּאִתְּעַר אִתְּעֲרוּתָא, נַקְטִין לָהּ שְׂמָאלָא בִּימִינָא, וּמְקַשְּׁרֵי לָהּ בְּגוּפָא, וּכְדֵין נָגִיד מִשְׁחָא עִלָּאָה, וְלָקְטָא לֵיהּ, עַל יְדָא דְּצַדִּי״ק. וְע״ד בָּעֵי לְמֶעְבַּד אִתְּעֲרוּתָא דְּסֹלֶת בְּמִשְׁחָא, וְאִתְקַשָּׁר כֹּלָּא כַּחֲדָא, וּכְדֵין עֲדוּנָא וְנַיְיחִין דְּיִחוּדָא חַד, וְלָקְטִין עֲדוּנָא וְנַיְיחָא דְּיִחוּדָא, כָּל אִינּוּן כִּתְרִין, וְאִתְקַשָּׁר דָּא בְּדָא, וְאִתְנְהֵיר סִיהֲרָא, וְאִתְקַשְּׁרָא בְּשִׁמְשָׁא, וְיָתֵיב כֹּלָּא בְּעֲדוּנָא.

793. The bread of fine flour, which is Malchut, THE NUKVA, was roused by the stirring BELOW. THE NUKVA IS CALLED 'BREAD', ACCORDING TO THE SECRET MEANING OF THE VERSE: "SAVE THE BREAD WHICH HE DID EAT" (BERESHEET 39:6). She is taken by left and right, and attached to the body, NAMELY ZEIR ANPIN CALLED BODY. Then supernal oil is poured FROM ZEIR ANPIN and She receives it through the Righteous, YESOD OF ZEIR ANPIN. Therefore, awakening below should be performed with fine flour in oil. All is attached together, and there is delight and pleasure in the unison, and the crowns, THE SFIROT OF THE NUKVA, receive that delight and pleasure of the unison. ZEIR ANPIN AND THE NUKVA are attached to each other; the moon, THE NUKVA, shines and joins the sun, and all settled delightedly.

794. וּכְדֵין קָרְבַּן לַיי׳, וְלָא לְאָחֳרָא, וְעַל דָּא, בַּבֹּקֶר יֹאכַל עַד, וְלָא לְאָחֳרָא, יֹאכַל עַד, וְיִתְעֲדָן וְיִתְקַשָּׁר בְּקִשּׁוּרֵיהּ בְּקַדְמֵיתָא. אֵימָתַי, בַּבֹּקֶר. דְּבָעֵי לְאִתְבָּרְכָא שְׁמָא קַדִּישָׁא בְּקַדְמֵיתָא, וּלְבָתַר יִתְבָּרְכוּן אָחֳרָנִין.

794. This is the sacrifice unto Hashem, WHEN THE NUKVA IS BROUGHT UNTO HASHEM and to no one else. Therefore "in the morning he shall devour the prey (Heb. *ad*)"; AD SHALL EAT IN THE MORNING, WHICH IS ZEIR ANPIN CALLED 'AD', and none other. THE VERSE TEACHES US that first Ad, ZEIR ANPIN, shall eat and be delighted in his union in the morning, WHEN CHASSADIM RULE, for the Holy Name should be the first to be blessed. Then will the others be blessed, AS IT SAYS, "AND AT NIGHT HE SHALL DIVIDE THE SPOIL" (BERESHEET 49:27), AS WILL BE EXPLAINED.

795. וְעַל דָּא, אָסִיר לֵיהּ לְבַ"נ לְבָרְכָא לְחַבְרֵיהּ בְּצַפְרָא, עַד דִּיבָרֵךְ לְקוּדְשָׁא בְּרִיךְ הוּא, דְּאִיהוּ בָּעֵי לְאִתְבָּרְכָא בְּרֵישָׁא, וְהַיְינוּ בַּבֹּקֶר יֹאכַל עַד. וּלְבָתַר יִתְבָּרְכוּן אָחֳרָנִין, וְלָעֶרֶב יְחַלֵּק שָׁלָל. דְּהָא קָרְבָּנוֹת דַּהֲוָה בְּרֵישָׁא, כֹּלָּא אִתְקְרַב לְקוּדְשָׁא בְּרִיךְ הוּא, וְאִתְעֲרוּתָא סַלְקָא תַּמָּן. וּבְגִין דְּהָא הוּא אִתְבָּרַךְ, הֲוָה מְקַשֵּׁר קְשָׁרִין לְכָל שְׁאָר חֵילִין עִלָּאִין, וּמְפַלֵּיג לוֹן בִּרְכָאן, לְכָל חַד וְחַד כִּדְקָא חֲזֵי וְיָאוֹת לֵיהּ, וּמִתְבַּסְּמָן עָלְמִין, וְאִתְבָּרְכָאן עִלָּאִין וְתַתָּאִין.

795. This is why it is forbidden for a man to greet his neighbor in the morning before blessing the Holy One, blessed be He, who should be blessed first, as "in the morning he shall devour ad" (or: 'ad shall devour'), WHICH IS ZEIR ANPIN. The others shall be blessed later; NAMELY "at night he shall divide the spoil" for the first sacrifices are offered entirely to the Holy One, blessed be He, and the stirring BELOW rises thither. Once he is blessed, he links by knots all the other supernal armies and confers blessings, each according to his worth. The worlds are sweetened and the upper and lower are blessed.

796. וְהַיְינוּ רָזָא דִּכְתִיב, אָכַלְתִּי יַעֲרִי עִם דִּבְשִׁי וְגוֹ', בְּקַדְמֵיתָא, לְבָתַר פָּלֵיג לְכֻלְּהוּ, וַאֲמַר אִכְלוּ רֵעִים שְׁתוּ וְשִׁכְרוּ דּוֹדִים. אָרֵיק בִּרְכָאן לְכֻלְּהוּ, וּמְפַלֵּיג לוֹן, לְכָל חַד וְחַד כִּדְקָא חֲזֵי לֵיהּ, וְעַל דָּא וְלָעֶרֶב יְחַלֵּק שָׁלָל. דְּהָא שְׁמָא קַדִּישָׁא יִתְבָּרַךְ בְּקַדְמֵיתָא, וְהַשְׁתָּא פָּלֵיג בִּרְכָאן לְכֻלְּהוּ עָלְמִין. דְּלָא תֵימָא דְּקָרְבָּנָא מִתְקָרֵיב לוֹן, וְלָא לְשׁוּם חֵילָא אָחֳרָא, אֶלָּא כֹּלָּא מִתְקְרַב לְקוּדְשָׁא בְּרִיךְ הוּא, וְהוּא אָרֵיק בִּרְכָאן, וּמְפַלֵּיג בִּרְכָאן לְכֻלְּהוּ עָלְמִין, וּבְגִין כָּךְ קָרְבָּן לַיְיָ', וְלָא לְאָחֳרָא.

796. This is the secret of the verse, "I have drunk my wine with my milk" first. Then, dividing amongst them all, he says, "Eat, O dear ones, and drink; drink deep, O loving companions" (Shir Hashirim 5:1), thus conferring blessings upon them all and allotting each with his fitting share. Therefore, "at night he shall divide the spoil" for the Holy Name is blessed first and then imparts blessings amongst all the worlds. Do not say that the sacrifice is offered them nor to any other force, but all is offered to the Holy One, blessed be He, who bestows blessings and divides them to all the worlds. Therefore it is a sacrifice to Hashem, and to no other GRADE.

797. אֲמַר ר"ש, בְּרִי, שַׁפִּיר קָא אֲמַרְתְּ. תּוּ אִתְעֲרוּתָא אָחֳרָא דְקָרְבָּנָא, כֹּלָא בְּגִין לְאַמְשָׁכָא בִּרְכָאן, וּלְאִתְעָרָא בִּרְכָאן, דְּיִתְבָּרְכוּן כֻּלְּהוּ עָלְמִין. בְּקַדְמֵיתָא קָרְבָּן לַיי', וְלָא לְאָחֳרָא, הַשְׁתָּא תַּקְרִיבוּ אֶת קָרְבַּנְכֶם, דְּיִתְקַשְּׁרוּן כֻּלְּהוּ עָלְמִין כַּחֲדָא, וְיִתְחַבְּרָן וְיִתְבָּרְכוּן עִלָּאֵי וְתַתָּאֵי.

797. Rabbi Shimon said: You have spoken well, my son. There is another awakening brought about by the sacrifice, that draws and incites blessings so that all the worlds shall be blessed. But first there is the sacrifice unto Hashem, TO BRING THE NUKVA TO THE GRADE OF ZEIR ANPIN, and to no other. Now THAT THE UNISON WITH ZEIR ANPIN IS PERFORMED, "shall you bring your offering" (Vayikra 1:2), NAMELY so that the worlds will be connected together and the upper and lower shall be blessed.

79. "And this is what their father spoke to them"

A Synopsis

Rabbi Aba inquires why a passage of Scripture refers to the twelve tribes as "All these," as opposed to "These are the twelve tribes." The word "All," we learn, signifies the mechanism by which the twelve tribes are connected to the source of all blessings, the world of Malchut.

Moreover, it indicates the Lower World's connection to the Upper World.

We are then told that the upper realm, called Zeir Anpin [Male], correlates to "voice," whereas the physical dimension of Malchut [Female] equates to speech. Thus, male and female [Upper and Lower Worlds] are unified – just as voice and speech are unified when words are spoken, through the sacred text. "That which (he) spoke." Next, we learn that all blessing issues from both the Male and Female principles, or the union of Zeir Anpin and Malchut.

The Relevance of this Passage

Here, the Upper and Lower Worlds are enjoined so that we may be the recipients of many blessings. This Light of blessing can flow freely if we do not allow negativity from the twelve signs to influence us. This effect is illustrated within this passage through the mystical power of the twelve tribes, which help us ascend over the twelve signs.

798. פָּתַח רְבִּי אַבָּא, וַאֲמַר קְרָא אֲבַתְרֵיה, כָּל אֵלֶּה שִׁבְטֵי יִשְׂרָאֵל שְׁנֵים עָשָׂר וגו', כָּל אֵלֶּה שִׁבְטֵי יִשְׂרָאֵל, אֵלֶּה שִׁבְטֵי יִשְׂרָאֵל מִבָּעֵי לֵיה, מַאי כָּל אֵלֶּה. אֶלָּא, לְאַחֲבְּרָא לוֹן, בַּאֲתַר דְּכָל בִּרְכָאן מְרִיקִין תַּמָּן. שְׁנֵים עָשָׂר. שְׁנֵים עָשָׂר וַדַּאי, קְשָׁרִין דְּתִקּוּנֵי מַטְרוֹנִיתָא, וְאִיהִי אִתְחַבְּרַת בַּהֲדַיְיהוּ, הַהֵ"ד שְׁנֵים עָשָׂר. וְזֹאת אֲשֶׁר דִּבֶּר לָהֶם אֲבִיהֶם וַיְבָרֶךְ אוֹתָם, דְּהָא בַּאֲתַר דָּא, דִּבּוּר שַׁרְיָא.

798. Rabbi Aba opened the discussion with the following verse: "All these are the twelve tribes of Yisrael..." (Beresheet 49:28). HE ASKS: Why say "All these?" Should it not have been, 'These are the twelve tribes.' What means "All"? HE ANSWERS: It attaches the tribes to the place whence all blessings issue from, NAMELY THE NUKVA. IT THEREFORE SAYS, "All THESE." Indeed there are "twelve" knots in the implements of the Matron, THE NUKVA, and she herself is attached to them, ACCORDING TO THE

SECRET OF THE VERSE "AND THE SEA WAS SET ABOVE UPON THEM" (I
MELACHIM 7:25). Hence it says, "Twelve...and this is that which their
father spoke to them, and blessed them" (Beresheet 49:28), SINCE THE
NUKVA CALLED "THIS" JOINED THE TWELVE TRIBES. For in this place
speech dwells, AS ZEIR ANPIN IS CALLED VOICE AND THE NUKVA
SPEECH.

799. תּוּ אֲשֶׁר דִּבֶּר, הָכָא קִשְׁרָא חַד, לְאִתְחַבְּרָא מִתַּתָּא לְעֵילָא,
וּמֵעֵילָא לְתַתָּא. מִתַּתָּא, בְּאִלֵּין תְּרֵיסַר שִׁבְטִין, וְזֹאת, אִתְחַבְּרָא
בַּהֲדַיְיהוּ. אֲשֶׁר דִּבֶּר, הָא חִבּוּרָא דְכַר וְנוּקְבָא, קְשׁוּרָא לִתְרֵין סִטְרִין,
מִתַּתָּא וּמִלְעֵילָא, לְסוֹף קָשַׁר לוֹן בַּאֲתַר דִּלְעֵילָא, דְכַר וְנוּקְבָא כַּחֲדָא.
הה"ד אִישׁ אֲשֶׁר כְּבִרְכָתוֹ וְגו'. מַאי כְּבִרְכָתוֹ. אֶלָּא כְּבִרְכָתוֹ בַּת זוּגוֹ.
אִישׁ אֲשֶׁר כְּבִרְכָתוֹ תַּרְוַוייְהוּ כַּחֲדָא.

799. We should explain the words: "That which (he) spoke" (Beresheet
49:28). There is a link here which connects the lower to the upper and the
upper to the lower. HE EXPLAINS, The lower TO THE UPPER via the twelve
tribes, ACCORDING TO THE VERSE, "ALL THESE ARE THE TWELVE TRIBES
OF YISRAEL" AND THE UPPER TO THE LOWER BY THIS, THE NUKVA, which
was attached to them FROM ABOVE. "That which he spoke" indicates the
union between male and female, FOR THERE IS NO SPEECH WITHOUT
VOICE, ZEIR ANPIN. It is attached to two sides from below, THE SECRET
OF TWELVE, and from above, THE SECRET OF THIS. Finally, he connected
them to the supreme place, male and female FROM THE CHEST UPWARD,
WHERE THEY ARE TOGETHER, AND THE FEMALE IS INCLUDED WITHIN
ZEIR ANPIN IN THE SECRET OF THE CHASSADIM IN HIM. Hence it says
"every one according to his blessing..." HE ASKS: What is "his blessing"?
HE ANSWERS: "His blessing" is his spouse, NAMELY THE NUKVA CALLED
SPOUSE. "Every one according to his blessing" means they are both as one,
AS ZEIR ANPIN AND THE NUKVA ARE INCLUDED TOGETHER.

800. פְּתַח וְאָמַר, יְבָרֶכְךָ יי' מִצִּיּוֹן וּרְאֵה בְּטוּב יְרוּשָׁלַָם וְגו', יְבָרֶכְךָ יי'
מִצִּיּוֹן, דְּמִנֵּיהּ נָפְקִין בִּרְכָאן, לְאַשְׁקָאָה לְגִינְתָּא, וְהוּא כָּלִיל כָּל
בִּרְכָאן, וְיָהִיב לָהּ, וּלְבָתַר וּרְאֵה בְּטוּב יְרוּשָׁלַָם. לְאַחֲזָאָה דְּכָל בִּרְכָאן
אַתְיָין מִדְּכַר וְנוּקְבָא. כְּגַוְונָא דָּא יְבָרֶכְךָ יי' וְיִשְׁמְרֶךָ. יְבָרֶכְךָ יי'

מִדְּכוּרָא. וְיִשְׁמְרֶךָ מִנּוּקְבָא. יְבָרֶכְךָ יי' מִזָּכוֹר. וְיִשְׁמְרֶךָ מִשָּׁמוֹר. וְכֹלָּא
חַד מִלָּה, בְּגִין דְּמִתַּרְוַוייהוּ נָפְקִין בִּרְכָאן לְעָלְמִין. וְעַל דָּא, אִישׁ אֲשֶׁר
כְּבִרְכָתוֹ בֵּרַךְ אוֹתָם.

800. He opened the discussion saying: "Hashem shall bless you out of Zion: and you shall see the good of Jerusalem" (Tehilim 128:5). "Hashem shall bless you out of Zion," for from it all blessings come forth to water the garden, and it includes all blessings and passes to it. Then "you shall see the good of Jerusalem," to show that all blessings issue from male and female. Similarly, "Hashem bless you, and keep you" (Bemidbar 6:24). "Hashem bless you" by the male, "and keep you" by the female, FOR KEEPING COMES FROM THE NUKVA. All this is one, for blessings issue from both into the world. Therefore "every one according to his blessing he blessed them."

80. "And Jacob made an end of commanding his sons"

A Synopsis

Rabbi Yehuda explains that Jacob "commanded" his sons to be attached to the Shechinah, referencing the cave where Adam is buried, a place near the Garden of Eden. We're told that four couples are buried there: the three Patriarchs, their wives, and Adam and Eve. The Zohar explains that four are required to make up a Holy Chariot. The Creator, however, linked King David to the three Patriarchs to form the chariot. So why, Rabbi Yehuda asks, does Adam rest in the cave with the three Patriarchs while King David is buried elsewhere?

We are then told that Adam was allotted 1000 years of life, but 70 of his years were transferred to King David to allow for his physical existence.

Therefore, both King David and Adam signify Malchut, which represents Female. The three Patriarchs embody Zeir Anpin, which is Male. Thus, Adam could be the fourth aspect, "substituting" for David, allowing the Upper Worlds [the Patriarchs] and the Lower World [David or Adam] to be united. It is then explained that the cave where King David is buried corresponds to the male energy of the Upper World, whereas King David embodies the female energy of Malchut. Hence, spiritual balance between the supernal and mundane worlds is achieved through this burial arrangement.

The Relevance of this Passage

The symmetry and perfection of the world and its inhabitants, which were brought into existence by The Creator, exist in all of us. This force of balance and union, ignited by our reading, allows the Light of the Shechinah and holy blessings to filter into our world. Our bond to the great Patriarchs, King David and root of our soul, Adam, is strengthened and enriched.

801. ר' יְהוּדָה פָּתַח קְרָא וְאָמַר, וַיְכַל יַעֲקֹב לְצַוּוֹת אֶת בָּנָיו וגו'. וַיְכַל יַעֲקֹב לְצַוּוֹת אֶת בָּנָיו, לְצַוּוֹת, לְבָרֵךְ מִבָּעֵי לֵיהּ. אֶלָּא דְּפַקִּיד לוֹן לְגַבֵּי שְׁכִינְתָּא, לְאִתְקַשְּׁרָא בַּהֲדָהּ. תּוּ, דְּפַקִּיד לוֹן עַל עִסְקֵי מְעַרְתָּא, דְּהִיא קְרֵיבָא לְגַן עֵדֶן, דְּתַמָּן הוּא אָדָם הָרִאשׁוֹן קָבוּר.

801. Rabbi Yehuda opened the discussion with the verse: "And Jacob made an end of commanding his sons" (Beresheet 49:33). HE ASKS: It says "commanding," but wouldn't one expect 'blessing'? HE REPLIES: He

commanded them to be attached to the Shechinah, and commanded them concerning the cave, which is close to the Garden of Eden, where Adam is buried.

802. תָּא חֲזֵי, הַהוּא אֲתַר אִקְרֵי קִרְיַת אַרְבַּע. מ״ט. בְּגִין דְּתַמָּן אִתְקְבָרוּ אַרְבַּע זוּגוֹת: אָדָם וְחַוָּה. אַבְרָהָם וְשָׂרָה. יִצְחָק וְרִבְקָה. יַעֲקֹב וְלֵאָה. הָא קוּשְׁיָא הָכָא, דְּתָנִינָן, אֲבָהָן אִינוּן רְתִיכָא קַדִּישָׁא, וּרְתִיכָא לָאו פָּחוֹת מֵאַרְבַּע, וְתָנִינָן קוּדְשָׁא בְּרִיךְ הוּא אַחֲבַּר לְמַלְכָּא דָוִד בַּהֲדַיְיהוּ, וְאִתְעֲבִידוּ רְתִיכָא שְׁלֵימָתָא, הה״ד, אֶבֶן מָאֲסוּ הַבּוֹנִים וגו׳. דְּדָוִד מַלְכָּא אִתְחַבַּר לְמֶהֱוֵי רְתִיכָא שְׁלֵימָתָא בַּהֲדַיְיהוּ. אִי הָכִי דָוִד בָּעְיָא לְאִתְקְבָּרָא בְּגוֹ אֲבָהָן, וְיֶהֱוֵי קִרְיַת אַרְבַּע בַּהֲדֵיהּ, מ״ט לָא אִתְקְבַּר בַּהֲדַיְיהוּ.

802. Come and see: this place is called Kiryat Arba (lit. 'city of four') because four couples were buried there: Adam and Eve, Abraham and Sarah, Isaac and Rivkah, and Jacob and Leah. There is a difficulty here. We learned that the Patriarchs are a Holy Chariot, yet a Chariot consists of no less than four. We also learned that the Holy One, blessed be He, joined King David with THE PATRIARCHS, and they formed a complete Chariot OF FOUR. The meaning of: "The stone which the builders rejected has become the head stone of the corner" (Tehilim 118:21) is that King David joined them and formed with them a complete Chariot. David was then supposed to be buried with the Patriarchs so together with him it will be a city of four. Why was he not buried with them?

803. אֶלָּא, דָוִד מַלְכָּא אֲתַר מִתְתַּקַּן הֲוָה לֵיהּ כִּדְקָא יָאוֹת, וּמַאן הוּא. צִיּוֹן, לְאִתְחַבְּרָא לֵיהּ כַּחֲדָא. וְאָדָם דְּאִתְקְבַּר בְּגוֹ אֲבָהָן, הָא אִינוּן אִתְקְבָרוּ בַּהֲדֵיהּ, בְּגִין דְּאִיהוּ מֶלֶךְ קַדְמָאָה הֲוָה, וְאִתְעֲבַר מִנֵּיהּ מַלְכוּ, וְאִתְיְהִיב לְדָוִד מַלְכָּא, וּמִיּוֹמוֹי דְּאָדָם, אִתְקַיַּים דָוִד מַלְכָּא, דְּאָדָם אֶלֶף שְׁנִין אִתְגְּזַר עֲלוֹי, וְאִתְעֲבָרוּ מִנֵּיהּ שַׁבְעִין שְׁנִין, יוֹמֵי דְּדָוִד מַלְכָּא, וְהוּא יָהִיב לוֹן, וַאֲבָהָן הֵיךְ יְקוּמוּן עַד דְּיֵיתֵי דָוִד מַלְכָּא, אֶלָּא זָכָה לְאַתְרֵיהּ, כִּדְקָא חֲזֵי לֵיהּ, בְּגִינֵי כָּךְ לָא אִתְקְבַּר לְגַבֵּי אֲבָהָן.

803. HE REPLIES: A place was prepared for King David, Zion, YESOD OF ZEIR ANPIN, with which to be united as one; and Adam was buried with the Patriarchs. They were buried with him, since he was the first king, from whom kingdom was removed and transferred to King David. King David lived with Adam's days, for it was decreed that Adam should live a thousand years, but seventy were removed from him to form King David's life and he gave them to him. ADAM WAS THEREFORE CONSIDERED TO PERTAIN TO MALCHUT, AND HE COMPLEMENTED THE CHARIOT OF THE FATHERS TO A FOURSOME. OTHERWISE, how could the Patriarchs rise TO HAVE A COMPLETE CHARIOT before the time of King David? OF NECESSITY DID ADAM COMPLEMENT THEM. DAVID WAS NOT BURIED WITH THEM, but merited a place worthy of him, WHICH IS ZION. Hence, he was not buried with the fathers.

804. תּוּ, אֲבָהָן בַּאֲתַר דִּדְכוּרָא שַׁרְיָין, וְדָוִד בַּאֲתַר דְּנוּקְבָא, וַאֲבָהָן נוּקְבָן אִתְקְבָרוּ בַּהֲדַיְיהוּ. וְדָוִד אִתְקְבַּר וְאִתְחַבַּר בַּאֲתַר דִּדְכוּרָא, מִלָּה כִּדְקָא חָזֵי לֵיהּ.

804. Moreover, the Patriarchs dwell in a male place, TO WIT, THEY ARE CHESED, GVURAH AND TIFERET OF ZEIR ANPIN, WHICH ARE MALES. David, WHO IS A CHARIOT TO MALCHUT, is in a female place. Hence the fathers were buried with their wives, and David was buried and attached to a male place, ZION, each as befits him.

81. "And he expired, and was gathered to his people"

A Synopsis
Among the many mysteries expounded upon in this passage, we learn that Jacob never died, but rather "expired," just as the sun expires every evening, leaving the moon to reflect its light. The intimate connection concerning the events that take place in Scripture, the characters that populate the Biblical stories, and the structure of the Upper World, are explored in detail by the Zohar. The underlying objective of this complex passage is to demonstrate how the male and female principles, Zeir Anpin and Malchut [the Nukva], are enjoined for the purpose filling all reality with the blessed Light of The Creator. The Zohar stresses the spiritual perfection of Jacob, whose existence positively influences all generations and unites the Lower and Upper Worlds.

The Relevance of this Passage
We are connected to the intricate structure of the supernal worlds and the processes by which the Lower and Upper worlds [Male and Female] are interlocked. This connection allows the Light of The Creator and the perfection of Jacob to freely flow into our lives, bringing blessing and removing the force of death from our midst.

805. וַיֶּאֱסוֹף רַגְלָיו אֶל הַמִּטָּה, בְּגִין דְּהָא אִיהוּ בַּאֲתַר דְּחַיִּין יָתֵיב. כַּד בָּעָא לְאִסְתַּלְּקָא מֵעַלְמָא, נָחִית רַגְלוֹי לְגַבֵּי מִטָּה, וְאִתְכְּנֵישׁ וְאִסְתְּלַק מֵעַלְמָא, הֲדָא הוּא דִכְתִיב וַיִּגְוַע וַיֵּאָסֶף אֶל עַמָּיו.

805. "He gathered up his feet into the bed" (Beresheet 49:33) because he dwelt in the place of the living, BEING A CHARIOT TO ZEIR ANPIN, THE TREE OF LIFE. Therefore, when he wanted to depart from the world he put his feet down upon the bed, THE SECRET OF THE NUKVA, and was gathered and gone from the world. TO WIT, HE WENT UP TO MAYIN NUKVIN (FEMALE WATERS) TO BE INCLUDED WITHIN THE UNION OF MALE AND FEMALE. Hence it says that he "expired and was gathered to his people," BUT NOT THAT HE DIED, FOR HE ASCENDED TO BE PART OF THE SUPERNAL LIFE.

806. פְּתַח וְאָמַר, נִכְסְפָה וְגַם כָּלְתָה נַפְשִׁי לְחַצְרוֹת ה', מִלָּה דָא הָא אוּקְמוּהָ חַבְרַיָּיא, אֲבָל תָּא חֲזֵי, אִית מָדוֹרִין תַּתָּאִין, וְאִית מָדוֹרִין

עֶלָּאִין, בְּעֶלָּאִין לָאו שָׁרְיָין תַּמָּן, וּמַאן אִינוּן, אִינוּן בָּתֵּי גַּוָּאֵי, וּבָתֵּי בָּרָאֵי. אִינוּן אִקְרוּן חַצְרוֹת ה', בְּגִין דְּאִינוּן קַיְימֵי בִּרְחִימוּ וְתֵיאוּבְתָּא לְגַבֵּי נוּקְבָּא. תָּא חֲזֵי, כַּד נִשְׁמָתָא סַלְקָא אִתְעַר כֹּלָּא לְגַבֵּי נוּקְבָּא, דְּהָא אִיהִי אִתְאַחֲדַת בִּתֵיאוּבְתָּא שְׁלֵימָתָא וְאִתְקַשְּׁרַת בֵּיהּ.

806. He opened the discussion saying: "My soul longs, indeed, it faints for the courts of Hashem" (Tehilim 84:2). A DIFFICULTY IS RAISED WHY HE DOES NOT LONG FOR THE HOUSE OF HASHEM, BUT TO HIS COURTS. HE SAYS, This has already been explained by the friends, yet come and behold: there are lower stories IN BRIYAH, YETZIRAH AND ASIYAH and upper stories IN ATZILUT. There are no SOULS in the upper ones, FOR SOULS DWELL ONLY IN BRIYAH, YETZIRAH AND ASIYAH. The stories are the inner houses IN ATZILUT and outer houses IN BRIYAH, YETZIRAH AND ASIYAH. The outer houses are called the courts of Hashem, because they are filled with love and desire for the female. DAVID SAID: "MY SOUL LONGS...FOR THE COURTS OF HASHEM" BECAUSE SOULS HAVE NO HOLD HIGHER THAN BRIYAH, YETZIRAH AND ASIYAH, CALLED THE COURTS OF HASHEM. BUT WHEN BRIYAH, YETZIRAH AND ASIYAH RISE UP TO ATZILUT, THE SOULS OF THE RIGHTEOUS ASCEND WITH THEM. Come and behold: when the soul rises, all stirs, ALL THE HOSTS OF BRIYAH, YETZIRAH AND ASIYAH, AND THEY RISE to the Nukva, WHO IS united THROUGH THEIR RISING TO HER with a complete desire WITH ZEIR ANPIN, and is attached to him.

807. יַעֲקֹב לָא מִית, בְּג"כ לָא אִתְמַר בֵּיהּ מוֹתָא, אֶלָּא וַיִּגְוַע וַיֵּאָסֶף אֶל עַמָּיו. חָמֵי מַה כְּתִיב, וַיֶּאֱסֹף רַגְלָיו אֶל הַמִּטָּה, דְּאִתְכְּנִישׁ שִׁמְשָׁא לְגַבֵּי סִיהֲרָא, שִׁמְשָׁא לָא מִית, אֶלָּא אִתְכְּנִישׁ מֵעַלְמָא, וְאָזֵיל לְגַבֵּי סִיהֲרָא.

807. Jacob did not die and therefore it does not say so, only that he "expired, and was gathered to his people." Look at the words "he gathered up his feet into the bed," WHICH IS THE NUKVA. IT MEANS that the sun, JACOB, was gathered to the moon, THE NUKVA. The sun does not die. It is merely gathered from the world and goes to the moon.

808. תָּא חֲזֵי, בְּשַׁעְתָּא דְּאִתְכְּנִישׁ יַעֲקֹב, אִתְנְהֵיר סִיהֲרָא, וְתֵיאוּבְתָּא

דְשִׁמְשָׁא עִלָּאָה אִתְּעַר לְגַבָּהּ, בְּגִין דְשִׁמְשָׁא כַּד סָלֵיק, אִתְּעַר שִׁמְשָׁא אָחֳרָא, וְאִתְדַּבַּק דָּא בְּדָא, וְאִתְנְהֵיר סִיהֲרָא.

808. Come and see: When Jacob was gathered, the moon shone, and the desire of the Supernal Sun, ZEIR ANPIN, was awakened for her. For when the sun, JACOB, arises, another sun is awakened, ZEIR ANPIN, and they cleave to each other; ZEIR ANPIN CLINGS TO THE NUKVA, and the moon, THE NUKVA, shines FROM ZEIR ANPIN.

809. אֲמַר ר"ש, שַׁפִּיר קָא אֲמַרְתְּ, אֲבָל הָא אִתְּמַר, דְעִלָּאָה עַלְמָא דִּדְכוּרָא, אִתְקַשַּׁר בְּתַתָּאָה, דְּאִיהוּ עַלְמָא דְנוּקְבָא, וְתַתָּאָה אִתְקַשַּׁר בְּעִלָּאָה, וְכֹלָּא דָּא כְּגַוְונָא דָא.

809. Rabbi Shimon said: You have spoken well. We also learned that the upper beings, the world of the male, NAMELY BINAH, is linked to the lower, the world of the female, NUKVA OF ZEIR ANPIN, and the lower is linked to the upper. So they all resemble each other.

810. וְהָא אִתְּמַר תְּרֵין עָלְמִין נִינְהוּ, כִּדְכְתִיב מִן הָעוֹלָם וְעַד הָעוֹלָם. וְאע"ג דִּתְרֵין נוּקְבֵי נִינְהוּ, חַד מִתְתַּקָּן בִּדְכוּרָא, וְחַד בְּנוּקְבָא. דָּא שֶׁבַע, וְדָא בַּת שֶׁבַע. הָא אֵם, וְדָא אֵם, דָּא אִקְרֵי אֵם הַבָּנִים. וְדָא אִקְרֵי אֵם שְׁלֹמֹה, כִּדְכְתִיב צְאֶנָה וּרְאֶנָה בְּנוֹת צִיּוֹן בַּמֶּלֶךְ שְׁלֹמֹה וגו'. בַּמֶּלֶךְ שְׁלֹמֹה, בַּמֶּלֶךְ דְּכָל שְׁלָמָא דִילֵיהּ. דָּא אֵם שְׁלֹמֹה, כִּדְכְתִיב, בַּת שֶׁבַע אֵם שְׁלֹמֹה.

810. We have learned that there are two worlds, as it is written: "from the world to the world" (I Divrei Hayamim 16:36)-BINAH AND THE NUKVA. And though both are females, SINCE BINAH TOO IS A FEMALE, yet BINAH is established by the male, FOR IN GREATNESS SHE IS CONSIDERED A MALE, and THE NUKVA OF ZEIR ANPIN is established by a female. BINAH is called seven and THE NUKVA daughter of seven (Bathsheba). Both are mothers, BINAH is "mother of children" and THE NUKVA is the mother of Solomon, as it is written: "Go forth, O daughters of Zion, and behold King Solomon with the crown with which his mother crowned him" (Shir Hashirim 2:11). King Solomon is the king that the peace (Heb. *shalom*) is his, NAMELY ZEIR ANPIN, WHOSE MOTHER, BINAH IS THE MOTHER OF CHILDREN. The mother of Solomon, as it is written: "Bathsheba the mother of Solomon" (I Melachim 1:11) IS THE NUKVA, FOR HERE IT DOES NOT SAY 'KING SOLOMON'.

811. וּכְתִיב וַתֵּרֶב חָכְמַת שְׁלֹמֹה. חָכְמַת שְׁלֹמֹה, דָּא אֵם שְׁלֹמֹה, דִּכְתִיב דִּבְרֵי לְמוּאֵל מֶלֶךְ מַשָּׂא אֲשֶׁר יִסְּרַתּוּ אִמּוֹ. דִּבְרֵי לְמוּאֵל מֶלֶךְ, הַאי קְרָא לָאו אִתְיְידַע מַהוּ סְתִימָא דִילֵיהּ. אֶלָּא, דִּבְרֵי לְמוּאֵל מֶלֶךְ: דְּבָרִים דְּאִתְּמַר בְּגִין אֵל דְּאִיהוּ מֶלֶךְ, וּמַאן אִיהוּ. דָּא אֵל זוֹעֵם בְּכָל יוֹם. וְאֵל שַׁדַּי. כְּמָה דְּאִתְּמַר.

811. It is written: "And Solomon's Wisdom excelled" (I Melachim 5:10). Solomon's Wisdom is Solomon's mother, NAMELY THE NUKVA, in accordance with the verse: "The words of King Lemu'el, the prophecy, that his mother taught him" (Mishlei 31:1). "The words of King Lemu'el": This verse is not clear, FOR WE DO NOT KNOW WHO KING LEMU'EL IS. But "the words of King Lemu'el" means the words which were spoken to El, who is King. Who is he? The one of whom it says "and El who has indignation every day" (Tehilim 7:11) and "and El Shadai" NAMELY THE NUKVA, as has been explained.

812. לְמוּאֵל כְּד"א לְמוֹ פִי. לְמוּאֵל מֶלֶךְ, דְּאִיהוּ בַּת שֶׁבַע. מַשָּׂא אֲשֶׁר יִסְּרַתּוּ אִמּוֹ, כַּד אִתְגְּלֵי עֲלוֹי בְּגִבְעוֹן, בַּחֲלֹמָא דְּלֵילְיָא.

812. Lemu'el, as in the verse "to my mouth (Heb. lemo fi)" (Iyov 40:4) MEANS HERE "TO (LIT. 'EL') EL." King Lemu'el is Bathsheba, THE NUKVA; "the prophecy, that his mother taught him," when he appeared before him in Givon in the vision of the night, IS "AND IF YOU WILL WALK BEFORE ME, AS DAVID YOUR FATHER WALKED" (I MELACHIM 9:4).

813. תָּא חֲזֵי יַעֲקֹב אִתְכְּנֵישׁ לְגַבֵּי סִיהֲרָא, וְעָבֵיד בָּהּ פֵּירִין לְעַלְמָא. וְלֵית לָךְ דָּרָא בְּעַלְמָא, דְּלָא אִית בֵּיהּ אִיבָּא דְיַעֲקֹב, בְּגִין, דְּהָא אִיהוּ אִתְעַר אִתְעֲרוּתָא לְעֵילָא, בְּגִין דִּכְתִיב, וַיֶּאֱסוֹף רַגְלָיו אֶל הַמִּטָּה, דְּאִיהוּ מָטָתֵיהּ דְּיַעֲקֹב וַדַּאי.

813. Come and see: Jacob was gathered to the moon, THE NUKVA, BY RAISING MAYIN NUKVIN (FEMALE WATERS) TO ZEIR ANPIN AND NUKVA WHEN HE PASSED AWAY, thus producing fruits by her, BY BRINGING UNION BETWEEN MALE AND FEMALE IN GREATNESS, WHICH PRODUCES SOULS CALLED THE FRUITS OF MALE AND FEMALE. There is no generation in the world without Jacob's fruit, THE SOULS WHICH ARE BORN OF THE MATING OF MALE AND FEMALE IN GREATNESS, WHICH JACOB BROUGHT BY RAISING MAYIN NUKVIN. For he caused stirring above, A UNION BETWEEN MALE AND FEMALE as it says, "he gathered his feet into the bed," the bed of Jacob BEING THE NUKVA.

814. זַכָּאָה חוּלְקֵיה דְּיַעֲקֹב, דְּהָא אִשְׁתְּלֵים לְעֵילָא וְתַתָּא, דִּכְתִיב וְאַתָּה אַל תִּירָא עַבְדִּי יַעֲקֹב נְאֻם ה' כִּי אִתְּךָ אָנִי. כִּי אִתִּי אַתָּה לָא אִתְּמָר, אֶלָּא כִּי אִתְּךָ אָנִי, וְהָא אִתְּמָר.

814. Happy is the portion of Jacob who was made perfect above and below, as it is written: "Fear you not, O Jacob My servant, says Hashem: for I am with you" (Yirmeyah 46:28), not 'you are with Me' but "I am with you." FOR HE WAS MADE PERFECT BELOW TOO THROUGH THE SHECHINAH.

82. "The mourning of Egypt"

A Synopsis

Rabbi Yitzchak sheds light on the term, "the mourning of Egypt." We are told that when Jacob resided in Egypt, "the land was blessed, waters flowed and famine ceased." For this reason, scripture reads, "the mourning of Egypt" and not "the mourning of Israel [Jacob]."

Next, the significance of the word "utter" is examined in a particular verse of Torah. *Yemalel*, the Hebrew word for "utter," denotes the concept of severance and cutting. In the context of verse quoted by the Zohar, the word "utter" signifies the annulment and cancellation of judgments that emanate from the Sfirah of Gvurah, the Left Column force of Judgment.

Thereafter, we discover that the Egyptians were adept in the black arts and sorcery. However, while Jacob lived in this physical world, no nation, no matter how well versed in magic, could rule over Yisrael. Moreover, upon Jacob's passing from this physical plane, the Egyptians realized that Judgment would still rain down upon them; hence the term, "the mourning of Egypt."

Rabbi Shimon then reveals that upon his merit, he can protect those who are destined for death as a result of their wicked deeds, specifically, two Roman informers. He chooses not to.

The Relevance of this Passage

Our connection to Jacob helps ensure that Light flows into our lives even during times of great Judgment and negativity. The additional spiritual influences arising herein, help annul Judgments that are handed down against us in the supernal courts. Finally, the exalted Light of the author of the Zohar, Rabbi Shimon, protects us from the Angel of Death, even though we might not merit exoneration.

815. רְבִּי יִצְחָק פָּתַח וְאָמַר, וַיָּבֹאוּ עַד גֹּרֶן הָאָטָד וגו', וּכְתִיב וַיַּרְא יוֹשֵׁב הָאָרֶץ הַכְּנַעֲנִי אֶת הָאֵבֶל בְּגֹרֶן הָאָטָד וגו'. הַנֵּי קְרָאֵי אִית לְאִסְתַּכְּלָא בְּהוּ, מַאי אִיכְפַּת לָן דְּאִינוּן אָתוּ עַד גֹּרֶן הָאָטָד. וּמ"ט אִתְכָּנַת אֲבֵלוּתָא דָּא לְמִצְרַיִם, דְּהָא אֵבֶל יִשְׂרָאֵל מִבְעֵי לֵיה, מ"ט לְמִצְרַיִם.

815. Rabbi Yitzchak opened the discussion with the verse: "And they came to the threshing floor of Atad...and when the inhabitants of the land, the Canaanite, saw the mourning at the floor of Atad" (Beresheet 50:10-11). We have to examine these verses. Why should it concern us that they came to the threshing floor of Atad, and why was it named "the mourning of Egypt." It should have been named 'the mourning of Yisrael,' so why Egypt?

816. אֶלָּא, הָכֵי אֲמֶרוּ, כָּל הַהוּא זִמְנָא דַּהֲוָה יַעֲקֹב בְּמִצְרַיִם, אִתְבְּרַךְ אַרְעָא בְּגִינֵיהּ, וְנִילוּס הֲוָה נָפִיק וְאַשְׁקֵי אַרְעָא, וְעוֹד דְּפָסַק כַּפְנָא בְּגִינֵיהּ דְּיַעֲקֹב. וְעַל דָּא, מִצְרָאֵי עֲבָדוּ אֲבֵלוּתָא, וְאִתְכְּנֵי עֲלַיְיהוּ.

816. HE ANSWERS: So they said that as long as Jacob dwelt in Egypt, the land was blessed for his sake, and the Nile used to rise and water the land. Moreover, the famine ceased due to Jacob. Hence the Egyptians mourned, and the mourning was named after them.

817. פָּתַח וַאֲמַר, מִי יְמַלֵּל גְּבוּרוֹת ה' יַשְׁמִיעַ כָּל תְּהִלָּתוֹ, הַאי קְרָא אוֹקְמוּהָ. אֲבָל מַהוּ יְמַלֵּל יְדַבֵּר מִבָּעֵי לֵיהּ. וְאִי תֵימָא דְּאָרְחֵיהּ דִּקְרָא הָכֵי הוּא, דְּהָא קְרָאֵי אִינוּן הָכֵי. לָא. דְּכֻלְּהוּ לְאַחֲזָאָה מִלָּה קָא אַתְיָין. אוּף הָכָא, לְאַחֲזָאָה מִלָּה קָא אַתְיָא, מִי יְמַלֵּל: כִּדְכְתִיב וְקָטַפְתָּ מְלִילֹת. גְּבוּרוֹת ה', בְּגִין דְּסַגִּיאִין אִינוּן, דְּהָא כָּל גְּזֵרָא דְּדִינָא, מִתַּמָּן קָא אַתְיָא, וְעַל דָּא, מַאן אִיהוּ דִיסַלֵּק וְיַעֲבַר גְּזֵרָה חֲדָא, מֵאִינוּן גְּבוּרָאן דְּעָבֵיד קוּדְשָׁא בְּרִיךְ הוּא.

817. He opened the discussion saying: "Who can utter the mighty acts (Heb. *Gvurot*) of Hashem? who can declare all His praise?" (Tehilim 106:2). This verse has been explained, yet why say "utter" instead of the usual "speak"? If, you say scripture is wont TO USE SYNONYMS FOR THE BEAUTY OF STYLE, it is not so. But all verses WITH SYNONYMS convey a specific meaning. Here, too, there is a specific meaning in "utter (Heb. *yemalel*)," as in the verse "pluck the ears (Heb. *melilot*)" (Devarim. 23:26), WHICH IS DERIVED FROM CUTTING AND SEVERANCE. "The Gvurot of Hashem" are numerous, since all verdicts come from thence, FROM THE GVUROT OF HASHEM, THE LEFT COLUMN. SCRIPTURE therefore SAYS: "WHO CAN UTTER GVUROT OF HASHEM," WHICH MEANS who will be able to cancel and annul one decree of the mighty acts performed by the Holy One, blessed be He.

818. תּוּ, מִי יְמַלֵּל, וִידַבֵּר, כֹּלָא חַד. יְדַבֵּר, דְּהָא כַּמָה וְכַמָה גְּבוּרָאן אִינּוּן, דְּלֵית לוֹן חוּשְׁבָּנָא, כַּמָה מָארֵי דְּדִינִין, כַּמָה מָארֵי תְּרֵיסִין, כַּמָה גַרְדִּינֵי נִמוּסִין, וּמִלוּלָא לָא יָכִיל לְמַלָּלָא לוֹן.

818. We should also add that 'utter' and 'speak' are the same and that UTTER MEANS speak. How numerous are the mighty acts, the prosecutors, the advocates and the executioners of those who break the Law. Speech cannot enumerate them, HENCE THE VERSE SAYS, "WHO CAN UTTER THE MIGHTY ACTS OF HASHEM."

819. וּבַמָּה יְדִיעָן, כֻּלְּהוּ בְּהַגָּדָה, דְּאִית בֵּיהּ רָזָא דְּחָכְמְתָא, דְּהָא בְּמִלוּלָא וּבַאֲמִירָה לָא יָכִיל לְמַלָּלָא לוֹן. לְמִנְדַּע לוֹן, אֲבָל בְּהַגָּדָה יְדִיעָן, כְּמָה דִכְתִיב, דּוֹר לְדוֹר יְשַׁבַּח מַעֲשֶׂיךָ וּגְבוּרוֹתֶיךָ יַגִּידוּ, בְּרָזָא דָא יָדְעִין, אֲבָל גְּבוּרָתֶךָ דְּהִיא גְּבוּרָה תַּתָּאָה, יְדַבֵּרוּ, דִּכְתִיב וּגְבוּרָתְךָ יְדַבֵּרוּ.

819. THE MIGHTY ACTS OF HASHEM are made known through recital, which contains the secret of wisdom, AND THROUGH WISDOM THEY CAN BE KNOWN. For through utterance and speech, there is no uttering and knowing them, only through recital, as it is written: "One generation shall praise Your works to another, and shall declare (recite) Your mighty acts" (Tehilim 145:4), through which secret they are made known; NAMELY BY RECITAL, THE SECRET OF WISDOM. But of Your Gvurah, the lower Gvurah WITHIN THE NUKVA, they shall talk, FOR IT CAN BE SPOKEN OF, as it is written: "and talk of Your Gvurah" (Ibid. 11).

820. יַשְׁמִיעַ כָּל תְּהִלָּתוֹ, דְּסַגִּיאִין אִינּוּן דִּינִין, דְּאִשְׁתְּמוֹדְעָן וּמִתְחַבְּרָן בְּתִהְלָה, וְכַמָה חֵילִין, וְכַמָה מַשִׁירְיָין דְּמִתְחַבְּרָן בָּהּ, כִּדְכְתִיב, הֲיֵשׁ מִסְפָּר לִגְדוּדָיו, וְעַל דָּא, מַאן יָכִיל לְאִשְׁתְּמַע כָּל תְּהִלָּתוֹ.

820. "Who can declare all His praise?" For many judgments are seen by it and are united in praise, and several hosts join in praise, as it is written: "Is there any number to His armies" (Iyov 25:3). Hence "who can declare all His praise?"

821. תָּא חֲזֵי, מִצְרָאֵי כֻּלְּהוּ חַכִּימִין הֲווֹ, וּמִסִּטְרָא דִּגְבוּרָה קָא נָפְקֵי, כַּמָּה חֵילִין וְכַמָּה מַשִּׁירְיָין, וְכַמָּה דַרְגִּין עַל דַּרְגִּין, עַד דִּמְטוֹ לְגַבֵּי דַרְגִּין תַּתָּאִין, וּמִצְרָאֵי הֲווֹ חֲרָשִׁין וְחַכִּימִין בְּהוֹ, וְיָדְעִין סְתִימִין דְּעָלְמָא, וְאִסְתַּכָּלוּ הָא, דִּבְזִמְנָא דְיַעֲקֹב קַיָּים בְּעָלְמָא, לָא אִית עַמָּא דְּשָׁלְטָא עַל בְּנוֹי, וְיָדְעוּ דְּהָא יִשְׁתַּעְבְּדוּ בְּהוֹ בְּיִשְׂרָאֵל זִמְנִין סַגִּיאִין.

821. Come and see: All the Egyptians were wise, on the side of Gvurah, NAMELY THE LEFT COLUMN, whence legions and hosts come forth and grades that reach the lower grades. The Egyptians, who were sorcerers, had knowledge of them, and knew of the undisclosed secrets in the world. They saw that as long as Jacob lived in this world, no nation could rule over his children, yet they knew that they would enslave Yisrael for a long period.

822. כֵּיוָן דְּמִית יַעֲקֹב חָדוּ, אִסְתַּכָּלוּ מַה יְהֵא בְּסוֹפָא, עַד דִּמְטוֹ לְגוֹרֶן הָאָטָד, דְּאִיהוּ גְּזֵרָא דְדִינָא שַׁלִּיטָא, אָטָ"ד בְּגִי' יַד, כְּד"א וַיַּרְא יִשְׂרָאֵל אֶת הַיָּד הַגְּדוֹלָה וגו', כֵּיוָן דִּמְטוֹ לַאֲתַר דָּא, חָמוּ גְּבוּרָאן דְּנָפְקֵי מֵהַאי אָטָד. אַמַּאי אִקְרֵי אָטָד. אֶלָּא, מַה אָטָד נָפְקֵי כּוּבִין לְהַאי סִטְרָא וּלְהַאי סִטְרָא, הָכִי נָמֵי יַ"ד, נָפְקֵי מִינָהּ אֶצְבְּעָאן, לְהַאי סִטְרָא וּלְהַאי סִטְרָא, וְכָל אֶצְבְּעָא וְאֶצְבְּעָא סָלֵיק בְּכַמָּה גְּבוּרָאן, בְּכַמָּה דִינִין, וּבְכַמָּה נְמוּסִין, כְּדֵין וַיִּסְפְּדוּ שָׁם מִסְפֵּד גָּדוֹל וְכָבֵד מְאֹד עַל כֵּן קָרָא שְׁמָהּ אָבֵל מִצְרָיִם, וַדַּאי אֵבֶל כָּבֵד זֶה לְמִצְרַיִם, וְלָא לְאָחֳרָא.

822. When Jacob died they rejoiced THAT NOW THEY WOULD BE ABLE TO ENSLAVE YISRAEL. They looked to see what would become of it and saw the threshing floor of Atad, the prevailing punishment, as 'Atad' has the same numerical value as 'hand', mentioned in the verse: "And Yisrael saw that great work (lit. 'hand') which Hashem did upon Egypt" (Shemot 14:31). When they came to this place, they saw the mighty acts coming from Atad UPON THEM, NAMELY THE TEN PLAGUES OF EGYPT AND THE PARTING OF THE RED SEA. Why is it called *Atad* (Eng. 'thorn-bush')? As the thorns grow on both sides of the thorn-bush, so do the fingers of the hand, each containing numerous Gvurot, punishments and decrees. Hence "they mourned with a great and very sore lamentation...so that the name of it was called the mourning of the Egyptians." This was truly a grievous mourning for the Egyptians, and no one else.

823. ר"ש פָּרֵישׁ פָּרְשָׁתָא. נָפְקֵי מִגּוֹ מְעַרְתָּא, אֲמַר חָמֵינָא דְּיוֹמָא דֵין יִנְפּוֹל בֵּיתָא בְּמָתָא, וְיַעְדְרוּן תְּרֵי רוֹמָאֵי מְקַטְרְגִין. אִי אֲנָא בְּמָתָא לָא יִנְפּוֹל בֵּיתָא. אַהֲדְרוּ לְגוֹ מְעַרְתָּא יָתְבוּ.

823. When Rabbi Shimon explained the verses, they went out of the cave WHERE THEY SAT. He said: I see that today a house in town will collapse, and two Roman informers will die there. If I will be in town, the house will not fall, FOR MY MERIT WILL PROTECT THEM. They returned to the cave, FOR HE DID NOT WISH TO RETURN TO HIS TOWN, AND THAT HIS MERIT WILL PROTECT THEM, BUT THAT THE HOUSE SHOULD FALL, AND THE INFORMERS BE KILLED. They sat down.

83. "Lift up your voice, O daughter of Galim"

A Synopsis
Rabbi Shimon discusses the importance of "praising The Creator" [uttering holy words that ignite awesome spiritual forces] with a pleasant voice. We learn that the "daughter of Galim (lit. 'waves')" refers to Malchut, our physical world, the fourth and completing aspect to the three Patriarchs who represent the Upper World dimension called Zeir Anpin. We then discover that the term "daughter of the waves" signifies the abundance of Light that flows from Binah into Malchut. This energy embodies the Light of the blissful World to Come. It is explained that Malchut was born from the side of judgment, and thus, has the power to break and triumph over the dark side. Malchut is called "poor," for like the moon, for she has no Light of her own. However, when our prayers and the singing from worlds above unite Male and Female, Malchut [the moon] shines with abundance and wholeness. Finally, the Zohar reveals that King David's spiritual endeavors elevated the world [moon] from spiritual poverty into wealth. Thus, when David left this world, Solomon assumed spiritual command over a world that was now spiritually whole.

The Relevance of this Passage
The spiritual Light that shines through these sacred verses sweetens our prayers with pleasantness and song so that they will be heard and well received above. The Light that awaits us in the World to Come is ignited and its warm rays illuminate the here and now. Our connection to King David helps unite our body and soul and the cosmic male and female principles, bringing wholeness and radiance to our existence.

824. פָּתַח ר"ש וַאֲמַר, צַהֲלִי קוֹלֵךְ בַּת גַּלִים וגו' צַהֲלִי קוֹלֵךְ, הַאי קְרָא לִכְנֶסֶת יִשְׂרָאֵל אִתְּמַר, בְּגִין דְּאִיהִי מְשַׁבַּחַת לֵיהּ לְקוּדְשָׁא בְּרִיךְ הוּא, בְּקָלָא מְשַׁבְּחָא, וְעַל דָּא צַהֲלִי קוֹלֵךְ. מֵהָכָא אוֹלִיפְנָא, כָּל מַאן דְּבָעֵי לְשַׁבְּחָא לְקוּדְשָׁא בְּרִיךְ הוּא בְּקָלָא, בָּעְיָא לֵיהּ קָלָא נְעִימוּתָא, דְּיֶעֱרַב לְאַחֲרָנִין דְּשַׁמְעִין לֵיהּ, וְאִי לָאו, לָא יָקוּם לְאַרְמָא קָלָא.

824. Rabbi Shimon opened the discussion saying: "Lift up your voice, O daughter of galim (lit. 'waves')..." (Yeshayah 10:30). "Lift up your voice" was addressed to the Congregation of Yisrael, which praises the Holy One, blessed be He, with a singing voice. Hence IT WAS SAID TO HER, "Lift up

your voice." From this, we learn that whoever wishes to praise the Holy One, blessed be He, aloud, should have a pleasant voice, which would be agreeable to the listeners. Otherwise, he should not raise his voice.

825. תָּא חֲזֵי, לֵיוָאֵי דְּאַתְיָין מִסִּטְרָא דָא, דִּכְתִּיב, וּמִבֶּן חֲמִשִּׁים שָׁנָה יָשׁוּב מִצְבָא הָעֲבוֹדָה וְגוֹ'. מ"ט. בְּגִין דְּקָלֵיהּ נָמִיךְ, וְלָא יֶעֱרַב לְאוּדְנִין, כִּשְׁאָר חַבְרוֹי, כְּדֵין מְעַבְרִין לֵיהּ מֵהַאי צְבָא הָעֲבוֹדָה דִּלְעֵילָא, דְּקַיְימִין לְנַגְּנָא לְגַבֵּי הַאי הָעֲבוֹדָה, וּלְיַקְּרָא שְׁמָא קַדִּישָׁא כִּדְקָא חָזֵי.

825. Come and see: It is written of the Levites, who come of the side OF SINGING AND PRAISING: "And from the age of fifty years they shall go out of the ranks of the service" (Bemidbar 8:25). What is the reason thereof? IN OLD AGE, the voice fails, and is not agreeable to the ear, as THE VOICE OF his companions. He therefore retires from the high ranks of service, whose service is to play and to glorify the Holy Name as befits.

826. חֵילִין לְעֵילָא, חֵילִין וּמַשְׁרְיָין לְגַבֵּי תַּתָּאֵי, לְשַׁבְּחָא שְׁמָא קַדִּישָׁא, וּלְזַמְּרָא לוֹן. וּבְגִינֵי כָּךְ יָשׁוּב מִצְבָא הָעֲבוֹדָה, וּבְגִין דְּכַנֶ"י קָא מְשַׁבְּחָא לֵיהּ לְקוּדְשָׁא בְּרִיךְ הוּא, אֲמַר קְרָא, צַהֲלִי קוֹלֵךְ בַּת גַּלִּים, בַּת אֲבָהָן.

826. There are legions above and legions below, which praise the Holy Name and sing to it. Since THE SINGERS BELOW ARE THE LIKENESS OF THE SINGERS ABOVE, "they shall go out of the ranks of the service." Since the Congregation of Yisrael praises the Holy One, blessed be He, scripture says "Lift up your voice, O daughter of galim," NAMELY the daughter of the Patriarchs, FOR THE NUKVA IS A FOURTH TO THE FATHERS, WHO ARE CHESED, GVURAH AND TIFERET. SHE IS THEN THE DAUGHTER OF THE FATHERS.

827. תּוּ, בַּת גַּלִּים, עַלְמָא דְּאָתֵי אִקְרֵי גַּלִּים, בְּגִין דְּכֹלָּא קַיְימָא בֵּיהּ, וְאִתְכְּלִיל בֵּיהּ תְּלֵי תְלִים, וְנַפְקָא מִנֵּיהּ לְכֹלָּא. תּוּ בַּת גַּלִּים, כִּדְכְתִיב, גַּל נָעוּל, וְכָל אִינוּן גַּלִּים וּמַבּוּעִין, כֻּלְּהוּ נָפְקֵי מֵעַלְמָא דְּאָתֵי, וּכְנֶסֶת יִשְׂרָאֵל אִיהִי בַּת גַּלִּים.

827. "Daughter of the waves" is also the World to Come, BINAH, which is called waves, since everything is found in it in heaps, LIKE THE WAVES IN THE OCEAN whence they come forth unto all FACES AND WORLDS. We can also interpret "daughter of the waves" as in the words "a fountain (Heb. *gal*) sealed" (Shir Hashirim 4:12), THE NUKVA'S MOCHIN BEING CALLED GAL, DERIVED FROM 'REVEAL (HEB. *GILUY*)'. All the waves and springs come out from the World to Come, BINAH, and the Congregation of Yisrael, WHICH IS THE NUKVA, THE RECIPIENT OF BINAH, is called the daughter of the waves (Heb. *galim*).

828. תָּא חֲזֵי, הַאי קְרָא קַשְׁיָא, בְּקַדְמֵיתָא כְּתִיב צַהֲלִי קוֹלֵךְ, דְהוּא בְּגִין לְזַמְּרָא וְלַאֲרָמָא קָלָא, וּלְבָתַר כְּתִיב, הַקְשִׁיבִי, אִי הָכֵי אַמַּאי צַהֲלִי קוֹלֵךְ, כֵּיוָן דִכְתִיב הַקְשִׁיבִי. אֶלָּא, צַהֲלִי, בְּגִין לְשַׁבְּחָא וּלְזַמְּרָא. תָּא חֲזֵי, אִי יִשְׂרָאֵל שָׁרָאן לְשַׁבְּחָא וּלְזַמְּרָא לְקוּדְשָׁא בְּרִיךְ הוּא, כְּדֵין כְּתִיב הַקְשִׁיבִי, מ״ט, בְּגִין דְיִשְׂרָאֵל אִינוּן מְשַׁבְּחָן וּמְזַמְּרָן בְּגִינָהּ לְקוּדְשָׁא בְּרִיךְ הוּא, וְעַל דָּא כְּתִיב צַהֲלִי קוֹלֵךְ, וּכְתִיב הַקְשִׁיבִי.

828. Come and see: this verse is difficult. First it says, "Lift up your voice," and then "hearken." Why should she then lift up her voice, when she is asked to listen, AS THERE IS NO NEED TO RAISE THE VOICE WHILE LISTENING? HE ANSWERS: It says, "Lift up your voice" to sing and praise; TO WIT, RAISING THE VOICE IS FOR THE SAKE OF THE BEAUTY OF SONG, NOT TO SPEAK. Come and see: when Yisrael start to sing and praise the Holy One, blessed be He, it says "hearken." Why? Because they praise the Holy One, blessed be He, for her sake, FOR THE SAKE OF THE NUKVA. Therefore it is written: "Lift up your voice" and "hearken." THE FORMER ALLUDES TO YISRAEL AND THE LATTER TO THE NUKVA, FOR WHICH SAKE THEY SING AND PRAISE.

829. לַיְשָׁה: בְּגִין דְאַתְיָא מִסִּטְרָא דִגְבוּרָה, כְּד״א לַיִשׁ גִּבּוֹר בַּבְּהֵמָה. וְהַאי לַיְשָׁה, גְּבוּרָה, לְתַבְרָא חֵילִין וְתוֹקְפִין. עֲנִיָּה עֲנָתוּת, בְּגִין דְאִיהִי אַסְפַּקְלַרְיָא דְלָא נָהֲרָא, עֲנִיָּה וַדַּאי, לֵית לָהּ נְהוֹרָא לְסִיהֲרָא מִגַּרְמָהּ, אֶלָּא מַה דְיָהֵיב לָהּ שִׁמְשָׁא.

829. "Layshah (lit. 'lioness')": HE ASKS ABOUT THE MEANING OF "HEARKEN LAYSHAH" (SHIR HASHIRIM 4:12) AND SAYS, Since THE

NUKVA comes from the side of Gvurah, SHE IS CALLED A LIONESS. As "a lion which is strongest among beasts" (Mishlei 30:30), so is the lioness strong and breaks the power and strength OF THE OTHER SIDE. "O poor Anatot" (Yeshayah 10:30), WHY IS THE NUKVA SO CALLED? Because She is the mirror which does not shine, and is indeed poor, for the moon, THE NUKVA, has no light except what is given her by the sun.

830. עֲנָתוֹת אִיהוּ חֲקַל, כְּפַר חַד, וְשָׁרְיָין בֵּיה כֹּהֲנֵי מִסְכְּנֵי, דְּאַהֲדְרָן עַל פִּתְחִין, וְלֵית מַאן דְּיַשְׁגַּח בְּהוֹ, בְּגִין דְּכָל אִינּוּן בְּנֵי הַהוּא כַּפְרָא, קְלִיסִין הֲווֹ בְּעֵינַיְיהוּ דְעַמָּא, וּבֵיתַיְיהוּ רֵיקַנְיָין יַתִּיר מִכָּל עַמָּא, בַּר מַה דְּיָהֲבִין לוֹן, כְּמִסְכְּנֵי קְלִיסִין דְּעַמָּא. בְּגִין כָּך, סִיהֲרָא לֵית לָה נְהוֹרָא מִגַּרְמָהּ, אֶלָּא בְּשַׁעֲתָּא דְּאִתְחַבַּר עִמָּהּ שִׁמְשָׁא אִתְנְהֵיר.

830. Anatot (Eng. 'poverty') is a village, where poor priests beg from door to door. But no one cares since all its inhabitants are scorned by the people, and their houses are more empty than THE HOUSE OF the people, except for what they are given, being the poorest of the poor. The moon is called Anatot too, for she has no light of her own, and shines only when the sun joins her.

831. תָּא חֲזֵי, דִּכְתִיב, וּלְאֶבְיָתָר הַכֹּהֵן אָמַר הַמֶּלֶךְ עֲנָתוֹת לֵךְ עַל שָׂדֶךָ כִּי אִישׁ מָוֶת אָתָּה. וְכִי עַל דְּזַמִּין לֵיה אֲדוֹנִיָּהוּ, אִישׁ מָוֶת אִקְרֵי. אֶלָּא, בְּגִין דַּהֲוָה מֵאֲתַר מִסְכְּנָא, דְּאִידְבַק בֵּיה סִיהֲרָא, דְּאִיהִי עֲנָיָה עֲנָתוֹת.

831. Come and see: It is written, "And to Evyatar the priest the king said: 'Get you to Anatot, to your own fields; for you are worthy of death'" (I Melachim 2:26). HE ASKS: Was he worthy of death because Adoniyahu summoned him TO HIS FEAST? HE ANSWERS: Because he came from a poor place, and the moon was attached to him, the poor Anatot.

832. וְאִי תֵימָא, וְכִי הִתְעַנִּית בְּכֹל אֲשֶׁר הִתְעַנָּה אָבִי, בְּגִינֵי כָּך זַכָּאה דְּלָא קָטִיל לֵיה. אֶלָּא אֶבְיָתָר, בְּגִין דַּהֲוָה מֵאֲתַר מִסְכְּנָא, זָכָה בֵּיה דָּוִד, עַד לָא סָלֵיק לְמַלְכוּ, כַּד הֲוָה מִכְמָאן לֵיה שָׁאוּל, וַהֲוֵי אָרְחוֹי כְּמִסְכְּנָא, אֶבְיָתָר כְּגַוְונָא דָא, וּלְזִמְנָא דְּשַׁלָּט שְׁלֹמֹה, סִיהֲרָא קַיְימָא

בְּאַשְׁלָמוּתָא, וַהֲוָה בְּחֶדְוָותָא דַעֲתִירוּ, דְּכֹלָּא הֲוָה לֵיהּ, לָא זָכָה בֵּיהּ
אֶבְיָתָר.

832. You may say, SINCE IT IS WRITTEN, "Because you have been afflicted in all my father's afflictions" (Ibid.), it was due TO HIS POVERTY then that he did not kill him, WHY THEN IS HE CALLED "WORTHY OF DEATH"? HE REPLIES: Since Evyatar came from a poor place, David took recognition of him before he became king, when Saul pursued him, for he acted like a poor man, and Evyatar too. ALSO WHEN HE BECAME KING, THE KINGDOM WAS NOT YET WHOLE. But when Solomon reigned, the moon, THE NUKVA, attained perfection. He rejoiced since all was his. Evyatar therefore could not join him.

833. וַדַּאי שְׂדֵה עֲנָתוֹת, רָזָא דְמִלָּה הֲוָה, וְיִרְמְיָה דְּקָנֵי לֵיהּ, כֹּלָּא הֲוָה, בְּגִין לְאַחְסָנָא רָזָא עִלָּאָה. תָּא חֲזֵי, כָּךְ שָׁלְטָא סִיהֲרָא, שְׂדֵה תַּפּוּחִים אִקְרֵי, כָּךְ אִיהוּ בְּמִסְכֵּנוּ, שְׂדֵה עֲנָתוֹת. בְּגִינֵי כָּךְ, תּוּשְׁבַּחְתָּא דִלְתַתָּא, עָבֵיד לֵיהּ עֲתִירוּ, וּשְׁלֵימוּתָא.

833. Assuredly, the field of Anatot contains this secret OF THE NUKVA UNDER THE REIGN OF THE LEFT. Jeremiah bought THE FIELD OF ANATOT to attain the supernal secret. Come and see: when the moon, THE NUKVA, reigns, NAMELY IN FULL ILLUMINATION, she is called 'an apple field.' When she is poor, she is called 'the field of Anatot.' For this reason, the singing above brings her abundance and wholeness, BY BRINGING ABOUT THE UNION BETWEEN MALE AND FEMALE.

834. כְּמָה דְּדָוִד, כָּל יוֹמוֹי אִשְׁתַּדַּל לְמֶעְבַּד שְׁלִימוּ לָהּ, וּלְנַגְנָא זַמָּרֵי, לְזַמְּרָא וּלְשַׁבְּחָא לְתַתָּא, וְכַד דָּוִד אִסְתַּלִּיק מֵעָלְמָא, שָׁבֵיק לָהּ בִּשְׁלִימוּ, וּשְׁלֹמֹה נָטַל לָהּ בְּעוּתְרָא, בִּשְׁלֵימוּתָא, דְּהָא סִיהֲרָא נָפְקָא מִמִּסְכֵּנוּ, וְעָאלַת לְעוּתְרָא, דִּבְהַךְ עוּתְרָא, שָׁלַט עַל כָּל מַלְכֵי אַרְעָא.

834. David strove all his days to perfect her by players who sang and praised her, FOR THROUGH THIS THE NUKVA ATTAINS PERFECTION. When David departed from the world, he left her whole and Solomon received her plentiful and whole. For the moon came out of poverty into wealth, through which he reigned over all the kings of the land.

84. "Silver was not accounted for anything in the days of Solomon"

A Synopsis
Here, the Zohar reveals the mighty power of the sun, Zeir Anpin, and its ability to transmute the dust of the world into gleaming gold. Moreover, we're told that the merciful Light of Zeir Anpin removes judgment from Malchut, thereby increasing gold. Such was the spiritual landscape during the reign of King Solomon. Because David had already perfected Malchut, Solomon's mystical power was directed at arousing wealth, love and Light. However, we learn that Solomon miscalculates the spiritual processes taking place in the Upper Worlds and rejects the Right Column energy of mercy [silver]. This action darkens the moon, allowing judgment to impact our world, hence the phrase, "Silver was not accounted for anything"

Moreover, because sacrifices are no longer offered in the temple, Judgment occurs each day of our lives. The Zohar then explains that the prayers of man can perfect the Upper and Lower World and remove the Left Column force of judgment.

The Relevance of this Passage
When we extend mercy to our friends and enemies, the Light of Zeir Anpin illuminates our own lives with mercy, transmuting judgments set against us into praise. When mercy is not part of our consciousness, Judgment is allowed to befall us every day. Hence, this passage awakens mercy within us, so that we may bestow it upon others. Our connection to these words helps perfect the Upper and Lower Worlds, whose union also removes judgment from own lives.

835. וְעַל דָּא אֵין כֶּסֶף נֶחְשָׁב בִּימֵי שְׁלֹמֹה. אֶלָּא כֹּלָּא דְהַב, דְּאִתְרַבֵּי דְהַב, וּבְהַהוּא זִמְנָא כְּתִיב, וְעַפְרוֹת זָהָב לוֹ, דְּהָא עָפָר דִּלְעֵילָא, הֲוָה מִסְתַּכֵּל בֵּיה שִׁמְשָׁא, וּבְאִסְתַּכְּלוּתָא דְּשִׁמְשָׁא וְתוֹקְפֵיה, עַפְרָא עָבֵיד וְאַסְגֵּי דְהַב.

835. For this reason, "silver was not accounted for anything in the days of Solomon" (I Melachim 10:21), but all was made of gold, and gold increased. At that time, it says, "And he had dust of gold" (Iyov 28:6), since the sun, ZEIR ANPIN, looked upon the upper dust, THE NUKVA, and through its strength, it turned the dust into gold.

836. תָּא חֲזֵי, מְטוּרֵי דִּנְהִירוּ, דְּתוֹקְפָא דְּשִׁמְשָׁא תַּמָּן, עַפְרָא דְּאַרְעָא

בֵּינֵי טוּרֵי, כֻּלְּהוּ עֲבְדֵי דְהַב, וְאִלְמָלֵא חֵיוָון בִּישִׁין דִּרְבִיאוּ תַּמָּן, בְּנֵי
נָשָׁא לָא הֲווֹ מִסְכְּנֵי, בְּגִין דְּתוּקְפָא דְשִׁמְשָׁא אַסְגֵּי דְהַב.

836. Come and see: where the dust of the earth turns into gold on the mountains, where the sunlight is strong everything turns into gold. And were it not for the wild animals which roamed there, people would not have been poor, because the power of the sun increases gold.

837. בְּג"כ, בְּיוֹמוֹי דִשְׁלֹמֹה, אֵין כֶּסֶף נֶחְשָׁב לִמְאוּמָה, דְּהָא תַּקִּיפָא
דְשִׁמְשָׁא אִסְתַּכַּל בְּעַפְרָא, וְאַסְגֵּי לֵיהּ דְּהַב. וְעוֹד דְּהַהוּא עַפְרָא סְטְרָא
דְדִינָא אִיהוּ, כַּד אִסְתַּכַּל בֵּיהּ שִׁמְשָׁא, נָטַל תּוּקְפָא וְאִתְרַבֵּי דַהֲבָא.
כֵּיוָן דְּאִסְתַּכַּל שְׁלֹמֹה בָּה, שַׁבַּח וְאַכְרֵיז וַאֲמַר, הַכֹּל הָיָה מִן הֶעָפָר
וְגוֹ'.

837. Hence in the days of Solomon, "silver was not accounted for anything," for the strength of the sun was upon the dust and turned it into gold. Also, the dust is of the side of Judgment, WHICH IS LEFT WITHOUT RIGHT, NOT ILLUMINATING, and when the sun, ZEIR ANPIN, looked upon it, NAMELY POURED CHASSADIM UPON IT, it removed the strength OF JUDGMENT FROM IT, and gold increased. When Solomon saw this, he praised it by saying: "All was of the dust" (Kohelet 3:20).

838. וְע"ד שְׁלֹמֹה לָא אִצְטְרִיךְ לְנַגְּנָא כְּדָוִד, אֶלָּא שִׁירָתָא דְּאִיהוּ
רְחִימֵי דְעוֹתְרָא, דְּהוּא נְהִירוּ וּרְחִימוּ דְּכָל תּוּשְׁבְּחָן דְּעָלְמָא בֵּיהּ הֲווֹ,
תּוּשְׁבַּחְתָּא דְמַטְרוֹנִיתָא כַּד יָתְבָא בְּכָרְסְיָיא לְקָבְלֵיהּ דְּמַלְכָּא קָאֲמַר.

838. Hence Solomon had no need of playing like David, SINCE THE NUKVA WAS ALREADY MADE PERFECT, but he sang SHIR HASHIRIM, which is love and wealth, light and love, for all the songs of the world were in SOLOMON'S SONG, who recited the song of the Matron, the NUKVA, when she sat upon her throne facing the King.

839. כְּתִיב וַיִּתֵּן הַמֶּלֶךְ אֶת הַכֶּסֶף בִּירוּשָׁלַם כָּאֲבָנִים, בְּגִין דְּכֹלָּא הֲוָה
דְהַב, וְעַפְרָא אִתְקַשַּׁר בִּשְׂמָאלָא, בְּסִטְרָא דִרְחִימוּ, כַּד"א שְׂמֹאלוֹ תַּחַת

לְרֵאשִׁי, וְשִׁמְשָׁא אִתְדַּבַּק בַּהֲדָה, וְלָא אִתְעֲדִי מִינָה.

839. It is written: "And the king made silver to be in Jerusalem like stones" (I Melachim 10:27). Because all was made of gold and the dust, THE NUKVA, was linked to the left on the side of love, NAMELY LOVER'S LOVE, THE LOVE OF THE LEFT, as it is written: "His left hand is under my head" (Shir Hashirim 2:6), the sun, ZEIR ANPIN, cleaved to her, and did not part.

840. שְׁלֹמֹה טָעָה בְּהַאי, דְּהָא חָמָא דְּאִתְקְרֵיב סִיהֲרָא בְּשִׁמְשָׁא, וִימִינָא מְחַבְּקָא, וּשְׂמָאלָא תְּחוֹת רֵישָׁא, כֵּיוָן דְּאִתְקְרִיבוּ דָּא בְּדָא, אָמַר הָא אִתְקְרִיבוּ כַּחֲדָא, יְמִינָא מַה הָכָא, דְּהָא יְמִינָא לָאו אִיהוּ אֶלָּא בְּגִין לְקָרְבָא, כֵּיוָן דְּאִתְקְרִיבוּ דָּא בְּדָא לְמַאי אִצְטְרִיךְ, מִיָּד אֵין כֶּסֶף נֶחְשָׁב בִּימֵי שְׁלֹמֹה.

840. Solomon made a mistake when he saw the moon attached to the sun, the right OF ZEIR ANPIN embracing her WITH CHASSADIM and the left OF ZEIR ANPIN under her head WITH THE ILLUMINATION OF CHOCHMAH. THE LEFT BECAME HER HEAD. As RIGHT AND LEFT were attached to each other, AND CHOCHMAH ON THE LEFT WAS ALREADY CLOTHED WITH THE RIGHT, he said: Now that they are linked together, what need is there for the right seeing that the function of the right, CHASSADIM, was to draw near ZEIR ANPIN AND THE NUKVA, SO THAT CHOCHMAH WITHIN THE NUKVA SHALL BE CLOTHED IN CHASSADIM OF ZEIR ANPIN? Now that they are together, there is no more need OF THE RIGHT, CHASSADIM. Straightaway "silver was not accounted for anything," FOR HE REJECTED THE SILVER, WHICH IS RIGHT, AS EXPLAINED.

841. א"ל קוּדְשָׁא בְּרִיךְ הוּא, אַנְתְּ דָּחִית יְמִינָא, חַיָּיךְ, אַנְתְּ תִּצְטְרֵךְ לְחֶסֶד בְּנֵי נָשָׁא, וְלָא תִּשְׁכַּח. מִיָּד סָטָא שִׁמְשָׁא מִלְקַבֵּל סִיהֲרָא, וְסִיהֲרָא שַׁרְיָא לְאִתְחַשְּׁכָא, וַהֲוָה שְׁלֹמֹה מְהַדַּר עַל פִּתְחִין, וַאֲמַר, אֲנִי קֹהֶלֶת, וְלָא הֲוָה מַאן דְּיַעֲבֵד עִמֵּיהּ חֶסֶד, מ"ט, בְּגִין דִּדְחָה דְּדָחָה יְמִינָא, וְלָא חָשֵׁיב לֵיהּ, הה"ד, אֵין כֶּסֶף נֶחְשָׁב בִּימֵי שְׁלֹמֹה לִמְאוּמָה.

841. The Holy One, blessed be He, said to him: 'You have rejected the right, WHICH IS CHESED. Upon your life, you shall yet need kindness

(Chesed) from people, but you shall not be offered any'. Immediately the sun, ZEIR ANPIN, declined from opposite the moon, THE NUKVA, and she began to darken. Solomon went begging, saying 'I am Kohelet,' but none did any kindness by him. Why? Because he rejected the right, CHESED, and did not consider it, as it says, "Silver was not accounted for anything in the days of Solomon."

842. וְעַ"ד, כָּל דְּאַסְגֵּי תּוּשְׁבְּחָן לְגַבֵּי קוּדְשָׁא בְּרִיךְ הוּא, אַסְגֵּי שְׁלָמָא לְעֵילָא, בְּגִינֵי כָּךְ הַקְשִׁיבִי לַיְשָׁה. כְּתִיב לַיִשׁ אוֹבֵד מִבְּלִי טֶרֶף וְגוֹ', לַיִשׁ הַיְינוּ לַיְשָׁה, כִּדְכְתִיב, חָק חֻקָּה. אוֹבֵד: כִּדְכְתִיב, וּבָאוּ הָאוֹבְדִים. מִבְּלִי טֶרֶף: בְּגִין, דְּאִיהִי תָּבְעָה עֲלֵיהּ לְמֵיהַב, כִּדְכְתִיב, וַתָּקָם בְּעוֹד לַיְלָה וַתִּתֵּן טֶרֶף לְבֵיתָהּ.

842. Hence, the more one praises the Holy One, blessed be He, THE RIGHT, peace abounds above. SCRIPTURE therefore SAYS, "Hearken Laysha," WHICH IS THE NUKVA WHEN SEPARATED FROM THE HOLY ONE, BLESSED BE HE, THE RIGHT. It is written: "The old lion (Heb. *layish*) perishes for lack of prey" (Iyov 4:11). Laysha is the feminine of *layish*, as *chok* (Eng. 'law') and *chukat* (Eng. 'ordinance'). THEY HAVE THE SAME MEANING, AS DO LAYISH AND LAYSHA. "Perishes (Heb. *oved*)": As in "who were lost (Heb. *ovdim*)" (Yeshayah 27:13), MEANS THAT IT IS LOST. "For lack of prey," since THE NUKVA demands FROM ZEIR ANPIN to give Her, as it says, "She rises also while it is yet night, and gives food (prey) to her household" (Mishlei 31:15).

843 וּבְנֵי לָבִיא יִתְפָּרְדוּ. בְּגִין, דְּכֻלְּהוּ חַיָּילִין, כַּד אִיהִי יְהִיבַת, לְהוֹן טֶרֶף, כֻּלְּהוּ מִתְחַבְּרָן כְּחַד, וְיָנְקִין כְּחַד. וְכַד אִיהִי יָתְבָא מִבְּלִי טֶרֶף, דְּגָרַם גָּלוּתָא, וַדַּאי בְּנֵי לָבִיא יִתְפָּרְדוּ, מִתְפָּרְשָׁן כֻּלְּהוּ, לְכַמָּה סִטְרִין וְאָרְחִין, בְּגִין לְאַשְׁכְּחָא לְמֶעְבַּד דִּינָא. וְעַ"ד, בְּזִמְנָא דְקָרְבָּנָא אִתְעֲבֵיד, כֹּלָּא מִתְתַּקְנָן, וּמִתְקַרְבִין כַּחֲדָא, כִּדְקָאַמְרָן, הַשְׁתָּא דְּקָרְבָּנָא לָא אִתְעֲבֵיד, וַדַּאי בְּנֵי לָבִיא יִתְפָּרְדוּ, וּבְגִינֵי כָּךְ, לֵית לָן יוֹם דְּלָא אִשְׁתַּכַּח בֵּיהּ דִּינָא, דְּהָא לָא מִתְעָרִין עִלָּאִין וְתַתָּאִין בִּשְׁלִימוּ עִלָּאָה כִּדְקָאַמְרָן.

843. "And the lion's whelps are scattered abroad" (Iyov 4:11), for all the armies, NAMELY THE ANGELS WHO ISSUE FROM HER, come together as

one when She gives them prey and feed together. But when She has no prey, on account of the exile, "the lion's whelps are scattered abroad" and Her armies go different ways and roads to find a place to execute judgments. So, when sacrifices are offered, everybody is in order, and they come together like we said. Now, IN TIME OF EXILE, when sacrifice is not offered, surely "the lion's whelps are scattered abroad." Therefore, not a day passes without judgment, since the upper and lower are not aroused by supreme perfection.

844. תָּא חֲזֵי, הַשְׁתָּא צְלוֹתָא דְּב״נ, אִתְעַר שְׁלִימוּ, לְעֵילָא וְתַתָּא, וּבְבִרְכָתָא דְּבָרֵיךְ לְקוּדְשָׁא בְּרִיךְ הוּא, מִתְבָּרְכִין עִלָּאִין וְתַתָּאִין. וְע״ד בִּצְלוֹתָא דְּיִשְׂרָאֵל מִתְבָּרְכָאן עָלְמִין. מַאן דִּמְבָרֵךְ לֵיהּ לְקוּדְשָׁא בְּרִיךְ הוּא, יִתְבָּרַךְ. מַאן דְּלָא בָּרֵיךְ לְקוּדְשָׁא בְּרִיךְ הוּא, לָא יִתְבָּרַךְ. הֲדָא הוּא דִכְתִיב כִּי מְכַבְּדַי אֲכַבֵּד וּבֹזַי יֵקַלּוּ.

844. Come and see: NOW IN THE TIME OF EXILE man's prayer causes perfection above and below, and the upper and lower are blessed by the blessing of the Holy One, blessed be He. Hence, Yisrael's prayer causes the worlds to be blessed. Whoever blesses the Holy One, blessed be He, shall be blessed, and whoever does not bless the Holy One, blessed be He, is not blessed, as it is written: "For them that honor Me I will honor, and they that despise Me shall be lightly esteemed" (I Shmuel 2:30).

85. The cup of blessing

A Synopsis
Rav Hamnuna Saba expounds upon the significance of a wine cup, the table, and the blessings made over the wine. The sage equates the cup to the receptive nature of Malchut and the wine to the supernal blessings that light our world. It is explained that both hands are used to receive the cup, signifying the Right and Left Columns which are required to create a circuit of spiritual energy. We're told that one should also bless the table to ensure sustenance, signified by the bread and wine that sit upon it.

The Relevance of this Passage
The tremendous Light that is awakened and drawn to this world through the blessing of wine is summoned forth, bringing us Light, balance, and sustenance.

845. רַב הַמְנוּנָא סָבָא, כַּסָּא דִבְרָכָתָא לָא יָהֵיב לֵיהּ לְב״נ אָחֳרָא לְבָרְכָא, אֶלָּא אִיהוּ אַקְדֵּים וְנָטֵיל לֵיהּ בִּתְרֵי יְדוֹי וּמְבָרֵךְ. וְהָא אֲמָרָן, דְּבָעֵי לְנַטְלָא לֵיהּ בִּימִינָא וּבִשְׂמָאלָא, וְאע״ג דְּכֹלָּא אִתְעָרוּ בֵּיהּ, שַׁפִּיר הוּא, אֲבָל כַּסָּא דִבְרָכָה הָכֵי אִצְטְרִיךְ כּוֹס, דִּכְתִיב כּוֹס יְשׁוּעוֹת אֶשָּׂא, דְּהָא בְּהַאי כּוֹס, אִתְנְגִידוּ בִּרְכָאן, מֵאִינוּן יְשׁוּעוֹת דִּלְעֵילָא, וְהוּא נָטֵיל לוֹן, וְכָנֵישׁ לוֹן לְגַבֵּיהּ, וְתַמָּן אִתְנְטֵיר חַמְרָא עִלָּאָה, וְאִתְכְּנֵישׁ בְּהַהוּא כּוֹס, וּבְעֵינָן לְבָרְכָא לֵיהּ בִּימִינָא, וּבִשְׂמָאלָא, וְחַמְרָא דְּאִיהוּ בְּהַאי כּוֹס כָּנֵישׁ, דְּיִתְבָּרְכוּן כַּחֲדָא, וּבְעֵינָן לְבָרְכָא פָּתוֹרָא, דְּלָא תְהֵא רֵיקַנְיָא מִנַּהֲמָא וְחַמְרָא כֹּלָא כַּחֲדָא.

845. Rav Hamnuna Saba (the elder) gave his cup of blessing to no one, but hastened to receive it with both hands and say the blessing. We have said that it should be received by both right and left. Even though others have explained it, and we agree with it. But the secret thereof is that for a cup of blessing we need a cup, as it is written "I will raise the cup of salvation" (Tehilim 116:13), NAMELY THE NUKVA CALLED THE CUP. By means of this cup blessings are drawn from the salvations above, AND THE CUP, THE NUKVA, receives and gathers them to it. There the supernal wine is preserved, THE ILLUMINATION OF THE LEFT FROM BINAH, and gathered in the cup, hence we need to bless it with both right and left; and the wine which is gathered in the cup will be blessed together, THAT IS, THE WINE

WHICH IS THE ILLUMINATION OF THE LEFT FROM BINAH, TOGETHER WITH THE CUP, BEING THE NUKVA. We should also bless the table, THE NUKVA, that it will not be without both bread and wine.

846. תָּא חֲזֵי, כְּנֶסֶת יִשְׂרָאֵל, כּוֹס שֶׁל בְּרָכָה אִקְרֵי, וְכֵיוָן דְּאִיהוּ כּוֹס שֶׁל בְּרָכָה, בְּעֵינָן יְמִינָא וּשְׂמָאלָא לְנַטְלָא לֵיהּ, וְהַהוּא כּוֹס אִתְיְיהִיב בֵּין יְמִינָא וּשְׂמָאלָא, וּבָעֵי דְּאִתְמַלְיָא חַמְרָא, בְּגִין חַמְרָא דְאוֹרַיְיתָא, דְּאִיהוּ נָפֵיק מֵעַלְמָא דְאָתֵי.

846. Come and see: the Congregation of Yisrael, THE NUKVA, is called a cup of blessing. Since it is a cup of blessing, we need both the right and left hands to receive it, for the cup is given between the right and left hands, CHASSADIM AND CHOCHMAH, AS HAS BEEN EXPLAINED. It should be filled with wine, because of the wine of the Torah, THE SECRET OF THE ILLUMINATION OF THE LEFT, which comes from the World to Come, BINAH.

847. וְתָא חֲזֵי, כּוֹס שֶׁל בְּרָכָה, בְּהַאי אִתְגַּלְיָין מִלִּין עִלָּאִין, הָכָא דַּאֲנַן בִּמְעַרְתָּא, אֵימָא הָכָא אִתְגַּלְיָיא רָזָא דִרְתִיכָא קַדִּישָׁא, כּוֹס שֶׁל בְּרָכָה בָּעֵי לְקַבְּלָא לֵיהּ בִּימִינָא וּשְׂמָאלָא, דָּא צָפוֹן וְדָרוֹם, וְכוֹס שֶׁל בְּרָכָה דִּיהֵא נָטִיל בְּרָכָה מִנַּיְיהוּ. מַאן כּוֹס שֶׁל בְּרָכָה, דָּא מִטָּתוֹ שֶׁלִּשְׁלֹמֹה, דִּבְעֵינָן דְּאִתְיְיהִיב בֵּין צָפוֹן לְדָרוֹם, וּבָעֵי לְאַנְחָא לָהּ בִּימִינָא, וְגוּפָא דְּיִתְתַּקַּן בַּהֲדַיְיהוּ, וְיִשְׁגַּח בֵּיהּ בְּהַהוּא כּוֹס, לְבָרְכָא לֵיהּ בְּאַרְבַּע בִּרְכָאן, בְּגִין דִּכְתִיב, תָּמִיד עֵינֵי ה' אֱלֹהֶיךָ בָּהּ וְגו'. אִשְׁתַּכַּח בְּכוֹס שֶׁל בְּרָכָה, רָזָא דִמְהֵימְנוּתָא, צָפוֹן וְדָרוֹם וּמִזְרָח וּמַעֲרָב, הָא רְתִיכָא קַדִּישָׁא כִּדְקָא חֲזֵי לֵיהּ.

847. Come and see: supernal things have been revealed here concerning the cup of blessing, while we stayed in the cave; here was revealed the secret of the Holy Chariot, CHESED, GVURAH, TIFERET AND MALCHUT. For the cup of blessing should be received with both right and left, which are north and south, CHESED AND GVURAH, and the cup of blessings receives its blessing from them. What is this cup of blessing? It is "his litter, that of Solomon" (Shir Hashirim 3: 7), NAMELY MALCHUT, which should be placed

between north and south, CHESED AND GVURAH, but CLOSER to the right. The body OF HE WHO BLESSES, TIFERET, should be prepared with them, and one should fix his eyes upon the cup and bless it with four blessings, since it says, "The eyes of Hashem your Elohim are always upon it" (Devarim 11:12). Thus there is a secret of faith in the cup of blessing; NAMELY north and south, east and west, CHESED, GVURAH, TIFERET AND MALCHUT. Here is a Holy Chariot worthy of it.

848. וּפָתוֹרָא בְּנַהֲמָא, בְּגִין דְּיִתְבָּרְכָא הַהוּא לֶחֶם דִּלְתַתָּא, וְיִתְבָּרַךְ לֶחֶם עוֹנִי, וִיהֵא לֶחֶם פַּנַּג, וְהָא אוֹקִימְנָא. וְיִשְׁתַּכַּח דִּכְנֶסֶת יִשְׂרָאֵל מִתְבָּרְכָא בְּד׳ סִטְרֵי עַלְמָא, לְעֵילָא וְתַתָּא. וְכוֹס שֶׁל בְּרָכָה, לְאִתְחַבְּרָא דָּוִד מַלְכָּא בַּאֲבָהָן, וְיִתְבָּרַךְ לְתַתָּא, דְּיִתְבָּרַךְ פָּתוֹרָא דְּב״נ, לְאִשְׁתַּכְּחָא בֵּיה מְזוֹנָא תָּדִיר.

848. There is bread upon the table, so that the lower bread, THE NUKVA, will be blessed, and the bread of poverty, THE NUKVA WHEN WITHOUT CHASSADIM, will be blessed and become millet bread WHEN HER CHOCHMAH IS CLOTHED IN CHASSADIM, AND SHE IS CALLED MILLET BREAD, as has been explained. The Congregation of Yisrael, THE NUKVA, is thus blessed above by the four directions of the world, CHESED, GVURAH, TIFERET AND MALCHUT, and above and below, NETZACH AND HOD. The cup of blessing brings the union between King David, THE NUKVA ABOVE THE CHEST, with the Patriarchs, CHESED, GVURAH AND TIFERET, WHENCE CHOCHMAH TAKES. And it is blessed below BY NETZACH HOD YESOD, AND THUS HAS CHASSADIM AS WELL, so that man's table be blessed that there will always be bread upon it.

849. קָמוּ כֻּלְּהוּ וּנְשָׁקוּ יְדוֹי, אָמְרוּ בְּרִיךְ רַחֲמָנָא דְּאָעֵילְנָא הָכָא, וּשְׁמַעְנָא מִלִּין אִלֵּין. נָפְקוּ מִן מְעַרְתָּא, וַאֲזָלוּ, כַּד עָאלוּ בְּמָתָא, חָמוּ עִיטְרָא דִּבְנֵי נָשָׁא דְּמִיתוּ, דְּנָפַל בֵּיתָא עֲלַיְיהוּ, יָתְבוּ וְחָמוּ דְּקָא סַפְדֵי לְאִינוּן דְּמִיתוּ, עִם אִינוּן רוֹמָאֵי.

849. They all rose and kissed his hands and said: Blessed be the Merciful One who brought us here to hear these words. They came out of the cave and went. When they reached the town, they saw dead men, upon whom a house fell. They sat and saw people who mourned those who died along with the Roman, FOR THE HOUSE COLLAPSED UPON JEWS AND GENTILES ALIKE.

86. "The threshing floor of Atad"

A Synopsis
Rabbi Shimon discusses the metaphor concerning the transference of earthly and spiritual power from Egypt to Yisrael. Next, we learn that Jacob's soul was the brightest since the Creation of the world. When Jacob departs this world from within the land of Egypt, which represents a domain of negativity, it is free from any influences issuing from the Other Side, and directly ascends to its proper place in the heavens.

The Relevance of this Passage
The ability to triumph over our Evil Inclinations [Egypt] and to transfer control and power to the will of our soul [Yisrael], is the great gift bestowed upon readers of this section. This action sets us on a course for greater spiritual growth, ensuring a lofty place in the World to Come and increased fulfillment in the here and now.

850. פָּתַח רִבִּי שִׁמְעוֹן וַאֲמַר, וַיָבֹאוּ עַד גֹּרֶן הָאָטָד, מַאן גֹּרֶן הָאָטָד. אֶלָּא, הָכָא אִתְרְמֵיז שָׁלְטָנוּתָא דְמִצְרָאֵי דְּאִתְעֲדֵי. גֹּרֶן הָאָטָד, דָא מְמַנָּא שׁוּלְטָנָא דְמִצְרָאֵי, דְּאִתְעֲדֵי מִקַּמֵּי שׁוּלְטָנוּתָא דְיִשְׂרָאֵל, דְּהָא חָמוּ גֹּרֶן כְּד"א מְלוּבָּשִׁים בְּגָדִים בַּגֹּרֶן, וְעַ"ד וַיִּסְפְּדוּ שָׁם מִסְפֵּד גָּדוֹל וְכָבֵד מְאֹד וְגו'.

850. Rabbi Shimon opened the discussion saying: "And they came to the threshing floor of Atad" (Beresheet 50:10). HE ASKS: What is the threshing floor of Atad? HE ANSWERS: It is an allusion to the dominion of Egypt, which is removed. The threshing floor of Atad is the dominion of Egypt which passed to give way to the dominion of Yisrael. For they saw a threshing floor, WHICH ALLUDES TO THE REIGN OF YISRAEL, like in "having put on their robes, in a threshing floor" (I Melachim 22:10). Therefore "they mourned with a great and very sore lamentation."

851. עַל כֵּן קָרָא שְׁמָהּ אָבֵל מִצְרַיִם עַד הַיּוֹם הַזֶּה, דְּוַדַּאי מִמִּצְרַיִם הֲוָה, אוֹף הָכָא לָאו דְּיוּדָאֵי נִינְהוּ אִלֵּין בַּכְיָין, אע"ג דְּמִיתוּ בֵּיהּ יוּדָאֵי, וְאִלֵּין יוּדָאֵי, אִלְמָלֵא הֲוֹו יוּדָאֵי, לָא מִיתוּ, וְכֵיוָן דְּמִיתוּ, קוּדְשָׁא בְּרִיךְ הוּא מְכַפֵּר חוֹבַיְיהוּ.

851. "So that the name of it was called the mourning of the Egyptians" (Beresheet 50:11): Assuredly the Egyptians MOURNED FOR THEIR DOMINION WHICH PASSED, but here also the weeping was not for Jews, though there were Jews among the dead. Had they been good Jews, they would not have been killed. But having died, the Holy One, blessed be He, pardons their sins.

852. אָמַר ר"ש תָּא חֲזֵי, דְּיַעֲקֹב אע"ג דְּנָפְקַת נִשְׁמָתֵיה בְּמִצְרַיִם, לָאו בִּרְשׁוּתָא אָחֳרָא נָפְקַת, מ"ט, כְּמָה דְּאִתְּמַר דְּלָא הֲוָה מִיּוֹמָא דְּאִתְבְּרֵי עָלְמָא, עַרְסָא שְׁלֵימָתָא, כְּהַהוּא עַרְסָא דְּיַעֲקֹב. בְּשַׁעְתָּא דַּהֲוָה סָלֵיק מֵעַלְמָא נִשְׁמָתֵיה מִיָּד אִתְקַשַּׁר בְּאַתְרֵיה, וְהָא אוּקִימְנָא.

852. Rabbi Shimon said, Come and behold: though Jacob yielded his soul in Egypt, it did not depart under the dominion of the other, NAMELY THE OTHER SIDE. Why? Because, as we learned, there has not been a bed more whole than Jacob's bed since the Creation of the world, FOR ALL HIS SONS WERE PROPER. As soon as he departed from the world, his soul joined its place, as has already been explained.

87. The embalming of Jacob

A Synopsis
The Zohar reveals the luminous power and influence of Jacob by recounting how the scents of the Garden of Eden and candlelight radiate in a cave during his presence. Next, we learn that the souls of the righteous pass through the cave of the Patriarchs to behold the spiritual deeds and Light they left behind. The process for embalming Kings is then expounded upon by Rabbi Aba and we learn that Jacob was embalmed to preserve both his body and soul so that he can join the Supernal Ark [Malchut]. Finally, it is revealed that Joseph is the chariot for Zeir Anpin, bridging Malchut with the Upper World. Hence, his keeping the covenant is deemed to have been accomplished in both worlds. This secret is alluded to by the two *yuds* יי in the word *Vayisem* (Eng: 'and he was put'). When Joseph left this world from the land of Egypt, it is said that he was put into two arks, or coffins. This means that he avoided the clutches of the Other Side and connected directly to the Shechinah [the upper Ark].

The Relevance of this Passage
If we read this passage with a contrite heart and soul, we can ignite the righteousness and spiritual power of Jacob and Joseph to help us rise above negativity in life [Egypt]. We are inspired to recognize the value of keeping the covenant, which ensures a connection to the Light of the Shechinah in this world and in the World to Come.

853. תָּא חֲזֵי, כַּד הֲוָה עָאל יַעֲקֹב בִּמְעַרְתָּא, כָּל רֵיחִין דְּגִנְתָּא דְעֵדֶן אִשְׁתְּכַח בִּמְעַרְתָּא, וּמְעַרְתָּא סָלְקָא נְהוֹרָא, וּשְׁרָגָא חַד דָּלִיק. וְכַד עָאלוּ אֲבָהָן לְגַבֵּי דְּיַעֲקֹב לְמִצְרַיִם, לְאִשְׁתַּכְּחָא עִמֵּיה, אִסְתַּלַּק נְהוֹרָא דִּשְׁרָגָא, כֵּיוָן דְּעָאל יַעֲקֹב בִּמְעַרְתָּא, הַדְרָא שְׁרָגָא לְאַתְרֵיה, כְּדֵין אִשְׁתְּלִים מְעַרְתָּא מִכָּל מַה דְּאִצְטְרִיךְ.

853. Come and behold: When Jacob entered the cave, all the perfumes of the Garden of Eden filled it. The cave was alight, for a candle burned THERE. When the Patriarchs came to Jacob in Egypt to be with him, the candlelight was gone FROM THE CAVE. When Jacob came into the cave, the candle returned. The cave was then perfected in all its needs.

854. וְעַד יוֹמֵי עַלְמָא, לָא קַבֵּילַת מְעַרְתָּא ב״נ אָחֳרָא, וְלָא תְקַבֵּל.

וְנִשְׁמָתִין דְּזַכָּאן אַעֲבָרָן מִקַּמַּיְיהוּ בְּבֵי מְעַרְתָּא, בְּגִין דְּיִתְעָרוּן, וְחָמִין זַרְעָא דְּשַׁבְקוּ בְּעַלְמָא, וְיֶחֱדוּ קַמֵּי קוּדְשָׁא בְּרִיךְ הוּא.

854. Never has the cave received any other man, and never will it. The souls of the righteous pass AFTER THEIR DEMISE before THE FATHERS inside the cave, so that they will awake and behold the seed they left in the world, and rejoice before the Holy One, blessed be He.

855. אֲמַר ר' אַבָּא, חֲנִיטָא דְּיַעֲקֹב מַאי אִיהוּ, א"ל זִיל שְׁאִיל לְאַסְיָא. תָּא חֲזֵי, כְּתִיב וַיְצַו יוֹסֵף אֶת עֲבָדָיו אֶת הָרוֹפְאִים לַחֲנֹט אֶת אָבִיו וַיַּחַנְטוּ הָרוֹפְאִים אֶת יִשְׂרָאֵל, ס"ד כִּשְׁאָר בְּנֵי נָשָׁא הֲוָה חֲנִיטָא דָּא. אִי תֵּימָא בְּגִין אוֹרְחָא הוּא דַּעֲבְדוּ, הָא כְּתִיב וַיָּמָת יוֹסֵף בֶּן וְגו' וַיִּישֶׂם בָּאָרוֹן בְּמִצְרָיִם, הָא לָא אַזְלוּ עִמֵּיהּ בְּאָרְחָא, דְּהָא תַּמָּן אִתְקַבַּר, וּכְתִיב וַיַּחַנְטוּ אוֹתוֹ.

855. Rabbi Aba said: What was the embalming of Jacob like? He said to him: Go and ask a physician. Come and see: it is written: "And Joseph commanded his servants the physicians to embalm his father: and the physicians embalmed Israel" (Beresheet 50:2). Could you possibly think that he was embalmed like other people? If you say that it was done due to the voyage, FOR THEY HAD TO PRESERVE HIM, it says, "So Joseph died...and they embalmed him, and he was put in a coffin in Egypt" (Ibid. 26). He was not taken away, but buried there, yet "they embalmed him."

856. אֶלָּא, אָרְחָא דְּמַלְכִין אִינוּן, בְּגִין לְקַיְּימָא גוּפַיְיהוּ, חֲנָטֵי לוֹן בְּמִשְׁחָא רְבוּת, עִלָּאָה עַל כָּל מִשְׁחִין, מְעוֹרָב בְּבוּסְמִין, וְשָׁאִיב לֵיהּ בְּגוּפָא, יוֹמָא בָּתַר יוֹמָא, בְּהַהוּא מִשְׁחָא טָבָא, אַרְבְּעִין יוֹמִין, דִּכְתִיב וַיִּמְלְאוּ לוֹ אַרְבָּעִים יוֹם כִּי כֵּן יִמְלְאוּ יְמֵי הַחֲנוּטִים. בָּתַר דְּאִשְׁתְּלִים דָּא, קַיְּימָא גוּפָא שְׁלִים זִמְנִין סַגִּיאִין.

856. It is the custom to embalm kings, in order to preserve the body FROM ROTTING. They are embalmed with anointing oil, superior to any other oil, mixed with spices. The good oil is absorbed in the body day after day for forty days, as it is written: "And forty days were fulfilled for him: for so are

fulfilled the days of those who are embalmed" (Ibid. 3). After this
procedure, the body is preserved for many days.

857. בְּגִין דְּכָל הַהוּא אַרְעָא דִּכְנַעַן, וְאַרְעָא דְּמִצְרַיִם, מְכַלָּה גוּפָא
וּמְרַקֵּב לֵיהּ לִזְמַן זְעֵיר, מִכָּל שְׁאָר אַרְעָא, וּבְגִין לְקַיְימָא גוּפָא עָבְדֵי
דָּא, וְעָבְדֵי חֲנִיטָא דָּא מִגּוֹ וּמִבָּרָא. מִגּוֹ דְּשַׁוְיָין הַהוּא מִשְׁחָא עַל
טַבּוּרָא, וְהוּא עָאל בְּטַבּוּרָא לְגוֹ, וְאִשְׁתָּאֵיב בִּמְעוֹי, וְקָאִים לֵיהּ לְגוּפָא
מִגּוֹ וּמִבָּרָא לִזְמְנִין סַגִּיאִין.

857. For the land of Canaan and the land of Egypt consume and corrupt the
body in a shorter time than other countries, and this is done in order to
preserve the body. The embalming is both for the internal part of the body
and the exterior. The oil is put on the navel, and it penetrates the inner part
of the body, is absorbed in the entrails and preserves it for a long time.

858. וְיַעֲקֹב הָכִי הֲוָה בְּקַיּוּמָא דְּגוּפָא, וְהָכִי אִצְטְרִיךְ, דְּגוּפָא דַּאֲבָהָן
אִיהוּ, וַהֲוָה בְּקַיּוּמָא בְּגוּפָא וְנַפְשָׁא. כְּגַוְונָא דָּא לְיוֹסֵף, דְּאִיהוּ דוּגְמָא
דְּגוּפָא, וּבְקַיּוּמָא דְּגוּפָא וְנַפְשָׁא הוּא. בְּקַיּוּמָא דְּגוּפָא, דִּכְתִיב וַיַּחַנְטוּ
אוֹתוֹ, בְּקַיּוּמָא דְּנַפְשָׁא, דִּכְתִיב וַיִּישֶׂם בָּאָרוֹן בְּמִצְרָיִם.

858. Jacob had need of the body and so it is appropriate: for he is the body
of the fathers, AS HIS FATHERS, CHESED AND GVURAH, ARE THE TWO
ARMS AND HE IS TIFERET, THE TORSO. Both his body and soul endured.
Joseph, too, resembles the body, FOR HE IS THE COVENANT, AND THE
COVENANT AND THE BODY ARE CONSIDERED THE SAME. He was
preserved in both body and soul: his body, as it is written: "And they
embalmed him" and his soul, as it is written: "And he was put in a coffin
(ark) in Egypt," WHICH MEANS THAT HIS SOUL JOINED THE SUPERNAL
ARK, WHICH IS THE NUKVA.

859. וּתְנִינָן תְּרֵי יוֹדִי"ן אֲמַאי. אֶלָּא, יוֹסֵף נָטַר לֵיהּ בְּרִית לְתַתָּא,
וְנָטֵיר לֵיהּ בְּרִית דִּלְעֵילָא, אִסְתַּלַּק מֵעַלְמָא, אִתְשַׁוֵּי בִּתְרֵי אֲרוֹנֵי,
בְּאָרוֹן לְתַתָּא, וּבְאָרוֹן לְעֵילָא. אָרוֹן דִּלְעֵילָא מַאן אִיהוּ. אֶלָּא, כְּד"א
הִנֵּה אֲרוֹן הַבְּרִית אֲדוֹן כָּל הָאָרֶץ, דְּאָרוֹן דִּלְעֵילָא אֲרוֹן הַבְּרִית אִקְרֵי,

דְּהָא לָא יָרֵית לֵיהּ אֶלָּא מַאן דְּנָטַר בְּרִית, וּבְגִין דְּיוֹסֵף נָטַר לֵיהּ לִבְרִית, אִתְּשַׁוֵּי בִּתְרֵי אֲרוֹנֵי.

859. We have learned why "*VAYISEM* (ENG. 'AND HE WAS PUT')" is spelt with two letters *Yud*. Joseph kept the covenant below and he kept the covenant above, BEING A CHARIOT TO ZEIR ANPIN. Therefore, when he passed away from the world, he was put in two arks (coffins), the ark above and the ark below. What is the 'ark above'? It is described by the words, "Behold, the ark of the covenant of (is) the master of all the earth" (Yehoshua 2:11). For the upper ark, THE SHECHINAH, is called 'the ark of the covenant'. It will be inherited only by him who keeps the covenant. Since Joseph kept the covenant, he was put in two arks.

88. "And he was put in a coffin in Egypt"

A Synopsis
The Zohar expands upon the wisdom concealed inside the verse "And he was put in a coffin (also: 'ark') in Egypt." Egypt, we're told, is the land of the Other Side, and though one may leave the world from this negative, foreign soil, the soul will merge with the Shechinah, as Joseph did, if it is righteous.

The Relevance of this Passage
The strength to rise above of the negativity and influence of our Evil Inclination [Egypt] is ignited, so that we may connect to the protective and nurturing Light of the Shechinah now, and in the World to Come.

860. וַיִּישֶׂם בָּאָרוֹן בְּמִצְרָיִם, הָכֵי הוּא וַדַּאי. וּקְרָא אוֹכַח רָזָא אָחֳרָא דְּאַף עַל גַּב דְּנָפְקַת נִשְׁמָתֵיהּ בִּרְשׁוּ אָחֳרָא, אִתְקַשַּׁר בִּשְׁכִינְתָּא, הֲדָא הוּא דִכְתִיב, וַיִּישֶׂם בָּאָרוֹן, לְעֵילָּא וּלְתַתָּא, בְּגִין דַּהֲוָה צַדִּיק, דְּכָל צַדִּיק יָרֵית אַרְעָא קַדִּישָׁא עִלָּאָה, כְּד"א וְעַמֵּךְ כֻּלָּם צַדִּיקִים לְעוֹלָם יִרְשׁוּ אָרֶץ נֵצֶר מַטָּעַי מַעֲשֵׂה יָדַי לְהִתְפָּאֵר.

860. "And he was put in a coffin (also: 'ark') in Egypt" (Beresheet 50:26). From this verse, we learn yet another secret. Though his soul departed in a foreign soil OF THE OTHER SIDE, it joined the Shechinah and "he was put in an ark," IN THE ARK above and IN THE ARK below. For he was righteous, and every righteous man inherits the Holy, Supernal Land, THE SHECHINAH, as it says, "Your people also shall be righteous: they shall inherit the land for ever; they shall be the branch of My planting, the work of My hands, that I may be glorified" (Yeshayah 60:21).

בָּרוּךְ ה' לְעוֹלָם אָמֵן וְאָמֵן.

Blessed be Hashem for ever and ever, Amen and Amen.

סְלִיק סֵפֶר בְּרֵאשִׁית

The end of the book of Beresheet

NOTES

NOTES

NOTES

NOTES

NOTES

NOTES

NOTES